D0769084

The Genoa Conference

The Genoa

Carole Fink

Conference

European Diplomacy, 1921–1922

The University of North Carolina Press · Chapel Hill and London

The publication of this work was made possible in part through
a grant from the National Endowment for the Humanities, a
federal agency whose mission is to award grants to support
education, scholarship, media programming, libraries, and
museums, in order to bring the results of cultural activities to
a broad, general public.

ISBN 0-8078-1578-0

Library of Congress Cataloging in Publication Data

Fink, Carole
  The Genoa Conference.

  Bibliography: p.
  Includes index.
  1. Genoa Conference. 2. Reconstruction (1914–1939)
3. Europe—Politics and government—1918–1945.
4. World War, 1914–1918—Influence. 5. Germany—
Foreign relations—Soviet Union. 6. Soviet Union—
Foreign relations—Germany. I. Title.
D727.F55 1984   940.5'1   83-14724

Designed by Naomi P. Slifkin

To Pauline Kallman

Contents

8

The Restoration of Europe *232*

9

The End of the Genoa Conference *258*

10

The Aftermath *281*

Conclusion

The Genoa Conference in Retrospect *303*

Illustrations

Preface

At Mars Hill College in October 1975, historians from the United States and Europe gathered at a conference organized by Dean David Knisley. Marking the fiftieth anniversary of the Locarno treaties, the meeting's purpose was to investigate the "Era of Locarno," from the Paris peace treaties to the first major steps toward their revision. In addition to the captured German documents, which for over two decades had supplied the basis for many important works on European diplomacy in the 1920s, scholars were now able to consult Austrian, Belgian, British, French, Italian, and League of Nations archives, the files of the United States and Canadian governments, a growing number of private papers, and an increasing quantity of printed official literature. The Mars Hill conference represented a unique forum for sharing archival information and creating international friendships of great value. In papers, articles, and books based on a broad, multinational perspective, its participants have reinterpreted the history of Europe during the ostensibly peaceful years between the end of World War I and the onset of the depression and of Hitler.

At Mars Hill I read my first paper on the Genoa Conference, comparing the handling of the European security problem in 1922 and 1925. The original suggestion to study Genoa came from Hans W. Gatzke, the foremost authority on German-Soviet relations in the 1920s and on Weimar Germany's leading statesman, Gustav Stresemann. Except for the brief and partisan contemporary accounts of the Genoa Conference by John Saxon Mills and Jean de Pierrefeu, there have been no full-length critical studies for the following reasons. First, historians have had difficulty until recently in obtaining the necessary archival sources, and second, Genoa was a failure. Though a number of historians have done research into its most spectacular subsidiary event, the Rapallo treaty, and though there have been good critical studies of the individual statesmen and nations that attended the conference, up to now no scholar has been able or willing to investigate this important event of 1922 in its entirety.

This work follows and has been inspired not only by the Mars Hill gathering but also by several distinguished studies of the interwar period. In *Locarno Diplomacy*, Jon Jacobson analyzed European diplomacy from a multinational perspective and discussed the enduring strains between Germany and the West; in *Politics and Diplomacy of Peacemaking*, Arno Mayer investigated the impact of the Russian Revolution; in their respective works, *La question des dettes interalliées et la reconstruction de l'Europe (1917–1929)* and *The Elusive Quest: America's Pursuit of European Stability and French Security, 1919–1933*, Denise Artaud and Melvyn Leffler filled an essential gap by examining American policy vis-à-vis Europe; in *The End of French Predominance in Europe*, Stephen Schuker elucidated the dynamics of international economic diplomacy as it affected both the reparations question and the problem of French security; and in *Recasting Bourgeois Europe: Stabilization in France, Germany, and Italy in the Decade after World War I*, Charles Maier demonstrated and compared the ties between domestic and foreign policy in the three nations. Though some of these books touch briefly on the Genoa Conference or the issues it encompassed, a gap nevertheless remains. We now have considerable insight into the process and results of peacemaking at Paris and into the subsequent crises over reparations that led to the Ruhr invasion, the Dawes Plan, and the Locarno treaties. However, the nature and meaning of the events of the relatively quiet year 1922 remain largely unexplored.

The Genoa Conference took place in the spring of 1922, between the much-heralded Washington Naval Conference, the Allied meetings over reparations in the late summer, and the Lausanne Conference in November. It occurred during a waiting period between crises in Europe and the Near East, a time of expectancy, when for various reasons the inclination toward conciliation and change temporarily outweighed the pressures to maintain and enforce the status quo. Though the Genoa Conference failed to produce palpable results, its extensive aims, its long six-week duration, and the importance of its failure all make it a subject worthy of study not only to "fill another hole" in our understanding of the 1920s but hopefully also to illuminate some larger questions, including the problem of failure in human affairs.

During the ten years of work on this study, I have incurred many debts and should like to acknowledge my gratitude to those who have helped me. First, I thank the American Council of Learned Societies for a Research Fellowship in 1978–79 that enabled me to complete the research for the book; its generosity and support also gave me time to reflect and explore new dimensions of this subject. I also wish to acknowledge the assistance of the National Endowment for the Humanities in contributing toward the publication of this book. I have received grants from the Penrose Fund of the American Philosophical Society in 1974, the Research Offices of the State University of New York at Binghamton in 1976, and the University of North Carolina at Wilmington in 1978, all of which helped defray the cost of research materials.

Canadian historian Susan Buggey and the staff of the Public Archives of Canada assisted me at the beginning of my research, as did Milton Gustafson and Robert Wolfe at the U.S. National Archives. In Britain I received help from A. J. P. Taylor, then the director of the Beaverbrook Library, who also granted me a memorable interview; from Martin Gilbert, who permitted me to see the Winston Churchill Papers; and from the staffs of the Public Record Office, the India Office, the University of Birmingham Library, and the Library of Churchill College, Cambridge University. In Brussels I greatly benefited from the guidance of the late Pierre Desneux and the assistance of André Dernelle.

My debts in Paris are considerable. At the archive of the French Foreign Ministry, I was given the utmost in cooperation from the staff and especially from Chief Archivist Maurice Degros and Ministers Plenipotentiary Jean Laloy and Martial de la Fournière. The late William Hawkins, founder and director of the Service Internationale de Microfilms, did expeditious work. In addition, I wish to thank Mlle Alice Guillemain at the archive of the Ministry of Economy and Finance, and General Porret, chief of the Historical Section of the archive of the French Army at Vincennes, for their assistance.

In Bonn, at the archive of the German Foreign Ministry, Dr. Klaus Weinandy and his staff provided their usual hospitality to American scholars, and Dr. Maria Keipert responded promptly to my later inquiries. In Koblenz Dr. Gregor Verlande gave me a thorough briefing and also helped with follow-up materials. I am grateful for the aid of Dr. Anna Benna of the Austrian Haus-Hof- und Staatsarchiv and Dr. Walter Winkelbauer of the Finanz- und Hof-kammerarchiv. Mr. Sven Welander, chief of the Historical Collections of the United Nations Library, was a most knowledgeable guide to the archives of the League of Nations; through his introduction, I met Mr. Evgeny Chossudovsky, who shared his research on Chicherin. In Rome the late Professor Rodolfo Mosca gave me valuable suggestions; the staffs of the Foreign Ministry archive and the Archivio Centrale aided my three visits. I profited from interviews with Henry P. Jordan, François Seydoux, Wolfgang Stresemann, and Louise Weiss, who gave personal recollections of the period.

I should like to acknowledge the loans of the microfilm editions of the Grigg Papers from Queens College, Kingston, Ontario, and of the Harding Papers from the Library of Congress, as well as the receipt of photocopies of the Hoover Papers from the Presidential Library in West Branch, Iowa. I thank Mr. Amory Houghton for permission to see the Alanson Houghton Papers in Corning, New York.

Rachelle Moore at Bartle Library of SUNY Binghamton provided cheerful and excellent assistance at the early stages of my work. Susan Clarvit and Maya Peretz helped with translations of Russian and Polish documents. The staff of the Humanities Reference Department at Wilson Library of UNC Chapel Hill have given me prompt and invaluable service. William Harris donated his efforts in executing the map. I express my deep gratitude for the expertise and dedication of my colleagues at Randall Library of UNC Wilmington, Sue Ann Hiatt, Louise Jackson, Debra Sewell, Philip Smith, Deborah

Sommer, Joanna Wright, and the director Eugene Huguelet, who have contributed generously to this book. At the University of North Carolina Press, Lewis Bateman has been a gracious and perceptive editor; Gwen Duffey and Pam Morrison guided the publication with great skill and courtesy. Finally, I end this long and incomplete list with thanks to my family, colleagues, friends, and students who over these many years have provided help, encouragement, and inspiration, and who have endured my enthusiasm for the events of 1921–22. I want to mention especially Seymour Fink, and Denise Artaud, Jacques Bariéty, Joel Blatt, Laurence Evans, Hans W. Gatzke, Paul Guinn, Jon Jacobson, Melton A. McLaurin, Marjorie Madigan, Sally Marks, Margaret Parish, Marta Petricioli, Stephen Schuker, Fred Stambrook, Olga Jiménez de Wagenheim, and Roberta Warman. I hope they recognize their contributions to this book. All errors and shortcomings are mine.

Wilmington, North Carolina
June 1983

Abbreviations

AA
Germany, Auswärtiges Amt (German Foreign Ministry)

ACP
[Joseph] Austen Chamberlain Papers, Birmingham

A Fin. Arch.
Austria, Finanz- und Hofkammerarchiv, Vienna (Austrian Finance and Exchequer Archive)

A HHSt
Austria, Haus- Hof- und Staatsarchiv, Vienna (Austrian Private, Court, and National Archive)

Akten-Wirth
Akten der Reichskanzlei . . . Die Kabinette Wirth I und II

BMA
Austria, Bundesministerium der Auswärtigen Angelegenheiten (Austrian Foreign Ministry)

BMAE
Belgium, Ministère des Affaires Étrangères, Brussels (Belgian Foreign Ministry)

BN
Bibliothèque Nationale, Paris

CrP
Eyre Alexander Crowe Papers, Public Record Office, London

CzP
George Nathaniel Curzon Papers, India Office, London

DBFP
Documents on British Foreign Policy, 1919–1939, 1st Series

DBPN
Documenten betreffende de Buitenlandse Politiek van Nederland, 1919–1945,
Period A, 1919–30, Vol. 3 (1 Sept. 1921–31 July 1922)

DVP SSSR
Documenty Vneshnei Politiki SSSR

FMAE
France, Ministère des Affaires Étrangères, Paris (French Foreign Ministry)

FMF
France, Ministère de l'Économie et des Finances, Paris (French Ministry of
Economics and Finance)

FO
Great Britain, Foreign Office

FRUS
Foreign Relations of the United States

GB BT
Great Britain, Board of Trade Papers, Public Record Office, London

GB CAB
Great Britain, Cabinet Papers, Public Record Office, London

GB Cmd.
Great Britain, Parliament, Papers by Command

GB FO 371
Great Britain, Foreign Office Records, Series 371, Public Record Office,
London

Germ. AA T-120
Captured Records of the German Foreign Ministry, Microfilm Series, T-120,
U.S. National Archives, Washington (designated by serial/roll/frame
numbers)

Germ. BA
Germany, Bundesarchiv, Koblenz (German Federal Archive)

Germ. Pol. Arch. AA
Germany, Politisches Archiv des Auswärtigen Amtes, Bonn (German Foreign
Ministry, Political Archive)

Grigg Papers
Edward Grigg Papers (microfilm edition)

Harding Papers
Warren G. Harding Presidential Papers (microfilm edition)

H.C. Deb.
Great Britain, House of Commons, *Parliamentary Debates*, 5th Series

Hoover/Comm.
Herbert Hoover Presidential Papers, Commerce Department Papers, West Branch, Iowa

HP
Maurice Hankey Papers, Churchill College, Cambridge

IMAE
Italy, Ministero degli Affari Esteri, Rome (Italian Foreign Ministry)

JO Ch. Déb. Par.
Journal Officiel de la République Française, Chambre des Députés, Débats Parlementaires

JP
Henri Jaspar Papers, Archives Générales, Brussels

LGP
David Lloyd George Papers, House of Lords Record Office, London

LGrP
Philip Lloyd-Greame [Viscount Swinton] Papers, Churchill College, Cambridge

LNA
League of Nations Archives, United Nations Library, Geneva

MAE
Ministère des Affaires Étrangères (Belgium, France); Ministero degli Affari Esteri (Italy)

MKP
William Lyon MacKenzie King Papers, Public Archives of Canada, Ottawa

PAC
Canada, Public Archives of Canada, Ottawa

PC-R
François Charles-Roux Papers, Ministère des Affaires Étrangères, Paris

PM
Alexandre Millerand Papers, Bibliothèque Nationale and Ministère des Affaires Étrangères, Paris

PMarg.
Pierre de Margerie Papers, Ministère des Affaires Étrangères, Paris

USDS
United States, Department of State Documents, National Archives, Washington

US MID
United States, Military Intelligence Division, National Archives, Washington

WSCP
Winston S. Churchill Papers, Oxford

The Genoa Conference

1

The Origins of the Genoa Conference

The Genoa Conference of 1922 took place as a result of certain events during the preceding year that challenged the structure and permanence of the Paris peace settlement and promoted revision. During 1921 Russia, Germany, and the United States—all opposed to the Versailles system and absent from the League of Nations—pursued independent policies that weakened Anglo-French leadership. The Entente Cordiale was withering because of Anglo-French differences over the German reparations question but also because of the wartime partners' mounting disagreements over the Near and Middle East, their relations with Russia, and the problems of security, disarmament, and economic recovery. To an extent, all of these problems were tied to their dependent relations with America. While the London government, which gave precedence to its imperial interests, favored certain modifications in the European status quo, Paris and its allies clung to the European settlement as the basis for their security.[1]

Just as the three outsiders launched their initiatives in 1921, Turkey under Mustafa Kemal Atatürk added a military and diplomatic challenge to the new Treaty of Sèvres, and the colonial world erupted with revolutionary, anticapitalist, and anti-Western ideologies. Britain and France were thus forced to defend, modify, or scrap the treaties they had created immediately after World War I: a peace settlement based on the unique conditions of 1918 that no longer existed. Public opinion, sobered from the euphoria of victory and the desolation of defeat, now began to question the durability of the postwar order.

1. On Anglo-French relations: Arnold Wolfers, *Britain and France between Two Wars: Conflicting Strategies of Peace since Versailles* (New York: Harcourt, Brace and Co., 1940); John Paul Selsam, *The Attempts to Form an Anglo-French Alliance, 1919–1924* (Philadelphia: University of Pennsylvania Press, 1936); and Neville Waites, ed., *Troubled Neighbors: Franco-British Relations in the Twentieth Century* (London: Weidenfeld and Nicolson, 1971). Also useful are: John C. Cairns, "A Nation of Shopkeepers in Search of a Suitable France, 1919–1940," *American Historical Review* 79 (June 1974): 710–43; and Samuel M. Osgood, "Le mythe de 'la perfide Albion' en France, 1919–1940," *Cahiers Historiques* 20 (1975): 5–20.

High unemployment, inflation, and economic stagnation were the hallmarks of the year 1921.[2] Though warfare ended in Eastern Europe, famine struck Russia in the spring. Its epidemics of typhus and cholera threatened to spread westward. Skirmishes between White Guard troops and Bolsheviks along the frontiers of the new Soviet state created unsettled conditions. In Western Europe, there was a general contraction of manufacture and trade. The governments faced reduced tax revenues, together with the shortage of private and outside capital investment, which threatened recovery and reconstruction, a lowering of living standards, and a reduction of national defense. The Center-Right coalitions in power since the war's end tended to sacrifice financial stability for national prestige and social peace. There was a markedly uneven development throughout Europe. This not only caused local suffering and uncertainty but also increasingly strained the wealthier producer, banking, and trading economies in Western, Central, and Northern Europe. The inability of the Entente to demonstrate the economic fruits of victory, indeed its helplessness to prevent the threatened collapse of its former enemy Germany, fueled the opposition to the Paris peace treaties.[3]

Treaty revisionism in the early 1920s had complex and widespread roots. Germany and its former allies, but also Soviet Russia, the United States, and the wartime neutrals, all questioned the political and economic clauses of the settlement. Italy and Japan, though belonging technically to the victors, felt themselves prejudiced by key details in the treaties. British Commonwealth leaders, whose populations had made great sacrifices in World War I, opposed the coercive apparatus that linked their future with obscure parts of Europe.

In Great Britain, with its ailing, aged industries and 2 million unemployed, there were perhaps the most articulate critics of the new international system. British bankers and manufacturers as well as the laborers in industries hurt by shortages of capital and raw materials, by closed export markets and controlled food imports, urged that their government work for "international conciliation," the code word for treaty revision. They had their counterparts in the industrial areas of Belgium and France. Finally, liberal and left-wing intellectuals and journalists in the Allied countries insisted that the decisions of

2. Derek H. Aldcroft, *From Versailles to Wall Street, 1919–1929* (Berkeley and Los Angeles: University of California Press, 1977), chaps. 3–5; Iván T. Berend and György Ránki, *Economic Development in East-Central Europe in the 19th and 20th Centuries* (New York: Columbia University Press, 1974), chap. 8; and Bernd Dohrmann, *Die englische Europapolitik in der Wirtschaftskrise, 1921–1923* (Munich and Vienna: Oldenbourg, 1980), chaps. 1–3.

3. The foremost spokesman was John Maynard Keynes, *The Economic Consequences of the Peace* (London: Macmillan, 1919); his second thoughts appear in *A Revision of the Treaty* (London: Macmillan, 1922). But see also: Francesco S. Nitti, *Peaceless Europe* (London and New York: Cassell, 1922); Gustav Cassel, *Money and Foreign Exchange after 1914* (London: Constable, 1922); and Erich Wüest, *Der Vertrag von Versailles in Licht und Schatten der Kritik: Die Kontroverse um seine wirtschaftliche Auswirkungen* (Zurich: Europa Verlag, 1962).

1919 were directly responsible for Europe's economic, social, and spiritual malaise.[4]

To be sure, the revisionist cause was selective: the German peace and the Allies' treatment of Soviet Russia and of each other were singled out or occasionally joined. The list of abominations produced by the treaties' critics covered a spectrum ranging from minor alterations to the total annihilation of the peace settlement. Most critics called attention to the new international organization, the League of Nations, which in its first year of existence had established a permanent secretariat in Geneva and an international civil service. However, the League of Nations Council, the forum of the Great Powers, met in various capitals and reeled from crisis to crisis. In its first meetings in Geneva, the League Assembly was the scene of complaints about the organization's limited membership, its bondage to the peace treaties and to the Allies, its limited functions, and the uncertainty of its future.[5]

The Genoa Conference was thus born in an atmosphere of revisionism that arose from diverse ideological, nationalist, economic, social, and political considerations. The British and French prime ministers, David Lloyd George and Aristide Briand, who sought to contain the whirlwind, respond to important diplomatic challenges, patch up their bilateral differences, and especially maintain themselves in power, ended the year 1921 with the decision to convene a world economic conference. For the first time, they invited their former enemies and Soviet Russia to attend as equals.

The Soviet Note of 28 October 1921

On 28 October 1921, People's Commissar of Foreign Affairs G. V. Chicherin sent a letter in the name of the Soviet government to the members of the Supreme Allied Council: Great Britain, France, Italy, Japan, and the United States.[6] The note was in response to the resolutions of the Brussels Conference (6 to 8 October), which had been convened by the Supreme Council to deal with the Russian famine. Twenty-one states, including Germany, had attended the Brussels meeting, along with representatives of private charitable organizations working to alleviate the famine. Russia had been excluded. The

4. Martin Gilbert, *The Roots of Appeasement* (New York: New American Library, 1966), pp. 78–82; Pierre Miquel, *La paix de Versailles et l'opinion publique française* (Paris: Flammarion, 1971); and Christoph Stamm, *Lloyd George zwischen Innen- und Aussenpolitik: Die britische Deutschlandpolitik 1921/22* (Cologne: Verlag Wissenschaft und Politik, 1977). The profound personal disillusionment of the postwar West European is echoed in T. S. Eliot's 1922 poem, "The Waste Land."

5. Cf. F. P. Walters, *A History of the League of Nations* (London: Oxford University Press, 1952), pp. 94–97, 149–51.

6. The text is in GB Cmd. 1546, and was printed in *Pravda*, 29 Oct. 1921.

Brussels Conference had recommended the granting of additional private and government aid to Russia but set two specific conditions: the Soviet government must recognize its existing debts and must establish a regime in which future credits would be secure.[7]

The Brussels terms were explicit: famine aid was to be linked to precise economic and political obligations. In accepting, Moscow added its own terms. Soviet dictator V. I. Lenin, who was chairman of the Council of People's Commissars (Sovnarkom) and head of the all-powerful politburo of the Central Committee of the Communist party, amended Chicherin's original letter to demand reciprocal concessions from the West.[8] Chicherin's 28 October message agreed to accept responsibility for the czarist government's *prewar* debts under three conditions: Russia expected substantial economic aid and foreign investment; it called for the cessation of all foreign intervention against the Bolshevik regime and for de jure recognition; and, finally, Chicherin proposed the "early convocation of an international conference" to mediate "reciprocal financial claims" and to "work out a final peace treaty" between Russia and the other powers.[9]

The Chicherin letter, a basic element in the origins of the Genoa Conference, represented the climax of important developments in Soviet foreign and domestic policy in 1921: the termination of foreign and civil war; the change from war communism to the New Economic Policy (NEP); the solidification of new Soviet institutions of government, finance, justice, and labor; and Moscow's attempt to control world revolution through the Communist Internationale. The transformation had begun in March, with the end of the war against Poland, the failure of the Communist offensive in Germany, and the suppression of the Kronstadt uprising. The new direction was signaled by the conclusion of trade pacts with Great Britain in March 1921 and with Germany in May, and by Russia's invitations to foreign capitalists to apply for concessions to develop mines, forests, oil, and other industries.[10]

7. Lloyd-Greame report, 14 Oct. 1921, *DBFP*, 20:782–85 (henceforth in *DBFP* either page or document numbers will be given); Hauschild memorandum, n.d., Germ. AA T-120 L636/ 4779/L201991–99; and reports in *New York Times*, 7, 11 Oct. 1921.

8. V. I. Lenin, *Collected Works* (Moscow: Progress Publishers, 1965–71), 45:683 (henceforth in *Collected Works* either page or document numbers will be given); Chicherin's 24 Oct. text and Lenin's corrections in ibid., pp. 356–58. Lenin: "The main thing: *our* claims to them should be stated *subtly* and precisely." (Italics in the original), p. 356.

9. Richard K. Debo, "George Chicherin: Soviet Russia's Second Foreign Commissar" (Ph.D. diss., University of Nebraska, 1964), p. 213, interprets Chicherin's initiative of offering reciprocal concessions to Britain and other powers as a means of expanding the authority of the People's Commissariat of Foreign Affairs (Narkomindel); E. M. Chossudovsky, "Lenin and Chicherin: The Beginnings of Soviet Foreign Policy and Diplomacy," *Millennium* 3 (Spring 1974): 7–9, stresses the collaboration between the two Soviet leaders.

10. E. H. Carr, *The Bolshevik Revolution, 1917–1923* (Baltimore: Penguin, 1966), 3: chap. 27.

Lenin's international maneuvers, which paralleled his struggle for NEP and the creation of small-scale agrarian capitalism under state control, were perceived both inside and outside Russia as a major retreat from Marxian orthodoxy: the "thermidorization" of the Russian Revolution. Foreign Trade Commissar Leonid Krassin, its spokesman abroad, conducted private negotiations with Western statesmen and industrialists. He made optimistic, occasionally exaggerated announcements to the press about potential offers and agreements, hoping to snare interested capitalists and to alarm their governments. Lenin hinted at additional internal changes to accommodate Western businessmen, for example, the possible alteration of Soviet laws dealing with labor, property, and the rights of foreign nationals. Until his first illness in December, Lenin directed almost every decision in domestic and foreign affairs, trade and economic development, politics and the military. Lenin worked energetically in 1921 to promote economic rapprochement with the West—the precondition, he believed, to the security and survival of the new Soviet state.[11]

Inevitably, there was opposition from the Communist party's left wing, the hard-liners who insisted that Russia had nothing to gain materially from cooperation with the West, stood for an "isolationist" economic policy, and feared foreign penetration.[12] Lenin thundered at his orthodox critics, as he had during the difficult Brest-Litovsk negotiations, that for the time being Moscow could not anticipate a world revolution. The events of 1921 had proved this. Instead of passively awaiting or promoting capitalism's coup de grace, Lenin wanted, at least temporarily, to use its technology, expertise, and particularly its capital, which had played so large a role in Russia's pre-1914 industrialization. Lenin's protégé, Gregory Sokol'nikov, announced that "[Europe's] salvation lies in Russia." The West, currently ailing with its inflation, unemployment, labor unrest, and stagnant capital, needed Russia's raw materials and vast market to export machinery and manufactured goods, and would therefore take all necessary steps to save itself, including the rebuilding of the Soviet state.[13]

11. "Two nineteenth century patterns blended in Lenin's mentality: balance of power politics and the primacy of economics in politics": Louis Fischer, *The Life of Lenin* (New York: Harper and Row, 1965), p. 557. Cf. I. Linder, "Lenin's Foreign Policy Activity," *International Affairs* 12 (1969): 46–51.

12. The major Bolshevik opponents included Leon Trotsky, economist Eugen Varga, Adolf Joffe, Karl Radek, E. A. Preobrazhensky, and also Joseph Stalin. Cf. Richard B. Day, *Leon Trotsky and the Politics of Economic Isolation* (Cambridge: Cambridge University Press, 1973), pp. 60–61; Eugen Varga, "Die Wendung in der Wirtschaftspolitik Sowjet-Russlands," *Die kommunistische Internationale* 18 (1921): 90; A. O. Chubaryan, "V. I. Lenin i Genua," *Istoriia SSSR* 2 (1970): 39–50; Karl Radek, "Die kapitalistische Welt und Sowjetrussland," in Karl Radek, *Die Liquidation des Versailles Friedens* (Hamburg: Kommunistische Internationale, 1922), pp. 22–33; Richard A. Day, "Preobrazhensky and the Theory of the Transition Period," *Soviet Studies* 2 (April 1975): 208–9.

13. Day, *Trotsky*, pp. 59–64.

Steering deftly between the Left and the Right of the party leadership, Lenin thus initiated a new form of East-West combat in 1921. Ideological differences between the Communist and capitalist worlds were to be submerged temporarily in practical economic and political discussions; the prevailing hostility between both sides would be overcome by calls for nonintervention, disarmament, and peace. Despite its acknowledged weakness, Soviet Russia still possessed advantages: there were material lures to dangle at Western capitalists and statesmen and lofty propositions to attract liberals and left-wing radicals, the unemployed and the disaffected. Under the banner of "peaceful coexistence," which by no means represented a capitulation, Lenin's Russia launched a new challenge to the West.[14]

The commencement of Soviet overtures to the West in mid-1921 coincided with a massive crop failure in the Volga region, which was caused by various miscalculations but also by a second successive year of drought. Threatened by widespread famine, Moscow looked to the West for assistance. On 13 July the writer Maxim Gorky appealed "to all honest people" for "bread and medicine." Lenin permitted establishment of the All-Russian Famine Relief Committee, which included prominent anti-Bolsheviks, to ask for contributions and supervise the distribution of relief supplies from domestic and foreign sources. Neither expectant nor frightened, Lenin assumed that this showpiece of collaboration with the old regime would produce a "couple of carloads of aid."[15] It also triggered a prompt, competitive reaction by Western governments.

First to respond was Herbert Hoover, secretary of commerce of the United States, on behalf of the American Relief Administration (ARA). This was the world's largest humanitarian organization; under Hoover's leadership, it had conducted major feeding operations during and after World War I. Four months earlier, the new Harding administration had rebuffed Moscow's request for a trade treaty similar to Britain's, posing conditions amounting to the dissolution of the Communist regime. However, Hoover's initiative in July was not un-

---

14. Lenin rejected Chicherin's suggestion that to appease Western sensibilities he and Trotsky resign from the Executive Committee of the Comintern: Lenin, *Collected Works*, 45:339–40. Compare E. M. Chossudovsky, "Genoa Revisited: Russia and Coexistence," *Foreign Affairs* 50, no. 3 (April 1972): 557–62, with Franklyn Griffiths, *Genoa Plus 51: Changing Soviet Objectives in Europe* (Toronto: Canadian Institute of International Affairs, 1973), pp. 23–32.

15. *FRUS, 1921*, 2:805. Also Charles M. Edmondson, "The Politics of Hunger: The Soviet Response to Famine, 1921," *Soviet Studies* 29, no. 4 (October 1977): 506–18; Lenin to People's Commissar for Public Health Semashko, 12 July 1921, in *Collected Works*, 45:208–9. The Cheka (the All-Russian Extraordinary Commission that served as the Bolsheviks' secret police force to root out "counterrevolution") monitored the famine committee's activities, and one of its members, Politburo member Lev Kamenev, also headed Pomgol, a newly created state-controlled relief office designed, if necessary, to replace the show committee. Also see Memorandum, 5 Sept. 1921, USDS 861.48/1673; and Jerome Landfield, "The Relief of the Starving Russians," *The American Review of Reviews* 64 (September 1921): 270.

welcome in Washington. The offer to provide aid through the ARA included specific demands for the release of Americans being held prisoner in Russia and also for guarantees of the complete independence of ARA officials. As one of the main architects of the administration's anti-Bolshevik policy, Hoover could represent this new and considerable relief effort as a means of strengthening the barriers against communism: America's humanitarian concerns could be assuaged by helping starving Russian children and its anti-Communist sentiments appeased by withholding control over supplies from Bolshevik officials. In the hoped-for eventuality that Lenin soon would be overthrown, the ARA would provide the United States with useful information and influence.[16]

America's example was followed by other private organizations, inc'"ding the Red Cross and groups of Russian emigrés. Lacking Hoover's resources and personnel, they were forced to rely on the cooperation of the current rulers of Russia.[17] The first European government to respond to Russia's call for help was its former ally, France, which had over 1 million bondholders whose investments in the czarist regime had been repudiated by the Bolsheviks. In view of the British and German trade treaties with Moscow and the proffered American action, Paris was threatened with isolation. Other creditor states—Switzerland, Belgium, Holland, and the Scandinavian countries—showed signs of joining the scramble for Soviet concessions.[18] Paris had to avoid being excluded from Europe's mounting involvement with Russia, curb competitive bidding for the Bolsheviks' favor, and ensure that any funds destined for famine relief be withheld from the Kremlin's control.

The Supreme Council met in Paris between 8 and 13 August. Its principal task was to decide on the fate of Upper Silesia. The plebiscite of March 1921 had resulted in a majority favoring retention by Germany; but French resistance and a Polish uprising in May forced the Allies to consider the possibility of partitioning the rich industrial province. Anticipating British and Italian support for Germany, Briand tried unsuccessfully to woo Berlin with a vague invitation to join an anti-Bolshevik bloc of France, Britain, and America.[19]

16. Benjamin Weissman, *Herbert Hoover and Famine Relief to Soviet Russia, 1921–1923* (Stanford: Standford University Press, 1974), pp. 17–49; and *FRUS, 1921*, 2:768, 798–808.

17. See, e.g., Comité des organisations russes réunies pour le secours aux affamés, *Mémoire rélatif à la famine en Russie* (Brussels: n.p., 1921).

18. See Raymond Poincaré, "Chronique de la quinzaine," *Revue des Deux Mondes* (15 July 1921): 209: "If the world will not listen to us and if, despite us, they head for Moscow, shall we remain permanently, self-pityingly back on the side of the road? Temporization is no policy." Prime Minister Briand's cautious policy outlined in an unsigned memorandum of 5 Aug. 1921, FMAE Z Russ. 348. Cf. Hoesch to AA, Paris, 4, 11 Aug. 1921, Germ. AA T-120 L636/4779/L201584–87, L201635–38.

19. F. Gregory Campbell, "The Struggle for Upper Silesia," *Journal of Modern History* 43, no. 3 (September 1970): 380.

During the council meeting Briand held firm, despite Lloyd George's bombast and sarcasm. Forced to leave early because of a crisis over Ireland, Lloyd George grasped the Italian suggestion to break the deadlock on Upper Silesia by submitting the question to the Council of the League of Nations. Briand readily agreed. And after Lloyd George departed, he presented his case for the creation of an international commission to deal with Russia's famine. Based in Paris, this body would investigate conditions in Russia, distribute aid via the All-Russian Famine Relief Committee, and work in cooperation with the ARA and the Red Cross.[20]

Despite Briand's efforts to create an aura of unity, there were significant differences in the Allies' Russian policies. The American representative remained conspicuously silent; the Japanese questioned whether the Bolsheviks would permit foreigners to dictate and dispense aid. Britain and Italy (the latter currently seeking a trade pact with Moscow) agreed to Briand's proposal but insisted that any Allied aid must be funneled through the "existing machinery of the present Soviet regime." France and Belgium, on the other hand, wanted the commission to form the basis of an international authority that would supervise relief work and, by supporting the All-Russian Famine Relief Committee, promote a political alternative to Lenin's government. The Supreme Council agreed on only two points: there could be no aid unless the Soviet government recognized all its existing obligations; and all strongly desired America's participation in any projected venture.[21]

Faced with the prospect of international inquiries and stiff conditions, the Soviet government accepted the ARA's terms on 19 August 1921. Lenin at first regretted the concessions necessary for this agreement but soon realized the importance of an initial contact between Russia and America.[22] On 29 August Dr. Fridjof Nansen, the famed Norwegian explorer and humanitarian representing the International Red Cross, signed a pact in Moscow with Lev Kamenev, a member of both the All-Russian Famine Relief Committee and the politburo, providing for a twelve-million-dollar fund-raising campaign. The German Red Cross soon followed with a more modest agreement.

By the time France organized and convened the meeting of its International Commission, presided over by Joseph Noulens, former French ambassador to czarist Russia, its purpose was doomed. The ARA refused to submit to the commission's control. The Red Cross decided to work directly with the Bol-

---

20. *DBFP*, 15: nos. 95 and 103. Lord Hardinge to Crowe, Paris, 10 and 13 Aug. 1921, *DBFP*, 20: nos. 390 and 392.

21. Harvey to Hughes, London, 23 Aug. 1921, *FRUS, 1921*, 2:818.

22. The ARA agreement in ibid., pp. 812–17; final negotiations in Weissman, *Herbert Hoover and Famine Relief*, pp. 48–73. Cf. Lenin, *Collected Works*, 45:250–51, 253–54, 262–63, 290, 339–40.

sheviks. The British were unenthusiastic. Finally, and significantly, Moscow, which suddenly dissolved the All-Russian Famine Relief Committee and arrested its anti-Bolshevik members, rejected the commission's decision to dispatch an investigatory committee to Russia.[23]

American relief, splendidly organized and lavishly funded under Hoover's energetic direction, supervised the feeding of over 10 million Russians during the next year. Notwithstanding criticisms of Hoover's autocratic methods, no one could question the ARA's efficiency or the spectacular results.[24] With the Americans dominating the arena of food supplies, the Allies continued to focus on the economic and political ramifications of Russia's catastrophe. The League of Nations made a feeble and futile effort to participate in aid relief. During its second assembly, Nansen asked the fifty-one member states to contribute 30 million pounds sterling for Russian aid; but his appeal was defeated by loud cries of poverty and by accusations against the Bolsheviks. Moreover, the Allies had decided to head off any possible League action and to thwart Nansen's work by calling their own meeting in Brussels.[25]

Great Britain now took the lead that had earlier been grasped by France. Lloyd George, consumed by the Irish question and irritated by the Kremlin's anti-British maneuvers in the Near East and in Asia, had let Russian affairs drift through the summer and early fall. London had observed the Briand, Hoover, and Nansen moves passively. Lenin's emissaries then dangled alluring bait: a potential purchase of 10 million pounds worth of British goods secured by the Export Credits scheme, which authorized the British government to guarantee transactions to stimulate foreign trade. To make matters clearer, the Kremlin placed British manufacturers in competition with American and German producers and hinted it would begin leasing nationalized properties. Former British owners, prospective investors and traders, and Whitehall itself

23. Lloyd-Greame report, 3 Sept. 1921, *DBFP*, 20:734–40; Chicherin's rejection of the commission's proposal, 7 Sept. 1921, *DVP SSSR*, 4:307–11; Allied response: *DBFP*, 20:751. The dissolution of the All-Russian Famine Relief Committee by the Cheka in Carr, *Bolshevik Revolution*, 1:185–88.

24. See Hoover's report to President Harding on the work of the ARA, 9 Feb. 1922, Harding Papers, roll 181; also US MID 2070:2151, 2161, 2167, 2169, 2175, 2185, 2187–88, 2192, and 2202; Weissman, *Herbert Hoover and Famine Relief*, pp. 74–202; and Lenin, *Collected Works*, 45:671, n. 317: "The staff of this organization, consisting mainly of U.S. army officers engaged in espionage, gave support to counter-revolutionary elements in Russia." ARA relief work peaked in Aug. 1922; then its activities (and Soviet cooperation) were gradually reduced, and the mission formally ended in June 1923.

25. Walter, *League of Nations*, p. 150; and Kathryn W. Davis, *The Soviets at Geneva* (Geneva: Geneva Research Center, 1934), pp. 32–34. The Allies' opposition to Nansen's efforts in Mueller to AA, Berne, 4 Oct. 1921, Germ. AA T-120 L636/4779/L201970–76 and *DBFP*, 20:751–54, 775.

appreciated the importance of asserting British leadership in the Russian market.[26]

Lloyd George's coalition government, dominated by the Tories, contained two outspoken anti-Bolsheviks: Foreign Secretary Lord Curzon and Colonial Secretary Winston Churchill.[27] Yet this government could not ignore the material realities, namely, the prospects of expanded trade with Russia, oil and mining concessions, and control of the diplomacy on the Russian question. On 9 September Chicherin sent word to Lloyd George (deliberately bypassing the Foreign Office) that Russia was prepared to recognize its debts subject to commensurate concessions from the West.[28] This gave London the opportunity to seize the reins and recoup Noulens' failure, Hoover's victory, and Nansen's crusade. The latter threatened to place substantial, unsecured credits in the hands of the Soviet rulers.

Sir Philip Lloyd-Greame, the Conservative head of the Department of Overseas Trade, which administered the Export Credits scheme, supported the organization of some form of international aid to Russia. For Britain it was essential to establish a united front at once, to prevent Moscow from forcing the West into a costly bidding contest to restore the ruined Russian economy.[29] France went along with the British initiative. The International Commission issued an invitation to twenty-one governments to meet in Brussels in early October to coordinate their financial and political dealings with Soviet Russia. Britain put pressure on Germany to participate, fearing a gap in the Western camp. Berlin reluctantly sent a delegate, who, like the American representative, abstained from voting.[30]

26. "Note of interview with . . . Russian Trade Delegation at 10 Downing St.," 5 Aug. 1921, minutes of meeting on relief for Russian famine held at the Board of Trade, 6 Aug. 1921, Hodgson to Curzon, Moscow, 23 and 25 Aug. 1921, and Curzon to Hodgson, London, 25 Aug. 1921, *DBFP*, 20:704–6, 721–23. On trade and concessions: Hodgson to Curzon, Moscow, 14 Aug. 1921, Curzon to Hodgson, London, 1 Sept. 1921, ibid., pp. 717–18 and 732; and L. A. Paish commentary, London, 24 Aug. 1921, GB BT 90/17.

27. See, e.g., minutes of meeting, 15 July 1921, of Interdepartmental Committee on Bolshevism, O'Malley to Berzin, London, 29 July 1921, Curzon to Hodgson, London, 7 Sept. 1921 (a protest against anti-British activities in India, Persia, Turkestan, Ankara, and Afghanistan), Hodgson to Curzon, Moscow, 17 and 30 Sept. (with Chicherin's replies), and Curzon to Hodgson, 27 Oct. (his counterreply), *DBFP* 20:698–701, 741–49, 766–67, 779–81, and 795–98. Also Martin Gilbert, *Winston S. Churchill* (Boston: Houghton Mifflin, 1975), 4:760–61.

28. Chicherin's instructions in *DVP SSSR*, 4:306. A. J. Sylvester to Lloyd George, 9 Sept. 1921, LGP F 58/2/25, communicating the offer.

29. Hardinge [Lloyd-Greame] to Curzon, Paris, 15 Sept. 1921, *DBFP* 20:760–61. See also Lloyd-Greame to Lloyd George, 3, 27, and 29 Sept. 1921, and Lloyd George to Lloyd-Greame, 26 Sept. 1921, LGP F 46/3/3, 5, 6, 7. Chicherin, mistaking London's purpose, protested against its plotting to set up still another "commission of inquiry": *DBFP*, 20:741, n. 4.

30. Behrendt to Sthamer, Berlin, 29 Sept. 1921, Germ. AA T-120 L636/4779/L201885;

The Brussels meeting produced indications of agreement and disagreement. The Allies were all committed to demanding debt recognition from the Russians and also wanted to torpedo Nansen's independent mission. They nevertheless diverged on important questions. The French were still hoping for a political arrangement that would keep the brakes on closer contact with the Bolshevik regime; the British desired a major credit action that would far transcend famine relief and link the entire capitalist West. Italy broke with its partners on the principle of full debt recognition. Germany, the outsider, similarly opposed any form of political pressure on the Soviet state.[31]

The Brussels Conference nonetheless represented a success for British policy. It somewhat balanced what it considered an adverse decision by the League of Nations on the boundaries of the partition of Upper Silesia.[32] At Brussels London obtained agreement on a collective offer of credits to Russia and the specific terms. For the moment a united front had been maintained. Britain had become the catalyst for this action, and Germany, despite the misgivings of Joseph Wirth's government, had been snared. Lloyd-Greame exuded confidence that the work of the Brussels Conference would continue. The signal was beamed at Moscow. On 28 October Chicherin officially responded with Russia's terms for dealing with the West.

Now Lenin had to face the results of Chicherin's note—an emerging British-led coalition turning famine relief into an economic and political offensive. The United States neither joined the coalition nor drew closer to Moscow. Despite Russia's efforts to attract American investors, the United States remained officially aloof and the Kremlin eventually had to submit to even stiffer conditions from the ARA.[33] After the Brussels meeting, as Western concessionaires began investigating possibilities in Russia, Joseph Stalin warned darkly in *Pravda* in December 1921 that the country would soon be overwhelmed with foreign missions and spies. Around them a "ring-fence"—from the Far East through India, Afghanistan, Persia, Turkey, Rumania, Poland, and Finland—would be tightened and new White Guard offensives plotted.[34] Le-

---

Curzon to D'Abernon, London, 3 Oct. 1921, *DBFP*, 20:781–82; and Dufour to AA, London, 28, 29 Sept. 1921, Germ. AA T-120 L636/4779/L201886, L2011911–12.

31. Hauschild to AA, Brussels, 6, 7 Oct. 1921, and undated memorandum summarizing the Brussels meeting, Germ. AA T-120 L636/4779/L201942–43, L201951–53, L201991–99, and his notes on the Brussels Conference, Germ. Pol. Arch. AA Abt. Pol. IV (Russland 811/4). Also Lloyd-Greame report, 14 Oct. 1921, *DBFP*, 20:782–85; and "Conférence de Bruxelles," 6–8 Oct., FMAE Z Russ. 395.

32. *New York Times*, 11 Oct. 1921, and analysis in *Le Temps*, 9 Oct. 1921.

33. Lenin, *Collected Works*, 45:362–64, 368, and 416–17; Weissman, *Herbert Hoover and Famine Relief*, pp. 101–2; and H. H. Fisher, *The Famine in Soviet Russia, 1919–1923* (New York: Macmillan, 1927), pp. 195–205.

34. Quoted in Carr, *Bolshevik Revolution*, 3:349.

nin, despite the heavy burdens of office, deteriorating health, the often con-
founding silence of Lloyd George, and the forebodings of Stalin, appeared
undiscouraged. Still preaching the virtues of peaceful coexistence with the
capitalist world, he meant to break the fence, widen the divisions of the West,
and win victory for Russia. The Treaty of Versailles would be a most useful
target.

Germany: From Wiesbaden to London

Reparations, one of the most complex problems of the interwar period, affected not only Germany's relations with the Entente but also the entire dimen-
sion of American-European and East-West relations.[35] Berlin was aware of this
and frequently linked its controversial payments burden with its diplomacy and
with domestic politics. Still shrouded in propaganda and nationalistic rhetoric,
and further complicated by the hyperinflation of 1922–24 and the Franco-Belgian invasion of the Ruhr, the reparations issue far transcended the issues of the
Genoa Conference. Nevertheless, the second essential factor in the origins of
the Genoa Conference was the German initiative in late 1921 for a reparations
moratorium and the powers' response.[36]

On 10 May 1921 Joseph Wirth formed a coalition cabinet in response to the
government crisis over the London Ultimatum of 5 May, which contained the

35. The most helpful source is Étienne Weill-Raynal, *Les réparations allemandes et la France*
(Paris: Nouvelles Éditions Latines, 1947), vol. 2. More recent works include: Peter Krüger,
Deutschland und die Reparationen, 1918/1919 (Stuttgart: Deutscher Verlags-Anstalt, 1973);
David Felix, *Walther Rathenau and the Weimar Republic: The Politics of Reparations* (Baltimore:
Johns Hopkins University Press, 1971); Dieter B. Gescher, *Die Vereinigten Staaten von
Nordamerika und die Reparationen, 1920–1924* (Bonn: L. Röhrscheid, 1956); Stamm, *Lloyd
George*; Jacques Bariéty, *Les relations franco-allemandes après la première guerre mondiale*
(Paris: Éditions Pedone, 1977); and Marc Trachtenberg, *Reparation in World Politics* (New
York: Columbia University Press, 1980). The subject is concisely summarized in Sally Marks,
"The Myths of Reparations," *Central European History* 17, no. 3 (1978): 231–55, and reviewed
in Peter Krüger, "Das Reparationsproblem der Weimarer Republik in fragwürdiger Sicht,"
Vierteljahrshefte für Zeitgeschichte 29 (January 1981): 21–47.

36. Except for Ludwig Zimmermann, *Deutsche Aussenpolitik in der Ära der Weimarer
Republik* (Göttingen: Musterschmidt-Verlag, 1958) and Heinrich Euler, *Die Aussenpolitik der
Weimarer Republik 1918/1923* (Aschaffenburg: Pattloch-Verlag, 1957)—both dated and flawed
—there are no critical studies of Weimar foreign policy.

For German diplomacy during this period, the most useful sources are: Ernst Laubach, *Die
Politik der Kabinette Wirth*, 1921/1922 (Lübeck and Hamburg: Matthiesen, 1968); László
Zsigmond, *Zur deutschen Frage, 1918–1923*, trans. P. Felix (Budapest: Akadémiai Kiadó,
1964); and Jean-Claude Favez, *La Reich devant l'occupation franco-belge de la Ruhr en 1923*
(Geneva: Droz, 1969). Two valuable contemporary works are: Carl Bergmann, *The History of
Reparations* (London: E. Benn, 1927); and Rudolf Hilferding, "Die Weltpolitik, das Repara-
tionsproblem, und die Konferenz von Genua," *Schmollers Jahrbuch* 46, nos. 3–4 (1922): 1–28.

Allies' reparations demands.[37] One day later, just before the deadline, Germany accepted the London Schedule of Payments that included the formal obligation to pay 132 billion gold marks to its former enemies. Wirth, a left-wing Centrist with little support in his own party, was chosen by Socialist President Friedrich Ebert to accept the ultimatum because he possessed the confidence of the German Left; he also appeared capable of gaining the cooperation of the German People's party (the DVP), a party with close ties to German industry, whose agreement was essential to levying the taxes necessary to pay reparations. A somewhat colorless politician and parliamentarian, an indifferent bureaucrat and negotiator, Wirth was also known as a staunch German nationalist. The main characteristic of his year-and-a-half chancellorship, according to one historian, was a "perpetual trimming . . . a constant, exhausting search for political equilibria. Industry was balanced against the Socialists, Russian possibilities against Western, a rhetoric of fulfillment against a constant effort to evade reparations, the search for fiscal reform against the wearied acceptance of inevitable inflation."[38]

Wirth adopted the policy of fulfillment (*Erfüllungspolitik*) of his close friend and Centrist colleague, Matthias Erzberger, as opposed to the hard-liners in Germany who preached defiance and revisionism. "Fulfillment" for the Germans was a practical, purposeful, if also a duplicitous policy. Once the Entente had specified the reparations sums in May 1921, Berlin had little to lose (except risk the histrionic complaints of the German Right, which had considerable value at the diplomatic negotiating table) and much to gain by a policy of ostentatious compliance.[39] This ended a year-long policy of drift and passivity. It enabled the Reich government to demonstrate before the world its good faith but also the crippling results to the economy of Germany and the Allied countries of the "insensate" reparations demands. Finally, formal acceptance of the London Schedule was considered indispensable to maintain Germany's territorial integrity: in March 1921 Allied troops had occupied Düsseldorf and Ruhr-

37. Rudolf Morsey, *Die Deutsche Zentrumspartei, 1917–1923* (Düsseldorf: Droste Verlag, 1966), pp. 379–92.

38. Charles S. Maier, *Recasting Bourgeois Europe: Stabilization in France, Germany, and Italy in the Decade after World War I* (Princeton: Princeton University Press, 1975), p. 249. Wirth's nationalism and his resentment of the Allies' reparations policies are not emphasized by Laubach or Felix; but see Stephen A. Schuker, *The End of French Predominance in Europe: The Financial Crisis of 1924 and the Adoption of the Dawes Plan* (Chapel Hill: University of North Carolina Press, 1976), p. 16.

39. The announced figure, 132 billion gold marks, was divided into three payment parts (Series A, B, and C) of which only 50 billion gold marks (the totals of Series A and B) were expected to be paid. For political reasons, French critics leaped on the fictitious sum of 132 billion as inadequate. Britain, the United States, and the neutrals deemed it exorbitant. Germany obtained valuable evidence of the Allies' ambivalence more than their greed. Cf. Felix, *Rathenau*, pp. 21–24.

ort and seized customs offices to collect reparations. Had Germany rejected the London Ultimatum, Allied troops might have occupied the entire Ruhr. Moreover, on 3 May there was a pro-Polish uprising in Upper Silesia. German volunteers (*Freikorps*) fought the Poles, and Berlin feared the Allies' decision on the fate of the province. *Erfüllungspolitik*, a policy of submission and realism, was designed to save the Reich from further dismemberment. In addition, stressing the danger of bolshevism and the threat of Germany's internal collapse and insisting that a weak, truncated Reich could not recompense the Allies, themselves heavily indebted to the United States, Berlin's *Erfüllungspolitik* became a platform to urge the *scaling down* of reparations payments, which menaced Germany, Europe, and the world.[40]

Erfüllungspolitik was instituted simultaneously with the Wirth government's establishment of closer economic ties with Soviet Russia. Just as Germany aimed at splitting the Entente, it sought also to exploit the chasm between the West and Moscow, using Russia's isolation to subvert the military clauses of the Treaty of Versailles.[41] The Allies were helpless to prevent German activities—the buildup of Soviet armaments, the production of proscribed weapons in Russia, and the ties between the Reichswehr and the Communist leadership —all of which were accompanied by discussions between German industrialists and the Kremlin.

The Berlin government was ambivalent about the Soviet connection. Although the East offered seemingly unlimited opportunity for nationalist and economic goals, it nonetheless presented a danger of ideological subversion and offered only questionable economic advantages at present. Germany needed Western capital to stabilize its inflation-riddled economy; and it had no funds to invest in Russia. Russia needed German technology, goods, and manpower; but it had no means to pay. Since Bismarck's time, German policymakers had debated the role of Russia in the Reich's overall economic as well as strategic policies. Now, under Weimar, the "Easterners" regarded Moscow as a primary area of concentration, but the "Westerners," impressed with the Entente's power and its demands, tended to minimize Moscow's significance.[42]

40. Maier, *Recasting Bourgeois Europe*, pp. 243–44, 248–49; Felix, *Rathenau*, pp. 67–68. Also cf. the more sympathetic Erich Eyck, *A History of the Weimar Republic* (Cambridge, Mass.: Harvard University Press, 1962), 1:193–95; and Laubach, *Kabinette Wirth*, pp. 58–69.

41. Horst-Günter Linke, *Deutsch-sowjetische Beziehungen bis Rapallo* (Cologne: Verlag Wissenschaft und Politik, 1970), gives much detail. See also Gerald Freund, *Unholy Alliance* (London: Chatto and Windus, 1957); Herbert Helbig, *Die Träger der Rapallo-Politik* (Göttingen: Vandenhoeck and Ruprecht, 1958); and Gustav Hilger and Alfred G. Meyer, *The Incompatible Allies* (New York: Macmillan, 1953).

42. Laubach, *Kabinette Wirth*, pp. 107–11; Hartmut Pogge von Strandmann, "Grossindustrie und Rapallopolitik: Deutsch-sowjetische Handelsbeziehungen in der Weimarer Republik," *Historische Zeitschrift* 222 (April 1976): 288–91; Theodor Schieder, "Die Entstehungsge-

German industry, with only few exceptions, had set itself adamantly against the policy of fulfillment while simultaneously opposing democracy, socialism, and the trade unions at home.[43] The Rhine-Westphalian magnates organized themselves into the Reichsverband der deutschen Industrie (RDI), a powerful pressure group vis-à-vis the German government. The RDI criticized the "politically-motivated" Versailles treaty and the "cabinet politics" of the postwar era; echoes of Lenin and John Maynard Keynes could be heard in its warning that France and Britain would soon rue the "economic realities" these had produced. Indeed, the Allies and neutrals were already suffering from German dumping, the export of the Reich's inflation, and the blatant lack of cooperation with Western traders on the part of German business. The RDI calculated that the resentment would be directed more against Paris than Berlin.

German industry's case for an "objective" (i.e., revisionist) European economic system was to some extent encouraged by the actions of the United States. On 25 August 1921 America and Germany signed a peace treaty in Berlin that normalized their relations. Washington, which possessed unofficial representation on all the Allied councils, including the Reparations Commission, made known its displeasure with the London Schedule and its preference that reparations payments be set according to "Germany's capacity to pay." However, when America in early August announced the convening of a conference on the Pacific that would deal also with disarmament, Washington became virtually inactive in European affairs, not venturing beyond its announced general disapproval of the Entente's reparations policies.[44]

The Wirth government thus embarked on a policy of ostensibly meeting its

---

schichte des Rapallo-Vertrags," ibid., 204 (June 1967) 550–55; and Gordon H. Mueller, "Rapallo Reexamined: A New Look at Germany's Secret Military Collaboration with Russia in 1922," *Military Affairs* 40 (1976): 109–17, which revises Hans W. Gatzke, "Russo-German Military Collaboration during the Weimar Republic," *American Historical Review* 63 (April 1958): 565–97.

A useful collection of documents is: Ministerium für Auswärtige Angelegenheiten der DDR/Ministerium für Auswärtige Angelegenheiten der UdSSR, *Deutsch-sowjetische Beziehungen von den Verhandlungen in Brest-Litovsk bis zum Abschluss des Rapallo-Vertrages* ([East] Berlin: Staatsverlag der DDR, 1971).

43. See especially Bernd Weisbrod, *Schwerindustrie in der Weimarer Republik* (Wuppertal: Hammer, 1978). Also see Georges Soutou, "Der Einfluss der Schwerindustrie auf die Gestaltung der Frankreichpolitik Deutschlands, 1919–1921"; Peter Krüger, "Die Rolle der Banken und der Industrie in den deutschen reparationspolitischen Entscheidungen nach dem Ersten Weltkrieg"; and Hermann J. Rupieper, "Industrie und Reparationen: Einige Aspekte des Reparationsproblems, 1922–1924," all in Hans Mommsen, Dietmar Petzina, and Bernd Weisbrod, eds. *Industrielles System und politische Entwicklung in der Weimarer Republik* (Düsseldorf: Droste Verlag, 1974), 2:543–51, 568–92. The political dimensions are ably discussed in John Williamson, *Karl Helfferich* (Princeton: Princeton University Press, 1971), pp. 344–64.

44. Robert H. van Meter, Jr., "The United States and European Recovery, 1918–1923," (Ph.D. diss., University of Wisconsin, 1971), pp. 284–305.

reparations obligations in the face of fairly widespread domestic opposition (even the Socialists believed that the payments were impossible), America's detachment, and Anglo-French differences that were risky to exploit. Through a perilous combination of foreign loans and currency manipulation, Germany was in the process of completing the required payment of one billion marks in late August 1921, when domestic violence erupted in the assassination of Erzberger. The first result was to impede the DVP's entry into the government. It also incited the German National People's party (the DNVP) to militate against *Erfüllungspolitik*. Abroad, critics such as Keynes insisted that Germany would be incapable of meeting its payments in 1922, a sentiment Wirth's government endorsed. Pessimistic over the fate of Upper Silesia, Berlin searched for an alternative strategy to reduce its payments; one possibility was to attempt a direct rapprochement with Paris.

On 27 August Germany and France completed the Wiesbaden agreement, which represented an important departure in both governments' policies.[45] The agreement was negotiated on 12 and 13 June at Wiesbaden between Germany's newly named minister of reconstruction, Walther Rathenau, and France's minister of the liberated regions, Louis Loucheur. The initiative had come from Berlin. Before resigning over the uproar created by the Allies' reparations demands, the Fehrenbach government on 23 April had offered to provide equipment and workers for French reconstruction. After accepting the London Schedule, the Wirth government renewed the proposal in a speech by Rathenau before the Reichstag on 2 June.[46]

Paris responded promptly and positively. During the lengthy conversations at Wiesbaden, Loucheur transformed the simple German proposal into a complex scheme of deliveries- and payments-in-kind that required almost three months of follow-up negotiation. Paris needed cash. However, it was not scheduled to receive anything from the first billion-mark payments of 1921, and France suspected that Germany might default in 1922. The Wiesbaden policy, promoted by Jacques Seydoux, under secretary for commercial relations in the Quai d'Orsay, represented the revival of his earlier 1920 plan; this envisaged direct Franco-German cooperation as the core of Western European reconstruction, cooperation that would eventually lead to collective action in Eastern Europe and Soviet Russia. France, seeking to lessen its dependency on Britain and America, by no means viewed Wiesbaden as a partnership between equals: during his talks with Rathenau, Loucheur refused to link the reparations negotiations with possible concessions regarding Germany's disarma-

---

45. Weill-Raynal, *Réparations*, 2:29–52; Louis Loucheur, *Carnets secrets, 1908–1932* (Brussels: Brepols, 1962), pp. 84–95; and Walther Rathenau, *Tagebuch, 1907–1922*, ed. Hartmut Pogge von Strandmann (Düsseldorf: Droste Verlag, 1967), pp. 243–56.

46. Felix, *Rathenau*, pp. 73–75; and Laubach, *Kabinette Wirth*, pp. 73–79.

ment or the future of Upper Silesia. Briand's government intended to base the Franco-German economic entente on Berlin's recognition of the permanency of its Versailles obligations and on France's right to impose sanctions if these not be met.[47]

Neither Wirth nor Rathenau was optimistic about the fruits of the Wiesbaden talks; faced with domestic troubles and an uncertain diplomatic situation, they nonetheless recognized the merits of a partial solution. French and German industrialists were not unanimously favorable toward the plan. Also, as anticipated, Moscow and Washington took a dim view of the negotiations. Above all, France's wartime partners, Belgium, Italy, and particularly Britain, opposed Wiesbaden not only because it gave France a priority and potentially increased the French share of reparations receipts but also because it threatened to create a new continental bloc.[48] Less than a week after the final version of the Wiesbaden agreement was signed by Rathenau and Loucheur, the League of Nations announced the partition of Upper Silesia. It gave Germany over half the territory but divided the industrial triangle, leaving most of the mineral wealth, the principal industrial establishments, and 350,000 Germans on the Polish side. While the League celebrated its difficult decision and France and Poland acknowledged a limited victory, Germany and Britain, which had taken the latter's side, were both disgruntled.

Germany regarded Britain as a potential ally in its effort to reduce French dominance and obtain relief from the London Schedule.[49] Before signing the Wiesbaden accords, Rathenau had sent a signal to the British of his willingness to conclude a similar pact.[50] Because German deliveries-in-kind would scarcely be helpful to Britain's ailing industrial economy, Rathenau proposed

47. Georges Soutou, "Die deutschen Reparationen und das Seydoux-Project, 1920/21," *Vierteljahrshefte für Zeitgeschichte* 23, no. 3 (1975): 237–70; Jay L. Kaplan, "France's Road to Genoa: Strategic, Economic, and Ideological Factors in French Foreign Diplomacy, 1921–1922" (Ph.D. diss., Columbia University, 1974), pp. 225–59; and Walter A. McDougall, *France's Rhineland Diplomacy, 1914–1924* (Princeton: Princeton University Press, 1978), pp. 140, 165–66.

48. Reactions to Wiesbaden in Weill-Raynal, *Réparations*, 2:52–56; Kaplan, "France's Road to Genoa," pp. 259–88; and Stamm, *Lloyd George*, pp. 153 and 210.

49. On 7 Sept. Wirth told the RDI confidentially that Britain anticipated a revision of the London Schedule that winter: *Akten-Wirth*, 1: no. 82 (henceforth in *Akten-Wirth*, either page or document number will be given). A day later, Britain's ambassador to Germany, Lord D'Abernon, reported by telephone that though the German situation was "satisfactory," the popularity of Britain and Lloyd George and the prestige of the Wirth government would be enhanced by demonstrable "advantages" of following London's "advice." D'Abernon urged a British counteroffer to the Wiesbaden agreements and warned about "disturbances" over Upper Silesia: A. J. Sylvester to Lloyd George, 8 Sept. 1921, LGP F 93/4/3.

50. Viscount Edgar D'Abernon, *Versailles to Rapallo, 1920–1922: The Diary of an Ambassador* (Garden City, N.Y.: Doubleday, Doran and Co., 1929), p. 217. Communications between Berlin and London in Stamm, *Lloyd George*, pp. 154–55.

an elaborate scheme involving expanded German exports to Russia, the profits of which would eventually be turned over to London as reparations. Significantly, this proposal coincided with talks under way between German and British capitalists to discuss joint ventures in Eastern Europe; Rathenau, as head of the Allgemeine Elektrizitäts-Gesellschaft (AEG), had participated in these talks.[51]

This German initiative provided Lloyd George with a means to counter France's conception of a "political" grouping of Western nations that could dictate conditions to Russia. Germany and England could head a quasi-laissez-faire arrangement, sanctioning the entry of government-supported *private* capitalists in the East.[52] On 23 November Lloyd George met with the German industrialist Hugo Stinnes, who brought a proposal for an international financial consortium, consisting of Britain, Germany, France, and the United States, that would coordinate the reconstruction of Russia. The Stinnes proposal arrived concurrently with serious discussions in Britain as a result of the Soviets' note of 28 October. In addition, Moscow had suddenly broken off negotiations with the British industrialist Leslie Urquart.[53] The German ideas thus found a ready audience in London.

The Rathenau and Stinnes initiatives coincided with a change in British policy: Lloyd George had decided that the London Payments Schedule was impossible, that Germany must be granted a moratorium, and that the questions of reparations, interallied debts, and Russian reconstruction would have to be combined into a policy of "European reconstruction." Britain, a major creditor to Europe but also a major debtor to the United States, was in a unique

---

51. Anglo-German collaboration in Russia, first urged by Keynes in 1919, was strongly supported by the commercial secretary of the British embassy in Berlin, F. Thelwell (see, e.g., memorandum, 9 Feb. 1921, GB BT 90/17). The Foreign Office and the Board of Trade preferred private initiatives and international syndicates (such as the ties established between Urquart, Krupp, and Deutsch in the summer of 1921: Linke, *Deutsch-sowjetische Beziehungen*, p. 142), to formal and official government action: Hilton Young to Grigg, 25 Oct., 9 Nov. 1921, Grigg Papers, roll 1.

52. "Wanted: A Policy of World Reconstruction," *Daily Chronicle*, 10, 11, 12 Oct. 1921, whose author, Stamm suggests, was possibly Philip Kerr.

53. Euler, *Aussenpolitik*, pp. 309–10; Frances Lloyd George, *Lloyd George: A Diary*, ed. A. J. P. Taylor (New York: Harper and Row, 1971), p. 239. Discussion of the "Stinnes plan" in *Morning Post*, 21 Nov., 1 Dec. 1921; *The Times*, 30 Nov. 1921; *Daily Telegraph*, 23 Nov. 1921; *Manchester Guardian*, 22 Nov. and 6 Dec. 1921; and *The Spectator*, 26 Nov. 1921. Urquart, negotiating on behalf of the Russo-Asiatic Consolidated Corporation, was attempting to obtain long-term leases over four of its former mining properties; Lenin, who earlier had encouraged the Urquart-Krassin negotiations, suddenly ordered a halt, demanding a loan in return for the concession and ordering an investigation of the mines held formerly by the British company: Lenin, *Collected Works*, 45:261, 339, 354–55, 359, and 371; and Thomas S. Martin, "The Urquart Concession and Anglo-Soviet Relations, 1921–1922," *Jahrbücher für Geschichte Osteuropas* 20 (1972): 551–59.

position to take leadership. Lloyd George had earlier tried and failed to win Woodrow Wilson's support for a great economic enterprise to restore all of Europe. Now he would act alone.[54] France's separate agreement with Kemal's Turkey hardened his attitude toward Paris. The opening of the Washington Conference made a British initiative in Europe all the more opportune. Lloyd George was spurred on by Treasury officials; British bankers; Britain's ambassador to Germany, Lord Edgar D'Abernon; his former secretary, Philip Kerr; and his current secretary, Sir Edward Grigg, to link a moratorium for Germany with the impending negotiations with Russia. No doubt the fall of the mark in October produced tremors in British financial circles. Moreover, adding relief for Germany to the new and controversial approach to Russia to some extent mitigated the political perils of the latter, especially in the cabinet.[55]

Wirth, who had anticipated the British move, on 26 October formed a new government in the wake of the Upper Silesian crisis. Though prevented by his Democratic party from joining, Rathenau remained a key actor in Germany's contacts with London for reparations relief. He arrived in Britain just after Stinnes, on 28 November, presumably on the initiative of British officials, and he met with people at the Treasury and at the Bank of England.[56] Rathenau displayed some enthusiasm for a projected world economic conference that would combine Europe's most pressing problems. During their private talk on 2 December, Lloyd George assured Rathenau that Britain wanted a "strong, healthy, and flourishing Germany" and would do all in its power to rehabilitate the Reich. Together they discussed their hopes for America's cooperation and the ways to overcome France's probable objections to Stinnes's proposals.[57]

The French were indeed apprehensive over the visits by Stinnes and Rathenau but could obtain no clarification from the Foreign Office, which was also

54. Gisela Bertram-Libal, *Aspekte der britischen Deutschlandpolitik, 1919–1922* (Göttingen: Kummerle, 1972), pp. 67–71; Stamm, *Lloyd George*, pp. 135–200; Konrad von Zwehl, *Die Deutschlandpolitik Englands von 1922 bis 1924* (Augsburg: Blasatitsch, 1974), pp. 20–21; and also the very partisan Kenneth O. Morgan, *Consensus and Disunity: The Lloyd George Coalition Government, 1918–1922* (Oxford: Clarendon Press, 1979), pp. 140–45.

55. James R. M. Butler, *Lord Lothian, Philip Kerr, 1882–1940* (London: Macmillan, 1960), pp. 80–108. Kerr's influence in: draft letter to Wilson (Mar. 1920) on the importance of European "appeasement"; opposition to Ruhr occupation (19 Feb. 1921); conveying reaction of "City and Industrial circles" to pressure on Germany (29 Apr. 1921); solution to Britain's industrial-labor problems by taking initiative for European reconstruction, hopefully with U.S. cooperation (23 June 1921); and urging a major British initiative (22 Sept. 1921), LGP F 60, 90/1/38; F 90/1/43; F 34/3/2; and F 34/2/8. Churchill was similarly though more cautiously in favor of a policy of reconciliation with Germany: Gilbert, *Churchill*, pp. 608–9, 791, 895–96. Also see Alan J. Sharp, "The Foreign Office in Eclipse," *History* 61, no. 202 (June 1976): 198–218.

56. *Akten-Wirth*, 1: Chefbesprechung, 12 Dec. 1921, no. 166; and Rathenau, *Tagebuch*, pp. 263–73.

57. Dinner, Friday, 2 Dec., at Philip Sassoon's with Lloyd George and Sir Robert Horne: Rathenau, *Tagebuch*, pp. 266–70.

scantily informed.[58] Briand returned from his tumultuous and not very successful Washington trip on 2 December. Suddenly, on 5 December, France's ambassador to Britain, Count de Saint-Aulaire, most likely on his own initiative, presented Curzon with a proposal for a bilateral defensive alliance that involved not only the defense of France against a German invasion but the defense of Poland as well. He explained that such a Franco-British alliance would facilitate some degree of French disarmament, which Britain long had been urging; would ease Germany's entry into the League of Nations, which London strongly favored; would stabilize Europe; and would make it possible for France to join the proposed consortium for the reconstruction of Russia.[59]

While the diplomats tried to orient themselves, Lloyd George proceeded in a different direction. The Irish question was for the time being settled; on 6 December an agreement was hammered out establishing a new state with dominion status in southern Ireland. Now his government could concentrate on the problems of the Continent.[60] The Bank of England on 2 December had, not unexpectedly, refused to grant Germany either short- or long-term credits because of the uncertain financial situation arising from the London Schedule; Wirth's *Erfüllungspolitik* had produced this "confirmation" that the Allies' reparations policies stood in the way of a solvent, paying Germany.[61] The British government promptly responded. Speaking in Manchester on 5 December, Sir Robert Horne, chancellor of the exchequer, urged a moratorium because Germany's collapse would menace all of Europe. That same day Lloyd George summoned Loucheur to London. At his country house in Chequers on 8 December, he confronted Briand's close friend and colleague with a combination of toughness and guile. He threatened that if France reacted to a German default by invading the Ruhr, "it would be the end of the alliance" between their two countries. Drawing a gloomy picture of Europe's economic future unless Russia were reintegrated through the joint action of German, British,

58. Unsigned memorandum, Paris, 23 Dec. 1921, FMAE Z GB 61. Earlier: Montille to MAE, London, 22, 26 Nov. 1921, tel. #1033 and #1048–50; Charles Laurent to MAE, Berlin 27, 29 Nov. 1921, tel. #2525–27 and #2529; Peretti to Montille, Paris, 24 Nov. 1921; and Seydoux note, Paris, 29 Nov. 1921, all in FMAE Z All. 468. The Belgians and Italians were also alarmed by the Anglo-German talks (*DBFP*, 16: nos. 749, 751, 753–55), but the irritated, uninformed Curzon could not enlighten them.

59. Saint-Aulaire–Curzon interview in FMAE, *Documents Diplomatiques, Documents relatifs aux négociations concernant les garanties de sécurité contre une agression de l'Allemagne, 10 janvier 1919–7 décembre 1923* (Paris: Imprimerie Nationale, 1924), pp. 90–93; and GB Cmd. 2169, pp. 208–9. On the origins, see Georges Suarez, *Briand: sa vie, son oeuvre* (Paris: Plon, 1941) 5:336–46.

60. Thomas Jones, *Whitehall Diary* (London and New York: Oxford University Press, 1971), 3:180–84.

61. Rathenau, *Tagebuch*, 1 Dec. 1921, p. 264: "City ablehnend. Davon abhängig alles weitere." Cf. Wirth statement to minister-presidents of the German *Länder*, 20 Jan. 1922: *Akten-Wirth*, 1: no. 192.

French, and American capitalists, he expressed "absolute certainty" that the present Russian government was prepared "in all sincerity" to recognize the czarist debt. He offered to cancel debts and reparations owed to Britain and to ease other financial pressures on France to the same extent that the United States would be willing to make similar concessions to Britain. Finally, he claimed that his private sources of information indicated America's willingness to "join in an examination of the world situation."[62]

Loucheur was not cowed by this torrent of threats and vague information. He reminded Lloyd George that France and Germany had already discussed the possibility of joint enterprises in Russia at Wiesbaden. He recommended that they both sound out Washington, preferring that America take the initiative in convening a world economic conference. Like Noulens and Briand, Loucheur stated his preference for coordinated, intergovernmental action vis-à-vis Russia.[63] But he was too late; Britain had already decided to respond to the signals from Moscow and Berlin.

Lloyd George also invited Briand to ply the route to Britain. In the meantime, he induced Loucheur to meet with Rathenau, who was conveniently still in London. The German received extensive information from British officials on the Chequers talks, on the "British" program, and on Loucheur's recognition that further German reparations deliveries were now impossible. Rathenau had won the confidence of the British and also gained invaluable support for his future reentry into the Wirth government.[64]

Thus, a half year later, the Wiesbaden partners were reunited in London at the behest of Lloyd George. The British government anticipated a revision of the London Schedule based on neither an expanded Anglo-French partnership nor renewed negotiations between Germany and the victor states but rather on a complex, multinational action involving Russia and the United States. However, the Soviets had not given firm assurances; and Washington's cooperation, even more vital, would be still more elusive. The Harding government, making a dazzling international debut, was reluctant to become involved with Russia, reparations, or war debts in the manner Lloyd George had devised.

Germany, which officially requested a moratorium on 14 December 1921, had won a striking victory. Great Britain had demonstrated to the world its commitment to treaty revision. France, despite remnants of independence and

62. Loucheur, *Carnets*, pp. 185–88.

63. Denise Artaud, *La question des dettes interalliées et la reconstruction de l'Europe (1917–1929)* (Lille: Atelier Reproduction des Thèses, Université de Lille III, 1978), 1:375–81, compares the French and British "Chequers plans" for combining debts and reparations: the French proposed a new mechanism for German payments, but Lloyd George insisted on a moratorium. Also see Kaplan, "France's Road to Genoa," pp. 301–3.

64. Rathenau, *Tagebuch*, pp. 271–73; and his report to the cabinet: *Akten-Wirth*, 1:463–64 (12 Dec. 1921).

resistance, could be towed along in the hope of its obtaining a pact with Britain. Wirth's policy, not without danger, dictated a prolonged, agile balancing act on the domestic and diplomatic fronts.[65] For the time being, the Reich had loosened the ties of Wiesbaden, promoted its case for further reducing its reparations, and won friends in London. Germany's goal of eroding the Versailles treaty and Lloyd George's new-found mission for European conciliation became linked.

The Washington Conference and Europe

The Washington Conference on the Limitation of Armaments represented the Harding administration's first major venture into international diplomacy. Studied primarily for its decisions regarding the Far East and naval construction, this conference also expressed the emerging United States policy toward Europe, Europe's reactions to signals from across the sea, and the limits of the "new diplomacy."[66]

Instead of the old, imprecise term of "isolation," it would be more correct to describe America's European policy in the early 1920s as an active, equilibrist diplomacy: a product of compromises between domestic industries and pressure groups, government institutions and agencies, the executive branch and Congress.[67] The first elected peacetime administration after World War I had to conciliate a Congress jealous of its budgetary power, highly organized agricultural, business, and banking constituencies that demanded the revival of "prosperity," and large segments of the American population that were un-

65. British support for the moratorium was not entirely disinterested since a payments default would harm the London banks that had invested 5 to 6 million pounds in credits to German importers: Maier, *Recasting Bourgeois Europe*, p. 267. Sir John Bradbury, Britain's chief delegate to the Reparations Commission and a critic of French and Belgian resistance to a moratorium, was also impatient with the stubborn RDI: "I do not want to have to grant a moratorium without making the industrials bleed" (quoted in ibid., pp. 266–67).

66. Robert H. van Meter, "The Washington Conference of 1921–1922: A New Look," *Pacific Historical Review* 46 (1977): 603–24; Roberta Allbert Dayer, "The British War Debts to the United States and the Anglo-Japanese Alliance, 1920–1923," ibid. 45 (1976): 569–95; Donald S. Birn, "Open Diplomacy at the Washington Conference of 1921–2: The British and French Experience," *Comparative Studies in Society and History* 12 (July 1970): 297–319; and Roger Dingman, *Power in the Pacific: The Origins of Naval Arms Limitation* (Chicago and London: University of Chicago Press, 1976), pp. 139–219. Documentation in : U.S. Department of State, *Conference on the Limitation of Armament, Washington, Nov. 12, 1921–Feb. 6, 1922* (Washington: Government Printing Office, 1922); and FMAE, *Documents Diplomatiques, Conférence de Washington, juillet 1921–février 1922* (Paris: Imprimerie Nationale, 1923).

67. Denise Artaud, "Aux origines de l'atlantisme: la recherche d'un équilibre européen au lendemain de la première guerre mondiale," *Relations Internationales* 10 (1977): 115–26; William A. Williams, "A Note on American Foreign Policy in Europe in the Nineteen Twenties,"

affected by big business's profits during the war and now feared the loss of their jobs, property, and savings in the wake of the short but sharp postwar depression.[68]

Republican foreign policy, though rooted in Wilsonianism, lacked its predecessor's undisputed executive leadership, its vision of America's role in the world, and especially a consistent conception of America's relationship to Europe. President Harding, Secretary of State Charles Evans Hughes, Commerce Secretary Herbert Hoover, Treasury Secretary Andrew Mellon, and many key American diplomats in Europe all wanted to mold relations between the United States and Europe. Bankers such as Benjamin Strong, governor of the Federal Reserve Bank of New York, and J. P. Morgan and his partners, Thomas Lamont and Dwight Morrow, often acted as unofficial spokesmen for Washington, as did the various agents assigned to international commissions, like James Logan, who was attached to the Reparations Commission.[69]

Republican foreign policy toward Europe was based on an inner contradiction. Though committed to promoting the reconstruction of a stable European market for American exports, the United States had made an ostentatious retreat from Europe's political affairs. The exclusion of the League of Nations from the Washington Conference underlined America's preference for ad hoc expedients and Great Power initiatives over participation in the structures that had been established at the Paris Peace Conference.[70]

In the Treaty of Berlin of August 1921, the United States had nonetheless obtained identical privileges vis-à-vis Germany that had been included in the Treaty of Versailles.[71] There were American observers not only on the Reparations Commission but also on the Supreme Council and the Conference of

Science and Society 22 (Winter 1958): 1–20; and D. C. Watt, "American 'Isolationism' in the 1920s: Is It a Useful Concept?" *British Association for American Studies Bulletin*, no. 6 (1958): 3–19.

68. Van Meter, "United States and European Recovery," chaps. 4–7.

69. Melvyn P. Leffler, "American Policy Making and European Stability, 1921–1933," *Pacific Historical Review* 46 (May 1977): 207–28.

70. Walters, *League of Nations*, pp. 137–38, gives the following examples of the Harding administration's change of America's posture from "aloofness to hostility" toward the League: Washington's refusal to answer League communications, its vetoing of League supervision of international health or drug questions, its delaying the establishment of the mandates system "until it had secured its interests in the oil of Mesopotamia and the cable station of Yap, not by the quick and easy method of consultation with the Council but by individual correspondence with each of the principal Allied powers," and, for twelve months, thwarting the League's efforts to bail out Austria. Washington, because of the delay in setting up its war-debt policy, hesitated to release its liens against the Vienna government deriving from the relief loans between 1919 and 1921. Cf. Peter E. Schmidt, "The Relief of Austria, 1919–1922" (Ph.D. diss., Case Western Reserve University, 1977), pp. 356–61, 379–85, 412–19.

71. Text in *FRUS, 1921*, 2:29–32.

Ambassadors. Constrained by its own divisions and by Congress, the Harding administration assiduously avoided political responsibility for the issues that divided postwar Europe: reparations and security. Refusing to recognize the link between war debts and reparations or between the lapsed Anglo-American guarantee to France and France's spreading military alliances, Washington preached against Europe's "economic chaos" and called for "disarmament," as if its own decisive wartime intervention, its formidable role in the peace treaties, and its sudden withdrawal could be ignored.[72]

America's Russian policies were similarly contradictory. Washington refused to recognize the Bolshevik regime and its nationalization policy. It nonetheless allowed the ARA to act rapidly and effectively to alleviate the famine, thereby obtaining valuable information and eliminating European competition. Despite Lenin's pleas, the United States refused to include Russia in the Washington Conference, though acting as Moscow's spokesman, it put pressure on Japan to evacuate Siberia. The policy of nonrecognition, first practiced by Wilson toward revolutionary Mexico, was aimed at postponing normal, equal relations with a hostile, ideologically based regime. Washington's official disapproval served to dampen American industry's rather reserved attitude about expanding economic relations with Soviet Russia. It also shielded those European states that were ideologically opposed to bolshevism and, more important, lacked the capital to resume their enterprises in the East.[73] However, it did not discourage Europe's two industrial and trading powers, Germany and Britain.

America's German policy sheds further light on Washington's aims. A defeated Reich, which no longer threatened American shipping and no longer appeared capable of dominating the Continent, was now considered a key factor in the stabilization of Europe. Weimar Germany was considered a potential bulwark against communism as well as a balance against Allied preponderance. In order to revive its strength and economic potential, Germany's reparations had to be reduced, France's sanctions policy had to be curbed, and Germany's neighbors also had to disarm. Yet the German republic was to be the "object" of Washington's European policy, not a partner.[74]

72. Arthur Sweetser to League Secretary-General Sir Eric Drummond, Washington, 22 Feb. 1922, LNA 40 19170/1866. Also Sally Marks and Denis Dulude, "German-American Relations, 1918–1921," *Mid-America* 54, no. 5 (October 1971): 211–26.

73. Cf. William A. Williams, *American-Russian Relations, 1781–1947* (New York: Rinehart, 1952), pp. 191–99; Philip S. Gillette, "American Capital in the Contest for Soviet Oil, 1920–1923," *Soviet Studies* 24, no. 4 (April 1973): 477–90; and N. Stephen Kane, "American Businessmen and Foreign Policy: The Recognition of Mexico, 1920–1923," *Political Science Quarterly* 90 (1975): 293–313. Excellent detailed analysis of America's Russian policy in unsigned memorandum, 28 Dec. 1921, Germ. BA R 43 I/132.

74. Carl-Ludwig Holtfrereich, "Amerikanischer Kapitalexport und Wiederaufbau der deutschen Wirtschaft, 1919–1923 im Vergleich zu 1924–1929," *Vierteljahrsschrift für Sozial-*

When it refused to become involved with the reparations crisis in the spring of 1921, Washington temporarily lost the initiative to Briand, Rathenau, and Lloyd George. However, when the leaders of Europe began spinning international combinations, tied relief for Germany with a major German role in the exploitation of the Russian market, and urged America's participation in an international consortium to develop that market, the administration responded negatively. Hoover was especially outspoken against Germany's being assigned a "middle-man" function. America was unwilling to take part in any arrangement where its goods and its capital would be dispensed by either former enemies or friends.[75]

Britain, which had aspired to a special economic relationship with the United States in the postwar years, was quickly disappointed. The Anglo-Saxon powers became locked in a global competition for raw materials and resources not only in Latin America, the Middle East, and Asia, but also in Russia and Central Europe. Wherever American capital encountered British or British-dominated companies, the American press fulminated against London's "closed-door" mentality. The Anglo-French San Remo agreement of 1920 had to be reinterpreted immediately to ensure the "open door" to American oil companies in the former territories of the Ottoman Empire. Before obtaining Washington's agreement to its mandate over Palestine, Britain had to repeat assurances of the protection of private American interests in the Holy Land.[76]

Washington wielded powerful leverage over Britain and France with its war-debt policies and with control of access to its vast private credit markets.[77] While France under Briand procrastinated about funding its war debts (in the hope of eventual German reparations payments and, perhaps, of some reduc-

und Wirtschaftsgeschichte 64 (1977): 497–529; Frank Costigliola, "The United States and the Reconstruction of Germany in the 1920s," *Business History Review* 50 (1976): 477–502; Bernard V. Burke, "American Economic Diplomacy and the Weimar Republic," *Mid-America* 54, no. 4 (October 1972): 211–33; and Werner Link, *Die amerikanische Stabilisierungspolitik in Deutschland, 1921–32* (Düsseldorf: Droste Verlag, 1970), pp. 89–105.

75. See Hoover to Hughes, Washington, 3 Dec. 1921, Hoover/Comm./Russia: "For us to align ourselves with Germany today in any relationship with the Russians would negative [sic] any values that have been so carefully built up in the past." Hughes had been inclined to encourage the Berlin government provided "that the German middlemen play fair": confid. memorandum, 28 Nov. 1921, Hughes to Hoover, 1 Dec., ibid.

76. Carl P. Parrini, *Heir to Empire: United States Economic Diplomacy, 1916–1923* (Pittsburgh: University of Pittsburgh Press, 1969), esp. chap. 6; and Michael J. Hogan, *Informal Entente: The Private Structure of Cooperation in Anglo-American Economic Diplomacy, 1918–1928* (Columbia, Mo.: University of Missouri Press, 1977). Oil negotiations preceding U.S. agreement to the British mandate in Palestine in *FRUS, 1921*, 2:94–105.

77. Artaud, *Dettes interalliées*; and Melvyn Leffler, *The Elusive Quest: America's Pursuit of European Stability and France's Security, 1919–1933* (Chapel Hill: University of North Carolina Press, 1979), chap. 2.

tion), London began developing a plan of trade-offs. No one wanted to introduce the question of war debts at the Washington Conference; but London needed a prompt debt settlement, the prerequisite to restoring its currency and also its status as a major banking power. For this settlement, London was willing to pay dearly, even the cost of renouncing the alliance with Japan (which indeed was unpopular with the dominions) and of making substantial concessions at Washington on reducing naval armaments.[78]

At Chequers, Lloyd George had claimed to receive a positive signal that Washington welcomed a world economic conference. The signal was possibly Harding's 12 November speech, the current talks between the British Treasury and American bankers, the impending Anglo-American oil agreements, or simply his own hope that the Irish settlement would mollify American public opinion. Nevertheless, on 16 December Washington deflated Lloyd George's trial balloon by declining to call a European conference.[79] Lloyd George's even more fanciful plan, that Harding would invite him, Briand, and Loucheur to America for a preliminary conference on debts and reparations, was similarly frustrated by poor preparation and press leaks. The British government thus faced the prospect of embarking without prior American support on new reparations discussions, on the effort to secure France's agreement to the proposed Russian consortium, which was based on the flimsiest Soviet commitment to repay its debts, and on the demand for debt recognition from the Bolsheviks without being prepared to offer credits or de jure recognition—all with the crushing problem of interallied debts still pending.[80]

The Washington Conference did have significant repercussions for Europe. Its "Pacific first" orientation, which Harding underlined on a number of occasions, did not hide Washington's interest in Europe's prompt stabilization. The Four Power Pact of 13 December 1921, set up to supersede the expiring Anglo-Japanese alliance, was considered by some a model for the Europeans to emulate. Clothed in fairly vague, nonbinding terms, this ten-year agreement provided for joint discussion and peaceful adjustment of problems in the Pacific. Unlike the League Covenant, the Four Power Pact called simply for "full and frank communication" in the face of aggression to arrive at an understanding as to the "most efficient measures to be taken, jointly or individually,

78. Ian Nish, *Alliance in Decline: A Study in Anglo-Japanese Relations, 1908–1923* (London: Athlone, 1972), pp. 354–82; Dayer, "British War Debts," pp. 569–95; and Michael G. Fry, *Illusions of Security: North Atlantic Diplomacy, 1918–1922* (Toronto: University of Toronto Press, 1972), pp. 187–92.

79. Harvey to Hughes, 13 Dec. 1921, USDS 550 E1/–; Harvey to Harding, 29 Nov., 12 Dec. 1921, Hoover to Harding, 16 Dec. 1921, Christian to Hughes, 22 Dec. 1921, Harding Papers, rolls 234, 144, 205. Also Jones, *Whitehall Diary* 1:185; Link, *Amerikanische Stabilisierungspolitik*, pp. 110–11.

80. Cabinet meeting, 16 Dec. 1921, GB CAB 23/27; Stamm, *Lloyd George*, pp. 220–21.

to meet the exigencies of a particular situation." No sanctions were envisaged, and there was no commitment to collective security. Ignoring the League, America, Britain, France, and Japan would police their interests in the Pacific.[81]

The Washington Conference set a precedent with its self-denying ordinances among the victors of World War I.[82] On 6 February the naval disarmament agreement established a ten-year moratorium on the construction of capital ships and the ratio (10:10:6:3.5:3.5) between the United States, Britain, Japan, France, and Italy. However, because of French resistance, America failed to extend the agreement to curtail the building of submarines or to take up the question of land armaments; none of the powers was prepared to limit its use of military aviation in wartime. The United States also succeeded in achieving the Nine Power Pact of 6 February, guaranteeing China's integrity and independence, ensuring the open door to interested powers, and holding out the possibility of China's eventually regaining its full sovereignty. Yet this too underscored divergencies among the former Allies, and between the West and Japan, that generous phrases could not hide.

The Washington Conference illustrated how public opinion could be riveted to a fairly technical diplomatic gathering. The American press raged over Britain's naval building, France's army, and Anglo-French colonial acquisitions during and after the war. France came off especially badly. The most striking case was that of Briand, whose miscalculations and maladroit performance were exaggerated by American, British, and Italian journalists, and thus blown up still more in Paris. Italy, lauded for its "cooperativeness," came off better; indeed, it alone could increase its navy. Britain, ably represented by Arthur James Balfour, steered a cautious though consistent path between the Europeans and America. Having achieved parity with America's navy, London could hope for a more extended, if unequal, partnership.[83]

The Washington Conference was a triumph for the proponents of peace through disarmament, but it left serious, unanswered problems for Europe. Britain more than France sought America's sympathy and support and was willing to pay a high price. France, labeled by the American press the "*gendarme* of Europe," was too vulnerable economically and militarily to endorse a Washington-style solution for Europe. During the closing moments of the Washington Conference, Congress quietly asserted its authority over war

81. Sweetser memorandum, "The Washington Conference and the League of Nations," Washington, 25 Feb. 1922, LNA Spec. Circ. #157.

82. Schanzer to MAE, Washington, 11 Jan. 1922, IMAE 49 (1922).

83. Ferdinand Siebert, *Aristide Briand: Staatsmann zwischen Frankreich und Europa* (Zurich and Stuttgart: E. Rentsch, 1973), pp. 248–50; Matteo Pizzigallo, "L'Italia alla Conferenza di Washington (1921–1922)," *Storia e Politica* 14, nos. 3-4 (July–Sept., Oct.–Dec. 1975): 408–48, 550–89; and Hankey to Grigg, Washington, 25 Nov. 1921, Grigg Papers, roll 1.

debts, thus reducing the possibility of relief for the Europeans.[84] Finally, the very success of Harding's conference made his administration loath to risk the sort of European gathering contemplated by Chicherin, Rathenau, and Lloyd George. Senate ratification of the Washington accords would require a struggle, an "isolationist backlash" was feared, and 1922 was an election year.

Mésentente Cordiale: The London Talks of December 1921

Anglo-French disaccord had become the leitmotif of the last half of 1921. The former wartime partners opposed each other on the key issues of reparations, security, and disarmament. Whereas the maintenance of the London Schedule was both a political and economic necessity for France, an immediate moratorium on reparations was deemed essential for Britain's return to prosperity. France sought security through military alliances, like the March 1921 pact with Poland. By contrast, Britain sought economic recovery by means of the Anglo-Soviet trade agreement that same month. The Washington Conference revealed the gap between British and French views on increased building of submarines, military aircraft, and land armaments. In addition, the former Entente was repeatedly jarred by disputes over war debts, Upper Silesia, Tangier, mandates, oil, and the Near East; the last became exceptionally acrimonious when France on 20 October signed a separate agreement with the Kemalists that essentially promoted the revision of the Treaty of Sèvres.[85] The presses, diplomats, and politicians of the two democracies frequently exaggerated their differences and misunderstandings in full view of their former enemies and allies, the neutrals, and their overwhelming creditor, the United States.[86]

Premiers Lloyd George and Briand had much in common. Born in the Celtic lands of Wales and Brittany, rising through traditional political channels with semipopulist slogans and reformist reputations, and gradually securing close ties with bankers and heavy industry, both had led their nations in wartime. Indeed, both were in power in 1916—the fateful year of Verdun, the Somme, and the Brusilov offensive, when victory had eluded the Allies and the chance for a negotiated peace was lost. Afterwards, Russia collapsed into revolution; America's entry counterbalanced Germany's victory in the East and gave the

---

84. Melvyn P. Leffler, "The Origins of Republican War Debt Policy," *Journal of American History* 59 (December 1972): 591–95.

85. GB Cmd. 1570.

86. Hines Hall III, "Lloyd George, Briand, and the Failure of the Anglo-French Entente," *Journal of Modern History* 50, no. 2 (December [June] 1978): Supplement D1123–25; and Alfred Fabre-Luce, *La crise des alliances: Essai sur les relations franco-britanniques depuis la signature de la paix (1919–1922)* (Paris: B. Grasset, 1922).

Allies their costly triumph. Both Lloyd George and Briand had considerable experience with economic mobilization and planning and also with the problems of interallied coordination. Both veterans of wartime conference diplomacy, they had become accustomed to brief, frequent, authoritative contacts between statesmen rather than exchanges of notes between lower-level bureaucrats. The war had taught them the usefulness of rapid decision making, which well suited their personalities.[87]

But there were critical differences between the two leaders. Lloyd George, in power uninterruptedly since 1916, headed a motley coalition of Liberals and Unionist Tories, a perpetuation of the wartime coalition that had enabled him to win the "coupon election" of November 1918. This was an uneasy, artificial entity, united by his leadership but frayed by the vocal criticism of influential Conservatives and Liberal Asquithites who stayed outside. Indeed, the chief beneficiary of the three tumultuous postwar years under Lloyd George was the Labour party, whose platform of European pacification and domestic reforms challenged and goaded the embattled coalition.[88] Lloyd George tended to neglect the House of Commons, and he remained aloof from all but his closest friends. His chosen field of action was European diplomacy, where, with the disappearance of Woodrow Wilson, he sought to inherit the mantle of the chief spokesman for peace and a new world order.

Briand, the more astute and skillful parliamentary politician, headed a minority Center-Left government in a Chamber dominated by the rightist Bloc national. After an absence of over three years from public affairs, Briand was appointed head of government and foreign minister in January 1921 by President Alexandre Millerand and charged with the mandate of enforcing the payment of German reparations. During the next twelve months until his dramatic resignation, French politics and public debate were concentrated to an extraordinary extent on foreign affairs. With his political adversary Raymond Poincaré at the head of the Senate Foreign Affairs Commission, Briand had to constantly demonstrate his fidelity to the "twin pillars" of Paris's policy: security and reparations. These often collided with Britain's twin pillars of disarmament and European reconstruction, and with America's insistence on disarmament and debt repayment.[89]

87. Ludwig Zimmermann, *Frankreichs Ruhrpolitik von Versailles bis zum Dawesplan* (Göttingen: Musterschmidt-Verlag, 1971), p. 29 and Maier, *Recasting Bourgeois Europe*, pp. 236–37.

88. Maurice Cowling, *The Impact of Labour, 1920–1924* (Cambridge: Cambridge University Press, 1971), pp. 15–128; and Michael Kinnear, *The Fall of Lloyd George: The Political Crisis of 1922* (London: Macmillan, 1973), chap. 1.

89. Édouard Bonnefous, *Histoire politique de la Troisième République*, 2d ed. (Paris: Presses Universitaires de France, 1968), vol. 3; F. H. Leonhardt, "Aristide Briand und seine Deutschlandpolitik" (Inaugural diss., Heidelberg University, 1951); and, especially, the critical comments in August Saint-Aulaire, *Confessions d'un vieux diplomate* (Paris: Flammarion, 1953) pp. 549, 576, and passim.

France and Britain differed on the future of their relationship. The initiative of 5 December by Saint-Aulaire signified France's wish to transform the Entente into a full-scale reciprocal alliance on the pattern of its treaties with Poland and Belgium, thereby creating a permanent counterforce against Germany as well as a possible Russo-German combination. Britain realized the importance of the Entente, if only as a counterweight against American domination and a defense against revolutions in Africa, Asia, and the Near East. London nonetheless resisted a formal alliance. The nation's opposition to a standing army; the constitutional restraint against foreign military commitments (except for those relating to the empire); the growing stress on governmental economy, epitomized by the "Geddes ax"; the dominions' lack of enthusiasm for an Anglo-French alliance that was militarily binding; and, perhaps most important, the realization that Britain was "overcommitted" economically, militarily, and politically—all these caused London to resist the basic French demands. Britain wished to go no further than to acknowledge its obligation to defend France's eastern frontier from another unprovoked German attack. Indeed, leading Britons accused France and its "excitable" allies of provoking Germany and Russia; at least for public consumption, Britain's leaders portrayed France as tough, inflexible, and militaristic.[90]

Public opinion in the two nations had grown mutually hostile after the war. In *Good-bye to All That*, Robert Graves emphasized how the fellowship of the trenches had deeply estranged their people. Keynes's vicious pen portraits of Georges Clemenceau at Paris and H. G. Wells's barbed criticisms of Briand's performance at Washington were matched by *Le Temps'* intemperate attacks on Lloyd George. Anti-French sentiment permeated all political segments in Britain: the Left opposed France's anti-Soviet stance; the Liberals believed its reparations policy was ruining the European economy; and the Tories, deploring its submarine and aircraft production, feared Paris's ability to make mischief against the British Empire, thus adding to the burdens of American competition, colonial nationalism, and Communist subversion. French politics were similarly colored by anti-British attitudes: the Left deplored London's "atrocities" in India and Ireland and its creation of troubles in Palestine; the middle parties regretted Britain's aloofness from Europe and its obsession with establishing a special relationship with America; and the Right attacked Britain's "softness" toward Germany and Soviet Russia.

France nevertheless had to appeal for a pact with Britain (a government about to shed an ally at the Washington Conference). Without London, France had no hope of collecting reparations and, in the long run, of shielding itself against German revenge. British and Russian aid had been decisive in September 1914, in stark contrast to the outcome of September 1870. A war-weakened

---

90. Selsam, *Anglo-French Alliance*, pp. 18–24.

France could not exist in splendid isolation, and there was no alternative to seeking a British commitment to help defend the peace treaties. Russia and Germany were inevitably revisionist, Italy resentful and unfriendly, and the new East European governments disunited and poor. The United States showed little sympathy for the French position. Therefore, as in 1904, France had both to acknowledge the areas of their worldwide competition and to make practical accommodations to the stronger British neighbor as the price for its security.

Briand arrived in London on 18 December and faced a difficult encounter with Lloyd George. There was doubt about Briand's political survival if he returned home empty-handed.[91] The portents were not favorable. Germany had already made its request for a moratorium. Rathenau's return to London for consultations on the reconstruction of Russia had already raised alarm in Paris. With America's refusal to consider cancellation of war debts, the British government grew stiffer toward France on economic and political questions. Belgium and Italy worried over an Entente deal at their expense while Millerand and Poincaré fretted at the price, namely, that France might be forced to recognize Russia, agree to the moratorium, and accept an inferior position alongside Britain.[92]

Briand had to make three choices: first, whether to demand the precise fulfillment of the London Schedule, which France itself had already modified at Wiesbaden, or agree to scale down reparations; second, whether to maintain an uncompromising attitude toward dealing directly with Soviet Russia, at the risk of France's exclusion from an Anglo-German consortium, or go along with Lloyd George's reconstruction schemes for the East; finally, whether to press doggedly for a specific Anglo-French alliance, at the possible cost of alienating its allies and America as well as Britain, or incorporate an Anglo-French pact into a larger framework of European reconciliation that also included Germany. To achieve the pact, which was Briand's essential aim, he was prepared to give way, prudently, on the first two issues, Germany and Russia.[93]

The talks between the two premiers began on 19 December. Despite Lloyd George's hope for an extended, conclusive conversation, they ended abruptly three days later with Briand's departure to face an interpellation in parliament on his foreign policy.[94] The tone of the discussions, less acrimonious than in August, was nonetheless far from cordial. Lloyd George was in a commanding position and he drove Briand hard on reparations. He offered to accept the Wiesbaden agreements and balance France's gain by reducing the Belgian pri-

91. GB CAB 23/27.

92. Suarez, *Briand*, pp. 347–49; Siebert, *Briand*, pp. 254–56; and Kaplan, "France's Road to Genoa," pp. 297–313.

93. Cf. Bonnefous, *Troisième République*, 3:274–75, which gives a similar analysis of Briand's choices.

94. *DBFP*, 15: nos. 106 and 108 (19, 21 Dec. 1921).

ority *if* France agreed both to a de facto moratorium and the convocation of an economic conference for the opening of Russia. On Russia he insisted that the Allies must help Lenin battle against "extremism" and dismissed Briand's cautions against dealing with the Bolsheviks. He reminded Briand that Mille-rand as prime minister in June 1920 had agreed to commence relations if Moscow recognized its foreign debts; furthermore, by signing with Kemal, France had already relinquished many of its principles.[95] Citing Italy's anxiety over their bilateral talks and the need to consult their allies over any major decisions, Lloyd George urged that a meeting of the Supreme Council be convened within two weeks at Cannes "to discuss the general economic situation in Europe"; Briand agreed.[96]

To underscore Lloyd George's aims, there were concurrent meetings of French and British financial experts, joined by Rathenau, to formulate a new reparations plan and discuss the outlines for an international syndicate to rebuild Russia; Krassin, also in London, was kept informed of the Anglo-German and Anglo-French talks, as was the ambassador of Italy.[97] Lloyd George and Briand agreed that Allied experts would reconvene in Paris to prepare a memorandum for the Supreme Council meeting at Cannes.[98]

Anticipating a new year of international conferences to treat the problems of Germany and Russia, Lloyd George and Briand expressed markedly different views, no doubt colored by the expectations of their two nations. While both recognized Germany's responsibility for its muddled finances and imminent default, they drew opposite conclusions on how to proceed. Briand argued for making the moratorium conditional on the imposition of strong external controls over the Reich's finances, which Lloyd George unequivocally opposed. Lloyd George warned that the British "public" would not tolerate any violent actions to collect reparations and that France, by ignoring this, risked alienating Britain, America, and Italy. Briand countered that *his* public would oppose any official display of amiable consultations between the Allies and the errant Reich, and that Rathenau should be barred from the Supreme Council meeting in Cannes unless Germany produced a satisfactory payments proposal to the Reparations Commission. Although both accepted the political necessity of demonstrating a measure of accommodation toward the Soviet regime, Briand did not share Lloyd George's clever but wishful argument that Lenin was will-

95. Ibid., nos. 105–9 (19, 20, 21 Dec. 1921); and notes prises au cours [des] conversation[s], 19, 20, 21 Dec. 1921, FMAE Y 684.

96. *DBFP*, 15: no. 108 (21 Dec. 1921); and Berthelot to Vignon [Secretary-General to Millerand], London, 21 Dec. 1921, FMAE Y 684.

97. *DBFP*, 15: no. 107–9 (20–21 Dec. 1921); Rathenau, *Tagebuch*, p. 272; *DVP SSSR*, 4:579–80, 605; and De Martino to Della Torretta, London, 20, 21 Dec. 1921, IMAE Amb. Lond. B 539–1.

98. *DBFP*, 15: no. 111 (22 Dec. 1921) and apps. 1 and 2.

ing and able to pay debts and restore private property; he thus asked for a specific commitment from Moscow.[99]

By far their most significant disagreement was over the pact, which Briand raised on 21 December when he proposed "a broad alliance in which the two Powers would guarantee each other's interests in all parts of the world, act closely together in all things, and go to each other's assistance whenever these . . . were threatened."[100] Lloyd George countered with a simple guarantee of France's eastern frontier against another German invasion. He insisted that the British people would not accept obligations involving the "unstable and excitable" populations of Eastern Europe and cited "Poland, or Danzig, or Upper Silesia" as examples of quarrels "whose rights and wrongs . . . might be hard to disentangle." Briand envisaged that the core Franco-British relationship would then be broadened with three or four European powers (including Germany) who would pledge to preserve peace and consult each other in the event of threats to the status quo. He thereby joined his alliance proposal with the Washington idea of a Great Power condominium. This arrangement would not only allow a measure of French disarmament but would also stabilize the German republic and curb its propensity for revenge. Grudgingly accepting this idea, Lloyd George nonetheless warned that the Allies might drive Germany and Russia into a more powerful alliance that could easily overturn the status quo.[101]

The London Conference ended on an inconclusive note. On Briand's request, the carefully worded press communiqué indicated that all major decisions would be postponed until the Allies met at Cannes. In the meantime, the locale shifted to Paris. Rathenau proved an uncooperative interviewee before the Reparations Commission, failing to answer its questions on what guarantees the Reich was willing to offer in return for a moratorium. Germany too would wait for Cannes.[102] The meeting of the Allied Financial Experts to establish a consortium for Russia ended in a deadlock when French and British delegates disagreed over the currency to be used for reconstruction projects.[103]

Briand had been maneuvered by Lloyd George into holding an immediate meeting of the Supreme Council on Germany and Russia. This created prob-

99. Ibid., nos. 108–9 (21 Dec. 1921), no. 111 (22 Dec. 1921). Also telephone message from Vignon [Millerand], warning against a "disguised or indirect recognition of the Soviet government," 21 Dec. 1921, FMAE Y 684. Briand therefore requested that Russia not be mentioned specifically in the official communiqués regarding the reconstruction of Europe.

100. *DBFP*, 15: no. 110 (21 Dec. 1921).

101. Ibid.

102. Rathenau, *Tagebuch*, p. 275; Laubach, *Kabinette Wirth*, pp. 139–40; and Weill-Raynal, *Réparations*, 2:105–6.

103. *DBFP*, 15: nos. 112–17 (29–31 Dec. 1921) and apps. 2–4; and "Reconstitution économique de l'Europe," 29–31 Dec., FMAE Y 29.

lems at home, where he had to answer questions in parliament on the London talks and defend his policies against charges of "sacrifice." Briand refused to make specific statements to the Chamber and insisted on a free hand at Cannes. But while Briand proceeded to draft his pact proposal, London gave no encouraging signs. Lloyd George remained unresponsive. Curzon, even more opposed to an Anglo-French alliance, was interested in what Paris was willing to offer.[104] Neither France nor Britain had as yet made any significant concessions; Briand, the supplicant, was the more vulnerable.

There were uncertainties regarding the three outsiders, whose initiatives in 1921 had strained the Entente and roused it to action: would the United States join the enterprise for the reconstruction of Central and Eastern Europe? Believing it would, the Allies held open a 20 percent share in the consortium for America. Would Russia meet the Allies' stiff political and economic terms? Though Krassin had hinted to the British that it might, Moscow was in fact unready to make "premature" concessions. Would Germany embark on the collective venture in the East for the benefit of its reparations account? Already during his second visit to London, after receiving negative signals from Berlin and Moscow, Rathenau grew less favorable toward the project, doubting his government's ability to raise sufficient capital to participate.[105]

Lloyd George and Briand, still acting within a Wilsonian framework, displayed a surprising confidence in the prospects of the conference diplomacy that they had planned for 1922. The strong, obstinate public opinion that both claimed to represent: could it be guided and redirected into the essential channels of international conciliation and cooperation? Could the other side—Germany and Russia—be persuaded or coerced to make sacrifices for the good of Europe? Would the United States, now attaining an imposing stature in the postwar era, welcome this development? At London the heads of the French and British governments took the first steps that led to the Genoa Conference. However, they were not ready to unify their policies. It was not evident that their need for each other's support in the great venture ahead superseded all other interests and alternatives.

104. Hardinge to Curzon, Paris, 23 Dec. 1921, CzP; Bonnefous, *Troisième République*, 3:276; Curzon to Lloyd George, London, 20 Dec. 1921, LGP F 13/2/63, 64; Curzon to Hardinge, 24 Dec. 1921, CzP; Crowe, "Notes Respecting the Possible Conclusion of an Anglo-French Alliance," 26 Dec. 1921, FO 800/243; Hardinge to Curzon, 27 Dec., CzP.

105. Parrini, *Heir to Empire*, pp. 151–54; Lenin, *Collected Works*, 45:426, 705–6; Rathenau, *Tagebuch*, pp. 272–73; D'Abernon, *Versailles to Rapallo*, p. 249; Schieder, "Entstehungsgeschichte," pp. 555–56; Moritz Schlesinger, *Erinnerungen eines Aussenseiters im diplomatischen Dienst* (Cologne: Verlag Wissenschaft und Politik, 1977), pp. 271–82.

2

Genoa Convoked

The Supreme Council, the deliberative organ of the victors, met for the sixteenth time on 6 January 1922 in the French Mediterranean resort city of Cannes.[1] Belgium, though not technically a member, sat on the council; this had become customary because much of the agenda dealt with Germany. There was also an American observer; and a representative of Germany was later invited to attend. During a week of intensive talks that accompanied the council's meetings, statesmen and financial experts discussed but did not resolve the three basic issues: Germany, Russia, and the Anglo-French pact. When the Cannes Conference ended abruptly, no decisions had been made on a reparations moratorium and the distribution of the first payments, on the terms under which Russia would renew its ties with the West, or on the Anglo-French pact. Instead, the outcome was the convocation of a world economic conference to be held two months hence, on 8 March 1922, in Genoa.

Cannes

Lloyd George and his entourage arrived early in Cannes. After a brief stopover in Paris for talks with Briand, he played golf and rested in the early winter sunshine after the strenuous Irish negotiations.[2] Lloyd George appeared confident and optimistic; he was bearing a plan for a summit conference that, modeled on Washington, would deal with all major aspects of European reconstruction and also produce a European peace pact. Briand, arriving on 4 January after a hectic but not unsuccessful parliamentary session, had less confidence and, except for the pact, no major goals.[3] Both the French press and the British press trumpeted the debate over a possible alliance. *Le Temps*

1. Harold Nicolson, *Curzon: The Last Phase, 1919–1925* (Boston: Houghton Mifflin, 1934), pp. 188–89, reviews the fifteen Allied conferences of 1920–21.
2. A. J. Sylvester, *The Real Lloyd George* (London: Cassell, 1948), pp. 68–69.
3. Hardinge to Curzon, Paris, 30 Dec. 1921 and 1 Jan. 1922, GB FO 371 W4, W31/4/17. The Briand government obtained a substantial vote of confidence on its handling of the bankruptcy of the Banque Industrielle de Chine; see Édouard Bonnefous, *Histoire politique de la Troisième République*, 2d ed. (Paris: Presses Universitaires de France, 1968), 3:270–73.

warned on 5 January against paying too high a price. On 4 January the *Times* criticized France's obstruction of European reconstruction, and the Liberal and Labour presses were hostile to any formal British ties with Paris. Briand seemed prepared to make some concessions on the Near East, submarine building, and Tangier, and to accept Lloyd George's summit conference in return for a pact. The still-unresolved reparations question provided France with some measure of influence in its dealings with Britain.[4]

The Anglo-French tête-à-tête in London had raised interest in Berlin, Moscow, and Washington, as well as anxiety in Brussels and Rome. Belgium was justly worried that the British might sacrifice its reparations receipts in France's favor, and Italy was also concerned over how much Britain would offer Briand.[5] Lloyd George had both encouraged the latter's fears and used them to induce Briand to call a prompt meeting of the Supreme Council in Cannes. Though it is possible that the British premier was prepared to go slightly further than the Foreign Office in meeting France's security requirements, there is no evidence that he wanted to turn the clock back to 1904 or 1914. Rather, he appears to have envisaged a complex series of steps that would subordinate the problems of reparations and French security to the larger questions of European reconstruction and rapprochement with Soviet Russia. He thus hoped to attract the United States to agree to a generous debt settlement with its former allies. Finally, Britain would sponsor a program for general disarmament in Europe.[6]

At first things went smoothly at Cannes. Even though Lloyd George had an evasive, even negative attitude toward an Anglo-French pact and the Allies had failed to agree on some key points, Briand was completely obliging about commencing the meeting of the Supreme Council without delay.[7] Italian Premier Ivanoe Bonomi, stressing his government's desire to work alongside Lloyd George on Russia and German reparations, urged that the forthcoming economic conference be held at Genoa. Since he needed Rome's support against

4. Hardinge to Curzon, Paris, 23 Dec. 1921, Curzon to Hardinge, London, 24 Dec. 1921, Hardinge to Curzon, 26 Dec. 1921 and 3 Jan. 1922, CzP; Curzon to Lloyd George, 20 Dec. 1921, LGP F 13/2/63, 64; Hardinge to Curzon, 5 Jan. 1922, GB FO 371 W193/50/17; and cf. Saint-Aulaire to MAE, London, 31 Dec. 1921, FMAE B81, 1, 4 Jan. 1922, FMAE Z GB 48.

5. Moncheur to Curzon, London, 26 Dec. 1921, LGP F 13/2/62, and Jaspar to De Gaiffier, JP 214; Della Torretta to De Martino, Rome, 14 Dec. 1921, De Martino to Della Torretta, London, 20, 21 Dec. 1921, and Lago to De Martino, Rome, 21 Dec. 1921, IMAE Amb. Lond. B 539–1.

6. See article by "Politicus" [Philip Kerr] in *Daily Chronicle*, 14 Dec. 1921, with the main outlines of Lloyd George's plan, and also Grigg to Thomas, 19 Jan. 1922, Grigg Papers, roll 2. Also see the Foreign Office's objections to Lloyd George's design in Tyrrell to Grigg [at Cannes], London, 2 Jan. 1922, Grigg Papers, roll 9; and Christoph Stamm, *Lloyd George zwischen Innen- und Aussenpolitik: Die britische Deutschlandpolitik 1921/1922* (Cologne: Verlag Wissenschaft und Politik, 1977), pp. 211, 217–21.

7. *DBFP*, 19: nos. 1 and 3 (4, 5 Jan. 1922).

the probable Franco-Belgian resistance to his plans, Lloyd George agreed to award the honor of host to Italy. The Genoa location had three advantages. The selection of an industrial port would emphasize the Allies' seriousness in the face of recent charges that their prior meetings had been convened primarily in resorts; it dealt a blow at the League, whose headquarters in Geneva was rejected; and it avoided London, where the fallout of a major world conference that included the Bolsheviks might have politically damaging effects.[8]

The meeting of the Supreme Council opened on Friday, 6 January, at 11 A.M.[9] Colonel Harvey, the American ambassador to Britain, was present as an observer. The prime ministers of Belgium, France, and Italy, and the Japanese ambassadors to Paris and London were in attendance. Lloyd George dominated the opening session with his proposal to summon what he described as "the most important of the series of conferences held since the armistice."[10] His long speech was designed to disarm the criticisms of the French Right, specifically, its "cheap" attacks that he was "soft" on the Germans, that his dealings with the Bolsheviks were more heinous than France's pact "with the murderers of the Armenians," and that the Allies would be forced to deal even if the Soviets acted in bad faith. Finally, he expressed his desire for a generalized peace pact modeled on Washington. It was a masterful statement; his sentiments on peace and reconstruction were warmly endorsed by Belgium, Italy, and Japan.

Briand, the council's acting president, was in the awkward position of the accused. He lamely cautioned against precipitate steps, against allowing "sentimental prejudice" to prevail over the "grave interests of the present time" and "causing to spring up in the hearts of the various peoples hopes, the non-realization of which would be dangerous." Briand's pleas and, more specifically, his political weakness had their effect. The Supreme Council limited the flow to the press of any detailed information on the impending conference. Moreover, it agreed to separate its deliberations on the reparations problem from the issue of European reconstruction, turning the former over to a special commission.[11]

On the afternoon of 6 January, the Supreme Council adopted Lloyd George's proposals with a few minor amendments. The six Cannes Resolutions formed

---

8. Giannini to Cabinet, Cannes, 6 Jan. 1922, IMAE 49. The choice of Genoa is still a mystifying subject, and the Lloyd George–Bonomi conversation sheds little light: *DBFP*, 19:16 (5 Jan. 1922). Given Lloyd George's antipathy toward the League, it is doubtful that he, as some have claimed, confused "Gênes" for "Genève."

9. The Supreme Council met at Le Cercle Nautique, a former gambling hall that was hurriedly restored. Villa owners lent palms, rugs, paintings, and decorations, and workmen feverishly installed telephones, hanging maps, and tables; see *New York Times*, 4 Jan. 1922.

10. *DBFP*, 19:19–25.

11. Ibid., p. 29. The reparations discussions at Cannes in FMAE B 81.

the basis for the reestablishment of economic and, eventually, political ties
with Soviet Russia. They were as follows:

1. Nations can claim no right to dictate to each other regarding the principles on which they are to regulate their system of ownership, internal economy and government. It is for every nation to choose for
   itself the system which it prefers in this respect.
2. Before, however, foreign capital can be made available to assist a
   country, foreign investors must be assured that their property and the
   rights will be respected and the fruits of their enterprise secured to
   them.
3. The sense of security cannot be re-established unless the Governments of countries desiring foreign credit freely undertake—
   (a) That they will recognize all public debts and obligations which
       have been or may be undertaken or guaranteed by the State, by
       municipalities or by other public bodies, as well as the obligation
       to restore or compensate all foreign interests for loss or damage
       caused to them when property has been confiscated or withheld.
   (b) That they will establish a legal and juridical system which sanc-
       tions and enforces commercial and other contracts with
       impartiality.
4. An adequate means of exchange must be available, and, generally,
   there must be financial and currency conditions which offer sufficient
   security for trade.
5. All nations should undertake to refrain from propaganda subversive
   of order and the established political system in other countries than
   their own.
6. All countries should join in an undertaking to refrain from aggression
   against their neighbors.

   If, in order to secure the conditions necessary for the development of the
   trade in Russia, the Russian Government demands official recognition,
   the Allied Powers will be prepared to accord such recognition only if the
   Russian Government accepts the foregoing stipulations.[12]

The Cannes Resolutions contained deliberate and significant contradictions
and ambiguities. Briand noted the inconsistency between the coexistence formula of paragraph 1 and the rigorous requirements of paragraphs 2, 3, and 4.
Lloyd George explained that this was intentional because governments seeking
foreign capital must "bow to the conditions" of property rights that existed
abroad.[13] According to Lloyd George, the strictures concerning subversive
propaganda and aggression (paragraphs 5 and 6) were similarly aimed at the

12. Ibid., p. 36.
13. Ibid., p. 32.

supplicant, Soviet Russia, and did not bind the West.[14] The final statement emphasized that these were the minimum terms for de jure recognition of the Soviet state. The Cannes Resolutions were therefore a clarification of the future course of relations between famine-plagued Russia and the West.[15] The Supreme Council decided to invite Germany, Austria, Hungary, and Bulgaria, along with all the nations of Europe and the United States, to a world economic conference at Genoa.

A new alignment in Europe was being prepared, and Lloyd George encouraged Bonomi to seek a leading place for Italy.[16] The Italian sent the telegram inviting Soviet Russia to the Genoa Conference. On 8 January Chicherin responded: his government would participate. Moscow's chief delegate, either Lenin or a comparable figure, would come with full powers to conduct definitive negotiations.[17]

Lloyd George, who dominated the proceedings, was overconfident and arrogant. He persuaded a reluctant Briand to invite German representatives to Cannes to speak before the council. Terming France a "nervous beast" that needed control through a treaty of guarantee lest it continue to bully the Germans,[18] he bullied Briand beyond the latter's capacity to make concessions and offered too little in return. The prospects of negotiations with Moscow, of the Allies' granting Germany an unconditional moratorium, and of Britain's vague and open-ended peace pact that threatened to usurp the fledgling League of Nations—all would possibly have been acceptable to Paris had the two leaders not reached an impasse over an Anglo-French alliance. The agreement Lloyd George offered Briand on 10 January, based on specific instructions from London, asked France to surrender on many key issues in order to receive a simple guarantee against unprovoked aggression.[19]

Briand was forced to depart on 11 January, just as Rathenau arrived, because

14. Ibid., p. 33. Millerand to Briand, Paris, 7 Jan. 1922, FMAE Z All. 378, asked if the nonaggression clause might in any way limit France's treaty right to take sanctions against Germany.

15. *DBFP*, 19:34.

16. Giannini to Cabinet, Cannes, 6 Jan. 1922, and Della Torretta to Contarini, Cannes, 6 Jan. 1922, IMAE 49. Also Marta Petricioli, "L'Italia alla Conferenza di Cannes," in *La Conferenza di Genova e il Trattato di Rapallo (1922), Atti del covegno Italo-Sovietico, Genova-Rapallo, 8–11 guigno 1972* (Rome: Edizioni Italia-URSS, 1974), pp. 394–434.

17. *DVP SSSR*, 5:47; French text in *DBFP*, 19:74; and English translation in Jane Degras, ed., *Soviet Documents on Foreign Policy* (London and New York: Oxford University Press, 1951), 1:287–88.

18. Conversation with Bonomi and Della Torretta, Cannes, 10 Jan. 1922, *DBFP*, 19:88.

19. At the beginning of their talks (ibid. [4 Jan. 1922], p. 7), Briand had confided French Senator Ribot's warning before he left Paris: "Ah, Briand, vous êtes déjà allé à Canossa. Prenez garde que vous n'alliez pas à Cannes aussi!" Lloyd George nonetheless chose to treat Briand heavy-handedly, exaggerating the statements imputed to him by the *Étoile Belge* (ibid., pp. 56–57, and Sylvester, *Real Lloyd George*, p. 70) and showing a marked lack of sympathy

of anxious telegrams from Millerand and Poincaré about the impending reparations decision. He met with his cabinet. After defending his policies before the Chamber, he dramatically resigned on 12 January, paving the way for the long-expected Poincaré government.[20]

The announcement of Briand's resignation occurred at the very moment that Rathenau was speaking to the Allied powers. With the fall of Briand, the Cannes Conference had to end. Lloyd George hotly denied the suggestion of the American ambassador that the convocation of the Genoa Conference was now in question. How could the new Paris government disavow its predecessor's commitment to its Allies while at the same time demanding that Moscow honor the czar's obligations?[21] The words had a hollow ring. Except to the Russians, Bonomi had not issued any invitations; the date had not been set precisely, nor had the agenda been clearly drafted. Whether a world conference would indeed materialize would depend largely on Britain.

The Cannes meeting affected the outsiders as well as the Allies. The divided Supreme Council decided to give the Germans a provisional reparations moratorium under stringent conditions. Rathenau had nonetheless won a sympathetic hearing, achieved Germany's inclusion in the projected Genoa Conference, and established his credentials as an effective spokesman for the Reich.[22] For Russia, Cannes was the consummation of its year-long efforts to reestablish political ties with the West, and it considered the invitation tantamount to recognition. Moscow was not asked for and did not volunteer an explicit acceptance of the Cannes Resolutions.[23] Harvey reported to Washington without much enthusiasm for the proceedings. He stressed Lloyd George's pleas that

---

when a snowstorm and the subsequent breakdown of telegraphic wires impeded the receipt of instructions from Paris, *DBFP*, 20:87.

The most sensational incident took place on Sunday, 8 Jan. 1922, when Lloyd George invited Briand and Bonomi to the Cannes Golf Club, where his extensively photographed and reported golf lesson to Briand caused an uproar in Paris; see Jules Laroche, *Au Quai d'Orsay avec Briand et Poincaré, 1913–1926* (Paris: Hachette, 1957), pp. 151–57. Details of the abortive pact negotiations in *DBFP*, 19: nos. 1, 3, 10, and 17; British cabinet minutes, 10 Jan. 1922, GB CAB 23/29; and Jules Laroche, "La grande déception de Cannes (Souvenirs de 1922)," *La Revue de Paris* (June 1957): 46–49.

20. Georges Suarez, *Briand: sa vie, son oeuvre* (Paris: Plon, 1941), 5:390–410; also De Gaiffier to Jaspar, Paris, 9, 10, 11, 12, and 13 Jan. 1922, BMAE Fr. (1922).

21. *DBFP*, 19:130 (12 Jan. 1922).

22. Ibid., pp. 131–36; Étienne Weill-Raynal, *Les réparations allemandes et la France* (Paris: Nouvelles Éditions Latines, 1947), 2:112–24; and David Felix, *Walther Rathenau and the Weimar Republic: The Politics of Reparations* (Baltimore: Johns Hopkins University Press, 1971), pp. 123–24.

23. Though the invitation may have caused "uneasiness" in Moscow (Richard K. Debo, "George Chicherin: Soviet Russia's Second Foreign Commissar" [Ph.D. diss., University of

the United States participate in the Genoa Conference but recommended an aloof response.[24]

For Italy, the forthcoming conference promised an opportunity to become a full-fledged member of the Entente or at least to be a junior partner closely aligned with Great Britain. This prospect held great merit for Bonomi's weak coalition government.[25] Belgium had also improved its position, regaining its priority on reparations payments and maintaining its place as a regular participant in Great Power conclaves, at the cost of performing occasionally difficult mediation tasks between Britain and France.[26]

Had he survived, Briand could have considered the Cannes Conference *his* success, the climax of his political and economic efforts to forge a rapprochement with Britain after steering a complicated course via Ankara, Berlin, Moscow, and Washington. With Briand's fall, however, France no longer celebrated the decisions at Cannes.[27] These became an embarrassment, and Paris was now forced to salvage both its interests and its honor in an enterprise on which it hesitated to embark.

Lloyd George had succeeded in implanting his vision of European peace *à l'anglaise* and had gained the Allies' acceptance for a huge summit conference. With Italy's help, Britain had buried France's lame effort to have the League organize the Genoa Conference;[28] and it had secured preliminary agreement to establish an international corporation with its headquarters in London to secure "better economic conditions in Europe."[29] Now Lloyd George would try openly to grasp the Wilsonian mantle of peacemaker in Europe. He appeared insouciant about the perils of Briand's political demise, Rathenau's elevation, Soviet calculations, the strength of American isolationist feeling, and, most important, his own growing political weakness.

Nebraska, 1964], p. 225), the Soviet government trumpeted it as a triumph: Schmidt-Rölke to AA, Moscow, 13 Jan. 1922 (2 tels.), Germ. AA T-120 3398/1733/D737893, D737907–8, and Grove to Curzon, Moscow, 20 Jan. 1922, GB FO 418/57 N944/472/38. Briand had fought unsuccessfully for a prior acceptance of the Cannes conditions (*DBFP*, 19:90–93), and France acknowledged its defeat (Fromageot note, Paris, 19 Jan. 1922, FMAE PM XIV).

24. Harvey to Hughes, Cannes, 6, 12 (2 tels.) Jan. 1922, USDS 550 E1/4, 5, 7.

25. Giannini to MAE, Cannes, 12[?] Jan. 1922, IMAE 49; also Prittwitz to AA, Rome, 14 Jan. 1922, Germ. AA T-120 K528/4153/K151529.

26. Margerie to MAE, Brussels, 13 Jan. 1922, FMAE PMarg. 361, 19 Jan. 1922, FMAE Z Belg. 50; and Grahame to Curzon, Brussels, 25 Jan. 1922, GB FO 371 W927/158/4.

27. André Chaumeix, "Le nouveau ministère," *La Revue de Paris* 29, no. 1 (February 1922): 663–72; and Ferdinand Siebert, *Aristide Briand: Staatsmann zwischen Frankreich und Europa* (Zurich and Stuttgart: E. Rentsch, 1973), pp. 267–76.

28. *DBFP*, 19:69–70 (9 Jan. 1922).

29. Ibid., nos. 8, 13, 16, 19, 20, and 25.

Aftermath

PARIS

Briand's resignation occurred a year after the fall of his predecessor, for the second time demonstrating France's acute attention to the direction of its diplomacy. His fall brought about the expected shift in French leadership to a Center-Right government under Raymond Poincaré. The former French president, head of the Senate Foreign Affairs Commission, and author of outspoken foreign-policy statements in the *Revue des Deux Mondes*, Poincaré had waited patiently for his opportunity during the past year. He took over both the premiership and the Ministry of Foreign Affairs. He appointed a conservative aristocrat, Emmanuel Peretti de la Rocca, as head of the Quai d'Orsay; designated an anti-German hard-liner, Charles de Lasteyrie, as finance minister; and formed a nonpartisan cabinet of *hommes de confiance*, of whom eleven of the nineteen had served in the Briand government. Louis Barthou, suspected as one of the principal authors of Briand's downfall, switched from the Ministry of War to the Ministry of Justice.[30]

Poincaré, commanding a strong parliamentary majority and responding to the nation's aroused fears of both desertion by its allies and surrender to its enemies, is traditionally viewed as a "resolute enforcer" of the Treaty of Versailles, even at the cost of military sanctions: *Poincaré-la-guerre* replaced Briand, *l'homme de la paix*, and the road to the Ruhr crisis a year later thus was opened.[31] Like many stark contrasts, this is vastly oversimplified. Poincaré did not possess overwhelming influence in the nation or in the Chamber, nor was he resolved in January 1922 to go into the Ruhr. Informed observers of Paris predicted little change from Briand's cautious policy. The once fiery journalist-politician would now be vulnerable to attacks by the increasingly vocal French

30. See Pierre Miquel, *Poincaré* (Paris: A. Fayard, 1961), pp. 428–29, on the return to power. Barthou, widely suspected of responsibility for the publication of Millerand's 10 January telegram to Briand, admitted: "I have never conspired against a ministry to which I did not belong"; quoted in Stephen A. Schuker, *The End of French Predominance in Europe: The Financial Crisis of 1924 and the Adoption of the Dawes Plan* (Chapel Hill: University of North Carolina Press, 1976), p. 205.

31. "Poincaré-la-guerre," the epithet of the French Left, in De Gaiffier to MAE, Paris, 23 Jan. 1922, BMAE Fr. (1922). The contrast was underlined by their contemporaries; see Jean de Pierrefeu, *La saison diplomatique: Gênes (Avril–Mai 1922)* (Paris: Éditions Montaigne, 1928), pp. 8–12; Emmanuel Peretti de la Rocca, "Briand et Poincaré (Souvenirs)," *La Revue de Paris* (16 Dec. 1936): 767–88; Georges Bonnet, *Le Quai d'Orsay sous trois républiques, 1870–1961* (Paris: A. Fayard, 1961), pp. 58–61; and Louise Weiss, *Mémoires d'une européene* (Paris: Payot, 1969), 2:158–61: "Raymond sait tout et ne comprend rien. Aristide comprend tout et ne sait rien" (p. 160). It was stressed in Richard D. Challener, "The French Foreign Office: The Era of Philippe Berthelot," in *The Diplomats*, edited by Gordon A. Craig and Felix Gilbert (New York: Atheneum, 1967), 1:52–57.

Left, the Radicals who advocated a more flexible policy toward Germany and Russia, and the Clemencistes who supported a firm defense of national interests and opposed any concessions to Britain. Even more than Briand, Poincaré was a man devoted to the Entente. Lacking any personal responsibility for recent Anglo-French disagreements over Tangier, Turkey, submarines, and aircraft, he could trade certain concessions (the ultimate being his agreement to cooperate over Genoa) to obtain London's agreement for a real alliance between their two nations to form the core of future European politics.[32]

En route to London from Cannes, Lloyd George requested an interview with the French premier-designate on 14 January.[33] It was an exceptionally tense two-hour encounter that took place in British Ambassador Lord Hardinge's study. Poincaré appealed more to Entente solidarity than to comradeship between the two political leaders. Rejecting the draft pact that Britain had proposed at Cannes, he suggested a bilateral military convention of a minimum of ten years' duration. On Genoa he was blunt: France would honor the former government's pledge to attend but only under stringent conditions. The Soviet government would have to adhere to the Cannes Resolutions, and there could be no discussion of reparations or any other clauses of the Versailles treaty at the conference. He cut short Lloyd George's plea to delve into the unsettled reparations problem before Genoa, insisting that smooth relations depended on their working through channels rather than face to face. He nonetheless pledged that the Entente would operate better than ever.[34] Lloyd George deplored the encounter. Neither arguments nor threats had prevailed against the dour French leader. Poincaré had rebuffed an "illusory" and controlling British guarantee for the real thing: a bilateral alliance.[35]

On 19 January Poincaré's "France first" program received a 472 to 107 vote of approval by the French Chamber.[36] J. L. Garvin, one of Lloyd George's

32. Bonnefous, *Troisième République*, 3:285–86; Renata Bournazel, *Rapallo: Naissance d'un mythe. La politique de la peur dans la France du bloc national* (Paris: Fondation Nationale des Sciences Politiques, 1974), pp. 58–66; and Walter A. McDougall, *France's Rhineland Diplomacy, 1914–1924* (Princeton: Princeton University Press, 1978), pp. 180–83, all give a more balanced picture of Poincaré.

33. Laroche to MAE, Cannes, 13 Jan. 1922, FMAE Z GB 48.

34. British Secretary's Notes of a Conversation between Lloyd George and Poincaré, British Embassy, Paris, 14 Jan. 1922, GB CAB 29/95. Also Hardinge to Curzon, Paris, 15 Jan. 1922, CzP; Charles Hardinge, *Old Diplomacy* (London: J. Murray, 1947), pp. 266–67; Sylvester, *Real Lloyd George*, p. 76; and George Allardice Riddell, *Lord Riddell's Intimate Diary of the Peace Conference and After, 1918–1923* (London: Gollancz, 1933), p. 394.

35. As reported to the German and Italian ambassadors: Sthamer [Dufour], Aufzeichnung über Besprechungen mit Sir Edward Grigg und Philip Kerr, 18 Jan. 1922, Germ. BA R 38/329; and De Martino to MAE, London, 19 Jan. 1922, IMAE 52/4 (Eng.)

36. Bonnefous, *Troisième République*, 3:285. The Socialists and Communists voted against; the majority of the Radicals and a few Clemencistes abstained.

strongest supporters, had predicted in the *Observer* on 15 January that Poincaré's advent probably meant "the end of the Entente." The Swiss journalist Albert Oeri, a more objective analyst, stressed in the *Basler Nachrichten* on 21 January how moderate Poincaré's attitudes actually were; he challenged the British prime minister (whose own reputation as a mediator had been weakened by Briand's fall) to let the British people decide "for or against" Poincaré's version of an Anglo-French pact.[37]

LONDON

On 19 January Sir Edward Grigg, Lloyd George's secretary and one of the main spirits behind the Genoa Conference, wrote: "We really got something done at Cannes."[38] Yet that same day there was a major political setback. Austen Chamberlain, Conservative leader, cabinet member, and a hitherto leading supporter of Lloyd George, announced that elections would not be scheduled in the near future. Armed with his great conference, Lloyd George had hoped to call a snap election on his return from Cannes, campaign on a platform of European pacification, and, with the expected victory, build a new cabinet dominated by a "National Liberal" grouping. The Conservatives, especially Sir George Younger, opposed the premier's "opportunism," which quite likely would have permanently split the Tories, leaving many of them in the sterile opposition camp with the Asquithites, Labourites, and Ulster men.[39]

Lloyd George was thereby stopped by his Conservative partners from going to the country with his Irish treaty, his cabinet's efforts at economy, the successes at Washington and Cannes, and the impending Genoa meeting. Normally diffident toward foreign affairs, the British public would probably have given him a favorable response, especially since the emerging Lloyd George coalition was presenting itself not only as a vigorous peacemaker abroad and as a staunch advocate for the revival of free trade and prosperity but also as the only effective bulwark against British socialism. The Tories indeed wanted to end their mariage de convenance with the ambitious Welshman but on their own terms and in their own good time. In the meantime, they had sufficient power in the cabinet to deny the prime minister a national vote of confidence before Genoa.[40]

37. Saint-Aulaire to MAE, London, 15 Jan. 1922, FMAE Z GB 48; and Mueller to AA, Berne, 21 Jan. 1922, Germ. AA T-120 L990/5411/L285649–50.

38. Grigg to Thomas, London, 19 Jan. 1922, Grigg Papers, roll 2.

39. Davidson to Bonar Law, London, 13 Jan. 1922, in J. C. C. Davidson, *Memoirs of a Conservative*, ed. Robert R. James (London: Weidenfeld and Nicolson, 1969), p. 111; Stamm, *Lloyd George*, pp. 236–39; Maurice Cowling, *The Impact of Labour, 1920–1924* (Cambridge: Cambridge University Press, 1971), pp. 131–37; and also Sthamer Aufzeichnung, 18 Jan. 1922, Germ. BA R 38/329.

40. Lord Beaverbrook, *Decline and Fall of Lloyd George* (London: Collins, 1963), pp. 14–29.

Like Briand, Lloyd George could have resigned, and indeed he threatened to do so.[41] This would have destroyed the prospects of Genoa; even had he personally represented Britain, he would not have possessed the power that he himself at Cannes had insisted all delegates must bring to the conference. Indeed, there was a considerable amount of support for the forthcoming meeting: the banking community was favorable, and the Labour party endorsed the cause of European pacification at its Manchester meeting at the end of January. Lloyd George bowed to necessity, accepting the delay of general elections until after Genoa. With so many troubles—Egypt, India, Iraq, Palestine, the Near East, and the ever-present possibility of a recurrence of violence in Ireland—a precious opportunity to strengthen Lloyd George's hand had been lost.[42]

Because of Genoa's political importance and the resistance to it in certain quarters, Lloyd George drastically reduced the role of Curzon and the Foreign Office in the preparations. He made extensive use of his secretaries and of personal contacts with Russian, German, and Italian representatives, and at least once bypassed regular channels to reach Paris. Moreover, the decision to give Italy a major responsibility for the invitations and the agenda (which were handled through the Italian embassy in London) increased Lloyd George's control.[43]

One element that eluded his grasp, the most crucial of all, was the cooperation of the United States. On many occasions he admitted that America's participation would be essential to Genoa's success. How could Washington be lured into the impending summit that had been called to establish the basis for Russia's reintegration into the European and world economy?[44]

WASHINGTON

America's response to its invitation to participate in the Genoa Conference was unpredictable.[45] No doubt there was a reluctance to refuse Italy outright since the Rome government was acting in a most cooperative manner during the Washington Conference. Also, there was marked disagreement in the gov-

---

41. Riddell, *Intimate Diary*, pp. 350–52.

42. Frances Lloyd George, *Lloyd George: A Diary* (New York: Harper and Row, 1971), pp. 240–41; Stamm, *Lloyd George*, pp. 239–42; but also see John Gallagher, "Nationalisms and the Crisis of Empire, 1919–1922," *Modern Asian Studies* 15, no. 3 (1981): 355–68, for the growing external problems.

43. De Martino to MAE, London, 22 Jan. 1922, IMAE Amb. Lond. 538.3. Also Sthamer to AA, London, 26 Jan. 1922, Germ. AA T-120 L999/5412/L286790–93.

44. De Martino [Giannini] to MAE, London, 28 Jan. 1922, IMAE Amb. Lond. 538.3.

45. On 10 Jan. 1922 the National Civic Federation and on 12 Jan. 1922 the American Federation of Labor protested Soviet representation at Genoa: Hoover/Comm. and Ricci to MAE, Washington, 15 Jan. 1922, IMAE 52/4 (USA).

Christian Herter, Harding's secretary, wrote to Charles Herring in Berlin on 12 Jan. 1922: "We are not any of us quite clear in our minds as to what role America would play and whether or not she would have more to lose than to gain by such a conference," copy in Hoover/Comm.

ernment as to whether America should attend. The Harding administration contented itself with announcing that it must delay any decision pending the conclusion of the conference on the Pacific and naval disarmament.[46]

American leaders had not ignored the discussions taking place in Europe. On 4 January 1922 Commerce Secretary Hoover had formulated his own plan for European economic stability based on severe reduction of armaments, a five-year reparations moratorium, a foreign loan raised by the Germans for the reconstruction of Belgium and northern France, reduction of the Army of Occupation on the Rhine, reorganization of Germany's finances, and stabilization of the German and all other European currencies back to the gold standard. This "moderate" program, costing no more than five hundred million dollars, was aimed at saving Europe from "social chaos" [bolshevism], increasing chances of peace and international harmony, and improving America's trade and competitive position in the European markets. For these "blessings," America could award a holiday on interest payments for five years to all countries except the United Kingdom. It is likely that Hoover hoped in one capacity or another to attend the Genoa Conference. He held strong views on debts and reparations, and had already spoken out against any plan funded by American capital that would allow Germany to act as a middleman in Russia.[47]

There were valid arguments in favor of America's attending the Genoa Conference. One was the fear that Britain and Germany would exclude the United States from Russia, a fear that Krassin craftily tried to aggravate.[48] Also, Genoa represented the opportunity to find out once and for all what the Soviets would concede to the West. Finally, it complemented the Washington Conference.

Yet there were equally compelling reasons to stay out. The underlying linkage of political controls and economic interests, as epitomized in the international corporation, was anathema to Washington. The deliberate contradiction in paragraphs 1 and 2 of the Cannes Resolutions offended American sensibilities; it could not accept even the transactional coexistence formula or the

46. De Martino to MAE, London, 18 Jan. 1922, Ricci to De Martino, Washington, 26 Jan. 1922, IMAE Amb. Lond. 538.3. Also Hankey to Curzon, Washington, 20 Jan. 1922, CzP; Lang to AA, Washington, 16 Jan. 1922, Germ. AA T-120 L998/5412/L286312–14; Jusserand to Poincaré, Washington, 27 Jan. 1922, FMAE Z É-U 62; Saint-Aulaire to MAE, London, 28 Jan. 1922, and Barrère to MAE, Rome, 30 Jan. 1922, FMAE PM G/I.

47. Hoover to Harding, 4 Jan. 1922, Hoover/Comm; also unsigned report [by Harrison or Philips], 23 Jan. 1922, USDS 550 E1/361; E. D. Durand memorandum, 2 Feb. 1922, "Participation of the United States in the Genoa Conference," Hoover/Comm.; and Werner Link, *Die amerikanische Stabilisierungspolitik in Deutschland, 1921–1932* (Düsseldorf: Droste Verlag, 1970), pp. 106–13.

48. Consul General Skinner to Hughes, London, 20 Jan. 1922, USDS 861.01. Because of Russia's acute need for food, Krassin had just been ordered to buy 15 million *poods* of grain in Jan. and Feb.: Lenin to Krassin, 12 Jan. 1922, and to Stalin, 19 Jan. 1922, in V. I. Lenin, *Collected Works* (Moscow: Progress Publishers, 1965–71), 45:430, 440–41.

implied commitment to eventually recognize Lenin's Russia.[49] There was also a general disinclination to become involved with "Europe's troubles": "to plunge into the morass of political, racial, religious and economic rivalries and animosities."[50] American bankers hesitated to coordinate investments or monetary policy with Britain or make foreign commitments that might risk domestic inflation. The farm bloc resisted any potential expenditures that might only benefit eastern banks; and the veterans' lobby fought for its bonus rather than for European reconstruction. The anti-French attitudes that worked against Genoa were based on France's allegedly huge military budget, its unwillingness to make financial sacrifices, and its harsh attitudes toward Germany. Finally, anti-German sentiments, particularly opposition to supporting Stinnes's *Drang nach Osten*, and the old anti-British feelings, which were strengthened by both Lloyd George's pretensions and his precarious political situation, became reasons for *not* participating.[51]

The Harding administration was resolved on an eventual conference to develop the theme of European reconstruction, but early March 1922 was not a propitious time. European recovery as framed at Cannes did not appeal to the administration, which was faced by a Senate jealous of its own power and suspicious of the Old World. On 31 January the Senate had established the World War Foreign Debt Commission as a means of controlling the funding of Allied war debts. This action, coupled with its reservations about the use of American force to uphold the Four Power Pact, represented a decisive setback to the activists in the administration, Hughes, Hoover, and Mellon. No one wanted to experience Wilson's humiliation: to have international commitments repudiated by the Congress. It was thus easy to credit the doubting and negative reports on Genoa from American diplomats in Europe. Richard W. Child, the new ambassador to Italy, insisted that the time was not ripe for another international conference.[52]

BERLIN

On 20 January Chancellor Wirth announced to a meeting of the minister-presidents of Weimar Germany's seventeen *Länder* that his year-long fulfillment

49. The [White] Russian ambassador warned of the danger that "Lenin might give wholesale concessions as had been done in China. A succeeding government would naturally oppose these concessions. It will therefore be in the interest of the Powers benefitting from the concessions to keep the Bolshevik Government in power"; see Dearing to Hughes, 12 Jan. 1922, *FRUS, 1922*, 1:386–87.

50. Anti-Genoa editorial in *The Independent and the Weekly Review*, 21 Jan. 1922, Hoover/ Comm.

51. Castle to Hughes, Washington, 25 Jan. 1922, USDS 550 E1/72; Bulletin économique, no. 21, pt. 1, 26 Jan. 1922, FMAE B 85; and Cartier to MAE, Washington, 27 Jan. 1922, BMAE 10991.

52. Child to Hughes and Harding, Rome, 30 Jan. 1922, USDS 550 E1/23.

policy had been crowned with success.[53] Political rather than economic considerations had guided the Reich's diplomacy, and he had finally been able to demonstrate conclusively that Germany had exhausted its capacity to meet the demands of the London Schedule. He cited the letter of 3 December, from Montagu Norman, governor of the Bank of England, to Reichsbank President Rudolf Havenstein, that refused short- or long-term credits to Germany because of the priority of reparations claims. Bankruptcy threatened. But now Berlin had "objective proof" that the Allies were responsible for thwarting the aid that would save Germany, and all of Central Europe, from economic chaos. Rathenau then outlined his recent missions to London, Paris, and Cannes, which had produced the temporary and partial moratorium and the invitation to Germany to join the international corporation and participate as an equal in the Genoa Conference.[54]

Cannes thus represented a major step in the destruction of the London Schedule, which Wirth's government had accepted eight months earlier.[55] Rathenau and his entourage had been treated as honored guests by the French government. The Reich's representative had spoken at length before the Supreme Council, had stressed the discrepancy between the Allies' demands and Germany's "ability to pay," and, with the exception of the French, had received a cordial hearing. Most important, close ties with the British had been maintained. Lloyd George sent word that he liked Rathenau's overlong speech; and afterwards his secretaries supplied Germany's representatives in London with advice and with details of the Lloyd George–Poincaré discussions.[56]

Nonetheless, contrary to Wirth's expectations, the Cannes meeting had not produced a definitive solution to the reparations problem. The advent of Poincaré, who insisted that reparations be excluded from Genoa, vastly diminished the forthcoming conference in German eyes. America's irresolution created another uncertainty because its capital was essential for both a German loan and European reconstruction. Moreover, Britain's support was far from unconditional: London demanded budget and currency improvements as the price for a reduction of reparations. At Cannes Germany had accepted the obligation to produce within a fortnight a report to the Reparations Commission detailing its internal reforms and payment proposals in order that the moratorium be extended beyond 15 February. Wirth now faced a difficult political problem: to

53. *Akten-Wirth*, 1: no. 192.

54. Terver to Briand, Breslau, 12 Jan. 1922, FMAE B 81, reported the accolades in the Socialist and the DVP press for Rathenau's "victory at Cannes."

55. On 9 Jan. 1922, Wirth had announced to the party leaders that this was his goal, *Akten-Wirth*, 1: no. 184. He considered the "broadening" of the reparations question into the wider problem of European reconstruction a "masterstroke," D'Abernon to Curzon, Berlin, 6 Jan. 1922, GB FO 371 C311/99/18.

56. Sthamer [Dufour] Aufzeichnung, London, 18 Jan. 1922, Germ. BA R 38/329.

increase taxes and reduce expenditures, maintain to the world the image of a bankrupt Germany, and defend his government against Poincaré's charges that Germany could and must pay. Most of the German press viewed Cannes as a step forward, but critics on the Left and Right pointed out the "illusion" under which the government was operating: that Germany could exploit interallied politics to liberate itself.[57]

Wirth headed a weak minority government of the Center and Social Democrats that was tacitly supported by the Democrats and occasionally by the Independent Socialists. This was insufficient to ram a convincingly tough tax compromise through the bourgeois-dominated Reichstag. The government hesitated to take decisive action either by levying the heavy direct taxes on income and property demanded by the Socialists to cover its mounting expenses or by levying largely indirect taxes and reducing government expenditures, which the industrialists advocated. Any tax reform was entwined with the reparations issue but also with the often violent ideological and class conflict in German society. The Wirth government had hitherto covered its deficits by printing large quantities of money, thereby inflating the currency and spreading economic chaos abroad. It essentially bowed to the requirements of heavy German industry and up to that time had still not hurt labor. Now the Reich urgently needed a stabilization loan, but none could be granted without reparations relief. This the Allies at Cannes had made conditional on a demonstration of sacrifice on the part of Germany and also on its compliance with the British scheme to participate in the reconstruction of Russia.[58]

Cannes thus gave Wirth both the challenge and the opportunity to strengthen his leadership. By threatening that the government would fall, he pressed the Socialists to accept a reduced, forced loan of 1 billion gold marks and to drop their other demands to tax the wealthy. He negotiated with the DVP, whose assent was required for increased taxes, promising it a ministerial chair when his government would eventually be broadened into a "Great Coalition."[59] With the tax compromise assured, the government met the 28 January deadline and sent the Reparations Commission a lengthy report on its expected income and payments, but it also stressed the necessity of a significant foreign loan. As expected, there was no immediate response from the Reparations Commission and a prompt revival of Anglo-French disaccord.[60]

57. Ernst Laubach, *Die Politik der Kabinette Wirth, 1921/1922* (Lübeck and Hamburg: Matthiesen, 1968), pp. 144–45.

58. Ibid., pp. 145–47; D'Abernon to Curzon, Berlin, 16 Jan. 1922, GB FO 371 N676/646/38; D'Abernon to Lloyd George, 20 Jan. 1922, and to T. E. Jones, 27 Jan. 1922, LGP F 54/2/14, 15.

59. Felix Pinner, "Das Kompromiss," *Berliner Tageblatt*, 26 Jan. 1922. The Great Coalition consisted of the original Weimar partners, the Socialists, Democrats, and Center, plus the DVP.

60. Weill-Raynal, *Réparations*, 2:124–25; Laubach, *Kabinette Wirth*, pp. 161–63.

A confident Wirth spoke out publicly on 26 January criticizing Poincaré and exhorting the Allies to concentrate not on coercing Germany but on reviving the world's economy.[61] Five days later, the appointment of Walther Rathenau as Germany's foreign minister was announced. It was not unexpected.[62] Ever since Rathenau had left the government and commenced his unofficial role as diplomat-negotiator, there had been predictions of his imminent return to office. The prospect of Genoa and important reparations negotiations in 1922 made his selection seem logical. Rathenau's personal ties with Wirth, his liaisons with the British and French, and his business contacts with the Russian world made him a natural choice to lead German diplomacy; his own party agreed.[63] A prominent participant at Wiesbaden and Cannes, a gifted orator and successful industrialist, he symbolized a "Western orientation" that fit in well with Wirth's continuing efforts to bury the London Schedule.

Rathenau's appointment had important political implications, for it blocked Gustav Stresemann's bid for power and his long effort as DVP leader to form a Great Coalition cabinet.[64] One of the outstanding political figures of the Weimar Republic, Stresemann wielded considerable strength as chairman of the Reichstag's Foreign Affairs Committee, head of a party with close ties to heavy Ruhr industry, and an individual with close contacts to the British, French, and Americans.[65] Wirth knew of Stresemann's ambition to be chancellor, twice frustrated in May and October 1921, but also of Stresemann's heavy liabilities: a hawkish war record, and his party's official opposition to fulfillment and reluctance to follow Britain's lead in Russia. By appealing to Stresemann's patriotism and demonstrating the independent Russian policy he had advocated, Wirth outmaneuvered the liberal leader so that he would smother his disappointment and wait patiently a few more months.

Wirth had not renounced control over foreign policy. In November 1921 he appointed Baron Ago von Maltzan to the Russian desk at the Foreign Ministry

61. *Verhandlungen des Reichstags, Stenographische Berichte* (Berlin: Reichsdruckerei, 1922), 352:5557; *Vorwärts, Frankfurter Zeitung, Vossische Zeitung*, and *Germania*, all on 27 Jan. 1922; and Della Faille to MAE, Berlin, 27 Jan. 1922, BMAE 10991.

62. Frassati to Della Torretta [in Cannes], Berlin, 9 Jan. 1922, IMAE 49, reported Wirth's announcement that Rathenau would take over the Foreign Ministry after Cannes.

63. D'Abernon to Curzon, 31 Jan. 1922, GB FO 371 C1526/725/18; D'Abernon to Hankey, 3, 7 Feb. 1922, LGP 54/2/6, 17; Felix, *Rathenau*, pp. 265–66; and James Joll, *Three Intellectuals in Politics* (New York: Pantheon, 1960), pp. 116–21.

64. *Akten-Wirth*, 1: no. 201 (Besprechung mit Vertretern der DVP, 6 Feb. 1922); Rudolf Morsey, *Die Deutsche Zentrumspartei, 1917–1923* (Düsseldorf: Droste Verlag, 1966), pp. 445–46; and Henry A. Turner, *Stresemann and the Politics of the Weimar Republic* (Princeton: Princeton University Press, 1963), p. 96.

65. Stresemann, Nachlass, 241, Germ. Pol. Arch. AA. Also see Germ. AA T-120 6696H/3109/H141141–341; Della Faille to Jaspar, Berlin, 10 Jan. 1922, BMAE 10991; and Laurent to MAE, Berlin, 13, 29 Jan., FMAE Z All. 385.

and intended to maintain strong links with Moscow[66] while Rathenau exhibited mild interest in the Western-sponsored international corporation. Indeed, one might ask whether Rathenau was a stand-in for Stresemann, Wirth's court Jew acceptable to British and Dutch bankers, tolerated by the French, and raising the appropriate misgivings in Moscow. His appointment and his expected dealings with all the unpleasantness Germany had to face—reparations, military control, the final partition of Upper Silesia—would make him, like Erzberger, the target of German nationalistic hatred.[67] Germany's postwar republic had not found a means whereby the voice of the majority for peace and social justice would be heard above that of an inordinately influential and defiant minority, which counted on the Reich's strength and economic power, the Allies' divisions, and a "Soviet strategy" to overcome the Entente's temporary predominance.[68] In this context, Wirth's appointment of Rathenau shortly after the Cannes meeting represented a statement that Germany would engage in a *Befreiungspolitik* in the public spotlight of 1922, regardless of the domestic and diplomatic consequences.

MOSCOW

The invitation to the Genoa Conference also represented a challenge to Lenin's leadership. On 23 December 1921 he had addressed the Ninth All-Russian Congress of Soviets on a most optimistic note: neither frost nor famine nor his own fatigue and ill-health dulled his conviction that Russia was progressing with internal reforms and foreign triumphs. NEP had transformed Russian society and would ultimately revive the production of food and raw materials. Internal and foreign trade would ensue. In the meantime, Western concessionaires would compete and strive to develop Russia's resources and modernize its industry, and their governments would soon follow with the extension of com-

---

66. Della Faille to MAE, Berlin, 25 Jan. 1922, BMAE 10991. Radek had just arrived in Berlin, joining Soviet representative Krestinsky, for talks with government officials and businessmen: D'Abernon to Lloyd George, 20 Jan. 1922, LGP F 54/2/14; also Gunter Rosenfeld, *Sowjetrussland und Deutschland, 1917–22* ([East] Berlin: Akademie-Verlag, 1960), p. 335, and Moritz Schlesinger, *Erinnerungen eines Aussenseiters im diplomatischen Dienst* (Cologne: Verlag Wissenschaft und Politik, 1977), pp. 271–77.

67. "What can a single individual do in the face of this torpid world, with enemies at his back and conscious of his own limitations and weakness?" Rathenau to a friend, 31 Jan. 1922, quoted in Count Harry Kessler, *Walther Rathenau: His Life and Work* (New York: Harcourt, Brace and Co., 1930), p. 301; Wirth's explanation to German party leaders in *Akten-Wirth*, 1: no. 205.

68. Cf. warning in Berthelot to Briand, Paris, 29 Jan. 1922, quoted in Suarez, *Briand*, pp. 429–30. On Wirth's politics, also see Charles S. Maier, *Recasting Bourgeois Europe: Stabilization in France, Germany, and Italy in the Decade after World War I* (Princeton: Princeton University Press, 1975), pp. 265–72. The stalemated November revolution is well illustrated in the government's handling of the sudden railroad strike: Laubach, *Kabinette Wirth*, pp. 153–57.

mercial and political ties.[69] He hoped that American relief, gratefully acknowledged, would stimulate more permanent economic relations.

Lenin also announced that the past year had witnessed the virtual extinction of "organized political opposition to bolshevism" along with a severe purge of dissident party members.[70] The Communist party had extended its control over the entire state apparatus, and the state was becoming increasingly centralized under NEP. In addition, Communist rule had been consolidated in the border republics, most recently (and violently) in Georgia, whose independence, for strategic reasons, would be eroded by Moscow.[71]

Although his policies since March 1921 had not followed a preconceived plan, Lenin was step by step laying the basis for a dictatorship, for state planning, and for russianization. The most visible result at the time, however, was the provocation of a fiery debate between the fundamentalist revolutionary ideology (which Lenin, as in 1918, denounced as "infantile Leftism") and the practical policy that Lenin and others justified, as they had during Brest-Litovsk, as a necessity to save, consolidate, and modernize the Soviet state and ensure its transformation to true socialism. The chief metaphor was "retreat" —either tactical or deplorable, depending on the spokesman—which affected not only Russia's domestic policy but also the revolutionary government's relations with the rest of the world.[72]

It is unlikely that Lenin ever planned to attend the Genoa Conference personally. Chicherin's telegram of 8 January warned of the "pressures of work, particularly in connection with the famine," that might prevent the Soviet leader from participating.[73] Because of the failure to change the conference site (an effort caused by Krassin's warnings of the danger in Italy from both Fascist and White Guard assassins) and especially in anticipation of the crucial Eleventh Party Congress that was scheduled at the same time as Genoa, Lenin decided not to make his first diplomatic foray abroad, nor to appoint Trotsky in his place.[74] Despite severe illness, he would keep a tight leash on Chicherin's

69. Report of the All-Russian Central Executive Committee and the Council of People's Commissars, 23 Dec. 1921, in Lenin, *Collected Works*, 33:143–83. Lenin's preparations in ibid., 45:409–13.

70. Letter to Politburo members, 19 Dec. 1921, in ibid., 33:138; also E. H. Carr, *The Bolshevik Revolution* (Baltimore: Penguin, 1966), 1:177–200.

71. Richard Pipes, *The Formation of the Soviet Union*, rev. ed. (New York: Atheneum, 1968), chaps. 5–6; also "Memo to J. V. Stalin . . . on the Formation of a Federation of Transcaucasian Republics," 28 Nov. 1921, in Lenin, *Collected Works*, 33:127.

72. Franklyn Griffiths, *Genoa Plus 51: Changing Soviet Objectives in Europe* (Toronto: Canadian Institute of International Affairs, 1973), pp. 28–30.

73. Degras, *Soviet Documents*, 1:287–88.

74. I. Linder, "Lenin's Foreign Policy Activity (Oct. 1921–Mar. 1922)," *International Affairs* 12 (1969): 48; Grove to Curzon, Moscow, 20 Jan. 1922, GB FO 418/57 N944/472/58 (no. 41); Schmidt-Rölke to AA, Moscow, 18 Jan. 1922, Germ. AA T-120 L998/5412/L286283–85; and Quarton report, "Interpretation of Recent Political Developments in Soviet Russia," Viborg, Finland, 27 Jan. 1922, USDS 550 E1/40.

preparations; he was also the author and coordinator of the Soviet maneuvers in January 1922 to split a united Western front at Genoa.[75]

Like Lloyd George, Lenin was counting on a quick decision at Genoa to cement his political position. He interpreted the discrepancy between paragraphs 1 and 2 of the Cannes Resolutions as an invaluable and exploitable symptom of Western indecisiveness or hypocrisy. Yet Lenin, like Wirth, was well aware of the necessity of demonstrating a minimal amount of conciliation: internal legislation, hints of dissolving the Cheka, new legal codes, steps to establish more orthodoxy in public finance, the subordination of the labor unions, the showy announcements of demobilization, and Moscow's public campaign for world disarmament were all designed to appease foreign capitalists and their governments, and incidentally to appease Western middle-class liberal and pacifist opinion.

Though Lenin's leadership was secure and his authority unquestioned, this did not prevent a sharp internal debate over the specifics of his policies. At the March congress, trade-union leader Alexander Shlyapnikov would voice the mounting resentment that industry was being sacrificed to agriculture under NEP.[76] Trotsky was the main spokesman for those who had opposed the dismantling of war communism during the past ten months, the suspected *embourgeoisement* of the Russian Revolution (widely welcomed in the Western press but a deep embarrassment in world revolutionary circles), and the creation of new economic "freedoms" within the context of the Soviet state. Trotsky doubted NEP, distrusted the concessions policy, and viewed Russia's weakness and isolation more as a *challenge* to communism's organization, strength, and ingenuity than an excuse to engage in dangerous negotiations with the West.[77]

Lenin had many allies against Trotsky and his supporters. Lev Kamenev, who had dealt with Hoover, insisted on Russia's dependency on foreign capital and admitted that industrial progress had to come at the expense of either "the peasant or the worker." Leonid Krassin was an ardent advocate of Western concessions. Karl Radek urged closer ties with Germany, especially its heavy industry, and Alexei Rykov was a proponent of economic modernization. Even

75. V. Buryakov, "Lenin's Diplomacy in Action," *International Affairs* 5 (1972): 93: "The policy of utilizing diverse imperialist contradictions stemmed from Lenin's well-known proposition that the more 'powerful enemy can be vanquished only by exerting the utmost effort and by the most thorough, careful, attentive, skillful and obligatory use of any, even the smallest rift between the enemies, any conflict of interests among the bourgeoisie of the various countries and among the various groups or types of bourgeoisie within the various countries.'" See Lenin to Molotov, 16, 20 Jan. 1922, in Lenin, *Collected Works*, 45:434, 446–48, proposing unofficial secret talks with all the designated foreign representatives to the Genoa Conference and calling a meeting to discuss Soviet strategy to "divide the Powers."

76. Carr, *Bolshevik Revolution*, 2:313, 320, 322.

77. Richard B. Day, "Trotsky and Preobrazhensky: The Troubled Unity of the Left Opposition," *Studies in Comparative Communism* 10, nos. 1–2 (Spring–Summer 1977): 69–86.

as staunch an ideologist as Nikolai Bukharin admitted the desirability of a "civil truce" between industry and the countryside; and Comintern head Georgi Zinoviev accepted the idea of eclecticism in Russia's economic planning.[78]

The most controversial figure was Gregory Sokol'nikov, who became finance commissar early in 1922. An old party member with a French doctorate in law and economics, he had returned with Lenin in the sealed train, signed the treaty of Brest-Litovsk, and in 1921 directed the "integrationist" policy that had led Russia to Genoa.[79] Capable and ambitious, he represented the extreme to which the Soviet leadership might go, including the formation of "mixed companies" established jointly with foreign capitalists to secure desperately needed capital. Sokol'nikov also made an abortive attack on *Vneshtorg*, the state's external trading monopoly.[80]

Lenin still held the pivotal position in Russia's power structure. The party faithful, despite their reservations over NEP, considered him the main protector against counterrevolution and Western interventionism. Indeed, Japanese troops remained in Siberia, the White Guard units in Eastern Europe had not all been disbanded, and the Mensheviks had not been completely subdued; also, the Hoover operation was regarded with fear and distrust.[81] For the moderates, only Lenin's prestige and tenacity kept Russia's interests foremost over the theorists of the Third Internationale. Lenin of course needed his warring followers to strengthen his bargaining position at home and abroad. He encouraged neither Sokol'nikov's administrative ambitions nor Chicherin's attempts to play the independent diplomat; he supported the "central planners" and still needed the Cheka. He gave Sokol'nikov "concrete tasks" but reassured Trotsky that "state capitalism" (modeled on the German war economy) would survive. He could lash out at the metalworkers for criticizing his pragmatic tactics but could also defend the power interests of the Soviet state ferociously, as he had during the Kronstadt mutiny a year before.[82]

78. Ibid., pp. 103–4; Carr, *Bolshevik Revolution*, 2:310; Richard B. Day, *Leon Trotsky and the Politics of Economic Isolation* (Cambridge: Cambridge University Press, 1973), pp. 95–96; William P. Morse, Jr., "Leonid Borisovich Krassin" (Ph.D. diss., University of Wisconsin, 1971), pp. 70–119; Marie-Luise Goldbach, *Karl Radek und die deutsch-sowjetischen Beziehungen, 1918–1923* (Bonn-Bad Godesberg: Verlag Neue Gesellschaft, 1973); Stephen F. Cohen, *Bukharin and the Bolshevik Revolution: A Political Biography, 1888–1939* (New York: Knopf, 1973), p. 147; and Georgi Zinoviev, *Die Taktik der kommunistischen Internationale gegen die Offensive des Kapitals* (Hamburg: Kommunistische Internationale, 1922).

79. Day, *Trotsky*, pp. 118–24, and Carr, *Bolshevik Revolution*, 2: chap. 19.

80. Though deeming it cumbersome and inefficient, Lenin backed Krassin against Sokol'nikov to save it: Lenin to Krassin, 12, 19 Jan. 1922, to Stalin, 19 Jan. 1922, and to Kamenev, 3 Mar. 1922, all in Lenin, *Collected Works*, 45:430, 441, 440–41, 496–99, and 725–26 (n. 606).

81. Lenin to Trotsky, Molotov, Zinoviev, and Unschlicht, 21, 30, 31 Jan. 1922, in ibid., pp. 443–44, 456–58.

82. Lenin to Sokol'nikov, 22 Jan. 1922, to Kamenev and Stalin, 25 Jan. 1922, in ibid., pp. 444–46, 450; *The Trotsky Papers, 1917–1922*, ed. J. M. Meijer (The Hague and Paris:

Flexible, though like Lloyd George occasionally ruthless and impatient, Lenin faced the opportunity and the danger of the Genoa Conference. Between the steely Soviet leader and the dedicated, aristocratic Chicherin a close collaboration developed. While the officials prepared the materials for Genoa and proceeded also to seek contacts with individual Western governments, Lenin kept watch for any signs of too blatant and damaging a retreat.[83]

ROME

The Italian leaders returned from Cannes as the designated hosts to a great international conference to be held in less than two months. The diplomatic initiatives of the Bonomi–Della Torretta cabinet since 1921,[84] its active role at the Washington Conference, its preliminary economic agreement with Russia in December, and its more vigorous participation in reparations discussions now seemed to bear fruit. The result of Cannes also wiped out the obloquy of Rome's exclusion from the Anglo-French conversations of December in London. Italy was to participate in the international corporation as an equal to the French and British. The much-feared Franco-British pact had not materialized. Italy had given loyal support to Lloyd George at Cannes and indeed credited its former premier, Francesco Nitti, with the original idea of "European reconstruction." The attempted rapprochement between the West and Russia might improve the prospects of the troubled, newly acquired Adriatic port of Trieste. Finally, the Genoa Conference was popular with Italian industrialists and workers, and presaged a more active Mediterranean policy.[85]

With the opening of parliament on 2 February 1922, Italy plunged into one of the worst political crises of its history, which had not only devastating political effects but also shaped its role at the Genoa Conference. The Bonomi government, formed in June 1921, had suffered almost continuous domestic turmoil. The elections of May 1921 resulted in a dramatic decline of the sorely divided liberals, made the Socialists and Catholic Popolari strong voices in Italian politics, and brought thirty-five Fascists into the legislature. The struggle for "legality" was undermined because almost half of the parliament espoused an antiliberal program. Proportional representation, introduced in 1919, had ended the old balancing act perfected by the aged master of *trasformismo*, Giovanni Giolitti. Heretofore, the bourgeois liberal parties had see-

Mouton, 1971), 2: no. 749; and speech to the metalworkers, 6 Mar. 1922, in Lenin, *Collected Works*, 33:212–26.

83. Lenin, *Collected Works*, 45: nos. 585, 586, 599, 602, 605, 623, 628, 630, 637, and 649.

84. Child to Harding, Rome, 11 Oct. 1921, Harding Papers, roll 208.

85. Kwiatkowski to Schober, Rome, 16, 22 Jan. 1922, A HHSt 687; Beyens to MAE, Rome (Vatican), 30 Jan. 1922, BMAE 10991; and Prittwitz to AA, Rome, 30 Jan. 1922, Germ. AA T-120 L990/5411/L285660–61. For a critical review of Nitti's internationalism, see Frank J. Coppa, "Francesco Saverio Nitti: Early Critic of the Treaty of Versailles," *Risorgimento* 2 (1980): 211–19.

sawed in power while class and confessional parties had remained subdued in the background. Now, in the presence of Mussolini's revolutionary followers on the Right, the Socialists and Catholics possessed disproportionate influence and the factious liberals lost prestige, confidence, power, and responsibility. Bonomi, a reformist Socialist little involved in foreign affairs, concentrated mainly on the menace of fascism and the growing number of strikes.[86]

Bonomi's foreign minister, the Sicilian aristocrat and career diplomat Marquis Pietro Tomasi della Torretta, steered a cautious course among the three directions of traditional Italian liberalism: the independent nationalism of the Salandrans; the flexible, relatively pro-French orientation of Giolitti and former Foreign Minister Carlo Sforza; and the anti-French, pro-British "internationalist" policy of the Nittians. Italy's foreign policy was further complicated by the Vatican's strong and active efforts to seek better relations with the kingdom, by ambitious Catholic politicians, and by militant Socialists, generally pro-German and anti-French, who were willing to follow industry's lead and tilt toward Russia as well. The net result was a policy under Della Torretta in which Italy had rejected isolation, searched for allies, drawn closer to Turkey, Russia, and Germany, and aligned itself with Britain and America and against France. Although the conservative Della Torretta was personally uncomfortable about Italy's rapprochement with Moscow, it was a logical outcome of Rome's new orientation.[87]

Italy's domestic crisis actually began on 22 January, when Pope Benedict XV died. The Socialists attacked the government for its unusual attentions on this occasion, its efforts to establish even closer relations with the successor, Pius XI, and especially its inability to control the increasing violence of the Fascists. Heavy industry, creditors, and account holders were alienated when the government failed to avert the long-anticipated crash of the Banca Itaiiana di Sconto. Giolitti criticized Bonomi's ineffectual financial policies, and his followers called for a more authoritative leadership at the Genoa Conference. When parliament opened, a motley combination of liberals declared no confidence, whereupon Bonomi wearily resigned. Nitti was unable to form a new government. Giolitti, who blocked him, similarly refused. For almost a month, Italy was without leadership, and it seemed impossible to produce a *combinazione* that could satisfy a majority in parliament. The solution, announced on 26 February, was another weak coalition headed by Luigi Facta, a

---

86. Maier, *Bourgeois Europe*, pp. 328–32; Danilo Veneruso, *La vigilia del fascismo: Il primo ministero Facta nella crisi dello stato liberale in Italia* (Bologna: Il Mulino, 1968), pp. 11–58; Italien-Innere Politik, Germ. AA T-120 K528/4153/K151505–52.

87. Prittwitz to AA and German Consul General, Trieste, to AA, 10 Dec. 1921, Germ. BA R 38/306; Prittwitz to AA, 27 Dec. 1921, Germ. AA T-120 9235H/3493/H253453–54; Barrère to MAE, Rome, 19 Jan. 1922, FMAE Z GB 48.

Giolittian lieutenant from Turin, and consisting of Catholics, liberals, and two members of the Salandran Right.[88]

The new Facta government, generally regarded as a stopgap, was a symbol of the danger to Italian democracy. Real politics now existed outside Rome and the parliamentary chambers: in the streets, factories, and hill villages. Though the new government advertised its anti-Marxist credentials, the real force behind it belonged to the Right, and there was little organized defense of Italian democracy. The small group of hard-line Communists, on orders from Moscow, held themselves aloof from the reformist Socialists. Except for their followers' street skirmishes with the Fascists, the radical Left took no formal steps to avert the catastrophe. Indeed, Communist loyalists were afraid that their Moscow confreres might succumb to the wiles and domination of bourgeois capitalist power at the Genoa Conference. The failure of any sort of liberal fusion in February 1922 meant the eventual demise of Italy's parliamentary form of government; and while the liberals continued their quarreling, Mussolini emerged as an increasingly vocal analyst of international affairs.[89]

Thus the events of early 1922 created a chaotic beginning to Italy's work on the Genoa Conference, a situation that the British greatly deplored.[90] Once freed from official responsibility, Della Torretta admitted his misgivings about the uncoordinated, potentially dangerous international gathering Italy was soon to host. Facta had originally wanted to be represented by Tommaso Tittoni, the colorless, pro-French former foreign minister, but Giolitti vetoed this. Thus Carlo Schanzer, a former cabinet minister and senator who had recently distinguished himself at the Washington Conference with his pro-British and anti-French stance, took over the post of minister of foreign affairs. With the retiring Facta, he would lead the delegation at Genoa.[91] There would be no sudden changes; the retention of Salvatore Contarini at his secretarial post in the foreign ministry ensured this.

The chaos in Rome shifted weight and importance to individuals in the Ital-

---

88. Naval Attaché report, 8 Mar. 1922, US MID 2657E (2095). Background in reports of Austrian Ambassador to the Vatican, 23 Dec. 1921, 7 Jan., 3 Mar. 1922, A HHSt 710; Graham to Curzon, Rome, 26 Feb. 1922, GB FO 371 C2939/366/12; and Veneruso, *La vigilia*, chap. 1.

89. Report, Sûreté Générale, Rome, 26 Feb. 1922, FMAE B 109; Renzo De Felice, *Mussolini* (Turin: G. Einaudi, 1965), vol. 2, pt. 1, pp. 233–37; Giorgio Rumi, *Alle origini della politica estera fascista (1918–1923)* (Bari: Laterza, 1968), pp. 166–74; Edgar R. Rosen, "Mussolini und Deutschland, 1922–1923," *Vierteljahrshefte für Zeitgeschichte* 5 (1957): 17–19.

90. Graham to Curzon, Rome, 27 Jan. 1922, GB FO 371 C1469/458/62; Graham to Crowe, 27 Jan. 1922, GB FO 800 CrP; Graham to Curzon, 3 Feb. 1922, CzP; but also Stefani communiqué on extensive preparations in Genoa, 8 Feb. 1922, GB FO 371 C2429/458/62.

91. On Schanzer: Hardinge to Curzon, Paris, 1 Mar. 1922, Graham to Curzon, Rome, 2 Mar. 1922, GB FO 371 C3058, C3146, C3315/366/12; Barrère to MAE, Rome, 28 Feb. 1922, FMAE B 88; and François Charles-Roux, *Souvenirs diplomatiques: Une grande ambassade à Rome, 1919–1925* (Paris: A. Fayard, 1961), p. 164.

ian embassy in London. There the economic expert, Dr. Francesco Giannini, played a leading role. Giannini had also been to Washington and Cannes; he was on close terms with top British officials and knew Lenin's close friend, Jan Antonovich Berzin, the Soviet envoy in London.[92] He and the anglophile ambassador de Martino maintained a very close liaison with British planners; they made the principal decisions about the invitations, the agenda, and the arrangements for the conference until Schanzer, returning from Washington, assumed his post at the Consulta in early March. The result of the prolonged political crisis was not only a painful period at home and the subsequent delay of the Genoa Conference but also the weakening of Rome's international position: Italy grew utterly subservient to Great Britain and once more was vulnerable to the Entente's known exclusionary tactics.

BRUSSELS

Belgian Prime Minister Georges Theunis had attended the Cannes Conference and displayed a generally favorable attitude toward Genoa. In fact, he had chaired the committee that had drafted the resolution establishing the international corporation to coordinate investments in Russia.[93] Belgium's citizens held 3.5 billion gold francs in holdings in prerevolutionary Russia and possessed a financial influence far out of proportion to the country's size and population; they had invested heavily in mines, metallurgical industries, glass works, railways, oil fields, and public service enterprises in Russia's cities. Brussels was therefore extremely interested in Britain's plans for reviving private enterprise in the East.[94]

Lloyd George's schemes dictated some caution because the mainspring involved *new* investments in the East rather than restoration of old ones. The Cannes Resolutions mentioned restoration *or* compensation of confiscated foreign interests. The British were casual about the exact form of restitution or repayment to be demanded from Moscow, about Russia's right to consolidate former holdings and award these as new concessions, and about the political guarantees that would be required in return for the Soviets' obtaining credits, new investments, and recognition from the West.

Belgium was split internally over the Genoa Conference. The former owners were wary of further despoilment by Anglo-German syndicates taking over their former properties; but Belgian export industries were interested in a revival of trade. The francophile press generally took Poincaré's side and echoed

92. Officially head of Italy's commercial delegation in London, Giannini was an experienced negotiator on oil and reparations questions; see note, 8 Jan. 1922, IMAE 49, and De Martino to MAE, 24 Jan. 1922, IMAE Amb. Lond. 538.3.

93. *DBFP*, 19:26–27, 97–98.

94. Comité de Défense des Interêts Belges en Russie to MAE, Brussels, 29 Dec. 1921, BMAE 10991; Fletcher to Hoover, Brussels, 29 May 1922, Hoover/Comm.

his reservations while Flemish and Socialist journalists supported Lloyd George. Foreign Minister Henri Jaspar admired Britain. Belgium was hoping to sign its own guarantee pact with London, and Brussels also owed Britain and the United States a huge postarmistice debt.[95] The safest policy was to follow Britain's lead, with due concern for Belgium's own welfare.

Theunis's Catholic-liberal coalition government, formed in December 1921, led a divided and still-devastated country. It had to proceed cautiously to maintain a hard-fought right to sit with the Great Powers. Belgium was, after all, a very small country with a disproportionately dominant group of industrialists and deep-seated ethnic divisions. The cause of European reconstruction interested Belgium as long as it did not interfere with its own difficult rebuilding.[96] Though Theunis was cognizant of the dangers of dealing with Soviet Russia and sitting between the bickering parties to the Entente, he nevertheless had to try.

GENEVA

The League of Nations, only two years old, was deliberately excluded from the three main diplomatic conferences of 1922: Washington, Genoa, and Lausanne. As a former official complained, while "the whole stage of international affairs was occupied by . . . great conferences . . . the Council, the Secretariat, and the regular organs of the League, continuing to transact their ordinary, unspectacular business, watched with a mixture of hope, anxiety, and jealousy the efforts of the powers to carry out the purposes of the Covenant without accepting its principles or using its institutions."[97]

Lloyd George was primarily responsible for the League's exclusion from the Genoa Conference. He had once endorsed the founding of the international organization. However, by 1921 he and his supporters attacked the fledgling League as cumbersome, competitive, and even a dangerous threat to the British Empire, and he vaguely threatened to replace it with a more congenial body. Lloyd George disliked the identification of the League with the Versailles treaty, with France and its allies. Britain and the dominions had misgivings about Article X of the Covenant, which obliged members to take on economic and military commitments in response to "aggression," which was a nebulous concept under the immediate postwar conditions. Finally, the

95. Delacroix to Jaspar, Brussels, 31 Dec. 1921, note pour M. le Ministre, 8 Jan. 1922, and Minister of Finance to Jaspar, 19 Jan. 1922, BMAE 10991. Also see Margerie to MAE, Brussels, 2 Feb. 1922, FMAE B 85, and Grahame report, Brussels, 28 Jan. 1922, Grigg Papers, roll 1.

96. On Theunis's government, see Carl-Henrik Höjer, *Le régime parlementaire belge de 1918 à 1940* (Uppsala and Stockholm: Almquist and Wiksells, 1946), pp. 125–32. Postwar Belgian foreign policy is ably covered in Sally Marks, *Innocent Abroad: Belgium at the Paris Peace Conference of 1919* (Chapel Hill: University of North Carolina Press, 1981), chap. 8.

97. F. P. Walters, *A History of the League of Nations* (Oxford: Oxford University Press, 1952), p. 162.

League's decision to partition Upper Silesia in the fall of 1921 demoted the institution entirely in Lloyd George's esteem.[98]

To protect its interests and maintain its worldwide empire, Britain under Lloyd George aspired to a special relationship with the United States, which had rejected any participation in League activities. Britain was thus forced to carry on onerous international tasks alone, even risking Washington's non-cooperation and opposition. When the United States refused to include the League in the Washington Conference, its exclusion from Genoa was automatic. Lloyd George assumed that the Americans and Russians would refuse to enter a League-sponsored meeting. Thereafter, he spared no effort to ensure the League's exclusion.[99]

The League could do little to fight back.[100] Only moderately endowed with funds to publicize or promote its work, it had scarcely gained an international audience and remained a marginal, relatively powerless, yet controversial organization. Germany, Russia, and America, all determined outsiders, had launched their diplomatic initiatives in 1921 well outside the League's auspices. The Supreme Council, the Reparations Commission, the Allied Military Control Commission, and the Conference of Ambassadors all controlled the major postwar political decisions. The League dealt regularly with very general problems: intellectual cooperation, international finance and transport, and health and labor questions. It also assumed, involuntarily, the burden of the most delicate problems emanating from the peace treaties: the Saar, Danzig, the protection of minorities, and disarmament. The contested decision on Upper Silesia was a good example of the limits and achievements of Geneva's work.

Despite the League's weakness, it had partisans within internationalist circles. League officials argued wishfully that its very existence indicated an improvement in the climate of European diplomacy; had it been there in 1914, there would have been no war. The well-financed and influential British League of Nations Union and its various continental counterparts published pro-League propaganda. Because many Britons had an almost religious reverence for the Covenant, Lloyd George was restrained from openly destroying the institution.[101]

98. Harvey to Harding, London, 29 Nov. 1921, Harding Papers, roll 231. On Upper Silesia, see Drummond to Balfour, Geneva, 29 June 1921, Drummond to Kerr, 20 Oct., 21 Nov. 1921, Kerr to Drummond, 17 Nov. 1921, LNA P33/3, 5.

99. Observations, Paris, 17 Jan. 1922, FMAE PM G/I; Directors' meeting, 18 Jan. 1922, LNA.

100. Drummond to Grigg, 24 Jan. 1922, Grigg Papers, roll 1; Haniel to German Consul General Geneva, Berlin, 25 Jan. 1922 and reply 4 Feb. 1922, Germ. AA T-120 L998/5412/L286290, L286398–400; and "Pourquoi la S.d.N. est-elle tenue à l'écart?" *Journal de Genève*, 4 Feb. 1922.

101. Telegram by British League of Nations Union to Secretariat, London, 12 Jan. 1922, LNA 10/18574/18574.

France could have exploited the League's popularity among the British masses and defended it from Lloyd George's threats, but it did not. French civil servants in Geneva were conspicuously reluctant to expand the organization's functions and authority. Poincaré shared Lloyd George's mistrust of the League. France was unwilling to diminish the treaty-enforcement rights of the Great Powers in favor of the new organization. Indeed, there was some concern in Paris that the League in the future might well be dominated by an anti-Versailles majority that advocated treaty revision. Except for insisting that none of the League's existing functions be usurped, Poincaré did not defend Geneva against the threat posed by the Genoa Conference. He did use the opportunity to spar in the press over how blatantly it could be ignored.[102]

In Geneva the young, utopian officials in the Secretariat were dismayed that their vision of peace and economic reconstruction was not credited by the Great Powers in or outside the institution. The League played no major role in organizing the Genoa Conference. Later Italy, burdened with the enormous tasks and expense of the world's first economic summit, at the last minute accepted technical help from the outcast organization.[103]

EXCURSUS: THE NEAR EAST

The abrupt ending of the Cannes Conference also had important implications for developments in the Near East. A key element in Lloyd George's offer of a guarantee to Briand was a proposal to settle Franco-British differences over the long Greco-Turkish conflict.[104] For over a year, Allied policies had diverged, and this was exacerbated by Soviet machinations, America's noncommittal policies, and especially Turkey's diplomatic and military triumphs alongside the disastrous policies of the Greeks.

The previous July the Greeks had launched an attack from Smyrna aiming to conquer Ankara and even Constantinople, goals far beyond the resources and strength of their Allied-sanctioned landing in Anatolia in 1919. The Turks had cleverly withdrawn beyond the Sakarya River. Then, in eight bloody days of fighting in early August, while the Supreme Council was meeting in Paris, they routed the Greeks and threatened their continued presence in Asia Minor.

102. Coolness toward the League was urged in Saint-Aulaire to MAE, London, 17 Jan. 1922, FMAE PM G/I; see also Hanotaux (France's council representative) to Poincaré, 24 Jan. 1922, FMAE Y 1204, and to Millerand, 24 Jan. 1922, BN PM/7. Daily Press Bulletin, 3 Feb. 1922, FMAE B 85; Poincaré to Couget (Prague), Paris, 4 Feb. 1922, and Couget to Poincaré, Prague, 6 Feb. 1922, FMAE PM G/I; Montille to MAE, London, 6 Feb. 1922, FMAE B 86; and Monnet to Seydoux, Geneva, 11 Mar. 1922, FMAE B 89.

103. Attolico memorandum, S.d.N. e la Conferenza di Genova, Jan. 1922, IMAE 52/51; Carlo Schanzer, "L'equivoco fondamentale della Società delle Nazioni," *Nuova Antologia* 232 (Nov. 1923): 3–16.

104. *DBFP*, 19:5. Also memorandum, The Proposed Alliance and the Eastern Question, 1 Feb. 1922, Grigg Papers, roll 9; De Martino to MAE, London, 1, 8 Feb. 1922, IMAE Amb. Lond. 531.3.

Faced with Turkish militancy, the Allies became convinced of the inevitability of their having to revise the 1920 Treaty of Sèvres.[105] Next to the German question, the Near East was a major focus of Allied diplomacy and disagreement.

Turkish Nationalist leader Mustafa Kemal was in many respects like Lenin: a forceful, flexible revolutionary leader and theoretician who had been forced by events to reshape his earlier doctrinal commitments. Once a Young Turk and victorious Ottoman general during the Dardanelles campaign, in 1920 he created a new movement and a national pact aimed at salvaging what he could from the ruins of the defeated empire. He accepted the loss of the Arab lands but none of the other territorial or economic clauses of Sèvres that would reduce the sovereignty and viability of a future Turkish state. Unlike Germany or Austria, Kemal's Turkey feared neither bolshevism nor the Allies' power; it also lacked much political opposition at home. By exploiting the humiliation of the former political and religious leadership now held in virtual captivity in Constantinople, Kemal set out to weld a new nationalism and extend Turkey's power in all of Anatolia and Thrace. Having renounced Ottoman imperialism, he set out to dominate and "turkify" what was left: this meant driving the Greeks out of Smyrna and Thrace, reconquering Armenia, and especially regaining full control over the nation's finances and economic resources. To this end he demonstrated remarkable diplomatic prowess and political leadership. Though largely secular, his movement commanded the loyalty of Moslems even outside Turkey, a force he could wield against Russia, France, and particularly the British Empire. Like Gandhi in India and De Valera in Ireland —though in a more militant and spectacular way—Kemal represented the birth of a new national leadership in the former colonial world.[106]

Under its new Bolshevik government, Russia, the traditional enemy, attempted to make Turkey a protectorate. This was an anti-British policy designed not only to establish security along the Soviet borders but also to ultimately extend Moscow's influence toward the Straits and the Middle East. Moscow and Ankara conquered and divided Armenia. On the same day as the conclusion of its trade pact with Britain, 16 March 1921, Russia signed a treaty

---

105. Salahi Ramsdan Sonyel, *Turkish Diplomacy, 1918–1923* (London and Beverly Hills, Calif.: Sage, 1975), pp. 113–35; Gotthard Jäschke and Erich Pritsch, *Die Türkei seit dem Weltkriege, Geschichtskalender: 1918–1928* (Berlin: Deutsche Gesellschaft für Islamkunde, 1929), pp. 43–57; A. J. Frangulis, *La Grèce et la crise mondiale* (Paris: F. Alcan, 1926), 2:119–327; and Michel Paillarès, *Le kémalisme devant les alliés* (Paris: Édition du "Bosphore," 1922), chap. 2.

106. There is as yet no scholarly biography of Kemal; Lord Kinross, *Atatürk: A Biography of Mustafa Kemal, Father of Modern Turkey* (New York: William Morrow, 1965), is the work of an able journalist. See also Michael M. Finefrock, "Atatürk, Lloyd George, and the *Megali* Ideal," *Journal of Modern History* 52 (Mar. 1980): Supplement D 1047–66.

of friendship and alliance with Turkey. Both signators had misgivings: Kemal was concerned about the growing number of native Turkish Communists, the paucity of Soviet military support, and the possibility that Russia would eventually make a deal with the West at his expense. Moscow similarly distrusted the Turkish overtures to the West, but also questioned whether Kemal would actually prevail. The verdict at the Sakarya River clarified matters. In November Turkey signed treaties with the three Soviet states in the Caucasus. At the same time the Russians, nudged by the Franco-Turkish pact, sent a mission to negotiate a peace between Turkey and the Ukraine and provide increased economic and military support; both sides discussed a joint policy vis-à-vis Rumania.[107] Despite residual elements of mistrust between their historically opposed states, the basis for an active Kemalist-Soviet entente had been laid.

The United States, which had not ratified the Treaty of Sèvres but was nevertheless interested in the Near East, took no active role in the Allied mediation efforts in 1921.[108] Washington recognized the strategic importance of the Straits, the problem of Soviet expansion toward the Mediterranean, and the significance of the Anglo-French duel over the oil-rich parts of the former Ottoman Empire. However, the Harding administration maintained a studied neutrality toward the fighting, revealing more sympathy for Turkish nationalism than for Greek imperialism.

Italy made the first switch. Rome had initially gone along with the Allies' pro-Greek policies; indeed, the 1919 Tittoni-Venizelos agreement was based on Italy's renunciation of its own claims to Rhodes, the Dodecanese, and Smyrna on Greece's behalf. But a year later, in June 1920, Sforza renounced the agreement and pursued a popular, pro-Turkish course that his successors, including the Fascists, would follow. On 12 March 1921 Sforza signed a secret agreement in London with the Turkish emissary Bekir Sami. Ankara rejected the pact because of its overtones of an exclusive Italian sphere in Adalia. Rome nevertheless began planning its withdrawal from Asia Minor and allowed arms to be sent through its occupation zone to the Nationalists. This policy, though risking London's ire, was less costly to Italy than one of building up Greek power in the Eastern Mediterranean or of allowing France alone to dominate the area. In return, Rome hoped for economic concessions from the Turks.[109]

107. Xenia J. Eudin and Robert C. North, *Soviet Russia and the East: A Documentary Survey, 1920–1927* (Stanford: Stanford University Press, 1957), pp. 109–13; Carr, *Bolshevik Revolution*, 3:295–304; and Lenin, *Collected Works*, 45: no. 551.

108. Adam memorandum, U.S. and the Revision of Sèvres, 20 Dec. 1921, *DBFP*, 17: no. 491; and Laurence Evans, *United States Policy and the Partition of Turkey, 1914–1924* (Baltimore: Johns Hopkins University Press, 1965), pp. 357–67.

109. C. J. Lowe and F. Marzari, *Italian Foreign Policy, 1870–1940* (London and Boston: Routledge, 1975), pp. 186–87; Sonyel, *Turkish Diplomacy*, pp. 119, 141–43; Carlo Sforza, "How We Lost the War with Turkey," *Contemporary Review* 32 (Nov. 1927): 587–89.

France had grudgingly acquiesced in the enforcement of the Treaty of Sèvres; however, when the pro-Allied Venizelos fell in late 1920 and the disliked King Constantine returned to the throne in Athens, and when a month later Briand returned to power, things began to change. To protect its mandate in Syria, Paris needed to end the border struggle with Kemal's army in Cilicia. It could thereby liberate needed French troops for Europe; but Kemal would then liberate troops for use against the Greeks or possibly against the British in Iraq. Briand appreciated the advantages of vying with the Bolsheviks as well as the British for influence in the Near East. French prestige there had always been high; France also held 60 percent of the former Turkish debt. On 9 March 1921 France signed with Bekir Sami and again Ankara vetoed. In June Briand sent the turkophile Senator Henry Franklin-Bouillon to Ankara to discuss an armistice. After the Turkish victory at Sakarya, Franklin-Bouillon went back and signed an accord with the Nationalists on 20 October.[110]

This pact represented a triumph for Kemal: Turkey's first equal treaty with a major Western power. It alarmed Moscow and infuriated the British. It also spurred the Italians to dispatch a negotiator to Ankara, though Rome, under severe pressure from London, hesitated to conclude a final accord with the Turks before the Allies' meeting at Cannes.[111]

Britain ultimately held the key to a Near Eastern settlement.[112] It had been the major guarantor of the Ottoman Empire for over a century, and its World War I military victories in the Near East had led to the great partition that split the Allies and aroused the native peoples. Now that Kemal had demonstrated a successful resistance to Greek expansion, London too would have to come to terms with Ankara. Britain was the only state strong enough to counterbalance the Soviet potential to dominate the Straits. London had to reconsider its commitments to Athens and to the remnants of the sultan's government in Constantinople. Both commitments, held in reserve, were important bargaining points.[113]

110. Henry H. Cumming, *Franco-British Rivalry in the Postwar Near East* (London: Oxford University Press, 1938), pp. 129–61; Suarez, *Briand*, p. 221.

111. Sonyel, *Turkish Diplomacy*, pp. 135–43; *DBFP*, 17: nos. 432, 434, 437, 452, 455, 456, 465, 470, 471, and 490 (on France); nos. 433, 434, 435, 436, and 462 (on Italy). After Curzon berated Saint-Aulaire about the Franklin-Bouillon agreement, he could not answer the latter's request "for information about the visits of Herr Stinnes and Rathenau to this country"; see *DBFP*, 17: no. 465.

112. Karl G. Larew, "Great Britain and the Greco-Turkish War, 1912–1922," *The Historian* 35, no. 2 (Feb. 1973): 256–67; Briton Cooper Busch, *Mudros to Lausanne: Britain's Frontier in Asia, 1918–1923* (Albany: State University of New York Press, 1976), pp. 321–27.

113. Note of conversation at the Villa Valetta, Cannes, 12 Jan. 1922 (Lloyd George, Curzon, Grigg, Vansittart, and Gounaris), *DBFP*, 17: no. 504. Cf. A. E. Montgomery, "Lloyd George and the Greek Question," in *Lloyd George: Twelve Essays*, ed. A. J. P. Taylor (London: Hamilton, 1972), pp. 279–80.

London's difficulties were largely outside its control: Soviet machinations, France and Italy's imminent defections, and the impending Greek collapse. Britain, with its still-precarious hold on Iraq, feared a possible Turkish onslaught against the oil-rich Mosul with the compliance of America or France. Finally, Britain, like France, was particularly sensitive to Moslem world opinion, especially in India.[114] When Greek Prime Minister Demétrios Gounaris came to London in October 1921 to seek aid, his visit provoked a pro-Turkish eruption in India, where Gandhi had just convened the national congress at Ahmedabad. While rapping Paris's hands for its insensitivity to the future rights of Christian minorities in the Near East, London, with its numerous Moslem subjects, could not afford to be accused of leading a crusade against Islamic Turkey.

By late 1921, the Near East problem had split the British government. Lloyd George remained firmly pro-Greek, but after Sakarya he was less ardent. He still hoped for a permanent Hellenic presence in Thrace and Asia Minor, and even considered the establishment of a consortium of Western capitalists in Greek-held territory.[115] From Constantinople, British High Commissioner Horace Rumbold deprecated the Kemalists, spun schemes with supporters of the sultan, and made generally ineffectual attempts to influence policy in London. The third and weightiest side, represented by the India, Colonial, War, and Foreign Offices, deplored the risks and expense of Britain's support of the Greeks. The decisive voice was that of Curzon, who later would be responsible for brilliantly extricating London from its quandary.[116]

In June 1921 Curzon's proposal for the internationalization of Smyrna was refused by the Greeks on the eve of their great offensive. In December he revived the plan. It was approved by the British cabinet but balanced by the government's decision to permit Greece to raise a loan of 15 million pounds from British bankers. Curzon convinced Lloyd George to take his Near East peace proposal to Cannes, where it was presented to Briand. When the latter fell, its was delivered on 16 January to Poincaré, who gave it a cool reception, treated the Greek emissaries harshly, and demanded the complete withdrawal of Athens' forces from Asia Minor.[117] Since time was on Kemal's side, it was to France's benefit to wait.

---

114. Harry N. Howard, *The Partition of Turkey* (Norman, Okla.: University of Oklahoma Press, 1931; New York: Fertig, 1966), pp. 265–66; and Busch, *Mudros to Lausanne*, pp. 327–30.

115. Project designed to develop new Greek "territories" by an international corporation, sent to Lloyd George, 22 Oct. 1921, on Gounaris's arrival, Grigg Papers, roll 9.

116. Busch, *Mudros to Lausanne*, pp. 323–27; Larew, "Greco-Turkish War," pp. 266–67; Frangulis, *La Grèce*, 2:312–22; and Nicolson, *Curzon*, pp. 246–68.

117. Conversation between Curzon and Poincaré, Quai d'Orsay, 16 Jan. 1922, *DBFP*, 17: no. 508; Frangulis, *La Grèce*, 2:325–27.

The convocation of the Genoa Conference and Britain's leading role in it gave London some leverage. Ankara, worried over the possibility of Soviet rapprochement with the West, asked Moscow to secure it an invitation. Whitehall had a moment of malicious pleasure when it dismissed Krassin's appeal on behalf of Kemal as a "piece of impertinence." Germany refused to help the Turks. Italy, pressed by Ankara, also appealed to London. The British replied that since Turkey was an "Asian Power" [*sic*] and "still at war with the Allies," it would be inappropriate for it to attend the Genoa Conference.[118]

This was only a minor triumph. Britain still had to take an initiative before long because the Greeks were faltering and suffering. An Allied conference on the Near East was delayed until late in March due to unanticipated events: the controversy that erupted in the India Office, Curzon's illness, and the fall of the Italian government, as well as Poincaré's continued indifference. The Great Powers had nonetheless embarked on a revisionist course in the Near East, with no support from the United States and with considerable concern over Soviet and German machinations. London had to find some means of maintaining Allied unity long enough to end the war in the Near East without a politically damaging defeat in the face of a concerned public opinion. Unlike France, which had earlier cut its losses to concentrate primarily on Europe, Britain remained preoccupied with the eastern Mediterranean and the Straits. Cannes and the impending Genoa Conference had given Lloyd George leadership in Europe; but Franco-British differences over the Near East and also over Tangier and Palestine[119] underlined London's dependency on France and even on Italy. Whitehall therefore had to pursue peace in Europe, maintain its important interests elsewhere, and keep control over the linkage between these.

118. Sonyel, *Turkish Diplomacy*, pp. 132–33; Schmidt-Rölke to AA, Moscow, 10 Jan. 1922, Germ. AA T-120 L991/5411/L285184; Krassin to Crowe, 13 Feb. 1922, Crowe memorandum, undated, and Waterlow minute, 27 Feb. 1922, GB FO 371 C2170/458/62. The sultan's government also made an abortive attempt to be represented at Genoa, GB FO 371 C1244/458/62.

119. Tangier, an ancient port at the southern entrance to the Mediterranean, had superb docks and potential aerial facilities. Before World War I, Britain, fearing that it might threaten Gibraltar, had obtained an agreement by all the powers that it be internationalized, but the pact was never implemented. After the war, when the German threat to North Africa was removed, France wanted only to maintain the status quo, namely, that Tangier, an enclave within Spanish Morocco and overwhelmingly Spanish in culture, would continue to be ruled by its puppet, the French-controlled sultan. Curzon came to Cannes with another plan to internationalize Tangier, which Briand seemed willing to accept. Poincaré was less accommodating, and Curzon resented the growing signs of veiled French control over the port; see GB FO 371 C5922/458/62.

Palestine, a far more complicated issue, involved Allied negotiations, primarily in the League of Nations, for the establishment of the British mandate, the terms under which Christian minorities would reside, the protection of holy places, extraterritorial rights, etc. Imperiale to MAE, Geneva, 10 Jan. 1922, IMAE 49, reports significant British "concessions." See also Walters, *League of Nations*, p. 213.

In Tangier, Palestine, and the Near East, Italy's interests tended to resemble France's more than Britain's.

3

Genoa Delayed

One of the primary areas of contention between Britain and France was the timing of the Genoa Conference. Exploiting the advantages of public interest and diplomatic momentum, London wanted to move quickly to the conference table; fearing the costs and therefore demanding adequate preparation and guarantees, France applied the brakes. The postponement of a major international conference was a serious undertaking, risking the weakening of Lloyd George's position and the encouragement of his opponents. The postponement question was eventually transformed from an Anglo-French power struggle into an international debate over Genoa itself.

Whither the Anglo-French Pact?

One significant result of the Cannes Conference was to further alienate French and British opinion from the institution of the Supreme Council as a forum for mediating their differences. Both sides evaluated the future of their relationship. The French were weary of international conferences at lush pleasure spots. Such conferences, which occasionally stooped to the frivolity of picnics and games of golf, gave Lloyd George a distinct advantage and frequently sacrificed Paris's interests.[1] France had been apprehensive over the last meeting; instead of a pact and a new reparations agreement, Cannes had simply given the Germans a platform and the Russians a precious invitation to Genoa. Poincaré preferred to return to more traditional channels of diplomacy but was not yet ready to give up a pact. On 13 January the *Petit Parisien* announced that the new ministry's first duty would be to "dispel the misunderstandings" with London; that evening *Le Temps* pleaded for the conclusion of a bilateral pact. Two days later, Poincaré wrote in *Revue des Deux Mondes* that the pact, though still indispensable, must consist of a real military commitment between the two partners.

Lloyd George too was weary of the Supreme Council; Grigg portrayed the institution as laying down "the law, like a remote and inaccessible Sanhe-

1. Hardinge to Curzon, Paris, 13 Jan. 1922, GB FO 371 W457/4/17. Henceforth all dates, unless otherwise indicated, are in 1922.

drin."[2] But the British premier wanted it replaced not with the "old" diplomacy but the "new." The Genoa Conference represented a chance to revive the Concert of Europe, with the remote possibility of including the United States; with the Washington Conference winding down, London believed that Paris would not risk isolation by insisting on a special relationship only with Great Britain.[3] Indeed, Ambassador Hardinge, Curzon, and especially Lloyd George were all convinced that Poincaré could be "bullied."[4]

In Paris the situation was perceived differently. Poincaré was determined to avoid Britain's using the pact (in the words of Saint-Aulaire) to "portugalize" France. The Belgian ambassador reported that the Quai d'Orsay was working day and night to prepare its position, and the German embassy predicted a prompt commencement of Anglo-French negotiations.[5] Following an interview where Saint-Aulaire presented Curzon with specific proposals, Poincaré dispatched his "modifications" of London's offer of a treaty between France and Britain. These contained his bargaining terms: reciprocal military engagements, with both sides guaranteeing the other against invasion and maintaining continuous staff talks; a broad definition of aggression that reinforced Britain's commitment to the demilitarization of the left bank of the Rhine; a plan for common action in the event of aggression in Eastern Europe; and a pact with either an unlimited duration or a duration of at least thirty years.[6] Significantly, there was no mention of the issues that concerned Britain: the Near East, Tangier, and French aircraft and submarine production. France presented its desiderata, as Lloyd George had at Cannes, though Poincaré was not as uncompromising and domineering as contemporary and later critics have asserted.[7]

London was unwilling to accept these terms before the Genoa Conference. A positive response might have alarmed Italy and Germany, on whose cooperation Genoa depended, and might also have worried Russia and America. The

2. Grigg to Thomas, 19 Jan., Grigg Papers, roll 2.

3. Grigg to Lloyd George, 1 Feb., LGP F 86/1/18; Sthamer to AA, London, 26 Jan., Germ. AA T-120 L999/5412/L286790–93.

4. Hardinge to Curzon, Paris, 20 Jan., CzP: "You have the whip hand with the Pact [which is] absolutely essential to his policy [and without which] his government will fall." Also Hardinge to Curzon, 21, 27 Jan., and 1 Feb., ibid., 27 Jan., GB FO 371 W916/916/17, 10 Feb. minute, GB FO 371 W1347/4/17; Curzon to Hardinge, 28 Jan., GB FO 371 W937/50/17; and Grigg to Lloyd George, 1 Feb., Grigg Papers, roll 9. De Gaiffier to MAE, Paris, 21, 27 Jan., BMAE Fr., reported Hardinge's information that "L'Angleterre obligera bien M. Poincaré à mettre de l'eau dans son vin."

5. De Gaiffier to MAE, Paris, 25 [?] Jan., BMAE Fr., and Mayer to AA, Paris, 24 Jan., Germ. AA T-120 3398/1733/D737926.

6. Texts in GB FO 371 W937, W963, W1162/50/17.

7. Ludwig Zimmermann, *Frankreichs Ruhrpolitik von Versailles bis zum Dawesplan* (Göttingen: Musterschmidt-Verlag, 1971), p. 53, presents the standard anti-Poincaré interpretation.

governments of the British Empire had, the last July, expressed their unwillingness to make specific military commitments to Europe. Even the Tories, including the francophile Austen Chamberlain, shrank before Poincaré's proposals.[8] Curzon, who disliked the prospect of a double alliance to enforce the Versailles treaty, insisted on the precedent of 1904: that there must be a prior settlement of all the outstanding issues France had evaded—Turkey, Tangier, and French arms—before the two governments could move toward any final agreement step by step. For Lloyd George there was no possible benefit from hobbling the Genoa Conference beforehand with any special commitment to France or the Versailles treaty.

Thus the last chance for an Anglo-French pact was dissipated. Curzon announced that there would be "no time" to work on a settlement with France before the scheduled opening of the Genoa Conference on 8 March. Though Poincaré was willing to make substantial compromises, London was unwilling to accommodate him. Because of personal animosity between the French and British statesmen, Lloyd George's ambitions for the Genoa Conference, and the vague hope both sides inspired in the other that the Entente could be superseded by something more substantial, France and Britain did not proceed to formalize their relationship before Genoa.[9]

The Politics of Postponement

Poincaré worried about the scope and implications of the impending Genoa Conference. The Cannes Resolutions voted on 6 January were vague and deliberately contradictory. Lloyd George had refused (and Briand had not opposed him) to force Moscow to give unconditional acceptance even to these general statements by the Supreme Council. The agenda, already distributed to all the invitees, was equally vague. A five-member committee, which was to have met after Cannes to draft a detailed program, had not been convened. The French government believed it needed a long period for adequate preparations —a minimum of three months. Paris began receiving word of extensive British preparations and, all the more disturbing, of continued Anglo-Russian contacts that seemed to presage an imminent and unconditional recognition of the So-

---

8. See Austen Chamberlain's letters to his sister Hilda throughout Jan. that criticize France's alliance scheme, ACP 5/1/22; also Balfour to Lloyd George, Washington, 12 Jan., GB FO 371 W388/50/17, which opposed an Anglo-French pact.

9. See the revealing exchange of telegrams between Lloyd George and Poincaré, 16–17 Jan., GB FO 371 W546/50/17; also De Gaiffier to MAE, Paris, 4 Feb., BMAE Fr.; Christoph Stamm, *Lloyd George zwischen Innen- und Aussenpolitik: Die britische Deutschlandpolitik 1921/1922* (Cologne: Verlag Wissenschaft und Politik, 1977), pp. 250–52; Piotr Wandycz, *France and Her Eastern Allies* (Minneapolis: University of Minnesota Press, 1962), p. 255.

viet regime.[10] Though Poincaré knew of the tense relations between Downing Street and the Foreign Office, and the lack of coordination of the plans for Genoa between London and Rome, he feared the 8 March deadline and a sudden British coup. On 3 February the *Daily Chronicle* printed a violently anti-French article by Philip Kerr.[11]

The Genoa Conference represented many dangers for France. The city itself, with its array of Fascists and Communists and its poor communications and security, seemed like a singularly bad choice for an international gathering.[12] The invitation to wartime neutrals who had not signed the Versailles accord, to the former enemy states, and, without any conditions, to the Soviet government threatened to produce embarrassing discussions about treaty revision and reparations, sanctions, and disarmament. The established balance between the functions of the Allies and the League of Nations could be undermined by a conference whose purpose was advertised as the formulation of "new diplomatic principles." Moreover, the ranks of France's allies had been weakened; fearing to anger Great Britain and indeed anticipating some positive results, Belgium and Poland were outwardly favorable to Lloyd George's initiative. The normally francophile states bordering on Soviet Russia favored an international pact with Moscow as a means of legitimizing their independence; and even anti-Soviet Rumania and Yugoslavia accepted the Genoa Conference with good grace.[13]

Though most of the invitees deemed the original agenda too general, the conclusion was that the Western powers must coordinate their policies. France therefore could not create a bloc that opposed "European reconstruction" nor risk the isolation it had experienced at Washington. Journalists from the United States, Britain, Italy, and the former neutrals joined pro-German and Communist organs in attacking Paris's "negativism" and France's "hegemonial" policies. But France actually had no program for Genoa save to allay the worst, namely, to prevent concessions to Germany that would reduce reparations and French security; to block concessions to Soviet Russia that would injure French creditors and endanger France's East European allies; and to modify Britain's grandiose credits scheme that threatened to establish either British or Anglo-

10. Saint-Aulaire to Poincaré, London, 24 Jan., 7 Feb., FMAE B 105; Saint-Aulaire to MAE, 28 Jan., FMAE B 85; and Martel to MAE, Riga, 28 Jan., FMAE Z GB 61.

11. Protested in Curzon to Kerr, 5 Feb., GB FO 800/150. French fears expressed in Poincaré's marginal notes to Saint-Aulaire telegram of 24 Jan., FMAE B 105, and in Avenol to Minister of Finance, London, 8 Feb., FMAE B 87.

12. Unsigned note, "Inconvenance du choix de Gênes comme siège de la conférence pour la restauration économique de l'Europe," Paris, 6 Feb., FMAE B 86.

13. Margerie to MAE, Brussels, 2 Feb., FMAE B 85; Panafieu to MAE, Warsaw, 20 Jan., 1 Feb., FMAE B 105, B 85; Daeschner to MAE, Bucharest, 1, 5 Feb., and Clement Simon to MAE, Belgrade, 2 Feb., FMAE PM G/I. Cf. Young to FO, Belgrade, 10 Feb., GB FO 371 C2208/458/62.

German economic predominance in Europe, a scheme that extended to ambitious oil plans for the Caucasus, and potential British domination of the Straits.[14] The Quai d'Orsay dismissed London's lament of a "broken Europe." Poincaré instigated a publication in which Britain was held responsible for the current economic crisis.[15]

French public opinion was considerably focused on the Genoa Conference. After 18 January *Le Temps* printed a daily "Avant Gênes" column, and most of the major French publications devoted special articles or editions to European reconstruction. Leading French politicians and political groupings spoke out against a summit strategy that could only benefit Germany and Russia. President Millerand, planning a politically important trip to North Africa, opposed any appeasement of Soviet Russia, as did such influential politicians as Alexandre Ribot, Gaston Doumergue, and Georges Leygues, former premier and current president of the Senate Foreign Affairs Commission. The extreme Right condemned the Genoa Conference as representing German, Russian, and "Jewish-dominated" diplomacy.[16] The radicals, Socialists, and Communists, who in principle were dedicated to "European reconciliation," stayed silent; their internal factionalism, their uncertainties about the present German and Soviet regimes, their policy of waiting in the wings until the Bloc national could be defeated, and, finally, the negative example of Briand's demise—all were factors that explained why no French statesman, not even Briand, stepped forward to defend France's participation at Genoa.

With the exception of a few provincial chambers of commerce, France's business community, led by the influential Association of Former French Investors in Russia, which was headed by Senator Noulens, was opposed to any dealings with Moscow, at least until the present Soviet regime had disappeared. The powerful French colonial lobby feared complications from Lloyd George's pronouncements on free trade. French industrialists recognized Germany's advantages in the East and resented its policies, which gave the appearance of an impoverished treasury while enriching its capitalists at France's

14. Seydoux note, 14 Feb., FMAE B 112; Jacques Bardoux, "Les risques de Gênes," *L'Opinion*, 18 Feb.; discussions of the Commission Centrale d'Experts, 15 Feb., FMAE B 112, and the Commission Interministerielle Russe, 16 Feb., FMAE PM G/II.

15. The theme of a book written by "Celtus" [André François-Poncet, from the Economic Section of the MAE; Guillaume de Tarde, from the Ministry of Commerce; and Jean Benoist from the Ministry of Public Works], *La France à Gênes: Un programme français de reconstruction économique de l'Europe* (Paris: Plon, 1922). Though published privately, it was distributed on the eve of the Genoa Conference to French representatives abroad.

The accusation of Britain's responsibility for the current economic crisis (like America, Britain cut off government credits to its allies in 1919) was made in a speech by Loucheur and reprinted in the *Journée Industrielle*, 21 Feb.

16. De Gaiffier to Jaspar, Paris, 16 Feb., BMAE 10991; also "Sous le règne d'Israël," *Libre Parole*, 4 Mar.

expense. Echoing Center and Right politicians, French businessmen suggested
that the best way to reconstruct Europe was to start with devastated France;
they even advocated that the best way to collect reparations payments was
through a coup de main in the Ruhr.[17]

The French parliament warned the government against surrendering any
"rights." Poincaré therefore had a mandate to stage a defense against any and
all dangers but had no clear and positive program to offer.[18] Thus a duel began
between the French and British premiers. The United States was preoccupied
with the winding down of the Washington Conference; Italy was disconcerted
by its government crisis; and Germany and Russia, both the objects of the
Franco-British struggle, opposed a postponement of the Genoa Conference but
could only affect the dialogue negatively. Poincaré took the initiative, dis-
patching a series of messages and notes to Great Britain and France's allies,
and making ample use of the press to ventilate his views. He worked also to
recapture support from France's allies and from the neutrals.

Poincaré's basic strategy was threefold: to postpone the Genoa Conference
as long as possible, to forge strong Allied unity, and to create ironclad restrictions on the scope of the impending summit meeting. The first was the most
critical. The expected absence of the United States, the still-pending question
of a reparations moratorium, and the imminent commencement of war-debts
negotiations—all made prudence dictate a long adjournment. For France it was
Germany first, Russia second; the Genoa Conference, which was to be cen-
tered on the latter, could wait. France tried and failed to win America's support
for a joint effort for postponement. Washington, though sympathetic with the
French maneuver, could not act because it had not yet responded to Italy's
invitation.[19]

17. Seydoux, Note sur la régime économique de l'Allemagne, 25 Feb., FMAE B 88. There
had been talks after Wiesbaden about Franco-German collaboration in Russia (FMF 30/1074,
especially 27 Dec. 1921 interview with Rathenau); after Cannes, the Marquis de Lubersac met
Stinnes in Essen (15 Jan., FMAE B 105). French businessmen concluded that their interests were
not parallel with Germany's; cf. "La conférence de Gênes et les intérêts allemands en Russie,"
Bulletin Quotidien [organ of the Comité des Forges, directed by André François-Poncet], 20 Jan.;
meeting at the Quai d'Orsay, 16 Feb.; FMAE B 106; and Tirard note, 31 Mar., FMAE B 93.

France feared to dilute the reparations problem in the larger issue of reconstruction: Lucien
Romier, "À quoi pensent les Allemands?" *Journée Industrielle*, 2–3 Apr., and E. Labarthe, "La
Conférence de Gênes," *Réveil Économique*, 15 Apr.: "Allez de glissades! Les Boches n'ont pas
pu passer à Verdun. Ils ne doivent pas passer à Gênes!" On Center and Rightist opposition, see
Renata Bournazel, *Rapallo: Naissance d'un mythe. La politique de la peur dans la France du
bloc national* (Paris: Fondation Nationale des Sciences Politiques, 1974), pp. 79, 82.

18. Leygues to Poincaré, 10 Feb. (transmitting the Viviani resolution of 9 Feb.), FMAE B 86.
Also Mayer to AA, Paris, 10 Feb., Germ. AA T-120 L998/5412/L286358–60, and Hardinge to
FO, Paris, 10 Feb., GB FO 371 C2003, C2019/458/62.

19. Poincaré to Jusserand, Paris, 2 Feb., FMAE B 85, and Jusserand to Poincaré, Washington,
n.d. (received 10 Feb.), n.d. (received 14 Feb.), and 25 Feb., FMAE PM G/II.

Allied solidarity was important to Poincaré, who dutifully reported to London on the Soviet overtures to Paris.[20] He also insisted on the inclusion of members of the Little Entente in any preliminary Allied discussions, a gesture that had a positive impact on Eastern Europe. There was a prompt response from Czechoslovakia's prime minister, Eduard Beneš, a young, respected statesman and protégé of the esteemed President Thomas Masaryk. Soon after the Cannes meeting, Beneš announced his desire to visit Paris, London, and Rome, and to work for close Allied cooperation.[21]

Finally, Poincaré made repeated requests for "clarification." He insisted that a formal agenda committee be convened in Paris and urged Britain to pledge its adherence both to the existing treaties and the League of Nations. He cleverly demonstrated how the Cannes Resolutions could be turned against the Allies: the "full debt repayment" demanded of Russia could be demanded *by* America; and the statement against aggression could be interpreted by former enemies as nullifying the treaty clauses that enabled the Allies to take sanctions against Germany and Hungary.[22]

The British Foreign Office, to which Poincaré's notes, messages, and requests for postponement were directed, responded warily. Junior officials conceded that all the French premier's points were valid; indeed, the Italians had similar misgivings.[23] Their chiefs, Crowe and Curzon, who did not admire Lloyd George's Genoa scheme, nonetheless scored Poincaré for "wrecking" the conference and were impatient and sarcastic with his emissary, the Count de Saint-Aulaire. To maintain Rome's spirits and diligence, London refused a postponement and insisted on an 8 March opening. Curzon vetoed the Little Entente's participation in any preliminary meeting, for this would establish a privileged coterie that would be resented by outsiders. Finally, the foreign sec-

20. Poincaré's marginal notes on note pour le Président du Conseil, 7 Feb., FMAE B 86: "Comme je l'ai indiqué à M. Peretti, prevenir Londres des demarches *multiples* dont nous avons été l'objet . . . et faire savoir que nous n'avons pas voulu les accueillir, pour ne pas nous séparer de nos alliés dans la préparation de la Conférence de Gênes, que nous croyons cette préparation entre alliés de plus en plus nécessaires." Cf. Poincaré to French Ambassadors in London and Rome, to Ministers in Prague, Warsaw, Belgrade, and Bucharest, Paris, 9 Feb., FMAE Z Russ. 349, and Peretti to all missions, 11 Feb., FMAE PM G/II. Also Crowe note, 10 Feb., GB FO 418/57, no. 52 N1338/646/38.

21. Couget to MAE, Prague, 23 Jan., and Saint-Aulaire to MAE, London, 23 Jan., FMAE B 85.

22. Note communicated by the French chargé d'affaires, 5 Feb., and minutes by Gregory and Waterlow, 8 Feb., GB FO 371 C1830/458/62; Waterlow to Curzon, 9 Feb., GB FO 371 C2000/458/62; minutes by Waterlow and Crowe, 9 Feb., GB FO 371 C2024/458/62; and Curzon to Hardinge, London, 16 Feb., GB FO 371 C2392/458/62.

23. Report of interdepartmental committee, 9 Feb.: Memorandum on the French note of 5 Feb., GB FO 371 C2041/458/62. Also Romano Avezzana to De Martino, Rome, 20 Feb., IMAE 52/2.

retary ridiculed Paris's sudden display of interest in Genoa's program, when its own preparations, as compared with Whitehall's, were so meager.[24]

On 11 February Curzon invited the governments who had attended the Cannes meeting to send experts to London for the purpose of "dissipating doubt and ambiguity" before the Genoa Conference.[25] Belgium, Italy, and Japan promptly accepted. France held back, awaiting a formal reply to its lengthy note of 5 February, which, much to Curzon's irritation, it published. When no answer came from London, Paris acted. On 18 February it formally asked the Italian government to postpone the Genoa Conference for three months.[26] The Little Entente, Japan, Switzerland, and the Netherlands, all informed in advance, did not second the request, but Czechoslovakia did.

Beneš began shuttling between Paris and London. On departing Prague, he had announced that he was opposed to the Genoa Conference.[27] Czechoslovakia—ethnically divided and surrounded by hostile, perhaps irredentist German and Hungarian neighbors—was beginning to establish a foreign policy designed to maximize its security and independence. Its existence was based on the Paris peace treaties, its future on maintaining the status quo. Beneš had recently completed delicate economic agreements with the neighboring states, Austria and Poland,[28] both of which he hoped to draw closer to the Little Entente, which was still a frail and divided organism. The announcement of the Genoa Conference had cut short the promising commercial talks between Prague and Moscow; the latter anticipated more substantial advantages from Genoa than the Czechs alone could offer.[29] The Czechoslovak government was resolutely anti-Bolshevik, flanked as it was by the anti-Soviet National Democrats led by Karel Kramář. It was frightened by the possibility of political recognition of Lenin and his minions, who could, in collusion with Germany, overwhelm or subvert the new East European order. Unlike France, there were no Czech creditors of the Bolshevik regime. In fact, the exploits of the Czech

24. Curzon to Saint-Aulaire, 11, 14 Feb., GB FO 371 C2041, C2243/458/62.

25. Curzon to Hardinge (Paris), Grahame (Brussels), and Italian Ambassador De Martino (London), 11 Feb., GB FO 371 C2041/458/62.

26. Poincaré to French Ambassadors in London and Rome, Paris, 17, 18 Feb., FMAE PM G/II, and to all French missions, 18 Feb., ibid. He sent Saint-Aulaire a list of nine "fundamental" questions unanswered by London.

27. Note, Paris, 17 Jan., on talks between Laroche and Czech Minister Osuský, FMAE B 85. Also Couget to MAE, Prague, 23, 31 Jan., ibid; Koch to AA, Prague, 28 Jan., 2 Feb., Germ. AA T-120 L998/5412/L264338–40, L286442–43; Einstein to State Dept., Prague, 18 Jan., USDS E1/11; and Bordanaro to MAE, Prague, 4 Feb., IMAE 52/4 (Czech).

28. On the Austro-Czech Treaty of Lány, 16 Dec. 1921: Marek to BMA, Prague, 12 Jan., A HHSt 479; on the Beneš-Skirmunt pact of 6 Nov. 1921: Aufzeichnung, 15 Nov. 1921, Germ. AA T-120 K367/3999/K118060, and Wandycz, *France and Her Eastern Allies*, pp. 248–53.

29. Cecil to Curzon, Prague, 11 Jan., GB FO 418/57, no. 22 N377/242/38, and E. R. W. McCabe report, 7 Feb., US MID no. 635, 2657 (Czech).

legion at the end of World War I made the Prague government liable for a part of Moscow's expected claim for damages by the Allies.

In some respects the highly industrialized Czechoslovakia had interests more parallel to Britain than to France. With its high-valued currency (painfully separated from the devalued German mark), Czechoslovakia was also suffering from shrinking markets, unemployment, and the need for a foreign loan.[30] The Genoa Conference promised a general economic revival and new markets in Eastern Europe; but it also threatened to give Czechoslovakia's large neighbor, Germany, the edge in the East with Britain's blessings, in order that the Reich could pay its reparations. Because of a German minority of 3 million, Beneš's government could not appear too ardently germanophobe, too hostile to Lloyd George's grand design; but the Czech leader was not enthusiastic about his country's prospects at Genoa. Like most Western statesmen, Beneš regarded Soviet Russia as a "ruined" land, although offering potential economic opportunities. (Indeed, except for the propaganda of the Third Internationale and sporadic threats against the White Russian and Ukrainian refugees that had settled in Prague, Russia posed little threat to Czechoslovakia's security, unlike the threat to its neighbors, Poland and Rumania.) Finally, there was a small but troublesome feature of the Genoa Conference: Britain's emphasis on free trade. Prague feared this as an attempt to revise some of the economic clauses of the Treaty of Saint-Germain that favored the succession states and as an effort to liberate Austria from its burdens without compensatory advantages to Czechoslovakia and its allies.

For Czechoslovakia, as for France, the chief problem would always be the German problem. The long-term danger was an Anschluss, a question not entirely buried in the beginning of 1922.[31] Accordingly, Beneš tried to solidify the status quo: to facilitate a prompt settlement on German reparations by favoring both a moratorium and a loan to Germany, to stabilize the economies of Central Europe and build up the Little Entente, and, of the utmost importance, to solidify the Anglo-French entente. All of these took precedence over creating a *barrière de l'est* against the weak and warring Bolsheviks.

To accomplish this, Beneš assumed the role of intermediary and carried a program to Paris and London. A dogged, energetic emissary, he pleaded for Allied solidarity to combat Russian bolshevism, insisting that the West could better the ARA's record, "penetrate" the Russian market, but evade any political commitments to the Soviet regime. Ultimately, he argued, the Soviet leadership would be compelled to make concessions to Western liberal values. He was willing to follow Britain's lead and establish economic ties with Moscow

30. Koch to AA, Prague, 2 Feb., Germ. AA T-120 L998/5412/L286338–40.

31. Rosenberg to AA, Vienna, 12 Dec. 1921, Germ. AA T-120 K362/3996/K115969–70, and Riedel to BMA, Berlin, 4 Jan. A HHSt 479.

but stopped short, with France, at political ties. As to Germany, Beneš shared France's dread of Teutonic economic dominance. While arguing for sane and practical solutions to the reparations stalemate, he pleaded that Weimar democracy would be encouraged more if Stinnes and company did not receive privileged hearings in London.[32]

The Beneš journey was a mixed success. Paris appreciated the main parts of his German program and all his pleas to maintain Austria's independence; it was less sympathetic with his willingness to broaden commercial ties with the Soviets.[33] In London, despite massive efforts to ingratiate himself with Lloyd George, Beneš encountered substantial opposition to his germanophobia, his pleadings for the League, his hopes for a Little Entente presence during the Allies' preliminary talks, and his attempt to secure a large British government loan.[34] He did make one point with his proposal to establish stages in the West's approach to Soviet Russia: first economic penetration, then a trial period, and finally full political ties. He established no personal *amitié* with Lloyd George, who had no sympathy with the East European succession states (whose patron, Wickham Steed, was the barbed voice editor of the hostile *Times*). The British premier disliked Prague's francophilia, its economic aspirations, and its high-handed attitude toward land reform and minorities. Beneš, in his turn, not only insisted that the Little Entente would maintain complete solidarity with France but also leaked the talks in the press; they appeared in the *Evening Standard* on 20 February.[35]

Contrary to various reports and to his own conviction,[36] Beneš brought no message from Lloyd George to Poincaré, though he did provide Paris with a great deal of information. He confirmed the Quai d'Orsay's fears that Britain desired a quick and decisive meeting at Genoa; then, after Easter, having presented his budget to parliament, Lloyd George intended to call a general election. Beneš predicted that reparations would probably be on the agenda at Genoa. He returned glumly to Prague, having canceled an announced trip to Rome, to face his Little Entente partners with empty hands and his nation with no new financial or diplomatic support.[37]

32. Beneš, "Les conférences en vue de la reconstruction de la Russie et de l'Europe," *Gazette de Prague*, 28 Dec. 1921; Bure to MAE, Prague, 8 Feb., BMAE 10991; Seydoux note, Paris, 13 Feb., FMAE B 82; "M. Beneš," *L'Europe Nouvelle*, 25 Feb.; Namier to Kerr, London, 15 Feb. (forwarded to Grigg), on Namier's talks with Masaryk and Beneš, Grigg Papers, roll 2.

33. Pertinax in *Echo de Paris*, 23 Feb.

34. Saint-Aulaire to MAE, London, 20 Feb., FMAE B 87. Beneš had two meetings with Lloyd George, 17, 20 Feb., GB FO 371 C2675, C2739/458/62; returning to Paris, he sent the British premier a list of suggestions, GB FO 371 C2931/458/62, with Gregory and Crowe minutes. Negative reaction to Beneš: Grigg to Lloyd George, 24 Feb., LGP F 86/1/89, and Sthamer to AA, London, 22 Feb., Germ. AA T-120 L998/5412/L286505–8.

35. Sthamer to AA, London, 23 Feb., Germ. AA T-120 4597H/2370/E188294–98.

36. See Beneš to Lloyd George, Paris, 22 Feb., LGP F 49/9/3.

37. Koch to AA, Prague, 27 Feb., Germ. AA T-120 L998/5412/L286590–93, but cf. (the

Lloyd George had decided to meet directly with Poincaré. After an exceedingly difficult interview with Krassin, he realized that the Genoa Conference could not succeed without France.[38] His message to Poincaré was routed to Saint-Aulaire through the former ambassador to Paris, Lord Derby, either in an attempt to spare Curzon the embarrassment of a negative French reply or to irk the haughty foreign secretary.[39] Poincaré agreed at once. Italy's isolation and Beneš's trip had benefited France, whose press was exultant over the "necessary" meeting.[40]

On 24 February Rome suddenly announced there would be a short postponement. Contrary to his repeated assurances, Della Torretta declared that the prolonged ministerial crisis that was about to end made it impossible for the Genoa Conference to open as scheduled in less than two weeks.[41] One day later, on 25 February, Lloyd George crossed the Channel, landed at Calais, and took a car sent by Poincaré to the prefecture at Boulogne-sur-Mer, where the two leaders were to meet. He was accompanied by the cabinet secretary, Sir Maurice Hankey, who had been summoned back early from Washington to coordinate the arrangements for the Genoa Conference; there was no one from the Foreign Office. Poincaré was attended by Peretti de la Rocca from the Quai d'Orsay.

Boulogne

For the second time in six weeks, Lloyd George and Poincaré met in France to discuss their differences and clear the path for the Genoa Conference. The leaders of Western Europe's two democracies and vast overseas empires, the wartime allies and peace-treaty makers, both faced parliaments and publics that were greatly incensed over foreign affairs and especially over their rela-

---

more optimistic) Einstein to State Dept., Prague, 27, 28 Feb., USDS E1/55, 124. The loan that Czechoslovakia obtained in April was decidedly in the Anglo-Germans' favor: Lockhart memorandum, Prague, 14 Apr., GB FO 371 C5637/388/12.

38. Decision to meet Poincaré: Derby to Lloyd George, London, 18 Feb., LGP F 14/5/38; meeting (Lloyd George, Chamberlain, Curzon, Hankey and Grigg, while Beneš was still in London), 20 Feb., GB FO 371 C2674/458/62; and Saint-Aulaire to MAE, London, 21 Feb., FMAE PM G/I. The abortive Krassin interview with Lloyd George and Curzon (during which the Russian refused to give unconditional acceptance to the Cannes Resolutions, which, Lloyd George admitted, made Poincaré's "exit easier"): Krassin to Chicherin, London, 13 Feb., *DVP SSSR*, 5: 102–3.

39. Derby to Lloyd George, London, 20 Feb., LGP F 14/5/40; Saint-Aulaire to MAE, London, 27 Feb., FMAE Z GB 48; Curzon's protest [Feb. 1922], never sent, CzP; see Alan J. Sharp, "The Foreign Office in Eclipse," *History* 61, no. 202 (June 1976): 206–8, for details.

40. *Le Temps*, 21 Feb., and *Echo de Paris*, 23 Feb.

41. Della Torretta to De Martino, Rome, 24 Feb., IMAE Amb. Lond. 538.3; De Martino to Crowe, 24 Feb., GB FO 371 C2769/458/62.

tionship to each other.[42] It was a tense, dramatic, but inconclusive encounter, which nonetheless shaped the Genoa Conference: when it would be held, what would be discussed, and the anticipated nature of Allied cooperation.

Lloyd George was tired. Although he was still in vital health at sixty, he had lost some of his ebullience since Cannes. The fall of the French and Italian governments had cast a shadow on his own political future. His Tory-Liberal coalition was challenged by its inner contradictions. More funds were urgently required for unemployment compensation, but industry demanded a reduction in taxes. The Geddes committee of antiwaste businessmen recommended severe reductions in armaments, threatening Britain's overseas and European commitments; a cabinet committee chaired by Churchill insisted on smaller reductions, particularly in naval armaments. The government was thus vulnerable to criticism both from the economizers and the spenders.[43]

Lloyd George took the position that the "appeasement of international rivalries" was the key to Britain's domestic ills, and he intended to achieve the first steps at the Genoa Conference.[44] It was nevertheless clear that the prime minister had been considerably weakened since Cannes. Poincaré knew this. But he knew also that Lloyd George had not quit. Indeed, in addition to maintaining contacts with the Russians, there had been extensive Anglo-German conversations.

These talks took place initially between Ambassador Friedrich Sthamer, Albert Dufour-Feronce, the counselor of the German embassy, and various members of Lloyd George's entourage: Kerr, Grigg, and the Russian expert Edward F. Wise. This group fed the Germans a steady stream of anti-French material together with occasional warnings of the premier's contemplated retirement. In addition to this special channel, Sthamer maintained close ties with the British Foreign Office, and Dufour with the governor of the Bank of England, Montagu Norman, and the editor of the *Observer*, J. L. Garvin.[45] Back in Berlin, Rathenau poured out his fears of a postponement of the Genoa Conference, France's obstructionism, and the Reich's probable exclusion from any prelimi-

42. "Lloyd George et Poincaré," *Le Matin* (Brussels), 20 Feb., and "L'indispensable accord," *L'Europe Nouvelle*, 25 Feb.

43. Cabinet meeting, 21 Feb., GB CAB 23/29; also Martin Gilbert, *Winston S. Churchill* (Boston: Houghton Mifflin, 1975), 4:768–70; and Stamm, *Lloyd George*, pp. 247–49.

44. This was in the text of George V's speech on 7 Feb. at the opening of parliament, *H. C. Deb.*, 150: cols. 6–7. See also Frances Lloyd George, *Lloyd George: A Diary* (New York: Harper and Row, 1971), pp. 240–41; George Allardice Riddell, *Lord Riddell's Intimate Diary of the Paris Peace Conference and After, 1918–1925* (London: Gollancz, 1933), pp. 350–56; Dufour Aufzeichnung, London, 16 Feb., and Schubert to Rathenau, Berlin, 25 Feb., Germ. AA T-120 4597H/2370/E188366–68 and E188305–6.

45. Sthamer to AA, London, 19, 27 Jan., 23 Feb., Germ. AA T-120 3398/1733/D737918, D737940, D738083, and 26 Jan., Germ. AA T-120 L999/5412/L286790–93; and Dufour, three Aufzeichnungen, London, 16 Feb., Germ. AA T-120 4597H/2370/H188360–68.

nary talks to the sympathetic D'Abernon, who communicated them promptly to London. Rathenau pleaded for direct Anglo-German negotiations. He also encouraged the German embassy to bypass the Foreign Office and contact his friend at the Treasury, reparations expert Sir Basil Blackett.[46]

The Germans were alarmed at how much Lloyd George would "give way" to Poincaré to obtain French participation in the Genoa Conference. Under the terms of the provisional moratorium agreed to at Cannes, Germany had to produce 31 million gold marks every ten days. If the Genoa Conference were delayed or if reparations were entirely excluded, Berlin feared an economic catastrophe. The Germans dispatched emissaries to London: Hamburg banker Carl Melchior spoke with Sir Robert Horne, chancellor of the exchequer, and also with Lloyd-Greame, who could give no encouragement regarding Germany's prospects at the Genoa Conference. Franz Kempner and Carl Bergmann, who were sent to represent Germany in the talks to found an international corporation, conducted their own soundings: Kempner spoke with Hankey, Norman, and Reginald McKenna, president of the British Bankers' Association and an influential independent Liberal. Bergmann conferred with Blackett and Grigg.[47]

The British apparently did little to calm the Germans' fears. McKenna suggested that if the mark were ruined, British and American public opinion would rally to Germany's side; and Grigg insisted that the City would refuse a loan to Germany until a "final solution" was made on reparations. The independent Bergmann opposed both the suicidal policy that was being advocated for Germany and one that was totally passive. He even suggested that Germany might yet avert bankruptcy by raising a loan internally, something neither London nor Berlin had in mind.[48] The net result of these talks, on the eve of the Boulogne meeting, was to keep the Germans at a feverish pitch with fear and expectation of some sudden change in their fortune. It was an empty ploy. Lloyd George hoped to find the key to European reconstruction and German reparations in Washington. However, despite all that had recently occurred, their British informants admitted to the Germans that Washington still sympathized with France and was reluctant to assume additional European burdens at the moment.[49]

46. Rathenau to Sthamer, Berlin, 13 Feb., Germ. AA T-120 L999/5412/L286877–78; D'Abernon to Hankey, Berlin, 7 Feb., LGP F 54/2/17; and D'Abernon to Curzon, 16 Feb., GB FO 371 C2328/725/18.

47. Schubert Aufzeichnung, Berlin, 25 Feb., Germ. AA T-120 4597H/2370/E188304; Melchior Notiz, Hamburg, 25 Feb., Germ. AA T-120 3398/1734/D738120; Rathenau to Sthamer (for Bergmann), Berlin, 25 Feb., Germ. AA T-120 4597H/2370/E188151; Schubert Aufzeichnung, 27 Feb., Germ. AA T-120 4597H/2370/E188286–87.

48. Schubert Aufzeichnung, Berlin, 2 Mar., Germ. AA T-120 4597H/2370/E188281–82.

49. Sthamer to AA, London. 2 Mar., Germ. AA T-120 4597H/2370/E188253–63.

Britain could not face the Russians and Germans at Genoa without America or France. By plying the route to Boulogne, Lloyd George faced reality, but he was scarcely a supplicant. Having sharpened his teeth on Beneš, he was prepared to put considerable pressure on Poincaré to honor France's commitment at Cannes. Otherwise he, with the Germans, Russians, Italians, and assorted defectors, would make peace without France. Nonetheless, arriving alone at Boulogne, without the thundering Curzon or a representative of Italy or Belgium to echo his sentiments, Lloyd George was also the vulnerable politician, asking an old partner for help with a tricky and difficult operation on which his political future depended. His recent cavalier dismissal of Poincaré's pleas for a pact did not facilitate his mission.

The meeting began inauspiciously. The aged car sent to meet Lloyd George at Calais barely made the trip to Boulogne, and Poincaré had made no luncheon arrangements for his guest, who dined spartanly at the railroad station.[50] The meeting opened at 2:45 P.M. Since neither party could speak the other's language, the Quai d'Orsay's translator, Maurice Camerlynck, gave a rapid and precise rendering of the heated conversation.[51] Both parties were correct but scarcely polite during the four-hour exchange, after which Poincaré departed abruptly by train before Lloyd George had left. In addition to the contradictory recollections of participants and their confidants, there are three resumés of the Boulogne meeting, which, even after mutual corrections, do not entirely agree.[52]

Host Poincaré opened the talks. Though the records differ considerably, he apparently announced that there were two "unrelated" subjects they would discuss: Genoa and the Anglo-French alliance. Lloyd George preferred to start with Genoa, and they never got to the second item. Both parties shot preliminary salvos. Poincaré posed what he considered to be the most important points that needed their agreement before the Genoa Conference:

1. There would be no encroachment on the League of Nations Covenant or on its prerogatives.
2. There would be no discussion of the clauses of the Paris peace treaties.

50. A. J. Sylvester, *The Real Lloyd George* (London: Cassell, 1948), pp. 77–78; Viscount Edgar D'Abernon, *Versailles to Rapallo, 1920–1922: The Diary of an Ambassador* (Garden City, N.Y.: Doubleday, Doran and Co., 1929), p. 274; and Dufour Aufzeichnung (conversation with Garvin, Kerr, Gregory and Poliakoff), London, 2 Mar., Germ. AA T-120 4597H/2370/ E188257–63. The British reported that not only was there no official reception for Lloyd George but also they had to prevail on their host to substitute the prefecture for a small, uninhabited tenement as the meeting place.

51. Emmanuel Peretti de la Rocca, "Briand et Poincaré (Souvenirs)," *La Revue de Paris* (15 Dec. 1936): 783–84.

52. The French version is in FMAE B 88. The English, "Revised after comparison with

3. There would be no discussions of reparations.

These were undoubtedly his strongest demands.[53] Significantly, he omitted any caution against the de jure recognition of Russia. Even Beneš had recognized this as a lost cause.

Lloyd George launched the charges that there were 2 million unemployed in Britain, where public opinion had grown increasingly hostile to the Versailles treaty and was convinced that Russia must no longer be excluded from Europe. France was now conceived as the enemy, as illustrated in the recent bielection defeat of three "pro-French" candidates. He warned that the Entente was in danger; were general elections to be held soon, the new parliament might press for "separate arrangements with Germany and Russia." Deploring the greatest rift between the two powers "since Fashoda," he pleaded for France's cooperation before it was "too late" and the pact was doomed.[54] Unintimidated, Poincaré challenged whether Britain meant to enforce the Versailles treaty it had helped to create. Lloyd George backed off, pleading for "understanding," warning that their failure would be "disastrous" for Europe and underlining the role he was playing at Boulogne as a missionary for peace.[55]

Having finished with their opening sparring, they got down to business. Poincaré suggested starting with his first point, the League of Nations; but Lloyd George preferred to handle reparations, one of their more important disagreements. The French and British texts show that they both concurred that since neutrals would be present at the Genoa Conference, it would be inappropriate to discuss either the principle or the amount of German reparations. They also agreed that in a conference devoted to the restoration of the European economy and particularly to the problems of foreign exchange and trade, the reality of reparations could scarcely be eliminated. Here their agreement ceased.

Lloyd George mentioned a communication from Italy that allegedly insisted on the "impossibility" of removing reparations entirely from the Genoa Conference.[56] Poincaré retorted: if the French Chamber did not receive absolute

---

French notes," GB CAB 29/95, I.C.P. 236, is reproduced in *DBFP*, 19:170–92. Hankey's preliminary text is in FMAE B 88. The reconstruction below is based on a composite of the three.

53. In the French text, Poincaré acknowledged Britain's assurances and felt they were already "in agreement" on all three points.

54. This is in the English text. In the French, Lloyd George's threats and complaints are much stronger and his lament is omitted.

55. In the French text, Poincaré is more polite. In the English, he remarks that "he could not doubt [this negative characterization of British public opinion] . . . since Lloyd George had said it," which does not appear in the French.

56. There is no record of this: *DBFP*, 19:174. Lloyd George told the cabinet on 24 Feb. that he had received it (GB CAB 23/29); a memorandum by Grigg on 24 Feb. alludes to it (LGP F 86/1/19); but there is no mention in De Martino to MAE, London, 22 Feb., IMAE Amb. Lond. 538.3, which discussed a conversation with Lloyd George on 21 Feb.

guarantees that there would be no public discussion of this question, France would not go to Genoa. Lloyd George yielded, acknowledging that only the Reparations Commission was competent to deal with the question. Both sides claimed victory. Poincaré insisted that France had secured all the guarantees it required; but Grigg encouraged the Germans to hope that the question could still be handled in the larger context of "European reconstruction." In fact, London simply, though wrongly, calculated that the Reparations Commission would settle the problem before Genoa.[57]

The two premiers then clashed over the date for Genoa: Lloyd George wanted a three-week postponement, Poincaré wanted three months. Poincaré pleaded that France needed more time for its preparations, adding that Italy, the Little Entente, and the neutrals were of a similar mind. Lloyd George expostulated that Britain's 2 million unemployed could not wait. What would have happened if London had so delayed in 1914?[58] He threatened to go to Genoa alone and make separate arrangements. During an ugly interlude, they squabbled about what each had contributed to the common cause in World War I and what they still owed the other. Poincaré offered one month. Unmollified, Lloyd George threatened to join Germany and Russia. Poincaré recalled his rebuff to Moscow's overtures and the fact that he had the entire Chamber behind *his* policy.[59]

They decided on the month, with Genoa to open in early April. Lloyd George urged that Poincaré attend personally. They could "settle principles" during the first fortnight and leave minor questions to the experts. He intended to return to London immediately after Easter to present the budget, which had to be passed before 4 May. Poincaré had his own constitutional problem: Millerand, scheduled to leave for Algeria, would be on the sea between 5 and 6 April. He therefore proposed that the Genoa Conference open on 10 April, when he could be in telegraph contact with the French president. Despite Lloyd George's plea, he made no personal commitment to appear at Genoa. He had

57. Hankey's original draft was extensively amended to include the insertion of a common verbal text: "The question of reparations must not be settled by the Genoa Conference, but through the machinery set up by the Treaty of Versailles." Lloyd George's "Je suis d'accord" in the French version is absent from the English. Though Poincaré was convinced that the question had been thoroughly eliminated ("L'entrevue de Boulogne," 25 Feb., FMAE B 88), Grigg told the German ambassador it had not (Sthamer to AA, London, 27 Feb., Germ. AA T-120 L989/5411/L285280).

58. In the French, not the English version. In the English text, Lloyd George's arguments are fuller and angrier than in the French.

59. Hankey's original omitted Poincaré's expressions of loyalty and included an innuendo, not in the French, that his "political difficulties . . . necessitated delay." In both versions Poincaré denied political considerations and stressed his support in parliament.

the plausible excuse that the simultaneous absence of the president and the premier while the Chamber was sitting would paralyze the government. Beneath this was the memory of Briand's demise at Cannes.[60]

Poincaré put up a lame fight for the League of Nations and accepted the reasons for its exclusion from a major role at Genoa. He nonetheless urged that its representatives sitting "at the edge of the Conference" be allowed to provide technical assistance and needed documentation. More important, he insisted that Genoa not become a permanent institution or spawn institutions that might compete with Geneva. In the past, the League had dealt with problems pertaining to both nonmembers Russia and Germany. In fact, he admitted "there would be no reason" to exclude both nations as soon as Moscow obtained recognition and the Reich manifested its intention to apply the Treaty of Versailles.[61]

Lloyd George ignored this and deprecated the League's usefulness in conducting any of the follow-up work after Genoa. Poincaré agreed that the financial and economic reconstruction of Russia might be entrusted to an ad hoc committee of "concerned nations." They both concurred that Genoa itself would not survive in any form whatsoever. Poincaré failed to dispute Lloyd George's insinuations that League members such as Spain and Brazil could make but a minimal contribution to European recovery as compared with nonmember (and the League's chief opponent) America. Lloyd George nevertheless admitted that he had no new world organization in mind.

They came to a prompt agreement on the inviolability of the Versailles, Saint-Germain, and Trianon treaties; the Treaty of Sèvres, still not ratified, would of course be excluded. The Genoa Conference would not touch upon other agreements, such as those signed recently between Russia and its immediate neighbors, that contained no "advantages" to the Western powers.[62]

Poincaré brought up a new subject: the announced Russian intention to demand reparations from the Allies for damages caused by their intervention during the civil war. He considered this a maneuver to outflank the West's claims to full repayment of the Russian debt. Lloyd George's solution was to reduce Russia's war debt and the interest charges against the claims for the damages caused by Kolchak, Denikin, and company; he did not, however, believe that the Soviet government would ever pay even a reduced sum. Poincaré spoke for the 1.2 million small French bondholders who had invested their

60. "He could not to undertake to be there personally, but France would be there" is the original English version amended by the French.

61. This French version superseded Hankey's original.

62. Poincaré's warning against discussing these treaties is in the English and not the French version.

savings to help their prewar ally. Lloyd George did not dispute their rights.[63] They did agree that the complex question of interallied war debts was not at all covered by the Cannes Resolutions.[64]

The discussion was less harmonious when they turned to the question of recognizing the Soviet regime. Lloyd George introduced a new version of Beneš's suggestion, proposing that recognition depend on the results achieved by the Genoa Conference and, more specifically, on how the Russians behaved at the meeting.[65] Poincaré, wondering whether "good talkers" would become wise and honorable commercial partners, proposed a delay of six months before the Allies granted de jure recognition. Lloyd George urged a more prompt decision because British financiers would never lend money without the security provided by agents, consuls, and diplomatic representation. He had received a telegram from London that the committee to plan the international corporation had strongly urged that all the participating governments guarantee the capital their private lenders would commit.[66] Britain and Italy had already agreed. Would France do so?

Poincaré, impeded by French law from giving such assurances, evaded the snare. He would reserve his freedom of action in both instances: de jure recognition and a government guarantee of private capital. Here there remained a considerable gap between British expectations and French hesitations. Paris felt it had retained a free hand on the recognition question: *on jugera sur les faits*.[67]

Then to the attack, Poincaré added disarmament to reparations as another forbidden subject. This problem belonged to the League. France's "means of defense for its soil" could not be discussed before the world, or else he would refuse to attend. Lloyd George again improvised. Somewhat untruthfully, he denied any "desire whatsoever to raise the [disarmament] question" but also insisted that the issue could not be entirely excluded. At Washington Briand himself had declared that the Russian military menace prevented France from discussing disarmament in Europe; with the appearance of the Bolsheviks at Genoa, the issue was likely to be revived. As with the reparations question, each side believed that it had won its point.[68]

Lloyd George satisfied Poincaré with his explanation of the proposed non-aggression pact, mentioned in Article 6 of the Cannes Resolutions. He said that

63. In the French his support is stronger than in the original or final English version.

64. Poincaré's arguments for this point are presented more strongly in the French than in the English versions.

65. Omitted from the French version.

66. Omitted from the French version.

67. The two versions are entirely different. Lloyd George's acquiescence is not recorded in the English version; Poincaré's agreement is not in the French.

68. There are a large number of discrepancies in the texts, but the conclusions are similar.

its intent was to bind Germany and Russia with an obligation similar to Article X of the League Covenant. It contained no limitation of France's right to take sanctions under the Treaty of Versailles.

Content with their political agreement, Poincaré conceded that the experts could begin to tackle the technical and economic questions. Lloyd George reluctantly agreed to delay the opening until 10 April and to ask the Italian government to make this change on behalf of France and Britain. In exchange, he asked Poincaré to draft a very positive press communiqué about the results of the Boulogne meeting to inform their attentive audience that Franco-British *amitié* had been restored.[69]

During the final moments, one of them raised the second item, the pact. Lloyd George was willing to discuss it, but Poincaré made an uncharacteristically casual response, and the question was left hanging.[70] Boulogne thus ended on an ambiguous note. The French were delighted with the results, and Peretti himself predicted that there would be a formal Anglo-French alliance before 10 April. The reality was less glowing. There were still many wrinkles to be worked out, as Poincaré's emissary, Jacques Bardoux, soon discovered in London.[71]

Both sides claimed a triumph at Boulogne. Poincaré stood firm on many issues critical to France.[72] Yet Lloyd George, exuding new confidence, boasted: "We got all we wanted. . . . The little man put up no fight and gave way at every point."[73] Genoa was saved; the Entente had survived another tense episode; and now London and Paris had to face the repercussions of their icy tête-à-tête.

69. Text in *DBFP*, 19:192.

70. The two versions differ markedly. In the English, Poincaré raised the question of the pact; Lloyd George seemed amenable but cautioned that "it would be easier for him to carry the Pact to Parliament when all the other questions had been regulated." In the French, Lloyd George brought up the pact, and Poincaré apologized that his departure, delayed by a half-hour, made it impossible to regulate this question as they had settled the political questions pertaining to Genoa. To Lloyd George's remark that now it would be "easy" to settle the pact and his invitation to London, Poincaré responded that though he would like to go, such a visit was no longer necessary "puisque tous nous deux sommes parfaitement d'accord." Whether one believes Lloyd George remained so obdurate or Poincaré so casual, it seems obvious that the two statesmen had quite different conceptions of what they had just accomplished.

71. De Gaiffier to MAE, Paris, 27 Feb., BMAE Fr.; Hardinge to FO, Paris, 26 Feb., GB FO 371 C2832/458/62; and "L'heureuse entrevue," *Le Temps*, 27 Feb., all give Poincaré's version. On the Bardoux mission to London, Paris was alerted that any Liberal or Conservative successor to Lloyd George would be an equally difficult negotiating partner, if not more so; see Saint-Aulaire to Poincaré, London, 2, 7 Mar., FMAE Z GB 48.

72. Barrère to Poincaré, Rome, 3 Mar., FMAE B 88.

73. Riddell, *Intimate Diary*, pp. 359–60, and Charles Prestwick Scott, *The Political Diaries of C. P. Scott, 1911–1928*, ed. Trevor Wilson (London: Collins, 1970), pp. 421–44.

In the Wake of Boulogne

ROME

As anticipated, Italy resented its exclusion from the Boulogne meeting.[74] The Italians felt that this cavalier treatment ill-suited their dignity as host to the Genoa Conference. Moreover, it emphasized Rome's isolation during the three-week cabinet crisis, and it threatened the reinstitution of an Anglo-French entente, which frequently ignored Italy's interests on both European and Mediterranean questions. Beneš eliminated his side trip to Rome; his visits to London and Paris, signaling a potential elevation of the Little Entente, also made Rome uncomfortable.

Italy's troubles were underscored when, on the night of 2 March, there was a Fascist coup in the free city of Fiume. This once more placed in the forefront the problem of the unratified Treaty of Rapallo and Italy's relations with Yugoslavia.[75] Schanzer, returning from his successful mission at the Washington Conference, inherited a difficult task: Italy had taken on a large burden, with considerable danger and no foreseeable benefits.

Things began more smoothly than expected with the French. Despite the ill feeling over Washington, Schanzer's reception in Paris was friendly. Poincaré even agreed to send him a copy of the record of the conversation at Boulogne.[76] While awaiting the official text, the Rome government weighed the meaning of the Boulogne decisions. The month postponement of the Genoa Conference evoked a fiery response from Chicherin, who threatened to withdraw the Soviets' acceptance. London and Paris decided to ignore the "impertinent" telegram, forcing Schanzer to bear the brunt of Moscow's anger.[77] Italy's formal announcement of the postponement quite likely triggered the negative American response.[78] The new date, 10 April (which was the begin-

74. British cabinet meeting, 24 Feb., GB CAB 23/29; De Gaiffier to MAE, Paris, 28 Feb., BMAE Fr.; Graham to Curzon, Rome, 27 Feb., 3 Mar., GB FO 371 C2767/366/22 and C3320/458/62.

75. US MID Report, 16 Mar., no. 1243, 2657E (Italy). The November 1920 treaty between Italy and Yugoslavia had established a free city in Fiume. Italian nationalists subsequently disputed this "concession" and wanted to annex the city. Rome, which had hesitated to implement the treaty and failed to submit it to the Chamber for ratification, was nevertheless embarrassed by the Fascists' coup de main.

76. Bonin to MAE, Paris, 1 Mar., IMAE 52/4 (France); Hardinge to Curzon, Paris, 1 Mar., GB FO 371 C3058/366/22; Poincaré to Barrère, Paris, 1 Mar., FMAE B 88.

77. Chicherin telegram to Italian, French, and British governments, Moscow, 26 Feb., IMAE 52/4 (Russia). Also Crowe memorandum, London, 7 Mar., GB FO 371 N2256/646/38; Barrère to Poincaré, Rome, 28 Feb., and Poincaré to Barrère, Paris, 4 Mar., FMAE B 88.

78. Schanzer sent a telegram to Washington on 5 Mar.; Hughes gave the negative reply to

ning of Holy Week), was embarrassing for the new Facta government, which was trying to establish better relations with the Vatican and the Popolari. Because the British insisted "it was time to get down to work," there was little chance for any further delay.[79]

Rome was uncomfortable with the list of "forbidden subjects" that Poincaré and Lloyd George had agreed on at Boulogne. The elimination of reparations, disarmament, and the main peace treaties, as well as the exclusion of the whole area of interallied debts because of America's absence, meant that Italy was about to host a "sterile" gathering before the entire world. Furthermore, it would be conducted under the eyes of the intensely divided Italian public.[80] Like France, Italy felt that the agenda was "repetitive and ambiguous." Italian industrialists shared their neighbors' hesitations about dealing with Soviet Russia and also about the perils of multinational cooperation led by London.[81] Rome nonetheless was committed to lead the conference. Its own negotiations with Moscow for a permanent commercial treaty were not discontinued, but obviously all would depend on the outcome of Genoa.

After Boulogne, relations between London and Rome grew less amicable, especially because of Schanzer's futile pleas for a further postponement of the Genoa Conference. Whitehall, after badgering Poincaré to hurry, only grudgingly agreed to Schanzer's request to delay the meeting of Allied experts until 20 March.[82] Lloyd George, ailing and politically harried, was silent; and the Foreign Office, particularly the acerbic Curzon, had little patience with Italy's efforts to coordinate strategy.[83] The French were less indifferent. Poincaré, who was well aware of developments in London, alternately wooed Sforza, the new, somewhat sympathetic Italian ambassador, with the moderateness of his

Italian ambassador Ricci on 7 Mar.; and it was published a day later. Cf. Lang to AA, Washington, 28 Feb., 7 Mar., Germ. AA T-120 L998/5412/L286560, L286690.

79. Graham to Curzon, Rome, 4 Mar., *DBFP*, 19:196–98.

80. Ibid.; and Barrère to Poincaré, Rome, 5 Mar., FMAE B 88.

81. Romano Avezzana (who was secretary general of the Genoa Conference) to De Martino, Rome, 20, 23 Feb., and De Martino to Romano Avezzana, London, 9 Mar., IMAE 52/2; also see *Verbale* of the five meetings of Romano Avezzana's commission that included major Italian industrialists, IMAE 52/37.

82. Wigram memorandum, London, 8 Mar., GB FO 371 C3450/458/62. Graham to FO, Rome, 9 Mar., GB FO 371 C3727/458/62, described Schanzer as "nervous and apprehensive"; Schanzer to De Martino, 10 Mar., IMAE Amb. Lond. 538.3, agreed finally to the 10 April opening.

83. Waterlow memorandum, 28 Feb., GB FO 371 C2967/366/22; Grigg memorandum, 10 Mar., GB FO 371 C3727/458/62; Grigg to Vansittart, 11 Mar., GB FO 371 C3981/458/62; Curzon memorandum, London, 3 Mar., GB FO 371 C3146/366/22 ("Is there any Italian capable of standing up?"); Grigg to Lloyd George, 14 Mar., LGP F 86/1/26; and Hankey to Lloyd George, 15 Mar., LGP F 26/1/14 ("I have turned on the FO to drive the Italians").

aims and ordered his ambassador in Rome, Camille Barrère, to keep pressure on Schanzer to accept the exclusion of "forbidden subjects."[84] Schanzer, still hoping for a special relationship with Britain, evaded any commitment.[85]

After Boulogne, the Italian Right dominated Italian politics. There were now 250,000 Fascists, with a vocal leadership and well-financed press.[86] In early March Mussolini departed for Berlin to orient himself on foreign policy questions. Italian nationalists criticized the government for its subservience to Great Britain.[87] Yet despite Sforza's accusations of Schanzer's "Nittianism," this new government and its spiritual father had deserted the Left for the Right of Center. Nitti himself, once an ardent advocate of European reconstruction and treaty revision, was now hesitant about Genoa and advocated that Italy strike a "realistic balance" between London and Paris.[88]

Schanzer attempted a delicate balancing act. Boulogne had resurrected the specter of an Anglo-French directorship that could always thwart Italy's aspiration to function as a great power. America's self-exclusion and the removal of reparations meant that economic subjects critical to Rome had virtually been eliminated. Soviet Russia, now the single main focus of the Genoa Conference, was scarcely expected to be a docile partner. Finally, East European questions, over which Italy exerted no independent control, might well surface at Genoa. An experienced politician and diplomat, Schanzer made careful preparations for Genoa, attempting to formulate as realistic a policy as possible. After Boulogne, Rome's anglophilia and francophobia were both considerably reduced.

BERLIN

Rathenau was even more embittered over the Boulogne meeting. Indeed, he requested the new German ambassador in Rome, Baron von Neurath, to sound out Schanzer discreetly about the prospect of an Italo-German collaboration.

---

84. Unsigned note, Paris, 9 Mar., FMAE B 89; Schanzer to De Martino and Sforza (about discussions with Barrère), Rome, 9 Mar., IMAE Amb. Lond. 538.3.

85. Aide-mémoire of Schanzer-Barrère talks of 11 Mar., IMAE Amb. Lond. 538.3, which were reported immediately to London, 11 Mar., GB FO 371 C3935/458/62.

86. France, État Major de l'Armée, 16 Mar. (Italie: fascisme), FMAE B 89.

87. *Il Mondo* and *Corriere della Sera*, 4 Mar.; and France, Sûreté Générale, Menton, 8 Mar., FMAE B 89.

88. Charles-Roux to MAE, Rome, 13 Mar., FMAE B 89; German Consul General Milan to AA, 18 Mar., Germ. AA T-120 L1468/5118/L415789–90; Prittwitz to AA, Rome, 27 Mar., Germ. AA T-120 L989/5411/L285365–66; and cf. Veneruso, *La vigilia*, pp. 409–10.

On the eve of the Genoa Conference, 3 Apr., the merchant ship *Carniola* made its much-delayed departure from Trieste to Odessa, a trip Rome viewed hopefully as the beginning of its entry into the market of southern Russia. Background in Giorgio Petracchi, "Ideology and Realpolitik: Italo-Soviet Relations, 1917–1933," *Journal of Italian History* 2, no. 3 (1979): 488–94.

He wrote, "It would be of vital interest to us to be able to convince the Italians to use their chairmanship and direction of the Genoa Conference not to limit discussion of questions that are crucial for us."[89] Encouraged by the germanophile Italian ambassador, Alfredo Frassati,[90] Rathenau insisted that Genoa would be "strangled" if it eliminated the crucial questions of interallied debts and reparations. However, Neurath found Schanzer "extremely reserved." Rathenau, whose initiative in Rome coincided with Poincaré's, thus learned that Germany could expect "little support" from Italy.[91]

Turning to London, he found little consolation. Lloyd George evaded his pleas for a personal interview. On 1 March the wily premier did grant an interview to Krupp official Otto Wiedfeldt, the newly designated German ambassador to Washington, and thereby relayed to the Germans his empty reassurance that reparations had actually *not* been banned from the Genoa Conference. This was accompanied by a threat: if Germany hesitated over Genoa, the Allies would proceed to recognize Russia, and the Reich would be excluded from these negotiations.[92] Sthamer made little headway in obtaining information from the Foreign Office. D'Abernon lent his assistance, with a request for a "clarification" of the Boulogne accord plus his own urgings for Anglo-German talks.[93] The growing split between the Foreign Office, the Treasury, and Downing Street seems not to have helped the Germans' case. On the instigation of Lloyd George and against Curzon's warnings, Berlin sent two representatives to London for "consultations"; but when State Secretary Ernst von Simson and Bergmann arrived, there was no one to speak with. All the important people had departed for Paris for talks among the Allied finance ministers on reparations and also to allay French suspicions about the Genoa Conference. Lloyd George was in the country. In order "not to waste their time completely," the Germans called on the governor of the Bank of England, who

89. Rathenau to Neurath, Berlin, 2 Mar., Germ. AA T-120 L999/5412/L286915–16.

90. Frassati to Schanzer, Berlin, 4 Mar., IMAE 52/20; also Frassati to Giolitti, 25 Jan., 24 Feb., in Giovanni Giolitti, *Quaranti' anni di politica italiana* (Milan: Feltrinelli, 1962), 3:357–60.

91. Neurath to Rathenau, Rome, 7 Mar., Rathenau to Sthamer, Berlin, 11 Mar., and to German Ministers in Paris, Brussels, and The Hague, 15 Mar., Germ. AA T-120 L999/5412/L286978–80. However, on 14 Mar. Neurath reported Romano Avezanna's statement that "if Lloyd George brought up the reparations question, Italy would loyally support him," Germ. AA T-120 L989/5411/L285302.

92. Wiedfeldt report, 4 Mar., Germ. AA T-120 3398/1734/D738145–46. These are some symptoms of the strains and contradictions in British policy: Crowe admitted to Saint-Aulaire his ignorance of the purpose of Wiedfeldt's visit, memorandum, 3 Mar., GB FO 371 C3351/458/62; nevertheless, on 7 Mar. Curzon advised D'Abernon to discourage a "highly inconvenient" visit by Rathenau, GB FO 371 C3173/458/62.

93. Sthamer to AA, London, 1 Mar., Germ. AA T-120 L999/5412/L286921–25; D'Abernon to FO, Berlin, 25 Feb., 3 Mar., GB FO 371 C2824, C3173/458/62.

predicted there would be no American or British loans to Germany until the London Schedule was revised.[94]

The Germans also learned that they would not be included in any of the Allied discussions of reparations.[95] Between 8 and 11 March, the Allies came to substantial agreement in Paris on subjects such as occupation costs, the distribution of cash receipts and deliveries-in-kind, the Belgian priority, and the Wiesbaden accord. Also, their final conclusions stressed the "exclusive" prerogatives of the Reparations Commission and, on French insistence, the necessity of establishing "concrete solutions" both for effective control over Germany's chaotic finances and to make Germany pay. Berlin now braced for a message from the Reparations Commission.[96] At the same time, Rathenau complained of receiving more than one hundred notes from the Allied Military Control Commission citing minor violations of the treaty.[97] Finally, Curzon cut off Germany's informal channels of communication with Grigg and Treasury officials. Germany was moving from the status of favored collaborator to an object of Allied control.[98]

Britain's ability to help Germany had been severely curtailed by America's actions: its refusal to attend the Genoa Conference, its request for a share in the occupation costs, and, above all its announced desire to negotiate a prompt debt-funding arrangement with London. Blackett and Giannini had worked out reparations plans all based on calculations involving a degree of cancellation of interallied debts. But Germany itself had thwarted the Anglo-Italian plan when Rathenau declined to negotiate a "final settlement" as the price of an international loan. Rathenau preferred an interim solution that would facilitate his

94. Sthamer to AA, London, 7 Mar., Simson to Rathenau, London, 9 Mar., Germ. AA T-120 L998/5411/L285938, 4597H/2370/E188236–41; Waterlow memorandum, London, 7 Mar., GB FO 371 C3513/458/62.

There was the usual Anglo-German squabble over a short-term versus a long-term reparations settlement and whether the Germans had paid anything at all: Simson to Rathenau, London, 9 Mar., Germ. AA T-120 4597H/2370/E188236–41. In another unproductive meeting on 9 Mar. with Garvin, the main topic of discussion was Lloyd George's political weakness, Germ. AA T-120 4597H/2370/E188221–22.

95. Schubert Aufzeichnung, Berlin, 13 Mar. 1922, Germ. AA T-120 3398/1734/D738148–51. Cf. memorandum by Sir Sidney Chapman, Permanent Secretary of the Board of Trade, London, 10 Mar., GB FO 371 C3683/458/62.

96. Étienne Weill-Raynal, *Les réparations allemandes et la France* (Paris: Nouvelles Éditions Latines, 1947), 2:125–34; Horne to Lloyd George, 14 Mar., LGP F 27/6/55; Sthamer [Bergmann] to Rathenau, London, 16 Mar., and Rathenau to Bergmann, Berlin, 18 Mar., Germ. AA T-120 4597H/2370/E188223–24, E188218.

97. Rathenau to Lucius [The Hague] [for Bergmann], Berlin, 18 Mar., Germ. AA T-120 4597H/2370/E188216–17. See D'Abernon's support for Germany's complaints in D'Abernon to Lloyd George, Berlin, 20 Mar., Grigg Papers, roll 10.

98. Schubert Aufzeichnung, Berlin, 21 Mar., Germ. AA T-120 4597H/2370/E188208.

nation's recovery over the next few years but not commit it too far beyond that.[99]

On 22 March the Reparations Commission meeting in Paris answered Germany's note of 28 January. While granting Germany a provisional moratorium, it posed rigorous conditions, including a sixty-billion-mark increase in taxes, a reduction in the Reich's expenditures, the establishment of an independent Reichsbank, and the setting up of a committee of guarantee in Berlin—all to be accomplished by 31 May. The Berlin government observed bitterly that the British representative, Sir John Bradbury, had pressed for higher taxes; he later explained to Treasury officials that this was the price for preventing the Reparations Commission from creating stronger surveillance mechanisms.[100] A sharp fall in the mark immediately ensued.

Blackett counseled the Germans to bluff,[101] and they followed his advice. On 24 March Rathenau reported to the cabinet. Stressing Lloyd George's current political difficulties and Genoa's importance to Britain, he recommended that it was a good time for a no. While still upholding the policy of fulfillment, which Wirth claimed had "saved the Ruhr," Rathenau proposed a defiant stance that he hoped would force the Allies into negotiations. Wirth underscored the political importance of the negative response and minimized the diplomatic risks. Ebert agreed with this strategy.[102]

Thus four days later, the chancellor and the foreign minister faced the Reichstag. Unafraid of the storm their refusal would cause in France, confident that many in Britain regarded the London Schedule as *unsinnig*, and still hopeful that Genoa offered "opportunties," both pronounced their no loudly and clearly. Rathenau used the occasion to mock the British premier for caving in to Poincaré at Boulogne.[103] In its official response, Germany rejected the new

99. Dufour Aufzeichnung, London, 15 Mar., Germ. AA T-120 4597H/2370/E188201–7; Sthamer to AA, London, 6 Apr., Germ. AA T-120 4597H/2370/E188138–45. Rathenau refused a reduction to 110 billion marks, which would likely be reduced by another 65 billion, because the remainder was "too high."

100. Text in Weill-Raynal, *Réparations*, 2:148–58. Bradbury to Blackett, 17, 23, 24 Mar., quoted in Stamm, *Lloyd George*, p. 277; Schubert to Rathenau, Berlin, 1 Apr., Germ. AA T-120 4597H/2370/E188184–91.

101. Sthamer to AA, 6 Apr., Germ. AA T-120 4597H/2370/E188138–45: "You Germans are much too honest. Even the French are much too honest. In any event you do not understand the game we must play as well as we Englishmen. We also want to be honest, but sometimes have to employ disagreeable methods in order to achieve a goal we believe to be right. The basic situation we are in is like a poker game. At the moment it is necessary for the opponent and the partner to bluff."

102. Cabinet meeting, 24 Mar., *Akten-Wirth*, 1:630, 634–35, 639.

103. St. Quentin to MAE, Berlin, 27 Mar., FMAE B 90. Walther Rathenau, *Gesammelte Reden* (Berlin: S. Fischer, 1924), p. 377: "Poincaré nahm dem Kampf gegen England auf, und Boulogne hat uns gezeigt, dass dieser Kampf nicht ganz erfolglos gewesen ist." Lloyd George's

taxes and any form of control over the Reich's finances, and proposed Allied-German talks over its mounting financial plight and its need for an urgent international loan. The response reached the Reparations Commission on 9 April, the eve of the opening of the Genoa Conference.

MOSCOW

Boulogne also cast its shadow on Moscow. From 17 January through 1 March, Lenin was absent from Moscow because of illness and fatigue, and stayed at a state farm in the nearby village of Kostino. Scarcely inactive, he remained concerned about the progress of NEP, famine relief, the writing of the new civil code, problems of internal and party politics, and especially preparations for the Genoa Conference. There is no doubt he was disappointed with the postponement. He personally ordered Chicherin to dispatch a "super-insolent" note protesting the adjournment and insisting that the meeting be held at the latest on 15 March 1922. The Soviet press echoed the fear, anger, and disappointment at Genoa's postponement and accused certain powers of "sabotage."[104]

Lenin returned to Moscow after his recuperation to face the hard-liners, the opponents of both NEP and Genoa. Trotsky announced that the Red Army was in readiness if France should unleash her satellites in Bucharest, Warsaw, Reval, and Helsinki; also, if Genoa took place at all, Russia would resist being treated like Germany at Versailles.[105] America's refusal to attend weakened the moderates, especially because of the importance of the ARA mission and the temporary strain in its relations with Moscow over transport problems.[106] Washington's absence removed not only a crucial mediating force between Russia and the Entente but also the major source of credits, the largest number of Western capitalists capable of helping Russian reconstruction, and the most important government, whose recognition could stabilize Lenin's regime.

In the wake of these two disappointments, Lenin chose to demonstrate

---

resentment in Thomas Jones, *Lloyd George* (Cambridge, Mass.: Harvard University Press, 1951), pp. 184–85.

104. V. I. Lenin, *Collected Works* (Moscow: Progress Publishers, 1965–71), 33:546, 45:485–86, 42:404. *Pravda*, 1 Mar., with Trotsky's attack on the critics of Chicherin's telegram; *Novy Put*, 2 Mar., on sabotage. Reviews of Soviet press in Wiedenfeld to AA, Moscow, 19 Feb., Germ. AA T-120 3398/1734/D738090; Martel to MAE, Riga, 2 Mar., FMAE B 88; and GB FO 371 N2924/472/38.

105. Young to State Dept., Riga, 6 Mar., USDS 550 E1/153; Wiedenfeld to AA, Moscow, 10 Mar., Germ. AA T-120 3398/1734/D738179; Quarton to State Dept. Viborg (Finland), 17 Mar., USDS 550 E1/176; and Wiedenfeld to AA, Moscow, 13 Mar., Germ. AA T-120 L998/5412/L286654–61.

106. Young to State Dept., Riga, 17 Mar., USDS 550 E1/186; also Benjamin Weissman, *Herbert Hoover and Famine Relief to Soviet Russia, 1921–1923* (Stanford: Hoover Institution Press, 1974), pp. 114–17.

toughness, a "leftist" and hard stance that he alone could express. On 6 March he delivered a long, repetitive speech to a meeting of the Communist group of the All-Russian Congress of Metalworkers; it was entitled "International and Domestic Situation of the Soviet Republic."[107] Conceding that Genoa remained "in the forefront of the problems of our international politics," he admitted that the situation had changed and that there was considerable doubt whether it would take place. But Russia was prepared.[108] Ringing defiance at both left-wing and right-wing Bolsheviks, he insisted: "We were going there as merchants, because trade with capitalist countries (as long as they have not entirely collapsed) is absolutely essential to us; we realized that we were going to Genoa to bargain for the most proper and most advantageous and politically suitable terms for this trade, and nothing more."[109]

The Western capitalist states had begun to shrink from their commitment and were playing "according to all the rules of the obsolete art of bourgeois diplomacy." But they would have to trade with Russia, or their "disintegration [would] continue. . . . After more than three years of effort, after their glorious victories, they cannot cope with the very simple task of restoring the old, let alone building anything new."[110]

Lenin boasted of the "increasing number of trade agreements" between Moscow and individual capitalist states. Needling the Boulogne partners, he said he was unafraid to appear personally at Genoa but would submit to no "test," such as the one Beneš had proposed. Alluding to the "suspicious" instability of the Allied governments, Lenin underscored Trotsky's threat that Genoa's postponement could be interpreted as a "danger signal of war": "Hardly a man of the Red Army . . . does not know . . . war . . . crop failures, appalling hunger and ruin, hellish poverty, and he knows what causes them. . . . There can scarcely be a desire so deeply ingrained in him as the desire to repel those who forced the war waged by Kolchak and Denikin and supported it."[111]

Admitting that NEP represented a retreat, Lenin announced: "Enough. We shall not retreat any further. We shall set about deploying and regrouping our forces properly."[112] By dallying, the capitalists would obtain no greater concessions. Over and over, he proclaimed: "The retreat has come to an end . . . The Genoa game, the game of leap-frog that is going on around it, will not

107. Text in Lenin, *Collected Works*, 33:212–26. Background in Brenna to MAE, Reval, 25 Mar., IMAE 52/4 (Russia); Grove to Curzon, Moscow, 21 Mar., GB FO 371 N2924/472/38; and Renseignements, Stockholm, [n.d.] Apr., FMAE Grenard Papers.

108. London had copies of its position papers: GB FO 371 N350/646/38.

109. Lenin, *Collected Works*, 33:213.

110. Ibid., p. 214.

111. Ibid., p. 218.

112. Ibid., p. 221.

compel us to waver in the least. They cannot catch us now. We shall go to the merchants and agree to do business, continuing our policy of concessions; but the limits of these concessions are already defined."[113]

The often-quoted speech of 6 March was more for political than diplomatic consumption. "Regrouping" was the term for the scaling down of the institutions and tactics of NEP and for asserting the need for purges, even of heretic Bolsheviks. "Executive control" meant that Soviet officials were to act efficiently and resolutely in conformity with the needs of the Soviet state. Lenin began to turn away from his protégé Sokol'nikov and to side publicly with Krassin on maintaining *Vneshtorg*, Russia's foreign-trade monopoly. He also tightened up control over new foreign concessions and foreign loans.[114] The crisis atmosphere in Moscow throughout the month of March culminated in the meeting of the Eleventh Party Congress, the last that Lenin attended. It was a stormy session, with Lenin presenting scathing criticisms of the Communists' inefficiency and advocating an "improved Communist culture."[115] The increased centralization of the Soviet state was manifested in the announcement that one delegation would represent all the constituent republics at the Genoa Conference.[116]

To the West, however, Lenin prepared a different signal. Despite Trotsky's threats of a spring offensive, the government was actually reducing the size and changing the nature of the Red Army;[117] during this critical changeover period, Moscow launched a peace offensive aimed at demobilizing its dip-

113. Ibid., pp. 223, 225.

114. Ibid., pp. 225–26; also 42:405–6, and 45:480–81, 495–500, 506, 513, 518, 523. On the new atmosphere of crisis and "realism" in Moscow: Martel to MAE, Riga, 12 Mar., FMAE B 108; Frassati to MAE, Berlin, 17 Mar., IMAE 52/4 (Russia); Grove to Curzon, Moscow, 21 Mar., GB FO 371 N2924/472/38; Marcetti Ferrante to MAE, Helsinki, 30 Mar., IMAE 52/4 (Russia); Paul Scheffer, "Unternehmer Staat," *Berliner Tageblatt*, 1 Apr., reprinted in *Augenzeuge im Staate Lenins: Ein Korrespondent berichtet aus Moskau, 1921–1930* (Munich: R. Piper, 1972), pp. 107–14; and Wolfdieter Bihl, "Die Sowjetunion aus der Sicht eines österreichischen Diplomaten (Apr. 1922)," *Österreichische Osthefte* 17, no. 3 (Aug. 1975): 217–24.

115. "We do not know how to keep house . . . any better than the capitalists." He then described how the import of canned foods from a French national required the intervention of Politburo members Krassin and Kamenev. Text of speech in *Pravda*, 28 Mar.

116. Grove to Curzon, Moscow, 13 Mar., GB FO 418/57, no. 64 N2393/646/38, superseding Graham to Curzon, Rome, 2 Feb., GB FO 418/57, no. 46 N1149/646/38, that the eight republics would each have their own representation.

117. Grove to Curzon, Moscow, 17 Mar., GB FO 418/57, no. 64 N2922/646/38; Wilton to Curzon, Reval, 17, 25 Mar., GB FO 418/57, no. 68 N2569/29/55 and FO 371 N2868/1171/38; Muller to Curzon, Warsaw, 15 Mar., GB FO 418/57, no. 65 N2501/29/55; Grove to Curzon, Moscow, 24 Mar., GB FO 371 N2843/29/33; and Rennie to Curzon, Helsinki, 31 Mar., GB FO 371 N3100/246/38, all discuss the alleged "war scare" from the Red Army should Genoa miscarry. But cooler heads deprecated these alarms: see, e.g., Hodgson to Curzon, Moscow, 11 Apr., GB FO 418/57, no. 85 N3623/246/38.

In truth, the Soviet government was in the process of reducing the Red Army in 1922, from

lomatic opponents. Lenin instructed the Genoa delegation to eliminate references to the inevitability of world wars and the bloody overthrow of the capitalist world, "frightful words that play right into the hands of the adversary." He proposed an appeal for a united front with the European Left advocating a pacifist Genoa program that included abolition of all war debts, revision of the Versailles treaty, and elimination of all military accords. Russia accordingly drew up a program recommending, among other things, a new League of Nations that would promote general world disarmament, the internationalization of all major railway routes, and an international unit of gold.[118]

If this plan—Moscow's response to Boulogne—seemed fanciful and provocative, it also reflected Lenin's strategy: to prevent the "enslavement" of Russia. The Genoa Conference held many dangers, including threats to the security of the Soviet delegates. Yet Chicherin's protest of 15 March in response to the delay was genuine; having committed itself to go to Genoa, Lenin's government wanted very much for the conference to take place.[119]

WASHINGTON

On 8 March, two days after Lenin's speech to the metalworkers, the United States government formally declined the invitation to attend the Genoa Conference; this occurred immediately after receiving the Italian announcement of the postponement and having submitted the Washington treaties to the Senate. Secretary of State Hughes not only refused but also added two strong criticisms. First, it was "not primarily an economic conference," and second, "questions appear to have been excluded from consideration without the satisfactory determination of which the chief causes of economic disturbance must continue to operate."[120]

With this slap at Britain and France for the Boulogne exclusions of repara-

---

1,600,000 in Mar., to 800,000 in Aug., and 600,000 in Dec.; see Walter C. Clemens, Jr., "Origins of the Soviet Campaign for Disarmament" (Ph.D. diss., Columbia University, 1961), pp. 74, 85–94.

118. Letter to Chicherin, 13 Mar., in Lenin, *Collected Works*, 45:506–12; I. Linder, "Lenin's Foreign Policy Activity (Oct. 1921–Mar. 1922)," *International Affairs* 12 (1969): 49; Franklyn Griffiths, *Genoa Plus 51: Changing Soviet Objectives in Europe* (Toronto: Canadian Institute of International Affairs, 1973), pp. 24–25.

119. Chicherin to British, French, and Italian governments, in Jane Degras, ed., *Soviet Documents on Foreign Policy* (London and New York: Oxford University Press, 1951), 1:293–94; Berzin to Curzon, London, 17 Mar., Maxse comment, 20 Mar., GB FO 371 N2548/646/48. Reaction in Hodgson to Curzon, Moscow, 16, 31 Mar., Grove to Curzon, Moscow, 27 Mar., GB FO 371 N3431/3431/38, N2924/472/38, N3116/646/38; Seydoux note, Paris, 17 Mar., FMAE B 108, *Le Journal* and *Le Temps*, 19 Mar.; Contarini to Schanzer, Rome, 23 Mar., IMAE 52/4 (Russia); Barrère to Poincaré, Rome, 27 Mar., FMAE B 90; and Marcetti Ferrante to MAE, Helsinki, 30 Mar., IMAE 52/4 (Russia).

120. Hughes to Ricci, 8 Mar., *FRUS, 1922*, I:392–94; Ricci to MAE, Washington, 8 Mar., IMAE 52/4 (USA); and Geddes to FO, Washington, 9 Mar., GB FO 371 C4166/468/62.

tions and disarmament—questions Washington regarded as central to European reconstruction—Hughes deplored what was left to Genoa. The Russian question raised "political" questions "in which the United States could not helpfully participate" until the fall of the Soviet regime.[121] After two months of study and worry, Washington had been convinced by Boulogne that it was better to stay out.[122]

The refusal was extremely popular. Lloyd George was not trusted in the United States. There was widespread resentment that he had sprung the Genoa Conference on America to emulate the Washington Conference. He was widely faulted by liberal journalists for "capitulating" to Poincaré at Boulogne; the anti-British Hearst press speculated both on his imminent fall and his possible successor. The same writers chided "militarist" France. Finally, there was considerable relief in having evaded the danger of sitting at the same table with the Bolsheviks.[123]

Hughes's refusal almost coincided with the first anniversary (4 March) of the Harding administration. The negative decision on the Genoa Conference gave Washington the opportunity to elaborate its own policies toward Britain, France, Germany, and Russia. Genoa had posed the unwelcome prospect of sharing political and economic leadership with the British, which the government, bankers, and businessmen all wished to avoid. Now Washington could continue its pressure on London for the "open door" in Britain's mandates and especially for equality of opportunity for American oil companies throughout the world. Having ended the Anglo-Japanese alliance, the United States would similarly oppose new forms of British "exclusivism" in Eastern Europe and Russia, again with the powerful weapon of the war debt.[124]

As to France, also a considerable debtor, the Harding administration could turn the screw against the nation that had acted so independently at the Wash-

121. " . . . the establishment of the essential bases of productivity in Russia."

122. Harding to Harvey, Washington, 22 Mar., Harding Papers, roll 228.

123. *New Republic*, 8, 15, 22 Feb., 22 Mar.; *Washington Post* editorial, 10 Mar.; Robert Dell, "The Genoa Fiasco," *The Nation*, 19 Apr. On Britain: Kerr to Grigg, New York, 22 Apr., Grigg Papers, roll 2; on France: "M. Poincaré, Genoa and the United States" and "M. Poincaré's Right and Left Hands," *The Nation*, 1, 22 Feb.; on Russia: Lang to AA, Washington, 27, 28 Feb., 7, 10 Mar., Germ. AA T-120 L1468/5118/L415977–80, L998/5412/L286560, L286590, L286637; and Cartier to MAE, Washington, 9 Mar., BMAE 10991: "Despite its republican form of government, the United States is one of the most conservative countries in the world and regards the political theories of Lenin and Trotsky as execrable."

124. Carl Parrini, *Heir to Empire: United States Economic Diplomacy, 1916–1923* (Pittsburgh: University of Pittsburgh Press, 1969), pp. 256–58; Denise Artaud, "Aux origines de l'atlantisme: La recherche d'un équilibre européen au lendemain de la première guerre mondiale," *Relations Internationales* 10 (1977): 115–26; Melvyn P. Leffler, *The Elusive Quest: America's Pursuit of European Stability and French Security, 1919–1933* (Chapel Hill: University of North Carolina Press, 1979), pp. 56–57; Roberta Allbert Dayer, "The British War Debts to the United States and the Anglo-Japanese Alliance, 1920–1923," *Pacific Historical Review* 45 (1976): 586–95.

ington Conference. On 15 March Logan, the American representative to the Reparations Commission, spoke with Seydoux; after voicing the repetitious criticisms of Genoa, he chided France for expecting reparations from Germany and full debt payment from Russia while procrastinating over the repayment of its loans to the United States.[125] America's anti-French stance was connected with domestic issues: debt repayment was exceedingly important for a Republican administration soon to face midterm congressional elections after submitting a program for higher taxes and reduced farm subsidies. Two other issues—disarmament and the rehabilitation of Germany—aggravated Franco-American misunderstanding. Washington wanted its former allies to disarm; but it shrank from coordinating policies with them to combat the dangers they faced from Germany and Soviet Russia.[126] It also refused to link reparations with war debts and hesitated to associate itself with British or French strategies regarding the Soviets. Indeed, because of his vigorous defense of France's interests under the peace treaties and insistence on a firm line against Moscow, Poincaré was a convenient target and excuse for America's disassociation from Genoa.

On Germany, America's policy was well defined. The United States considered the Reich responsible for rebuilding the devastated regions of Belgium and France but wanted no role in enforcing this. It opposed any form of coercion that would destroy Germany's economy and hence its own growing investments. The business community, particularly J. P. Morgan, favored a major loan to rehabilitate the Reich's finances. This was the origin of America's proposal to break the reparations deadlock by establishing an international bankers' committee. Working outside of Genoa's anticipated "political entanglements," this solution was proposed as a means of preventing Germany's economic collapse. Washington believed, unrealistically and prematurely, that it could coax France to accept a "businessmen's solution."[127]

One indication of Germany's growing importance to America was the dispatch in early April of Ambassador Alanson Houghton. The Corning Glass magnate and former member of the House Foreign Affairs Committee was

125. Seydoux, Note pour le Président du Conseil, Paris, 15 Mar., FMAE B 89. Seydoux asked Logan why the United States was demanding 1 million dollars from its allies in occupation costs. See also Hoesch to AA, Paris, 11 Mar., Germ. AA T-120 3398/1734/D738152–54, and Lang to AA, Washington, 15 Mar., Germ. AA T-120 L1468/5118/L415803–6.

126. Child to Hughes, Rome, 16 Mar., USDS 550 E1/108, and Thomas Jones to Lloyd George, London, 16 Mar., LGP F 26/1/26.

127. Herrick to State Dept., Paris, 5 Apr., USDS 550 E1/168. Also Schubert Aufzeichnung, Berlin, 5 Apr., Germ. AA T-120 4597H/2370/E188147–48; Delacroix to Theunis, Paris, 6 Apr., BMAE 10991; Werner Link, *Die amerikanische Stabilisierungspolitik in Deutschland, 1921–1932* (Düsseldorf: Droste Verlag, 1970), pp. 124–25; and John M. Carroll, "The Paris Bankers' Conference of 1922 and America's Design for a Peaceful Europe," *International Review of History and Political Science* 10 (August 1973): 39–42.

fluent in German and favorably disposed toward his new host government. On his farewell visit, he promised Harding to keep in mind "the hundred years of friendship and good will that existed between Germany and the United States [more] than the few years of bitterness that had separated them."[128] Paris was duly concerned with this new addition to the assemblage of sympathetic diplomats in Berlin.

As to Soviet Russia, the United States had two objects in mind. First, as with the precedent in Mexico, nonrecognition was to serve as a cautious waiting policy, balancing the ambitions of businessmen and bankers with the government's policy of asserting the rights of private property. Second, the State Department insisted on an independent American policy toward Moscow, charging that the projected international corporation was a European "monopolistic" effort to exploit Russia.[129]

America's interest in Russia diverged sharply from that of the Europeans. There had scarcely been any loans to Russia before 1917 and hardly any direct ownership of Russian properties. Standard Oil had acquired the properties of Nobel in the Caucasus *after* the nationalization decrees of late 1917. Therefore Washington had little sympathy for the French and Belgian prewar investors and considerable suspicion of British and German capitalists who were now investigating short-term concessions drawn from confiscated holdings. Like Beneš, the leaders of the United States were convinced that Bolshevik Russia had nothing to sell or buy. Unlike the Europeans, to whom Russia represented an alternative to America's closed markets, the United States, with its rich resources and huge domestic commerce, could be patient and persevere with the long-term goal of eliminating the Bolsheviks. In the meantime, Genoa represented a perhaps dangerous stopgap, a reward for Lenin and Trotsky's defiance. Although the United States had a free and decisive hand in Latin America, there were strong competitive governments and groups of industrialists in Europe prepared to challenge and defy Washington's aloof posture toward Russia. The Boulogne meeting and its aftermath, which kept Genoa alive even without American participation, thus led to a period of watchful uncertainty on both sides of the Atlantic.

---

128. Harding reportedly answered, "That's a good thought. Say it as often as you can"; quoted in Fred G. Stambrook, " 'Resourceful in Expedients'—Some Examples of Ambassadorial Policy Making in the Inter-War Period," *Historical Papers* (1973): 305. Also Jusserand to MAE, n.d. (received 3 Apr.), FMAE Y 412.

129. On 10 May Hughes told the national convention of the U.S. Chamber of Commerce that if countries refused to recognize valid titles acquired in accordance with existing laws, international commerce would collapse: N. S. Kane, "American Businessmen and Foreign Policy: The Recognition of Mexico, 1920–1923," *Political Science Quarterly* 90 (1975): 307. Also Dawson to State Dept., Mexico City, 12 May, USDS 550 E1/224, 229, on linkages between the Old World and the New; U.S. consuls in Sidney, [n.d.] Mar., and in Natal, 13 Mar., USDS 550 E1/66, 220, on American "isolationism"; and unsigned memorandum, "Les relations avec la Russie," Paris, 25 Mar., FMAE Grenard Papers.

Old Business: The International Corporation

One issue that figured largely among Genoa's opponents was the proposed central international corporation that had been discussed during the London and Paris meetings in December and the Cannes Conference in January. On 10 January the Supreme Council had voted to establish an international corporation as a means of providing financial resources and expertise for the reconstruction of Eastern Europe. It had voted also to establish an organizing committee to meet in London, make all the preliminary arrangements, and report to the Genoa Conference.[130]

The scheme of an international corporation had a complex history. It bore some resemblance to a plan that the Dutch banker K. E. Ter Meulen had presented to a conference in Brussels in September 1920 that was sponsored by the League of Nations. Ter Meulen had proposed to mobilize private capital for European reconstruction through special state guarantees of credits to importers under the League's supervision.[131] The corporation envisaged for the Genoa Conference originated with Stinnes's proposals in November 1921 that a group of private industrialists hoping to trade in Soviet Russia be covered by the support of their respective governments.[132]

The international corporation then developed into a British scheme. It answered the problem of high unemployment, sluggish export industries, the unwillingness of the City's bankers to take risks to increase foreign trade, and America's reluctance to join in European recovery. Moreover, it added the assumptions that reparations had produced the financial chaos of Europe's markets and that some form of Anglo-German collaboration would provide a fruitful solution. Finally, it hypothesized that France would willingly go along with this scheme because it would benefit from German prosperity and future reparations payments.[133]

Britain had already taken some preliminary steps in 1921: its Export Credits Act was meant to stimulate foreign trade through government guarantees to private traders. Individual British capitalists had approached their German counterparts; and the Russians had been encouraged to offer concessions in London. However, these uncoordinated efforts had not produced palpable results; this was why Lloyd George and his entourage were convinced that an international solution had to be sought at Genoa.[134]

Initially there was not much acceptance of the "Stinnes plan." Loucheur

130. *DBFP*, 19:81–87, 97–99; Vermerk, Berlin, 26 Jan., Germ. AA T-120 L991/5411/L285688–89.

131. Ter Meulen plan, BMAE 10991; also *DBFP*, 19:238.

132. Heinrich Euler, *Die Aussenpolitik der Weimarer Republik, 1918–1923* (Anschaffenburg: Pattloch-Verlag, 1957), pp. 309–12, and F. Lloyd George, *Lloyd George: A Diary*, p. 239.

133. Stamm, *Lloyd George*, pp. 205–10.

134. Ibid., p. 210.

had succeeded in broadening the scheme from a consortium for Russia alone to a European body pledged to rehabilitate all of Eastern Europe; neither he nor Briand wanted to stress aid to the Bolsheviks without the accompanying political conditions.[135] There was conflict from the very start. Where Rathenau was primarily interested in reviving Russian railways, Loucheur focused on the importance of reviving former European industrial concerns. Briand tried to dilute Germany's participation by stressing the importance of Belgian and American contributions.[136] Lloyd George repeatedly insisted that the prerequisite to the industrialists' support of the corporation idea was the de jure recognition of the Soviet regime.

There was marked disagreement over the capital to be committed. The British had originally proposed a private corporation based in London and possessing resources of 20 million pounds. The members would include France (contributing 20 percent), Britain (20 percent), the United States (20 percent), Germany (20 percent), Belgium (5 percent), and Italy (5 percent); the remaining 10 percent would be apportioned among smaller powers, including the Netherlands, Czechoslovakia and Switzerland. Loucheur preferred a smaller corporation, with 2 million pounds sterling and with subsidiary national corporations formed for particular reconstruction projects.[137]

Underneath, this disagreement was over the risks. France was reluctant to commit a fixed sum in a higher valued currency because it feared that a rise in the exchange to prewar parity could wipe out as much as 50 percent of its citizens' investments. Paris could not undertake to guarantee their security nor could it alone take such a risk. The British defended their scheme by invoking Germany's willingness to subscribe in sterling. Moreover, a corporation established for the rehabilitation of Europe would scarcely be convincing to potential recipients without a substantial capital in a solid currency. Despite British accusations of France's lack of "cooperativeness," Paris held out until the Cannes meeting.[138] There, finding no support from Belgium or Italy, Britain had to back down.

At Cannes the Supreme Council accepted Loucheur's lower figure of 2 million and decided that a central corporation in London would control all the supporting companies, which would be capitalized in the members' currencies up to a total of the 20 million pounds. The decision did not specify what forms of "control" would be exerted. Although the international corporation was to

135. Delacroix to Jaspar, Paris, 31 Dec. 1921, BMAE 10991; *DBFP*, 15:777.

136. *Journée Industrielle*, 3 Jan.

137. *DBFP*, 15:806–35; also "Reconstitution économique de l'Europe," 30, 31 Dec. 1921, FMAE Y 29.

138. Note pour le Président du Conseil, Paris, 17 Jan., FMAE B 81; Dubois note (Conférence de Cannes), 19 Jan., FMF F 30/1275; De Gaiffier to Jaspar, Paris, 3 Jan., BMAE Fr.; and *DBFP*, 19:44–51, 65–69.

be "free from government control," its very birth at the hands of the Supreme Council revealed its official status. On 10 January the council asked all its members to contribute ten thousand pounds to an organizing committee, to give it all the support and assistance in their power, and to give the same support and assistance to the corporation when it was formed. Two days later, just after the announcement of Briand's resignation, Rathenau, in the course of his peroration about Germany's dire financial problems, emphasized Germany's right and qualifications to participate in the international corporation and in the reconstruction of Eastern Europe.[139]

Immediately after Cannes, the British did the preliminary work to create the central international corporation, stressing the private nature of the enterprise.[140] The Russians were suspicious. Though some considered the scheme a veiled attempt to give the Germans a "free hand in Russia," the German government had misgivings, fearing to be entangled in a British-dominated scheme, but also fearing an exclusion the British scarcely anticipated.[141]

The organizing committee finally met in London on 21 February. Delegates from the Supreme Council attended, and the United States had an unofficial observer. At the opening session, Britain dropped a bombshell with the announcement that His Majesty's government had decided to guarantee the entire 4 million pounds to be raised by its national corporation, and the Italians, forewarned, said they would do likewise. British delegate Lord Inverforth responded to French and Belgian expressions of dismay with a recollection that Loucheur had promised that his government would make such a guarantee.[142]

This opening scene made it all the easier for the British to keep faith with the Germans; and thus it came about that Kempner and Bergmann, who were conveniently in London, were invited to attend the organizational meeting of 23 February. This caused a sensation in Paris. *Le Matin* reported that the Germans had been included in the preparatory talks for Genoa itself, a charge that Poincaré, preparing for Boulogne, had to hurriedly deny. Rathenau, though wary of the corporation, allowed his representatives to join Britain and Italy in agreeing to a government guarantee of private investors; Germany's real purpose in London was to obtain relief on its reparations.[143]

139. *DBFP*, 19:84, 89, 126.

140. Howarth to Crowe, London, 17 Jan., and Ferguson to Crowe, 18 Jan., GB FO 371 C797, C890/458/62.

141. Herrick to State Dept., Paris, 27 Jan., USDS 550 E1/22; *Deutsche Tageszeitung* and *Deutsche Allgemeine Zeitung*, 27 Jan.; Sthamer to AA, London, 4, 13, 14, 15 Feb., Prittwitz to AA, Rome, 6 Feb., Mayer to AA, Paris, 15 Feb., and Simson to Sthamer, Berlin, 18 Feb., Germ. AA T-120 L991/5411/L285695, L285702–3, L285700, L285708–18, L285727.

142. Saint-Aulaire to MAE, London, 21 Feb., FMAE PM G/II; Moncheur [Cattier] to Theunis, London, 21 Feb., BMAE 10991.

143. Sthamer [Kempner and Bergmann] to Rathenau, London, 21, 22 Feb., Germ. AA T-120 L991/5411/L285730–31, L285734–36.

The meeting of the organizing committee was not amicable. Contrary to British hopes that every company would participate in every reconstruction venture, French, Belgian, Italian, and German sentiment favored giving the national corporations a considerable amount of autonomy. The Italians argued that no national company should secure a monopoly. The Germans, assessing their opportunities for profit as the most promising of all, were reluctant to pool profits. France had to bow to Britain in agreeing to exclude Poland. Switzerland, Denmark, the Netherlands, and of course the United States and Japan would all be invited to participate.[144]

The central international corporation would be a private company located in London and managed by the firm Binder, Hamlyn and Company; it would have an initial capital of ten thousand pounds (made up of the two-thousand-pound contribution by each of the Supreme Council members and Germany); finally, it would be an independent international organization, exempt from British taxation. However, it was informally agreed that its chairman would be a Briton. Draft articles for the national companies were drawn up. Owing to French reservations, the final report of the organizing committee contained the provision that the corporation would not involve itself in any country that refused to recognize its public debts and obligations, failed to establish a legal system that facilitated and enforced freedom of trade and the honoring of contracts, and provided for security of trade and commerce. These three specific conditions were to be imposed on Soviet Russia.[145]

To put pressure on Paris and Brussels, the organizing committee set the date of 11 March as the deadline for making the initial contribution of two thousand pounds and committing a government guarantee for the capital of each private company. When three governments accepted, the corporation would be formed. French delegate Sergent brought back the bad news to Paris: the guarantee of a popular subscription of 200 million francs would be a burden to Poincaré's government; British control over the international corporation seemed dangerous, particularly in view of London's vagueness about its ultimate purpose, the machinations of capitalists such as Urquart, the prospect of flooding Russia with pounds and of allowing German control over Russia's railways. On the other hand, there was no basis to believe the Russians would accept the corporation's help, and Seydoux observed critically that there was no specific reconstruction plan. Paris and Brussels decided to wait until Genoa, and so did the Germans.[146]

144. Rathenau to Sthamer, Berlin, 27 Feb., Germ. AA T-120 L991/5411/L285737–38; Sthamer [Kempner and Bergmann] to Rathenau, London, 25 Feb., Sthamer to Rathenau, 27, 28 Feb., Germ. AA T-120 L991/5411/L285739, L285740–46, L285749–50.

145. Sthamer to Rathenau, London, 28 Feb., Germ. AA T-120 L991/5411/L285761–67.

146. Saint-Aulaire to Poincaré, London, 25 Feb., FMAE PM G/II; Seydoux-Sergent conversation, Paris, 28 Feb., FMAE PM G/III; Saint-Aulaire to MAE, London, 22 Mar., FMAE B 90;

Thus no corporation was established before the Genoa Conference. Despite the alarms of the Russian emigré Boris Savinkov and despite Louis Fischer's accusations, the West had created no consortium to exploit Russia.[147] Lloyd George had nonetheless accomplished his goal: even if the original conception had been thwarted and modified, the Allies had created a useful instrument to manifest a certain amount of sympathy toward Russia along with a measure of coercion.[148] The corporation had the extra advantage of keeping the Germans in tow, maintaining pressure on Paris and Brussels, and worrying Washington. It remained for the Genoa Conference or, as one French diplomat suggested, the Reparations Commission to deliver the coup de grace to the central international corporation.

Aufzeichnung (unsigned), Berlin, 20 Mar., Germ. AA T-120 L991/5411/L285813; and Securité Générale, note, 1 Mar., FMAE Z Russ. 349.

147. Savinkov letter, 7 Apr., in the *Times*, accusing Lloyd George of using the Germans and Bolsheviks to pillage Russia's wealth; and Louis Fischer, *The Soviets in World Affairs* (Princeton: Princeton University Press, 1951), 1:326–29.

148. Seydoux note, 16 Mar., FMAE B 115; Saint-Aulaire to MAE, London, 20 Mar., FMAE B 90; Saint Quentin to MAE, Berlin, 4 Apr., FMAE Y 161. The *Financial Times* on 5 Apr. reported Lloyd George's "delight" with the corporation's progress.

4

Final Preparations

In place of a multinational conference in March 1922 at Genoa, there were meetings of the major groupings of Europe: the East Europeans, the neutrals, the Germans and Russians, and the Allies. All responded to the forthcoming gathering, discussed their strategies, and solidified their aims. During the month delay before the Genoa Conference—a damaging postponement according to its partisans—the skeptics and opponents of Lloyd George's plan tried to erect barriers against the perceived dangers. The adherents, their leader largely silent, worked assiduously to maintain public support for Genoa and the momentum for eventually breaking down the existing blocs.

Preconference Meetings

AN EASTERN BLOC?

The prospect of the Genoa Conference shook the new states of Eastern Europe. All had been carved or expanded from the ruins of the former Hohenzollern, Habsburg, Romanov, and Ottoman realms and, as such, were creatures and adherents of the status quo: antirevisionism was at the core of whatever foreign policy they devised.[1] Yet the "status quo" was not universally agreed upon in 1922. The states that bordered on Soviet Russia, Rumania, Poland, and the Baltic states, had acquired territory after hostilities had ceased in the West. Their new boundaries were not yet recognized by the Great Powers; indeed, one of the powers (Japan) was itself still in Siberia. The national consolidation of these East European states depended on recognition of their frontiers, which indeed necessitated a general political settlement between the West and Soviet Russia. On the other hand, Czechoslovakia and Yugoslavia, which had no contiguous borders with Soviet Russia, were less impatient about an East-West

1. Dodge to State Dept., Belgrade, 7 Feb., USDS 550 E1/60. Also see Henry L. Roberts, "International Relations between the Wars," in *Challenge in Eastern Europe*, ed. C. E. Black (New Brunswick, N.J.: Rutgers University Press, 1954), pp. 179–95; C. A. Macartney and A. W. Palmer, *Independent Eastern Europe: A History* (London: St. Martin's, 1966), chaps. 3, 4, and 6; and Joseph Rothschild, *East Central Europe between the Two World Wars* (Seattle: University of Washington Press, 1974), pp. 4–11, 33–34, 76–86.

agreement or about acknowledging the northern territorial arrangements. (Yugoslavia was officially termed the Serb-Croat-Slovene state until 3 October 1929; however, Yugoslavia will be used throughout this book.)

Lloyd George's grand design for the reconstruction of Russia and the economic rehabilitation of Central and Eastern Europe had little appeal to East European leaders. In 1922 they faced acute internal problems: land redistribution, transport and currency problems, ethnic disunity, and the struggle to control their raw materials while seeking access to foreign trade and capital—in short, fledgling efforts to establish autonomous national economies and independent state power. Newly liberated, they scarcely welcomed the Supreme Council's announcement of a Western-sponsored action, with heavy German participation, to restore the lands of Eastern Europe. These foreign investments would have a political and economic price: pressure to stabilize their currencies, coordinate their transportation systems, balance their budgets, reduce their armaments, lower tariffs, buy more goods from the West, and relinquish financial control to the Great Powers.[2] The ill-fated Porto Rosa Conference had demonstrated Eastern Europe's resistance to efforts to "coordinate" their economies.[3]

The aftermath of Cannes created a new problem: the specter of Anglo-French disunity.[4] With America's withdrawal from its political role as guarantor of the Paris peace settlement and with Great Britain indicating its disinterest in the controversial border problems of Poland, Czechoslovakia, Rumania, and Yugoslavia, the menaces of German expansionism, Hungarian irredentism, Italian incursions, and the Anschluss all resurfaced. There were legitimate fears that British bankers were counting on Berlin, Vienna, and Budapest to act as conduits for British economic expansion in the East.[5] Security was another problem. Without a unified Entente to guarantee their independence, the new states would require even larger armies on their exposed, unguaranteed borders, thus raising budgets, aggravating class and ethnic antagonisms, and further delaying economic development.

The Little Entente was formed in 1920–21 for the specific purpose of block-

2. Young to FO, Belgrade, 23 Feb. (also 10 Feb.), GB FO 371 C2896, C2208/458/62: "Mr. Popović's favorite expression to me was that they are not Persians." Similar expressions in Clement-Simon to Poincaré, Belgrade, 28 Mar., FMAE B 90: "They conceive of Genoa as divided into blacks and whites, rich and poor, lenders and borrowers . . . "

3. The Porto Rosa meeting of Oct.–Nov. 1921 had represented a major Italian effort to ease the barriers and restrictions that had been established by all the succession states of the former Habsburg monarchy: Giorgio Marsico, "L'Italia e la preparazione della Conferenza di Portorose (24 ott.–23 nov. 1921)," *Risorgimento* 30 (June 1978): 55–75. On its meager results, see "Die Konferenz von Portorosa," 9 Dec. 1921, and Aufzeichnung, Berlin, 2 Mar., Germ. AA T-120 K362/3396/K115958–64, K115982–84.

4. See, e.g., Freytag to AA, Bucharest, 16 Feb., Germ. AA T-120 L998/5412/L286610–13.

5. Lockhart memorandum, Prague, 14 Apr., GB FO 371 C5637/388/12.

ing a Habsburg restoration in Hungary.[6] One goal of Beneš's mission in February was to assert this group's interest in maintaining Allied unity and also, if possible, to claim the Little Entente's right to participate in the Entente's decision making. When Boulogne failed to end the Anglo-French *mésentente* and when Eastern Europe faced the imminence of an international conference in Italy that would include as principal participants both formerly dominant powers, Russia and Germany, it seemed necessary to coordinate the diplomatic strategy of "the lands in between."

Of all the East European states, Poland was the most threatened by the goals of the Genoa Conference. Warsaw had watched the Beneš mission with great interest and some degree of envy; it had also closely observed the Soviet overtures in London, Paris, and Berlin.[7] The controversy over Genoa and the ostensible split in the Entente provided Warsaw with the opportunity, indeed the necessity, to formulate its own plan of action.

Under Foreign Minister Konstanty Skirmunt, Poland was developing a new and flexible foreign policy despite a series of weak cabinets dependent on the nationalist-dominated Sejm (Chamber). The policy was based on the French alliance of March 1921 but also on loyal fulfillment of the 1921 Treaty of Riga with Soviet Russia, an attempt at detente with Czechoslovakia, and efforts to establish closer ties with Yugoslavia and Rumania. At the same time, Poland tried not to antagonize its old friends, Hungary and Italy.[8]

This ambitious diplomacy drew fire at home and abroad. Marshal Joseph Piłsudski, in temporary political eclipse, opposed Skirmunt's pro-Russian, anti-German orientation. The Polish Left and the minorities wanted a more pro-British stance and were uncomfortable about the demarches toward the Little Entente. The Polish Right, only nominally francophile, preferred "splendid isolation."

France did not endorse Poland's ambition to build new East European combinations. It had little sympathy for Poland's eagerness, after the signature of

---

6. "Die 'Kleine Entente,' " n.d., Germ. AA T-120 3398/1734/D738158–77; Eduard Beneš, "The Little Entente," *Foreign Affairs* 1 (September 1922): 66–72.

7. Piotr S. Wandycz, *France and Her Eastern Allies, 1919–1925* (Minneapolis: University of Minnesota Press, 1962), pp. 258–59; and Sergiusz Mikulicz, *Od Genui do Rapallo* (Warsaw: Książkà i Wiedza, 1966), pp. 49–76.

8. On Skirmunt, a former Lithuanian landowner in czarist Russia, see Muller to Curzon, Warsaw, 21 Feb., and unsigned note, London, 1 Apr., GB FO 371 N1905/1876/55, N8397/8034/55; Thaw to Hughes, Warsaw, 2 Mar., USDS 550 E1/152; and especially Schoen to AA, Warsaw, 28 Jan., 19, 25 Feb., Germ. AA T-120 L998/5412/L286309–10, 3398/1734/D738069, 6192H/2910/E465351–52. Also Wandycz, *France and Her Eastern Allies*, p. 242; Zygmunt J. Gasiorowski, "Poland's Policy towards Soviet Russia, 1921–1922," *Slavic and East European Review* 53, no. 131 (April 1975): 235; and "Polens Aussenpolitik zwischen Versailles und Locarno: Runderlass des polnischen Aussenministers Skirmunt an alle Missionen (Warschau, 2 Aug. 1921)," *Berliner Monatshefte* 18 (January 1940): 17–23.

the Riga treaty, to convince others of the importance of establishing formal diplomatic relations with ' oviet Russia;[9] it frustrated the Poles' effort to act as a mediator between Paris and Moscow.[10] Beneš was predictably opposed to Polish competition. Although he had signed a pact with Skirmunt in November 1921, their two governments and peoples remained divided by territorial disputes and political differences. London, on the other hand, welcomed Poland's willingness to expand ties with Soviet Russia; however, Whitehall took a dim view of an enlarged, more activist Little Entente. Finally, the Russians opposed Warsaw's renewed diplomatic activity and prepared to counter it where Moscow had the most influence—in the Baltic.

Aside from Skirmunt's vain aspiration to snatch the middleman role from Beneš, Poland's main goal was security. It was assumed that the Germans would play the preponderant role in rebuilding Russia's transportation system and industries and extracting its raw materials. Poland nonetheless hoped that the West, regarding it as a crucial bridge, would finally ratify its borders: the border with Russia, established at Riga, which gave the republic control over large amounts of White Russian territory far to the east of the so-called Curzon line; the border with Lithuania, including the city of Vilna, which it formally annexed in March 1922; and, finally, the vast province of Eastern Galicia, once part of Austria-Hungary, which Piłsudski had occupied in June 1919 and over which Poland intended to maintain control.[11]

The Allies were unready to ratify these borders for a number of reasons. They hesitated to sanction Poland's domination of more Ukrainian, White Russian, Lithuanian, and Jewish minorities or to provide Moscow with an irredenta and a possible pretext to attack Poland once more. In addition, the West was reluctant to take any action that would imply political recognition of Soviet Russia: Poland's eastern borders had been set with Soviet compliance and without the Allies' agreement. Hoping for the eventual collapse of the Soviet regime, the West was in no hurry to sanction the mutilation of former czarist Russia on Poland's behalf. Paris maintained this position strongly, despite the

9. Poincaré to all missions, Paris, 10 Mar., FMAE B 89. Despite Polish complaints of insufficient consultation with Paris over the Genoa Conference (cited in Wandycz, *France and Her Eastern Allies*, p. 258), the Quai d'Orsay appears to have kept the Polish minister informed: cf. notes, 25 Feb., FMAE B 106, 27 Feb., FMAE B 88, and 11 Mar., FMAE PM G/IV.

10. Unsigned note, Paris, 23 Feb., FMAE B 107, on the meeting in Berlin on 11 Feb. between Polish Foreign Ministry officials Juliusz Łukasiewicz and August Zaleski and Soviet representatives Radek and Nikolai Krestinsky.

11. Zygmunt J. Gasiorowski, "Polish-Czechoslovak Relations, 1918–1922," *Slavonic and East European Review* 35 (1956): 172–93; Mikulicz, *Genui do Rapallo*, pp. 73–79, 144–46; Macartney and Palmer, *Independent Eastern Europe*, pp. 112–14; and the informative though biased article by Stephen Witwitsky (head of the Ukrainian-Galician delegation to the Paris Peace Conference), "L'indépendence de la Galicie Orientale," *L'Europe Nouvelle* 5 (April 1922): 490–92.

anxiety it created in Warsaw.[12] Indeed, Czechoslovakia, Yugoslavia, and Rumania also did not recognize any of Poland's eastern borders. Skirmunt thus was committed to an uphill fight to gain support, and his only backing, to be sure opportunistic in nature, came from Moscow.

Warsaw began its attempt at a collective East European action on the occasion of the betrothal of King Alexander of Yugoslavia to Princess Marie of Rumania, which was celebrated in Bucharest with the arrival of the aged Serbian leader Nikola Pašić. On 22 February the Polish minister to Bucharest, Count Aleksander Skrzyński, met with Pašić, Rumania's Prime Minister Ionel Brătianu, and the Czechoslovak minister as well. Neither of the Balkan states displayed much interest in the Genoa Conference or about holding preliminary talks. Rumania and Yugoslavia, narrowly based regimes still led by prewar liberal leaders who were attempting to unify and centralize their enlarged states, faced serious internal unrest at that moment. After the disappearance of their former respective enemies, czarist Russia and the Habsburg monarchy, new and more aggressive antagonists, Soviet Russia and Italy, were now on the scene. The Bucharest meeting did produce agreement that Poland and the Little Entente would send expert representatives to a conference in Belgrade to coordinate their plans for the Genoa Conference.[13]

Beneš, returning from Paris, sought to reassert his leadership. Prague, unlike Warsaw, wanted the Genoa Conference to concentrate primarily on commercial questions and desired that no political questions be raised. Masaryk insisted that the problem of Russia's borders was much too delicate for an international conference. Beneš, then as later, would rely on his statesmanship and his confidence in the West for security, rather than promoting specific territorial arrangements. He met with Yugoslav Foreign Minister Momčilo Ninčić at Bratislava on 2 March to share details of his Western journey and explain his cancelled trip to Rome. He also pleaded against including Poland in the Little Entente and tried to soothe Ninčić's pique over Czechoslovakia's pretension to have spoken for the three members in Paris and London.[14]

12. Wandycz, *France and Her Eastern Allies*, p. 358. Paris also insisted that all the succession states to czarist Russia were responsible for a portion of the latter's prewar debts: Poincaré to all missions, Paris, 10 Mar., FMAE B 89.

13. Vollgruber to BMA, Bucharest, 23 Feb., A HHSt 687; Freytag to AA, Bucharest, 23 Feb., Germ. AA T-120 L998/5412/L286531; Keller to AA, Belgrade, 25 Feb., Germ. AA T-120 6192H/2910/E465347; and Dodge to State Dept., Belgrade, 28 Feb., USDS 550 E1/122.

14. Young to FO, Belgrade, 1 Mar., GB FO 371 C3087/458/62; Dodge to State Dept., Belgrade, 5 Mar., USDS 550 E1/121; Conférence de Gênes: Échanges de vues et accords préliminaires, Paris, 15 Mar., FMAE B 89; Alena Gajanová, "La politique extérieure tchécoslovaque et la 'question russe' à la Conférence de Gênes" (based on the archives of the Foreign Ministry of Czechoslovakia, including reports of the Czechoslovak minister in Warsaw, Prokop Maxa), *Historica* (Prague) 8 (1964): 154–55; Piotr S. Wandycz, "Foreign Policy of Edvard

The prospects for a quadruple alliance quickly diminished. The Belgrade Experts' Conference was scheduled to open on 5 March, but the Rumanian representatives came four days late. Tired of meetings, wary of Beneš, and hoping for a signal from London, Brătianu took his time. The host Yugoslav government was distracted by its own problems. The Croat parliamentary bloc had prepared a manifesto for the Genoa Conference complaining of Serb-dominated centralization; the Italians were intriguing in Montenegro; and Hungary and Bulgaria were instigating minority petitions for the conference. Further, there would be a difficult effort to dislodge the Italians from Fiume and bring the Rapallo treaty of 1920 to life. Finally, both Balkan governments, like Czechoslovakia, had recently been turned down for loans in London.[15]

Little was accomplished at the Belgrade meeting, which took place between 9 and 13 March. Poland decided not to ask, and no other government offered to bring up the question of border guarantees at the Genoa Conference. On Russia there was no policy save "expectancy." On reparations, now officially excluded by the Boulogne agreement, there was curiosity about when and how much money might eventually flow to Eastern Europe. However, no bloc was formed at the Belgrade gathering, and no definite program for Genoa was announced save a vague pro-French and pro-treaties orientation. Poland's failure to achieve a quadruple entente was underscored when the announced foreign ministers' conference, which was to have taken place on the eve of Genoa, never materialized.[16]

On 13 March there was a meeting of the foreign ministers of Poland, Latvia, Estonia, and Finland in Warsaw. Having failed with the Little Entente, a reshuffled Polish government (with Skirmunt still at the helm of the Foreign Ministry) tried another approach—the formation of a Baltic bloc to secure its eastern frontiers. This was an audacious plan, bound to raise the ire not only of

Beneš, 1918–1938," in *A History of the Czechoslovak Republic, 1918–1948*, edited by Victor S. Mamatey and Radomír Luža (Princeton: Princeton University Press, 1973), pp. 216–37.

15. On Rumania: Daeschner to MAE, Bucharest, 22, 24 Feb., FMAE PM G/II and B 87; De Martino to Schanzer, London, 9 Mar., IMAE Amb. Lond. B 539.2; and Freytag to AA, Bucharest, 6, 25 Mar., 14 Apr., Germ. AA T-120 K367/3999/K118108–9, K118138–40, L998/5412/L286678–79. On Yugoslavia: Keller to AA, Belgrade, 20, 28 Feb., 10 Mar., Germ. AA T-120 L998/5412/L286511–27, L286614–19, L989/5411/L286335–37; Clement Simon to MAE, Belgrade, 2 Feb., FMAE PM G/I, 17 Feb., FMAE PM G/II, 20 Feb., FMAE B 87; Young to FO, Belgrade, 23 Feb., GB FO 371 C2896/458/62; and Dodge to State Dept., 6 Apr., USDS 550 E1/212. On unsuccessful loans: Young to Curzon, Belgrade, 16 Mar., GB FO 371 C4078/458/62.

16. Dodge to State Dept., Belgrade, 11, 18 Mar., USDS 550 E1/146, 162; Keller to AA, Belgrade, 13 Mar., Germ. AA T-120 L992/5411/L285898–901; Young to FO, Belgrade, 13, 16 Mar., GB FO 371 C3800, C4078/458/62; Troutbeck memorandum, "Little Entente and Genoa," 20 Mar., GB FO 371 C4208/458/62; and Mikulicz, *Od Genui do Rapallo*, pp. 150–53.

Russia but of Britain and Germany as well. France, which presumably encouraged the gathering of Poland and its immediate neighbors, nonetheless realized the dangers of provoking an armed Soviet response, of encouraging Poland to take an aggressive action that might conflict with Paris's other allies, and of further antagonizing Britain.[17]

On 17 March an accord was signed in Warsaw providing for political and economic cooperation among the four states as well as concerted measures in the event one were attacked. London took this development with equanimity, hoping Warsaw would contain its "pan-Gallic imperialism" and exuberance in order not to endanger Genoa's prospects.[18] Moscow, which sent an observer to the last day of the Warsaw meetings, was less detached. It invited all the participants to a follow-up session at Riga to be held at the end of the month to discuss reconstruction and security.

After some hesitation, Poland, Latvia, and Estonia accepted. The Finns, reportedly restrained by Paris, sent only an observer.[19] The Riga meetings of 29–31 March resulted in a triumph for Moscow. In addition to making general statements on commerce and local concerns, the final accord called for recognition of Soviet Russia. The Poles were embarrassed. The Riga meeting left a bad taste all over Eastern Europe of the fruits of collective action, of the diminishing prospects of Soviet moderation, and of the dangers if Genoa failed.[20]

The British, though pleased with the Riga line, lamented Poland's month-long, frenetic efforts: London believed that all the informal diplomacy should have been left to the Great Powers. France, except for its Communists, was furious with the Poles for allowing the Russians a forum at Riga to preach disarmament, reconstruction, and de jure recognition of the Soviet state. Skirmunt had difficulty explaining the Riga episode to his critics in the Sejm, and Polish military and diplomatic officials protested that "appeasement" had gone too far.[21]

Finally, from 20 to 28 March, Poland was host to an international health

17. Martel to MAE, Riga, 4 Mar., FMAE PM G/III; Benndorf to AA, Warsaw, 15 Mar., Germ. AA T-120 L993/5411/L285907–9; and John W. Hiden, "The Significance of Latvia: A Forgotten Aspect of Weimar *Ostpolitik*," *Slavonic and East European Review* 53, no. 30 (January 1975): 399–400, 405–6.

18. Muller to Curzon, Warsaw, 24 Mar., Wilton to FO, Riga, 25 Mar., and Roberts minute, London, 28 Mar., GB FO 371 N2909, N2869/82/63.

19. Mikulicz, *Od Genui do Rapallo*, p. 157; Goppert to AA, Helsinki, 20, 22, 23 Mar., Germ. AA T-120 L998/5411/L286691–92, L993/5411/L285911, L995/5412/L286018; Ribot to MAE, Helsinki, 12 Apr., FMAE B 93. The Finns, who were involved neither in the czarist debt nor German reparations, preferred to be considered one of the neutrals.

20. Text of the Riga protocol in *DBFP*, 19:231–32. Analysis in: GB FO 371 N3107/82/63; Wurzian to BMA, Lvov, 1 Apr., A HHSt 687; and Gajanová, "Politique extérieure tchécoslovaque," pp. 157–58.

21. Mikulicz, *Od Genui do Rapallo*, p. 167.

conference called at the request of the League of Nations Council to deal with the typhus epidemic spreading from Russia into Eastern Europe. The list of invitees included Germany, Russia, and the Soviet Ukraine, and German was added to French and English as an official language. Paris fretted that Warsaw was usurping the League's prerogatives and was unhappy with Skirmunt's decision to submit the conference's decision to Genoa.[22] Paris regarded the Poles as too adventuresome. Indeed, Skirmunt had tried and failed to win Lloyd George's support for a territorial guarantee for Poland before the Genoa Conference.[23]

Despite its failure, Poland's diplomatic activity did succeed in calling the Great Powers' attention to Eastern Europe on the eve of Genoa. Skirmunt had posed alternatives to the existing alignments. Until 1922 France had defended the status quo and the security of the new and enlarged states.[24] However, their prosperity no doubt also depended on British, American, and neutral bankers, German industrialists, and the opening of Russia. Lacking either unity or broadly based governments, Eastern Europe faced the opening of the Genoa Conference as its first major diplomatic challenge since the Paris peace treaties; and especially for Poland this represented both a danger and an opportunity.

A NEUTRALS' BLOC?

There was a counterpart to Poland's abortive efforts to organize the East European states before Genoa: Sweden tried to form a neutrals' bloc. Whereas certain East European states felt insecure because of their unrecognized borders, many of the neutrals were insecure about the state of their economies, which they blamed on the territorial and economic "disruption" caused by the Paris peace settlement. The Swiss, Dutch, and Scandinavian economies had boomed in wartime. Now the general contraction of trade, German dumping, and the unstable state of international exchanges had produced high levels of unemployment and labor unrest. With the exception of Spain, the neutrals were governed by coalitions—moderate Left in Scandinavia and the moderate Right in the Netherlands and Switzerland. Fiercely independent, they were nonethe-

22. Conferenza sanitaria di Varsavia, 20–28 Mar., LNA 12B 20690/18972; Commert note, 31 Mar., exchange of letters between Poincaré and Minister of Public Health Paul Strauss, Paris, 7, 13 Apr., and note analyzing Warsaw resolutions, n.d., FMAE B 91, 94, 92; cf. British Minister of Health Sir Alfred Mond to Lloyd George, London, 4 Apr., LGP F 37/2/11, which supported the Warsaw resolutions.

23. The only record of this meeting is Lloyd George's statement to the cabinet on 5 Apr., in GB FO 371 N3308/64/55. Skirmunt's optimistic reaction in Margerie to MAE, Brussels, 9 Apr., FMAE Z GB 49. The Poles realized, however, that Britain would risk little on their behalf: Mikulicz, *Od Genui do Rapallo*, p. 77.

24. Unsigned article, "La Petite Entente et la Conférence de Gênes," *Revue des Balkans*, 4 (1 March 1922): 59–60.

less all members of the League of Nations, which they hoped to make the forum for the views of small democratic states as well as the Great Powers. Genoa thus posed a challenge: the Western-sponsored, London-based consortium and the presence of Germany and Russia would all affect their economies and political futures.[25]

Was there any need to form a neutrals' alignment? Members of the bloc had little in common except for the fact that they had not fought in the war, signed the treaties, or been involved directly either with reparations or the tangle of interallied debts. Some, like the Dutch and Spanish, had overseas empires and worldwide commercial or cultural interests, whereas the others were oriented mainly toward Europe. Sweden and Norway, both governments dependent on the radical Left, had established trade ties with the Soviets, but the Dutch and Swiss were resolutely anti-Bolshevik. The neutrals' orientation toward the Entente similarly varied: Norway, Sweden, Spain, and Switzerland generally stood behind Britain, the Danes and Dutch behind France, but these positions were not rigid. Sweden competed with Britain for Russian concessions; Denmark wavered between Britain and France; Switzerland and Spain vacillated between Britain and Germany; and the Dutch, because of their commercial and banking interests, gravitated toward Britain on the reparations question.

Neither Britain nor France welcomed a neutrals' bloc, London because it felt such alignments would obstruct matters at Genoa, France because the neutrals' ideology, anti-Versailles and antireparations, was directed against Paris's policies. Germany was thus understandably in favor of any initiative to coordinate policies among the neutrals because they could create a counterweight to the Entente with their still-considerable financial resources.[26] The neutrals proved capable of resisting pressures from the Great Powers. For example, France failed to persuade the Swiss to join in a demarche to postpone the Genoa Conference. Germany similarly failed to convince Dutch Foreign Minister Jonkheer Herman van Karnebeek to work actively against a postponement.[27] Nevertheless, when Boulogne was followed by America's refusal to attend the Genoa Conference, the neutrals realized the necessity of unified action. They felt anxious over the continued Anglo-French quarrel but concluded that without the help of America's power and prestige, they could do little themselves.[28]

Sweden nonetheless tried. The government of Hjalmar Branting put forward

---

25. *DBFP*, 19:285–88, analyzes each of the neutrals.

26. Gevers to Karnebeek, Berlin, 27 Feb., *DBPN*, no. 179; also Rathenau Aufzeichnung, Berlin, 25 Feb., Lucius to AA, The Hague, 18 Mar., Simson to Lucius, Berlin, 20 Mar., Germ. AA T-120 L989/5411/L285279, L995/5412/L285983, L285986–88.

27. Lacroix to Seydoux, Berne, 25 Jan., FMAE PM G/I Allizé to MAE, Berne, 6, 13, 21 Feb., FMAE PM G/II, and Renseignement, Paris, 15 Mar., FMAE B 89; also Lucius to AA, The Hague, 23 Feb., Germ. AA T-120 L998/5412/L286480–81.

28. Grew to State Dept., Berne, 14, 29 Mar., USDS E1/139, 180.

a severe deflationary policy in the face of an acute unemployment of 160,000 (one-third of Sweden's trade-union members) and sought to establish an independent voice for European reconstruction. Indeed, Branting sought to surpass Lloyd George's flagging leadership of the "progressive cause."[29] This was heralded in a series of articles by the Swedish economist Gustav Cassel, who advocated that the neutrals reject the Entente's "destructive" economic and political policies. Cassel called for reinstitution of the gold standard, lowering of tariffs, encouragement of international trade, and especially the immediate revision of the reparations clauses of the Treaty of Versailles.[30]

There was mild approval by the British minister in Stockholm, some support from Norway, and an immediate positive reaction in Berlin; indeed, Rathenau invited Cassel to visit, as a guest of the German government, to discuss credit and currency.[31] Despite Danish and Dutch apathy, Branting, who was attempting a grandiose action to silence domestic criticism, convened a conference of neutrals in Stockholm on 18 March. The gathering consisted of the Swedish and Norwegian prime ministers and the diplomatic representatives of the Netherlands, Switzerland, Denmark, and Spain. It passed some general resolutions supporting the League of Nations, free trade, and the gold standard, and also indicated an interest in participating in the international corporation.[32]

The Dutch government, whose representative arrived ostentatiously late in Stockholm, was disgruntled with the gathering; Karnebeek feared the meeting's anti-Entente overtone and particularly the announced flirtation with the Soviets. The Netherlands and Denmark were both far less hurt by the industrial crisis than the other neutrals and more interested in Germany than in Russia. Each opposed the formation of a bloc that could cause serious complications with its immediate neighbors, especially in the case of the Hague government.[33]

29. Sholes (U.S. Consul) to State Dept., Goteborg, 28 Feb., USDS E1/120; Mueller to AA (für R. M. persönlich), Berne, 5 Mar., and Nadolny to AA, Stockholm, 9 Mar., Germ. AA T-120 L995/5412/L285955, L285957–58.

30. Translations of Cassel's articles in *Norges Hangels og Sjöfastidende* and *Svenska Dagbladet*, Germ. AA T-120 L995/5412/L285964–69, L285956; May to Jaspar, Stockholm, 20 Mar., BMAE 10991; and Renseignement, Paris, 22 Mar., FMAE B 90.

31. Barclay to FO, Stockholm, 15, 16, 17 Mar., GB FO 371 C4152, C4253, C3994/458/62; U.S. Minister in Norway to State Dept., Christiana, 21, 28 Mar., USDS E1/188. Cassel's visit to Berlin: Germ. AA T-120 L995/5412/L285972, L285976–78, 3398/1734/D738194–97, L995/5412/L286005, L286010–12, L286021–23, L286025–26, L286033; and Ernst Laubach, *Die Politik der Kabinette Wirth, 1921/1922* (Lübeck and Hamburg: Matthiesen, 1968), p. 177.

32. Nadolny to AA, Stockholm, 19 Mar., Germ. AA T-120 L995/5412/L285989; Barclay to Curzon, Stockholm, 21 Mar., GB FO 371 C4586/458/62.

33. *DBPN*, nos. 187, 192, 193, 207, 214; also Marling to Curzon, The Hague, 21 Mar., GB FO 371 C4358/458/62; Siegfried to MAE, The Hague, 28 Mar., FMAE B 90; Philips to State Dept., The Hague, 21 Mar., and Prince to State Dept., Copenhagen, 5 Apr., USDS 550 E1/179, 206.

There was another neutrals' meeting in Berne consisting of a preliminary session attended by experts on 5 April and a ministers' meeting between 8 and 10 April, on the very eve of Genoa. There were no significant results. This time there was only guarded discussion of Russian reconstruction. The Dutch and Swiss opposed de jure recognition of Moscow, and the Scandinavians followed the more liberal British position. However, the Dutch and Swiss split over the international corporation. Because of the urgings of their bankers and industrialists, the latter were willing to participate; but the former refused. As a result of Cassel's pessimistic report of his stopover in Berlin, the neutrals predicted German bankruptcy. There was discussion of the possibility of an international loan, but they reserved this question "until Germany was rendered solvent," the code expression for a new reparations settlement.[34]

Genoa, with its broad and vague agenda, had brought the neutrals together twice to voice their collective uneasiness; but they had no solutions. The majority was in favor of negotiation with Russia and treaty revisionism toward Germany; but an influential minority resisted the creation of a formal neutrals' bloc. Without the United States, they remained weak, isolated, internally and externally divided, and ultimately vulnerable to the pressures and decisions of the Great Powers. The best they could achieve was a collective commitment to goodness, generosity, and internationalism, but because of the risks, they shrank from defending these together.[35]

GENOA OR GENEVA?

After Boulogne, the role of the League of Nations in relation to the Genoa Conference came again to the fore. Lloyd George seems to have modified his original intransigent position as a result of several factors: Beneš's visit, Poincaré's insistence, the pro-League element of British public opinion, and the growing realization in Rome and Whitehall of the need for technical help in organizing so large an international gathering. Returning from a visit to London, Secretary-General Sir Eric Drummond informed a directors' meeting in early March that the British premier had agreed to the League's handling the follow-up work of the Genoa Conference. The organization's confidence was reviving. The current negotiations in Geneva between Germany and Poland for a convention on Upper Silesia, the convocation of an international health conference in Warsaw, and the increased involvement of the council with the Vilna issue—all seemed harbingers of the League's increased prestige. While the

34. Seydoux, Note pour le Président du Conseil, Paris, 30 Mar., FMAE B 90; Mueller to AA, Berne, 1 Apr., Germ. AA T-120 L995/5412/L284034–36; Benoist to MAE, The Hague, 4 Apr., FMAE B 92; Grew to State Dept., Berne, 7, 8 Apr., USDS 550 E1/171, 211; Allizé to MAE, Berne, 7, n.d. Apr., FMAE B 92, 94.

35. Peltzer to MAE, Berne, 10 Apr., BMAE 10991; Scott to Curzon, Berne, 11 Apr., GB FO 371 C5460/458/62; Lacroix to MAE, Berne, 13 Apr., FMAE B 93.

League would not be formally represented at the Genoa Conference, it would also not be excluded. It now seemed likely that it would supervise whatever needed to be implemented afterwards.[36]

Even its opponents recognized that the League of Nations had amassed considerable documentation and expertise in the handling of economic, financial, transport, and disarmament questions. Its supporters viewed Genoa as primarily a follow-up of the 1920 Brussels Conference.[37] It thus seemed logical to put League materials and personnel at the service of the Genoa Conference; but in what capacity? Poincaré interpreted the Boulogne accord not only as protecting the League's prerogatives but also as permitting some form of League representation at Genoa. This would underscore Lloyd George's pledge not to create a rival organization and also impede the discussion of forbidden subjects.[38]

While Lloyd George was resting in the Welsh countryside and planning his next political moves, Schanzer and Poincaré made inquiries in London to clarify the question of League representation at Genoa. Curzon, deferring to the premier's wishes, flatly rejected anything other than a consultative role for Geneva's personnel. Insisting the League was not a sovereign entity, he announced that it was inappropriate for it to have official representation alongside the other delegates. Poincaré, expressing indignation at this deprecation of the League but also anticipating the British refusal, had taken another step: he had requested an emergency session of the League of Nations Council in Paris to deal with the problem of the forthcoming Genoa Conference.[39]

It was a very tense session; in addition to Genoa, it also covered such subjects as the Saar and disarmament. On 25 March French delegate Léon Bourgeois quoted the Boulogne text in presenting the French case: the League must be entrusted with the "application and execution" of the work of the Genoa Conference. The British delegate, H. A. L. Fisher, acknowledged French fears of the League's displacement but openly displayed his reservations about the young world organization. Curzon, who was in Paris for the Near Eastern negotiations, transmitted the Bourgeois proposal to Lloyd George, who cabled his assent with the proviso that nothing be binding on the Genoa Conference. He wanted to maintain control as to which parts (if any) of the Genoa Confer-

36. Minutes of directors' meeting, Geneva, 3 Mar., LNA.
37. Haas note, Paris, 9 Feb., LNA 40A 20136; "The Relation of the Genoa Conference to the Work of the League," n.d., GB FO 371 C4621/458/62; Jean Goût, Note pour le Président du Conseil, 1 Mar., FMAE Y 1205.
38. Bourgeois to Poincaré, Paris, 6 Mar., FMAE PM G/III; Poincaré to Bourgeois, Saint-Aulaire, and Hardinge, 7 Mar., and Bourgois note, n.d., FMAE Y 1205.
39. Saint-Aulaire to Poincaré, London, 18 Mar., FMAE B 89; Curzon to Hardinge, London, 19 Mar., and De Martino, 21 Mar., in *DBFP*, 19:241–46; Poincaré to Drummond, Paris, 15 Mar., FMAE B 89, and to French Ambassadors in London, Brussels, Rome, and Madrid, 21 Mar., FMAE Y 1205; De Martino to Crowe, London, 19 Mar., GB FO 371 C4270/458/62.

ence would be handed over to the League. The French, by contrast, wanted things spelled out in advance: that Geneva would be the sole administrator of all of Genoa's decisions.[40]

Italy, in its role as conference manager, chose the British view over the French. After his conference with Lloyd George in London on 27 March, Schanzer went to Paris, where he formed an Anglo-Italian-Japanese alignment on the League Council. On 28 March the Bourgeois proposals were defeated. In place of a forceful resolution on the Genoa Conference, the council took note of an Italian request that the Secretariat send individuals who would contribute their documentation and competence on request. The isolated Bourgeois made a statement for the record of his government's determination that the League be charged with the "application and execution" of all subjects for which it was competent, including the key and forbidden question of disarmament.[41]

Despite the formal outcome, it was a victory of sorts for the League. Related organs, the International Labor Organization and the International Institute of Agriculture, were to send technical representatives, and Minorities Section Chief Erik Colban intended to go as well.[42] When the directors met on 30 March, Drummond announced confidently that no competing organization would emanate from the Genoa Conference and that Germany and perhaps Soviet Russia might eventually become members.[43]

Drummond pleaded that day for an international esprit among his colleagues, for a feeling transcending purely nationalist orientation. Colban planned to work among the neutrals to stimulate more pro-League sentiment. Yet Geneva was anxious. Would there really be no more Genoas? How far could their incipient internationalism progress before it collided with the resistance of the Great Powers?[44] So far the League had proved prudent and efficient in handling purely technical matters but less astute on politics. It would again be assigned minor questions at Genoa, and the great matters might still remain outside Geneva's purview. The League's champions either had insufficient power or simply regarded it as a bastion of the status quo. Genoa, with its vague suggestion of new alignments of the powers and possible change, underscored the League's weakness.

40. Bourgeois to Poincaré, Paris, 25 Mar., FMAE Y 1205; Fisher to Curzon, Paris, 26 Mar., CzP; telephone message, Curzon to Prime Minister, Paris, 26 Mar. and response that day [via Crowe] from Lloyd George, GB FO 371 C4581/458/62; directors' meeting, Geneva, 30 Mar., LNA; Mayer to AA, Paris, 31 Mar., Germ. AA T-120 L989/5411/L285404–7.

41. Aide-mémoire sur la 17. session du Conseil (S.d.N.), Brussels, 1 Apr., BMAE 10991. Belgian delegate Paul Hymans presided over the meeting.

42. ILO, 20 Mar., and IIA, 4 Apr., in GB FO 371 C5154, C5038/458/62. On Colban's mission: directors' meeting, Geneva, 30 Mar., LNA, and LNA 41 18841/10503.

43. Minutes of directors' meeting, Geneva, 30 Mar., LNA.

44. Monnet to Bourgeois, Geneva, 7 Apr., FMAE B 93.

NEAR EAST CEASE-FIRE?

The Genoa Conference and the struggle to control Anatolia and the Straits were interconnected. Turkey, fearing a Soviet agreement with the West, tried unsuccessfully to obtain an invitation. Greece, distracted by the effort to maintain itself in Smyrna, made meager preparations for Genoa; domestic discord prevented Athens from accepting the suggestion that it collaborate with the Little Entente. Finally, the rift between Britain and France, and Italy's effort to move into the breach had their effect as well.[45]

As early as October 1921, when the Greeks were routed at Sakarya, the Allies had agreed on a foreign ministers' conference on the Near East. Briand accepted this during his visit to London and Poincaré during Curzon's visit to Paris in January. The fall of the Italian government delayed matters; but the Near East remained an important item on the Allies' agenda. Neither Britain nor France considered referring the question of a peace settlement with Turkey to the League of Nations. It was the responsibility of the Great Powers both to formulate and enforce a revision of the Treaty of Sèvres.[46]

Britain's position in March 1922 was noticeably weak. Under Poincaré, Paris was entirely pro-Turk, and Italy, though seemingly reliable, was subject to pressure from Ankara. There was a nasty scandal in London. The secretary of state for India, Edwin Montagu, was forced to resign because he authorized the publication of a telegram from the viceroy of India appealing for a pro-Turk policy to pacify nationalist and Moslem public opinion in India.[47] With Montagu gone and Gandhi arrested on 11 March, Britain had to formulate peace terms for the Near East before the Greeks utterly collapsed. The Turks remained intransigent, refusing Curzon's conditions with respect to the protection of Christian minorities under their future realm, and London was unable to dictate a solution. At the cabinet meeting of 20 March, both Churchill and Curzon complained that the absent Lloyd George's policies had produced an unenforceable treaty, Turkish-Bolshevik collusion, and threats to Mosul and Iraq. Curzon, about to leave for Paris for the long-delayed talks, was pessimistic. He promised to "yield as little as possible."[48]

Despite his forebodings, Curzon was fairly successful at the Allied foreign ministers' conference and ceded very little. On the first day, Britain, France, and Italy agreed that the current lull in hostilities should be converted into a

45. German Minister to AA, Athens, 13 Mar., 4 Apr., Germ. AA T-120 L998/5412/ L286681–82, L286753–54; A. J. Frangulis, *La Grèce et la crise mondiale* (Paris: F. Alcan, 1926), 2:324–35; Salahi Ramsdan Sonyel, *Turkish Diplomacy, 1918–1923* (London and Beverly Hills, Calif.: Sage, 1975), pp. 133–34.

46. Crowe memorandum, London, 3 Mar., *DBFP*, 17:643–44.

47. Briton Cooper Busch, *Mudros to Lausanne: Britain's Frontier in Asia, 1918–1923* (Albany: State University of New York Press, 1976), pp. 327–34.

48. GB CAB 23/29.

formal armistice between Greek and Turkish forces; a note was dispatched to the belligerents. However, when Curzon, Poincaré, and Schanzer proceeded to discuss the terms of an armistice, their essential disagreement resurfaced. Curzon had very few cards save the timing of the Greek withdrawal from Smyrna. For political reasons, he had to fight for the neutralization of the Straits, the rights of Christian and Armenian minorities, and a Greek presence in Thrace. Poincaré stuck tenaciously to the revisionist position: the Treaty of Sèvres had to be entirely scrapped; there must be no form of coercion against the Turks, who were to be allowed to maintain a conscript army; and, in the matter of minorities, there should be nothing beyond what the League of Nations had already established for the new states of Eastern Europe, or, possibly, there could be a population exchange.[49]

Schanzer's position was the most precarious. He supported the British, although his heart was with Poincaré. Indeed, Italy's needs still lay elsewhere, namely, in securing the economic benefits promised in the Tripartite Accord of 1920, which had accompanied the Sèvres treaty and which neither of his partners now wished to honor. Schanzer said little and sacrificed much. There was a considerable amount of acrimonious speech among the Allies and, as at Boulogne, bickering over the past and the present.[50]

The Allied foreign ministers' conference in Paris did represent a new form of peacemaking: the substitution of diplomacy for pronouncements by the Supreme Council. Unlike their tactics with Germany or Russia, the three Western powers were commencing the process of negotiation with a former enemy. They were dismantling the coercive apparatus they had established at Sèvres and, though Britain and France had already considerably profited, were sacrificing various interests, including the rights of minorities. This was the result of the total collapse of the Greek military enterprise but also of Kemal's strength and underlying, long-standing Allied rivalries.[51]

At Paris the Great Powers temporarily submerged their differences. They offered the belligerents an armistice in place and proposed a subsequent peace conference where they would present a new, more pro-Turk settlement. Athens accepted a cease-fire but reserved judgment on the peace terms. Kemal promptly refused, correctly understanding that the Allies' formula contained no guarantee of a final Greek withdrawal from Thrace and Anatolia. Again there was a deadlock.[52]

Britain, hobbled by Lloyd George's grecophilia and stubbornness, was not ready to make an unconditional peace with Kemal and clung to any shred

49. Conversations, 22–26 Mar., *DBFP*, 17:668–756.

50. Ibid., pp. 672–74, 676, 680, 681, 683–85, 687, 689, 695, 702–3, 705–6.

51. Pronouncement by the three powers, 27 Mar., GB Cmd. 1641.

52. A. E. Montgomery, "Lloyd George and the Greek Question," in *Lloyd George: Twelve Essays*, ed. A. J. P. Taylor (London: Hamilton, 1972), pp. 280–81; Frangulis, *La Grèce*, 2:358–84.

of Sèvres. Poincaré considered good relations with Turkey an excellent lever against London and the Bolsheviks and also vis-à-vis the restive Moslem population of the French empire. France was thus the ardent revisionist in the Near East, using a language of reconciliation with Nationalist Turkey and opposing Allied efforts to dictate a peace settlement. Until the debacle in the fall, Curzon remained in a constant fury over how France, so militant in Europe, was so staunchly oriented toward appeasing Kemal's Turkey. He was equally impatient with Italy's efforts to keep communications open with Ankara.[53]

The continuing uncertainty over the outcome of the Greco-Turkish struggle undoubtedly affected the Genoa Conference. The Allies were divided over the prospect of having eventually to formulate terms for the revision of a peace treaty; there were ample opportunities for propaganda and intrigue. The United States openly disapproved of any attempt to dictate a Near Eastern settlement.[54] In the end, Ankara would force a solution with its military victories in the late summer of 1922. But in the meantime, there was a sense of danger and frustration in London. As long as Lloyd George's policies prevailed, Whitehall realized that the outcome depended not only on the adversary's moves but also on Britain's difficult championship of Allied solidarity in the Near East. To this end, Curzon insisted on removing this forbidden subject from any open discussion at Genoa.[55]

The London Report

Allied representatives finally met in London between 20 and 28 March to prepare for the Genoa Conference. It was a meeting of Belgian, British, French, Italian, and Japanese experts, with Germany, the neutrals, and the Little Entente specifically excluded. Lloyd George, still absent in Wales except for a brief, stormy session with his cabinet and a meeting with Schanzer, was kept informed of the proceedings by Grigg, Hankey, and Wise.[56] The French delegation, headed by Seydoux, worked closely with the Belgians. The experts had

53. Hardinge [Curzon] to FO [for cabinet], Paris, 24 Mar., *DBFP*, 17:698. Debates on Smyrna: ibid., pp. 675–76; debates on Christian minorities: ibid., pp. 687–89; Italy's claims: ibid., pp. 797–800, 806–12, and 821–24.

54. Laurence Evans, *United States Policy and the Partition of Turkey, 1914–1924* (Baltimore: Johns Hopkins University Press, 1965), pp. 362–65.

55. Curzon to Gregory [at Genoa], London, 21, 25 Apr., *DBFP* 17:780–81, 794–95.

56. Grigg to Lloyd George, London, 14, 15 Mar., Hankey to Lloyd George, 15, 16, 20, 21, 24 Mar., LGP F 86/1/26, 27, 14–15, 19–20, 23. E. F. Wise is described as "a man of decidedly left-wing views" by Kenneth O. Morgan, *Consensus and Disunity: The Lloyd George Coalition Government, 1918–1922* (Oxford: Clarendon Press, 1979), p. 113. Wise, a former official in the Ministry of Food, was a confidant of Lloyd George and an active figure in the 1920–22 Anglo-Soviet trade negotiations; he urged closer ties with Russia: see LGP F 149/2/3, F 197/7/4, F 149/2/11. The "ubiquitous Wise" was resented by the Foreign Office as representing the

no mandate to make binding agreements or even recommendations for the Genoa Conference. This was underscored not only by Poincaré's instructions but also by Giannini's repeated statements that Italy would not limit its future dealings with Russia or place any burdens on the Genoa Conference. Although political questions were excluded from the discussions, it soon became evident that even "technical" matters divided the Allies.[57]

London and Paris had made substantial preparations. Working through inter-ministerial commissions, which included bankers and industrialists along with government and colonial officials, both had drawn virtually opposite conclusions about the prospect before them at Genoa. The British Foreign Office had drafted a treaty for the reestablishment of diplomatic relations with Russia. It listed a series of stringent conditions, including full compensation to foreign creditors under the aegis of a debt commission (half of whose membership would be non-Russian); pledges to refrain from hostile propaganda against the West; and the establishment of an extraterritorial regime for Western capitalists reentering the Soviet state. The British draft contained a few elements of reciprocity, including mutual recognition of all existing treaties—the Treaty of Versailles but also, contrary to the Boulogne agreement, all treaties signed by the Soviet government since the war. The British draft also anticipated Russian claims against the West.[58]

In their long, arduous preparatory meetings in Paris, the French had debated in what manner to attempt the restoration of the Soviet economy: whether simply to lay down general principles of reconstruction for the entire area or to divide the former czarist "empire" into spheres of influence and to work for the intensive revival of its productive capacity in stages—agriculture, transportation, and eventually industry—that would be directed and controlled by selected, experienced foreign capitalists. France's final report represented a conclusion, by no means unanimous, in favor of the second procedure; it also acknowledged the inevitability of a major German role in Russia's reconstruction as well as the importance of oil.[59]

---

worst of Lloyd George's personal entourage: Saint-Aulaire to Poincaré, London, 27 Mar., FMAE B 115. After Lloyd George's resignation in Oct., Wise worked briefly for the Soviet trade agency in London and then drifted back into British left-wing politics. See Maltzan to Brockdorff-Rantzau, Berlin, 24 Apr. 1923, Germ. Pol. Arch. AA, Brockdorff-Rantzau Papers, and E. F. Wise, "Anglo-Russian Trade and the Trade Agreement," *Empire Review* 38 (September 1923): 995–1004. The Wise papers have been lost or destroyed (communications to the author by T. F. Wise and W. K. Struthers, Dec. 1973). There are no records on Wise available in the FO files of the PRO.

57. Saint-Aulaire [Seydoux] to Poincaré, 20 Mar., FMAE B 115.

58. Text in *DBFP*, 19:199–206.

59. Rapport, Paris, 3 Mar., FMAE PM G/III; Resumé, 6 Mar., FMAE Grenard Papers; meetings and preparations in FMAE B 112–13, and Cheysson, "La reconstruction de la Russie," 27 Dec., 1921, FMF F 30/1074.

Neither the French nor the Belgians, whose preparations were similar to the French,[60] had anticipated that the British would have no economic plan at all but would merely lay down terms for a quick political settlement with Moscow. The two continental delegations were surprised and alarmed. Poincaré instructed his representatives to "hold firm." They did; and though Wise and Giannini fought for the British plan, the commission's chairman, Sir Sidney Chapman, had recently traveled to Paris and showed marked sympathy for the French position.[61]

Behind the two positions lay domestic realities. Britain and Italy, seeking to appease their leftist opinion, had decided that the time was ripe for nominal recognition of the Soviet government. They had already established personal contacts with Bolshevik emissaries and trade representatives, who had encouraged London and Rome to expect an eventual erosion of leftist communism in Moscow and its hostility to the West. Both governments sought to win over industrialists *and* workers to their appeasement policy, carrying the pro-German element also in tow. On the other hand, in France, with its 1.2 million dispossessed Russian bondholders exerting a heavy weight on the Poincaré government, there was considerable pressure to insist on the priority of the past: before France agreed to recognize the Communist state, Moscow would have to recognize its debts. Belgium, more influenced by its bankers and industrialists, who had invested heavily in prewar Russia's mines, oil fields, factories, and public utilities, stressed the conditions of restitution of nationalized properties. Unlike Great Britain, the United States, or the neutrals, neither France nor Belgium had much new capital to invest in Russia or a significant amount of goods to sell. Thus, their main emphasis was in restoring Russia's "productivity" in order for the French to retrieve their interest payments and the Belgians their property.

These opposing opinions were set out in the opening debate.[62] When they got down to business, the British draft treaty was converted into a set of Allied conditions, though the French and Belgians resisted any formula that would automatically provide recognition. They all agreed that Russia should repay all its debts, except those to Germany; however, they disagreed on procedures. France's position on rejecting reciprocal claims between Russia and the West prevailed. However, for lack of Belgian support, the French had to back down on the issue of broadening the powers of the debt commission to control the

60. Commission d'études pour la Conférence de Gênes, Feb.–Mar., BMAE 10991. Summary in *Le Soir*, 12 Mar.

61. Seydoux notes, Paris, 14 Mar., FMAE PM G/IV, 16 Mar., FMAE B 115; Lasteyrie to Poincaré, Paris, 16 Mar., FMAE B 113, Poincaré to Seydoux, Paris, 18 Mar., FMAE B 89, and Saint-Aulaire [Seydoux] to Poincaré, London, 21 Mar., #312, #317–20 (henceforth #s identify more than one telegram per day), FMAE B 115.

62. Compte rendu, London, 20 Mar., FMAE B 115.

finances of the Russian government. Consequently, when the compensation question arose and Belgium urged a very liberal interpretation of "foreign" ownership of Russian companies that had been nationalized in November 1917, France withheld its support. The result was that only companies with sizable holdings by foreign nationals were deemed eligible for restitution. Britain and Italy blocked Franco-Belgian efforts to build the debt commission entirely of foreign creditors and to identify specific assets as security for the Soviet debt. On private debts, the Europeans objected in principle to Britain's proposal to convert these into public obligations. Finally, despite Chapman's repeated assurances, there was no explicit statement in the report to satisfy the Franco-Belgian concern that property would be restored (compensated only on the former owner's initiative) and that no despoilment by other nationals would be allowed.[63]

Turning to the future, everyone agreed to the British proposals pertaining to "good administration of justice," adequate conditions of residence for foreigners, and respect for treaties and conventions facilitating the resumption of trade, investment, and industry. However, when the Belgian delegate urged specific guarantees for capitalists reentering Russia and a testing period of Russia's good faith, Wise and Giannini objected so violently that he had to back down. Seydoux played the mediator, drafting seven final articles under the innocuous heading, "Measures by Which the Immediate Restoration of Russia Would Be Facilitated."[64]

Neither side had budged; the Allies had simply decided to focus on details and in so doing had exposed their internal differences. Unlike Hughes, who a year earlier had expounded general principles and rejected any contact with the Bolshevik state, the Allies were trapped by their own political and diplomatic needs: they attempted to spell out conditions that would both satisfy their various publics and at the same time elicit the Russians' obedience. The London meeting made no attempt to deal with critical problems such as the breakdown of Russia's transport system, which was frustrating Hoover's relief efforts. They could not formulate a draft convention over France and Italy's objections. Instead, they formulated a series of terms that were harsh, demanding, and contradictory.

According to the London Report, Russia was to assume all its past debts and could make no claims for damages on the Allies. The debt commission would appoint mixed arbitral tribunals to mediate claims between former creditors and despoiled owners and the Soviet government. Russia was to adopt internal

63. Chapman report, London, 28 Mar., GB FO 371 C4781/458/62; Rapport, délégation belge, Brussels, 28 Mar., BMAE 10991; Seydoux to Poincaré, Paris, 30 Mar., FMAE B 115; and Jung and Giannini rapporto, n.d., IMAE 52/8.

64. Grigg to Lloyd George, London, 23 Mar., Grigg Papers, roll 9, expressed disgruntlement with the French maneuver to delay recognition of Russia.

reforms on behalf of foreign capitalists that would have amounted to the extinction of the Communist regime. On the other hand, the Allies reserved Russia's right to obtain reparation from Germany under Article 116 of the Versailles treaty; France remained insistent that Poland and the other succession states be forced to assume a portion of the czarist debt; and Italy and Japan wanted the Ukraine and the Far Eastern Republic included in any Allied-Soviet agreement. If Moscow agreed to the West's terms, the Allies were willing to bestow on Russia some formal prerogatives of the old regime.[65]

The second part of the London Report dealt with general principles for the economic and financial restoration of all of Europe. Both sides compromised. London pressed for a statement advocating a return to gold, an association of central banks, and an international monetary convention establishing a preliminary gold-exchange standard. When the French resisted, these proposals were transformed into general recommendations for the future. France and Belgium similarly resisted pressure to commit their governments to guarantee private investors in the international corporation. France watered down Britain's proposal to remove artificial controls over exchanges. Italy's demand for universal most-favored-nation treatment was squashed. The rest of the general items—on customs and transport—caused little difficulty.[66]

Again, there was no attempt to produce a binding convention. The recommendations on economics, finance, and transport contained general, internationalist principles couched in discreet diplomatic language. The French felt they had checked the most dangerous British ideas and protected their own and their allies' interests. But all was not safe. As the experts wound up their deliberations, there was another reminder that London and Rome controlled the formal preparations for the Genoa Conference.[67]

Schanzer met Lloyd George on 27 March; he found the premier rested, vigorous, well prepared, and impatient with Rome's hesitations.[68] Lloyd George wanted Genoa to last no more than a month, to be conducted expeditiously in a "businesslike" manner, and to produce prompt "results," all of

65. The text, in three sections, in *DBFP*, 19:260–69. Analysis in Chapman memorandum, ibid., pp. 257–59; Sthamer to AA, Germ. AA T-120 4597H/2370/E188149; Poole memorandum for Hughes, Washington, 13 Apr., USDS 550 E1/285.

66. Text, "Restoration of Europe," was also in three sections: Financial (Currency, Credits, and Exchanges); Economic (Customs, Treatment of Foreigners, Protection of Industrial Property and Copyrights); and Transport, in *DBFP*, 19:269–76. Saint-Aulaire [Seydoux] to Poincaré, London, 24, 25 Mar., #333, #338, FMAE B 115; Chapman report, *DBFP*, 19:259–60.

67. Poincaré to Saint-Aulaire (for Seydoux), Paris, 23 Mar., #644, and Saint-Aulaire [Seydoux] to Poincaré, London, 27 Mar., #341–43, FMAE B 115; Hankey to Lloyd George, London, 23 Mar., Grigg memorandum, 23 Mar., LGP F 26/1/26, F 86/1/37.

68. Riassunto della conversazione, 27 Mar., IMAE 52/2; notes of the meeting, *DBFP*, 19:247–55. Lloyd George was accompanied by Hankey and Grigg; Schanzer by Giannini and his assistant for the Genoa Conference (another veteran of Washington), Giovanni Visconti Venosta.

which belied the current cautious Allied negotiations. Schanzer had a more general plan: a conclave of "victors and vanquished" where all the work would be done in large committees. Lloyd George of course prevailed. He insisted on public speeches on the opening day by Italy, Britain, France, Germany, and Russia: the Great Powers of Europe. Then the Genoa Conference would get down to business. It would divide into four commissions: political (the Russian question), economic, financial, and transport, whose membership would follow a bloc system laid out in advance.

The British conception was modeled loosely on the Paris Peace Conference, though now the Little Entente and the neutrals would have representation along with the Great Powers. It was a conscious change both from the Washington Conference, which had lasted three months working solely through the powers' meetings, and from the procedures followed by the League of Nations, whose assembly and commissions included all members. The Genoa procedure followed Lloyd George's penchant for public speeches and quick, authoritative decisions. He did not shrink from separating the great and small powers or from including Germany and Russia among the former. Above all, he wanted Genoa to have a real working structure, handle real problems, and reach quick conclusions.

Schanzer yielded to Lloyd George's prearrangements, after lamely defending a more democratic conference. He agreed that the "inviting powers"— Belgium, France, Great Britain, Italy, and Japan—would meet a day before the opening session, on 9 April, to discuss the procedure.[69] Poincaré's fears were revived: there would be insufficient discipline against the raising of "forbidden subjects," the recognition question would resurface, and, most of all, a "Political Commission" containing Russian, German, and neutral members would dominate the Genoa Conference. The French delegates had held their own during the London experts' meetings; but Poincaré was not at all confident that the Welsh magician would not spring new surprises at Genoa.[70]

Prelude to Rapallo:
The Russo-German Meetings in Berlin

Fresh from its success at the Riga Conference, the Soviet delegation stopped over in Berlin on 1 April, still hoping to avoid facing a unified Allied camp as

69. Saint-Aulaire to Poincaré, London, 28, 29 Mar., FMAE B 115, B 90; De Martino to MAE, London, 29 Mar., IMAE 52/1.

70. Poincaré to Saint-Aulaire, Paris, 30 Mar., and to De Margerie (Brussels) and Barrère (Rome), 5 Apr., FMAE B 90, B 92; Barrère to Poincaré, Rome, 3, 6 Apr., FMAE B 91, B 92; Engelhardt [Lagarde] to MAE, Genoa, 6 Apr., FMAE B 92; and Sauerwein to *Matin*, Rome, 6 Apr., FMAE B 92. Seydoux had warned earlier (see n. 67) that Lloyd George might well whip

supplicants. Chicherin issued a defiant statement, insisting that Russia would not cave in at the Genoa Conference. To add substance to its propaganda, the Soviet government hoped to conclude a model political agreement with Germany, establishing full diplomatic relations and rejecting any claims for compensation caused by the Bolsheviks' nationalization of private property.[71]

Karl Radek, who had arrived earlier to begin negotiations with the German Foreign Ministry, now turned to another task: the meeting of the Executive Committee of the Three Internationales that was held in the Reichstag building between 2 and 5 April. This was an interesting rehearsal for the Genoa Conference, for the Kremlin now encountered unexpected responses to its appeal for leftist support for the Soviet state. Convened by the "Second and a Half" Internationale (the International Working Union of Socialist Parties, also known as the Vienna Union), this curious gathering joined the three international working-class movements: the old Second Internationale, represented primarily by Belgian and British delegates; the Third Internationale, dominated by Radek and Bukharin, with Clara Zetkin speaking for the Germans; and the Vienna group, Lenin's despised "Zimmerwald majority," that had opposed the war *and* bolshevism. The Vienna group was led by the Austrians Viktor Adler and Otto Bauer, and had delegates from France, the British Independent Labour party, and the Russian Mensheviks. The Executive Committee was called officially to "combat the growing strength of capitalism" and to forge joint tactics.[72]

Radek and the Germans stood together, attacking the Versailles treaty and particularly its reparations clauses. The Second Internationale responded. Belgian delegate Émile Vandervelde defended his government and the peace settlement. Both he and Ramsay MacDonald criticized Moscow for the overthrow of the Menshevik regime in Georgia and warned against applying the death penalty in the impending trial of the Social Revolutionaries. Radek, in the face of overwhelming opposition and in order to secure his main mission of obtaining support for a resolution calling for "assistance and the reconstruction of

---

out a pact at Genoa—granting the "moral consecration" of recognition but withholding urgent credits.

71. E. H. Carr, *The Bolshevik Revolution* (Baltimore: Penguin, 1966), 3:370–71. Report on the Riga meeting in *DVP SSSR*, 5:173–75. Chicherin's warning quoted in Richard K. Debo, "George Chicherin: Soviet Russia's Second Foreign Commissar" (Ph.D. diss., University of Nebraska, 1964), pp. 231–32; also interview in *Vossische Zeitung*, 4 Apr., GB FO 371 N3399/646/38.

72. [Communist Internationale], *Protokoll des internationalen Executivkomitees in Berlin vom 2. bis 5. April 1922* (Vienna: Kommunistische Internationale, 1922); also Carr, *Bolshevik Revolution*, 3:404–9; Marie-Luise Goldbach, *Karl Radek und die deutsch-sowjetischen Beziehungen, 1918–1923* (Bonn-Bad Godesberg: Verlag Neue Gesellschaft, 1973), p. 110; and especially R. A. Leeper memorandum, "Meeting in Berlin . . . of the 2, 2½, and 3 Internationales," London, 20 June, GB FO 371 N6003/6003/38.

Soviet Russia," dropped his demand for a condemnation of Versailles, which probably would not have passed. He agreed to allow observers to attend the trials of the Social Revolutionaries in June. Lenin, furious with the volatile Radek, wrote angrily in *Pravda* on 11 April, "We Have Paid Too Dearly": the "bourgeoisie" had outwitted the Comintern; united-front tactics with Western fraternal parties had failed.[73]

On 4 April, two days after the closing of the stormy Eleventh Party Congress where Lenin had undergone severe criticism by the leftists, *Pravda* had announced: "The Central Committee elected by the Eleventh Congress of the Russian Communist Party had confirmed the secretariat of the Central Committee as follows: Comrade Stalin (General Secretary), Comrade Molotov, and Comrade Kuibyshev."[74] Though presented in a low-key manner, the occurrence was both unusual and significant. In place of three coequal party secretaries, Stalin had been made a chief with two assistants. Preobrazhensky had already challenged Stalin's accumulation of party and government offices.[75] The growing fusion of the party and the state in 1922, the conjuncture of Moscow's diplomatic and Comintern initiatives, and Lenin's failing health (his stroke was less than six weeks off) all made Stalin's newest appointment noteworthy. Lenin had presided over the three months' debate since Cannes between the hard-liners and the moderates over Soviet Russia's internal policies and foreign relations; Stalin now joined him at the helm.[76]

Stalin represented a new synthesis of the extremists' views. As Lenin's candidate, he had defended the establishment of better relations with the capitalist world, deprecated the strength of Europe's Communist and Socialist parties, and doubted the imminence of world revolution.[77] Nonetheless, he questioned

73. Lenin to Molotov for Politburo, 9 Apr., *The Trotsky Papers, 1917–1922*, ed. J. M. Meijer (The Hague and Paris: Mouton, 1971), 2: doc. 767. The Comintern also rejected the Berlin meeting and repudiated Radek's promises. The Second and Second and a Half Internationales made plans to merge, and did so by 1923. The Third Internationale, which was excluded, seceded from the follow-up Berlin meeting on 23 May. Vandervelde and Theodor Liebknecht, representing the more moderate Internationales, attended the trials of the Social Revolutionaries, which took place between 8 June and 7 Aug., but when the prosecutors and Bukharin declared the Berlin agreement void and when the accused "agreed," the Western socialists were forced to leave Russia on 14 June. Twelve of the thirty-three defendants were sentenced to death; on Trotsky's initiative, these were commuted to ten-year prison terms, ibid.; also Leeper memorandum, "Meeting in Berlin," London, 20 June, GB FO 371 N6003/6003/38.

74. Carr, *Bolshevik Revolution*, 1:218–19. On the congress: Adam B. Ulam, *Lenin and the Bolsheviks* (London: Collins, 1969), pp. 716–17.

75. Carr, *Bolshevik Revolution*, 1:219.

76. Leeper memorandum, London, 17 June, GB FO 371 N5755/3416/38; Ulam, *Lenin*, pp. 720–22; and Teddy J. Uldricks, *Diplomacy and Ideology: The Origins of Soviet Foreign Relations, 1917–1930* (London and Beverly Hills, Calif.: Sage, 1979), pp. 128–30.

77. For the first time in 1922, the customary May Day slogans of the Russian Communist party made no mention of "world revolution": Carr, *Bolshevik Revolution*, 3:408.

whether the Soviet system could survive, much less prosper, in a peaceful symbiosis with the West without destroying the power structure currently being erected in Moscow. Moreover, unlike Lenin, Stalin, the former commissar of nationalities and conquerer of his homeland, separatist Georgia, was an ardent proponent of Soviet Russian nationalism.[78]

Stalin's suspicions of the West and his chauvinism, even more than his accommodations to the Leninist line, were present at the beginning of his rise to power. Undoubtedly this affected Kremlin policy at the Genoa Conference, although in the absence of Soviet documents this cannot be precisely verified. A new strain of realpolitik emerged within the Soviet leadership. It was bolstered by the sectarians' scruples and Great Russian nationalism, as well as by the visible setbacks since Cannes for the new diplomacy of peaceful coexistence with the West.[79]

Chicherin was head of the Genoa delegation and one of Stalin's important adversaries. He had largely prepared the Soviet program with Lenin and now made a final effort to redeem his initiative of October 1921. Even more than his mentor and protector, the aristocratic diplomat counted on splitting the capitalist West with a specific strategy: competing with London and wooing Weimar Germany.[80] Despite the failure of the Russo-German talks in January, the advent of Rathenau, and the stalemate in March, Chicherin still hoped to convince Berlin to reach an agreement before the Genoa Conference. The Allies had reinforced the Kremlin's persuasiveness by raising the specter of Article 116 of the Versailles treaty.

Germany had few remaining hopes for the Genoa Conference since the reparations question had virtually been removed and the Entente seemingly patched up. Nevertheless, Rathenau expected that prominent bankers and financial experts would attend, and he hoped that Genoa's technical commissions would provide him a forum to promote his theories of the causes of Germany and Europe's current economic malaise. He was encouraged by Cassel's visit to plead for a conference on reparations between the Allies and Germany. However, there now was a 31 May deadline for Germany to comply with the newest demands from the Reparations Commission; failing this, Germany (which was

---

78. Richard Pipes, *The Formation of the Soviet Union*, rev. ed. (New York: Atheneum, 1968), pp. 266–82; David M. Lang, *A Modern History of Soviet Georgia* (New York: Grove, 1962), pp. 234–42.

79. J. V. Stalin, *Works* (Moscow: Foreign Languages Publishing House, 1954), 10:128–29, 394. The sudden rise of Great Russian nationalism noted in Wiedenfeld to AA, Moscow, 20 Mar., 10 Apr., Germ. AA T-120 L998/5412/L286697–707, L1468/5118/L415816–20; Prussian Staatskommissar für Öffentlichen-Ordnung, Berlin, 24 Apr., Germ. BA R 43 I/132 (reporting increase of orthodox clericalism and anti-Semitism); also Carr, *Bolshevik Revolution*, 1:374–77.

80. E. M. Chossudovsky, "Lenin and Chicherin: The Beginnings of Soviet Foreign Policy and Diplomacy," *Millennium* 3, no. 1 (Spring 1974): 4, 6–8, 10–13.

Four Bolsheviks in Berlin before the Genoa Conference. (*Left to right*)
Chicherin, Radek, Litvinov, and Bratmann-Grodovski (courtesy of
H. Roger Viollet, Paris).

about to send a defiant reply) might be threatened with sanctions and a possible
French invasion of the Ruhr. Genoa thus represented a chance, however meager, for Rathenau to repeat his successes at London and Cannes when he had
represented his nation's case with persuasiveness and eloquence.[81]

But Russia, not Germany, was the central issue of the Genoa Conference.
Lloyd George, insisting on the link between Germany's ability to pay reparations and his schemes for restoring Russia, expected Berlin to participate fully
and wholeheartedly in the international corporation. This not only antagonized

81. Saint Quentin to MAE, Berlin, 27, 30 Mar., FMAE B 90; Dard to MAE, Munich, 1 Apr.,
FMAE B 91; Viscount Edgar D'Abernon, *Versailles to Rapallo, 1920–1922: The Diary of an
Ambassador* (Garden City, N.Y.: Doubleday, Doran and Co., 1929), pp. 302–3; US MID
Intelligence Summary, XVIII (1922): Germany; and Count Harry Kessler, *Walther Rathenau: His
Life and Work* (New York: Harcourt, Brace and Co., 1930), pp. 303–4.

Moscow but also provoked domestic criticism. Stresemann warned during the Reichstag debate of 29 March against the "enslavement of Russia" and urged the government to act independently in regard to Moscow.[82]

Ostpolitik divided the Berlin cabinet. Wirth advocated an independent, pro-Soviet stance to counterbalance French pressure and also as a continuation of his year-long military, economic, and political strategy. This was also the policy of influential military and government officials. On the other side, Ebert and the moderate Socialists were resolutely anti-Soviet. Rathenau, almost in the middle, considered the present Russia of minor importance to Germany, except as a bargaining object in German-Entente negotiations. Despite rumors of Russian dealings with France over Article 116 of the Versailles treaty and the known links between Moscow and London, Rathenau little feared a sudden revival of the 1914 coalition.[83]

Maltzan, the chief Russian expert in the German Foreign Ministry, was convinced of the importance of reaching agreement with Moscow before Genoa. In a letter to Radek on 10 March (the day before the deadline for Germany's adherence to the international corporation), Maltzan indicated that Reich leaders were not wholehearted about Lloyd George's project and would consider reviving an independent *Ostpolitik*.[84] After Germany received the note of 21 March from the Reparations Commission, Maltzan was permitted to resume negotiations with Radek and Bukharin. Soon the old Russo-German differences reemerged: Moscow refused to liquidate its foreign-trade monopoly, and Germany's industrialists were reluctant or unable to invest substantial amounts of capital in Russia. Russia was unwilling to compensate former owners of nationalized property; but Germany, as a member of the international corporation, was committed to participate in the collective effort to restore or provide restitution to former owners. The talks broke down, pending Chicherin's arrival.[85]

Rathenau undoubtedly had no intention of consummating an agreement with the Russians before the Genoa Conference, but he had the opportunity to encourage the Russians and worry the British that he might.[86] Just after Chicherin arrived in Berlin, he wrote pleadingly to Lloyd George to help Germany

---

82. *Verhandlungen des Reichstags, Stenographische Berichte* (Berlin: Reichsdruckerei, 1922), 354:6647–48; Theodor Schieder, "Die Entstehungsgeschichte des Rapallo-Vertrags," *Historische Zeitschrift* 204 (June 1967): 567–68. The German Communists also picked up the "enslavement" theme.

83. Cabinet meeting, 5 Apr., *Akten-Wirth*, 2:674–89.

84. Maltzan to Radek, Berlin, 10 Mar., Germ. AA T-120 L311/4255/L096693–96. This warm communication coincided with the commencement of talks between Poland and the Baltic states.

85. Maltzan Aufzeichnung, Berlin, 27 Mar., Germ. AA T-120 L311/4255/L096693–96.

86. Schieder, "Entstehungsgeschichte," p. 568; Laubach, *Kabinette Wirth*, pp. 192–93; and Russian reports in *DVP SSSR*, 5:188–90, 202–7.

in its weakness. A day later, the British premier dampened his hopes by announcing to the House of Commons that Britain would stand resolutely behind France; the Versailles reparations provisions would not be scrapped at Genoa.[87] Rathenau thus decided to play his Russian card.

Even before the arrival of Chicherin and Maxim Litvinov, deputy chief of the Narkomindel, the Germans had made two very conciliatory gestures. The Russians were shown Germany's copy of the London Report, and the German cabinet decided unanimously to restore the czarist embassy building on Unter den Linden to the Soviet government.[88] On 2 April, the first day of the Russo-German talks, Maltzan was alone, and he was unable to prevail over the resolute Chicherin. Little was accomplished except the pronouncement of the German and Russian formulas for a political and economic agreement. A day later Rathenau made his appearance, impetuously offered concessions, and hinted at an immediate pact. It was a bluff. No word came from London, but there was good news from Paris that the Reparations Commission had voted to establish an experts' committee to examine a project for an international loan to help stabilize the German currency. Urged for some time by Rathenau, this was a small but significant advance.[89]

Faced with reality, Germany pulled back. When the Russians presented a draft treaty (almost identical to the one signed two weeks later[90]) and offered to sign at once, the Germans raised many objections. Frightened about prejudicing its relations with the West, Berlin drew the line on symbolic issues: on the granting of de jure recognition to Moscow and on obtaining most-favored-nation treatment should the Soviets cave in at Genoa. Maltzan further explained that there was insufficient time for his government to examine all the serious "financial" considerations involved.[91]

The Russians were angry, but Rathenau was content and even smug at the outcome of these talks. He nourished hopes for a *Vermittlungsmission* (a mission as arbiter) between the Allies and Russia at the Genoa Conference. These hopes were unrealistic: Germany had not only been excluded from the London meetings but would not be present at the forthcoming talks among the inviting powers. Berlin had done little to ingratiate itself recently either with the Allies or with the Russians. Finally, as the Beneš mission had proved, Lloyd George had little use for foreign middlemen.

The Russians departed from Berlin with a treaty ready for signature, when-

87. Rathenau to Lloyd George, Berlin, 2 Apr., GB FO 371 C5100/99/18; D'Abernon, *Versailles to Rapallo*, p. 303; and cabinet meeting, 5 Apr., *Akten-Wirth*, 2:675.

88. *Akten-Wirth*, 2:681; Maltzan Aufzeichnung, Berlin, 1 Apr., Germ. AA T-120 L311/4255/L096719; and Debo, "Chicherin," p. 240.

89. *DVP SSSR*, 5:203; Maltzan Aufzeichnung, Berlin, 3 Apr., Germ. AA T-120 L311/4255/L096742–44; *Akten-Wirth*, 2:694–96; and Schieder, "Entstehungsgeschichte," pp. 604–7.

90. Schieder, "Entstehungsgeschichte," pp. 604–7, compares the two.

91. Rathenau's report to cabinet, 5 Apr., *Akten-Wirth*, 2:688; Wirth to Reichstag, 29 May, *Verhandlungen des Reichstags, Stenographische Berichte*, 355:7676.

ever the Germans could be convinced to agree.[92] Chicherin had taken the measure of the Germans and found them nervous and divided. This could easily be exploited. Both sides promised to stay in contact, to provide information and mutual support. This would benefit the Russians more than the Germans. Chicherin was preparing to make his debut on the world stage. Still relying on Lenin's waning power and on his own determination, skill, and conviction, he was unafraid of the consequences. Indeed, noting Lloyd George's appeal for world disarmament in his speech to the House of Commons, the Russian pledged that this too was part of the Soviet program.[93]

Rathenau, on the other hand, was part of a weak, presumably interim government that was morbidly sensitive to any and all consequences of its foreign policy.[94] For the Soviets, a German treaty was a desirable "model"; for the Germans, however, any arrangement with Russia would be exceptional and solve none of the Reich's immediate problems. Rathenau could plan no major initiatives for the Genoa Conference. There were vague hints of British or Russian pronouncements on disarmament, which posed the remote possibility of easing the current pressure on Germany to cut its military in complete conformity to the Allies' demands, and forcing Paris to defend its alliances and armaments. But Germany itself had little power to affect the outcome of Genoa, except by trying to alter the basis on which it was to operate or by promoting its failure.

On the Eve: The Entente

The press was alive with discussions of the Genoa Conference. The *Manchester Guardian Commercial* published twelve issues dedicated to European reconstruction. These were edited by John Maynard Keynes, author of the recently published *Revision of the Treaty*, a sequel to his 1919 book, *The Economic Consequences of the Peace*. The special issues, translated into five languages and circulated throughout the world, were intended as an authoritative

92. The Russo-German talks were scarcely secret: cf. Renseignement, Stockholm, 2 Apr., FMAE B 91; Saint Quentin to MAE, Berlin, 4 Apr., and Chateauneuf to MAE, Copenhagen, 7 Apr., FMAE B 92; Frassati to MAE, Berlin, 7 Apr., IMAE 52/20; Willems to MAE, Hamburg, 1 Apr., Della Faille to MAE, Berlin, 4, 7 Apr., BMAE 10991. Also D'Abernon, *Versailles to Rapallo*, pp. 302–3.

93. D'Abernon to Curzon, Berlin, 4 Apr., GB FO 371 N3234/646/38.

94. Unsigned memorandum respecting the German political situation, Berlin, 4 Apr., GB FO 371 C5152/725/18. Questioned by Reichstag deputy Graefe about the high percentage of Jews in the German delegation (33 percent, compared with a total Jewish population of 1 percent, and even with the recent migration of *Ostjuden*, no more than 2 percent), the government in at least one instance deliberately removed a non-Aryan from its list of experts for Genoa: Loebe to AA, Berlin, 8 Apr., Germ. AA T-120 L989/5411/L285546–58; Moritz Schlesinger, *Erinnerungen eines Aussenseiters im diplomatischen Dienst* (Cologne: Verlag Wissenschaft und Politik, 1977), p. 298.

guide to European recovery; they included an array of charts, documents, and commentaries written by leading European statesmen as well as economic, financial, and commercial experts. The French replied with the officially inspired *La France à Gênes*, which appeared on the eve of the conference. In it they attacked the British ideas for reconstruction and discreetly promoted a "zones" plan for Russia as the most promising of all projects.[95]

The British and French presses both divided along ideological lines in their expectations for Genoa. The Right opposed the conference and any commitment to de jure recognition of Soviet Russia. The Left regarded the establishment of ties with Moscow as indispensable; they were joined by groups of businessmen in Britain and France who, despite an improved trade climate in the spring of 1922, believed in the psychological benefits of a world summit. Moderate opinion was less convinced either of the necessity of the Genoa Conference or of its perils. After Boulogne, some observers questioned whether the looming German question and the problems of disarmament, interallied debts, an Anglo-French pact, and European security should be sacrificed for a potentially academic debate over restoring Russia to its place in the European system.[96]

British politics on the eve of the Genoa Conference were dominated by the crisis of Lloyd George's leadership. Returning from Boulogne, he faced a threat from the Tories, the majority party in his cabinet, who had quashed his hopes for immediate elections after Cannes. Taking advantage of Unionist discomfort with Lloyd George's domestic and foreign policies, the Die-Hards (Tories outside the cabinet), led by Sir George Younger, urged the Conservative party to reunite and prepare to run separately in the coming post-Genoa elections. Younger praised the "French system"—every party for itself—which he wished to substitute for the powerful, durable Lloyd Georgian regime; he favored weak, ephemeral coalitions dependent on parliamentary votes and at the mercy of party chiefs. Churchill noted that the country was "longing to get back to party conflict, but cannot afford it."[97] Lloyd George was the target and opponent of these longings.

Although he was tired, Lloyd George was still a vigorous and ambitious

95. *The Collected Writings of John Maynard Keynes*, ed. Elizabeth Johnson (London and New York: Macmillan, 1977), 7:317–53; Seydoux, "Reconstruction de l'Europe: Entreprise internationale du *Manchester Guardian Commercial*," Paris, n.d., FMAE B 90; documentation on *La France à Gênes* in FMAE B 91, 96.

96. John Maynard Keynes, "Reconstruction in Europe," *Manchester Guardian Commercial*, Supplement 18 May, pp. 66–67; Wertheimer to AA, Paris, 6 Mar., Germ. AA T-120 L999/5412/L286992–96; Stempel to Minister of Reconstruction, Berlin, 27 Mar., Germ. BA R 38/324; and Mayer to AA, Paris, 28 Mar., Germ. AA T-120 L998/5412/L286711.

97. Martin Gilbert, *Winston S. Churchill* (Boston: Houghton Mifflin, 1975), p. 774; Michael Kinnear, *The Fall of Lloyd George: The Political Crisis of 1922* (London: Macmillan, 1973), pp. 105–7.

leader who had dominated British politics for sixteen years. He called the Tories' bluff by threatening to resign and hand power and the burdens of office to Austen Chamberlain.[98] Chamberlain declined. The prime minister withdrew to his home at Criccieth in Wales for almost an entire month, allowing the opposition to vent its rage and observing foreign governments and Whitehall prepare for Genoa. Scarcely inactive, he rallied his friends and wooed selected Tories for his cause. To the loyal Grigg, he was Napoleon, "fighting the most brilliant campaign of his whole history" against the Die-Hards, who represented the "old reactionaries of Europe in 1814." Lloyd George preferred the analogy of William Pitt, who in 1797 had fashioned ill-fated peace proposals to an enemy whose doctrines he personally loathed for the benefit of England, Europe, and mankind.[99]

Lloyd George's cabinet survived the scandal over Montagu's resignation from the India Office and the embarrassingly lengthy search for a replacement.[100] Indeed, attacks by the Die-Hards, the Liberal Wee Frees led by Asquith, and the Northcliffe and Rothemere press all became increasingly ineffectual. They simply shifted public sympathy to the beleaguered Lloyd George. The most serious threat came from Winston Churchill, the prime minister's protégé, friend, and fellow cabinet Liberal, who was appalled at the specter of rapprochement between the British Empire and Soviet Russia. Armed with evidence of massive Soviet violations of the trade pact of March 1921 and of Moscow's subversive activities that continued up to the very moment, Churchill exceeded the Tories in his public and private denunciations of the "tyrannic Government of these Jew Commissars, at once revolutionary and

98. A. J. Sylvester, *The Real Lloyd George* (London: Cassell, 1948), pp. 78–79; Frank Owen, *Tempestuous Journey: Lloyd George, His Life and Times* (New York: McGraw-Hill, 1955), pp. 602–3.

99. A series of articles in the *Daily Chronicle* written by a "special correspondent" from Criccieth leaked the text of Lloyd George's letters: Owen, *Tempestuous Journey*, p. 611. Cf. Beaverbrook to Lloyd George, 13, 15, 19, 20, 30 Mar., and Lloyd George to Beaverbrook, 15, 23 Mar., Beaverbrook Papers; Evans to Lloyd George, 21 Mar., LGP F 16/2/11; Garvin to Grigg, 21 Mar., LGP F 86/1/34; Horne to Lloyd George, 23, 26 Mar., LGP F 27/6/59; McCurdy to Lloyd George, 23 Mar., LGP F 35/1/43; Grigg to Lloyd George, 26 Mar., LGP F 86/1/35; Munro to Lloyd George, 25 Mar., LGP F 1/7/56; Lee to Lloyd George, 26 Mar., LGP F 31/2/69; also Grigg to Balfour, 6 Mar., Grigg Papers, roll 1; and George Allardice Riddell, *Lord Riddell's Intimate Diary of the Paris Peace Conference and After, 1918–1923* (London: Gollancz, 1933), p. 368 (Criccieth, 23 Mar.).

Historical analogies in Grigg to Lloyd George, 17 Mar., LGP F 86/1/29, and Lloyd George statement to cabinet, 27 Mar., GB CAB 23/29, app. 1, and to House of Commons, 3 Apr., *H.C. Deb.*, 152: cols. 1897–98.

100. Peter Rowland, *David Lloyd George: A Biography* (New York: Macmillan, 1975), pp. 568–69; Owen, *Tempestuous Journey*, pp. 603–6; Thomas Jones, *Whitehall Diary* (London and New York: Oxford University Press, 1969), 1:193; Gilbert, *Winston Churchill*, p. 773; Morgan, *Consensus and Disunity*, pp. 320–31. Though the removal of the Liberal Montagu was

opportunist, who are engaged not only in persecuting the bourgeoisie, but are carrying on a perpetual and ubiquitous warfare with the peasants of Russia."[101]

Churchill's fury was no doubt bolstered both by Poincaré's hesitations and by his own political ambitions. It was widely believed that he hoped to assume leadership over the Unionist Conservatives, though at least one inside observer doubted that the Tories would "kill the king merely to put a lesser prince in his place, even if it were under their suzereinty." The *Sunday Express* criticized Lloyd George for consorting with too many Jews. An undercurrent of anti-Semitic sentiment reinforced a long-standing upper- and middle-class antipathy to the Welsh outsider, who was reputedly in the "hands of the Jews, Boches, and Bolsheviks."[102]

But who would take his place? Britain's unemployment had mounted persistently; in March the cabinet had to decide whether and how to fund supplementary benefits. The government was divided along ideological lines over textile import duties, the new violence in Ireland, and defense spending, not to mention the still-unsettled questions of a pact with France, German reparations, and peace in the Near East. There was no ready replacement for Lloyd George. He appealed to the nation "not on high politics but on high policy" in the hope that peace in Europe would restore Britain's lost prosperity.[103] The long period between Boulogne and the opening of the Genoa Conference gave the opposition the chance to revive "politics" and thus forced him to do the same.

First, Lloyd George conducted his own massive press campaign, using the *Daily Chronicle* to expose his side of the argument. He revealed his willingness to part with his "dearest political friends" in the fight for Genoa. He released his resignation letter to Chamberlain and also published the still-secret Fontainebleau memorandum of March 1919, in which he had warned that ill treatment by the Allies would eventually drive Germany and Bolshevik Russia together.[104] He castigated his enemies and rallied his friends, insisting to Lord Beaverbrook: "I mean to go wherever the policy of European pacification leads me. There is nothing else worth fighting for at the present moment. The

---

considered a victory for the Tories, Lloyd George was relieved to be rid of a nagging critic of his Near East policies: cf. David and Frances Lloyd George, *My Darling Pussy: The Letters of Lloyd George and Frances Stevenson, 1913–1941*, ed. A. J. P. Taylor (London: Weidenfeld and Nicolson, 1975), p. 36.

101. Gilbert, *Winston Churchill*, p. 760; Churchill to Chamberlain, 18 Mar., WSCP; Chamberlain to Lloyd George, 23 Mar., LGP F 7/5/22.

102. Beaverbrook to Lloyd George, 15 Mar., and correspondence 30 Mar.–1 Apr. on press attacks, Beaverbrook Papers; also Wilson to Squib, 29 May, copy in WSCP.

103. Christoph Stamm, *Lloyd George zwischen Innen- und Aussenpolitik: Die britische Deutschlandpolitik 1921/1922* (Cologne: Verlag Wissenschaft und Politik, 1977), pp. 256–70; Morgan, *Consensus and Disunity*, pp. 278–79.

104. Text in David Lloyd George, *Memoirs of the Peace Conference* (New Haven: Yale University Press, 1939), 1:266–74; Chamberlain to Lloyd George, London, 25 Mar., LGP F 7/5/24, protesting the leaks.

office is certainly not worth a struggle apart from what you can accomplish through it."[105]

He rejected Chamberlain's cautions about pursuing an independent policy toward Soviet Russia and refused to tie Britain "to the chariot wheels of France" to gain Unionist support. He accused Churchill not only of stalking for a "Rightist party" but also of seeking to blemish Britain's word: "If Winston, who is obsessed by the defeat inflicted on his military projects by the bolshevik armies is determined that he will resign rather than assent to any recognition, however complete the surrender of the Communists and whatever the rest of Europe may decide, then the Cabinet must choose between Winston and me."[106]

He argued less persuasively that European reconstruction was impossible without Russia, that the French business community entirely supported his Genoa plan, and that, "if conditions change," America might soon fall in line. He also revealed his inherent motive and concern. Like Lenin, he feared to remain inactive in the face of the nation's suffering and the threat of a leftist uprising. "If, with all this great unemployment which will last for some time in spite of all we do there is a failure through our fault in the project of European cooperation to restore trade, there will be such a revolt amongst the working classes of this country that no government could withstand it, and our great industrial leaders will sympathize with that revolt."[107]

Urged by his followers, Lloyd George demanded a vote of confidence from the House of Commons. First, he had to face his own cabinet, which had not discussed his Genoa policy or Russia since December.[108] Returning refreshed from Wales, he promised to fight for "peace, appeasement, and reconstruction" against the "doctrines of intervention, ascendency, and vengeance." It was old-fashioned liberalism against the forces of reaction, staged before the watchful eyes of Poincaré. Bolstered by the report from Stanley Baldwin, Conservative head of the Board of Trade, about the dismal prospects for recovery in 1922, he appeared ready to fight for Genoa. It would be "the real test of whether [the] coalition is to be progressive or reactionary."[109] The meeting with Schanzer on 27 March reinforced Lloyd George's instinctive combativeness; the Italian gave way on every point.

But Churchill would not retreat in the face of the "bolshevik and communist

105. Lloyd George to Beaverbrook, 23 Mar., Beaverbrook Papers.

106. Lloyd George to Chamberlain, 22 Mar., ACP 23/6/10.

107. Ibid. In Sept. 1921 George V had warned that rising unemployment might "lead to serious trouble": Owen, *Tempestuous Journey*, p. 608.

108. Chamberlain to Lloyd George, 23 Mar., LGP F 7/5/22; Chamberlain memorandum, n.d., Chamberlain to Curzon, 24 Mar., and Curzon to Chamberlain, 25 Mar., ACP 23/6/2, 21, 35.

109. Baldwin memorandum, 23 Mar., ACP 23/6/28. Also Lloyd George to Chamberlain, 24 Mar., LGP F 7/5/23; and Lloyd George, *My Darling Pussy*, p. 39.

menace."[110] He rallied the cabinet behind his refusal to give Lloyd George a free hand at Genoa to offer the Bolsheviks recognition and credits. Curzon did accept the spirit and letter of the Cannes Resolutions, admitting that "if details were worked out," there could eventually be recognition. However, Poincaré and Beneš's strategy had worked: the recognition would be a probationary one, with a Russian chargé d'affaires conducting business but not received at court. Finally, the cabinet insisted that there could be no progress at all in Britain's diplomatic relations with Moscow unless the latter accepted the terms of the Cannes Resolutions.[111]

Lloyd George returned to north Wales. For the first time in his career, he had been dictated to by the cabinet. His supporters observed that he "seemed to be losing his punch and grip." Believing three-quarters of the cabinet were now disloyal, Grigg wanted him to resign. Beaverbrook deplored his continuing; for the sake of a few more months in power, he had pledged the future and thus become "the sport of fate."[112] Lloyd George's speech to the House on 3 April was "restrained and cautious," lacking his customary "fire and energy." It reassured the Belgians and French, worried the Germans and Italians, and pleased President Harding with its "courage."[113] Chamberlain easily stopped a Die-Hard move to bring down the government. The cabinet's program for Genoa won an overwhelming vote of confidence, 379 to 84.

Though Lloyd George did not receive a free hand from his government or from parliament, he had not been beaten. Despite the strident criticisms of the right-wing press, Lloyd George had maintained, indeed enlarged, the divisions within the Tory ranks, because there was as yet no alternative to the present government and its policies.[114] He kept the Left behind him as well, though

110. The *Times*, 27 Mar., reporting Churchill's long-awaited Northampton speech.

111. Cabinet meeting, 28 Mar., GB CAB 23/29. Also Jones, *Whitehall Diary*, 1:195–96; and cf. *Lloyd George Family Letters, 1885–1936*, ed. Kenneth O. Morgan (Cardiff and London: University of Wales Press, 1973), p. 193: "Crisis is distinctly off. Carried the Cabinet. Winston put up a fight, but I got F. E. [Unionist lord chancellor, Lord Birkenhead] so Winston was left alone and realised it."

112. Lord Beaverbrook, *The Decline and Fall of Lloyd George* (London: Collins, 1963), pp. 141–42; Grigg to Brand, 30 Mar., Grigg Papers, roll 1; Jones, *Whitehall Diary*, 1:197; Saint-Aulaire to Poincaré, London, 30 Mar., FMAE B 90; Lloyd George to Cabinet, 2 Apr., GB CAB 23/29, app. 3; and Hankey to Curzon, 3 Apr., LGP F 26/1/28, confirming the cabinet's "instructions."

113. *H.C. Deb.*, 152: cols. 1885–1904; *Review of Reviews* (April 1922): 290–91; Moncheur to MAE, London, 4 Apr., BMAE 10991; Tirard to MAE, Koblenz, 4 Apr., FMAE B 92; Graham to Curzon, Rome, 7 Apr., GB FO 371 C5287/458/62; Harding to Harvey, Washington, 6 Apr., Harding Papers, roll 228; and Chilton to Curzon, Washington, 7 Apr., GB FO 371 C5655/458/62.

114. Jones, *Whitehall Diary*, 1:94; Moncheur to MAE, London, 4 Apr., BMAE 10991; Saint-Aulaire to Poincaré, London, 7 Apr., FMAE B 92; and especially De Martino to Schanzer, London, 6 Apr., IMAE 52/1.

not the extremists. He had used all the means at the disposal of politicians in a democracy—threats to resign, publicity, efforts at cabinet discipline, and an appeal to parliament—to obtain his mandate for the Genoa Conference. With all its limits, it provided real opportunities for the still indispensable, combative, and enterprising Lloyd George.

For Poincaré the days before Genoa were as complex and difficult as for Lloyd George. The French Right, like the British Die-Hards, was reluctant to enter into negotiations with the Soviets despite the Cannes Resolutions. There was a constant stream of pressure from Noulens and other former French investors in Russia to secure adequate guarantees if negotiations took place. Finally, the resolutely anti-Soviet Millerand, who had just departed for his important month-long trip to North Africa, maintained a close surveillance over the government's Genoa policy.[115]

Poincaré remained evasive about his own plans to attend while the president was outside the country. He disliked international conferences, feared the arrangements for Genoa, and, like the Russians, worried about his personal security in a relatively unfriendly country; it seemed prudent to stay in Paris in order not to encourage the Germans and to wait and see what the Russians would offer.[116]

Poincaré chose Barthou to head France's delegation; Barthou was one of a handful of cabinet members who had urged the premier to go to Genoa. A loquacious political veteran, he was to be assisted by Barrère, the ultraconservative ambassador to Rome, but also by Seydoux, the Quai d'Orsay's skilled commercial expert.[117] Lloyd George's delegation consisted largely of his close associates, a bevy of financial experts and a handful of junior Foreign Office representatives. Curzon would not be at Genoa because of a serious illness. Thus, neither Britain nor France had a leading diplomatic personality at Genoa to counterbalance Lloyd George; except for Seydoux, no one else had participated in the original discussions during the past winter.

The French parliamentary debate coincided with the British. In his opening speech on 1 April, Poincaré scarcely dispelled Lloyd George's concerns. Per-

---

115. Leygues to Poincaré, 15 Mar., FMAE Z Fr.-Russ. 349; Noulens to Poincaré, FMAE B 105, B 108. On Millerand: Reichskommissar für Überwachung der öffentlichen Ordnung, Berlin, 4 Apr., Germ. Pol. Arch. AA, DDG Frankreich/Russland. His trip to Algeria, Rabat, and Tunisia in Apr.–May, the longest trip ever by a French president, was ostensibly for the purpose of assuring the population of French control and leadership at a time of nationalist revolts stirred by the examples of Turkey and Egypt: Édouard Bonnefous, *Histoire politique de la Troisième République* (Paris: Presses Universitaires de France, 1968), 3:314; Charles-Robert Ageron, *Historie de l'Algérie contemporaine* (Paris: Presses Universitaires de France, 1979), 2:286–88. American intelligence suspected that another motive was to rally Moslem opinion behind France and against London: US MID Weekly Report (1922): 9348–50.

116. Hardinge to Curzon, Paris, 28 Mar., GB FO 371 C4611/458/62, 29 Mar., CzP.

117. Wertheimer to AA, Paris, 4 Apr., Germ. AA T-120 L998/5412/L286719–25.

haps he was responding to the message from London the day before; Britain, asked by America for interest on the October and November debt payments, now reserved the right to request the same from France. Just as Chamberlain had promised the House of Commons, Poincaré pledged to the Chamber that it would ratify all the decisions taken at the Genoa Conference. He vowed that there would be no recognition of Soviet Russia without debt repayment and promised that though certain details pertaining to the German economy might be discussed at Genoa, any substantive discussions of the Versailles treaty would be "verboten."[118]

The Socialists pleaded for a more conciliatory attitude toward Russia and Germany. The Right demanded firmness, a defense of France's rights, no concessions, and no debacles similar to what had happened at Washington. Resuming the platform, Poincaré assured the deputies that though France would not play the role of a "sulky onlooker" and would contribute what it could to Europe's restoration, there would be no retreat in respect to its treaty rights. His government also won a convincing vote of confidence, 484 to 78.[119] However, it was as inconclusive as Lloyd George's; parliament had tied Poincaré to the pledge that there would be no repetition of Washington or Cannes.

Paris was uneasy with its role as a potential spoiler, and it did not ignore the importance of European recovery to Britain or the gravity of Germany and Russia's problems. Nevertheless, Lloyd George's attempt at a soothing speech created another alarm in France with its deliberate reference to disarmament; everyone realized this was an unsubtle warning to Paris to cooperate with Britain.[120] France, excluded from the talks between Lloyd George and Schanzer, feared Italy's machinations and the talents and prestige of the British prime minister. Poincaré was uneasy about Genoa's organization, especially its Political Commission. The German note to the Reparations Commission reinforced Paris's fear and frustration with the burden of enforcing the Versailles treaty against Germany's obstruction and Britain's maneuvers. Poincaré had no plan for the Genoa Conference, for he had not wanted it to take place. It is nonetheless imprecise to fault him for an obstructionist policy. Given his delicate political situation, he faced a variety of hazards: Briand's fate; his partner's well-known ire; a possible German-Russian rapprochement; and new, possibly dangerous changes in Europe's structure.[121] He was no doubt moti-

118. *JO Ch. Deb. Par.*, 1 Apr., p. 1368.

119. Hardinge to Curzon, Paris, 2 Apr., GB FO 371 W2873/4/17, 3 Apr., CzP.

120. Saint-Aulaire to MAE, London, 4 Apr., FMAE B 92; Leeper minute, 6 Apr., GB FO 371 N3234/646/38; and Wertheimer to AA, Paris, 9 Apr., Germ. AA T-120 L989/5411/L285475–80.

121. De Gaiffier to MAE, Paris, 4 Apr., BMAE Fr.; Wertheimer to AA, Paris, 4 Apr., Germ. AA T-120 L998/5412/L286719–25; Jouvenel to Poincaré, Paris, 8 Apr., FMAE Jouvenel Papers. "Obstructionism" is stressed by Jay L. Kaplan, "France's Road to Genoa: Strategic, Economic, and Ideological Factors in French Foreign Policy, 1921–1922" (Ph.D. diss., Columbia University, 1974), pp. 346–47.

Lloyd George in Paris, en route to Genoa (courtesy of H. Roger Viollet, Paris).

vated by a desire to prevent these from occurring, not to torpedo the Genoa Conference.

At France's suggestion, Poincaré met Lloyd George for a final time before Genoa on 7 April, on a train connecting the Gare du Nord and the Gare de Lyon.[122] Lloyd George was accompanied by Ambassador Hardinge and by Hankey, who would serve as secretary at the Genoa Conference; Poincaré, by Barthou and the interpreter Camerlynck. It was another unfriendly discussion. When Poincaré recited his criticisms of the proposed conference structure, Lloyd George lashed out that every Liberal and Labour MP had denounced France during the recent House debate. To Poincaré's remarks that such feeling "had its counterpart" in Paris, Lloyd George blamed the French for originating all the hostile feelings. Poincaré pledged loyal collaboration but pleaded that France not be asked to make sacrifices at Genoa. He also warned against concessions to Russia and German "provocations." Lloyd George guardedly praised the spirit of the first part of the declaration, noting that Franco-British collaboration was essential to peace.

Lloyd George undoubtedly won the exchange. He had frustrated Poincaré's maneuver to include the entire Little Entente in all of Genoa's commissions,

122. Grigg to Lloyd George, 4 Apr., LGP F 82/2/1; Poincaré to Saint-Aulaire, Paris, 5 Apr., FMAE Z GB 49; and British secretary's notes of a meeting, Paris, 7 Apr., GB CAB 29/95.

and he had not given any promises in regard to Russia. Well aware of the pressures under which Poincaré was operating, Hardinge nevertheless boasted to London that France had been "tamed," at least for the moment.[123] Lloyd George en route to Genoa felt the burden of three months of preparations. Was a breakthrough near, and still possible?

123. Hardinge to Curzon, Paris, 9 Apr., CzP; Hankey to Adeline Hankey (hereafter "wife"), no. 1, Genoa, 9 Apr., HP; Wertheimer to AA, Paris, 7 Apr., Germ. AA T-120 L994/5411/ L285946-47; and De Gaiffier to MAE, Paris, 7 Apr., BMAE Fr.

5

The First Week

Genoa was a fitting place for a world economic conference. It was Italy's premier port and major industrial city, with a long, illustrious banking, mercantile, naval, and colonial history. Its colonial empire in the twelfth and thirteenth centuries had extended to the Crimea, and its citizens had pioneered double-entry bookkeeping, maritime insurance, and joint stock companies. The city was therefore representative of the enterprising spirit of early European capitalism; for three hundred years, it had played a major role in Mediterranean trade, war, and diplomacy.[1] Genoa was also important to modern Italian history as the probable birthplace of Christopher Columbus, as the home of composer and violinist Niccolò Paganini and of the spiritual father of the Risorgimento, Giuseppe Mazzini. Five miles to the east, in the Quarto dei Mille, Giuseppe Garibaldi, with his band of one thousand Red Shirts, had launched the expedition to liberate Sicily and Naples on 6 May 1860.

After unification, Genoa, known as *la superba* ("the proud"), became the natural gateway for the products of the Po valley, the industries of Lombardy and Piedmont, and, via the alpine tunnels and passes, of the goods of Switzerland, Germany, and Central Europe, for which it competed with Marseilles and the ports of northern Europe. It was the entry point for the lumber, cotton, and grain of northern Africa. Its industrial base, tied to the port, included the building and repair of ships and railways, iron, steel, munitions, and warehousing, along with the older enterprises of banking and insurance. There were light industries in the city's suburbs: food processing, tanning and textiles, and small artisanal factories. World War I produced boom conditions; the giant Ansaldo complex alone employed eighty thousand workers.[2]

By 1922 the postwar slump had visibly scarred Genoa. Ansaldo was dismembered, the Banca di Sconto collapsed, and there was a related wave of business failures. High unemployment, labor unrest, daily street fighting between Communist and Fascist gangs, the ravages of an influenza epidemic, and the severe water shortage of the preceding winter—all made Genoa a grim,

1. Robert Lopez, *Storia della colonie genovesi nei Mediterraneo* (Bologna: Zanichelli, 1938) and *Studi sull' economia genovese nel medio evo* (Turin: S. Lattes, 1936).

2. Allan L. Rodgers, *The Industrial Geography of the Port of Genova* (Chicago: University of Chicago Press, 1960), pp. 1–26.

perhaps dangerous environment for a thirty-four nation summit conference. The city was plagued by strikes; the idle ships in its port reflected the contraction of postwar trade. Like Marseilles, it suffered not only from antiquated equipment and the turmoil in the eastern Mediterranean but also from competition with the more modern harbors of Germany and the Netherlands.[3]

Genoa: The Setting

Genoa was cramped in an amphitheater between the sea and the foothills of the Ligurian Apennines. It was a picturesque city, with its vast, semicircular harbor, maze of narrow, winding streets, Romanesque churches, and tall Renaissance palaces, as well as the dramatic vistas from its steep staircases and bridges. Italy's second most congested city, it lacked the grand hotels, restaurants, and other amenities of the more spacious and modern metropolises or the resort towns of Europe.[4] Only the major delegations (the British, French, German, and Japanese), along with the Belgians and the Swiss, could be quartered inside Genoa. The British were given the high, massive Hotel Miramare; the disgruntled French were placed lower down, adjacent to the railroad station at the Savoy; and the Germans were lodged in the small but pleasant Eden Park. The heads of the British, French, Italian, and Belgian delegations were ensconced in the hilltop villas of the Genoese upper classes, which impeded communications with each other, their compatriots, and the other delegates.[5]

Outside Genoa was the Ligurian Riviera. To the west, a hilly, winding, narrow road led to famous health and bathing resorts; to the east, there was a more dramatic rocky coastline. The representatives of the neutrals, the Netherlands, Norway, Denmark, Sweden, and Luxembourg, were housed in Pegli, a small town just west of Genoa. The rest spread eastward. Lower members of the German contingent, along with the delegates of Austria, Bulgaria, Hungary, Poland, Albania, Portugal, and Spain, were located in Nervi. Yugoslavia and a small part of the Belgian delegation were assigned to Santa Margherita.

3. Graham to Crowe, Rome, 27 Jan., GB FO 800 CrP.

4. Ugo Giusti, *Le grandi città italiane nel primo quarto del XX^{mo} secolo* (Florence: Alfani e Venturi, 1925), p. 9; Virginia W. Johnson, *Genoa the Superb* (Boston: Estes and Lauriat, 1892); Italy, Ente Nazionale per le Industrie Turistiche, *Ten Towns of Italy* (Rome: ENIT, 1933); and glowing description in John Saxon Mills, *The Genoa Conference* (New York: Dutton, 1922).

5. Special telephone wires and a fleet of cars connected delegation headquarters with the Villa d'Albertis (Lloyd George), Villa Raggio (Barthou), Villa Raggi (Facta and Schanzer), and the Villa Fossati (Theunis and Jaspar). The Japanese, represented by persons of ambassadorial rank, apparently were not assigned a villa and stayed at the Hotel Isotta in Genoa. Though the Villa Fuckel was reserved for Wirth, he stayed with the delegation at the Eden Park. See Consul General Osborne to State Dept., Genoa, 14 Apr., USDS 550 E1/235.

America's unofficial observer, the Ambassador to Italy Richard W. Child, was assigned a comfortable suite of rooms at the Hotel Bristol in Genoa: Richard W. Child, *A Diplomat Looks at Europe* (New York: Duffield, 1925), p. 27.

Czechoslovakia, Rumania, Greece, Latvia, Lithuania, Estonia, and Finland were situated in Rapallo. Despite its protests about the lack of security along the long, treacherous route, the Soviet delegation was placed in the rambling, white marble Hotel Imperiale, on the road between Santa Margherita and Rapallo, which was well guarded by Italian security forces. Later, for convenience, the Russians rented additional space in the city at the Hotel de Gênes.[6]

Genoa was teeming with visitors. In addition to one thousand delegates and two thousand staff members and journalists, there were some seven thousand Italian police and army officers. It was an armed city, with cavalry patrols along the roads, the pavements permanently lined with *carabinieri* and infantry pickets every fifty yards.[7] Communication with the outside world was slow and cumbersome. Of almost 27 million lire expended for the conference, Italy spent 12 million for postal services, telephone, telegraph, and radio, and for refurbishing the conference press office. This nevertheless proved insufficient to expedite all the messages to and from the huge delegations and press corps.[8]

Despite the immense cost and effort, the city of Genoa prepared a festive appearance for the world summit conference. On one of its gates, built in 1160, there was the inscription: "If you bring peace, you may pass through this gate; if you mean war, you will go away sad and beaten."[9] Genoa, which had been invaded by the Moslems, Saracens, Spanish, Austrians, and repeatedly by the French, had been afflicted by the Black Death in the fourteenth century, and had suffered repeated civil strife throughout its history, was about to play host to a motley gathering that had raised considerable expectations and fears. The police arranged a temporary truce between the local Communists and Fascists. Genoa similarly hoped to provide the place where peace could be established between Soviet Russia and the West, which would revive its confidence and prosperity.

The Inviting Powers

Lloyd George traveled to Genoa by special rail coach. He was accompanied by Sir Robert Horne, chancellor of the exchequer; Sir Laming Worthington-Evans, secretary for war; his secretaries Sylvester and Grigg; Maurice Hankey,

6. Ispettorato Generale de Pubblica Sicurezza (hereafter IGPS), 9 Apr., IMAE 52/31; N. N. Lyubimov and A. N. Erlikh, "The 1922 Genoa Conference," *International Affairs* (Moscow) (June, August, September, October 1963): 69.

7. Osborne to State Dept., Genoa, 14 Apr., USDS 550 E1/235; Gregory to Lampson, Genoa, 14 Apr., GB FO 371 N3704/646/38; Édouard Herriot, *Jadis: D'une guerre à l'autre* (Paris: Flammarion, 1952), p. 100.

8. Note on Italian preparations, n.d., PAC MKP; Graham to Balfour, Rome, 18 June, GB FO 371 C9106/458/62; Child, *Diplomat*, p. 27; and especially Il Comune di Genova, *Bollettino Municipale Mensile*, 15 March.

9. Osborne to Hughes, Genoa, 21 Apr., USDS 550 E1/254.

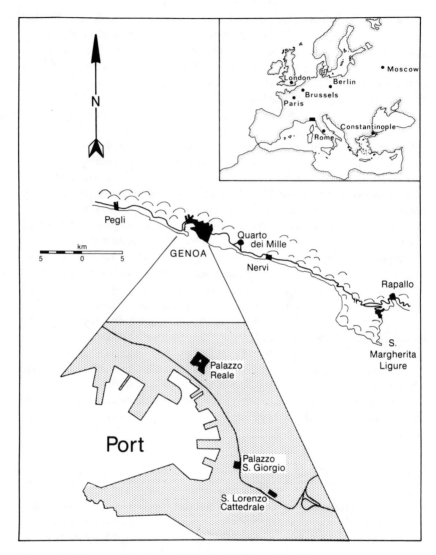

Genoa and Surrounding Areas (Map by William Harris).

conference organizer; and his wife, Dame Margaret, and his daughter, Megan. The prime minister's party arrived in the middle of the day on Saturday, 8 April. While the British Empire delegation took up quarters in the Miramare, Lloyd George established himself in the hills of the Quarto dei Mille, in the spacious villa of Count d'Albertis, an overly friendly host who stayed the entire afternoon. The trip revived Lloyd George's optimism, though he was

Città di Genova

CONCITTADINI,

Il 10 aprile 1922, inizio della Conferenza economica, resterà una data memorabile fra quelle che segnano le principali tappe dell' umano progresso. Genova, la cui storia è pure ricca di fatti grandiosi, mai fu testimone di evento così importante. Qui si affissano ansiosi gli sguardi di tutto il mondo in attesa della vera parola di pace.

Milioni di voci sembrano gridarci d' oltre tomba che non per creare un eterno disagio ai viventi furono immolate tante vite. Dopo l' immane guerra, la compagine della famiglia umana era rimasta spezzata: ma le ragioni della civiltà esigono che rifloriscano gli scambi, si ristabiliscano consuetudini e rapporti, riprenda ovunque il pulsare vigoroso della vita sociale.

La nostra Città che visse e prosperò nei traffici, che da tempi remoti corre sui mari e penetra nelle più lontane regioni, che fu madre di Chi aggiunse nuove genti all' umano consorzio, e di Chi proclamò i diritti dei popoli, sente tutta l' importanza dell' avvenimento ed è fiera d' esser sede del nuovo congresso ove convengono in un supremo intento di concordia gli alleati i neutri gli avversari di ieri, e tutte le nuove nazioni che in questi ultimi tempi si sono costituite.

GENOVESI,

Agli ospiti illustri diamo il benvenuto in nome di Genova, in nome dell' Italia. Nel cuore d' ognuno è l' augurio che questa sia vera Pasqua di pace. Offriamo a tutti la cordiale e dignitosa accoglienza che è tradizione nostra, e caratteristica dei popoli forti e gentili. Abbiamo fede sicura nei destini della patria e della umanità. Con noi è tutto il mondo civile.

Dal Palazzo Municipale, addì 7 Aprile 1922.

Il Sindaco
F. RICCI

Announcement to the Citizens of Genoa (courtesy of the Archivio di Stato di Genova).

disappointed at the absence of Lenin and Poincaré, and perhaps even more by that of his faithful secretary and mistress, Frances Stevenson.[10]

The Vatican, seeking a more active role in Europe, endorsed the Genoa

---

10. David and Frances Lloyd George, *My Darling Pussy: The Letters of Lloyd George and Frances Stevenson, 1913–1941*, ed. A. J. P. Taylor (London: Weidenfeld and Nicolson, 1975), p. 43; Hankey to wife, 9 Apr., HP; A. J. Sylvester, *The Real Lloyd George* (London: Cassell, 1948), pp. 80–81.

Conference. The local press on 8 April published a letter from Pius XI to the archbishop of Genoa hoping for its success. To Poincaré's chagrin and German delight, the new pope wrote that the best guarantee of peace is "not a forest of bayonets" but "mutual confidence and friendship." Secretary of State Cardinal Gasparri formulated a proposal for reducing Germany's total reparations to 50 billion marks by Britain's reduction of the French debt and waiver of its own reparation claims up to 25 billion marks and by a loan from the United States for the rest. An essential condition for the Vatican's plan was the termination of all military occupation and foreign control over Germany and the "establishment of normal peace conditions."[11]

Business began at once. Beneš, arriving early, checked in with the British and Austrian delegations. There was considerable traffic between Genoa and the Hotel Imperiale. Finally, on the evening of the eighth, Lloyd George and Schanzer conferred on Britain's projected nonaggression pact, still a vague proposal to bring peace to the borders of Soviet Russia.[12]

Schanzer commenced his role as messenger for Lloyd George. He visited Brătianu in order to counterbalance Czechoslovakia's influence and soothe Rumania's pique over British and Italian hesitancy to recognize its control over Bessarabia.[13] He journeyed to the Russian headquarters to urge Chicherin to make a "thoroughly conciliatory speech" during the opening session and particularly to accept the Cannes conditions. Chicherin, busy with long and exhausting interviews with journalists to explain his pacifist views, was happy to bargain. In return for meeting Lloyd George's requests, he reserved the right to add his own "supplementary principles." He was also promised a seat on every committee set up by the Genoa Conference.[14]

11. Reparations plan: De Salis to Curzon, Rome, 6 Apr., GB FO 371 C5319/458/62; Gasparri memorandum, n.d., LGP F 86/6/7; and Tirard to Poincaré, Koblenz, 10 May, FMAE B 117. Papal greetings to the conference discussed in Jonnart to Poincaré, Rome, 8, 9 Apr., Poincaré to Jonnart, Paris, 8 Apr., FMAE PM G/V; De Salis to Curzon, 6, 14 Apr., GB FO 371 C5319, C5975/458/62; Beyens to MAE, Rome, 10, 12 Apr., BMAE 10991; and review by German press, 8 Apr., Germ. AA T-120 L1468/5118/L415793–96. "Forest of bayonets" ostensibly referred to the French military-service law of 7 Apr., which, over the protests of the Left, set an eighteen-month term: De Gaiffier to MAE, Paris, 7 Apr., BMAE Fr.; Wertheimer to AA, Paris, 10 Apr., Germ. BA R 43/469.

12. Hankey to wife, 9 Apr., HP; Oppenheimer to BMA, Nervi, 10 Apr., A HHSt 687; conversation at the Villa d'Albertis, 8 Apr., *DBFP*, 19:302–4.

13. Background in Dering to Curzon, Bucharest, 30 Mar., GB FO 371 C4898/458/62; Sforza to MAE, Paris, 15 Mar., Martin Franklin to MAE, Bucharest, 8 Apr., Schanzer to Martin Franklin, Genoa, 12 Apr., IMAE 52/4 (Rumania): Alena Gajanová, "La politique extérieure tchécoslovaque et la 'question russe' à la Conférence de Gênes," *Historica* (Prague) 8 (1964): 151, 153; and Dov B. Lungu, "Soviet Romanian Relations and the Bessarabian Question in the Early 1920s," *South Eastern Europe* 6, no. 1 (1979): 40–41.

14. *DVP SSSR*, 5:206–7; Richard K. Debo, "George Chicherin: Soviet Russia's Second Foreign Commissar" (Ph.D. diss., University of Nebraska, 1964), pp. 242–43.

On Palm Sunday, 9 April, the "inviting powers" met in the newly renovated Palazzo Reale, the official seat of the conference.[15] This body consisted of Belgium, the British Empire, France, Italy, and Japan; by agreement between Lloyd George and Poincaré, it would form the directorate of the Genoa Conference. As anticipated, the first encounters produced Anglo-French sparring. Barthou admitted that he lacked plenipotentiary powers. Lloyd George grumbled that this would cause needless delays; "all those present were busy men and could not remain indefinitely, even in so beautiful a climate as that of Genoa." That afternoon Barthou's demand that the Germans and Russians be forced publicly to accept the Cannes Resolutions before being admitted triggered a lengthy, irrelevant argument about the war and the nature of interallied "cooperation." The dilemma over Cannes was settled by a compromise: the conference president would simply announce at the opening that the "fact that the Powers have come here shows that they have adopted the principles embodied in the Cannes Resolutions."[16]

There was more acrimonious discussion over the Political Commission and the small, selected subcommission that would do the actual work. Belgium joined Britain and Italy in agreeing to limit its membership. France refused to admit the Germans and Russians without also including the Little Entente and the neutrals. Poincaré's misgivings over the entire procedure involving a "political" commission were lost in the haggling. Barthou was overridden on the important points by Lloyd George's bantering and his own bluster and inattentiveness.[17] He appealed to Paris, but Poincaré refused to grant him full powers. His chief commiserated with Barthou's "good fight" over the subcommission and wished him good luck on a "difficult mission."[18]

The German delegation arrived Sunday evening at 8:15. Because of the Allied talks, there was no official greeting party. Facta and Schanzer later went to the Eden Park and gave a full résumé of the meetings of the inviting powers.[19] The Germans learned there would be but one plenary session, and then Lloyd George wanted the Genoa Conference to get down to business, which was precisely what all but the French desired.

15. Notes of informal meetings, 9 Apr., *DBFP*, 19:305–16, 317–31.

16. Ibid., p. 324.

17. Gregory to FO and Curzon, Genoa, 10 Apr., GB FO 371 C5202, C5332/458/62; Barthou to Poincaré, #2–6, #7–14, FMAE B 92, #19–21, FMAE B 93. Jaspar's lack of support appeared particularly painful to the French, who had blocked Italy's efforts to remove Belgium from the inviting powers: Schanzer to Sforza and De Martino, Genoa, 9 Apr., IMAE 52/1.

18. Barthou to Poincaré, Genoa, 10 Apr., #16–17, Poincaré to Barthou, 10 Apr., #4, FMAE B 93.

19. Unsigned tel. to AA, Genoa, 9 Apr., Germ. AA T-120 3398/1734/D738278–83, 10 Apr., Germ. AA T-120 L312/4255/L096836–40.

Palazzo San Giorgio, 10 April 1922 (courtesy of H. Roger Viollet, Paris).

Plenary No. 1: Palazzo San Giorgio

The Palazzo San Giorgio, reputedly the former headquarters of Europe's oldest bank and the present seat of Genoa's port authority, was lavishly decorated on 10 April. The area around it was cordoned off by military pickets and mounted patrols. "White gloved, red cockaded Royal guards lined the route . . . [which was] decked out with potted plants and red carpets." There were flags on all the houses, crowds at the windows, and a tingling air of expectancy and excitement.[20]

Inside the large rectangular hall, sunk deep into the wall and commanding the room, there was a marble statue of Columbus, to whose first voyage the bank allegedly had contributed. To his left, on a twelve-foot marble plaque mounted on the wall, there was a quotation from Machiavelli describing the bank's founding. On the right, there were two glowing and optimistic letters of about the same size: one from Columbus to Isabella of Castille, the other to the Commune of Genoa. At the opposite end of the hall, facing this display, was the press gallery, which had been limited to 200 of the 750 applicants. It included French Communist Marcel Cachin and the Americans Max Eastman and Ernest Hemingway, then a correspondent for the Toronto *Daily Star*. All

20. Harry Graf Kessler, *Tagebücher, 1918–1937* (Frankfurt-am-Main: Insel-Verlag, 1961), p. 288. The English translation, *In the Twenties: The Diaries of Harry Kessler*, trans. Charles Kessler (New York: Holt, Rinehart and Winston, 1971), is abbreviated (p. xvii).

Palazzo San Giorgio: The First Plenary Session (courtesy of UPI).

around the room filling the recesses in the walls, were large, ornate marble statues of Genoese notables; underneath one a motion picture camera was set up.[21]

Despite the broad daylight outside, the dark chamber was illuminated by an immense chandelier. Below it stood the traditional double horseshoe table covered with the green tablecloth. Behind, camp chairs had been arranged in rows for local personages, experts, secretaries, and lesser diplomats. A cardinal was seated directly behind the Soviet delegation. Sailors served as attendants.

The archbishop of Genoa appeared in wine-colored robes and skullcap carrying his warm message from Rome. The hall grew noisy with conversation and moving objects. Then the delegations began to arrive. The British Empire delegation arrived next to the last after a motorcade through the troop-lined streets of Genoa. Finally, the Russians came:

> Litvinov with a big ham-like face is in the lead. He is wearing the rectangular red insignia. After him comes Chicherin, with his indeterminate face, his indefinite beard, and his nervous hands. They blink at the

21. Ernest Hemingway, "Russian Girls at Genoa," *Toronto Daily Star*, 24 Apr., reprinted in *Hemingway By-Line: 75 Articles and Dispatches of Four Decades* (London: Penguin, 1968), pp. 46–47; Max Eastman (who misdates the plenary 23 Apr.), *Love and Revolution: My Journey through an Epoch* (New York: Random House, 1964), pp. 286–87; and Kessler, *Tagebücher*, p. 288.

light from the chandelier. Krassin is next. He has a mean face and a
carefully tailored Van Dyke beard and looks like a prosperous dentist.
Joffe is last. He has a long, narrow spade beard and wears gold-rimmed
glasses.[22]

The Germans had made a less ostentatious but equally important entry into the
palazzo, admitted for the first time on the basis of equality at a postwar diplomatic gathering. Seated halfway down one of the long tables, the striking,
bald-headed Rathenau and the undistinguished Wirth represented Genoa's
other looming question.[23]

Facta called the conference to order at 3 P.M.[24] Speaking in Italian, he welcomed the gathering on behalf of the Supreme Council and the Belgian government, and then read the greetings of King Victor Emmanuel III and a message
from Poincaré. After his formal election as conference president, Facta delivered a rambling and colorless speech stressing points that were important to
Italy: the economic troubles of the world, the need for all to sacrifice, and a call
for "equity, justice, and solidarity between peoples." He dutifully announced
that all those present "have . . . accepted the principles contained in the
Cannes Resolutions." But to France's chagrin, he had already insisted: "In this
place the memories of the hatreds and resentments of the war must be forgotten; here there are no longer friends and enemies, victors and vanquished, but
only men and nations striving in common for the attainment of a lofty ideal."[25]

Lloyd George, terming Genoa "the greatest gathering of European nations
which has ever been assembled on this continent," delivered a dramatic
speech.[26] "We meet on equal terms," he insisted, "to seek out in common the
best methods for restoring the shattered prosperity of this continent." Admitting the importance of the Cannes conditions, he nevertheless urged that their
main purpose was "peace, a real peace": "It is true that the actual fighting has
ceased, but the snarling goes on. . . . Europe is deafened with this canine
clamour. . . . It needs rest, quiet, tranquility. . . . It needs peace."

---

22. *Hemingway By-Line*, p. 48. Cf. Gregory to Lampson, Genoa, 14 Apr., GB FO 371
N3704/646/38, who described the Bolsheviks as "look[ing] like they had stepped out of a Drury
Lane pantomine, real melodramatic cut throats from Babes in the Wood. Chicherin looks like a
degenerate; he is and, of course, except for him and Krassin, I fancy that they are all Jews."
23. *Hemingway By-Line*, p. 48.
24. Lloyd George had proposed to open earlier in order that all the speeches appear in the next
day's papers, but Schanzer vetoed this for technical reasons. Hankey was nonetheless able to
obtain copies of the first three and summarize the rest in his press communication to London:
Hankey to wife, 12 Apr., HP. Minutes of the first plenary session in *DBFP*, 19:334–58.
25. *DBFP*, 19:338; entire speech, ibid., pp. 337–40. The addition of Italian as the third
official conference language, a gesture to the hosts and a conscious deviation from League
practices, was costly and time consuming: Sylvester, *Real Lloyd George*, p. 83.
26. *DBFP*, 19:340–43.

He urged a "common statesmanship of Europe" to guide its public opinion, to teach that "the good of another country is not necessarily an evil for its own." Though regretting America's absence, he cleverly combined a dose of over-optimism aimed at his European audience with a warning to the New World: "If we can set these things right at this conference, I feel sure that America will not merely come in, but come in gladly." In a modern reversal of Columbus's achievement: "Genoa once more will render another immortal service to humanity by rediscovering Europe to America." He challenged the delegates to fulfill the hopes that had been raised, to do their "duty manfully and fearlessly," to save Europe from further destruction and be worthy of the sentiments of peace and goodwill embodied in the sacred week before Easter. It was a most successful speech—vigorous, clear, practical, and idealistic—and it impressed even his most severe critics.[27]

Barthou, though a distinguished speaker and experienced parliamentarian, was at a pronounced disadvantage. He pledged France's "loyal cooperation" but cautioned against "vain words" or the hope that a "magic wand could rebuild on these shattered wounds the enchanted castle of our dreams." France, which knew well the horror of war, was "wholly, resolutely for peace" but would not permit Genoa to become a "court of appeal before which existing treaties are brought up, judged, and revised." It was a dour, uninspiring performance.[28]

Following two formal speeches by the Japanese and Belgian delegates, the two great invitees were given the floor. Wirth, in a tactless gesture, spoke in German.[29] He gave a long, rambling, fairly academic address enumerating the world's economic problems, stressing Germany's particular troubles, and combining deference with hints of defiance. The applause was more for the occasion than for its substance. Then the awaited moment: Chicherin spoke first in French, then in English. The entire hall was silent and attentive while the stooped Russian spoke in a high, shrill voice, with exotic pronunciations. Russia accepted the Cannes Resolutions and was prepared to collaborate in the "general reconstruction of the economic life of Europe." It adhered to the principles of peaceful coexistence and advocated cooperation between states representing the "two systems of property." He came "not with the intention of making propaganda . . . but in order to engage in practical relations": to open Russia's frontier to international transit, cultivate millions of its most fertile

27. Lloyd-Greame to wife, Genoa, 10 Apr., LGrP.

28. *DBFP*, 19:343–44. Louise Weiss, *Mémoires d'une européene* (Paris: Payot, 1969), 2:161, termed Barthou a "puppet among the 'Entities.'" Cf. Roger to Charles-Roux, Genoa, 16, 19 Apr., FMAE PC-R, and Siegfried to Goût, Genoa, 12 Apr., FMAE PM G/V.

29. Reichskanzlerrede, 10 Apr., Germ. AA T-120 3398/1734/D738296–300; Kessler, *Tagebücher*, p. 288, termed it "thin, sterile, and inoffensive"; see Lloyd-Greame to wife, 10 Apr., LGrP, on the frantic search for a translator.

acres for food, grant concessions of forests and mines, undertake joint agricultural and industrial enterprises with the West, and, as demonstrated in recent legislation, bring Russia's judiciary and administration in conformity with the specifications of Cannes.

Then he hurled his thunderbolts. "All efforts towards reconstruction . . . are vain so long as there remains suspended over Europe and the world the menace of new wars." Ostensibly seizing Lloyd George's cue, he announced his intention to propose a general limitation of armaments along with the absolute prohibition of "barbaric forms" of warfare such as asphyxiating gas and aerial bombardment. Russia was ready to disarm on a reciprocal basis with the West. He grasped two other Lloyd Georgian schemes: that Genoa be the first in a series of peace conferences and that a new "League of Peoples" emerge on the basis of universalism, equality, and full representation of workers and other minorities. Finally, if Russia's wealth were to be thrown open for the use of the whole world, there must also be a redistribution of the world's gold, industry, and resources.[30]

The speech was sensational. Barthou leaped from his seat and, following French parliamentary practice, scolded the "Honorable M. Chicherin" for remarks that exceeded the conference's agenda. Chicherin quoted Lloyd George, Briand, and Poincaré as authorities for his references to future conferences, the League, disarmament, and the vagueness of the Genoa agenda. Lloyd George played peacemaker. Summoning all his wit and persuasiveness, he implored Chicherin not to "overload" the Genoa Conference, and the audience applauded.[31]

Facta refused to allow either Chicherin or Barthou to speak again and briskly announced the rules of the Genoa Conference. They would divide at once into four commissions: political, financial, economic, and transport. All the assembled powers would be represented on them—two delegates for each of the inviting powers, Germany, and Russia, and one each for the rest. Each commission would elect a president, and these officers, along with the conference president, would form the presidential bureau of the Genoa Conference. The official languages would be Italian, French, and English. The deliberations of the commissions would be closed to the public. Official communiqués would be drawn up by the Secretariat, headed by Secretary-General Baron Camillo Romano Avezzana. Finally, a commission for the verification of credentials would begin work at once.

30. Text in *DBFP*, 19:348–51, and in Jane Degras, ed., *Soviet Documents on Foreign Policy* (London and New York: Oxford University Press, 1951), 1:298–301. See also Kessler, *Tagebücher*, pp. 288–89; and George Kennan, *Russia and the West under Lenin and Stalin* (New York: New American Library, 1961), p. 206.

31. *DBFP*, 19:351–56; Kessler, *Tagebücher*, pp. 289–91; Hankey to Chamberlain, 12 Apr., HP; and Lloyd George, *My Darling Pussy*, p. 43.

The first plenary meeting of the Genoa Conference ended at 7:10 P.M. The British were "well satisfied." Barthou, furious at Facta and Chicherin, was convinced that Lloyd George had taken his side. The Germans, neither jubilant nor depressed, viewed the opening proceedings soberly. The American observer was delighted to be free of Genoa's intrigue.[32]

Count Harry Kessler interpreted the opening session as

> one of the great scenes in political comedy in the manner of Aristophanes. . . . We have watched two small town actors, Barthou and Wirth, and two superb players, Lloyd George and Chicherin, with the former doubling as the secret producer of the whole affair. The opening performance has alone been worth the fare. To have been able to share in the feelings of the great producer, Lloyd George, would have been beyond price. Throughout Barthou's second and third speeches . . . he sat with his face resting between his hands. Inwardly he must have been hugging himself with satisfaction.[33]

Yet, except for a colorful drama, as a Belgian presciently noted, "Tout cela [est] très intéressant à observer, mais à mon humble avis toute opinion est encore prematurée."[34]

The Political Commission

The conference got down to work the next day. The delegates were pressed to expedite their deliberations, taking advantage of interest and timing. The press was hungry for every scrap of news. The parliaments of Europe were about to recess for Easter; during Genoa's first week, domestic politics underwent a temporary truce. With so many heads of government, experts, and businessmen there, Genoa became a world capital. Even the leader of the Genoa section of the Fascist party, who had declared a moratorium on demonstrations, expressed his sympathy with the conference.[35] Now perhaps Genoa would get down to "business."

---

32. Gregory to FO, Genoa, 10 Apr., GB FO 371 C5359/458/62; Grigg to Chamberlain, Genoa, 12 Apr., Grigg Papers, roll 1 ("It warmed one's heart to see how the whole of Europe rallied as if by common instinct to the British lead. . . . A revelation to the French!"); Barthou to MAE, Genoa, 10 Apr., #22–28, FMAE B 93; unsigned tel. for Ebert, State Secretary (AA) Haniel, and Press Section (AA), Genoa, 10 Apr., Germ. AA T-120 3398/1734/D738322; and Osborne to Hughes, Genoa, 11 Apr., USDS 550 E1/232.

33. Kessler, *Tagebücher*, pp. 291–92.

34. Davignon to Ramaix, Genoa, 11 Apr., BMAE 10991.

35. Unsigned tel. (special report from W.T.B.), Genoa, 11 Apr., Germ. AA T-120 3398/1734/D738325–28. On 10 Apr. the British cabinet suspended its deliberations on protectionist legislation until Lloyd George's return: Christoph Stamm, *Lloyd George zwischen Innen- und*

Or would it? Moments before the first meeting of the full Political Commission at the Palazzo Reale, Barthou asked to meet with Lloyd George. Poincaré, angered by Germany's recent defiant response to the Reparations Commission, had ordered the delegation to oppose the Reich's participation in the Political Commission.[36] Barthou pleaded for a suspension of the meeting in order that he might consult with Paris. In none-too-tactful tones, Lloyd George refused, denying that Poincaré could "push buttons" to control the Genoa Conference and threatening to complain publicly about France's obstructionism. Indeed, if France wished to *discuss* reparations, a subject it had excluded from Genoa's agenda, there were sufficient experts present to do so. Barthou readily backed down.[37]

The Political Commission opened with fireworks. Hungary's prime minister, Count István Bethlen, brought up another controversial subject, complaining about the mistreatment of 3 million Hungarian minorities by the governments of Czechoslovakia, Rumania, and Yugoslavia. He appealed to the commission to promote the loyal fulfillment of the minority treaties that the new East European states had been forced by the Allies to sign.[38] Beneš swept this aside, insisting that the surveillance of minority rights was the prerogative of the League of Nations, of which Hungary was not as yet a member. The evenhanded Facta did not throw out the Hungarian statement. He used it to launch his prepared announcement that there would be an eleven-member subcommission charged with formulating "suggestions" to the full Political Commission.

There was little difficulty choosing delegates: the subcommission would consist of the five inviting powers, plus Germany and Russia; Sweden and Switzerland, representing the neutrals; Rumania, representing the Little Entente; and Poland. Beneš, who did not want to participate, took credit for securing places for Poland and Rumania. Chicherin, who unsuccessfully protested the inclusion of Japan and Rumania (states still in "forceful occupation" of former Russian territory), was completely accommodating about Poland. Barthou remained silent about Germany.[39]

The subcommission convened that afternoon, and Schanzer was elected its president. Lloyd George formally presented the first half of the London Report

---

Aussenpolitik: Die britische Deutschlandpolitik 1921/1922 (Cologne: Verlag Wissenschaft und Politik, 1977), pp. 265–66. In Germany, except for the Gleiwitz incident, the continuing slide of the mark, and some rumblings in the Rhineland, everything was quiet: Haniel to Rathenau, Berlin, 11 Apr., Germ. Pol. Arch. AA, Bur. R.M., bd. 9.

36. Poincaré to Barthou, Paris, 10 Apr., #5, FMAE B 93.

37. Note of conversation, 11 Apr., GB CAB 31/S.G. 1; notes d'une conversation, 11 Apr., FMAE Y 29; Barthou to Poincaré, Genoa, 11 Apr., #30–32, FMAE B 93.

38. *DBFP*, 19:360–61. Background in Hohler to FO, Budapest, 8 Mar., John Balfour to Curzon, Budapest, 31 Mar., GB FO 371 C3525, C4866/458/62.

39. *DBFP*, 19:361–63; Barthou to MAE, Genoa, 11, 14 Apr., #35–38, #67, FMAE B 93.

pertaining to Russia, though the governments that had written it all stated that they were not "bound" by the document. Swiss Prime Minister Giuseppe Motta asked that it be distributed to all the delegates at Genoa. Chicherin, expressing "ignorance" of the report, asked for time to study its contents. Barthou icily agreed. Schanzer gave the Russians forty-eight hours to answer the Allies' nonbinding terms.[40]

The creation of the subcommission of the Political Commission was disturbing to Geneva and Paris and a source of satisfaction to Moscow and Berlin. League observers regarded the subcommission as a possible "permanent, extended Supreme Council" that might rival the world organization. In the *Echo de Paris* on 11 April, Pertinax termed the "eleven" an anticipation of "the end of the alliances of 1914."[41] Indeed, Moscow had been admitted without having undertaken any meaningful commitments and immediately had obtained substantial control over the outcome of the Genoa Conference. Moreover, the German press celebrated the Reich's "friendly reception" and France's "isolation."[42]

France was indeed isolated. The twin forbidden subjects, reparations and disarmament, hovered over Genoa and could not be entirely suppressed. Hungary had been allowed to introduce a third sensitive issue, the protection of minorities; this not only created difficulties for France's allies but also could be skillfully manipulated by Berlin.[43] Poincaré, who had insisted that reparations take precedence over the Russian question, refused to haggle with the Germans or the British at Genoa in front of the Bolsheviks and neutrals and without any American participation. France owed massive debts to Britain and America that were about to be called in. It smoldered over Germany's industrial prosperity, its blatant "evasions" of reparation payments, and its "illusory" disarmament. Paris realized that the disarmament issue, wielded selectively by Britain and the combined forces of Germany and Russia, would effectively separate France from most of the delegates at Genoa, who, at least for public consumption and Washington's approval, would have to support statements on behalf of arms reduction.[44]

40. *DBFP*, 19:364–67.

41. Directors' meeting, Geneva, 19 Apr., LNA; Hardinge to Curzon, Paris, 12 Apr., GB FO 371 W5444/458/62.

42. *Le Temps*, 16 Apr.; Wiedenfeld to AA, Moscow, 18 Apr., Germ. AA T-120 L312/4255/L096773–77; Della Faille to Jaspar, Berlin, 11 Apr., BMAE 10991; Saint Quentin to MAE, Berlin, 11 Apr., #670, FMAE Y 29; Laurent to MAE, Berlin, 12, 13 Apr., #676–77, #678, FMAE B 93; Müller Aufzeichnung, Genoa, 12 Apr., Germ. AA T-120 K1946/5372/K505538; and Mayer to AA, Paris, 14 Apr., Germ. AA T-120 3398/1734/D738377–78.

43. Simson Aufzeichnung, Genoa, 12 Apr., Germ. AA T-120 L795/5105/L233207–8; also IGPS report, 15 May, IMAE 52/31.

44. Barthou to MAE, Genoa, 11 Apr., #39, Poincaré to Barthou, Paris, 12, 13 Apr., #17, #23–27, Poincaré to Millerand, Paris, 13 Apr., and État-Major, Prague, 13 Apr., FMAE B 93.

To one observer at Genoa, France appeared "beaten" less than three years after Versailles; the subcommission seemed a crucial turning point, indicative of "genuinely far-reaching change." A "new Areopagus" had been created that included Germany and Russia over "rabid French opposition" but with the acquiescence of the neutrals, the Little Entente, and even Poland.[45] What would this new Areopagus accomplish?

Villa d'Albertis

During the next twenty-four hours, Genoa's three other commissions were convened to examine the second half of the London Report. As anticipated, each full commission was divided into smaller subcommissions according to the bloc methods. There were some surprises.

The Financial Commission, presided over by Horne, set up a subcommission consisting of the inviting powers, Germany, Russia, the Netherlands, Denmark, Czechoslovakia, and Finland. This body was divided into three units to study currency, exchanges, and credits. Experts were appointed to make recommendations on the first two matters; discussion of the third awaited the outcome of the Political Commission's negotiations with Russia.[46]

France was stopped by a "German-British-Italian" alignment in its effort to eliminate both the Germans and Russians from the financial subcommission. It received no help from Belgium.[47] Berlin and Moscow had high hopes for this forum. The Germans intended to plead their case with the bankers assembled at Genoa and gain their support for a loan. The financial subcommission was the place to forcefully and discreetly argue the causes of and remedies for Germany's ruined economy. Russia, represented by Rakovsky in the opening meeting, again preached a sermon for disarmament. The evenhanded Horne allowed the discussion of subjects only remotely related to the agenda but forbade proposals expressly excluded.[48] Finally, the experts set to work.

France's alarm monitored in Hardinge to FO, Paris, 14 Apr., GB FO 371 C5476/458/62, telephone call, 14 Apr., and cipher tel., 15 Apr., GB CAB 31/13 R/nos. 2–3; Wertheimer to AA, Paris, 12 Apr., Germ. BA R 43 1/469; Mayer to AA, Paris, 13, 14 Apr., Germ. AA T-120 L996/5412/L286050, 3398/1734/D738379–80; and De Gaiffier to MAE, Paris, 12 Apr., BMAE Fr.

45. Kessler, *Tagebücher*, p. 294.

46. Gregory to FO, Genoa, 13 Apr., GB FO 371 C5472/458/62; Barthou to MAE, Genoa, 14 Apr., #61–64, FMAE B 93.

47. Barthou to MAE, Genoa, 11, 12 Apr., #40–44, #51–53, FMAE B 93. Müller to Ebert, Haniel, and Press Section, Genoa, 12 Apr., Germ. AA T-120 3398/1734/D738333–34, on the "menacing character" of France's unsuccessful maneuver but urging no *Siegesgeschrei* because "The U.S., British, and neutral press will underscore our victory."

48. Müller to AA, Genoa, 14 Apr., Germ. AA T-120 3398/1734/D738369–75; Barthou to MAE, Genoa, 12 Apr., #51–53, FMAE B 93; Siegfried to Goût, Genoa, 12 Apr., FMAE PM

Next, the Economic Commission, headed by the French delegate Maurice Colrat, met on the morning of 12 April. It easily tabled a Hungarian proposal to establish a special subcommission to study economic relations among the succession states. A twelve-nation subcommission was formed, with Norway, Switzerland, and the Netherlands representing the neutrals, Yugoslavia and Latvia, the Little Entente and the Baltic states. Except for Germany, no former enemy states were included.[49]

Last, the Transport Commission, presided over by Belgian Prime Minister Georges Theunis, met in the afternoon. Its subcommission consisted of Portugal, Switzerland, Poland, Estonia, and Austria. To include more of the small states, it further divided into two bodies, one to study European railways (the Big Seven, plus Austria, Poland, Estonia, Czechoslovakia, and Yugoslavia) and one for Europe's waterways (the Big Seven, plus Rumania, Greece, the Netherlands, Norway, and Latvia), with a Belgian presiding over both.[50]

During the building of these subcommissions, several prominent features emerged: erosion of wartime distinctions, Anglo-Italian solidarity, lack of Franco-British cooperation, and the attempt of the Vierverband (the Little Entente and Poland) to function as one of the "Great Powers."[51] Consequently, the representatives of the League of Nations tried to play an active role in the technical discussions. Admitted to the meetings as observers, they worked to assert the League's interests and importance, and to secure Geneva's right to implement the decisions of the Genoa Conference. They also lobbied among the delegates to combat Russian threats to transform or to replace the League, to promote Germany's membership, and to increase the voice and authority of the small powers alongside the great.[52]

Politics were, of course, Genoa's main preoccupation. While the British, Italian, and German representatives plied the route to the Hotel Imperiale and the Hotel de Gênes, Lloyd George held court at the Villa d'Albertis. On 12 April he encouraged Schanzer's hope for an Anglo-Italian pact, presumably to spur Italy's efforts to make Genoa a success. The next day he met with Brătianu and Austria's Chancellor Johann Schober, giving encouragement to their political aims.[53] Despite the absence of Lord Riddell, the able press chief,

G/V; and Francis Conte, *Christian Rakovski (1873–1941), Essai de biographie politique* (Lille: Atelier de reproduction des thèses, Université de Lille III, 1975), 2:421–24.

49. Unsigned tel. to FO, Genoa, 12 Apr., GB FO 371 C5766/458/62; Barthou to MAE, Genoa, 12 Apr., #46–49, FMAE B 93.

50. Gregory to FO, Genoa, 12 Apr., GB FO 371 C5431/458/62; Barthou to MAE, Genoa, 15 Apr., #74–76, FMAE B 93.

51. Storck to BMA, Bucharest, 14 Apr., A HHSt 687; and especially Child to State Dept., Genoa, 15 Apr., USDS 550 E1/236.

52. Siegfried to Goût, Genoa, 17 Apr., FMAE PM G/V. The League observers met daily to discuss their work and to share information.

53. Conversation, 12 Apr., Schanzer Papers, I:IIv; Notes, Lloyd George–Brătianu conversa-

Grigg kept the British press apparatus functioning smoothly: the prime minister met with journalists every day.

Awaiting word from Moscow, Chicherin requested the postponement of the political subcommission until Saturday, 15 April.[54] Lloyd George was impatient for results.[55] Convinced that something must and could be accomplished, he decided to hold informal talks with the Russians. The news from his own informants and the Italians indicated that the Soviet government was prepared to accept only its prewar debts. It would not restore private property but would provide bonds or leases. In addition, the Russians intended to counterbalance the Allies' financial claims with a substantial bill for the intervention. Lloyd George believed he could exploit the conflicts within the Soviet delegation. Sensing flashes of independence in Barthou, he also thought he could win France over to his plan for informal negotiations.[56]

Barthou obligingly appeared at the villa in the late afternoon on 13 April. Belgian Foreign Minister Jaspar arrived soon thereafter. Barthou unexpectedly agreed to participate in private talks with the Soviet delegation. Seydoux also agreed, on the condition that these be only "semi official" (*officieuse*). An appropriate cover was devised for the inquisitive press; the Allies announced that the political subcommission would meet on 15 April.[57]

The Western powers realized that the Soviet delegation intended to hold firm against the rigorous details of the London Report. They were also aware of the growing force of Russian nationalism that might explode, as in Kemal's Turkey, if the Allies made immoderate demands. They nonetheless had little room for compromise either on basic principles or on details. The Allies did decide at the Villa d'Albertis that they were ready to deal directly with the Bolsheviks and were also prepared to exclude the Japanese (whose presence might irritate Chicherin) and, for their own reasons, the Germans, whose claims against Russia had not been recognized in the London Report.[58] Except in the question

---

tion, 13 Apr., GB CAB 31/S.G. 4; Notes, Lloyd George–Schober conversation, GB CAB 31/S.G. 5; and Bischoff Hausnotiz, 13 Apr., A HHSt 687.

54. Müller to AA, Genoa, 12 Apr., Germ. AA T-120 3398/1734/D738337.

55. Child to Hughes, Genoa, 12 Apr., USDS 550 E1/228; Canadian delegate Charles Gordon to MacKenzie King, Genoa, 11, 13 Apr., PAC MKP. However, in Churchill to Lloyd George, 12 Apr., LGP F 10/2/63, reporting Britain's improved economic prospects and the generally optimistic mood in the country, he warned, "I do hope and trust you don't take a wrong turn."

56. Lloyd George–Schanzer conversation, 13 Apr., *DBFP*, 19:367–71.

57. Notes of informal meeting, 13 Apr., ibid., pp. 371–80; Barthou to MAE, Genoa, 13 Apr., #58–64, FMAE B 93.

58. Annex II ("Determination of Claims"), no. 15, stated: "No claim shall be recognized in respect of rights which had ceased legally to exist before Mar. 1917." It thus eliminated German property expropriated by czarist Russia during World War I. Germany's exclusion emphasized in Barthou to MAE, Genoa, 14 Apr., #65, FMAE B 93; Japan's explained in Lloyd-Greame–Hayashi conversation, 13 Apr., GB CAB 31/S.G. 5.

of reparations, Franco-British cooperation, so essential to Genoa's success, seemed to be revived.[59] Nonetheless, by the evening of 13 April, the Areopagus had been reduced to five.

On Good Friday, 14 April, Soviet delegates Chicherin, Litvinov, and Krassin spent the entire day at the Villa d'Albertis in an essentially fruitless discussion.[60] A remarkably candid and moderate Chicherin admitted the limitations under which he was operating in terms of what he could concede to the Allies. He also warned them against hoping that the present Soviet government would soon be replaced. With surprising unity, Lloyd George, Barthou, Schanzer, and Jaspar stood together in demanding the complete fulfillment of the Cannes Resolutions: full repayment of prewar and wartime debts and the restitution of private property.

Toward 1:00 P.M., the meeting adjourned for lunch. To avoid the delay of the Russians' leaving for their quarters, Lloyd George invited them to dine with him. Barthou stiffly declined to join them; Schanzer and Theunis also refused; and thus Lloyd George, much to the consternation of members of his entourage, was left alone with the Russians.[61]

That afternoon Krassin, in an attempt to steer the Allies toward the future, outlined the extensive possibilities for Western investment in Russian agriculture, industries, raw materials, and transport. The Allies failed to grasp the bait, doubting that Russia's present laws could protect foreign enterprise. Litvinov and a most conciliatory Chicherin urged that they set up a committee to explore possible bases of agreement.[62] Lloyd George insisted they must first concur on the "fundamental question" of Soviet recognition of their debts. By evening they agreed to let a committee of Allied and Russian experts tackle the debt question the next day. If the experts were able to produce a formula, their discussions could resume in the afternoon. Another story for the press was devised, and the meeting of the political subcommission scheduled for the morrow was again officially postponed.[63]

The Russians were not happy with these talks.[64] Faced with a unified Allied front, they had been pressed to accept all the elements of the Cannes Resolu-

59. Barthou to MAE, Genoa, 15 Apr., #80–81, Seydoux note, 13 Apr., FMAE B 94, 96. Gregory to Lampson, Genoa, 14 Apr., GB FO 371 N3704/646/38, characterized Barthou's behavior as "lamb-like"; however, Hankey to Chamberlain, Genoa, 13 Apr., HP, complained that the French were intercepting British cables.

60. Notes of informal meeting, 14 Apr., *DBFP*, 19:380–404.

61. Hankey to wife, 15 Apr., to Chamberlain, 16 Apr., CzP; Lloyd-Greame to wife, Genoa, 16 Apr., LGrP.

62. Barthou to MAE, Genoa, 14 Apr., #70–73, FMAE B 93. Poincaré to Millerand, Paris, 13 Apr., FMAE PM Tel/2, based on an intercepted telegram from Moscow, analyzes Chicherin's offer.

63. Gregory to FO, Genoa, 14 Apr., GB FO 371 N3553/646/38.

64. Chicherin's account quoted in *Neue Zürcher Zeitung*, 11 Apr., 1962.

At the Villa d'Albertis. (*Left to right*) Barthou, Lloyd George, and Hankey (photo from Maurice Hankey Papers, by permission of the Master and Fellows of Churchill College, Cambridge University).

tions and were given no indication of what the West was willing to offer. There would be no further intimate talks unless the experts reached an agreement.[65] The only possible hope for the Russians was to divide the capitalist West.

Resumption of the Russo-German Talks

Good Friday had been a day off for the German delegation. Some, taking advantage of the fine weather, made automobile trips to the beach at Nervi, visited picturesque Portofino, where the kaiser once had a villa, or called at Rapallo.[66] That morning Rathenau composed a fifteen page letter to Reich President Ebert summing up his first impressions.[67] Curiously sanguine in tone, it lacked key details. Rathenau noted the conciliatory acknowledgment of Germany's latest note by the Reparations Commission on 13 April and reported on his talks with the bankers. However, he failed to mention that con-

65. Barthou to MAE, Genoa, 14 Apr., #70–73, FMAE B 93; Jaspar to MAE, Genoa, 15 Apr., BMAE 10991.

66. Hemmer to Wever, Genoa, 14 Apr., Germ. AA T-120 K1946/5372/K505535–37.

67. Rathenau to Ebert, Genoa, 14 Apr., Germ. AA T-120 3398/1734/D738344–58.

versations had taken place between Bergmann and Seydoux the day before, in which the French expert had firmly refused German overtures; nor did he share the anxiety of British and American observers that a crisis over reparations soon would explode.[68]

Though admitting some dissatisfaction with the London Report, Rathenau assumed that there would be a compromise and that a Genoa agreement would ensue.[69] Silent on the well-established liaison between the German and Soviet delegations,[70] he suggested that the Germans might conduct a mediating action to achieve a Genoa pact that would protect the Reich's interests. He gave little credence to the possibility of Germany's exclusion from the main "Russo-British" talks. To complete the optimistic picture, he described how the "little states" (presumably the neutrals and the Little Entente) were behaving less "pro-French" than expected and would probably continue to do so.[71]

Rathenau's strongest concern was the disunity of the German delegation. The day before, Hermann Bücher, an industrialist and spokesman for the RDI, had told a Swiss banker that he opposed an international loan until the reparations question was finally settled.[72] Rathenau had to clarify this statement immediately. The press was sensitive to every sign of conflict within the delegation; the Germans missed the Foreign Ministry's able press chief, Ulrich Rauscher, who remained behind in Berlin awaiting his new assignment in Warsaw.

Rathenau assured Ebert that he intended to lead the delegation and to end Germany's isolation by establishing contact with every delegation except the French and possibly the "very reserved" Japanese. Should he succeed, he hoped Germany might be relieved of the pressure from "those institutions which make life impossible for us," particularly the Conference of Ambassadors and the various scolding Allied commissions. There was one final revealing admission in an otherwise excessively confident report: he would not "know more until our first meeting with Lloyd George." Though their first encounter had been short and affable, he had not succeeded in obtaining a private interview.

During his first five days in Genoa, Rathenau had used a number of opportunities to promote Germany's interests. He had lectured the League's represen-

---

68. Kessler, *Tagebücher*, pp. 296–97; Wigram to Lampson, Genoa, 12 Apr., GB FO 371 C5538/458/62; Consul General Carrigan [Child] to State Dept., Milan, 15 Apr., USDS 550 E1/194.

69. Cf. Rathenau to Haniel, Genoa, 13 Apr., Germ. Pol. Arch. AA, DDG/Eng.-Russ., expressed stronger concern over the Allies' terms.

70. Reported in Müller to Ebert and Haniel, Genoa, 12 Apr., Germ. AA T-120 3398/1734/ D738335–36.

71. Also in prefect's report, 15 Apr., IMAE 52/31.

72. Aufzeichnungen, Genoa, 13, 14 Apr., Germ. AA T-120 3398/1734/D738360–68.

tatives on Berlin's grievances against Geneva. He had met with Swiss representative Edmond Schulthess, who subsequently delivered a blunt and helpful speech in the Economic Commission; ostensibly criticizing the dumping of goods practiced by the Reich, Schulthess urged that the commission tackle the "actual problems" necessary to achieve economic progress, the code words for reparations.[73] Rathenau also had friendly meetings with Skirmunt and Brătianu. Finally, while dining with his friends Keynes and Melchior on the evening of Good Friday, he announced that he was preparing a major document on economic reconstruction.[74]

In the late afternoon on Good Friday, the Germans learned of the Allied-Russian talks. Maltzan spoke with the Russians, who volunteered few details of the conversations at the Villa d'Albertis, suggested that France and Britain were anxious for a prompt settlement, and reminded the Germans that they "could have made an agreement . . . earlier in Berlin."[75] At 11 P.M. Giannini arrived at the Eden and asked to see Wirth. Later Rathenau, Simson, and Maltzan were summoned. Giannini, representing Schanzer, reported on the events of the day and described the Allied-Russian talks as successful. Queried by Rathenau whether the London Report would be the basis of the agreement, Giannini fell silent. When the Germans threatened to conclude their own pact with the Russians, the Italian made no response.[76] After Giannini left at mid-

73. League observers' meeting, 14 Apr., LNA 40A 20136/20136; Simson to AA, Ebert, and Press Section, Genoa, 15 Apr., Germ. AA T-120 3398/1734/D738382–83.

74. Rathenau to Haniel, Genoa, 13 Apr., Germ. Pol. Arch. AA, DDG/Eng.-Russ.; and Rathenau diary, 14 Apr., Germ. AA T-120 3398/1735/D739151–52.

75. Maltzan wrote two documents on the antecedents of the Rapallo treaty: "Letzte Vorgänge vor der Unterzeichnung des deutsch-russischen Vertrages," 17 Apr., Germ. AA T-120 3398/1735/D738893–98, and the more extended "Ausführliche Aufzeichnung über die letzten Vorgänge vor der Unterzeichnung des deutsch-russischen Vertrages," 17 or 18 Apr., Germ. Pol. Arch. AA DDG, bd. 18. The first, abbreviated version, stressing Germany's efforts to stay in contact with the British, was shown to D'Abernon, who included it in *Versailles to Rapallo*, pp. 311–15. The second version, probably intended as a more thorough explanation to Berlin, in 1928 was shown to Kessler, who omitted key passages and added recollections of his own in *Walther Rathenau: His Life and Work* (New York: Harcourt, Brace and Co., 1930), pp. 312–25. Complete texts of the "Letzte Vorgänge" and the "Ausführliche Aufzeichnung," along with indications of Kessler's omissions and a commentary on the two documents, are in Ernst Laubach, "Maltzans Aufzeichnungen über die letzten Vorgänge vor dem Abschluss des Rapallo-Vertrages," *Jahrbücher für Geschichte Osteuropas* 22, no. 4 (1975): 554–79.

76. The "Ausführliche Aufzeichnung," in Laubach, "Maltzans Aufzeichnungen," p. 568, contains no details of Giannini's message; it was described—with significant errors, including the misdating of the Allied-Russian talks as beginning on "Wednesday"—in the "Letzte Vorgänge," ibid., p. 562. There is more detail in Müller [Maltzan] to Ebert, Wever and AA Press Section, Genoa, 18 Apr., Germ. AA T-120 3398/1734/D738409–14: Rathenau allegedly said, "They have invited us to a lovely dinner, shown us the menu, but we will not be invited to eat." Kessler, who also saw this telegram in 1928, added Giannini's comment: "C'était seulement préparé pour nous," *Rathenau*, p. 318. Giannini had not attended the villa talks.

night, Rathenau told Maltzan they would at once resume the Berlin talks. Maltzan phoned Joffe, and they agreed to meet the next morning in the Palazzo Reale.[77]

Since Giannini's statements allegedly triggered the German decision to resume the talks with the Russians, one must examine this incident further. The principal evidence of his visit is in the accounts written afterward by Maltzan to justify Germany's subsequent actions. It is quite possible that Giannini's report was misunderstood or exaggerated by the apprehensive Germans, or that it was used later to justify an impulsive decision.[78] Certainly Italy had nothing to gain by frightening the Germans into a separate agreement with the Russians. Though Rome was conducting its own negotiations with Moscow, its best prospect was for a comprehensive East-West settlement. A German-Soviet treaty would hardly benefit the poorer Italians or the languishing port of Genoa; indeed, it would give Chicherin considerable advantage in his dealings with Rome. Schanzer promptly denied rumors that a "Signor X" had misled Rathenau; and objective observers confirmed his chagrin that Germany had stolen a march on the Allies.[79]

Some have suspected that Giannini, who enjoyed close relations with both the Bolsheviks and the British, was acting on their behalf on the night of Good Friday. Again, there is no basis to support this. The Russians were mystified and irritated at Rathenau's excuse that Giannini was the cause of his decision; and Lloyd George had no reason to frighten the Germans at so early and delicate a stage in the villa negotiations.[80] How is one to judge the assertion that the British leader would promote any agreement (even one prejudicial to his own difficult labors) to put pressure on France to collaborate?[81] France was

77. "Ausführliche Aufzeichnung," in Laubach, "Maltzans Aufzeichnungen," p. 568.

78. In Rathenau's diary, 14 Apr., Germ. AA T-120 3398/1735/D739152, "Unterhaltung mit Giannini" was distinctly added afterwards. Kessler himself (*Tagebücher*, p. 300) questioned "what was it that Giannini said and how far was it admissible for Rathenau to rely on *him alone* without obtaining more information, or first making a protest" (italics in the original). Many historians, including Laubach, "Maltzans Aufzeichnungen," p. 562, have confused Amedeo Giannini, the head of the press section of the Italian Foreign Ministry who edited the documents of the Genoa Conference, with Francesco Giannini, the courier on 14 April.

79. Schanzer to De Martino, Genoa, 24 Apr., IMAE Amb. Lond. 538.3. On 28 Apr. the Italian embassy in London issued the following statement (ibid.): "Dr. Giannini was officially charged with the duty of keeping the German delegation informed of the negotiations that were proceeding between the Allies and the Russians. He carried out his instructions with complete faithfulness and clarity and to the satisfaction of the Italian government." Also Karnebeek diary, Genoa, 18 Apr., *DBPN*, no. 245, on Schanzer's irritation with the Germans.

80. Lyubimov and Erlikh, "1922 Genoa Conference," pp. 79-80; and John Maynard Keynes, in *Manchester Guardian*, 24 Apr.

81. Asserted in Francis Conte, "Lloyd George et le Traité de Rapallo," *Revue d'Histoire Moderne et Contemporaine* 23 (January-March 1976): 59-64.

already exceptionally cooperative with the Russians. On the first day of the talks, it was not Barthou but the Russians who had been obstreperous.

Regardless of the exact nature of Giannini's communication, the Germans now felt their isolation acutely. Despite all his efforts, Rathenau had not yet met privately with Lloyd George. The Germans had complained about the London Report to Wise and to John Gregory, a junior Foreign Office representative specializing in Russian affairs, but neither of them could provide much reassurance. Now they knew that talks between the Allies and Russians had commenced without them. Germany was indeed fully represented on all the technical commissions at Genoa; that very morning Rathenau had praised the conference's organization to Ebert. It was nevertheless clear that his dealings with the bankers, neutrals, and the world press lost significance in the light of Giannini's information.

Rathenau reacted with a decision he knew would lead to a separate treaty with the Russians and a falling out with the Allies. It is conceivable that his vanity was wounded once he learned from Giannini that Germany had been excluded from the villa talks. He had lost the chance to play his *Vermittler* role. Even more important, the Germans would have to wait passively until the main actors concluded their work, leaving them occupied only with the perhaps futile and divisive task of winning over the bankers.[82]

The Villa d'Albertis talks were the catalyst for Rathenau's decision to set up parallel negotiations with the Russians. Aware of how close Berlin and Moscow already were, he doubtless intended to beat the Entente at its own game. Officially the Germans always justified Rathenau's decision as having been provoked by the menace in the London Report—the threat to make Germany pay reparations to Russia and to sacrifice German property claims. Giannini's laconic and unsubstantiated report was added, perhaps to implicate Schanzer and Lloyd George in Rathenau's fearful, allegedly preventive behavior. It is of course also possible to interpret Rathenau's action in another way: if the villa talks were ultimately *unsuccessful* and Genoa broke up, Germany would have

82. Theodor Schieder, *Die Probleme des Rapallo-Vertrags* (Cologne: Westdeutscher Verlag, 1956), p. 39, and Karl Dietrich Erdmann, "Deutschland, Rapallo und der Westen," *Vierteljahrshefte für Zeitgeschichte* 11, no. 2 (April 1963): 125–30, both suggest Rathenau had lost hope in a loan, particularly because of America's absence from Genoa. László Zsigmond, *Zur deutschen Frage, 1918–1923*, trans. P. Felix (Budapest: Akadémiai Kiadó, 1964), p. 222, interprets Rathenau's decision as a form of *Machtpolitik*; this is supported in Koch to Rathenau, Berlin, 6 May, and Rathenau to Dr. Otto Boelitz, Genoa, 6 May, and to Koch, Genoa, 9 May, Germ. Pol. Arch. AA, Bur. R.M., bd. 11. The weight of domestic concerns, the gloomy political picture, the fear that a Russo-Allied agreement might revive German communism, and the German public's critical attitude toward Genoa are in Rauscher to German Delegation, Berlin, 14 Apr., Germ. AA T-120 L1468/5118/L415929–33.

The most balanced appraisal of Rathenau's decision in Gordon A. Craig, *From Bismarck to Adenauer: Aspects of German Statecraft*, rev. ed. (New York: Harper and Row, 1965), pp. 49–50.

relinquished an opportunity to strike a bargain with the Soviet state at the most propitious moment for the Reich.[83]

The decision to conclude an agreement with the Russians had many immediate advantages: it would heal one of the important splits in the German delegation, ensure German industry of a lead in the reconstruction of Russia, prevent an East-West arrangement prejudicial to the Reich, and also serve notice on the Entente (and especially on France) that Berlin had an alternative policy to being cowed by the Allied commissions. Did Rathenau weigh the impact of his decision on Lloyd George, the French, the bankers, or Europe, or was it a desperate or impulsive act? To what extent was he the helmsman and to what extent was he the reluctant implementor of Wirth and Maltzan's *Ostpolitik*? The answers can never be known with certainty. In any event, on the day before Easter, two private meetings took place almost simultaneously at Genoa, and neither was very successful.

Holy Saturday

Despite the Allies' precautions, the Genoa press was filled the next day with announcements of the secret talks at the Villa d'Albertis. Barthou called a special meeting to explain the proceedings to members of the Little Entente; only the Polish and Czechoslovak representatives appeared. The neutrals and other small powers railed against the revival of "Supreme Council" tactics that were contrary to the announced spirit of the Genoa Conference.[84]

Prior to the Russians' arrival, Allied experts assembled at the Villa d'Albertis to formulate the total of the Russian debt to their governments. They assumed there would be a reduction and thus established no precise figures until the Soviet delegates presented theirs.[85] Litvinov arrived, bringing a bill for 50 billion gold rubles, which represented the destruction of one-third of prewar Russia's wealth caused by the wars of intervention. This claim more than exceeded that of the Allies.[86]

83. Argued in Hartmut Pogge von Strandmann, "Rapallo—Strategy in Preventive Diplomacy: New Sources and New Interpretations," in *Germany in the Age of Total War*, ed. Volker R. Berghahn and Martin Kitchen (London: Croom Helm, 1981), pp. 136–37.

84. Barthou to MAE, Genoa, 16 Apr., FMAE B 94; Lloyd-Greame to wife, Genoa, 16 Apr., LGrP; Gregory to Lampson, Genoa, 14 Apr. (postscript 15 Apr.), GB FO 371 N3704/646/38.

85. Notes of informal meeting of experts, 15 Apr., 10 A.M., GB CAB 29/95 I.C.P. 238F. They estimated the total Russian indebtedness as follows: to Great Britain, 607,000,000 pounds; to France, 5,789,000,000 francs; and to Italy, 53,000,000 francs and 182,000,000 lire.

86. Notes of meeting of experts with Russia, 15 Apr., 11:30 P.M., GB CAB 29/95 I.C.P. 238G. Hankey to Chamberlain, Genoa, 16 Apr., HP: "The meeting was an absolute frost. Litvinov, who appears to be rather the villain of the piece (he is a horrible-looking brute, with a fat, sensual, clean-shaven, puffy face and very thick lips) went back on the whole thing and made the most preposterous claims on behalf of Russia."

The Russians obligingly stepped out to allow the Allied experts to ponder what Lloyd-Greame labeled Litvinov's "fantastic" figures. In view of Russia's devastation in the war and in order to smooth out the negotiations, Britain was willing to allow a 50 percent cancellation of Russia's war debt to the Allies. Seydoux preferred 33 percent. In any event, the experts decided not to formally consider the Russian claims at all but simply to offer a flat reduction of the Russian debt to their governments.[87] Litvinov stuck to his figure. He and Krassin argued that since Russia had received no benefits from the long struggle—no colonies, no reparations, no Alsace-Lorraine, and no Mesopotamia—he would not acknowledge any war debts, even if reduced by 100 percent. The impetuous Lloyd-Greame shouted that only Russia had repudiated war debts.[88]

That afternoon the Allied leaders met with their experts and learned of the negative results.[89] Lloyd George proposed that they make "clear proposals" that the Bolsheviks could telegraph to Moscow. However, he also took an uncompromising line, insisting on the principle of recognition of war debts, full repayment of private debts, full restitution or compensation for nationalized property, and rejection of Litvinov's insolent demand for "reciprocity." Schanzer pleaded for leniency, whereupon Barthou spoke even more harshly, insisting that their meeting with the Russians was concession enough. Indeed, he had restrained himself from bringing up the perfidy of Soviet Russia's desertion of its erstwhile allies with the Treaty of Brest-Litovsk. Lloyd George maneuvered the group into taking a "liberal" stance. Since the talks might break down and they would probably "never get either the interest or the war debt," he proposed a reduction of the latter and an offer to postpone payment on the principal and interest. The Allies would reject Russia's counterclaims and demand full repayment to private bondholders and compensation to property owners. Despite the remote chance that it might set a damaging precedent for interallied debt negotiations, Barthou agreed to the compromise, largely on Seydoux's advice that it conformed to the London Report.[90]

Chicherin, Litvinov, and Krassin arrived in the late afternoon, explaining that their delay was caused by long waits at level railroad crossings.[91] (It is conceivable that they had also oriented themselves on the morning's discussions with the Germans.) Lloyd George, in a long and heated polemic, ridiculed Litvinov's figures and the whole notion of presenting a bill for the Allied

---

87. Notes of meeting of experts, GB CAB 29/95 I.C.P. 238F.

88. Notes of meeting of experts with Russia, GB CAB 29/95 I.C.P. 238G.

89. Notes of informal meeting between Belgian, British, French, and Italian delegations, 15 Apr., 3:35 P.M., *DBFP*, 19:404–9.

90. Barthou to MAE, Genoa, 16, 17 Apr., #85–88, #95–96, FMAE B 94; Poincaré to Barthou, Paris, 16 Apr., ibid., gave approval.

91. Notes of meeting between British, French, Italian, Belgian, and Russian delegations, 15 Apr., 4:30 P.M., *DBFP*, 19:410.

intervention; such fantastic claims had been made recently by the Irish. The English and French revolutions had both been prolonged by lavish support from the outside, yet neither nation had sent bills to their adversaries. He reminded the Russians that the Allies had gone to war in 1914 over a "Slavic quarrel," had paid dearly and gained little ("Did M. Chicherin want . . . Mesopotamia?"); that Brest-Litovsk had violated the 1914 Allied agreement, thus making Moscow liable for Allied claims; and, finally, that the threatened repudiation of Russia's debts would fall hardest on the poor. Polemics over, the British premier crisply announced that the Allied terms would have to be met in order for Genoa to continue.[92]

Chicherin almost matched the power of Lloyd George's rhetoric.[93] He accused the Allies of virtually creating the White and interventionist armies. He reminded them that, according to the British leader's own words, World War I had originated in an Anglo-German quarrel, not a Slavic one; that Brest-Litovsk came as a result of Russia's collapse, which was caused to some extent by Western "shells that did not explode, or were sent to Italy"; and that Russia's withdrawal in 1918 was not unlike Britain's at Gallipoli. He deemed the whole issue of war debts one that solely concerned the Allies who had profited from the war. Russia, which had sustained 54 percent of the Entente's losses, expended 20 billion gold rubles, and then been almost crushed by the Allied intervention, was now emerging from revolution and the defeat of the White armies, and felt free of any obligation to its former allies.[94]

Chicherin again attempted to steer the discussion toward the future and the most useful means of reconstructing Russia. He pleaded that Genoa not break down and urged Lloyd George not to insist on restoring private ownership in the Bolshevik state.[95] Litvinov was more blunt, especially on debts, doubting the "innocence" of many private creditors; he did concede that some of Moscow's 50 billion claim could be used to pay off these supplicants. The practical Krassin asked about the confiscated Russian icebreakers and war vessels. Again, the Russians stepped out to allow the Allies to respond.

Lloyd George insisted to his colleagues that the most important issue was debt recognition. They could work out the precise mechanics according to the experts' formulas.[96] When the Russians returned, he said there would be no

92. Ibid., pp. 410–13; Hankey to Chamberlain, 16 Apr., HP.

93. *DBFP*, 19:414–16; Lyubimov and Erlikh, "1922 Genoa Conference," p. 100.

94. In the confidential print (GB CAB 29/95, I.C.P. 238D), Chicherin is quoted as saying, "What had Russia gained from the war. . . . She would be ready to receive Constantinople [cf. *DBFP*, 4:635–38] and to hand it over to the National Government of Turkey . . . to receive Eastern Galicia and to dispose of it according to the will of the people."

95. Lyubimov and Erlikh, "1922 Genoa Conference," pp. 100, 102, has Lloyd George twice rebutting the plea; there is nothing in the British résumé.

96. Notes of informal meeting of British, French, Belgian and Italian governments, GB CAB 29/95, I.C.P. 238E.

problem over the icebreakers. The Allies demanded complete debt recognition as a condition to granting a moratorium on debt payments and a reduction of the principal, and rejected any token of reciprocity. The Russians equivocated. Chicherin requested that the political subcommission reconvene to discuss the future, but Lloyd George refused. There could be no discussion of credits or foreign investments until the past was settled. Chicherin announced he would have to consult Moscow, and Lloyd George agreed to a delay of three or four days.[97] Barthou, who had tried unsuccessfully to set strict time limits and to pin Chicherin down, complained to Paris of the latter's "evasions" and of Lloyd George's "lassitude."[98]

The Allied-Russian talks had reached a critical stage. Lloyd George begged Chicherin not to stress to Moscow that the Allies had rejected Russia's claim to reciprocity but simply to convey the generous Western proposals. The Italians believed that there would be a positive response. Hankey, exhausted from two full days of villa meetings and four days of continuous stenography, bet six to four that the Russians would accept.[99] Others were less optimistic: Barthou lacked confidence in the Russians' ability to retreat. The American observer, Ambassador Child, was convinced that the Russians would either refuse or take evasive action. The Allies' troubles expanded when the Japanese delegation withheld its approval to the offer of 15 April; Japan, holding a forty-million-pound war debt from Russia, would not automatically acquiesce in a moratorium or a reduction.[100] The East-West talks were suspended. The press, however, was told that they were "proceeding" and was given no information on the crucial message to Moscow.[101]

Rathenau, after perusing the morning press reports of the villa talks, spent a busy Saturday meeting again with bankers, statesmen, and journalists.[102] On his instructions, Maltzan met with Adolf Joffe and Christian Rakovsky at the Palazzo Reale.[103] The Russians, conveying more precise information than the day before, admitted there were some problems between the Allies and themselves. Maltzan cautiously sounded them out on resuming the Berlin talks. However, he was not so convinced by Giannini's information that he was ready

97. *DBFP*, 19:417–21.

98. Barthou to Poincaré, Genoa, 16 Apr., FMAE Y 29. *L'Europe Nouvelle*, 25:226, noting the absences of Riddell and Stevenson, commented: "Il n'y a plus de fée dans la délégation britannique."

99. Hankey to Chamberlain, 16 Apr., HP; Lyubimov and Erlikh, "1922 Genoa Conference," p. 102, had felt so too.

100. Barthou to Poincaré, 16 Apr., FMAE Y 29; Carrigan [Child] to State Dept., Milan, 15 Apr., USDS 550 E1/194; Japanese Delegation to Facta, 18 Apr., *DBFP*, 19:421–22.

101. At Chicherin's request: *DBFP*, 19:421. See Barthou to MAE, Genoa, 16 Apr., #83–88, FMAE B 94.

102. Rathenau diary, 15 Apr., Germ. AA T-120 3398/1735/D739153.

103. "Ausführliche Aufzeichnung," in Laubach, "Maltzans Aufzeichnungen," p. 568.

to surrender.[104] In fact, he warned that if Russia concluded a separate agreement with the Allies, Berlin might not be able to revive the lapsed talks between German industrialists and the Soviet government. Germany would help *if* Russia agreed to renounce Article 116 and grant the Reich most-favored-nation treatment in the question of nationalized property. Joffe and Rakovsky, admitting they still wanted a pact with Germany, stressed that the question of recognition must be solved. Although they offered to promote Germany's arguments with Chicherin, they gave no indication that they felt compelled to modify their demands against Berlin.

Maltzan and Dufour went to the Miramare in search of their British contacts.[105] They left notes for Wise and Gregory, requesting an immediate conference. Wise arrived at the Eden Park in the late afternoon. There was a long heated discussion during which Maltzan revealed Giannini's report, Rathenau's instructions, and the talks with the Bolsheviks that day. He reproached the British for their menacing silence over the London Report. Barred from the villa talks, the Germans were frightened that their interests would be compromised by an Allied-Russian agreement. According to Maltzan, Wise tried to reassure them that Lloyd George was aware of their concerns. Moreover, he allegedly expressed no surprise at the talks that day in the Palazzo Reale, which he claimed were known also to the French and British delegations. Before departing, he repeated that the villa negotiations were going very well and would lead to a positive result.[106] Wise's statements, like Giannini's, are documented only by the Germans; once more an Allied emissary administered a dose of misinformation that, though laced with soothing rhetoric, raised the Germans' fears and propelled them toward the Bolsheviks.

Despite evidence to the contrary, the Reich delegation suspected that an East-West agreement that would sacrifice its interests was imminent. Italian journalists anticipated a positive response from Moscow. At a dinner given by the Cologne banker Louis Hagen, Wirth announced that the usually well-informed Beneš was convinced there would be an accord between the Allies and Russia. Finance Minister Andreas Hermes, who later opposed the Rapallo pact, urged Maltzan and Simson on the night of 15 April to take prompt action to stave off Germany's dangerous isolation.[107] The Germans grew more depressed. Around 11 P.M. Wise phoned, asked for details of what Germany found threatening in the London Report, and gave a casual reassurance. The

---

104. Maltzan to Dirksen, Genoa, 15 Apr., Germ. AA T-120 L312/4255/L096831–32; Schieder, "Entstehungsgeschichte," pp. 582–83.
105. "Ausführliche Aufzeichnung," in Laubach, "Maltzans Aufzeichnungen," p. 569.
106. Ibid., pp. 569–70.
107. Ibid., p. 570. Max Reiner, director of the political information service of the *Vossische Zeitung*, and Dutch banker Fentener van Vlissingen, both at the dinner, believed there was already an agreement.

Germans were not reassured; but they were not panicked either. A telegram was sent to Berlin discounting rumors that an Allied-Russian treaty had already been signed but also stating that Germany's main efforts were being directed at preventing an agreement from which it would be excluded.[108]

Around 1:15 A.M. Joffe phoned with news that the Russians were now prepared to resume negotiations and were inviting the Germans to the Imperiale at 11:00 A.M. the next morning. He admitted that there was as yet no Allied-Russian agreement, but the negotiations were expected to resume on either Monday or Tuesday. This was a lie because the villa talks were suspended until word came from Moscow.[109] In their famous pajama talk recounted by Maltzan, Rathenau, Wirth, and Simson decided that they would meet the Russians. They also decided to contact Wise once more.[110] Maltzan, after little if any sleep, phoned the Miramare at 7:30 A.M. and was told Wise was still in bed. He tried again at 9:30 and again before 10:00, when he learned that Wise had left. Maltzan, Rathenau, Simson, and Friedrich Gaus, the Foreign Ministry's legal expert, then departed for their rendezvous with the Bolsheviks.[111]

Finale

After a week of fine weather, it rained all day on Easter Sunday. That morning Wirth, Hermes, and other members of the German delegation attended mass at the Cathedral of San Lorenzo; they were greeted warmly by the archbishop and cheered by the crowds. Lloyd George attended Easter services in the English church; then with Lloyd-Greame he went to the Villa Raggi to dine with the Italians. Relieved of their official duties, Genoa's delegates scattered to the seashore or wrote letters.[112]

At noon Barthou sent a telegram and a lengthy letter to Paris summing up the impressions of his first week's work. Impatient and uncomfortable with the proceedings, irritated with the guile of his Italian hosts, he was nonetheless well satisfied that Lloyd George was keeping the pledges he had made at Bou-

108. Ibid., p. 571. Müller to AA, Cabinet, and Ebert, Genoa, 15 Apr. (there is no time of departure; it arrived in Berlin at 1:30 A.M.), Germ. AA T-120 3398/1734/D738386.

109. "Ausführliche Aufzeichnung," in Laubach, "Maltzans Aufzeichnungen," p. 571. Lyubimov and Erlikh, "1922 Genoa Conference," p. 80, state that the call was placed at 2:00 A.M. by A. V. Sabanin, chief of the Economic and Legal Department of the Narkomindel, and lasted "no more than three minutes." Which Russian phoned, and what exactly was said, remains a mystery: Laubach, "Maltzans Aufzeichnungen," p. 571, n. 81.

110. Kessler, *Rathenau*, pp. 322–23. Maltzan's "Ausführliche Aufzeichung" curiously omits Wirth from the meeting: Laubach, "Maltzans Aufzeichnungen," p. 571, n. 83.

111. "Ausführliche Aufzeichnung," in Laubach, "Maltzans Aufzeichnungen," p. 571; Kessler, *Rathenau*, p. 323.

112. Unsigned tel. to AA, Genoa, 16 Apr., Germ. AA T-120 L1468/5118/L415821; Lloyd-Greame to wife, Genoa, 16 Apr., LGrP; Kessler, *Tagebücher*, p. 297.

logne. But his chief, who also sent a telegram and letter at midday, was less complacent. Referring to the "extremely alarmed state" of French public opinion because of the Soviet statements on disarmament and the pressure to discuss reparations, Poincaré repeated his instructions and urged Barthou to "hold firm."[113] At about the same time, Wirth was sending a wire to Berlin that a Russo-German agreement was imminent.[114]

Toward noon the Germans, looking weary and anxious, arrived at the Imperiale.[115] While Rathenau conferred with Chicherin over the remaining points of dispute, his colleagues dined in Rapallo. Rathenau departed to visit a friend in Portofino. Maltzan, Gaus, and Litvinov continued the search for a formula for the knotty most-favored-nation issue. At 4 P.M. a phone call came in from the German delegation headquarters that Wirth and Rathenau had been invited to the Italians' villa to have tea with Lloyd George. Rathenau was unavailable, and Wirth, unwilling to go alone, declined.[116]

At 6:30 P.M. on 16 April, the foreign ministers of Germany and Russia signed the "Rapallo treaty." The agreement consisted of six articles providing for the immediate establishment of diplomatic and consular relations, the mutual repudiation of claims for war costs and damages, Russia's renunciation of any possible claims under the Treaty of Versailles, and Germany's waiver of claims for the nationalization of its citizens' property in Russia.[117] In a secret exchange of notes, Russia finally agreed to grant Germany equal status with the Allies if any settlement were reached subsequently on nationalized property.

Contrary to the Allies' program for Genoa, Germany had accorded Soviet Russia full and unconditional recognition. It agreed to Russia's demand to

113. Barthou to Poincaré, 16 Apr., #83–88, FMAE B 94, and letter, 16 Apr., FMAE Y 29; Poincaré to Barthou, 16 Apr., #44, FMAE Y 29, and letter, 16 Apr., FMAE PM G/V.

114. Wirth to AA (for Haniel), Genoa, 16 Apr. (no departure time; it arrived in Berlin at 2:40 P.M.), Germ. AA T-120 3398/1734/D738387.

115. Maltzan's "Ausführliche Aufzeichnung," in Laubach, "Maltzans Aufzeichnungen," p. 571, and his "Letzte Vorgänge," ibid., p. 561, give the arrival times as noon and 11:30 A.M. respectively; Lyubimov and Erlikh, "1922 Genoa Conference," p. 81, state they arrived at 11:00 A.M.

116. D'Abernon to Curzon, Berlin, 23 Apr., GB FO 371 N3995/646/38; Rathenau to Lloyd George, Genoa, 18 Apr., Germ. AA T-120 3398/1735/D738736–37. When he returned from Portofino and learned of the invitation, Rathenau allegedly "paced up and down once or twice, then turned to Maltzan and said, 'le vin est tiré, il faut le boire,' stepped into his car and drove off with Maltzan still pale with emotion on the front seat, to sign the treaty": Kessler, *Rathenau*, p. 324.

117. Text in Germ. AA T-120 3398/1735/D738919–22 and *DVP SSSR*, 5:223–24. Though the treaty said "done at Rapallo, 16 Apr.," the Imperiale was actually located within the borders of Santa Margherita. Ostensibly the Germans, who had used "Rapallo" from the beginning to describe the Russian headquarters, were responsible for misnaming the treaty after the larger municipality: cf. Lyubimov and Erlikh, "1922 Genoa Conference," p. 79.

extend the pact to all the federated republics, including the Ukraine, thus being the first government to recognize the unity of the Soviet state.[118] Moreover, both countries agreed to "mutually seek to meet [each other's] economic requirements . . . in a spirit of good will." This meant implicitly that Germany had withdrawn from the international corporation and had pledged to promote better economic relations between Reich industry and the Soviet government.

Except for the one small concession on the most-favored nation (which was a moot point anyway in view of Chicherin's statement the day before that Russia would resist restoring private property to former owners), Germany had gained little for its week's delay. The treaty represented a lopsided Soviet victory, caused by a combination of deceitfulness and ambition. Litvinov gloated to Moscow: "Our semi-private talks with the Supreme Council [sic] aroused fears in the minds of the Germans, and Rathenau, neither alive nor dead, came running to us yesterday and proposed right on the spot the same agreement which he refused to sign during our stay in Berlin."[119]

The German delegation, fearing the treaty's reception at home, stressed to Berlin the defensive nature of the agreement: it was a means of "preventing isolation."[120] Rathenau emphasized that the British had been kept "constantly informed." He sought to minimize the consequences and still anticipated a decisive encounter with Lloyd George, which had been delayed Sunday afternoon by the "Kämpfe von Rapallo." Returning from the Imperiale, he met Blackett and told him the entire contents of the treaty. The British reparations expert apparently accepted the news with neither anger nor astonishment. Early the next morning, Maltzan sent a copy to Wise.[121]

The formal reconciliation between Germany and Russia took few people by surprise because the Berlin negotiations had been well monitored by every capital. Poincaré deemed the Rapallo treaty not unexpected but "stupid." "Fortunately," he told an American journalist, "we can always count on Germany to make a blunder," isolating themselves "on the first occasion they were allowed to participate in a European conference."[122] Nevertheless, an explo-

118. "Ausführliche Aufzeichnung," in Laubach, "Maltzans Aufzeichnungen," p. 572.

119. *DVP SSSR*, 5:226. Intercepted by the British: LGP F 26/1/30.

120. "Letzte Vorgänge," 17 Apr., in Laubach, "Maltzans Aufzeichnungen," pp. 560–64; Müller to Ebert, Reichskanzlei, Press Section of AA, Genoa, 18 Apr., Germ. AA T-120 3398/1734/D738409–14; and Kessler, *Tagebücher*, p. 299: "The essential point for us was that we could wait no longer without the danger that the Entente would conclude an agreement with the Russians without consulting or *including* us. Also that the Russians demanded we sign *now*" (italics in the original).

121. Rathenau to Haniel, Genoa, 17 Apr., Germ. Pol. Arch. AA, Bur. R.M., bd. 10; Maltzan, "Letzte Vorgänge," in Laubach, "Maltzans Aufzeichnungen," p. 564; and Maltzan to Wise, Genoa, 17 Apr., Grigg Papers, roll 9.

122. Confidential talk, Paris, 18 May, LGP F 5/8/14.

sion erupted in Genoa and reverberated outside because a separate agreement had been signed in the midst of the tense first days of the conference. This triggered a search for accomplices. Lloyd George became the target of rumors that he had instigated or tolerated the Rapallo treaty as an alternative model to the stalled negotiations with the Russians. The French, already "very nervous" over what concessions might have to be made to the Bolsheviks, and the Germans, fearing the price of the Rapallo pact, both claimed that the British leader had a major responsibility for the bombshell. The French and Germans were convinced that even if Lloyd George had not known all the details in advance, he must have approved of the act.[123]

However, all evidence points not only to Lloyd George's surprise but also to his negative reaction to the fait accompli that he had long warned against and predicted.[124] Had he wished to intimidate Poincaré, he had more effective means of coercing the French than ruining his own diplomacy. To be sure, Paris was a convenient butt of his criticism because of its stiffness on reparations and disarmament, Barthou's gaffes, and the sheaves of telegrams from the "absent gentleman in Paris." But it stretches credulity to insist on Lloyd George's schadenfreude with a treaty that menaced France, its allies, and the still-new structure of postwar Europe.

To be sure, the hours before Rapallo indicated the weakness of the Lloyd Georgian system and its style of personal diplomacy; Wise's role, especially his nonchalance in the face of distinct German warnings, remains inexplicable, but again we have only the German side of these negotiations. Perhaps the Reich delegation relied too heavily on its customary channels, which this time failed to reach Lloyd George. Because he put a good face on almost immediately does not prove the accusation that Lloyd George's surprise and anger were in any way feigned. Britain regarded Berlin as a junior partner, but a competitor in the East. If memories of the Somme were fading, the anxiety over the German economic colossus was not.

Some members of the Allied camp did welcome the Rapallo treaty. Grigg thought that the view of the "precipice" exposed by the Russo-German agreement would force a prompt settlement at Genoa, but he also admitted that the

123. Lyubimov and Erlikh, "1922 Genoa Conference," pp. 82–83, quotes *Matin* correspondent Jules Sauerwein. For the Germans, see Dufour Aufzeichnung, Genoa, 16 May, Germ. AA T-120 L795/5105/L233209–14; Kessler, *Tagebücher*, pp. 298–99; and Ernst Laubach, *Die Politik der Kabinette Wirth, 1921/1922* (Lübeck and Hamburg: Matthiesen, 1968), p. 211, n. 222.

124. Even so astute an observer as Beneš confirmed this in a telegram to Masaryk: Gajanová, "Politique extérieure tchécoslovaque," p. 161. His first words, on hearing of the treaty, were, "Impossible; surely such a thing could not happen": Sylvester, *Real Lloyd George*, p. 81. Then he fumed, "Damn German stupidity": *My Darling Pussy*, p. 44. German historians (Erdmann, Stamm, and Pogge von Strandmann) contend that Lloyd George objected more to the timing of the Rapallo treaty than to its content.

Bolsheviks had now gained the upper hand. Similarly, an Italian diplomat's optimism that Rapallo would contribute to "equilibrium" was naive; the two signatories scarcely had any desire to stabilize the present structure of Europe.[125]

By going to Rapallo, Germany deliberately broke the West's solidarity versus Soviet Russia to gain its own advantage. On the pretext of a largely nonexistent threat—that a deal between the Allies and Russia would force Germany to pay reparations beyond what it was currently refusing to pay and would relieve the Russians of compensating German creditors, when it was refusing to recognize most foreign claims—Germany came to terms with the Russians and secured for itself a premier place in Russian reconstruction. There was also the hint of an accompanying military accord; though not signed at Genoa, this was well advanced in terms of the year-long collaboration between Berlin and Moscow. The Rapallo agreement thus exposed the vulnerability not only of Poland but of the entire East European settlement established after World War I. Finally, and perhaps most significant, the Rapallo treaty was meant to impress the German public. The German delegation at Genoa hoped that once they understood the circumstances that caused it to occur, the German people would recognize Rapallo as the Reich's first independent demarche since 1914.[126]

The Genoa Conference was distorted, but not destroyed, by the Rapallo treaty. It continued five more weeks. However, now Lloyd George was forced to demonstrate ingenuity, courage, patience, and leadership to salvage what could be saved. It would be a difficult and perhaps impossible task to overcome the shock of the event on Easter Sunday.

125. Grigg to Chamberlain, Genoa, 18 Apr., Grigg Papers, roll 1; Frassati to MAE, Berlin, 19 Apr., IMAE 52/37–38.
126. Hemmer to Wever, Genoa, 22 Apr., Germ. AA T-120 K1946/5372/K505560–63.

6

Genoa Continues

The second week of the Genoa Conference was largely devoted to the Rapallo culprits: devising a means of chastising Germany and, at almost the same time, trying to convince the Soviet representatives to give a satisfactory response to the Allied proposals of 15 April at the Villa d'Albertis. The locale of the negotiations changed abruptly. The inviting powers moved to Schanzer's villa, to the seat of the British Empire delegation at the Hotel Miramare, and finally back to the conference headquarters at the Palazzo Reale. New faces appeared and new groupings took part in the proceedings; both developments were unanticipated and unintended. In the wake of the Rapallo crisis, the second week of the Genoa Conference created intense conflicts among the major delegations and a growing mistrust outside. It was nevertheless a time for "action," on which Lloyd George thrived.[1]

Germany Chastised

On Monday morning, those members of the German cabinet present at Genoa met with their principal advisors for a placid session at the Eden Park Hotel. Rathenau reported on the preceding day's negotiations that had "produced the treaty with Soviet Russia." Weighing its impact on the Genoa Conference, he overoptimistically predicted that the British would support it and the Italians would follow Britain's lead. France would no doubt launch a "politically-motivated attack," but he expressed no concern over this. Wirth praised the foreign minister and his associates for consummating the deed, and there were no dissenting voices. Socialist Economics Minister Robert Schmidt said that the treaty would be welcomed by the Left and by heavy industry, and he anticipated no difficulty with the Right.[2] In this state of utter complacency, there was also no objection to Rathenau's announcement that he had advised Berlin to ignore the most recent message from the Reparations Commission, which firmly though tactfully answered all of Germany's objections to increasing taxes, accepting conditions for a foreign loan, and submitting to external controls. The

1. Hankey to Chamberlain, Genoa, 18 Apr., HP.
2. *Akten-Wirth*, 2: no. 246.

commission had also announced that there would be no further communication until the 31 May deadline.[3]

On Easter Monday morning, the Germans and Russians polished the text of their treaty and exchanged their confidential notes.[4] At noon Rathenau announced the agreement to the German press and distributed copies in ample time to make headlines that evening all over Europe. While continuing his own efforts to overcome Bücher's opposition to his loan negotiations, Rathenau sent Baron von Neurath, the German ambassador to Rome, with a personal message to Schanzer and to American Ambassador Child. Wirth's press chief visited the British delegation, told Hankey the Rapallo agreement was "harmless," and pledged Germany's cooperation with the work of the Genoa Conference, neglecting to mention that the treaty had just been published.[5] Late that afternoon, when Kessler was bringing congratulations on the news sweeping through Genoa, he found Rathenau in the Eden Park garden with Giannini, who was "not happy with the Russian negotiations."[6] All three gentlemen realized that the Rapallo treaty had damaged the Allies' bargaining position with the Soviets.

Although he was furious with the Germans for their misdeed and their arrogance, Lloyd George needed to display cool restraint in order to retain control over the Genoa Conference, achieve his aims, and ensure his prompt return to Britain. The night before he and Schanzer had invited the French, Belgians, and Japanese (who were disturbed over the offer to reduce Russia's war debts) to a meeting on Monday at 5 P.M. in Schanzer's villa. They intended to lead a discussion on their options if the Russians should accept, reject, or (what was considered most likely) give an equivocal response to Saturday's offer. Because of Rapallo, the meeting took another turn. Taking advantage of the group's bewilderment over the bombshell, Lloyd George expressed outrage mixed with prescience at an act of which he had been both "totally ignorant" and nevertheless expecting. Playing on their fears of all the consequences,

---

3. Ibid., pp. 706–7; Étienne Weill-Raynal, *Les réparations allemandes et la France* (Paris: Nouvelles Éditions Latines, 1947), 2:157–58; Poincaré to Barthou, Paris, 13, 16 Apr., #28, #44, FMAE B 93, 26 Apr., #178–80, FMAE B 95.

4. Russia granted Germany most-favored-nation status if an agreement on nationalized property were consummated with a third party, and Germany agreed to participate in the international corporation only after prior consultation with Moscow: Simson to AA, Genoa, 17 Apr., Germ. AA T-120 3398/1735/D738917–22.

5. Rathenau, diary, 17 Apr., Germ. AA T-120 3398/1735/D739155; Haniel to Rathenau, Berlin, 19 Apr., and Neurath to Wirth and Rathenau, Genoa, 19 Apr., Germ. AA T-120 L309/4255/L096197–98, L096245–47; Gregory to FO, Genoa, 17 Apr., GB FO 371 N3564/646/38; Hankey to Chamberlain, Genoa, 18 Apr., HP.

6. Rathenau diary, 17 Apr., Germ. AA T-120 3398/1735/D739155; Kessler, *Tagebücher*, pp. 297–98.

Lloyd George termed the rapprochement of the two pariahs a "very serious fact," adding that it menaced Britain less than the rest of Europe.[7]

Caught completely off guard and without instructions from Paris, Barthou made nasty inquiries to Schanzer about the Italo-Soviet liaison, charged that Rapallo violated both the Treaty of Versailles and the Cannes Resolutions, and vaguely threatened to withdraw from the Genoa Conference.[8] The Belgian and Japanese delegations echoed his shock and outrage. Responding to Schanzer's plea to save Genoa, Lloyd George genially proposed that they "sleep on the problem." But that was not all. He forced Barthou to drop his demand to call a plenary session to expel the two culprits from Genoa. He gave shape to the Allies' response by offering to draft a censorious letter to the Germans *alone*, who had violated the West's solidarity against the Bolsheviks. He recommended that a committee of jurists decide whether the Rapallo agreement violated the Treaty of Versailles. Finally, he thwarted Barthou's resolve to discontinue the semiofficial talks with the Russians. It was not only assumed these would go on, but Lloyd George also insisted that these were now an essential means of separating Russia from Germany. All Lloyd George conceded was the inclusion of representatives of the Little Entente and Poland—undoubtedly interested powers—in the protest note to Germany, and he agreed to postpone the technical commissions sine die.[9]

Hankey, Grigg, Horne, Worthington-Evans, and Lloyd-Greame worked through the night, producing at least five drafts of a strong protest note to Germany. Britain's strategy was to censure Germany, but not excessively. It did not wish to force the Germans to leave, provoke the Bolsheviks to act chivalrously in the Reich's defense, or offend the United States. The rebuke was intended to assuage Lloyd George's anger, reassure Barthou's superior, and allow Genoa to continue.[10] That night Lloyd George made a surprise appearance at a dinner given at the Hotel de Gênes by Albert Thomas, director of the International Labor Organization; there he publicly berated German State Secretary Julius Hirsch and accused Rathenau of duplicity. Neither the French nor the Germans entirely believed him. Rathenau prepared his defense.[11]

7. Notes of informal conversation, 17 Apr., *DBFP*, 19:522–30; Hankey to Chamberlain, Genoa, 18 Apr., HP; Gregory to Curzon, Genoa, 18 Apr. (2 tels.), GB FO 371 N3671, N3672/646/38.

8. Barthou to Poincaré, Genoa, 17 Apr., #103–7, FMAE B 116, ending: "Please send precise instructions."

9. Ibid.

10. Hankey to Chamberlain, Genoa, 18 Apr., HP; Lloyd-Greame to wife, Genoa, 19 Apr., LGrP.

11. Hirsch Privataufzeichnung, Genoa, 17 Apr., Germ. AA T-120 3398/1735/D738929–39; Poincaré to Barthou, Paris, 18 Apr., #62, FMAE Y 30; Hardinge to FO, Paris, 19 Apr., GB FO 371 N3699/646/38; Rathenau to Haniel, Genoa, 18 Apr., Germ. AA T-120 L640/4783/

On Tuesday morning a new ad hoc grouping met at the Villa Raggi to agree on a stiff note to the Germans. In addition to the inviting powers, Poland, Czechoslovakia, Rumania, Yugoslavia, and Britain's "oldest ally," Portugal, were present.[12] Facta, newly arrived from Rome, had learned of the crisis on the train. The Italians pleaded for moderation, prepared a lavish lunch, and urged them not to disband until they could face the press with a constructive statement. Facta's pleas were reinforced by the arrival of a deputation of Giolittians asking for information.[13]

During the talks, which lasted seven hours, the harsh British text was modified by the Italians. Germany was nonetheless condemned for

> secretly conclud[ing] a treaty with the Soviet government . . . in violation of the conditions to which [it] pledged [itself] in entering the conference. . . . By inviting Germany to Genoa and by offering representation to her on equal terms with themselves, the Inviting Powers proved their readiness to waive the memories of war and granted Germany the opportunity of honest cooperation with her former enemies in the European tasks of the conference. To that offer of goodwill and friendship Germany had replied with an act which destroys that spirit of mutual confidence which is indispensable to international cooperation.[14]

Lloyd George intended to dispose of the Rapallo treaty by issuing this clear reproach and by prohibiting Germany from further participation in the negotiations between the Allies and Russia. He insisted on continuing the negotiations. While awaiting the final draft, he guided the meeting into a discussion about Russia and the prospects of coming to an agreement with the Bolsheviks. Schanzer also used the opportunity to gain the delegates' support for resuming the suspended technical commissions. By evening the note was signed, sealed, and dispatched to the Reich delegation, in time for its publication in the morning newspapers of Europe.[15]

Barthou had suffered a major setback. Contrary to Poincaré's instructions, the protest made no explicit statement about Germany's violations of the Treaty of Versailles and the Cannes Resolutions. Ignoring Paris's advice, he had also

---

L203567–68; Harry Graf Kessler, *Tagebücher, 1918–1937* (Frankfurt-am-Main: Insel-Verlag, 1961), pp. 288–89; and Rathenau to Lloyd George, Genoa, 18 Apr., LGP F 53/3/14.

12. Notes of meeting, 18 Apr., 11 A.M., *DBFP*, 19:431–43; Hankey to Chamberlain, Genoa, 18 Apr., HP; Lloyd-Greame to wife, Genoa, 19 Apr., LGrP; Barthou to Poincaré, Genoa, 18 Apr., #115–21, FMAE B 116; Haniel to Rathenau, Berlin, 19 Apr., Germ. AA T-120 L309/4255/L096197–98.

13. *DBFP*, 19:443.

14. Ibid., pp. 444–45. In Lloyd George's original wording (p. 444): "Germany had replied with an act of disloyalty."

15. Notes of meeting, 18 Apr., 4:30 P.M., ibid., pp. 446–51.

consented to an unequal treatment of Germany and Russia. Notwithstanding all his bluster, he had been outmaneuvered by both Lloyd George and Schanzer. Even the inclusion of Poland, Rumania, Yugoslavia, and Czechoslavakia (of which Barthou boasted as a French victory) had not helped him; the small powers made it clear they would not follow France in causing a rupture. All Barthou gained was a "moral" victory; by manifesting a distinctive pliability, he was credited with allowing the Genoa Conference to continue, though he admitted it now held real dangers for France.[16]

Lloyd George had to convince the Germans to accept the Allies' note, relinquish their place on the Political Commission, but not leave Genoa. He invited them for the first time to the Villa d'Albertis. Abject but unrepentant, Wirth, Rathenau, Maltzan, and Dufour arrived at noon on 19 April. Lloyd George was accompanied by Lloyd-Greame, Hankey, and Grigg, and there was no one from the Foreign Office. For two hours they argued under a bright, blinding sun; a breeze blew Hankey's papers, and a sudden shower drenched his notes, adding to his discomfort with the company.[17]

Lloyd George, exploiting the developing schism within the Reich delegation over the merits of the Rapallo treaty, accused the Germans of having ruined his hopes for a "real [sic] talk" on reparations at the Genoa Conference. He claimed that despite Poincaré's resistance, he had almost obtained Barthou's agreement, but the German action had stifled his initiative. Indeed, "Dr. Rathenau had no idea how difficult it was to keep France from going into the Ruhr." Then he gave the Germans the choice of withdrawing the Rapallo treaty or accepting the Allies' note.[18]

Uncowed, Rathenau accused the Allies of ruining Germany with their interminable commissions and demands, and complained of the prime minister's aloofness during the first days of the Genoa Conference, which had caused "his own arrangement with Russia." When he threatened that instead of accepting either unpleasant alternative Germany might leave Genoa, Lloyd George taunted that such a gesture would neither appease the Reich public nor influence the outcome of the Genoa Conference. Rejecting Wirth's woeful

16. Poincaré to Barthou, Paris, 18 Apr., #58, FMAE Y 30, #59, FMAE B 94, #64, FMAE B 116, 19 Apr., #69–71, FMAE B 94; Barthou to Poincaré, Genoa, 18 Apr., #115–21, FMAE B 116; Barthou [Barrère and Seydoux] to Peretti, Genoa, 18 Apr., #113–14, FMAE B 116; and Hankey to Chamberlain, Genoa, 18 Apr., HP.

17. Hankey to wife, Genoa, 20 Apr., HP: "Rathenau the Foreign Minister is a horrible German Jew, very degenerate in appearance with a head shaped like an egg. The Chancellor was a fat . . . gemütlich kind of German, not a bad sort. But they were horribly shifty and equivocal, evading the point and making false insinuations. . . . Their personalities revealed all the troubles that led to the war. . . . They were impossible people to deal with."

18. Notes of meeting, 19 Apr., *DBFP*, 19:452–62; Aufzeichnung über eine Unterredung, 19 Apr., Germ. AA T-120 3398/1735/D739226–35.

tales and additional excuses for Rapallo and also evading Rathenau's plea to help Germany's "economic life" in return for its cooperation at Genoa, Lloyd George repeated that the price for their full participation was the annulment of the Rapallo treaty. He sent the Germans off to Santa Margherita on an essentially futile mission.[19]

Rathenau, angry and bitter at his treatment by the British leader, had been bluffing: he had no intention either of leaving Genoa or succumbing to Lloyd George's blackmail. Chicherin obligingly refused to rescind the Rapallo agreement.[20] Wirth, on the other hand, appealed for British sympathy, asked for help with the Russians, and deftly shifted the blame for all misunderstanding to Rathenau.[21] The latter conveyed the Russians' refusal to the British delegation. He then threatened the harried Schanzer to throw the Genoa Conference into disarray by issuing a formal rejection of the Allies' note. His price for accepting Germany's exclusion from the Political Commission was an indication of the Allies' willingness to consider concessions on reparations, a foreign loan, and the easing of military control. The Italians delivered a positive response, presumably from Lloyd George.[22]

On 21 April Wirth wrote to Facta formally accepting the Allies' conditions. Written in a querulous and tendentious tone, the letter justified the Rapallo treaty. Moreover, though agreeing to withdraw from the negotiations "on questions . . . already settled between Germany and Russia," Wirth stressed Germany's interest in all other questions to be handled by the Political Commission.[23] Lloyd George held a gala press conference that afternoon in the Palazzo San Giorgio to announce that the crisis was over.[24] Across town Wirth also met with journalists but was far less confident. The Germans, in obvious disarray, had made no progress on obtaining a loan or bettering their situation vis-à-vis the Reparations Commission. They had nevertheless been allowed by Lloyd

19. Ibid. The Italian, French, Belgian and Japanese delegations received a full report of the meeting: Barthou to MAE, Genoa, 19 Apr., #140, FMAE B 116.

20. Maltzan Aufzeichnung, 19 Apr., Germ. AA T-120 L640/4784/L203597: The Russians suggested conditions for delaying or enlarging Rapallo, which the Germans did not pursue; *Akten-Wirth*, 2:712–15.

21. Brand to Grigg, 20 Apr., Grigg Papers, roll 1; Grigg to Lloyd George, n.d., GB CAB 31/S.G. 10; Moritz Bonn, *Wandering Scholar* (New York: John Day, 1948), pp. 270–71.

22. Unterhaltung Rathenau–Lloyd-Greame, 19 Apr., Germ. AA T-120 3398/1735/D739236–39; *Akten-Wirth*, 2:714; Gregory to FO, Genoa, 20 Apr., GB FO 371 N3745/646/38; Unterredung Schanzer-Rathenau, 20 Apr., Germ. AA T-120 3398/1735/D739240–41; Unterhaltung Rathenau-Visconti Venosta, 20 Apr., Germ. AA T-120 3398/1735/D739142; Müller to AA, Haniel, Ebert, Wever, and Rauscher, Genoa, 21 Apr., and Müller to AA, 21 Apr., Germ. AA T-120 L1468/5118/L415860–61, 3398/1734/D738466–49; *Akten-Wirth*, 2:721–22.

23. Text in Germ. AA T-120 3398/1735/D738990–93 and *DBFP*, 19:505–6.

24. *Deutsche Allgemeine Zeitung* and *Daily Telegraph*, 21 Apr.; eyewitness accounts in Kessler, *Tagebücher*, pp. 303–4, and Jean de Pierrefeu, *Saison diplomatique: Gênes (Avril–Mai 1922)* (Paris: Éditions Montaigne, 1928), pp. 94–97.

George to escape with the mild-enough sanction of remaining excluded from the Allies' negotiations with the Russians.[25] These, however, were now sorely prejudiced by their separate treaty.

Lloyd George's clever acrobatics to save the Genoa Conference added to the puzzlement and anger in Paris, where the news of the Rapallo treaty struck like a bolt of lightning.[26] On 18 April *Le Temps* termed the pact a "preparation for war." Even members of the moderate Left urged the government to withdraw from the Genoa Conference, and there was pressure from the Right to convene parliament at once. The Poincaré cabinet, stressing the threat to Versailles, interpreted the crisis as a test of the Allies' willingness to enforce the peace. On 20 April *Le Temps* speculated that if they did not, Germany, like Prussia in 1762, 1813, and 1870, would rise in revanche with Russia's help and Italy's complicity. Paris observed the first surprised responses to Rapallo transformed into an acceptance of the fait accompli, into approval by the Italians and many of the neutrals, and into discreet celebrations by segments of the German press, accompanied by painful and widespread reproaches to France for having forced Germany into the arms of Soviet Russia.[27]

Poincaré was prodded by the Right to make an adequate response and vainly sought a means *outside of Genoa*—either through the Conference of Ambassadors or the Reparations Commission—to condemn the Rapallo treaty.[28] At the same time he bombarded Barthou with demands to annul the treaty. Barthou's only possible response was to send a letter to Facta complaining of Germany's provocative response to the Allies, though this exposed him to Lloyd George's anger and impatience and to charges that France was trying to "wreck" Genoa.[29] To maintain Allied solidarity in the renewed negotiations with the

25. *Akten-Wirth*, 2:722, 725; cf. *Tägliche Rundschau*, 21 Apr.

26. Mayer to AA, Paris, 18 Apr., Germ. AA T-120 3398/1734/D738406–7.

27. Tardieu to Poincaré, Paris, 19 Apr., Poincaré to Barthou, Paris, 19 Apr., #74–77, FMAE B 116, 20 Apr., #94, 21 Apr., #101, FMAE Y 30; Jean Goût to Millerand, Paris, 20 Apr., FMAE PM G/V ("Everyone here is counting up the Versailles articles that Rapallo has violated."); Mayer to AA, Paris, 20 Apr. (2 tels.), Germ. AA T-120 3398/1734/D738439–40, D738442–45. Foreign press reaction in: Jusserand to MAE, Washington, n.d. (arrived 19 Apr.), #493–95, and Charles-Roux to MAE, Rome, 18 Apr., #517–18, FMAE B 116; Saint-Aulaire to Poincaré, London, 19 Apr., FMAE Y 30; and summary of German, French, and Polish presses in Germ. AA T-120 3398/1735/D739034–36.

28. Mayer to AA, Paris, 20 Apr., Germ. AA T-120 3398/1734/D738450–51; Hardinge to FO and Delegation in Genoa, Paris, 20 Apr., GB FO 371 N3747/646/38; Sforza to Rome and Genoa, Paris, 22 Apr., IMAE 52/20. Abortive protests to Conference of Ambassadors: Saint-Aulaire to Curzon, London, 20 Apr., and Ovey to Saint-Aulaire, London, 26 Apr., GB FO 371 N3762/646/38. Also protests to Reparations Commission: Poincaré to Dubois, Paris, 21 Apr., and Dubois to Poincaré, Paris, 28 Apr., FMAE B 116, 117.

29. Barthou to Facta, 21 Apr., *DBFP*, 19:495; Poincaré to Barthou, Paris, 22 Apr., #109, FMAE Y 31; Barthou to MAE, Genoa, 22 Apr., #170–71, FMAE B 94; and note of conversation, 22 Apr., 11 A.M., GB CAB 31/S.G. 12.

Russians, Lloyd George and Schanzer reluctantly agreed to draft another censorious note to the Germans. Barthou said he would write one too.[30]

One week after Rapallo, on 23 April, the inviting powers, Little Entente, Poland, and Portugal reassembled at the Palazzo Reale.[31] Brătianu pleaded for Anglo-French solidarity; Facta urged them to work for Genoa's success; and Lloyd George denounced the "old spirits of conflicts and hatreds" that might drive British democracy away from its former allies. Barthou shrank from the Welshman's tantrum and perceived that France's solitary gesture was deplored by all present. Britain's draft was accepted with minor amendments. It rejected all of Germany's justifications for Rapallo but cited no specific violations of existing treaties, and then declared the incident "closed."[32]

Rathenau, forewarned by Schanzer, was unwilling to submit to another rebuke. Because it seemed imprudent to provoke France further, Wirth wrote a personal letter to Facta rebutting the new Allied statements, which, by prior agreement, would not be published. Lloyd George opposed this maneuver, whereupon Schanzer persuaded the Germans to desist. In the end Rathenau agreed, and he derived satisfaction from this token gallantry and from saving the Genoa Conference from another demonstration of French irascibility.[33]

The week-long divisive effort to chastise Germany undoubtedly strained Franco-British relations. Barthou, much to Paris's chagrin, lamented his "isolation."[34] Poincaré, "at the end of his patience" and losing confidence in his chief delegate, started the series of requests summoning Barthou back to Paris. Barthou, deeming his presence "crucial" during Genoa's continuing crises, demurred.[35] In spite of the urgings of Barthou and Saint-Aulaire, Poincaré refused to go to Genoa and be subject to Lloyd George's pressure.[36] As at

---

30. Meeting, 22 Apr., 4 P.M., *DBFP*, 19:495–504; Barthou to MAE, Genoa, 22 Apr., #171, FMAE B 116.

31. Meeting, 23 Apr., 10:30 P.M., *DBFP*, 19:508–12.

32. Text in ibid., pp. 513–14; Barthou to MAE, Genoa, 23 Apr., #182, #183–88, FMAE B 116; Gregory to Crowe, Genoa, 23 Apr., and Wigram to Waterlow, Genoa, 24 Apr., GB FO 371 N3592, N3919/646/38; Hankey to Chamberlain, Genoa, 23 Apr., HP.

33. Unterhaltung Rathenau-Schanzer, 22 Apr., Germ. AA T-120 3398/1735/D739254–55; Unterhaltung Rathenau–Romano Avezanna, 23 Apr., Germ. AA T-120 3398/1735/D739262–63; note of conversation with Dufour, 24 Apr., Grigg Papers, roll 9; Besprechung mit Venosta, Schanzer, und Facta, Genoa, 25 Apr., Germ. AA T-120 3398/1735/D739258–60; Rathenau to AA [i.e., Wirth to Ebert], Genoa, 25 Apr., Germ. AA T-120 L996/5412/L286129–32; and *DBFP*, 19:514.

34. Barthou to Poincaré, Genoa, 23 Apr., #197, FMAE Y 31; 26 Apr., #227, FMAE B 95.

35. Poincaré to Barthou, 22 Apr., #109, FMAE Y 31, 23 Apr., #123–24, FMAE B 94, 25 Apr., #151–53 ("The cabinet takes exception . . . to the term 'isolation' "), FMAE PM G/V. Also Barthou to Poincaré, Genoa, 22 Apr., #171, FMAE B 116.

36. Barthou to MAE, Genoa, 22 Apr., #170, FMAE B 94, and Saint-Aulaire to MAE, London, 24 Apr., #424–28, FMAE B 95.

Cannes, the French public viewed every aspect of the treatment of Germany as both a crucial test of the Entente and a dangerous trial for its prime ministers.

Lloyd George was dangerously impatient. Though he complained publicly of the two days' delay caused by France's protest, his entourage privately boasted of his growing mastery over Barthou and over the leaders of the Little Entente.[37] The British leader's compulsion to save the Genoa Conference made him arrogant and heedless of France's shock after Rapallo. His machinations to effect a quick, relatively benign slap at the Germans had nevertheless provoked additional defiant gestures from the Reich delegation to which France was challenged to respond. From the viewpoint of Paris, the virtually harmless chastisement of Germany for an act so grave underscored the dangers of the conference. The result was a growing tension and suspicion between Paris and Genoa that could do nothing but threaten the main part of Lloyd George's grand design.

Resumption of Talks with the Russians

The renewed negotiations with the Russians proved even more difficult and divisive for the Allies than the crisis over Germany. Indeed, they had come to Genoa precisely to negotiate an agreement with the Bolsheviks. On the docket there were two documents: the London Report with its rigorous terms and the note to Chicherin of 15 April insisting that Russia must recognize all its debts in order for Genoa to continue. Lloyd George interjected into the discussions of 18 April the warning that though the Germans had "stolen a march" on them, they must not "accept defeat." Indeed, as Barthou had anticipated, he urged that they "do [their] best to seduce Russia from the arms of Germany."[38]

Theunis attempted to move things along by proposing that they discuss the outstanding questions regarding Russia "en bloc, instead of taking one point at a time," leaving aside, of course, the question of de jure recognition.[39] There were immediate hesitations. The French and Japanese delegates opposed even a discussion of de jure recognition. The Rumanian delegate made the first in his series of announcements concerning the "special problems" his government had to settle before resuming relations with Soviet Russia.[40]

Beneš, who was at the meeting only to sign the condemnatory statement

37. Hankey to Chamberlain, Genoa, 23 Apr., HP.
38. Meeting, 18 Apr., *DBFP*, 19:447; Barthou to Poincaré, Genoa, 17 Apr., #103–7, FMAE B 116.
39. Meeting, 18 Apr., *DBFP*, 19:449.
40. Bessarabia, the Rumanian treasure in Moscow, and the security of Rumania's eastern frontier: ibid., pp. 449–50.

The Allies at Genoa. (*Front row, left to right*) Barrère, Schanzer,
Worthington-Evans, Lloyd George, Facta, and Barthou (courtesy of UPI).

against Germany, also tried to break the deadlock. He urged the Allies to
cooperate in developing a strong and positive economic program to reconstruct Russia. Should the Bolsheviks accept the Allies' terms, this would form
the basis of an immediate *economic* agreement; should Moscow refuse, the
West could demonstrate with their "elaborate and concrete program" their
solidarity, their superiority to Germany, and a useful propagandistic weapon
against the Communists.[41]

41. Ibid., p. 450. Background in Koch to AA, Prague, 20 Apr., Germ. AA T-120
L1468/5118/L415869–73; unsigned Aufzeichnung, Prague, 3 May, Germ. BA R 43 I/132;

Beneš's remarks went to the heart of the dilemma. Aside from de jure recognition (which France had virtually ruled out), what could the Western governments acting in concert actually offer the Russians? Indeed, Germany had grappled with this problem since January. In the end, Berlin had accorded immediate, nonconditional recognition but no meaningful guarantee of private or government credits. The Allies still had an opportunity to accomplish something at Genoa if they could provide a tangible offer to Moscow.

Chicherin was still interested in this possibility. He invited a junior Foreign Office representative, Commander Maxse, to the Hotel de Gênes on 19 April and announced that he had received a definitive reply from the Soviet government to the Allies' note of 15 April. His instructions, signed by Lenin and Trotsky, authorized him to accept the Allies' terms with certain reservations concerning the length of the moratorium and the restitution of confiscated factories, but the main condition was that the Russian government receive "substantial credits for reconstruction purposes." After conferring with Lloyd George, Maxse assured Chicherin, Litvinov, and Krassin that credits would be available through the international corporation and Britain's Trade Facilities and Export Credits Acts but admitted that his government was unable to obtain specific funds from parliament or make practical arrangements at Genoa. All Maxse could propose was a prompt and formal debt recognition by the Russians, which would open the varied private sources of capital to them.[42]

Convinced of Chicherin's keenness to settle, Lloyd George, hosting a luncheon of the inviting powers on 20 April, proposed a new procedure: a small committee of experts to discuss the details of the anticipated positive Soviet note.[43] He argued that the smaller group could "thrash out" details of the moratorium for debt repayment, restitution of private property, providing security for future investments, and "giving concrete shape to what could be done by Europe for the reconstruction of Russia." Barthou was unhappy about a small committee having so extensive a mandate and so many possible snares, but he could not overcome Lloyd George's persuasiveness and the consensus of the group. He succeeded only in enlarging the experts' committee to include a representative of the neutrals and the Little Entente. Lloyd George insisted on commencing the informal talks at once. In his long diplomatic experience, he had found these crucial to achieving "practical results."[44]

The British had far overestimated their persuasiveness with the Russians.

Masaryk to Beneš, Prague, 18, 24 Apr., *Dokumenty e materialy po istorii sovetsko-chekhoslovakskikh otnoshenii* (Moscow: Ministerstvo Inostrannykh Del, 1973), 1:492–93, 494–95.

42. Maxse memorandum, Genoa, 20 Apr., Grigg Papers, roll 9. The two-thousand-word telegram from Moscow (intercepted by the Italian secret service) in Attolico report, Genoa, 20 Apr., LNA 40A 20136/20226.

43. *DBFP*, 19:463–71.

44. Ibid., pp. 468–69, 471; Barthou to MAE, Genoa, 20 Apr., FMAE Y 30.

Chicherin sent a note that reversed the priorities and demanded immediate and substantial help as a condition of debt recognition and restitution or compensation for nationalized property.[45] Lloyd George invited the Russians to the Villa d'Albertis and exerted all his talents for cajolery, but he achieved only limited modifications.[46] Chicherin wrote a new note to the Allies on 21 April. He accepted Russia's prewar debts, subject to a moratorium; agreed to the Allies' rejection of Soviet counterclaims; substituted "writing down" for his originally worded statement that Russia intended to "write off" its war debts; and agreed to offer owners the use of nationalized or withheld property in the form of long-term leases, and, where this was not possible, "to satisfy the just claims of former owners." However, he remained insistent that debt repayment and compensation for nationalized property were predicated on Russia's receiving both immediate financial help from the West and de jure recognition.[47] This was the bitter fruit of Rapallo.

On 21 April the subcommission of the Political Commission (minus Germany and Russia) held its first meeting in ten days at the Palazzo Reale. Its members received copies of the 15 April note and the Russian reply that had arrived at the Villa d'Albertis that morning. Lloyd George directed the meeting. Though criticizing important details in the Russian note, he declared that the document did not justify a "rupture of negotiations" and urged them to convene the informal experts' meeting he had suggested the day before. Duly hesitant over plunging into talks with the Bolsheviks, who kept raising the dangerous matter of de jure recognition, Barthou formally objected to the procedure. Lloyd George won him over with assurances that *he* did not accept the Russian note and that the informal meeting with the experts was simply for the purpose of clarifying the points on which they and the Russians disagreed.[48]

That afternoon, when the Russians rejoined the political subcommission, Barthou engaged in another verbal duel with Chicherin over the meaning of the Cannes Resolutions.[49] But the die was cast. France had agreed to continue the negotiations in a new and unchartered forum. Barthou, filled with apprehensiveness, found the situation "difficult and dangerous," and suspected an Anglo-Italian plot to spring the recognition question by surprise. Appealing to Paris for help, he found Poincaré adamant against a trip to Genoa. To add to his troubles, he had infuriated the British with his ineffectual but "provocative remarks."[50]

45. Chicherin to Lloyd George, Genoa, 20 Apr., GB FO 371 N3936/646/38.

46. Conversation, 20 Apr., 5:30 P.M., *DBFP*, 19:474–77.

47. Letter from M. Chicherin, 20 [21] Apr., *DBFP*, 19:477–78; Hankey to Chamberlain, Genoa, 23 Apr., HP.

48. Meeting, 21 Apr., 10:30 A.M., *DBFP*, 19:478–87.

49. Meeting, 21 Apr., 3:30 P.M., ibid., pp. 487–91.

50. Barthou to MAE, Genoa, 21 Apr., #159–61, Poincaré to Barthou, Paris, 22 Apr., #106–8, FMAE B 94; Hankey to Chamberlain, Genoa, 23 Apr., HP.

The experts' committee got to work early the next morning, on 22 April.[51] Presided over by Worthington-Evans, it included single representatives of Belgium, Czechoslovakia, France, Italy, Japan, and the Netherlands. However, Soviet delegate Christian Rakovsky, chairman of the People's Commissars of the Ukraine, was accompanied by Krassin, Litvinov, and trade union leader Ian Rudzutak. The beginning was unpropitious. Rakovsky corrected Chicherin's note by insisting that Russia intended to write *off*, not write down, its war debts. To everyone's annoyance, he asked for an adjournment to enable the Soviet delegation to attend the king of Italy's reception,[52] and he announced that he would prepare an agenda for the experts' deliberations.

France retaliated in the afternoon. Seydoux withdrew because of irritation at a statement by Rakovsky that rebutted all the points in the London Report (which not only had been distributed to all the delegates but also had been spread throughout the streets of Genoa); his departure thus closed the session.[53] The next morning the group meeting in the Palazzo Reale for the purpose of concluding the chastisement of Germany also took up the Rakovsky incident. Schanzer soothed the troubled waters. The saving device was to declare Rakovsky's letter formally "non-existent," return to the texts of 15 and 21 April, and have the experts meet again with the Russians.[54]

However, when they reconvened that afternoon, Litvinov, Rakovsky, and Krassin refused to renounce the "non-existent" document, denounced the London Report, and refused to submit to the Allies' conditions.[55] The next day they returned demanding immediate recognition and credits. In exchange, they were willing to recognize prewar debts but demanded a thirty-year moratorium on payment of the interest and the exclusion of Russia's obligations not only to citizens of Germany but also to those of Japan and Rumania.[56] War debts and most private loans contracted during the war were to be annulled. Private property of foreign citizens that had been nationalized or requisitioned could be restored under conditions established by the Soviet government in the form of concessions; and if restoration were impossible, Moscow was willing to compensate "just claims." Finally, the Russians demanded the return of all former czarist property.

The Allies' experts, faced with so bold and uncompromising a stance by the

51. Meeting of committee of experts, 22 Apr., 10:30 A.M., *DBFP*, 19:491–93.

52. The Soviet appearance at the royal festivity created a sensation, especially after the Italian Communist party had publicly asked Chicherin to refrain: *New York Times*, 23 Apr.

53. Meeting of committee of experts, 22 Apr., 4:30 P.M., *DBFP*, 19:506–8. Rakovsky memorandum, ibid., pp. 518–28; Barthou to MAE, Genoa, 22 Apr., #172–75, FMAE B 116.

54. Meeting, 23 Apr., 11:30 A.M., *DBFP*, 19:515–18.

55. Meeting of committee of experts, 23 Apr., 4:00 P.M., ibid., pp. 529–39.

56. Note by the Russian delegation, Genoa, 24 Apr., ibid., pp. 553–54. Germany was excluded according to the terms of the London Report (its citizens were not "claimants in possession of obligations on 1 Mar. 1917"). The Russians added Rumania and Japan because their citizens inhabited states with "unsettled territorial disputes" with Soviet Russia.

Soviet representatives, questioned them sharply. Belgian representative Felicien Cattier led in the effort to define basic areas of divergency. Rakovsky blithely admitted that a Brussels banker would have to release to the new Soviet state bonds that had been deposited as security for loans to czarist Russia; yet he would have to acquiesce in the confiscation of his property in Russia if it could not be restored. Furthermore, in one very specific illustration, the former Belgian participants in oil concessions in Grosny, which were now consolidated by the Soviet government into a huge trust, would be forced to contribute fresh capital to secure a "preferential right" to take part in a new concession comprising their former interests. The Bolsheviks refused to recognize any absolute right of former proprietors or shareholders, either for new concessions or for compensation. When queried about the conditions under which Western capitalists would operate in the future, Krassin merely boasted "that the Russian government had already acquired a certain amount of experience."[57]

Rakovsky attempted to present the committee with a note asking for specific forms of financial assistance, but Worthington-Evans brusquely dismissed the Russians. Over Giannini's protest, he announced that the experts now had sufficient information to report to their governments.[58] Cattier proposed that they draft an ultimatum to bring matters to a head. The experts decided only to compile a report that contained the minutes of the last two turbulent sessions.

The meetings with the Russians intensified the divergence among the Allies.[59] Theunis departed for Brussels, where, greeted with an outcry from Belgian owners of nationalized Russian properties, he instructed Jaspar to hold firm.[60] Faced with Poincaré's demands that he return to Paris for consultations, Barthou on 24 April dined with an angry Lloyd George, who reproached France once more for trying to "wreck" Genoa. The occasion for his rancor was Seydoux's latest refusal to reduce Russia's war debts; however, in view of the talks with Rakovsky and company, this was a moot point indeed.[61]

The resumption of the talks with the Russians after Rapallo intensified the difficulty of the Allies' task. The Entente was not very cordial. The Germans, now excluded, played the role of wary and interested observers. If Kessler was correct—that Lloyd George had intended to use the Genoa Conference to disengage from France by maneuvering Barthou into displaying "a cloven hoof among a company of angels"—Germany and Russia had "spoiled his design by not behaving immaculately either."[62] In any event, the results of the experts' committee gave Lloyd George very little basis for hope.

57. Meeting of committee of experts, 24 Apr., 5 P.M., *DBFP*, 19:539–54.
58. Meeting of committee of experts, 24 Apr., 6:45 P.M., ibid., pp. 554–57.
59. Barthou to MAE, Genoa, 23 Apr., #183–88, FMAE B 116.
60. Grahame to Curzon, Brussels, 27 Apr., GB FO 371 C6429/458/62; Margerie to MAE, Brussels, 27 Apr., FMAE B 110.
61. Note on Anglo-French relations, Genoa, 24 Apr., *DBFP*, 19:557.
62. Kessler, *Tagebücher*, p. 306; Rathenau to AA, Genoa, 22 Apr., unsigned tel. to AA,

Wirth, Krassin, and Chicherin; *far right*, Joffe (courtesy of UPI).

Nonaggression Pact

It is essential that the division of the European nations into two mighty camps should not be perpetuated by narrow fears on the part of the victor nations or secret projects of revenge on the part of the vanquished. It is essential that the rivalries generated by the emancipation of nations since the war should be averted from the paths of international hatred and turned to those of cooperation and good will. It is essential also that the conflict between rival social and economic systems which the Russian revolution has so greatly intensified should not accentuate the fears of nations and culminate in international war.[63]

Genoa, 24 Apr., and Rathenau diary, 24 Apr., Germ. AA T-120 3398/1734/D733480, D738523–24, 3398/1735/D739164.

63. Lloyd George to Briand, Aide-mémoire of statement, 4 January 1922, Cannes, France, in MAE, *Documents Diplomatiques, Documents relatifs aux négociations concernant les garanties de sécurité contre une agression de l'Allemagne (10 jan. 1919–7 déc. 1923)* (Paris: Imprimerie Nationale, 1924), p. 99.

In the above statement to Briand at Cannes, Lloyd George introduced the idea of a European nonaggression pact modeled on the recent agreement on the Pacific concluded at Washington. There were obvious differences between what could be accomplished at Washington under an undisputed American leadership and through compromises achieved among former World War I allies and what could be accomplished at Genoa: a summit meeting of thirty-four nations that included Russia, Germany and other former enemies, and neutral states but that lacked the United States.

Like Hughes at Washington, Lloyd George wanted to make a dramatic breakthrough toward a general European disarmament. Britain, like the United States, needed to convince its public that all means were being exhausted to lessen its tax burden, increase trade and jobs, expedite the return to prosperity, and still maintain national security. In Europe, as in the Pacific, the obstacle was not only the enemy of World War I and revolutionary Russia but also former Allies, whose struggle over the spoils, attempts to enforce the peace treaties, border quarrels, and growing armies, submarines, and air power prevented the establishment of a real peace. Lloyd George proposed a general compact that would ratify the territorial status quo in Europe, renounce all forms of aggression, and thereby lead to prompt and extensive disarmament.[64]

Lloyd George's original proposal at Cannes contained both a narrow and a broad conception. The narrow one was to establish a safety belt around Soviet Russia: "If we insist that Russia shall not attack her neighbors, we must also insist that her neighbors shall not attack her."[65] This idea was confined to Europe. He reassured the Japanese that his nonaggression formula and the whole Cannes document applied only to those countries that would participate in the economic reconstruction of Europe; the Tokyo government would not be vulnerable to any Soviet reproaches for its prolonged occupation of Siberia. This caused Jaspar to comment that "the rest of the world could [thus] be at war."[66]

There was also a larger vision in Lloyd George's proposals, which was revealed in his talks with Briand on 5 and 8 January 1922. Both leaders were convinced of the importance of a "general European Entente . . . like the Pacific Pact" that would be based primarily on the Anglo-French entente. Despite some significant differences in Lloyd George and Briand's interpretations of the nature and goals of their future relationship, they did agree on the following: that Anglo-French cooperation would be at the center of a future all-European nonaggression pact; that disarmament was necessary both to reduce their

---

64. US MID, 28 Feb., no. 4876 (Belg./Pol.).
65. Lloyd George statement to Supreme Council, Cannes, 6 Jan., *DBFP*, 19:24.
66. Ibid., p. 33.

domestic burdens and win America's support; and that the present League of Nations, weakened by Germany and Russia's absence, needed to be supplanted by a new structure establishing peace in Europe.[67]

By the time Genoa was convened, the areas of Anglo-French agreement had evaporated. Poincaré's insistence on a straightforward Anglo-French military alliance was rejected by London, and this altered one essential condition of Lloyd George's plan. Furthermore, Paris demonstrated unexpected support for the prerogatives of the League of Nations, resisted vague calls for disarmament that would benefit Germany more than France, and suspected that a generalized nonaggression pact might curtail Paris's rights to take sanctions under the Treaty of Versailles.[68] On a broader scale, the United States exhibited little interest in helping to secure the status quo in Europe or participate in European reconstruction. Finally, even the more narrow conception of pacification around Russia's borders was threatened by the sudden bellicosity of the Soviet press on the eve of the Genoa Conference and by Trotsky's bold statements to the Red Army. Without stable, recognized borders and guarantees from the Great Powers, the new small states bordering Soviet Russia could scarcely submit to a British scheme to disarm.[69]

With Briand gone, Lloyd George inherited the sole responsibility for promoting the nonaggression pact at Genoa. It immediately created fear and misunderstanding; it was the stimulus for Chicherin's provocative remarks at the opening session and for concern by France and its allies about what forbidden subjects might surface. On 16 April the *New York Times* published Grigg's version of Lloyd George's plan for a ten-year European truce, a plan developed on the day the Rapallo treaty was signed: it was a simple program in which the nations of Europe would renounce aggression and pledge to collaborate if any act of aggression should take place.

To dispel rumors, expectations, and apprehensions, the actual text was unveiled a week later, on 23 April:

> (List of Contracting States)
>
> Being desirous of establishing on a firm and lasting basis the peace and security of Europe,
>
> Recognizing that the inviolability of the territory of another Power is a fundamental and universal principle of international law, and as such is binding on all civilized States,

67. Ibid., p. 13 (5 Jan.), p. 58 (8 Jan.).

68. Note, Paris, 31 Jan., FMAE B 85; Sûreté Générale, Menton, 9 Apr., FMAE B 92, Prague, 13 Apr., FMAE B 93; Barthou to MAE, Genoa, 13 Apr., #54–55, FMAE Y 29; and Poincaré to Barthou, Paris, 13 Apr., #23–27, FMAE B 93, 22 Apr., FMAE Y 31.

69. Crowe memorandum, London, 20 Mar., GB FO 371 C4346/458/62.

> Being pledged in many cases by the terms of the Covenant of the
> League of Nations to resist all acts of external aggression against the ter-
> ritorial integrity of other members of the League,
>
> Having resolved to facilitate the cause of disarmament by a pledge to
> refrain from all acts of external aggression, and
>
> Having decided to conclude convention to this effect have appointed
> their plenipotentiaries who have agreed as follows: —
>
> 1. Each of the high contracting parties pledges itself to refrain from
> any act of aggression against the territorial integrity of any other of the
> high contracting parties.
>
> 2. In the event of any act of aggression being committed in breach of
> article 1, each of the high contracting parties pledges itself to make use
> of all means at its disposal and to resort to any organization which may
> be available for the discussion, consideration and adjustment *by peaceful
> means* of the dispute out of which the act of aggression arose.[70]

Lloyd George's position on peace and war was stated starkly in this document. Willing to accept though not guarantee the present territorial settlement,
he viewed the foremost danger to be "external aggression" of any kind. His
position was based on a prewar conception that wars began by attacks that were
resisted; it was shaped even more by the traumatic experience of World War I,
where such attacks had led to automatic participation by all the Great Powers.
Like the Washington Pact for the Pacific, Lloyd George's nonaggression formula envisaged the peaceful settlement of all disputes, the abandonment of all
military alliances, and the halting of all national rivalries, but it was predicated, of course, on Russia's acceptance of the Allies' conditions.

From the otherwise sympathetic Italians there came the first important criticisms.[71] Vittorio Scialoja, the former foreign minister, pointed out that the
proposed peace pact was based on a primitive interpretation of "aggression": a
direct attack to seize another state's territory. This contingency was already
covered in Articles XI and XVII of the League Covenant. There were, however, at least two conceivable cases of "aggression" not clarified—incursions
on the territory of a neighbor as a limited form of self-defense or as fulfillment of a treaty obligation and an aggression "without war," where the invaded state did not mount its own forces for defense. These grey areas were
indeed the chief foreseeable causes for war after 1919. Article X of the Covenant,[72] although not an ironclad guarantee because of the League Council's

---

70. *DBFP*, 19:571, emphasis added.

71. Osservazioni sul progetto Lloyd George, Genoa, n.d., IMAE 52/34.

72. "The Members of the League undertake to respect and preserve as against external
aggression the territorial integrity and existing political independence of all Members of the
League. In case of any such aggression or in case of any threat of danger of such aggression, the

rule of unanimity, was sufficiently specific about recognizing and defending the "territorial integrity and political independence" of all members to alienate the United States in 1919 and draw continuous opposition from Britain and its empire. Lloyd George's peace pact represented an implicit retreat from the burden of Article X by stressing "peaceful means" as the sole appropriate response to "external aggression."[73]

Scialoja was also concerned that the draft pact, a "moral declaration without a practical component," would create a dangerous illusion.[74] It entailed no commitment on the part of the signators to arbitration, to sanctions, or to collective security. This was precisely what Lloyd George wanted: a high moral declaration that would reassure the United States, Britain, the pacifists of Europe, and the Bolsheviks that he meant to limit and not extend the causes of another war.[75] His version of "peace" was to rule out situations where generalized hostilities might erupt in Europe for any reason, even for the enforcement of the Paris peace treaties, which significantly were not mentioned at all in his pact.

While the German delegation gave cautious support to Lloyd George's proposal, France and its allies were predictably alarmed. Poincaré viewed a nonaggression pact as encouragement for Soviet threats to Poland and German defiance against the Allies; indeed, the Reich delegates on Genoa's technical commissions routinely issued statements rejecting all proposals that were "in conformity with the Versailles Treaty."[76] Beneš took the lead at Genoa in combatting the peace pact, whereupon he would earn Lloyd George's deep resentment. He insisted that the pact would be ineffectual without a prior strengthening of Anglo-French ties; he opposed any formal commitment to the present borders of Poland and also stressed the role of the Little Entente in maintaining peace in Eastern Europe. The Czech proposals, leaked in the Genoa press, contradicted Lloyd George's original intention.[77] They were based on a more partisan and practical view of international affairs.

Council shall advise upon the means by which this obligation shall be fulfilled": F. P. Walters, *A History of the League of Nations* (London: Oxford University Press, 1952), p. 48.

73. Hurst to Crowe, London, 16 Mar., Wigram memorandum, 18 Mar., Lampson, Crowe memoranda, 20 Mar., Crowe to Hankey, 24 Mar., Hankey to Crowe, 25 Mar., GB FO 371 C4356, C4543/458/62; Gregory to Crowe, Genoa, 23 Apr., Leeper, Ovey, Curzon minutes, London, 26 Apr., FO to Gregory, London, 27 Apr., GB FO 371 N3592/646/38.

74. Osservazioni, Genoa, n.d., IMAE 52/34.

75. "Gênes et le pacte européen," *L'Europe Nouvelle*, 16 Apr.

76. Unsigned Aufzeichnung, Berlin, 24 Mar., Germ. AA T-120 L312/4255/L096873–77; Poincaré to Barthou, Paris, 22 Apr., #111–12, #119–20, FMAE B 116, B 94; Barthou to MAE, Genoa, 22 Apr., #168, FMAE B 94; *DBFP*, 19:511.

77. Grigg, notes of conversation with Beneš, Genoa, 21 Apr., Grigg Papers, roll 9; Lloyd George–Beneš conversation, Villa d'Albertis, Genoa, 26 Apr., *DBFP*, 19:565–71; Beneš to Lloyd George, n.d., LGP F 199/3/5; Barthou to Poincaré, Genoa, 25 Apr., #213, 28 Apr.,

On 24 April France responded. Poincaré delivered a militant speech at the opening of the Conseil Général de la Meuse in his birthplace, Bar-le-Duc, which was just a few miles from the still-devastated regions of eastern France.[78] Denouncing the "German-Bolshevik" Treaty of Rapallo,[79] he discussed the possibility of a German default on 31 May, insisted on the prerogatives of the Reparations Commission to vote sanctions, and also posed the prospect of an isolated punitive action by France. The speech sent shock waves through London, Berlin, and Genoa.[80] Two days later, though in slightly more moderate tones, Millerand spoke at Philippeville about the trials facing France and its allies, and he encouraged his audience to fight loyally for its mother country.[81]

Both leaders' speeches, undoubtedly aimed at reassuring French public opinion, failed to mollify either the Right or the Socialists: the former wanted stronger statements and the latter were distressed by their harshness.[82] Poincaré also hoped to impose moral pressure on Britain and to renew the Allies' solidarity after the shock of Rapallo; but Lloyd George responded by inviting him to Genoa to discuss the problem of reparations. This threw him into disarray. A timid individual and a staunch partisan of the Entente, Poincaré had no intention of leaving Paris for Genoa's dangerous climate, of prolonging or enlarging the conference agenda, or of leading the opposition to Lloyd George's "peace pact." He wanted a Franco-British pact first, and his speech at Bar-le-Duc was a blustering attempt to revive the dialogue that had lapsed since Boulogne and that for him took precedence over the confusion at Genoa.[83]

#279–81, Poincaré to Barthou, Paris, 28 Apr., #213–14, FMAE B 95; Wigram memorandum, Genoa, 1 May, Grigg Papers, roll 9; Wigram to Waterlow, Genoa, 2 May, GB FO 371 C6652/458/62.

78. Text in *La politique française en 1922* (Paris: Dunod, 1923), pp. 29–32.

79. Jay L. Kaplan, "France's Road to Genoa: Strategic, Economic, and Ideological Factors in French Foreign Policy, 1921–1922" (Ph.D. diss., Columbia University, 1974), p. 377, considers this a clever tactic to distinguish the "Bolsheviks" from Russia itself.

80. Saint-Aulaire to MAE, London, 25 Apr., FMAE Z GB 49; Laurent to MAE, Berlin, 23 Apr. (2 tels.), FMAE B 116, Y 31; Mayer to AA, Paris, 22, 24 Apr., Germ. AA T-120 3398/1734/D738491–92, D738511–20; A. J. Sylvester, *The Real Lloyd George* (London: Cassell, 1948), p. 94; Louise Weiss, *Mémoires d'une européene* (Paris: Payot, 1969), 2:168–69; Pierrefeu, *Saison diplomatique*, pp. 153–55; Kessler, *Tagebücher*, p. 307.

81. Text in *La politique française*, pp. 32–35.

82. Sforza to Schanzer, Paris, 25 Apr., IMAE 52/4 (France); De Gaiffier to MAE, Paris, 26 Apr., BMAE 10991.

83. Poincaré to Barthou, Paris, 27 Apr., #188–89, FMAE B 117; Peretti-Sforza conversation, Paris, 27 Apr., FMAE B 95; De Gaiffier to Jaspar, Paris, 28 Apr., BMAE 10991; Hardinge to FO, 27 Apr., GB FO 371 C6170/458/62; and Poincaré to Saint-Aulaire, Paris, 2 May, FMAE PM/59.

Lloyd George and Barthou met in the wake of Bar-le-Duc. The British premier was exasperated both at Beneš's maneuvers and Poincaré's show of independence. Barthou, himself under attack by the French press and admitting his differences with Poincaré, tried not to be cowed by Lloyd George's sarcasm. Lloyd George insisted that France and Britain "stand together." He nevertheless stressed the dangers ahead. First, Poland was menaced by a Russo-German combination; it could not be saved by the Western powers and would be "crushed like an egg shell." Second, with the deadline of 31 May approaching, the Allies had to meet at Genoa to discuss "what was going to happen." Barthou could not answer either point.[84] Poincaré, anxious over these confrontations, continued to insist that his chief delegate return to Paris.[85]

Lloyd George's announced peace pact, for all its vague and tentative nature, spread confusion and alarm.[86] *L'Europe Nouvelle* reported it was widely dubbed the "oui aggression" pact that encouraged threats from the revisionists. Neither the Russians nor Germans so conceived it. Lenin welcomed Lloyd George's plan (even in its "unsatisfactory form") as providing a breathing space along Soviet Russia's borders.[87] Rathenau fretted over Beneš's proposals, fearing that Germany might be forced to sign a document that acknowledged the Versailles treaty.[88] In truth, Lloyd George had no intention of doing more than testing the waters; until the Russians signed an agreement with the Allies, any talk of a European peace settlement was premature. Nevertheless, the nonaggression pact introduced at Genoa further widened the gap between Britain and its allies. It hinted at a new version of peace, a vision of European order based on reconciliation between victors and vanquished, and the renunciation of force and coercion. Perilously unmindful of the ambitions of former enemies and the apprehensions of former allies, Lloyd George weighed down the Genoa Conference with an added divisive burden.

---

84. Conversation, Villa d'Albertis, Genoa, 26 Apr., noon, *DBFP*, 19:572–78; Gregory to FO, Genoa, 26 Apr., GB FO 371 C6113/458/62; Hankey to Chamberlain, Genoa, 27 Apr., HP; and Barthou to MAE, 26 Apr., #231–39, FMAE B 109.

85. E.g., Poincaré to Barthou, Paris, 25 Apr., #135–40, 26 Apr., #168–69, FMAE B 95, 27 Apr., #188–89, FMAE B 117.

86. Poincaré to Barthou, Paris, 27 Apr., #186–87, FMAE B 95; Child to State Dept., Genoa, 29 Apr., USDS 550 E1/226.

87. Lenin to Chicherin, Moscow, 30 Apr., in V. I. Lenin, *Collected Works* (Moscow: Progress Publishers, 1965–71), 45:536–37. Martel to MAE, Riga, 24 Apr., FMAE B 116, reported that during the heated day-long discussions of the Rapallo treaty by the Central Committee of the Russian Communist party, Zinoviev, to quell concern over the possible military burden on Russia in the event of a war between the Entente and Germany, announced that the treaty could be annulled if the Entente, Poland, and the Baltic states "renounced aggression."

88. Rathenau diary, 26 Apr., Germ. AA T-120 3398/1735/D739166; Simson to AA, Genoa, 27 Apr., Germ. AA T-120 3398/1734/D738573–75.

Intermezzo

The conference is once more in serious peril. . . . I am working as I never worked in my life to save it. [Lloyd George, 19 April][89]

> Lloyd George, who is making noises against France, is covering up his main urge—to force us to pay debts in general . . . and to former owners in particular. [Lenin, 19 April][90]

The conference is still laboring heavily & without a boast I am the only man who can pull it through. [Lloyd George, 23 April][91]

> We have had a row. The P.M. is very anxious to give credits to Russia. [Lloyd-Greame, 23 April][92]

> Chicherin either has already made or is quite capable of making an obvious mistake and of violating a CC directive. [Lenin, 24 April][93]

I have had a simply diabolical day of work and worry. The conference is trembling on the edge of a precipice and I am doing all I can to save it. [Lloyd George, 26 April][94]

Lloyd George is fighting for his political life. . . . He has never hesitated on such occasions . . . to proceed with ruthless brutality. [Kessler, 26 April][95]

> Bear in mind the terms that were drawn up in London. [Curzon, 26 April][96]

> Lloyd George leads the conference with perfect ease, like Louis XIV. "He smiled at breakfast" and everyone is optimis-

89. David and Frances Lloyd George, *My Darling Pussy: The Letters of Lloyd George and Frances Stevenson, 1913–1941*, ed. A. J. P. Taylor (London: Weidenfeld and Nicolson, 1975), p. 44.

90. Note to Stalin, Kamenev, and Trotsky, with draft tel. to Genoa, in Lenin, *Collected Works*, 45:532.

91. Lloyd George, *My Darling Pussy*, p. 44.

92. Lloyd-Greame to wife, Sunday [23 Apr.], LGrP.

93. Letter to Stalin for members of the R.C.P.[B] C.C. Politburo, in Lenin, *Collected Works*, 45:533.

94. Lloyd George, *My Darling Pussy*, p. 45.

95. Kessler, *Tagebücher*, p. 308.

96. Private cipher wire to Gregory, GB FO 371 N4043/646/38.

tic. Because he wants success, he will make concessions.
[Siegfried, 26 April][97]

Except for Bar-le-Duc, the voice of the *grand chef* is
muted. The Quai d'Orsay does not know how long the divergence between the delegation and Poincaré can go on.
[Jacques Dumaine, French Foreign Ministry official,
27 April][98]

> Before reproaching us, Lloyd George should look to his
> own wiles. [Poincaré, 27 April][99]

The time has passed for those who may have
planned . . . to attempt to isolate France. The sentiment has
swung toward France, who long ago forecasted the dangers of
trading with Russia and . . . now . . . holds before the eyes
of smaller nations the real and imagined dangers of all the
plans of Lloyd George. [Child, 29 April][100]

> Do not in any case undertake the slightest financial obliga-
> tion, do not make even a semi-recognition of the debts and do
> not be afraid of a break up in general. [Lenin, 30 April][101]

Useless to make an accord which parliament and the country will reject. [Gaston de Ramaix, Belgian Foreign Ministry
official, 30 April][102]

> Everyone wants to leave Genoa. [*L'Europe Nouvelle*,
> 6 May]

Genoa and the Home Front

After three weeks, it appeared that the Genoa Conference would continue
for some time.[103] It had survived Rapallo and Bar-le-Duc; but the prospect for
an agreement with the Russians and the success of the meeting were unclear.
The Allies, having decided to respond to Rakovsky's challenge with an ultimatum to the Russians, disagreed over their future course in treating with the

97. Siegfried to Goût, Paris, FMAE PM G/V.
98. Dumaine to Charles-Roux, Rome, FMAE PC-R.
99. Tel. to Barthou, #186–87, FMAE B 95.
100. Tel. to State Dept., USDS 550 E1/226.
101. Tel. to Chicherin, in Lenin, *Collected Works*, 45:536.
102. Letter to Jaspar, BMAE 10991.
103. Hankey to Chamberlain, Genoa, 27 Apr., HP; and Lloyd George, *My Darling Pussy*,
pp. 44–47.

Bolsheviks. Germany, formally chastised, had not been eliminated from the proceedings, and its delegates maintained a vigorous schedule of appointments with American and neutral bankers, the Russians, and the press. Finally, Lloyd George's peace pact, which opened the problems of the undefined borders of Eastern Europe and of possible sanctions if Germany should default on 31 May, also clouded the atmosphere.

The atmosphere at Genoa grew less optimistic. Those excluded from the Great Powers' deliberations and the experts' talks grew restless and worried. Lloyd George paid more attention to the representatives of the smaller states, who, languishing in their hotels and cafés and ignored by the press, were grateful for his attention.[104] Some delegates began to leave. Horne's departure for London dashed the Germans' still-lingering hope of a talk on reparations. Theunis departed for Brussels, Schober to Vienna, Bethlen to Budapest, Branting to Stockholm, Enole to Helsinki, and Nincic temporarily to Belgrade. Barthou, Karnebeek, and Wirth received pleas to return to their capitals. The "spirit of Genoa," represented mainly by Lloyd George and the faithful Schanzer, had fewer partisans and more passive observers.

Outside, in Europe, conditions seemed to be improving. Spring planting in Russia promised a good harvest; the British economy appeared to be picking up; and, as Rathenau carefully observed, the German currency temporarily ceased its plunge. Following the Easter recess, parliaments reopened, budgets were prepared, and politics resumed. Genoa's distance from its delegates' capitals was exacerbated by a combination of poor communications over the overloaded telegraph wires and the all-too-profuse press reportage that gave a distorted view of the proceedings. A French delegate remarked that reading the Paris press, whose stories invariably originated in Genoa, was like experiencing "reality" when one removed a bathing cap. Theunis chided the Belgian press for its exaggerations. The government in Berlin pleaded with the delegation to send an emissary to give more accurate information about what actually was happening at Genoa. Moscow, more remote, received its "news" later still.[105]

Lloyd George pushed doggedly on, trusting Chicherin's ability and willing-

104. See, e.g., Ackers-Douglas to Curzon, Vienna, 14, 29 Apr., GB FO 371 C5559, C6643/458/62; John Balfour to Curzon, Budapest, 28 Apr., GB FO 371 C6423/458/62; Doucet to MAE, Budapest, 2 May, FMAE B 98; Findlay to Curzon, Christiana, 21 Apr., and Parr to Curzon, Copenhagen, 9 May, GB FO 371 C6026/458/62, N4769/646/38; Lucius to AA, The Hague, 19 Apr., 1, 3 May, Germ. AA T-120 L309/4255/L096268, L996/5412/L286151, L286160.

105. Siegfried to Goût, Genoa, 26 Apr., FMAE PM G/V; Landsberg to AA, Brussels, 27 Apr., Germ. AA T-120 L1468/5118/L415937-40; Grahame to Curzon, Brussels, 27 Apr., GB FO 371 C6439/458/62; Kempner to Delegation, Berlin, 16, 18 Apr., Wever to Hemmer, Berlin, 17, 18, 19, 21 Apr., Germ. AA T-120 K1946/5372/K505542, K505551-52, K505547-50, K505553, K505556-59; Hodgson to Curzon, Moscow, 18, 25 Apr., 2 May, GB FO 371 N3844, N4123, N4417/646/38.

ness to come to terms and his own gifts for managing the conference. His patience grew short. He was anguished by the criticism of the French press and the intermittent attacks by the Tories. He began voicing his "pessimism" on the repercussions of failure: Germany would dominate Russia, "international capital" would develop the Soviet state via Berlin and without the Allies' control, and the new Russo-German colossus would cause Poland to "crack like an egg."[106]

To spur Genoa on, Lloyd George sent an emissary to the Vatican, and the result was another papal letter to Gasparri. Pius XI termed the conference's work "important for Western Civilization" and recommended that the Catholic Church's diplomatic representatives give it their full support.[107]

Within his own entourage, Lloyd George was depicted as leading a crusade. As Grigg wrote to a friend:

We are having a terrific struggle here against all the accumulated hatred, suspicions, and prejudices of many centuries to get Europe started on a new orientation towards peace and reconstruction. France is appallingly difficult—not that she means to be obstructive, but her public men are so utterly blinkered and unable to look beyond the purely material side of French interests. In spite of France, I believe the P.M. will arrive at a Russian settlement and a European pact of Non-Aggression. It will be a great achievement and, if he brings it off, entirely his own.[108]

In London, where general elections were expected soon after the Genoa Conference, the politicians were relatively quiet but the press was active. Liberal and Labour newspapers fulminated against France's "war-mongering" while the Tory press complained about the prime minister's adventuresomeness in courting the Russians.[109] Churchill, who on 20 April suffered serious injury from a fall, raged privately at the ailing Curzon's absence from Genoa, at

106. Notes of conversation with Jaspar and Schanzer, 27 Apr., *DBFP*, 19:588. Similar sentiments in Hankey to Chamberlain, Genoa, 27 Apr., HP; also see Lloyd George's remarks at the Anglo-French press dinner of 26 Apr., Germ. AA T-120 3398/1734/D738553–56, and *Times*, 28 Apr. According to a French intelligence report from Menton on 5 May (FMAE B 97), Kamenev had boasted that Berlin would become the "real center of Russian commerce." An American intelligence report from Paris, forwarded on 13 June to Washington (US MID Weekly Summaries, XVII, 1922), stressed the importance of "international Jewish banking groups" in British policy.

107. Lloyd George, *My Darling Pussy*, p. 46; Gregory to Grigg, Genoa, 27 Apr., LGP F 86/6/7; De Salis to FO, Vatican, 30 Apr., and to Curzon, 4 May, GB FO 371 C6285, C6754/458/62; Richard Mayer to AA, Vatican, 1 May and Bergen to AA, Rome, 1 May, Germ. AA T-120 L1468/5118/L415866–67, 9236H/3493/H253678; and Lloyd George to Pius XI, Genoa, 6 May, LGP F 62/2/2.

108. Grigg to (Canadian jurist) Loring Christie, Genoa, 30 Apr., PAC Christie Papers.

109. Christoph Stamm, *Lloyd George zwischen Innen- und Aussenpolitik: Die britische Deutschlandpolitik 1921/1922* (Cologne: Verlag Wissenschaft und Politik, 1977), pp. 311–13.

the "monstrous birth [Rapallo]" that he believed Britain had midwifed, and against Lloyd George's baiting of France, which might lurch into the Ruhr.[110] Curzon and Chamberlain, who shared some of these apprehensions, could do little while their chief was abroad.

Barthou, with scarcely an admirer in his own entourage and an exacting master in Paris, was on more precarious ground.[111] He knew that his time at Genoa was short, and he tried to avoid collisions with the mercurial Welshman. He continued to display to the British the telegrams from Paris and to complain of Poincaré's criticisms. Indeed, Barthou demonstrated a considerable amount of independence, ignoring Poincaré's instructions to cease participating if Rapallo were not annulled, writing strongly in defense of his actions, and complaining of press criticism at home. Barthou and Seydoux were both infected by the "Genoa spirit"; they did not want France to be isolated or accused of wrecking the conference. Indeed, Seydoux persisted in his commitment to formulate a concrete plan for Russian reconstruction.[112]

Authority for France's decisions still remained in Paris, where Poincaré wanted Genoa to end promptly. He preferred that the Allies drop the sterile and dangerous negotiations with Russia and proceed with the more pressing problems of reparations and war debts. The Paris press reflected the government's fears and impatience with the Genoa Conference. After Rapallo, France wanted to make sure that the Russians, Germans, or British did not capitalize on the situation with further coups.[113]

The mood in the Russian headquarters at the Imperiale had turned pessimistic over the prospect of securing a large loan or of obtaining recognition from the West. Publicly the Russians blamed a "lethargic and nervous" Lloyd

---

Also Arthur Mann's critique in the *Yorkshire Post*, Leeds, 27 Apr., Bonar Law Papers: Lloyd George "seems like a gambler ready to stake present friendships on the apparently hopeless task of conciliating peoples who shew at every turn their ill-will and bad faith"; Mann also warned that "unless he smoked the Russians and Germans out," Unionist support would evaporate.

110. Churchill to Joseph Philip, 18 Apr., to Chamberlain, 19 Apr., to Northcliffe, Curzon, and Gwynne, 24 Apr., to Birkenhead and Sir Ian Hamilton, 25 Apr., and to Curzon, 26 Apr., WSCP; also Martin Gilbert, *Winston S. Churchill* (Boston: Houghton Mifflin, 1975), pp. 780–84.

111. Jean Roger to Charles-Roux, Genoa, 14, 16, 19, 21 Apr., Dumaine to Charles-Roux, 27 Apr., FMAE PC-R.

112. Barthou to MAE, Genoa, 20 Apr., #146, FMAE B 116, 23 Apr., #180–81, #189, FMAE B 94, 25 Apr., #214–15, 26 Apr., #226, FMAE B 95. Poincaré to Barthou, Paris, 1 May, FMAE PM G/VI, indicated that the articles "most embarrassing for us often originate in Genoa with the British or American press according to our intercepts of their telegrams." There was little the French government could do to rectify this. Seydoux's differences with Poincaré in *DBFP*, 19:559.

113. Poincaré to Millerand, Paris, 26, 28 Apr., FMAE PM/tel. 2; Poincaré to Barthou, Paris, 18 Apr., #55, 23 Apr., #122–24, FMAE B 94, 24 Apr., #136, 25 Apr., #169, FMAE B 95, 26 Apr., FMAE PM G/V.

Lloyd George and Barthou (courtesy of H. Roger Viollet, Paris).

George for succumbing to Poincaré and reneging on his earlier promise to Krassin.[114] Czech sources reported that the real cause of the Russians' gloom was the news (or lack of it) from Moscow: there were vague indications that the politburo was reexamining the concessions policy and rumors of Trotsky's appearance on the Russo-Polish border. Chicherin tried some alternatives, such as his inconclusive talk with the American banker, Frank Vanderlip. Still, like Lloyd George, Chicherin was committed to pursuing the Genoa negotiations and hoped for an agreement. On 28 April he sent a protest note to Facta against the suspension of the negotiations and threatened to withdraw his conciliatory message of 21 April.[115]

After the first surprise of Rapallo, there was a significant change in attitude in Moscow. Georgi Steklov's editorials in *Isvestia*, which were possibly dictated by Lenin himself, represented a definite hardening of the Soviet position

114. IGPS, Boll. no. 11, 26 Apr., IMAE 52/31; Berlin, 11 May: Ein Bericht der Sowjetdelegation in Genua, 27 Apr. [sent to Moscow, with copies to Soviet representatives in Britain, Germany, and the Baltic states, presumably intercepted in Berlin], Germ. AA T-120 6700H/3045/H118367–72; Lloyd George, *My Darling Pussy*, p. 49.

115. Osborne to State Dept., Genoa, 25 Apr., USDS 550 E1/268; Chicherin to Facta, Genoa, 28 Apr., *DBFP*, 19:658–59.

toward the West. Apprised of the division within the Soviet delegation over Chicherin's letter of 21 April, Lenin sent angry messages against both Chicherin and Krassin; he lambasted Lloyd George as a "capitalist tool" and hostage of the French. Like Poincaré, Lenin was unafraid of breaking off; nor did he shrink from disavowing and dismissing disobedient Soviet delegates. As he recuperated from the surgery that took place on 23 April, his foremost concern was the impending meeting of the All-Russian Executive Committee; he needed a positive report for the delegates.[116]

Germany, no longer central to the outcome of the Genoa Conference, also had a divided delegation. The news from home of the controversy created by Rapallo further added to Rathenau's problems. There was little for the foreign minister to do, except wait for the possibility of a *Vermittler* role between the Allies and Russia, and in the meantime maintain a statesmanlike posture above the melee of conflicting political interests. Though personally satisfying, this did not contribute to the solution of Germany's chief problem: reparations.[117]

The German government in Berlin was shocked by Rapallo; Berlin had little control over the "cabinet" sessions that were held in Genoa or over the text of the messages the delegation sent to the Allies. The news that arrived in Berlin was rife with sensationalism. The Reich government succeeded in toning down the press but not in conquering its own misgivings or answering the criticisms of important party leaders. Berlin welcomed Poincaré's speech at Bar-le-Duc for this alone: France now received almost as much criticism as Germany for the coming crisis of 31 May. However, the Germans also realized that the British were not aiding them vigorously, and Berlin retained few hopes for the remainder of the Genoa Conference.[118]

A weak Italian government, awaiting the convocation of parliament on 8 May, needed some dramatic breakthrough soon: a trade agreement with Russia, an oil concession by the Great Powers, a Near Eastern settlement, an agreement with Yugoslavia regularizing the status of Fiume, or even an economic arrangement with Germany, to redeem its great labors and expenditure for the Genoa Conference. Schanzer, loyal and diligent despite harsh criticism from the French and Belgian delegations, risked alienating the Italian public because of his subservience to Lloyd George. Even his patron Nitti criticized

116. Lenin, *Collected Works*, 45:536, 537; Wiedenfeld to AA, Moscow, 2 May, Germ. AA T-120 L309/4255/L096534; Louis Fischer, *The Life of Lenin* (New York: Harper and Row, 1964), pp. 599–600.

117. Child to State Dept., Genoa, 22 Apr., USDS 761.62/60.

118. Wever to Hemmer, Berlin, 18, 19, 21–23, 25, 27–30 April, Germ. AA T-120 K1946/5372/K505553–59, K505589–94, K505601–6, K505614–17; Laurent to MAE, Berlin, 27 Apr., #739–42, 1 May, #760–61, FMAE B 117; Houghton to State Dept., Berlin, 1 May, USDS 550 E1/294.

his slavish following of the British lead, and the Fascists stirred Italy's latent anglophobia by reciting dreams of expansion in the Mediterranean. The Left and the Right carefully scrutinized the negotiations with the Russians from their opposite perspectives. Thus, after Rapallo, Italy was in difficult straits, needing to keep the conference going but also needing to obtain some benefits on its own.[119]

The Belgians, unlike the French, relished conference diplomacy, especially when they had been awarded an honored place as they had at Genoa. Jaspar took the opportunity to conduct talks with many of the delegates, even opening another fruitless dialogue with the Dutch over unsolved questions from the Paris Peace Conference. Both Theunis and Jaspar had wanted to accommodate Lloyd George for the sake of a possible Anglo-Belgian pact; but the Belgians also were interested in regaining their extensive former properties in Russia.[120]

The Rapallo agreement created bewilderment and strong divisions in Belgian public opinion. The francophile press urged that the Entente be strengthened and Belgium remain the key member, while the Flemish press applauded the Russo-German pact and opposed France's "menace" but was also suspicious of Lloyd George's design where it represented the industrialists. Belgium, the factory of Europe, had little further capital to invest in Russia. The former owners lacked confidence in the present Soviet regime, feared spoliation by British and German capitalists, and rejected "compensation" in worthless Soviet bonds. Belgium's interests separated it from France and Britain, but it also did not make common cause with other small neutral states.[121] Indeed, it was the Belgian suggestion, in response to the impatient public opinion at home, to draw up an ultimatum that would bring matters at Genoa to a head. With Theunis gone, the impulsive and courageous Jaspar was increasingly exposed to the conference's pressures for a settlement with Russia.

The Japanese delegation was uncomfortable at Genoa. Excluded from the

119. Charles-Roux to Poincaré, Rome, 18 Apr., FMAE Y 30; Benjamin Crémieux, "L'Italie à Gênes," *L'Europe Nouvelle*, 6 May; Barthou to MAE, Genoa, 9 May, FMAE PM G/VII; Pagliano to Schanzer, Rome, 19 Apr., 2 May, IMAE 52/37/[38], 52/20; Danilo Veneruso, *La vigilia del fascismo: Il primo ministero Facta nella crisi dello stato liberale in Italia* (Bologna: Il Mulino, 1968), pp. 405–35; Giorgio Rumi, *Alle origini della politica estera fascista (1918–1923)* (Bari: Laterza, 1968), pp. 167–74; Renzo De Felice, *Mussolini* (Turin: G. Einaudi, 1965), 2:238.

120. Jaspar to MAE, Genoa, 24 Apr., BMAE 10991; Grahame to Curzon, Brussels, 17 May, Marling to Curzon, The Hague, 18, 19 May, and Grahame to Balfour, Brussels, 29 May, GB FO 371 W4256, W4369–70, W4577/838/4; *DBPN*, nos. 246–47, 258–59, 262, 265; Grahame to Curzon, Brussels, 25 Apr., GB FO 425/389 No. 2, W3836/158/4.

121. Grahame to Curzon, Brussels, 25 Apr., GB FO 371 C6166/458/62; Wadsworth to State Dept., Brussels, 2 May, USDS 550 E1/279; Jaspar to MAE, Genoa, 24 Apr., Jaspar to Theunis, Genoa, 25, 26, 29 Apr., BMAE 10991. Reports on the Flemish press, 24 Apr., IMAE 52/4 (Belg.) and Germ. AA T-120 6700H/3045/H118571–78.

private Allied talks with the Russians, it received regular briefings from the British. At home the conference excited little interest except for the question of the Russian debt, over which Japan had little control. The Tokyo press took a neutral position, occasionally scolding the French but also expressing a residue of distrust of the Anglo-Saxon powers after the Washington Conference. The most sensitive question was the still unsettled status of Japan's occupation of Siberia. The Dairen negotiations with the Chita government had been suspended pending the outcome of the Genoa Conference; Britain and America were urging an early Japanese withdrawal and were reputedly themselves interested in the oil of Siberia and Sakhalin. The Bolsheviks, working hard for recognition, indicated that they soon intended to extend their control over the Asian province. Thus Japan had problems that the Genoa Conference might influence but not solve decisively. Being represented was merely a prestige item, which still demanded caution, prudence, and vigilance.[122]

Skirmunt, the Polish delegate, tried to remain on good terms with both Lloyd George and Barthou. His aim was to play the "middleman" between the West and Russia in the hope of obtaining recognition of Poland's eastern frontiers and also of securing commitments for French and British loans. At home Skirmunt's supporters in the Foreign Ministry were not outwardly worried about the Rapallo agreement; they urged an active Polish policy that consisted of increased collaboration with Britain, a decrease in Poland's dependency on France, detente with Russia, and even some measure of rapprochement with Germany. However, the group around Piłsudski strongly opposed Skirmunt's experiments. Shocked by Rapallo, they advocated less conciliation, more "independence," and reliance on Poland's own resources rather than the mirage of European solidarity.[123]

The members of the Little Entente did little but guard their national interests at Genoa. Beneš was the most active at the conference. Because the German-

122. Note by Japanese delegation to Facta, 18 Apr., and Grigg conversation with Ishii, Genoa, 19 Apr., LGP F 200/3/5; Eliot to FO, Tokyo, 31 Mar., 8, 18, 25 Apr., 3 May, Leeper and Lampson minutes, London, 10, 17 June, GB FO 371 N4168/9/57, C5197/458/62, N3733, N5112, N5464/9/57; Solf to AA, Tokyo, 28 Apr., Germ. AA T-120 3398/1735/D739126; Claudel to MAE, Tokyo, 2 May, FMAE B 100. Background in: John Albert White, *The Siberian Intervention* (Princeton: Princeton University Press, 1950), pp. 372–418; and *DBFP*, 19:602, 631.

123. Busse to AA, Warsaw, 19 Apr., Germ. AA T-120 L640/4783/L203563–64; weekly report of Polish press, 15–22 Apr., Germ. AA T-120 L312/4255/L096782–83; Benndorf to AA, Warsaw, 29 Apr., Germ. AA T-120 L309/4255/L096477–79; Muller to Curzon, Warsaw, 26 Apr., GB FO 371 N4133/646/38; Barante to MAE, Warsaw, 26 Apr., FMAE B 117; Austrian Minister to BMA, Warsaw, 8 May, A HHSt 180; Unterhaltung Rathenau-Skirmunt, Genoa, 24 Apr., Germ. AA T-120 3398/1735/D739256–57; Sergiusz Mikulicz, *Od Genui do Rapallo* (Warsaw: Książkà i Wiedza, 1966), pp. 305–31.

Soviet pact challenged Czechoslovakia's economic aspirations and therefore created domestic repercussions, Beneš immediately approached Chicherin to resume talks on a bilateral trade treaty.[124] The Yugoslav delegation, the most limited in its action, hoped for a settlement with Italy over the Fiume question and worked successfully to suppress the Croat protest to the conference. Rumania was mainly concerned with obtaining the powers' support for its financial claims against Russia and the reduction of Soviet pressure on its borders.[125] In sum, the Little Entente did not play a significant collective role at Genoa. Its populations were involved only in specifically national issues. Its statesmen, like the neutrals, stood outside the important conclaves and decision making; but they feared Anglo-French bickering, the German-Soviet combination, and the prospect of a rupture. Unlike their roles at Paris after the war and in Geneva, they had little means or opportunity to contribute to the outcome of the Genoa Conference.

Child and Logan, representing the United States as unofficial observers, were severe critics of the events at Genoa. Child stressed the conference's "confusion," and Logan "came away with the firm conviction in our government's abstaining from participation," terming Genoa a "cess-pool of Machiavellian political intrigue and machinations."[126] At home the Rapallo treaty stirred little alarm. The administration was calm, and the press took a neutral stance. Nevertheless, the prolongation of the Genoa Conference could not be ignored, especially the possibility that something might be accomplished. Three issues concerned Washington: the festering Franco-German quarrel that might erupt on 31 May; the prominence of the Bolsheviks, which threatened to create embarrassing domestic consequences in America; and Lloyd George's repeated calls to the United States to help "save Europe," which struck a negative chord in the Harding administration. While the American public ignored the intricacies of Old World diplomacy, Harding himself watched the proceedings at Genoa closely; he believed that the outcome would necessarily influence America's next moves.[127]

---

124. IGPS, Boll. no. 14, 29 Apr., IMAE 52/31; Tschechoslowakisch-russische Handelsbeziehungen, Prague, 3 May, Germ. BA R 43 I/132; Diekhoff to AA, Prague, 6 May, Germ. AA T-120 L1468/5118/L415946–49; and Ovey to Lampson, London, 5 May, GB FO 371 N4378/242/38.

125. "La Petite Entente et la conférence," *L'Europe Nouvelle*, 29 Apr.; Dodge to State Dept., Belgrade, 1, 18 May, USDS 550 E1/228, 335; Dering to FO, Bucharest, 2 May, GB FO 371 N4233/246/38.

126. Child to State Dept., Genoa, 24, 29 (2 letters) Apr., USDS 550 E1/205, 226, 281; Child to Harding, 22 May, Harding Papers, roll 231; Logan to Harrison, Genoa, 28 Apr., USDS 550 E1/293.

127. *Washington Post*, 19 Apr., and *New York American*, 20, 22 Apr., both with cartoons

The gap between the Genoa Conference and the outside world was increasing. Lloyd George began to drive the delegates to reach an agreement, and the small powers had to line up behind the great. However, departures slowed the proceedings, news from the capitals began to overshadow events at Genoa, and advice, inquiries, and directives from their colleagues at home weighed on the delegates. Lloyd George's position was still relatively secure, but others were not. There was a growing fatigue and an abrasive quality in the environment at Genoa, which continued for a month after Rapallo. Its main activity—peace with Russia—was resumed under less than promising conditions.

---

entitled "Sammy and His Pals," depicting Genoa as sheer mayhem and the aloof American figure expressing relief at his exclusion; Cartier to MAE, Washington, 22 Apr., BMAE 10991; Kerr to Grigg, New York, 22 Apr., Grigg Papers, roll 2; Tyrrell to Curzon, London, 28 Apr., CzP; Harding to Harvey, 22 Mar., 4, 6, 24, 25 Apr., 3 May, Harding Papers, roll 228.

7

Peace with Russia?

Following six days of difficult, often acrimonious negotiations among the Allies over the document to be presented to the Russians, one of Genoa's labors was complete: on 2 May 1922 Schanzer sent Chicherin a brief covering letter and a memorandum consisting of a lengthy preamble and thirteen clauses.[1] This laboriously drafted, extensively edited, and carefully worded document represented the first collective effort by the Western powers to place their relations with Moscow on a new basis, in short, to make peace with the Soviet government.

The 2 May Memorandum

The deliberations on the memorandum were not conducted in a vacuum. The Rapallo agreement had distorted the political and diplomatic situation. Germany had granted recognition to Russia without demanding debt repayment, had accepted the Soviets' nationalization measures subject to treatment similar to any later agreement with third powers, had posed no political conditions such as the cessation of Bolshevik propaganda and subversion, and had promised to lend its efforts to promoting its capitalist enterprises in Russia. Moreover, when taking up the problem of war debts, the Allies had to consider the attitude of the United States, which had just issued invitations to individual debtor governments to send "financial representatives to Washington for the purpose of direct dealing."[2] Finally, with little control over events in the Far and Near East, and with strong disagreements over the looming reparations deadline of 31 May, the Allies scarcely entered their dealings with the Russians with unity or harmony.

The document of 2 May represented a significant accomplishment. It was a clear-cut statement of the terms under which the Western powers collectively were willing to resume relations with Soviet Russia: the Allies were willing to encourage and promote reconstruction *if* Moscow accepted their conditions of

1. Text in *DBFP*, 19:692–702; reprinted in GB Cmd. 1667, pp. 26–38, and in *FRUS, 1922*, 2:777–86.
2. *FRUS, 1922*, 2:399.

(1) full recognition of public and private debts, (2) restitution or compensation for nationalized property and cessation of subversion against other states, and (3) the establishment of a regime that enabled foreigners to do business freely. Shorter and less precise than the London Report, the document of 2 May was the outcome of Genoa's long deliberations and, even more, of Lloyd George's design.

What did he want? "Peace in Europe," he insisted; another "South Sea bubble," mocked the London *Times*. A "new orientation," chanted Grigg; a "dangerous adventure," warned *Le Temps*. The truth was somewhere in between. The British prime minister was juggling two great problems, Germany and Russia, and he sought a formula that would restructure European politics. He hoped for an agreement with Chicherin and a peace pact for Eastern Europe. A practical arrangement between the West and Moscow would eventually lead to formal recognition, increased trade and investments, border guarantees, a new world organization more universal than the League, and, finally, European disarmament. The German question was to be subsumed under the larger heading of Russian reconstruction. Berlin would develop a prominent role as trader, builder, and British copartner in the East, reparations payer in the West. France and its allies would contribute to and profit from European cooperation. Poland and Rumania would obtain security. International capital would follow London's direction. And Lloyd George would be ensured a long tenure at 10 Downing Street.[3]

How did this individual, highly political vision succeed in producing the first step, a collective offer to the Russians? Lloyd George's ideas had many advantages, not the least of which was the expectancy of the European public that something would be accomplished at Genoa. The conference had reinforced the hope that Russia could rejoin the community of nations and a lasting peace be restored. Britain used all its energy and persuasiveness to convince the delegates and the press of the soundness, "realism," and urgency of coming to terms with Moscow, and there was a ready audience for this message.

The Russia with which the West was dealing in the spring of 1922 was weak and impoverished, led by an ailing leader and a dictatorial minority party that strayed markedly from Communist orthodoxy, and bitterly divided over its future course. These facts made the Allies' decisions all the more difficult. At the time the West perceived three Russias.

First, they perceived the Old Regime and pre-Bolshevik Russia, represented primarily by its remaining adherents. This Russia had been an ultraloyal, indeed indispensable, World War I ally. Even more important, it was the former source of such critical raw materials as grain, timber, metals, and oil, and an

3. De Martino to Schanzer, London, 30 Apr., IMAE Amb. Lond. 538.3, stressed the impending general election.

extremely lucrative site of prewar Western holdings and investments; in addition, its government had borrowed and bought lavishly from the West.

Second, they saw the present government, with its motley ruling coalition, an ungainly mixture of leftist sectarianism and economic reformism. This government was the headquarters of the Third Internationale's world conspiracy but also the signer of treaties with a score of bourgeois governments. It held an incessant number of party, labor, municipal, state, and international congresses, and its press daily echoed fierce ideological disputes. But there was also a growing centralized power of the small Bolshevik leadership.

Third, they could see a "future Russia" where the clock would never turn back either to the czarist autocracy or to militant war communism but would *evolve* into a new state form: dissolve the Cheka, recall the Constituent Assembly, reform the system of justice and labor relations, and eventually join the League of Nations. In sum, they envisioned a "Thermidor," which hopefully would not produce a Bonaparte.

The first perception was the anti-Bolshevik vision of the militant Right but also that of Masaryk and Millerand, Churchill and Hoover, who believed the Bolsheviks might be replaced by the March 1917 leaders they had overthrown. The second was the pro-Leninist view of the Left, of the *Daily Herald* and *Humanité*, which exerted some influence on the democracies of Europe and America. The last was the "liberal" view of a Lloyd George who modeled himself on the pragmatic Pitt of 1797, the view of the *Manchester Guardian* and Europe's moderate press. Given the postwar economic problems of Europe and the fragile coalition politics on which almost all of the governments rested, these three views of Russia occupied a very real and practical place in day-to-day politics. The Right viewed the present regime as heinous and transitory; the Left opposed any attempt to alter or control Moscow; and the liberals expressed the hope that through negotiation and compromise Russia and Europe would save each other.

In their approach to the Soviets, the Western governments had four alternatives: two passive and two active. On the passive side there was first of all official ostracism and nonrecognition, which nevertheless permitted a certain amount of probing by private traders and humanitarian organizations. This was the policy of the anti-Communist governments in Washington, Paris, Prague, Berne, Brussels, and The Hague,[4] some of which even maintained diplomatic relations with representatives of the Old Regime or with the separatist governments deposed by the Bolsheviks. It was admittedly a do-nothing policy, vulnerable to criticisms by moderates and leftists at home and abroad. Also, it was

4. See, e.g., Richard K. Debo, "Dutch-Soviet Relations, 1917–1924: The Role of Finance and Commerce in the Foreign Policy of Soviet Russia and the Netherlands," *Canadian Slavic Studies* 4, no. 2 (Summer 1970): 199–217.

perpetually threatened by a breaking of ranks by governments seeking to acquire advantages for their citizens.

A second passive policy was laissez-faire, one that accepted, either willingly or through compulsion, the inevitability of establishing de facto or de jure relations with the Soviet state. Examples of countries following this policy were Russia's neighbors: Poland, the Baltic and Scandinavian states, Turkey, and, finally, Germany. This essentially paper transaction opened doors but caused as many problems as benefits for domestic leftist parties and gave few immediate advantages for individual capitalists. Moreover, laissez-faire fragmented Europe's solidarity and left unsolved the continuing menace of Moscow's hostility to the capitalist world and its weakness.

On the active side, the first alternative was "destabilization," the aggressively anti-Communist stance that Churchill had championed and Wilsonian liberals had joined in 1918, first against the Bolshevik treason to the Allies and then on behalf of Old Guard claimants. By 1922 even Japan, the last representative of wartime interventionism in Siberia, was willing to renounce such a policy as costly, internally divisive, and largely unsuccessful. Indeed, Western-sponsored counterrevolution, on which the hopes of restoring Old Russia had rested, proved more inept, less pliable, and more nationalistic than czardom.[5] The episodes of direct and indirect intervention had left a legacy of bitterness and ruin in Russia and huge counterclaims against the West, which the Allies at London had grudgingly acknowledged.[6]

Finally, there was a second active possibility, which might be termed "help and cooperation"; this policy represented the extension of the temporary famine relief operations of 1921 to a more permanent basis, using a combination of private capital and Western taxpayers' money to rehabilitate Russia's farms, industries, and transport, even at the risk of preserving the present Bolshevik regime. It involved few illusions about this regime, whose attempts at subversion were fully recognized.[7] Yet the alternatives—alliance with the warring czarist factions, renewed civil war and chaos, and do-nothing—were unattractive. Lenin's regime, if by his own admission still "inefficient," was a more adequate potential trading partner than Whitist generals or the Bolshevik radi-

5. Lloyd George statement, 26 Apr., *DBFP*, 19:576.

6. War Office to FO, London, 18 Apr., GB FO 371 N3676/646/38.

7. Chamberlain to Lloyd George, London, 1 May, GB FO 371 N4146/646/38, conveyed information that the Third Internationale had just allocated 5 million rubles for Communist propaganda against Britain and France, one-third of which was for the use of the delegation at Genoa. Hodgson to Curzon, Moscow, 15 May, GB FO 371 N4947/248/38, doubted such funds were available and noted that financial exigency had caused a cooling of relations between the government and the Internationale. Nevertheless, Lenin did recommend that the Third Internationale work with insurgents in South Africa: *Collected Works* (Moscow: Progress Publishers, 1967–71), 45:531. At Genoa Chicherin met with Arab and Indian revolutionaries: Secret Intelligence Service report (hereafter S.I.S.), 12 July, GB FO 371 N7227/6003/38.

cals who might succeed him. If one simply ignored Rakovsky's taunts and messages and concentrated on Chicherin's letter of 21 April, there were undoubtedly possibilities for progress in Soviet-Western relations.

Help and cooperation possessed the unique advantage among the two passive and two active policies of being the sole way of attracting support of the Right, Middle, and Left, at least *temporarily*, as Keynes's series "Reconstruction in Europe" had demonstrated. Businessmen were interested in gaining access to their former enterprises or at least in preventing others from obtaining preponderant advantages. Liberals wanted peace and trade. The radical Left wanted full employment and the survival of the Soviet state. Help and cooperation also fused the three visions—the "old Russia," dear to the Right; Lenin's Russia, defended by the Left; and the liberals' image of a progressively more democratic, open, and westernized Russia.

Help and cooperation thus became the basis for the memorandum dispatched to the Russians on 2 May. Instead of an ultimatum, the West decided to formulate a memorandum, a negotiating instrument, indicating that it was prepared to contribute to Russia's rehabilitation, to accept the fact that Moscow could not repay debts at once, and, in some form or other, to recognize the current regime: its government, laws, and system of property. In return, the Western powers had to formulate their conditions and specifications for peace with Russia. Despite their noisy disagreements, they accomplished this by 2 May.

Preamble: What the Allies Offered to Russia

When the Allied experts met in London in March, they had solemnly pronounced that the

> economic restoration of Russia is largely dependent upon her enlisting the support of foreign enterprise and capital. [However,] without a considerable transformation of the prevailing conditions foreigners will be reluctant either to return to their former undertakings or to start fresh undertakings. So long as precarious and unstable conditions continue, only speculators will be willing to venture on trade, and there is a fear that the chief result would be not the reconstruction but the exploitation of Russia and the Russian people, which it is the purpose of the Governments represented at Genoa to avoid.[8]

Carefully avoiding specific details concerning the "instruments" to be applied to Russian reconstruction or the "relation of any such instrument to existing trade agreements with Russia" (both political issues excluded from their deliberations), the Allied experts had drafted only the vaguest outline of how

8. *DBFP*, 19:260–61.

Russia was to be helped: agriculture would be the "foundation" of Russia's rehabilitation, followed by improvements in its industry and its transport.[9] There were only five short paragraphs dealing with the Allies' contribution to Russian reconstruction, as compared with two long chapters outlining the Allies' demands.

This was the document handed to the Russians on 10 April. It provided neither real nor symbolic incentives for the Soviets to sign, especially after Rapallo, and the Allied terms of 15 April added nothing more.[10] Sticking closely to the Cannes Resolutions, there was no promise of de jure recognition and no indications of specific forms of Western aid, either through direct government loans or government support of private lenders and capitalists. Yet despite Rapallo and the rumors that Berlin would be the guiding center of Soviet commerce, the Russians continued to hope that the West would bid higher than the Germans; they did not break off and asked what would be offered.[11]

Lloyd George was stopped by his own delegation from making a pledge of direct government credits to the Russians, a move that exceeded his mandate.[12] He therefore charged the British experts to draft a very elaborate aid proposal on behalf of the Allies. The result was a carefully written document addressed not only to the Bolshevik negotiators but also the European liberal and leftist public that needed evidence of the Allies' willingness to help and not plunder Russia. Russia, once "an important element in the economic system of Europe" but eliminated after 1918, was likely to be replaced as a supplier. Nevertheless, its current "privation, misery, and famine" constituted a "plague spot of increasing menace to the European system."[13]

The British draft promised that help would come from the West: supplies of food, clothing, medical stores, and other necessities of civilized existence, along with locomotives, wagons, fertilizers, agricultural implements, tools, machinery, and port supplies. But such aid was predicated on two conditions: the restoration of property to its former owners and the recognition of debts. Capital would flow into Russia through various sources: the Trade Facilities Act, the Export Credits scheme (in which 11 million pounds was not yet pledged), and the international corporation. Though it would begin with an admittedly meager initial capital of 20 million pounds, the corporation would be an important beginning: a union of private capital and public guarantees,

9. Ibid., p. 261.

10. Ibid., pp. 421–22.

11. Hodgson to Curzon, Moscow, 24 Apr., GB FO 371 N4119/155/38; Rapport, Sûreté Générale, Menton, 5 May, FMAE B 97.

12. Lloyd-Greame to wife, Genoa, Sunday [23 Apr.] and 25 Apr., LGrP.

13. *DBFP*, 19:592.

an international enterprise founded specifically for Russian reconstruction.[14] Lloyd George revealed these proposals on 27 April to the Italian and Japanese delegates, who concurred.[15]

The French produced their own proposals. Written by Seydoux and almost twice as long as the British, the French document was an implicit criticism of both Lloyd George and Poincaré's refusals to draft a specific plan for Russia's rehabilitation.[16] It harked back to the earlier lively discussions in February in the Quai d'Orsay and presented a blueprint for reviving the Russian economy through the action of foreign concessionaires. The international corporation would provide seed money, and then private lenders and special government credits might follow. Russian reconstruction would be supervised by Western "pioneers," bringing their expertise, machinery, and capital as the vanguard of foreign penetration.

The political subcommission met on 28 April. Barthou, opening with the announcement that contrary to rumors he was *not* leaving, made a weak presentation of the French proposal. Lloyd George disliked its tone and derided its "useless," "irritating," and "provocative" phraseology. Schanzer criticized it for stressing long-term solutions, unlike the British draft, whose "precise . . . financial section interested the Russians most." Lloyd George wooed France with soothing words on its "very special position" in regard to actual contributions to Russia's rehabilitation: all France's resources "were absorbed by the reconstruction of the areas devastated by the war." Schanzer broke the impasse by proposing the creation of a five-member drafting committee, consisting of representatives of Belgium, Britain, France, Italy, and Switzerland, to draw up a single preamble by the next morning reconciling the French and British statements.[17]

Lloyd George was delighted with the results, which contained 90 percent of the British text.[18] The preamble to the Allies' document, worded carefully, blamed Russia for its woes and minimized their effect on Europe. Russian reconstruction, "to be carried out in the interests of Russia itself," could not be achieved "without the help of the capital and the commercial experience of the Western countries." The purpose of these remarks was to answer by turn Trotsky's taunts of the West's weakness, the fears of both Left and Right that Russia would be plundered, and the liberals' insistence that "help and cooperation"

---

14. Ibid., p. 593.

15. Ibid., pp. 593–603; Attolico report, Genoa, 20 Apr., LNA 40A 20136/20226.

16. *DBFP*, 19:618–20; background in Saint-Aulaire [Seydoux] to MAE, London, 27 Mar., #341–43, FMAE B 115, and in *DBFP*, 19:559.

17. Meeting of subcommission of Political Commission, 28 Apr., *DBFP*, 19:603–12.

18. Worthington-Evans to Chamberlain, Genoa, 30 Apr., CzP; Lloyd-Greame to wife, Genoa, 29 Apr., LGrP.

be practical and meaningful. In the most general terms, Russia was promised supplies, capital, and the "initiative and experience of foreigners." These would be dependent, however, on Moscow's fulfillment of specific conditions set forth afterward.

The subcommission agreed to Schanzer's proposal that the specific list of aid begin with the international corporation. That afternoon a meeting was hurriedly arranged to organize the corporation formally along the lines approved in February in London.[19] Britain, France, Italy, Belgium, Germany, and Japan, along with Czechoslovakia, Canada, Denmark, Norway, Holland, Sweden, Switzerland, and Spain, would all participate. Every member had to deposit a contribution of five hundred thousand pounds within thirty days; all the members also had to acquiesce in Britain's demand that they guarantee their investors' capital and interest. The way for American membership was left open.[20]

The final version of the preamble contained a list of what Britain, France, Italy, Japan, and Belgium individually could contribute to Russian reconstruction; for reasons of brevity, the list was limited to the five, excluding the other members on the subcommission and the rest of the governments at Genoa. The document was vague on the possibility of direct government loans because none of the Allies could make a commitment there at Genoa. Indeed, participation in the international corporation was neither set nor obligatory.[21]

Were the terms in the preamble "pure eyewash," as one British official thought,[22] or did they contain the elements of help and cooperation? Krassin at once queried Lloyd George, who explained that the schemes could *eventually* work to Russia's advantage. He also pledged to raise and stimulate additional government and private credits, the "real help that Russia needed." But there could be no further promises. To add a measure of coercion, he threatened that if Moscow refused the Allies' terms, Britain might forget Europe and concentrate on "Eastern and Colonial trade." He also warned that the Germans in their poverty had little to offer and reminded Krassin that in response to leftist-revolutionary agitation, the "counter-revolutionary spirit was beginning to prevail" in Western Europe. From his perspective, the goal was "to turn the mind of the capitalists toward Russia." He was confident that the encounter would benefit both sides.[23]

19. Gregory to FO, Genoa, 29 Apr., GB FO 371 C6281/458/62; Ritter to Bergmann, Genoa, 2 May, Germ. AA T-120 L991/5411/L285839-43.

20. Child to State Dept., Genoa, 19 Apr., USDS 550 E1/200, warned that "a substantial U.S. investment . . . will fall under British control and management."

21. *DBFP*, 19:630–33, 637–40; Barthou to MAE, 20 Apr., #301–5, FMAE B 110; Dufour to Bergmann, Genoa, 2 May, Germ. AA T-120 L991/5411/L285038.

22. O'Malley minute, 8 May, *DBFP*, 19:702–3.

23. Informal meeting at the Villa d'Albertis, 5 May (Lloyd George, Worthington-Evans, Wise, and Krassin), ibid., pp. 751–55.

Russia's Obligations: Debts and Private Property

Now Lloyd George mustered all his energy and wiles to complete the document specifying what Russia would have to accept in order to receive the West's proffered aid. There were some easy decisions. The first clause, dealing with propaganda, was expanded so that the Soviet government would pledge "not to interfere . . . in the internal affairs" or "disturb the territorial and political status quo" of its neighbors, would curb the activities of the Third Internationale, and would "use all its influence to assist the restoration of peace in Asia Minor."[24] Aimed at the hard-liners on both sides, these were nevertheless secondary considerations.

The questions of debt repayment and restoration of private property aroused conflict among the Allies, indeed, brought the Genoa Conference to still another crisis point. On the question of debts, Britain insisted that they were committed to the concessions made in their note of 15 April, which Chicherin had forwarded to Moscow and which had been the basis of his response on 21 April. The Allies had promised a "substantial" reduction of Russia's war debts as well as a reduction of the interest and a moratorium on the repayment of Russia's prewar debts to private capitalists.

Poincaré had earlier given his approval to both these arrangements. The signing of the Rapallo treaty provided him with justification to back off, and he needed to, because he doubted that parliament would accept any reduction of France's claims; moreover, France and its allies would scarcely benefit from so generous a gesture toward Moscow unless the United States and Britain offered commensurate concessions in advance.[25]

Poincaré therefore instructed Barthou to refuse any reduction of Russia's war debts pending a comprehensive general settlement among all the World War I debtors and creditors. Unlike London, Paris was not anxious to solve the problem of extinguishing the Soviets' counterclaims against the Allies by reducing the total; in fact, the French were prepared to match the gigantic bill for the intervention by claiming damages caused by the Treaty of Brest-Litovsk. In view of the current reparations struggle with Berlin and the impending negotiations with London and Washington over its war debt, Poincaré felt it premature, even dangerous, to make a conciliatory gesture to Moscow.[26]

France's second important interest involved Russia's debts to private individuals. It had a powerful force of 1.2 million bondholders, whose shares were now of minimal value. The government was unwilling to take on the onus of

24. Ibid., pp. 633–36.

25. Poincaré to Barthou, 15 Apr., #40–41, 16 Apr., #47, 17 Apr., #55–56, 18 Apr., #56–57, 19 Apr., #78–80, 22 Apr., #113, FMAE B 94, 20 Apr., #[?], 21 Apr., #103, FMAE Y 30.

26. Poincaré to Barthou, 25 Apr., #[?], FMAE Y 31, 25 Apr., #137, #155, FMAE B 95.

waiving any part of their practically nonexistent claims. Seydoux, himself a bondholder,[27] did not oppose a moratorium but objected to the British scheme for canceling interest for five years and reducing it for the next ten. The key to this problem lay in the presence of the representatives of French bondholders in Genoa; Seydoux was in constant touch with them.

Finally, there was the question of restoration of private property. Britain had accepted the consequences of the Soviets' nationalization edicts, and it now sought to formulate the terms under which its capitalists and those of Europe could secure trade and concessions in the new Russia with adequate guarantees of personal and professional security. The neutrals, Germany, the Little Entente, and even France had originally been on Britain's side.[28] It was Belgium that took up the cause of the former owners, arguing that the conditions under which property would be restored might prejudice them. The jurist Cattier argued: "England possessed several forms of property. Thus, to substitute leasehold for freehold was not a very serious matter for an Englishman. On the Continent, on the other hand, there was only one recognized form of property. Consequently, they could not substitute leasehold for freehold without weakening the *whole idea of property*. It was the *social aspect* of the question that alarmed him."[29]

Belgian protests about the precarious legal and security conditions in Russia won little support.[30] European governments had regularly bent their values and principles to changing political circumstances resulting from wars, revolutions, and social upheavals. Lloyd George made a strong rebuttal: the Allies were already committed to the Cannes Resolutions, in which paragraph 1 allowed all governments to regulate their own systems of private property and paragraph 3 gave the Soviets the option of compensating rather than restoring former owners. Further, he argued, not only had the staunchly capitalist United States of America confiscated the private railroads during wartime but, closer to home, the governments of Czechoslovakia and Rumania, with their "agrarian reform" programs, had nationalized the property of foreign citizens with far more restrictive terms of compensation than the West was demanding of Russia; this had not prevented the Czechs, on the eve of Genoa, from finally succeeding in raising two major loans in Great Britain.[31]

Lloyd George's statements were disingenuous, for Soviet conditions were unique. During the past two years, Russia had consolidated smaller properties into huge trusts. Some were state-run and some were being converted into either mixed companies or foreign concessions in the hope of raising foreign

27. *DBFP*, 19:581.
28. Lloyd-Greame to wife, Genoa, 29 Apr., LGrP.
29. *DBFP*, 19:582.
30. Ibid., pp. 582, 585, 590–91.
31. Ibid., pp. 582–83, 590–91; the *Times*, 6, 7 Apr.

capital and attracting experts and machinery. Moscow's concessions policy was both erratic and internally controversial. It was essentially a means of stirring competitive bidding and rivalries among Western capitalists and governments and playing one side against the other.[32] The British-Belgian debate at Genoa reflected one of its results, pitting Lloyd George, representing the potential concessionaires, against Jaspar, representing the dispossessed.

Belgian capitalists, with little new money to invest in the concessions ostensibly offered by the Soviet government, were frightened at the prospect of seeing their former properties and leases assigned to more powerful groupings of British, Dutch, American, and German capitalists. Rakovsky had already admitted that former owners possessed no priority and would be "compensated" by being allowed to enter new trusts on a competitive basis. The Belgian firm Pétrole de Grosny, headed by the Antwerp banker Joseph Waterkeyn, had recently been refused a concession it had bid for. Waterkeyn wrote Jaspar on 26 April that it was necessary to find a formula on private property that would free the former owners from their "dependence" on the Soviet regime. Waterkeyn demanded that Belgium hold out for full restitution of property, rejected the concept of "enjoyment" in the form of a lease, and refused compensation in the form of bonds as "risky and valueless." Fearing fellow capitalists as much as the Russians, he pleaded that Jaspar resist any formula that was not "absolutely precise." There could be no loophole by which former properties could disappear into larger concessions. If restitution were physically impossible, Waterkeyn wanted compensation to be paid in gold rubles.[33] The Belgian government endorsed these demands.[34]

If Belgium had to be intransigent on this "issue of principle," France was in a more difficult position. Barthou was isolated and irritable. He had already faced Lloyd George's reproaches over France's volte-face on the war-debts issue. Constantly on the defensive, he was the butt of Lloyd George's sarcasm and helpless before the prime minister's indefatigable composers of memoranda.[35] France's friends were not always reliable. Barthou watched with misgivings Beneš's approaches to Chicherin after Rapallo to resume discussions of a Soviet-Czech trade pact. From the start, Belgium had given France noticeably little support. On the war-debt issue, Jaspar had declared neutrality; on

32. Lenin, *Collected Works*, 45:448–49, 452, 505, 506, 513, 522, 523–24; E. H. Carr, *The Bolshevik Revolution* (Baltimore: Penguin, 1966), 3: 277, 281–85, 353–54.

33. *DBFP*, 19:549; FO to Jaspar, [25] Apr., BMAE 10991; Waterkeyn to Jaspar, Antwerp, 26 Apr., 5 May, Jaspar to Waterkeyn, Genoa, 4 May, ibid.; Hodgson to Curzon, Moscow, 24 Apr., *DBFP*, 20:863–65, reporting the refusal of the Pétrole de Grosny concession.

34. Theunis to Jaspar, Ramaix to Jaspar, Brussels, 30 Apr., BMAE 10991; copy in Peretti to French Delegation, Paris, 3 May, #270–71, FMAE B 96.

35. IGPS, Boll. no. 14, Genoa, 29 Apr., IMAE 52/31; Lloyd-Greame to wife, 29 Apr., LGrP.; Hankey to Chamberlain, 27, 30 Apr., and Worthington-Evans to Curzon, 30 Apr., HP.

private bondholders, he had added only a limp defense.[36] The preconference Franco-Belgian cooperation had been eroded by Genoa's atmosphere, which meant there was no concerted resistance to Lloyd George's campaign to make concessions to the Russians.

In an attempt to coordinate their positions, Lloyd George and Barthou held a tête-à-tête at the Hotel Miramare on 29 April, just before the day-long meetings of the political subcommission.[37] Barthou asked for clarification of the possibility of reducing Allied war debts. Lloyd George merely repeated his proposal to Loucheur five months earlier: Britain was prepared to renounce all its war debts and its claims for pensions against Germany on the condition that France, Italy, and the rest drop their claims for pensions against Germany and on the even more remote contingency that the United States "wipe out its European debts." According to Lloyd George's scenario, Germany, having only to repair the devastation it had caused in the war (four-fifths of which would go to France), would be capable of raising an international loan sufficiently large to "start her own economic life." All was undoubtedly dependent on the United States, and America's main precondition was that "peace should be established in Europe." This could be commenced at Genoa. Lloyd George flattered Barthou's vanity and thereby convinced him to permit the jurists to handle the vexatious questions of debts and private property. The British premier gave Barthou the impression that he held the key to improved Franco-British relations, indeed European and world relations, in his own hands.[38]

Nevertheless, the meetings of the political subcommission were not entirely harmonious. Barthou did not meekly submit to Lloyd George's proposals. At one disagreeable juncture when they bickered over the meaning of the Boulogne conversations, Lloyd George threatened to submit the text to the scrutiny of jurists.[39] They argued over war debts. The Russians had demanded a total cancellation because of their vast counterclaims. Britain wanted a 50 percent reduction based ostensibly on Russia's immense war contributions but in reality as a means of eliminating any further discussion of Moscow's counterclaims. Lloyd George insisted that Poincaré had agreed to reduce Russia's war debts. Since Russia's loans from Britain had been five times greater than those from France, this reduction would be to the benefit of the French bondholders, whose principal (though not the interest) was to be fully recognized.[40] Japan

36. Barthou to MAE, Genoa, 26 Apr., #[?], FMAE B 109, 27 Apr., #[?], FMAE PM G/V, 1 May, #309, FMAE B 96, 2 May, #[?], FMAE Y 31.

37. Résumé, 29 Apr., FMAE Y 31; notes of meeting, *DBFP*, 19:624–29.

38. Barthou to MAE, Genoa, 1 May, #310, FMAE B 96; Gregory to Tyrrell, Genoa, 30 Apr., GB FO 371 C6588/458/62; Hankey to Chamberlain, Genoa, 30 Apr., and Worthington-Evans to Curzon, Genoa, 30 Apr., HP.

39. Meeting of subcommission of Political Commission, 29 Apr., 11 A.M., *DBFP*, 19:630–36; 4 P.M., ibid., pp. 641–49; Barthou to MAE, Genoa, 29 Apr., #293–97, #301–5, FMAE B 110.

40. *DBFP*, 19:643.

supported France in opposing any reductions whatsoever. The neutrals were uninterested in the debate; and Jaspar again stressed his unconcern.[41]

The political subcommission meetings were suspended over Sunday while the jurists worked on the intricate questions of debts and private property. When they reconvened on 1 May, it was announced that France had produced the solution to the least controversial question, Russia's debts to private investors: holders of securities or their representatives would deal directly with the Soviet government. There would be a fixed time limit of one year, after which an impartial tribunal would adjudicate any unsettled claims. The tribunal would also possess wide powers, including the right to recommend the postponement of interest payments. The French and British agreed on other details, including the elimination of the politically delicate references in the London Report to the establishment of a "special regime" for foreigners residing in Russia.[42]

The jurists had produced a brilliant compromise formula on war debts: Russia was to acknowledge its full debt to its former allies; however, in the interests of "facilitating the immediate reconstruction of Russia" and rehabilitating its credit, the Western powers agreed to defer their claims both on capital and interest. They rejected any liability for loss or damage suffered during and after the Russian Revolution. Finally, they held out the possibility of a future reduction of the war debt, conditional, to be sure, on Russia's renunciation of its counterclaims.[43]

This tour de force by the British and French legal experts, Sir Cecil Hurst and Henri Fromageot, had certain consequences. France, in order to put the whole issue of war debts (on which it stood virtually alone) on ice, had to make concessions to Britain elsewhere. In his speech accepting the compromise and agreeing to go back on their offer to the Russians, Lloyd George made France's obligation painfully specific.[44]

Barthou, after many pleas for delay, had to leave the following day for Paris. In addition to submitting a report to the government, Barthou had taken on a special mission: to secure Poincaré's agreement to Lloyd George's nonaggression pact and deliver Lloyd George's pleas for an Allied meeting on the reparations situation.[45] He was tormented by the "Cannes precedent," namely, that Briand's departure and resignation had torpedoed the last conference. Thus,

---

41. Ibid., p. 648.

42. Ibid., pp. 668–70.

43. Ibid., p. 661. Barthou to Poincaré, Genoa, 1 May, #317, FMAE B 110; Hankey to Chamberlain, Genoa, 2 May, HP.

44. *DBFP*, 19:651: "His consent was a provisional one, and his final assent would depend entirely upon the attitude adopted by other Governments towards other drafts settled by practically the same committees." See Barthou to Poincaré, Genoa, 2 May, #334–40, FMAE B 110.

45. *DBFP*, 19:629.

when the third and most difficult question of restoring private property came up on 1 May, he gravitated toward the British point of view. Given Belgium's earlier indifference to the debts issue, Russia's indubitable right according to paragraph 1 of the Cannes Resolutions to reorganize properties within its borders, and, most important, the agreement of groups of former owners there at Genoa to the formula drafted by the jurists, Barthou went along with the compromise formula. "Article 6" (later Article 7) of the Allies' proposals, prepared by Hurst, Fromageot, and Cattier, accepted the Soviets' expropriation of private property and consolidation into larger trusts and specified that compensation would be primarily through the issuance of bonds, but it also held out the possibility, should the award be deemed inadequate by an impartial tribunal, of a grant by the Soviet government of the "enjoyment" of the former owner's property.[46]

The more the sun of Anglo-French amity shone, the more visible one small dark cloud of Belgium's resistance appeared. Cattier had functioned only as an official observer during the jurists' meetings.[47] Brussels instructed Jaspar not to accept any text on private property that exposed Belgian property owners to a ruinous bidding contest with stronger nations. Rakovsky had already hinted and Theunis knew too of negotiations between various oil companies and other industrial concerns involving properties once owned by Belgians. Though sitting among the Great Powers, Belgium, a small nation impoverished by the war and strained by postwar economic, social, and ethnic problems, was unable to sacrifice its interests to Allied solidarity or "world peace."

Thus, on 1 May Jaspar presented the Belgian position to the subcommission of the Political Commission. He was willing to accept long-term leases as a possible substitute for full ownership. He nevertheless resisted the idea of consolidation and insisted on full restitution in all instances where the property could still be identified. Fearing to allow his countrymen to be completely at the mercy of Moscow, he demanded compensation in gold if the property had been destroyed or disappeared.[48] Furious, Lloyd George accused Belgium of trying to wreck the Genoa Conference. He harped on the theme of joint sacrifice: Britain, he claimed, had over four times Belgium's prewar investments in Russia and far heavier taxes and war costs than the Brussels government. He warned Jaspar against "pressing for something which would inevitably destroy the last chance of ever having a compact with Russia."[49]

In the afternoon, Barthou attempted to play the role of mediator. No one stood on Belgium's side, and Jaspar refused to accept any amendment.[50] The

46. Ibid., p. 662; Barthou to MAE, Genoa, 2 May, #334–40, FMAE B 110.
47. Jaspar to Theunis, Genoa, 29 Apr., 1 May, BMAE 10991.
48. Meeting of subcommission of Political Commission, 1 May, 11 A.M., *DBFP*, 19:651–54.
49. Ibid., pp. 654, 655.
50. Meeting of subcommission of Political Commission, 1 May, 4:30 P.M., ibid., pp. 671–72.

contradiction written in the Cannes Resolutions four months earlier came back to haunt the Allies: the coexistence statement in the first paragraph, a transactional formula never intended to stand alone, was now used as a weapon against a small friendly nation that could not accept or profit from the consequences of the Bolshevik revolution. To complete the day's irony, while the capitalist governments were arguing over their scruples at Genoa, Trotsky harangued the Red Army in his May Day address and pledged there would be no concessions on the part of the Soviets at all.[51]

Since the Allied note was virtually finished, Lloyd George urged the political subcommission to sign and hand it over to the Russians the next morning. Belgium refused to sign. Barthou, "very much struck" by Jaspar's remarks and reserving the right to discuss them with his government, nevertheless acquiesced in Lloyd George's plea that they hurry. Thereby Anglo-French harmony had been reestablished, and the memorandum could be dispatched to Chicherin the next day.[52]

Moments before Barthou's departure from Genoa, Lloyd George called on the French delegate for an amiable chat and also to reinforce the messages he was sending to Poincaré.[53] He again urged an Allied meeting on reparations, merely promising in return to say something "friendly" toward France in his meeting with British and American journalists. He was convinced that Barthou would obtain "full instructions to make peace with Russia."[54] This was an improbable hope, the product of weeks of strain, of difficulties with the Russians and Belgians, of dire warnings from London that he *had* to work in concert with the Allies, and, especially, of overconfidence.[55]

On 2 May, when the political subcommission reconvened to finish its work, Belgium was absent. There was a new surprise. Barrère, the acting head of the delegation, announced that instructions had arrived one hour earlier from Paris ordering him not to sign the memorandum. Because of "the divergence of opinion . . . between the Belgian delegation and the other delegations . . . the French delegation [had] to postpone its final adhesion until M. Barthou had had an opportunity of discussing the matter with the French Government."[56]

To add to the confusion, Seydoux proposed an amendment to Article 6 (7) in an attempt to reconcile the British and Belgian points of view on the property question within the context of the Cannes Resolutions: "In cases where the

51. Ibid., p. 770.

52. Ibid., p. 672; Barthou to MAE, 2 May, #334–40, FMAE B 110; Roger to Charles-Roux, Genoa, 6 May, FMAE PC-R.

53. Note of conversation, 2 May, *DBFP*, 19:673–80; Résumé, 2 May, FMAE Y 31.

54. David and Frances Lloyd George, *My Darling Pussy: The Letters of Lloyd George and Frances Stevenson, 1913–1941*, ed. A. J. P. Taylor (London: Weidenfeld and Nicolson, 1975), p. 45; Lloyd George to Curzon, 30 Apr., LGP F 13/3/18.

55. Chamberlain to Worthington-Evans, London, 3 May, ACP 23/6/32.

56. *DBFP*, 19:686; Poincaré to Barthou, Paris, 2 May, #248–50, #251, FMAE B 110.

Soviet Government cannot restore the property itself, it shall not be entitled to grant it afterwards to other concession holders. If the Russian Soviet Government proposes at a later date to make a draft of that kind, preference shall be reserved to the former owners."[57]

Lloyd George grudgingly accepted on the condition that they dispatch the memorandum to the Russians at once. He also added his own final paragraph to Seydoux's amendment: "If the exploiting of the property can only be ensured by incorporating it into a general group, the preceding provision shall not apply, but the former owner shall have the right to take part in this group in proportion to his former rights."[58] This vitiated Seydoux's improvement and, by restoring the initiative to the Soviet government and the advantage to major capitalist concerns, it assured Belgium's rejection.[59]

Caught between Lloyd George's stubbornness and his orders from Paris, Barrère gave way to the overriding sentiment on the subcommission and agreed to send the memorandum to the Russians. He succeeded only in including the notation that France had signed with reservations.[60] He justified his actions to Paris with the following reasons. First, he was impressed by Lloyd George's eloquent plea for solidarity between Britain and France. Also, the French delegation was irritated with Jaspar: his desertion on the debts issue, his stubborn refusal to compromise on the property question, and especially his reluctance to follow France's lead, which had raised tensions with Britain to an intolerable point. Further, Barrère feared that should the negotiations break off abruptly, Britain and Italy might well seek a separate agreement with the Soviets. Finally, and perhaps most important, Barrère shared Barthou's sensitivity to France's "isolated and difficult" situation at Genoa, which would have been exacerbated by a refusal to sign the memorandum. He asked Poincaré not only to approve his conditional adhesion but also to urge Brussels to persuade Jaspar to return to the fold.[61]

In their haste to finish their work, the political subcommission tabled Lloyd George's suggestion to draft an elaborate explanatory letter to the Russians that included references to the nonaggression pact and de jure recognition.[62] These would be discussed only if the Russians accepted. The group similarly ignored Barrère's proposal to set a time limit to the Soviet response. Thus, on 2 May, in just over four hours of discussion in the Palazzo Reale, the political subcommission—minus Germany, Russia, and Belgium—concluded its labors. The drafting committee worked past midnight, and at 3 the next morning, the

---

57. *DBFP*, 19:690; FMAE PM G/VII for text.

58. *DBFP*, 19:690.

59. Unsigned note, Genoa, 4 May (to Delacroix), BMAE 10991.

60. Barrère to MAE, Genoa, 3 May, #349–55, FMAE Y 32.

61. Ibid. Also Barrère to MAE, Genoa, 3 May, #364–65, FMAE B 110, 4 May, #370, FMAE Y 32.

62. Gregory to FO, Genoa, 3 May, GB FO 371 N4219/646/38.

memorandum, with a brief covering letter from Schanzer, was dispatched to the Russian delegation.[63]

First Fruits

Lloyd George, exultant over his victory in the "desperate struggle" with France and Belgium, was not optimistic about the Bolsheviks' reply. He wrote the patient and absent Frances Stevenson, "I hear contradictory accounts, but they all agree as to the Russian character. It will shrink from a clear and definite yes."[64] Indeed, the first unofficial Russian responses reinforced his fears. Chicherin's public statements were negative, and the hard-liner, Adolf Joffe, left mysteriously on 5 May for Moscow via Berlin.[65] The Soviet delegation was still divided between its hard-liners and its moderates. The noisy May Day celebrations were a warning to the latter; and Chicherin, though the most conciliatory of the delegates, continued to explore alternatives to caving in to the West.[66]

The reception of the memorandum of 2 May was overshadowed by Genoa's second sensational event: the "oil scandal."[67] The facts were simple. Since the previous fall, a Canadian speculator, Colonel J. W. Boyle, had been conducting negotiations with Krassin on behalf of the Royal Dutch Shell group of oil companies. The British government had given its approval as a way of bringing the giant trust into closer relationship with the state-owned Anglo-Persian company or at least of securing British control over Shell's activities in Russia. Government-backed credits for Shell's sale and distribution of Soviet oil appeared to promise economic benefits, including the reduction of Britain's high unemployment; it would also head off a possible agreement between Shell and its major competitor, the American Standard Oil Company.[68]

63. Hankey to Chamberlain, Genoa, 3 May, HP.

64. Lloyd George, *My Darling Pussy*, 3 May, p. 48; also Hankey to Curzon, Genoa, 2 May, CzP; Gregory to FO and Chamberlain, Genoa, 5 May, GB FO 371 N4362/646/38.

65. On Chicherin: statements in *Tribuna*, 4 May, and the *Times*, 5 May; Child to State Dept., Genoa, 6 May, USDS 550 E1/246; Barrère to MAE, Genoa, 5 May, #387, FMAE Y 32. On Joffe: Barrère to MAE, Genoa, 6 May, #400, FMAE Y 32; D'Abernon to FO, Berlin, 8 May (2 tels.), GB FO 371 N4549, N4563/646/38; Laurent to MAE, Berlin, 9 May, #795, FMAE B 111; Martel to MAE, Riga, 16 May, FMAE PM G/VIII; Hodgson to FO, Moscow, 19 May, GB FO 371 N4896/646/38.

66. IGPS, Boll. nos. 17–18, IMAE 52/31.

67. Described sensationally in Louis Fischer, *Oil Imperialism: The International Struggle for Petroleum* (New York: International, 1926), pp. 38–67; less so in E. H. Davenport and Sidney R. Cooke, *The Oil Trusts and Anglo-American Relations* (New York: Macmillan, 1924); and inaccurately in *The Autobiography of Lincoln Steffens* (New York: Harcourt, Brace and Co., 1931), p. 810.

68. Cheetham to FO, Paris, 2 May, and Gregory to FO, Genoa, 4 May, GB FO 371 N4194/50/38; Note sur les concessions de pétrole en Russie [8–9 May], FMAE B 111; Leslie

The Soviet government, fearing to be at the mercy of one big firm or government and hoping to wipe out the claims of all former owners, approached French, German, and especially American oil companies, inviting them to participate singly or in a huge trust.[69] Before the Genoa Conference, there were no substantive agreements. Oil men flocked to Genoa from all over the globe, cautiously awaiting the outcome of the negotiations. Their presence, plus the army of largely underemployed reporters, created a situation ripe for the creation of *fausses nouvelles*.[70]

On the morning of 1 May, *Oeuvre* correspondent Camille Lemercier cabled his Paris office and the Quai d'Orsay that the night before an agreement had been signed between the Russians and a multinational petroleum group headed by Shell.[71] It gave a monopoly for the production and sale of Russian petroleum, as well as a vast concession in the Baku and Grosny areas. The American Standard Oil Company, which in 1920 had purchased an equal interest in the extensive Nobel holdings in Russia that already had been nationalized, was reportedly "furious" at its exclusion from the race for concessions by its great rival.[72]

The announcement, with its lurid overtones of monopoly, despoilment, and British greed, flooded the world press on 2 May, almost simultaneously with the announcement of the terms of the Allied memorandum to the Russians.[73] It immediately drew attention to the compromise formula of Article 7, the amended Seydoux amendment that represented a license for consolidating and exploiting expropriated properties. Standard Oil's claims were eliminated because the Allies in their property clause defined former owners as those in possession before 1917; various French companies that had acquired Russian oil shares after the nationalization were similarly excluded. The proportionately small number of bona-fide Belgian owners of properties in the Caucasus would no doubt be eliminated from participation.[74]

The truth, however, was that no oil agreement was signed at Genoa, al-

---

Urquart, "The Real Facts about Russian Oil," *Financial Times* (London), 10 May. Background in Ovey to Krassin, London, 19 Oct. 1921, GB FO 371 N11704/10242/38; Hilton Young to Grigg, London, 31 Oct. 1921, LGP F 86/7/1; Boyle to Crowe, London, 10 Jan., GB FO 371 N380/380/38; Lloyd-Greame memoranda on Shell-Anglo Persian amalgamation, 6, 25 Jan., 7, 9 Feb., GB BT POW 33/92; meetings, 11, 13, 17, 21 Mar., 5, 7 Apr., GB FO 371 W2119/873/50; review of the eventually defunct proceedings in unsigned memorandum, 31 Dec., GB BT POW 33/349. Shell discussions in Lloyd-Greame to Hankey, London, 7 Feb., GB BT POW 33/92; O'Malley minute, London, 10 Oct., GB FO 371 N9265/50/38.

69. Unsigned memorandum, Washington, 31 Jan., USDS 861.8383/38.

70. Rapport du commissaire special de Menton: Conférence de Gênes, 22 Mar., FMAE B 90.

71. Lemercier to MAE, Genoa, 1 May, FMAE B 96.

72. Gregory to FO, Genoa, 7 May, GB FO 371 E4848/1294/59.

73. See, e.g., *Manchester Guardian* and *Daily News*, 3 May; Child to State Dept., Genoa, 4 May, USDS 550 E1/241; Osborne to State Dept., Genoa, 5 May, USDS 861.6363/66.

74. Leeper and Willert minutes, 4 May, GB FO 371 N4462/50/38.

though "texts" were displayed as far away as Brussels, The Hague, and London. Negotiations between Shell and the Soviets, restricted to the sale and distribution of Russian oil, were stalled. Moreover, they had not touched on the question of *ownership* of any fields. Where did the rumor originate, and why? Most likely it came from a member of the Russian delegation anxiously awaiting the Allies' deliberations, as a means of provoking fear and further disunity among the Western powers. The tactic that had worked on the eve of Rapallo succeeded all too well again. There were parties on both sides who were prepared to exploit fear, uncertainty, and greed.[75]

Roused from their lethargy, the excluded oil companies, especially Standard, prodded their governments into action. The specter of a new rivalry between Shell and Standard, after London had devoted months to appeasing the United States, spread gloom in Whitehall and jubilation in the Hotel Imperiale. Indeed, in a report to Moscow, Litvinov gloated that the oil rumors had enabled the Russians to seize the initiative on determining the fate of the Genoa Conference from a hesitant Great Britain and an intransigent France.[76]

Though he denied any official connection with the oil negotiations, the rumors may not have been unwelcome to Lloyd George. They put pressure on France and on other countries not to oppose an agreement with Soviet Russia and also to relent on the question of de jure recognition.[77] Indeed, the American government hesitated to escalate the incident beyond discreet diplomatic inquiries.[78] It was in Paris where the concatenation of events since Rapallo now produced the strongest response.

75. See, e.g., *L'Information*, 2 May, quoting an interview with Krassin on 30 Apr.; "Sous un voile humanitaire, la Conférence de Gênes a été en realité la conférence de pétrole" and "Krassin, Shell, Royal Dutch Company," *Journal d'Alsace*, 10 May; Max Hoschiller, "La pétrole à Gênes," *L'Opinion* 15 (13 May): 509–10; Jean Lepoutre, "La lutte pour la suprématie du pétrole," *Revue Économique Internationale* 14 (25 May): 246–74; and Alfred Vagts, "Petroleum-Politik," *Gesellschaft* 2 (July 1925): 49–65.

76. Child to State Dept., Genoa, 2 May, USDS 550 E1/230; Millspaugh to Harrison, Washington, 3 May, USDS 861.6363/64; Geddes to FO, Washington, 4 May, GB FO 371 4321/50/38; Bedford to Hughes, 5 May, USDS 861.6363/63; Kempner to Wirth, Berlin, 5 May, Germ. BA R 43 I/132. Also *FRUS, 1921*, 2:94–105; Geddes to Curzon, Washington, 20 Jan., GB FO 371 A904/177/45; Michael J. Hogan, "Informal Entente: Public Policy and Private Management in Anglo-American Petroleum Affairs, 1918–1924," *Business History Review* 48, no. 2 (Summer 1974): 187–205; and Philip S. Gillette, "American Capital in the Contest for Soviet Oil, 1920–23," *Soviet Studies* 24, no. 4 (April 1973): 477–90. Litvinov tel., 6 May, in S.I.S. report, Russia: Apr.–Aug., GB FO 371 N10682/246/38.

77. Barrère to MAE, Genoa, 3 May, #348, FMAE Y 32; Boyle to Poincaré, Genoa, 8 May, FMAE B 111; Avenol to Ministry of Finance, Genoa, 3 May, FMAE B 96; Geddes to FO, Washington, 4 May, GB FO 371 N4321/50/38; Tyrrell to Grigg, London, 4 May, and Grigg to Tyrrell, Genoa, 9 May, Grigg Papers, roll 3; O'Malley minutes, London, 9 May, GB FO 371 N4321, N4583/50/38.

78. Hughes to Child, Washington, 4 May, USDS 550 E1/230; Jusserand to Poincaré, Washington, 6 May, #533–34, FMAE Y 32; Cartier to MAE, Washington, 3 May, BMAE 10991.

Poincaré learned almost simultaneously of Lloyd George's heavy-handed treatment of Barthou, France's accommodation on the question of private property, Belgium's objections, and the *Oeuvre* report on the oil concession. On 2 May he called an emergency meeting of the cabinet and afterwards cabled the delegation at Genoa to withhold France's adherence to the Allies' memorandum to the Russians.[79] Barrère disobeyed, as we have seen, and pleaded with his chief that France "stay in." Lloyd George had also increased the pressure on the French delegation to bend on the question of de jure recognition for Russia. Poincaré may possibly have believed that the British government was implicated in the alleged oil concession. On first learning of it, he immediately sent his air minister and oil expert, Laurent Eynac, to Genoa to investigate and asked the French ambassador in London to investigate the rumors that Lloyd George's "son-in-law" was involved.[80]

More was at stake for France than *la lutte de pétrole* between the great oil companies. On the night of 2 May, there was a banquet given by the influential *Journée Industrielle*, attended by over four hundred guests, including the heads of France's largest industries. They expressed "unanimous excitement" at the news from Genoa: the oil rumors, the acts of "brigandage," France's recognition of compulsory expropriations, and its abandonment of Belgium— the "last defense of civilization."[81] Here was a chance to turn America's opinion in France's favor because the United States could not ignore concessions allegedly granted to the Russians *and* British at Genoa.

Even more important to France was the news that had arrived from Brussels, that the Belgians resented France's "desertion."[82] In a speech to parliament on 2 May, the influential Socialist leader Vandervelde warned of "retaliation": should a crisis erupt after 31 May over a German default, France might not expect Belgium to stand at its side. The Belgian parliament supported Jaspar's stand.[83] France therefore was possibly headed toward a rupture with an essential ally on the Reparations Commission.

Relations between the French and Belgian delegations at Genoa had not been

79. *DBFP*, 19:686; Poincaré to Barthou, Paris, 2 May, #248–50, #251, FMAE B 110.

80. Poincaré [Peretti] to Delegation, Paris, 2 May, #256, Poincaré to Delegation (secret, for Eynac), Paris, 4 May, #301–5, FMAE B 96, Barthou [Eynac] to MAE, Genoa, 8 May, #426–29, FMAE B 97, 14 May, #502–5, FMAE B 111, 15 May, #513, FMAE B 98; Lloyd-Greame interview with Eynac and Pineau, Genoa, 13 May, and minutes by Clarke, O'Malley, and Sperling, London, 16, 18 May, GB FO 371 N4969/50/68. On the brother-in-law: Poincaré to Saint-Aulaire, 5, 6 May, FMAE B 97, B 111. Saint-Aulaire to Poincaré, London, 9 May, #241, FMAE B 97, gave an accurate reconstruction of Anglo-Russian oil negotiations. British reaction to the insinuations: GB FO 371 N5146, N5147/646/38.

81. Goût to Millerand, Paris, 5 May, FMAE PM G/VI.

82. Margerie to MAE, Brussels, 3 May, #118–20, FMAE Y 32.

83. Telephone conversation of Jaspar and Theunis, 4 May, JP, 210; unsigned memoranda, Brussels, 3, 4 May, BMAE 10991.

smooth. Both Barthou and Barrère had resented Jaspar's lack of support over the debts issue. Even before the debates over private property, Jaspar had intimated that Belgium might not automatically stand by France on 31 May; its public opinion needed proof that all peaceful measures had been exhausted before the Allies would decide to impose sanctions. Jaspar, on his side, was frequently irritated with French pressure to stay in, and he complained of what he considered Barthou's high-handed tactics.[84]

Poincaré realized that without Belgium France would be truly "isolated." Security against a hostile Germany and, after Rapallo, a potentially hostile German-Russian coalition took precedence above all else.[85] He was therefore unmoved by his delegates' laments of their aloneness at Genoa, attentive to the reports of Russo-German military collaboration, and willing to wait longer for the indispensable alliance with Britain. An agreement at Genoa offered nothing but empty Soviet promises and a potential weakening of the Versailles system.

Though the French army had plans since 1921 for an invasion of the Ruhr,[86] there is no evidence that Poincaré contemplated a coup de main against Germany at the end of May. At the moment, he needed to manifest solidarity with Belgium and firmness against Britain in its obsession with appeasing Russia. On 4 May Lasteyrie predicted a four-billion-franc deficit in the 1923 budget, with no prospect of increased taxes or an international loan. France therefore had "overriding reasons" to adhere to Belgium and maintain its uncompromising stance on reparations, even at the cost of infuriating Lloyd George.[87]

Poincaré instructed the delegation to resist all Lloyd George's blandishments, including the newest, that France bend on the question of de jure recognition of Russia.[88] Despite Barrère's pleas, he ordered him to withdraw France's approval from the 2 May memorandum. He sent Barthou back to Genoa with directions to avoid further "improvisions" such as the Seydoux amendment. Poincaré refused any discussions of peripheral questions such as disarmament. He repeated his veto of an Allied meeting at Genoa or anywhere else over reparations before 31 May, and he also rejected the direct talks that Rathenau had proposed to stave off the crisis.[89]

84. Poincaré to Margerie, 3 May, #252, FMAE Y 32; Jaspar to Theunis, 1 May, BMAE 10991.

85. Sforza to Schanzer, Paris, 1 May, IMAE 66 (Russia); Schanzer to Sforza, Genoa, 4 May, IMAE 52/4; Sforza to Schanzer, Paris, 5 May, IMAE 52/37–38, 6 May, IMAE 52/4 (France).

86. Unsigned Aufzeichnung, Paris, 26 Apr. (initialed by Rathenau at Genoa, 13 May), Germ. AA T-120 L1466/5326/L415735–44; De Gaiffier to MAE, Paris, 2 May, BMAE Fr., 6 May, BMAE 10991, 11 May, BMAE Fr.

87. Poincaré to Delegation, Paris, 5 May, #307, FMAE Y 32.

88. Barrère to MAE, Genoa, 4 May, #374–77, FMAE Z Russ. 349; Poincaré to Barrère, Paris, 5 May, #306, FMAE B 97.

89. Poincaré to Millerand [at Ajaccio], Paris, 5 May, FMAE PM tel./2; Poincaré to Barthou,

Poincaré's moves did not immediately repair the Franco-Belgian breach. The Belgians were embarrassed and resentful of Paris's sudden support and were afraid of the cost.[90] Barthou smoothed Jaspar's feelings at Genoa. Brussels eventually accepted France's assurances that there were no strings attached and that Barthou would not deviate again on the question of property. As expected, Lloyd George and Schanzer, nervously awaiting the Soviet reply, were incensed by France's defection. Lloyd George sent a protest to Paris at the endless uproar over a much-denied oil agreement. The French blandly replied that their change of heart was based primarily on an issue of principle and on solidarity with their ally, Belgium.[91]

In the midst of these events came the sudden announcement of an Italian-Turkish trade agreement. Whitehall was exasperated, and members of parliament protested Italy's perfidy. Lloyd George, needing Italian help at Genoa, did not reprove Schanzer. But again Britain was burdened with the looming failure of its Near Eastern policies and with the difficulties of keeping its allies in line.[92]

Responding to an earlier German suggestion,[93] Lloyd George now turned to Wirth and Rathenau. He appealed to them to help save the Genoa Conference by inducing the Russians to sign. He was forced to hear another recitation of the Reich's perilous finances, complaints over French-sponsored autonomy schemes in the Rhineland, and, most painful, the Germans' barbed criticisms of the document of 2 May, which they termed unrealistic and ungenerous. Wirth, who had contemplated leaving in response to appeals from Berlin, agreed to extend his stay at Genoa. He and Rathenau promised to lend their support in return for an implicit but unspecified quid pro quo.[94]

Paris, 5 May, 6 May, #337, Poincaré to Barrère, Paris, 6 May, #330–31, FMAE B 97. Cf. Rathenau's meetings with Beneš, 2 May, and with Sauerwein, 6 May, Germ. AA T-120 3398/1735/D739281–82, D739300–1.

90. De Gaiffier to MAE, Paris, 6 May, BMAE 10991; Poincaré to Margerie, Paris, 5 May, #256–60, FMAE Y 32, 5 May, #281, FMAE B 111; Poincaré to Delegation, Paris, 4 May, #286–89, FMAE Y 32, 5 May, #310, FMAE B 97, 6 May, #332, #338–39, FMAE Y 32; Margerie to Poincaré, Brussels, 4 May, #129A, 5 May, #134–40, 6 May, #141–48, FMAE Y 32, 8 May, #165–68, FMAE B 111; and Poincaré to Delegation, Paris, 8 May, #364–65, FMAE B 97.

91. Lloyd George to Hardinge, Genoa, 4 May, Hardinge to Poincaré, Paris, 5 May, Poincaré to Hardinge, Paris, 5 May, GB FO 371 N4347/646/38; Hardinge to FO and Lloyd George, Paris, 5 May, GB FO 371 N4356/646/38; Poincaré to Hardinge, Paris, 7 May, GB FO 371 N4378/646/38.

92. Hardinge to Curzon, 5 May, CzP; Graham to Curzon, Rome, 5 May, ibid.; note of conversation [with Schanzer], Villa d'Albertis, 4 May, *DBFP*, 19:726–28; Lloyd George to Curzon, Genoa, 5 May, Grigg Papers, roll 10.

93. Dufour Aufzeichnung, 30 Apr. (conversation with Grigg, 29 Apr.), Germ. AA T-120 3398/1735/D739277–80.

94. Notes of conversation, 4 May, *DBFP*, 19:730–35; Wirth to Ebert, Genoa, 4 May, Germ. AA T-120 3398/1734/D738701–4; Hankey to Chamberlain, 4 May, HP.

The Allies were trapped with their problematic proposals on which they no longer agreed and which Chicherin indicated he probably would not sign. Lloyd George had pressed France far beyond its ability to compromise and far beyond his own ability to coerce Poincaré. He needed German help and Russian compliance to succeed. There was little left to celebrate about the memorandum the Allies had sent to the Russians.[95] In a terrible temper over the first "hot, fly-infested days," over intrigues back in London and the Germans' mischief, over waiting for Russia and waiting for Barthou's return, the usually ebullient Lloyd George almost lost heart, and the Genoa Conference stood before its moment of truth.[96]

95. John Maynard Keynes, "The Proposals to Russia," *Manchester Guardian*, 4 May; D. François, "La question russe à la Conférence de Gênes," *L'Europe Nouvelle*, 5 May.

96. Lloyd George, *My Darling Pussy*, pp. 49–50; also Lloyd-Greame to Baldwin, 6 May, LGrP; Hankey to Chamberlain, 7 May ("The conference is now at the crisis of its fate"), HP; Barthou to MAE, Genoa, 7 May, #410, FMAE B 111; Philippe Millet, "La Conférence de Gênes: Va-t-elle vers la rupture ou l'ajournement?" *L'Europe Nouvelle*, 6 May.

8

The Restoration of Europe

The second half of the London Report was entitled the "Restoration of Europe."[1] The Genoa Conference devoted a considerable amount of time and effort in this direction. In addition to examining the experts' recommendations on finance, economics, and transport, the delegates gave their attention to a number of technical and political problems that pertained to "restoration." As anticipated, these issues brought up the larger question: what role would the League of Nations, the still-fledgling world organization, play in the Genoa Conference? Representatives of the League were eager to participate fully, to use the meeting to expand Geneva's authority and prerogatives, at least in those areas where Genoa proved successful. Though the non-Russian deliberations took place in a quasi-isolated atmosphere, separate from the more important negotiations with the Russians, they were undoubtedly influenced by the currents surrounding them.

While awaiting the Russian reply, on 3 May the Genoa Conference held its second plenary session back in the Palazzo San Giorgio to adopt the reports of the Financial and Transport Commissions. The Economic Commission, which did not finish until 5 May, reported on the last day, two weeks later. The three commissions all presented their proposals in the form of nonbinding recommendations to all the powers assembled at Genoa. There was little new in their proposals. The significance of the non-Russian deliberations lay in the meetings themselves, what strategies and compromises were offered, and how the commissions' debates reflected the problems of European reconstruction in the spring of 1922.

The Financial Commission

> The resolutions come to by the commission which this conference is asked to adopt constitute a financial code no less important to the world than was the civil code of Justinian.[2]

1. *DBFP*, 19:269–76.
2. Ibid., p. 705.

This hyperbolic statement by Worthington-Evans, who had succeeded Horne as president of the Financial Commission, demonstrated both the extent of the commission's aspirations and the uncertainty of its achievement. Of Genoa's three technical commissions, this dealt with the most controversial issues of European reconstruction: the restoration of sound gold-based currencies, the reestablishment of smoothly functioning international exchanges, and the allocation of credits to needy areas. These issues not only divided the rich from the poor nations of Europe and the victors from the vanquished; they also divided the Allies themselves over how to reconcile their domestic requirements with the need to restore a smoothly functioning international economy.

Political considerations were by no means eliminated; the looming reparations deadline, the problem of interallied debts, and the current negotiations with the Russians all penetrated the discussions.[3] The presence of an observer from the League of Nations, the acting director of the economic and finance section, served to remind the delegates of Geneva's concern and its ambitions. In the commission's opening meetings, Germany and Russia tried to channel the discussions on their behalf: the Germans blamed their inflated currency on an "unbalanced budget" (their code expression for the reparations obligation) and Rakovsky reintroduced the Soviet proposal for disarmament. Horne, in a hurry to return to London, simply turned matters over to the experts.[4]

The Financial Commission divided into three subcommissions on currency, exchanges, and credits. This gave the impression that it was isolating small, manageable problems, whose interconnections and larger ramifications could temporarily be set aside.[5] The subcommissions drew on the resolutions of the Brussels Economic Conference of 1920 sponsored by the League of Nations, along with the recommendations drafted by the experts in London. The two subcommissions on currency and exchanges appointed a single committee of experts to draft their proposals; these consisted of all the assembled (primarily West European) government officials and financial authorities, all veterans of various postwar international gatherings. Sir Basil Blackett presided, Germany and Czechoslovakia were included, but there was no expert representative from Russia.[6]

A resolution on currency required a compromise among conflicting national orientations. Britain and the neutrals desired an early return to the gold standard, but they hesitated to act alone until the problems of reparations and war

3. Seydoux, Resultats des travaux des commissions techniques, n.d., FMAE B 99; Roger Picard, "Les questions financières à la Conférence de Gênes," *Revue d'Économie Politique* 36 (July–August 1922): 491; Siegfried to Goût, Genoa, 26 Apr., FMAE PM G/V.

4. Müller to AA, Genoa, 12, 13 Apr., Germ. AA T-120 3398/1734/D738339–43, D738369; Barthou to MAE, 12, 13 Apr., #51–53, #61–64, FMAE B 93; and meetings, 12, 13 Apr., Gregory to FO, Genoa, 13 Apr., GB FO 371 C5769, C5791, C5472/458/62.

5. Siegfried to Goût, Genoa, 17 Apr., FMAE PM G/V.

6. Barthou to MAE, Genoa, 14 Apr., #61–64, FMAE B 93.

debts were settled.[7] In the meantime, because of sustained high taxes, growing unemployment, and economic woes attributed to the chaotic international system, the strong-currency governments prodded their neighbors, as America was prodding Europe, to renounce their unsound monetary practices—their unbalanced budgets, high military expenditures, and rampant inflation—in other words, to assume the burdens and self-discipline required to restore international prosperity.[8]

France, Belgium, and Italy, though realizing the virtues of stabilizing their depreciated currencies, were in no hurry for "settlements" that either reduced Germany's reparations or acknowledged their immense obligations to Britain and America, because such settlements would primarily benefit those who had enriched themselves during the war, especially the neutrals. All three had substantial reconstruction costs. In time, they hoped to regain the prewar value of their currencies; they rejected any form of immediate devaluation, or "devalorization," that would mean a sacrifice of their national prestige and of the savings of their thrifty, politically important middle class. Such a move would also expose them to higher prices, unemployment, social unrest, and the onslaught of speculators.[9]

At the furthest extreme stood Germany and the other former Central Powers, which accepted the ultimate wisdom and desirability of the gold standard but in their day-to-day policies perpetuated the inflationary tactics of wartime to maintain social peace and evade their reparations payments.[10] It is indeed ironic that though these excesses were at the root of Britain's panic, London— as helpless to stop the Reich's printing press as to dissolve Russia's trade monopoly—made France the scapegoat. When Keynes railed against the three holdouts (France, Belgium, and Italy) for their unwillingness to pay the price for European solidarity and expiate their wartime "profligacy," and when Professor Cassel chided them for their "illusions," there was something phari-

---

7. D. E. Moggridge, *The Return to Gold* (Cambridge: Cambridge University Press, 1969), pp. 16–17.

8. Gustav Cassel, "The Economic and Financial Decisions of the Genoa Conference," *Manchester Guardian Commercial: Reconstruction in Europe* (hereafter *MGC:RE*), 15 June, p. 139.

9. Luigi Einaudi, "I risultati finanziari di Genova," in *Chronache economiche e politiche di un trentennio, 1893–1925* (Turin: G. Einaudi, 1966), 6:703–9; Louis Eisenmann, "L'oeuvre économique de la Conférence de Gênes," *Revue des Études Coopératives* 2 (April–June 1922): 280–81. "Devalorization" was considered a "kinder" word by contemporaries than devaluation.

10. Stephen A. Schuker, *The End of French Predominance in Europe: The Financial Crisis of 1924 and the Adoption of the Dawes Plan* (Chapel Hill: University of North Carolina Press, 1976), pp. 14–15. Cf. Jörgen Pederson, "Einige Bemerkungen zur deutschen Inflation von 1919–1923," *Zeitschrift für die gesamte Staatswissenschaft* 122 (July 1966): 418–30, and Carl-Ludwig Holtfrerich, *Die deutsche Inflation, 1914–1923* (Berlin and New York: W. de Gruyter, 1980).

saical about these accusations. Everyone had simply chosen the most appropriate form of postwar social peace. While the politicians paid homage to the theorists of their choice, the speculators profited.[11]

In the end, the old recommendations of the Brussels Conference, which stressed the restoration of sound currencies, the establishment of balanced budgets, and cooperation by central banks, were superseded by the Genoa Resolutions:[12] (1) The gold standard was declared the ultimate object of European stabilization. Governments were to take steps to stabilize their currency; those whose currencies were close to their prewar parity should make sacrifices to complete the deflation and those whose depreciation had proceeded too far should display courage and unselfishness and write down the prewar value of their monetary unit. (2) Whatever parity were chosen, governments should maintain "self-discipline" in terms of balanced budgets, adequate reserve requirements, and the avoidance of ruinous competition for gold supplies and political manipulation of central banks. (3) A gold-exchange standard would supplement the system by allowing countries to maintain some of their monetary reserves, not in scarce gold but in strong reserve currencies such as sterling or the dollar. (4) Finally, the experts recommended an international monetary convention to centralize and coordinate the demand for gold and maintain standards for each national currency. They proposed that the Bank of England promptly convene a meeting of central banks to promote these aims.[13]

The report on currency contained two revealing "conditions": first, that the question of international indebtedness, including the problem of reparations, had to be examined; and second, that no monetary convention could succeed without universal participation—a call to America. Herewith the Genoa delegates exposed their lack of realism. Reparations fell well outside their purview. Moreover, the United States refused to link reductions in reparations and war debts and opposed the formulation of multinational settlements.

These proposals contained other illusions, including nostalgia for an imagined smooth, self-regulating gold system before World War I and the myth of independent central banks. The health of the prewar system had depended largely on an unparalleled European economic expansion that hid many stresses and changes, including the rise of American and Japanese competitors and the emergence of economic strength and national consciousness in the colonial world. Moreover, in that largely misunderstood past, except for infor-

---

11. Cassel, "Economic and Financial Decisions," p. 139; John Maynard Keynes in *Manchester Guardian*, 20 Apr.; and Gabriel Hanotaux, "Economic Metaphysics," *MGC:RE*, 18 May, pp. 67–69. W. Lionel Fraser, *All to the Good* (Garden City, N.Y.: Doubleday, 1963), pp. 66–71, gives personal recollections of the period.

12. *DBFP*, 19:706–9, reviewed in Picard, "Questions financières," pp. 482–87.

13. Müller to AA, Genoa, 21 Apr., Germ. AA T-120 3398/1734/D738470–72; Siegfried to Goût, 21 Apr., FMAE B 94.

mal cooperation, there had rarely been an effort to band together collectively, as there now was at Genoa. The war, and especially the immediate postwar period, had stimulated new political and economic responses to the problems of European societies. Governments, worried about their electorates' grievances, were even less likely than they had been before 1914 to make sacrifices on behalf of an abstract gold standard or the international monetary system. Rather, the tone—extended after the war—was to delay what could be put off and make the other, especially the enemy, pay.[14]

Central bank cooperation, already practiced informally after World War I, was unlikely to be formally adopted. Whatever their common interests in European stabilization, the Bank of England and the Federal Reserve system, the two strongest institutions, had separate goals, based on different domestic priorities. The "little inflation" in America that Britain needed for its recovery was anathema to Benjamin Strong, governor of the Federal Reserve Bank of New York. Moreover, the close collaboration between the governor of the Bank of England, Montagu Norman, and his German counterparts, Reichsbank Presidents Rudolf Havenstein and Hjalmar Schacht, was resented in France. In the end, there was no central bank meeting in the summer of 1922. Despite an initially positive American reaction, Genoa's most ambitious proposal became another casualty of Anglo-French *mésentente*.[15]

The gold-exchange standard proposed by the British at Genoa contained few built-in protections against the ills it was designed to cure: speculation, inflation, unemployment, and runs on gold. It not only tended to be inflationary, but it also provoked Anglo-American rivalries and kept pressure on the weaker sterling. The use of British currency as a monetary reserve by other nations enabled London to continue to function as a major financial center in the 1920s and hide its growing trade deficits. However, when Britain went off gold in 1931 (as America did in 1971), governments holding the reserve currency suffered. Charles de Gaulle announced to a press conference on 4 February 1965 that the monetary difficulties of the sixties began at Genoa, with the gold-

14. E.g., Poincaré to Barthou, Paris, 19 Apr., #81–83, FMAE B 94.

15. Nixon to Drummond, Genoa, 24 Apr., LNA 40A 20311/20311; also *New York American* and *New York World*, 20 Apr., *New York Times*, 21 Apr., in Hoover to Hughes, Washington, 22 Apr. (copy to Child), USDS 550 E1/203; Dean Elizabeth Traynor, *International Monetary and Financial Conferences in the Interwar Period* (Washington: Catholic University of America Press, 1949), pp. 86–87; Stephen V. O. Clarke, *Central Bank Cooperation, 1924–1931* (New York: Federal Reserve Bank of N.Y., 1967), pp. 36–38; Melvyn P. Leffler, *The Elusive Quest: America's Pursuit of European Stability and French Security, 1919–1933* (Chapel Hill: University of North Carolina Press, 1979), pp. 56–57. Eleanor Lansing Dulles, *The Bank for International Settlements at Work* (New York: Macmillan, 1932), pp. 16, 445, considered the Genoa proposal the germ idea for the BIS.

exchange standard. This is an exaggeration. The gold-exchange proposal was halfheartedly and incompletely adopted, and the majority at Genoa still clung to the past, and to gold.[16]

Gold was still considered the "ultimate financial regulator." Keynes argued that its immediate reintroduction as the international standard would promote the revival of trade and production and would channel capital and international credit to where they were needed most. "One of the greatest elements of uncertainty would be lifted. One of the most vital parts of prewar organization would be restored. And one of the most subtle temptations to improvident national finance would be removed; for if a national currency had once been stabilized on a gold basis it would be harder (because so much more openly disgraceful) for a finance minister so to act as to destroy this gold basis."[17]

Russia agreed in theory. Despite its current considerable inflation, Moscow possessed hoards of gold and therefore placed itself on the side of traditionalism. Given the resistance of the other powers, the experts and politicians made only general palliative resolutions praising gold. While they thus clung to principle, they also avoided clashes. They thereby renounced the opportunity at Genoa to formulate an international plan of when, how, and at what parity European currencies would be stabilized. The resultant uncertainty and zigzagging of international exchanges intensified the problems Genoa had tried to solve.[18]

The experts also drafted recommendations regarding the European exchanges.[19] Following the London proposals that were based on the 1920 Brussels plan, they called for specific restraints on the East European governments: the abolition of their "futile and mischievous" exchange controls, such as licensing, differential pricing, and various forms of discrimination, as well as any other methods that interfered with free and unhindered commercial dealings. Turning to Western Europe, they criticized special restrictions aimed at imports from countries with depreciated currencies. One of the most important and original recommendations of the subcommission was to establish markets in forward exchanges: that central banks maintain the foreign balances and

16. Melchior Palyi, *The Twilight of Gold, 1914–1936: Myths and Realities* (Chicago: Regnery, 1972), p. 4. Also *New York Times*, 5 Feb. 1965, and Benjamin M. Rowland, ed., *Balance of Power or Hegemony: The Interwar Monetary System* (New York: New York University Press, 1976), pp. 30, 86, 235–36, 287.

17. *Manchester Guardian*, 20 Apr.; also "Stabilization of the Exchanges" and "European Banking," *MGC:RE*, 7 Dec., and Richard Meyer, *Bankers' Diplomacy: Monetary Stabilization in the 1920s* (New York: Columbia University Press, 1970), pp. 6–15.

18. John Maynard Keynes, in *Manchester Guardian*, 17, 27 Apr.; Palyi, *Twilight of Gold*, pp. 68–195.

19. *DBFP*, 19:709; also Picard, "Questions financières," pp. 487–88.

securities of smaller banks, which would be protected from taxation and other forms of coercion and would thereby ease trade and minimize the risks to merchants of exchange fluctuations.[20]

To implement the subcommission's recommendations, the Financial Commission impractically counted on both government compliance and the bankers' cooperation. It also hinted at a third possibility when it referred the knotty question of double taxation (taxation laid on profits or income first in the country where they were earned and then in the person's country of residence) to the Economic Commission; it was generally acknowledged that the latter would ask the League of Nations, which was already handling this question, to continue. This was Geneva's first victory, and no one raised an objection.[21]

Both the experts and the Financial Commission discussed the links between smoothly functioning exchanges and the need to settle debts, reparations, and the problems of European peace. Again, the call was for "discipline." However, some members of the commission resisted the idea of relinquishing all exchange controls; these had been effective in wartime and still benefited weaker-currency countries, such as Austria, as a means of centralizing control over and preventing the flight of their limited capital.[22] Because the Swiss protested so vehemently against Germany's dumping, the recommendation against exclusionary legislation had to be referred to the Economic Commission. Russia, as a matter of Communist principle, refused to renounce control over its exchange operations. Terming "stability of . . . exchanges . . . the indispensable preliminary to a new economic and technical progress and eventually to the maintenance of civilization itself," Rathenau used the occasion to plead for help for Germany and for "energetic, efficacious, and immediate cooperation."[23]

The credits subcommission met last.[24] This body represented one of the raisons d'être of the Genoa Conference: how to establish conditions whereby the countries with sound currency and surplus capital for investment could be induced to lend it to the devastated areas of Eastern Europe. The answers, neither revolutionary nor inspiring, represented some gains. The recommenda-

---

20. Eisenmann, "L'oeuvre économique," p. 287; Nixon to Drummond, Genoa, 24 Apr., LNA 40A 20311/20311; Sir Henry Strakosch (author of the proposal), "The Money Tangle of the Postwar Period," in *The Lessons of Monetary Experience*, ed. Arthur D. Gayer (New York: Farrar and Rinehart, 1937), pp. 153–59.

21. Ritter to AA, Genoa, 20 Apr., Germ. AA T-120 3398/1734/D738436–38; Picard, "Questions financières," p. 488; 6th meeting of League representatives, Genoa, 20 Apr., LNA 40A 20136/20226.

22. Nixon to Drummond, Genoa, 24 Apr., LNA 40A 20311/20311.

23. *DBFP*, 19:718–19.

24. Müller to AA, Genoa, 25 Apr., Germ. AA T-120 3398/1734/D738534–36.

tions involved conditions that would have to be met by borrowers, including the stabilization of their public finance and currency and the improvement of their budget practices, especially by eliminating the nefarious device of "extraordinary expenses." Loans to these countries would be made only for "productive purposes," not to maintain "emplois inutiles" or to lower artificially the price of commodities. Above all, borrowers were urged to renounce inflationary measures.[25]

Something new was added: borrowing countries not only were to offer real security and legal commitments in return for credits, but they also were obliged to furnish the creditor with "regular, precise, and abundant information" on the state of their public finances. The League of Nations would periodically publish collections of these documents, which were deemed indispensable for understanding between nations and for creating an atmosphere of "candor" favorable to the complete restoration of international lending.[26]

Once these terms were fulfilled, what credit mechanism could be offered that would be adequate, given the world situation, and what could be adapted to present needs? Government credits were difficult to obtain, and private lenders, despite favorable rates of return, were reluctant to take risks without the backing of their governments. Resolution 16.2 of the Financial Commission admitted that during the "transitory" situation a special system for lending had to be established. It simply proposed the establishment of an international corporation that would be composed of collaborating national corporations and would be responsible for studying and aiding European reconstruction. How it would be organized, under whose authority it would operate, and what financial means it would possess—these questions were left unanswered. Since there was as yet no East-West agreement, the Russians raised no objections on the Financial Commission, save to warn against "creating any form of monopoly."[27]

Despite the enthusiasm of the British,[28] there was little joy in those who had come to Genoa to be reconstructed. The problem of Austria provides an apt example. Premier Schober had hoped to raise credits at Genoa to save Austria's ruined currency and stave off bankruptcy. By the spring of 1922, all of Austria's assets had been charged as guarantees of its reparations, occupation costs, and relief credits. The liens were held not only by the Western Allies but by all the succession states. The latter were encumbered by "liberation payments" (their portion of the former Habsburg state debt) and were thus reluc-

25. Picard, "Questions financières," pp. 488–49.
26. Ibid., pp. 489–90.
27. *DBFP*, 19:709–10, 716.
28. Gregory to FO, Genoa, 3 May, GB FO 371 C6521/458/62.

tant to free the Vienna government from its charges for the requested twenty years. Beneš argued, how could they ask their parliaments to act generously without any compensation.[29]

Without a lifting of these liens, held by eighteen governments, and without the agreement of the Reparations Commission, Austria had no possibility of securing the long-term credits that would save it from collapse. The liberation payments, though largely fictitious, could not be suspended except by agreement among all the Allies; at least one (Italy) refused to grant these automatically because of its own financial problems. There were additional complications. The Vienna government needed to discipline itself by abolishing its costly domestic subsidies, reducing other government expenditures, and increasing taxation, all politically risky steps for Schober's fragile coalition. Austrian diplomacy was hobbled by pan-German agitation, especially in the army, for closer ties with the Reich, and also by Socialist agitation for detente with Russia. Outside, a fierce competition to control the beleaguered republic raged among its neighbors; there were moves by Czechoslovakia to bring Austria into the Little Entente, Italian counterefforts to gain dominance over its northern neighbor, and even alleged French efforts to win influence over the tiny Danubian state.[30]

Britain occupied a neutral position in the Austrian question. Despite Whitehall's misgivings about the ban on Anschluss in the Treaties of Versailles and Saint-Germain, Lloyd George warned Schober against incautious "experiments" with pan-Germanism. Though British Treasury officials deplored the shackles of the peace treaties, they assumed that an independent Austria should and would survive, if given prompt and generous international assistance.[31] Poincaré opposed allowing the Genoa Conference to handle the Austrian question because the League was about to formulate another rescue plan. In addition, Paris was reluctant on principle to broaden Genoa's agenda and, more important, to permit discussion of any clauses of the peace treaties.[32]

29. Sir William Goode (chairman of the Austrian section of the Reparations Commission), "The General Financial Position of Austria," *MGC:RE*, 15 June, p. 143.

30. K. W. Rothschild, *Austria's Economic Development between the Two Wars* (London: F. Müller, 1947), pp. 14–32; Eduard Hohenbichler, *Republik im Schatten der Monarchie* (Vienna: Europa Verlag, 1971), pp. 101–17; Heinrich Benedict, ed., *Geschichte der Republik Österreich* (Vienna: Verlag für Geschichte und Politik, 1954), pp. 116–22. Also Austrian Legation to Lloyd George, London, 25 Jan., LGP F 49/2/4; Ackers-Douglas to FO, Vienna, 1 Mar., 6, 14 Apr., GB FO 371 C3325/396/3, C5254, C6643/458/62; Pontalis to MAE, Vienna, 8 Feb., FMAE B 86; Jung-Schuller conversation, Rome, 16 Mar., and Orsini to MAE, Vienna, 7 Apr., IMAE 52/4 (Austria); and Programm für Genua, n.d., A HHSt 687.

31. Lloyd George–Schober conversation, 13 Apr., GB CAB 29/S.G. 4; Bischof Hausnotiz, 19 Apr., A HHSt 687; Goode, "Financial Position of Austria," p. 143; and Lampson, Crowe minutes, London, 2 June, GB FO 371 C7982/896/3.

32. Poincaré to Pontalis, 15 Feb., FMAE B 86; Eichoff to Schober, Paris, 5 Apr., A HHSt 687.

The Austrian delegation engaged in vigorous politicking at Genoa, attempting to exploit the powers' rivalries to place Austria's problems before the conference. Success seemed imminent when, during the plenary meeting on 20 April, Horne made a surprise announcement to the Financial Commission calling for a meeting the next day of the countries "interested in Austria."[33] Schanzer was named chairman of the ad hoc committee. With Genoa bogged down after Rapallo, the Austrians interpreted Horne's move as an attempt at one small breakthrough to raise the conference's prestige. More important, through the Austrian back door, the reparations question would enter the Genoa Conference.[34]

Austrian hopes rapidly evaporated. On 21 April the only meeting took place. A subcommittee of experts was appointed and charged with examining a draft proposal in which all of Vienna's creditors would waive their liens for twenty years. The experts never met because the Yugoslav and Rumanian representatives refused to consider renouncing their liens at Genoa. Beneš skillfully represented and defended his allies. Sensing defeat, Schober twice pleaded to see Lloyd George, but he failed.[35]

Schober returned from Genoa with vague promises of short-term French, Italian, and Czechoslovak loans and of possible concessions by Rumania and Yugoslavia on the liens. His government soon collapsed.[36] While crediting his tireless labor at Genoa, Austrian party leaders chose a tougher politician, Christian Socialist Dr. Ignaz Seipel, to head a new, purely bourgeois government. No doubt the hyperinflation and the budget crisis contributed to Schober's fall, but the collapse of the last Austrian coalition that had the cooperation of the Social Democrats was also caused by the "fatal disappointment" of the almost universal expectation that something would be accomplished at Genoa to save Austria.[37] Help came six months later through a combination of private loans, government guarantees, political pledges, Austrian self-discipline, and the supervision and surveillance of the League of Nations.[38]

33. Müller to AA, Genoa, 21 Apr., Germ. AA T-120 3398/1734/D738470–72; 6th meeting of League representatives, Genoa, 20 Apr., LNA 40A 20136/20226.

34. Schwartzwald to BMA, Genoa, 21 Apr., A Fin. Arch. 17; Hennet to Schober, Nervi, 20 Apr., ibid.

35. Schwartzwald to Ministry of Finance, Nervi, 21 Apr., ibid.; Schober to Lloyd George, Nervi, 4 May, Grigg Papers, roll 10; Barthou to MAE, Genoa, 11 May, #467, FMAE B 97.

36. Schonfeld to State Dept., Vienna, 22 May, USDS 550 E1/330; Ackers-Douglas to FO, Vienna, 19, 26 May, Cadogan and Waterlow minutes, 24 May, GB FO 371 C7444, C7821/396/3; Pontalis to MAE, Vienna, 31 May, FMAE B 100. Also Erich Zöllner, *Geschichte Österreichs* (Vienna: Verlag für Geschichte und Politik, 1970), pp. 503–4; Gottlieb Ladner, *Seipel als Überwinder der Staatskrise vom Sommer 1922* (Vienna: Stiasny Verlag, 1964), pp. 30–32.

37. Ladner, *Seipel*, p. 29.

38. Peter E. Schmidt, "The Relief of Austria, 1919–1922" (Ph.D. diss., Case Western

The other credit-hungry nations, though less desperate, were forced by West European bankers to pay high interest and adhere to stringent terms for loans; they thus obtained little satisfaction.[39] They had waited for three weeks to learn about potential aid, were preached at for their evil practices, and gained "no hopes of obtaining a penny of credit." The international corporation was obviously devised to deal primarily with Russia. The credits subcommission ignored a Belgian proposal based on the earlier Ter Meulen plan. It also refused to deal seriously with Italian proposals to establish viable controls over public finance. League officials observed with a mixture of relief and smugness that Genoa would not be referring any credit recommendations to Geneva.[40]

The credits subcommission did underscore Genoa's principle that reconstruction loans would emanate primarily from private sources. Government credits would be extended only in the most urgent instances for long- rather than short-term purposes. But how could private capital move into Eastern Europe, with its restrictions, inflation, unbalanced budgets, discriminatory practices, and high military expenditures, under terms that these new states could afford, and be "constructive" at the same time? Austria, Hungary, and most of the other governments of Eastern Europe needed substantial loans to ensure domestic peace no less than Russia. They were nevertheless reluctant to submit to the politicians' and bankers' conditions that would have provoked the opposite.

Though they recognized that the treaties had contributed to the economic disorder in Eastern Europe,[41] the Western powers hesitated either to guarantee the status quo or set up a mechanism for peaceful, orderly treaty revision. In the end, the Allies were well satisfied with the Financial Commission. The French felt relieved that there had been no real commitments at all. The British, awaiting a settlement with Russia, agreed. One observer wrote, "Those who hoped to get from Genoa a real reconstruction plan will be extremely disappointed; but those who feared it were reassured."[42]

Reserve University, 1977), pp. 426–521; F. P. Walters, *A History of the League of Nations* (London: Oxford University Press, 1952), pp. 206–10.

39. Clement-Simon to MAE, Belgrade, 27 Apr., FMAE B 99.

40. Nixon report, 13th meeting of League representatives, 27 Apr., LNA 40A 20136/20433; Attolico to Drummond, Geneva, 24 May, ibid., Spec. Circ. #186.

41. Goode, "Financial Position of Austria," p. 143; Wildner to Ministry of Finance, Vienna, 13 May, Goode memorandum, 16 June, Wildner memorandum, Vienna, 24 June, and subsequent correspondence on efforts with Allies and Reparations Commission to revise Article 190 of the Treaty of Saint-Germain, A Fin. Arch. 17; and Schmidt, "Relief of Austria," pp. 444–59.

42. Barthou to MAE, Genoa, 4 May, #366–67, FMAE B 96; Picard (deputy-governor of the Bank of France) rapport, Paris, 17 May, FMAE B 99; quotation is from Siegfried to Goût, Genoa, 3 May, FMAE PM G/VI.

The Transport Commission

Even if exchanges were stabilized and credits allocated, there was still the problem of moving goods physically across Europe, particularly over a continent whose frontiers had changed so dramatically.[43] There had been two earlier conferences on transit problems. One had been held at Barcelona in March and April 1921 under the auspices of the League of Nations; it included almost all the members of the League and Germany. The other took place at Porto Rosa in November 1921; it was called by the Italian government and attended by the succession states of the former Habsburg monarchy. Both had passed resolutions aimed at removing obstacles both to railway and water traffic. The Treaty of Versailles and the other peace treaties also contained provisions for the conclusion of an international regime of transit, waterways, ports, and railways.[44]

The London Report had incorporated the conclusions of Barcelona and Porto Rosa.[45] The Transport Commission, headed by Theunis and later Jaspar, appointed a twelve-member subcommission, which divided the work into two subcommittees, one for railways and one for waterways, in order to allow the largest possible number of small states to participate. A Belgian delegate presided over both. Throughout the proceedings, the representatives of the five inviting powers functioned as an informal drafting committee, first editing the London Report and then combining the two reports for final submission to the subcommission, the full Transport Commission, and the plenary session on 3 May.[46]

Once more politics entered the technical deliberations. Lithuania, for example, cited Poland's capture of Vilna as an impediment to "smooth transport relations" between two neighbors. Germany refused to recognize any of the transit clauses in the Versailles treaty; together with the Soviet delegate, it challenged the results of the Barcelona Conference because of its sponsorship by the League of Nations. Against the efforts of Austria, Hungary, and the West European powers, the Little Entente declined to promise ratification of the Porto Rosa accords that would unify transportation in the Danubian area. Russia and the Baltic states similarly opposed the powers' proposal to send

43. Reviewed in "Problems of Transit," *New Statesman* 17 (16 April 1921): 36–37.
44. Summarized in "Memorandum by the British Representatives on the Transport Commission," Genoa, 29 Apr., GB BT 90/18.
45. *DBFP*, 19:276 (articles 59, 61).
46. Barthou to MAE, Genoa, 15 Apr., #74–76, FMAE B 94; "Memorandum by British Representatives," 29 Apr., GB BT 90/18.

"experts" to survey their facilities and recommend improvements of their railways, ports, and waterways.[47]

On 3 May Jaspar reported to the plenary session on the Transport Commission's modest list of proposals.[48] Lloyd-Greame endorsed the report, adding a series of essential conditions: the importance of adequate facilities for unfettered transit of goods by land and sea, reciprocal use and exchange of rolling stock, reestablishment of direct international trains for both passengers and goods, inclusive tariffs, a single waybill for through transport without discrimination against foreign traders or carriers, elimination of delays at customs stations, and common frontier stations. In short, these were noncontroversial, nonbinding recommendations aimed at smoothing the flow of European trade.[49]

The Transport Commission adopted Germany's proposal to establish a unified administrative system for all European railways, such as the one that had existed informally under the Deutscher Verein prior to World War I. Germany's purpose was to block the League of Nations from assuming control over railway traffic.[50] To ensure French sympathy, the British delegate proposed Paris as the administrative center; since French railways were still privately owned, this also emphasized the "non-political nature" of the decision. Paris nonetheless considered this a victory, giving it a real economic and political advantage over Berlin.[51]

The French Railway Administration was asked by the Genoa Conference to summon a meeting of all European railways to consider the following:

1. The technical details of restoration of European railway traffic.
2. The possibility of creating a permanent Railway Administration Conference.
3. The special questions of impediments to international transport occasioned by exchange fluctuations.

The conference met that summer. The International Union of Railways (Union Internationale des Chemins de Fer), founded under French leadership, continues to this day as one of the enduring legacies of the Genoa Conference.[52]

47. "Memorandum by British Representatives," 29 Apr., GB BT 90/18; D. G. Franke, "Der Wiederaufbau des europäischen Verkehrswesens," *Deutsche Rundschau* 192 (August 1922): 116; Stieler to AA, Genoa, 20 Apr., Ritter to AA, Genoa, 22 Apr., Germ. AA T-120 3398/1734/ D738446–49, D738486–89.

48. *DBFP*, 19:720–22; the eight articles summarized on p. 725.

49. Ibid., pp. 722–23; also note by British Empire delegation, Genoa, n.d., GB FO 371 C6586/458/62.

50. Stieler to AA, Genoa, 19 Apr., Germ. AA T-120 3398/1734/D738426–29.

51. *DBFP*, 19:725; "Memorandum by British Representatives," 29 Apr., GB BT 90/18; Seydoux, Commissions techniques, FMAE B 99.

52. The board of directors of the eight independent French railways convened the founding

Despite the British delegate's praise for its past service and expertise, the League of Nations was assigned a minor place in the transport resolutions. Because of German and Russian obduracy, it was merely given the responsibility of periodically examining the "progress made in the execution" of the Transport Commission's recommendations.[53] Robert Haas, the French director of the League's transit committee, noted the irony in so vast and vague a mandate, as well as the underlying reality that Geneva was "not expected to do anything."[54]

The League nevertheless continued to assert its interest in transit questions. In November 1923 it drew up two international conventions, on maritime ports and on railways, that codified the work started before World War I and continued at the peace conference and at Genoa. Thereafter its role slackened as the three militant outsiders, the United States, Germany, and Russia, refused to cooperate. The new important area of international air traffic eluded its supervision. Though the League proved successful in matters of secondary importance and in providing technical help, information, and arbitration of intergovernmental disputes, even its members hesitated to endow it with powers to regulate the transit of people and goods.[55]

The Economic Commission

> The economic problems of the present day are of so wide and complicated a nature that the commission of which I had the honor to be president might well have found in its title an excuse for ambitious resolutions. . . . They have not judged it necessary, or even useful to offer a still-bruised Europe the cold comfort of those high-flown resolutions which fall from the lips of theorists with an air of oracular solemnity.[56]

The preliminary remarks of the French president of the Economic Commission, Maurice Colrat, illustrated the contrast with the Financial Commission in their outlook, leadership, and mandate. Where the Financial Commission was guided by the theoretical and commercial orientation of London, the Economic

---

conference. The union's first chairman, Alfred Mange (1922–40), was general manager of the Orleans Railway Company; its first secretary-general (1922–45) was Gaston Leverve: "International Union of Railways—UIC: 1922–1972" (Paris: UIC, n.d.).

53. *DBFP*, 19:725; "Memorandum by British Representatives," 29 Apr., GB BT 90/18, and cf. Attolico to Seydoux, Genoa, 15 Apr., FMAE B 94; Haas to Drummond, Genoa, 5 May, LNA 40A 20280/20466.

54. Haas, Questions de transport, Genoa, 5 May, LNA Spec. Circ. #185.

55. Walters, *League of Nations*, pp. 179, 260.

56. *DBFP*, 19:1004.

Commission was directed largely along the practical and political guidelines set by Paris. Colrat's report to the last plenary session on 19 May bore no resemblance to the idealism of Worthington-Evans and Jaspar two weeks earlier.

Colrat interpreted the economic ills of Europe:

> The economic harmony of the [prewar] world depended upon a just division of labor between peoples [that] has been destroyed by a blind and presumptuous megalomania which the nations must recognize and eradicate. . . . Almost everywhere the war has created industries which cannot continue to thrive. . . . Industries which were normal before the war have been developed to an abnormal and altogether excessive extent. There has thus arisen an economic nationalism which aims at producing everything, irrespective of the needs of consumption and without consideration of the costs of production.[57]

The solution called "neither for joint discussion nor for common action." In a perhaps unconscious parody of the coexistence formula in the first paragraph of the Cannes Resolutions, Colrat announced: "Each nation must resolve [the problems of its national economy] on its own account by the adjustment of its industry to its natural wealth and its acquired capabilities."[58] Colrat then presented twenty-four resolutions, a series of commonsense recommendations permitting the nations a "judicious adjustment to circumstances." He insisted on the importance of the Paris peace treaties and ended on a lofty note, invoking the majesty of Europe and the sacred soil of Italy.[59]

The Economic Commission had been divided into two subcommissions: the first dealt with practical problems such as tariff regulation; the second concerned itself with legal issues, industrial property, and problems of arbitration. Neither handed their entire mandate over to experts as did the financial subcommissions. Only when disputes or technical questions arose did they ask specialists to draft compromise formulas. There was lively discussion and often heated debate in the two subcommissions; however, leaks into the press were rare because the journalists were preoccupied with the outcome of the Allied-Russian negotiations. The resolutions of the Economic Commission represented compromises between the often diametrically opposed positions of the main capitalist governments. Of the three technical commissions, its resolutions strayed the furthest from the original London Report. Also, the Economic Commission delegated more of its follow-up work to the League of Nations and its subsidiaries than the other two commissions, and it created no new ad hoc institutions to complete its work.

57. Ibid., p. 1005.
58. Ibid.
59. The economic resolutions were then summarized, ibid., pp. 1006–8; "General Report . . . Economic Commission," n.d., GB BT 90/18.

All this reflected French influence: the distrust of high-flown theory and theorists; the scorn of "artificially maintained" wartime industry; the emphasis on agriculture, production, and labor; the concern with supplies of raw materials; the careful balancing of loyalty to one's own country, belief in the concept of Europe, fidelity to treaties, and a growing loyalty to the Covenant; and finally, the caution (which Britain shared) over the application of these economic resolutions outside Europe and to colonial areas.[60]

The first explosive issue in the Economic Commission again involved the Porto Rosa resolutions. The London Report had recommended that these be ratified without delay.[61] Because of Little Entente opposition, there had been no formal convention at Porto Rosa, but rather a recommendation that the following theses be submitted to each individual parliament for discussion and ratification: (1) that all import and export restrictions be lifted by 1 July 1922; (2) that trade treaties be negotiated among the succession states on the basis of equality; (3) that participating governments remove restrictions against foreigners such as the import-export permits and minimum export prices; and (4) that in any of their subsequent agreements there would be no clauses to prejudice the interests of outside powers.[62]

The Porto Rosa Conference had pitted Italy, Hungary, and Austria against the Little Entente on the issue of protectionism, with Britain and France on opposite sides.[63] Italy argued for the establishment of complete freedom of trade among all the succession states. The British supported this position. Czechoslovakia insisted on maintaining current tariffs and import-export restrictions because the "unsettled" conditions of Germany and Austria dictated "self-defense" by the new states. In truth, the Little Entente and France opposed any maneuver promoting the economic reunification of Danubian Europe under the tutelage of one or more of the powers.[64]

The Little Entente wanted to forget Porto Rosa, but Italy and Hungary hoped to stimulate "moral pressure" at Genoa to revive it.[65] The issue pitted Rome

60. Peretti to Barthou, Paris, 8 May, Barthou to MAE, 9 May, Poincaré to Barthou, Paris, 12 May, FMAE PM G/VII; résumé of work of Economic Commission, 15 May, FMAE B 98; Seydoux, Commissions techniques, FMAE B 99; Loveday, "Note . . . the Economic Commission," n.d., LNA 40A 20985/20356; "General Report . . . Economic Commission," n.d., GB BT 90/18; Hanotaux, "Economic Metaphysics," pp. 67–68; and Eisenmann, "L'oeuvre économique," p. 279.

61. *DBFP*, 19:292 (article 41).

62. Aufzeichnung, 8 Mar., Germ. AA T-120 K362/3996/K115982–84.

63. Marie-Luise Recker, *England und der Donauraum, 1919–1929* (Stuttgart: Klett, 1976), pp. 170–72.

64. Einstein to State Dept., Prague, 28 Feb., USDS 550 E1/124.

65. Tiedemann to AA, Budapest, 7 Feb., Germ. AA T-120 L998/5412/L286354, von Fürstenberg to AA, Budapest, 13 Mar., Germ. AA T-120 L999/ 5412/L287032–42; Doulcet to MAE, Budapest, 27 Apr., FMAE B 98; John Balfour to Curzon, Budapest, 28 Apr., GB FO 371 C6423/458/62.

against Prague, but also London against Paris. Germany shared the Little Entente's views in favor of certain forms of protectionism and thus encouraged its small neighbors to fight the battle against Italy. This gave Colrat the opportunity to mediate between the two sides. He succeeded in eliminating any substance or force from the Porta Rosa resolutions. The Economic Commission recommended that the "fully sovereign" succession states do whatever they could to reduce the impediments to their commerce according to the Porto Rosa principles; these, however, were demoted to but one example of exemplary action. Beneš and his allies claimed a victory; but the West European press underscored the political and economic dangers of the "balkanization" of Eastern Europe. Indeed, the cost of their economic self-protection weighed heavily on the area's economies.[66]

Italy's other initiative before the Economic Commission failed even more decisively. Rome brought a proposal, far stronger than the one in the London Report, challenging the current system of restrictions on the export of raw materials.[67] Britain, because of its empire, opposed this; the Little Entente did also because export restrictions were its members' major form of economic control. Krassin, the Soviet spokesman, was caught in a contradiction: officially, he sympathized with Rome's plight as a nonproducer of raw materials, and he advocated the universal sharing of resources. But he had to defend Moscow's trade monopoly as the permanent regulator of its exports. France sided with Italy; however, because it was neither in as dire need nor as prejudiced by the current conditions of supply, Colrat could again play the role of mediator. He found a formula for another compromise, again a masterpiece of innocuousness. While conceding every nation's right to dispose freely of its natural resources and protect itself from exaggerated demands from outside, the resolution nevertheless urged that a nation with a surplus neither refuse to sell nor do so in ways that discriminated against certain countries. The only acceptable controls over the export of raw materials were to be for "fiscal" reasons, when the proceeds of such sales would scarcely rise above the cost of production and thus would impoverish the producer. And although it recommended that this resolution be adopted as quickly as possible, the Economic Commission recognized that certain states, "in view of their exceptional condi-

66. Hirsch, "Niederschrift . . . Wirtschaftsexpertenkommission," Genoa, 21 Apr., Germ. AA T-120 K1946/5362/K505572–78; Müller, "Bericht . . . Unterausschuss der Wirtschaftskommission," 25 Apr., Germ. AA T-120 K1946/5362/K505583–87; Barthou to MAE, Genoa, 25 Apr., #216, FMAE B 95; Schwarzenberg to AA, Vienna, 15 May, Germ. AA T-120 K362/3996/K116049; Eisenmann, "L'oeuvre économique," pp. 274–75; Iván T. Berend and György Ránki, *Economic Development in East Central Europe in the 19th and 20th Centuries* (New York: Columbia University Press, 1974), pp. 201–9.

67. Müller to AA, Genoa, 20 Apr., Germ. AA T-120 3398/1734/D738452–54; "General Report . . . Economic Commission," n.d., GB BT 90/18; Eisenmann, "L'oeuvre économique," pp. 279–80.

tions," would not be able to implement it. Finally, though it urged against discriminatory export policies in general, the resolution upheld those that had been established by the Paris peace treaties.[68]

The argument for "commercial equality," centering on the principle of most-favored-nation treatment, produced the most explosive debate in the Economic Commission. Except for their lobbying for reparations relief, the Germans concentrated their main assault at the Genoa Conference here. They aimed specifically against Articles 264 through 267 of the Treaty of Versailles, which forced the Reich for five years to grant the signatories one-sided access to its markets while permitting them to close Germany out from theirs. The purpose had been to prevent German dumping on nations that it had devastated in wartime. In addition, the treaty stipulated that the League of Nations could extend the five-year period. This supported France's claim that its economically inferior position had to be redressed. The German delegation came to Genoa with Wilsonian and pragmatic arguments that its exclusion from certain markets and the discriminatory tactics against its producers had ruined the Reich's economy and currency. Germany's small neutral neighbors, though victims of its industrialists' ruthless dumping policy, rallied to the banner of "free trade" and especially a most-favored-nation policy as panaceas for the current crisis.[69]

Most-favored-nation, like the gold standard, was a seductively simple and seemingly positive step. Like its financial counterpart, it had a much misunderstood history, but it was generally more popular than gold. Most-favored-nation agreements favored advanced, industrialized trading nations over poorer ones. They also permitted loopholes, for which prewar Germany had been notorious, to retain wide areas of protection. In their worst form, imposed by the Western powers, they became the "open door," now fiercely resisted by the new East European states. After World War I, Wilson's Point III, which called for freedom of trade, had been substantially modified at Paris. The Allies had established many special forms of control and protection in the peace treaties not only to rebuild devastated areas but also to ensure the viability of the new order.[70]

After the treaties were signed, the Entente immediately disagreed over their implementation. France favored the principle of equality of benefits between trade partners (bilateralism); the British, opposing bilateralism as much as protectionism, argued for free trade. Paris argued for "equity" against London's demand for a "mechanistic equality." Therefore the struggle at Genoa was important. Had Germany, with the help of Britain, Italy, Japan, and the neu-

68. "Economic Resolutions," GB FO 371 C7217/458/62.

69. Seydoux, Commissions techniques, FMAE B 99; "General Report . . . Economic Commission," n.d., p. 4, GB BT 90/18.

70. Eisenmann, "L'oeuvre économique," pp. 276–78.

trals, succeeded in forcing through the adoption of the most-favored-nation principle, it would have represented both a symbolic and a real victory: undermining the Treaty of Versailles and increasing the Reich's potential access to the Allies' markets. The French were determined to resist.[71]

The Germans received no support from the Soviet delegation, who were committed to bilateralism. Britain, Italy, and Japan, despite their preferences for unconditional most-favored-nation agreements, had to acknowledge their adherence to the existing treaties. The Little Entente tried to mediate by proposing that the League of Nations function as watchdog over all forthcoming trade treaties; the Swiss representative caused some mirth by remarking that by the time international inquiries could be made, the situation would invariably have changed.[72]

Switzerland did contribute to the solution with another innocuous resolution recommending that future commercial treaties be based on the system of reciprocity adapted to "special circumstances" and that they also contain the most-favored-nation clause to the extent possible. In two appended notes, the majority voiced its support of the most-favored-nation principle and opposed bilateral treaties that established special rights and tariffs prejudicial to third parties. Colrat permitted this because the result was a signal French victory and a victory for "Versailles." After a bitter debate, nothing had changed.[73]

The "spirit of compromise" dominated the Economic Commission, which continued to bury challenges with bland statements. Germany was stopped from exploiting the issue of consular rights and the treatment of foreigners to score another propagandistic point. A subcommission buried its attempt to capitalize on the unemployment debate. Proposals brought by international labor and cooperative organizations were promptly and deftly disposed of.[74]

71. Hirsch, "Niederschrift," Genoa, 21 Apr., Germ. AA T-120 K1946/5372/K505572–78, Müller to AA, Genoa, 22 Apr., Germ. AA T-120 3398/1734/D738481–84; Barthou to MAE, Genoa, 21, 22 Apr., #150–52, #168, Poincaré to Barthou, Paris, 22 Apr., #119–20, Barthou to MAE, Genoa, 23 Apr., #169, #177, FMAE B 94, Barthou to MAE, 25 Apr., #218–20, Lucien Dior (minister of commerce) to Poincaré, Paris, 26 Apr., Poincaré to Barthou, Paris, 26 Apr., #166, FMAE B 95.

72. Loveday reports to League observers' meetings, Genoa, 25, 28 Apr., 2 May, LNA 40A 20136/20340, 20434, 20529. Disappointment with Russia in Müller to AA, Genoa, 20 Apr., Germ. AA T-120 3398/1734/D738452–54.

73. Barthou to MAE, Genoa, 3 May, #358–63, FMAE B 96; also résumé of the work of the Economic Commission, 15 May, FMAE B 98; Seydoux, Commissions techniques, FMAE B 99; "General Report . . . Economic Commission," n.d., p. 4, GB BT 90/18.

74. Montpetit to MacKenzie King, Genoa, 2 May, PAC MKP; Loveday, "Note . . . the Economic Commission," n.d., LNA 40A 20985/20356; "General Report . . . Economic Commission," n.d., pp. 6–7, GB BT 90/18; Seydoux, Commissions techniques, FMAE B 99; Eisenmann, "L'oeuvre économique," pp. 281–82; and "The Genoa Conference and the International Labor Office," *Industrial and Labor Information* 2, no. 9 (2 June 1922), in Hoover/Comm. (Genoa Conf.).

The Economic Commission issued unequivocal statements on several non-controversial matters. It unanimously recommended the publication of customs tariffs, their maintenance at specified levels so far as possible for long periods, their issuance in clear language, and the abolition of export-licensing systems. It recommended easing regulations on foreigners and adopting the as-yet-unratified proposals of the Paris Conference of 1920 to facilitate procedures and fees for passports and visas. It advised equal treatment of foreign nationals and firms; it also proposed adhesion to prewar conventions and the cancellation of wartime measures threatening the protection of industrial property and literary and artistic work. Finally, it called upon the League to investigate problems of dumping and differential export prices, to act as a channel for the publication of customs tariffs and import and export restrictions, and to continue its work on commercial arbitration.[75]

Thus, although it broke no new ground, the Economic Commission gave eloquent testimony to the divisions among the capitalist states of Europe at the very time they were attempting a rapprochement with Soviet Russia. There were more losers than gainers, particularly Italy. In the final plenary, the Giolittian, Teofilo Rossi, made an eloquent plea for freedom of trade. Rathenau, after enunciating four of his by now commonplace "truths" about the causes of Germany and Europe's ills, recited with passion Petrarch's phrase: "Lo vo gridando: O pace! pace! pace!" Chicherin tried to rekindle fireworks by complaining of the Economic Commission's indifference to the working class. Colrat, with the help of Motta, extinguished them, Lloyd George made no comment at all, and Facta brusquely closed the debate.[76]

In its technical discussions, Genoa was far more limited than the Brussels Conference. There the experts had felt free to range over every topic relating to the restoration of Europe, including debts, reparations, and disarmament. The governments at Genoa were committed to an ideology of encouraging the revival of private enterprise, especially when faced with the Soviet challenge in Russia. Where there was resistance to relinquishing government control over finance, transportation, and the economy, all of which had grown remarkably in wartime, the Genoa ensemble issued cautious suggestions for improvement: central bank cooperation and a gold exchange standard; international railway and waterway cooperation, and a list of trade reforms forming the basis of future work by the League of Nations.[77]

If the Genoa Conference was less bold than its critics desired, it had good

75. "General Report . . . Economic Commission," n.d., p. 8, GB BT 90/18; résumé of work of Economic Commission, 15 May, FMAE B 98.

76. Third plenary session, *DBFP*, 19:1008–17.

77. Loveday, "Note . . . Economic Commission," n.d., LNA 40A 20985/20356; Eisenmann, "L'oeuvre économique," pp. 261–66, 282–95; "General Report . . . Economic Commission," n.d., pp. 1–3, GB BT 90/18.

reason for its prudence. The impending reparations crisis, America's aloofness, and Russia's obstreperousness all overshadowed its technical labors. The result, like much international rhetoric in the twenties, was a call for international solidarity over national egotism. Discipline, self-sacrifice, compromise, and international cooperation were difficult to achieve even verbally under a spotlight of world attention, expectations, and distrust, where neither statesmen nor "experts" worked independently. Nevertheless, even if the Russian negotiations proved barren, the "Little Genoa" had frankly and hurriedly exposed the pervasive economic problems of Europe.

Geneva and Genoa

The myriad of technical issues handled at the Genoa Conference kept the team of League observers busy during the Conference. The group met almost daily to coordinate their work and were sensitive to the delicacy and importance of their role.[78] In addition to the routine German and Russian objections about handing the League any of Genoa's follow-up work, there were others who had misgivings about the representation of the world organization at the conference.

In Geneva there were two divergent opinions about the League. Jean Monnet, assistant secretary-general, cautioned: "The League is nothing but a group of rules and methods adopted by various governments to prepare or execute their common decisions. It thus cannot be represented officially at a gathering of sovereign states, of whom the majority are its members. Nothing would compromise the League's future more than to give the impression that there exists a political orientation or a program of the League separate and distinct from that of its individual members."[79]

His chief, Drummond, and Bernardo Attolico, head of the communications section, both disagreed with this narrow view. Drummond developed specific goals for the Genoa Conference: (1) All the continuing work was to be assigned to the League; no permanent rival organizations were to be established. (2) Germany was to be admitted to the League as soon as possible, and preferably by the assembly in September 1922. In the interval, Germany would participate fully on all League committees handling questions raised by the Genoa Conference. (3) Though the Russian question was more intractable, Drummond hoped for an outcome similar to that of Germany: if granted recognition at Genoa or soon afterwards, Russia should also be admitted to the League.[80]

78. There were twenty-five meetings of the League's representatives, a valuable though not unbiased record of the Genoa Conference: 14 Apr.–9 May, LNA 40A 20136/20136–20684.
79. Monnet to Bourgeois, Paris, 9 Mar., FMAE B 89.
80. Minutes of directors' meeting, Geneva, 30 Mar., LNA.

These contrasting goals to some extent reflected the views of Monnet's, Drummond's, and Attolico's home governments, with important distinctions. Poincaré was reluctant to expand Geneva's importance, but he also refused to allow it to be usurped by a rival organization. Neither Britain nor Italy wanted to strengthen the League, but they did want Genoa to succeed in ways parallel to Drummond's goals. Drummond and Monnet discreetly stayed away from Genoa. The League's observers were led by Attolico, who enjoyed close and cordial ties with his own government and with leading diplomats. The group had great enthusiasm and confidence, hoping to work behind the scenes to recoup the loss of prestige at the Washington Conference.[81]

The first information that reached Geneva produced mixed reactions from the Secretariat. The Rapallo treaty and the subsequent ostracism of Germany set back for the time being the League's hopes for Berlin's entry. Nonetheless, in the ensuing tumult over punishing Germany, the threat that Lloyd George might create a new anti-League power bloc was removed.[82] The Secretariat noted the neutrals' protests that the inviting powers dominated the conference, a more overtly unfair procedure than that practiced in Geneva. Paul Mantoux, the director of the political section, contrasted the disorganization and confusion that reigned at Genoa with the "calm, methodical work" carried on in Geneva. To emphasize its autonomy, the Secretariat ignored the powers' requests for a delay and deliberately scheduled a council meeting on 11 May as a showpiece of international decorum.[83]

Yet the League could not hope for Genoa's utter failure.[84] Geneva was dependent on Franco-British cooperation and vitally interested in the problems of Russia and European reconstruction. The technical commissions offered opportunities to increase the League's authority and further its goals. As has been seen, the Financial and Transport Commissions withheld the implementation of their key decisions from Geneva; but the Economic Commission, by referring certain tasks, acknowledged the League's ability to promote international trade.

Undeterred by Rapallo, the League's officials conducted soundings of the German and Russian delegates.[85] But though these meetings were amicable, there was little likelihood that either Germany or Russia could or would be-

81. Meetings of League representatives, Genoa, 29, 30 Apr., 1 May, LNA 40A 20136/20435, 20498, 20504; Drummond to Attolico, Geneva, 4 Apr., LNA 10 18574/19818.

82. Meeting of League representatives, 20 Apr., LNA 40A 20136/20226.

83. Mantoux, "La rôle de la S.d.N. dans la vie internationale," Geneva, 19 May, LNA Mantoux Papers P 31/4; Imperiali to Schanzer, Rome, 1 May, IMAE 52/21; minutes of directors' meeting, Geneva, 3 May, LNA.

84. Minutes of directors' meeting, Geneva, 26 Apr., LNA.

85. On Germany: Drummond memorandum (conversations with Simons), Geneva, 16 Mar., LNA Drummond Papers 33/5; Pelt to Drummond, Geneva, 4 Apr., LNA Spec. Circ. #173. On Russia: Slavik memoranda, 18, 28 Feb., 24 Mar., 27 Apr., LNA Spec. Circs. #148, #153, #165, #177.

come members in 1922. France opposed both candidacies until they had demonstrated their adherence to the treaties and the territorial status quo. Britain and Italy, which supported German membership, were stopped by the shock of Rapallo from pressing the case.[86] The two outsiders in their public statements gave the League little cause for hope. Rathenau nursed his grievance over the partition of Upper Silesia and echoed German rightist propaganda against Geneva. Russia raised the specter of a "counter-League," consisting of the Third Internationale, a "Union of Soviet Socialist Republics," representatives of disgruntled outsiders, such as Germany and Kemalist Turkey, and delegates from the colonial peoples of Asia, Africa, and the Near East.[87]

The League's representatives nevertheless found ways of operating on minor issues at the Genoa Conference to keep their work in the forefront. One example is their consuming preoccupation with the Warsaw Health Conference and their efforts to secure endorsement of its resolutions by the Genoa Conference. These called for a large, antiepidemic campaign in Eastern Europe costing 1.5 million pounds sterling and supervised by the World Health Organization in Geneva. Though Attolico admitted that the Warsaw resolutions had little to do with the agenda of the Genoa Conference, League representatives urged that Genoa attend to this humanitarian function that also would extend Geneva's activity and authority in Russia and Eastern Europe.[88]

The League's lobbyists strove to win the powers' interest and support. France disapproved of the Warsaw Conference, where both Russia and Germany had full representation and whose official languages were English, French, *and* German. It opposed the prospect of continuing meetings in such places as Kharkov and Moscow with German and Russian delegates, and protested against such expensive and "redundant" activities.[89] Germany, on the other hand, pledged its cooperation, and, aside from the de rigeur protests

86. Chamberlain to Lloyd George, London, 3 May, Grigg Papers, roll 10; Gregory [Lloyd George] to Chamberlain, Genoa, 9 May, Fisher minute, London, 9 May, and Chamberlain to Lloyd George, London, 10 May, GB FO 800 Chamberlain Papers; Aufzeichnung, 16 May (Schäffer-Wise conversation), Germ. AA T-120 3398/1735/D739305–7; Attolico to Schanzer, Genoa, 30 Apr., IMAE 52/21; meetings of League representatives, 14, 15, 17 Apr., LNA 40A 20136/20136, 20137, 20164.

87. Attolico to Drummond, Geneva, 24 May, LNA Spec. Circ. #186; meetings of League representatives, 15, 26, 27 Apr., 3 May, LNA 40A 20126/20137, 20385, 20529, 20567; Kathryn W. Davis, *The Soviets at Geneva* (Geneva: Geneva Research Center, 1934), p. 125. Because Soviet cooperation was desirable for the League, its officials used special prudence in dealing with Russia's new Baltic neighbors: Walters, *League of Nations*, pp. 123, 150; Colban to da Gama, Geneva, 10 Apr., LNA 41 18841x/10503.

88. Drummond's statement to directors' meeting, Geneva, 3 Mar., LNA.

89. Poincaré to Paul Strauss (minister of public health), Paris, 7 Apr., Strauss to Poincaré, Paris, 13 Apr., FMAE B 94; Barthou to MAE, Genoa, 23 Apr., #178, ibid., Poincaré to Barthou, Paris, 29 Apr., #216, FMAE B 96.

against the League's involvement, the Russians and Ukrainians supported the implementation of the Warsaw Resolutions.[90]

Ludwik Rajchman, the Polish head of the League's Health Organization, urged that the "innocuous" Warsaw Resolutions might rouse Genoa from its post-Rapallo lethargy and give the Political Commission a practical goal. He succeeded in winning British, Italian, and Japanese support. The inviting powers took up the question on 10 and 16 May. Lloyd George overrode Barthou's formal objections, and a resolution was drafted for the final plenary.[91]

The League received little reward for its labor. The resolution introduced on 19 May to adopt the Warsaw Resolutions was vague, unspecific, and—for practical reasons—deliberately ignored the League's role in alleviating epidemics. Chicherin proposed that a new international commission carry out the Warsaw Resolutions because Russia had not recognized, and therefore could not cooperate with, the League of Nations. No one answered these "disloyal reservations"; in fact, none of the closing speeches of the Genoa Conference mentioned the League of Nations.[92]

The League was also involved in the disposition of "memorials," the various complaints submitted to the Genoa Conference. Like international gatherings since the Congress of Westphalia, Genoa attracted a number of supplicants who raised issues only remotely connected with the agenda. The Italian port was temporarily a world capital, and an appeal to the conference was an invaluable form of publicity. Most of the petitions were disregarded, but the inviting powers discussed sixteen appeals.[93] The most important of these, pertaining to minority rights, fell definitely within the purview of the League.

The minorities issue was one of Geneva's most difficult problems. It had been handed over before the birth of the new world organization by the peacemakers in Paris. There were articles in the treaties with Austria, Hungary, and Bulgaria, and special treaties with all the new and enlarged East European states providing for the protection of minorities and guaranteeing their politi-

90. Comert mémorandum, Paris, 31 Mar., FMAE B 91.

91. Meetings of League representatives, 20, 21 Apr., 2, 4, 6, 8 May, LNA 40A 20136/20226, 20256, 20529, 20536, 20584, 20597; *DBFP*, 19:797–98, 940–41.

92. *DBFP*, 19:1027; Health conference at Warsaw, n.d., LNA 12B 20787/18972; Attolico to Drummond, Geneva, 24 May, LNA Spec. Circ. #186.

93. In addition to the Warsaw Health Conference, there was a protest from the Saar delegation, seven petitions from peoples and governments overthrown by the new Soviet state (the Ukrainian Democratic Republic, Georgia, Armenia, Azerbaijan), two involving peoples incorporated into Poland and Yugoslavia (Eastern Galicia and Montenegro), an urgent appeal for economic aid from the government of Albania, a protest by the Ankara government against its exclusion from the Genoa Conference, a letter from Lithuania contesting Poland's seizure of Vilna, and the appeals from Hungary and Bulgaria on behalf of their kin in neighboring states. Texts of the appeals taken up in *DBFP*, 19:812–46; discussion, 10 May, ibid., pp. 797–809. Petitions from the Croats of Yugoslavia and the Arabs of Palestine were suppressed.

cal, economic, religious, linguistic, and cultural rights, which were placed under the guarantee of the League of Nations. (Though Germany and Italy had substantial minority populations, they were deemed Great Powers and thus exempt from international minorities supervision.) To implement its obligation, the League had devised a procedure based primarily on the initiative of the individual council members. Up to the Genoa Conference, these members had been reluctant to take up the cause of minorities, which were mainly composed of former enemy nationals: Germans, Hungarians, or Bulgarians. In April 1922 the Minorities Commission of the ultraliberal International Union of League of Nations Societies met in Munich and protested the League's record of indifference to minority rights. The governments of Hungary and Bulgaria sent pleas to the Genoa Conference to urge the League to "ensure the effective protection of minorities in conformity with the treaties."[94]

In this instance Geneva's interest was to prevent open discussion of minority complaints at the Genoa Conference, to spare itself criticism and to protect those on whose cooperation the system depended. France and the Little Entente fought against Britain and Italy's inclination to air the grievances of Hungary and Bulgaria. Fatigued by the Russian negotiations, Lloyd George let the opportunity pass for a pro-minorities, anti-League manifestation before the Political Commission; the complaints were referred to Geneva.[95] The League's authority was reinforced when Colban paid a flying visit to Genoa, where he negotiated the terms of the minority treaties for Latvia and Estonia, the precondition for their entry into the League. Colban stressed the League's orientation: to enforce the minority treaties but also to protect the sovereign rights of its members in the face of claims by minority groups and their "defenders." Hungary and Bulgaria were therefore little consoled by the momentary attention at Genoa to the minorities' cause. The incident also intensified the Little Entente's resistance to increased international attention to the issue of minority rights.[96]

Afterwards, the Secretariat attempted to evaluate its role at the Genoa Conference. The pessimists stressed the dearth of new "living problems" handed over to the League, smarted at Chicherin's unanswered attack, complained how little the powers valued the institution, and doubted that its members would fight for its independence and survival. Because of German, Russian, and American hostility as well as Lloyd George's antipathy, the League had been deliberately excluded from any important proposals at Genoa. Finally,

94. Rosting memorandum, 23 Jan., Colban supplement, 28 May, LNA 41 20884/17333; Facchinetti to Attolico, n.d., Attolico to Drummond, 17 May, Attolico to Facchinetti, 31 May, ibid.; *DBFP*, 19:836–37, 838–40.

95. *DBFP*, 19:805–8, 938–39.

96. Memorandum, Geneva, 28 May, LNA 41 20884/17333; Couget to MAE, Prague, 5 June, FMAE Y 37.

there probably would be other Genoas, called for specific political purposes, in which Geneva would play a subordinate or nonexistent role and would be expected to perform purely technical tasks.[97]

More optimistic observers questioned this bleak judgment, claiming that the League had "saved" the Genoa Conference, performed valuable technical services, and disarmed its severest critics. The paucity of Genoa's final accomplishments rescued the League from responsibility for a failed cause, indeed, made its minor role all the more tolerable. However, Drummond and Attolico, who retained high ambitions for Geneva, considered Genoa a negative episode. There had been no setbacks, but there was also no progress toward giving the League a principal role in the settlement of important territorial and political problems. H. R. Cummings, head of the League's information section, wrote the following after his five weeks at Genoa: "I found it a salutary experience to move . . . in a distinctly non-League atmosphere and to realize, painfully, close at hand, that in the really first-class problems of the world, the League has not taken its proper place."[98]

In his postmortem on Genoa, Drummond counseled his staff that during the next few years he expected few repetitions of the "accident" of Upper Silesia. The Great Powers would undoubtedly make most of the important decisions themselves. The neutrals would fall in line and would remain, as at Genoa, only grudging supporters of the Paris peace settlement. The League's task was simply to remain alive until a more "settled world" emerged, at which point it might hope to assume a "dominant position."[99] Significantly silent on how the world would "settle" and whether its chief enemies would acquiesce, the League on this passive note closed its files on Genoa—another painful trial on the road to Locarno and finally to Munich.

97. Attolico to Drummond, Geneva, 24 May, LNA Spec. Circ. #186. Report of Italian representative, 22 July, in League of Nations, Third Assembly (1922), Supplement: Extract 28 Aug., LNA 40A 21463/21105, listing the specific questions turned over to the League.
98. "Genoa and the League," 24 May, LNA Spec. Circ. #184.
99. Minutes of directors' meeting, Geneva, 8 June, LNA.

9

The End of the Genoa Conference

The fragile fabric Lloyd George had put together began to unravel. He was not a patient man. The conflicts and contradictions he had hoped to surmount at Genoa with his charm and persuasiveness did not disappear. Above all, the nonaggression pact continued to raise apprehension and mistrust. The neutrals stressed their unwillingness to sign any document that either sanctioned the status quo or abridged the authority of the League of Nations. The Germans refused to give "fresh recognition" to the Versailles treaty. On orders from Moscow, Chicherin deliberately avoided making any commitments to Russia's present borders. Consequently Skirmunt ceased his efforts for an open discussion of Poland's frontiers; Warsaw and Paris preferred a "quieter atmosphere" for such important deliberations.[1] In spite of Schanzer's hope for a comprehensive treaty, Lloyd George recognized there could be no peace and no disarmament without a favorable Russian reply to the Allies' terms of 2 May.

Lloyd George grew angry and churlish, needling the Germans, driving the Italians, and threatening the loyal Schanzer and Skirmunt—and also Krassin —that if no agreement were signed at Genoa, Great Britain would forget Europe *and* Russia and withdraw into its island kingdom.[2] The Germans and Russians were uncowed; indeed, both explored alternatives to an exclusive British policy. Rathenau held conversations with the American ambassador. He also tried unsuccessfully to approach the French directly with a request for talks on reparations and other outstanding questions.[3] The Soviet delegate asked for more specific information on the Allies' note, whereupon Grigg and

1. *DBFP*, 19:634, 680–85, 688, 744–47, 749, 754; Wigram-Dufour talks, Genoa, 4 May, Grigg Papers, roll 10; Barthou to MAE, Genoa, 2 May, FMAE Y 31, Poincaré to Delegation, Paris, 3 May, #266–69, FMAE B 96, Barthou [Barrère] to Poincaré, Genoa, 7 May, #413–17, FMAE B 97.

2. *DBFP*, 19:726–29, 743–44, 753–54, 759–60; "Aufzeichnung . . . die Zusammenkunft zwischen . . . Wirth und Rathenau mit Lloyd George, Birkenhead, Worthington-Evans, Hankey, und Grigg," 4 May, Germ. AA T-120 3398/1735/D739288–95, Rathenau to Haniel, Genoa, 6 May, Germ. Pol. Arch. AA, Bur. R.M., bd. 11, Wirth to Ebert, Genoa, 4 May, Germ. AA T-120 3398/1735/D738701–4.

3. Rathenau to Haniel, Genoa, 6 May, Germ. Pol. Arch. AA, Bur. R.M., bd. 11; Beneš-

Wise, on their own, drafted a document explaining the terms under which Western capital would reenter Russia. The Russians were not impressed with this offering; in fact, it was written without the consent of key members of the British delegation and was later termed the "fraudulent prospectus" by the Foreign Office.[4] Krassin also sought out Child, who gave him little encouragement. However, Meyer Bloomfield, a labor expert who, with Harding's approval, was en route to Moscow to investigate conditions in Russia, stopped at Genoa where he had long friendly conversations with both Krassin and Litvinov.[5]

The prospects for Genoa's success deteriorated. The pronouncements of the technical commissions had failed to arouse great hope, and the nonaggression pact was virtually defunct. The original expectations that had brought statesmen from thirty-four countries, the need and ambitions that had attracted many to Genoa, had now degenerated into oil scandals and bankers' conclaves, hesitant, bickering statesmen with an inability to control the flow of capital, and capitalists frightened to act without their governments' support. At this point, disenchanted observers wrote off Genoa and began formulating their own panaceas for Europe's current economic ills.[6]

Anglo-French Contretemps

Barthou returned to Genoa on the morning of Saturday, 6 May, armed with instructions from the French cabinet. He first saw Jaspar and explained his conduct five days earlier when he had accepted the memorandum to the Russians despite Belgium's reservations. Now he pledged that France was solidly on Jaspar's side. His next interview was with Schanzer, who no longer expected Poincaré to make an appearance at Genoa but greeted Barthou's return as a pledge that France had no intention of torpedoing the conference.[7] Barthou then called at the Villa d'Albertis in the late afternoon, apologizing for his

Rathenau conversation in Aufzeichnung, n.d., Germ. AA T-120 3398/1735/D739281–82; Barrère to Poincaré, Genoa, 5 May, #388, FMAE B 97.

4. *DBFP*, 19:761–63; Lloyd-Greame to wife, Genoa, 8 May, LGrP; O'Malley memorandum, 6 Feb. 1923, CzP; Harry Graf Kessler, *Tagebücher, 1918–1937* (Frankfurt-am-Main: Insel-Verlag, 1961), pp. 311–13.

5. Child to State Dept., 4, 6, 10 May, USDS 550 E1/239, 247, 319; IGPS Boll. no. 17, 4 May, IMAE 52/31. Sent with official funds to Russia, Bloomfield wrote Harding a lengthy confidential report on his return: Harding to Fletcher, 11 Jan., Harding Papers, roll 224; Poole to Hughes, 20 Mar., Poole memorandum, USDS 550 E1/303, 309; and Bloomfield to Harding, 6 July, Harding Papers, roll 181.

6. See, e.g., Kessler, *Tagebücher*, pp. 315–16, and Child to State Dept., Genoa, 1 May, commentaries, 3, 4 May, USDS 550 E1/227, 228, 304.

7. Barthou to MAE, Genoa, 6 May, #396–97, FMAE Y 32; Jaspar memorandum, Genoa, 6 May, JP/210; Sforza to Schanzer, Paris, 6 May, IMAE 52/4 (France).

delay. The tense encounter opened with his statement that France adhered completely to Belgium's position. Armed with materials to support France's rejection of the 2 May memorandum, Barthou also alleged that America was "grateful" for Belgium's stand.[8]

Lloyd George affected great sadness for the occasion. He was gloomy over the Russians' hesitations, about the menace of Germany's eventual domination of Russia, and about the impossibility of finding a formula on private property that would overcome Belgium's scruples. "There was no doubt," he said, "that if this conference broke down, Great Britain and France would have to reconsider the whole European situation." What he meant to "reconsider," just four months after his agreement with Briand and twenty days after Rapallo, was not Russia's intransigency but France's sabotage. Should this "great European conference" fail, he threatened that "this might prove the turning point in Anglo-French relations." He characterized the conflict as pitting 1.2 million Russian bondholders in France against the 2 million unemployed in Britain. Lloyd George accused France of "ingratitude," of posing as the defender of Belgium against Great Britain, which had made tremendous sacrifices for the common cause during the last war. Barthou was moved but not overwhelmed. He coldly delivered Poincaré's final refusal of an Allied meeting before 31 May. On leaving, he began to prepare his defense against Lloyd George's expected accusations of France's sabotage.[9]

Lloyd George was convinced that he had once more bested the Frenchman with his combination of pathos and threats. The next day he announced to Wirth that he and Schanzer had with their firmness halted a unilateral French response if Germany defaulted on 31 May.[10] Lloyd-Greame, invited by Seydoux for a frank talk, spoke in a similarly arrogant way. He warned that the Entente partners were drifting apart, and if France's policy ran counter to Britain's, "we can't play." If France "broke on the Russian question" on a "point of prestige" rather than on the basic issues that had been decided at Cannes, then "all Englishmen will consider it as a willful break—and we shall break right through—reparations and all the rest." Lloyd-Greame deplored France's "mad" policy, caused by a "howling" press, and he threatened that France would be "isolated" in Europe for the sake of a momentary triumph—the alleged defense of Belgium. He added: "You may make a rally in the ruble. To what purpose? You won't balance your budget, or change fact."[11]

8. Note of conversation on the terrace of the Villa d'Albertis, 6 May (revised after comparison with French notes), *DBFP*, 19:764–76; Notes du secrétaire français, Genoa, 6 May, FMAE Y 32; Barthou to MAE, Genoa, 7 May, #400–403, FMAE Z GB 49.

9. Barthou to MAE, Genoa, 7 May, #411, FMAE B 97.

10. Hankey to Chamberlain, Genoa, 7 May, HP; Grigg to Chamberlain, 7 May, Grigg Papers, roll 1; Wirth to Ebert, Genoa, 8 May, Germ. AA T-120 3398/1734/D738712–14.

11. Lloyd-Greame to wife, Genoa, 8 May, LGrP; Barthou to Poincaré, Genoa, 8 May, #420–25, FMAE B 111, 9 May, #449, FMAE B 97.

The British, overwrought with their labors or unaware of their ineptitude, exaggerated their persuasiveness. Lloyd-Greame incorrectly assumed that Seydoux had concurred with his diatribe, that the French would cave in, go along with Britain's Russian policy, and rejoin the political subcommission when it resumed negotiations with the Bolsheviks. Back in Paris, Poincaré ordered his delegates to stand fast.[12] It was Lloyd George's punishing strategy that backfired. Early on 7 May, on the morning after his interview with Barthou, he boasted to Philippe Millet, correspondent for the *Petit Parisien* and director of the influential *Europe Nouvelle*, about the growing British disaffection with France. He produced "documents," including a letter from a cabinet member, to the effect that the "divorce should take place." A worried Millet wrote the story and communicated it to other French journalists; "Pertinax" repeated it to the *Times* editor, Wickham Steed, who was lodged with the French delegation in the Hotel Savoy. Steed, a defender of Anglo-French solidarity and a notorious opponent of Lloyd George, wrote on 8 May in the *Times* that Lloyd George had threatened Barthou to end the Entente.[13]

London erupted with questions, the stock market panicked, and Lloyd George not only had to assemble the British press that night to issue denials but eventually had to ask Barthou to write a denial as well.[14] No one benefited from this contretemps. British opinion sympathized more with the prime minister than his opponents because of the unfair and vicious sniping of the press. Yet there was a growing nervousness in Britain over his frequent private meetings with the Germans and Russians and about the break with Belgium.[15] Lloyd George had lost his dominance over the Genoa Conference at the moment Poincaré and Lenin were tightening the controls over their delegations. He could do little to help the Germans or the faithful Italians until the Russian question was settled. Child, who lunched with Lloyd George on 6 May, described him as a "defeated and baffled man."[16]

12. Poincaré to Barthou, Paris, 8 May, #369–71, FMAE B 111, 9, 10 May, #385, #388, FMAE B 97.

13. Louise Weiss, *Mémoires d'une européene* (Paris: Payot, 1969), 2:170–71.

14. Barthou to Lloyd George, Genoa, 8 May, LGP F 51/3/15; Barthou to MAE, 9 May, #433–34, FMAE B 97; Cabinet, 10 May, GB CAB 23/30; A. J. Sylvester, *The Real Lloyd George* (London: Cassell, 1948), pp. 95–97.

15. Saint-Aulaire to MAE, London, 9 May, #235, FMAE B 97; Peretti note, Paris, 10 May, Saint-Aulaire to MAE, 11, 12 May, FMAE Z GB 49.

16. Diary, 7 May, in Richard W. Child, *A Diplomat Looks at Europe* (New York: Duffield, 1925), p. 45. Also Gordon to King, Genoa, 10 May, PAC MKP; David and Frances Lloyd George, *My Darling Pussy: The Letters of Lloyd George and Frances Stevenson, 1913–1941*, ed. A. J. P. Taylor (London: Weidenfeld and Nicolson, 1975), 9 May, pp. 50–51: "The Russians difficult—hesitating with their judgement warped in doctrine. The French selfish—the Germans impotent—the Italians willing but feeble—the little countries scared. The *Times* devilish. . . . I am fighting the most difficult battle of my life—& the most decisive. . . . Grigg works hard —but now & again gets depressed. So do they all & our dinners are occasionally like funeral feasts."

The Russian Reply

During the nine days between the completion of the Allied memorandum of 2 May and the Russian reply, there was considerable activity and dissension in the Hotel Imperiale. Joffe's mysterious departure intensified the divisions among the Russians. Chicherin, Krassin, and Vorovsky all allegedly supported a compromise with the West. Aware of Lloyd George's waning power, they believed that were this moment to pass, none other might come. No other Western leader had the authority, energy, and motivation to attempt another Genoa. Vorovsky, the Soviet representative in Italy, was also conscious of Rome's quest for an agreement. The hard-liners, Preobrazhensky in Genoa, Radek in Berlin, and Joffe en route to Moscow, opposed the Allied memorandum, feared its costs, and urged rejection. Litvinov and Rakovsky apparently occupied the middle ground. Litvinov, with his impeccable orthodox credentials, sought to prevent a rupture, and Rakovsky feared to break off contacts with the West.[17]

The form and content of the Allied memorandum did not ease the task of the Soviet moderates. There was no way of masking the fact that Lloyd George's pockets were empty and that the Allies' terms amounted to a form of capitulation, much like Brest-Litovsk. But four years later, Russia had changed. Moscow needed security and credits, and Genoa promised neither. Lloyd George's peace pact guaranteed no easing of pressure on Russia's borders. Without a stabilization of the international status quo, the Red Army, which consumed one-fourth of the budget and possessed a considerable influence in internal affairs, could not be reduced.[18] Even to gain the vague promise of eventual recognition and credits, Soviet Russia had to make pledges that renounced the basis of its revolution.

Russia urgently needed financial aid from the West. Observers in the spring of 1922 noted that while the urban centers were humming and a good harvest was expected, there were enormous industrial problems: factories, plagued by poor transport, bureaucratic inefficiency, and low productivity, were operating at a reduced capacity of 20 to 30 percent. Short of raw materials and machine tools, some were months behind in paying wages and were even laying off their workers. The government was willing to grant favorable terms to foreigners. But thus far Europe had given Russia no substantial credits and sold goods only for cash, which depleted the dwindling gold supply that had largely been plundered from the Russian Orthodox church and the Rumanian treasury.[19]

17. Wise to Grigg, Genoa, 12 May, Grigg Papers, roll 10; IGPS Boll. nos. 15, 18, 21, and 21A, for 1, 5, 8, 9 May, IMAE 52/31; S.I.S. report, Russia, Apr.–Aug., GB FO 371 N10682/246/38.

18. V. I. Lenin, *Collected Works* (Moscow: Progress Publishers, 1965–71), 33:139; 34:536–37.

19. Bloomfield confidential report, 6 July, Harding Papers, roll 181.

Lenin was busy preparing for the impending meeting of the All-Russian Central Executive Committee of Soviets (CEC), a state governing body just below the increasingly more powerful Council of People's Commissars. The CEC, consisting of some three hundred delegates—largely officials, many of whom were not Bolsheviks, workers, or peasants—was scheduled to meet in the Imperial Palace of the Kremlin from 12 to 21 May. The main work at hand was the drawing up of the new civil and criminal codes. The former was showpiece legislation for the West; it consisted of property, contract, and arbitration law designed to lure capitalists back to Russia. The latter was a weapon against the remaining Menshevik and Social Revolutionary opposition.[20]

Lenin worked tirelessly on these two pieces of legislation but also de lt with other problems: the oppressive dualism between the Communist party and the Soviet government, his months-long battle with bureaucratic inefficiency, his defense of the foreign trade monopoly, and his struggle with Russia's raging inflation. At the same time, he was also promoting the visit of a young American businessman, Armand Hammer, in whom he placed exaggerated hopes for an opening with the United States. Still ailing, Lenin relied heavily on the party apparatus and the Stalin-dominated Politburo to transmit his wishes to Genoa.[21]

Moscow received meager, sometimes confusing and contradictory communications from the Soviet delegation. After the surprise of the Rapallo treaty Lenin attempted to hold the delegation on a tight leash, since he needed to prepare an authoritative report on Genoa for the CEC. Lenin disapproved of Chicherin's note of 21 April and insisted there could be no concessions on the return of nationalized property without a "very advantageous and immediate loan."[22] He rejected a full recognition of debts and warned Chicherin not to fear a rupture. His letter of 2 May, demanding the return of three delegates to help in the preparation of his report for the CEC, probably precipitated Joffe's departure.[23]

Once he learned of the text of the Allies' memorandum of 2 May, Lenin ordered an immediate break ("a better opportunity will not be found"). He also recommended a "highly circumspect flirtation with Italy separately" to assuage Rome's disappointment and make capital of the Rapallo treaty. Yet Lenin was not inflexible. When Litvinov asked for instructions and described in detail the delegation's efforts to prolong the negotiations with the West, Lenin consented to continuing because the eventual breakup was "pre-determined."

20. V. I. Lenin, *Selected Works, 1922* (Moscow: Progress Publishers, 1967), pp. 358–59, 560–63; Krassin to Child, London, 7 June, Hughes Papers.

21. Lenin, *Collected Works*, 45:530–34, 537, 539–41, 549, 740–41; numerous complaints about Soviet officialdom in ibid., pp. 423, 432–33, 436, 440, 442, 444–46, 450, 454, 464, 466, 467–68, 470–73, 478, 480–81, 482, 489–90, 493–94, 496–99, 500, 503–4, 521–22.

22. Ibid., p. 537; intercepted by Italian secret service, IGPS report, 8 May, IMAE 52/31.

23. Lenin, *Collected Works*, 45:537–38.

He left it up to the delegation's discretion to find the most "suitable" moment for the break.[24]

Chicherin and Krassin rejected the credit package offered by members of Lloyd George's entourage, which consisted of an illusory combination of private investments backed by government guarantees. They insisted on the following two principles: that credits from the West be based on an agreement between both sides and that Russia receive a specified sum (1 million pounds credit during the next three years) or be granted a seven-year moratorium on the repayment of its old debts. Reciprocity and equality formed the basis of Chicherin's negotiations. The Russians were willing to recognize their prewar obligations and, under certain conditions, restore or compensate former owners; but they were unwilling to capitulate to the West on essential principles or financial needs.[25] The Soviets' bargaining position had slightly improved since Rapallo. The subsequent negotiations with Italy, Czechoslovakia, Yugoslavia, and also with representatives of the Vatican created an aura of independence, and the threatened split in the Entente increased Russia's room for maneuver.[26] Yet in the end, Chicherin gained little. The memorandum of 2 May held out Moscow's sole prospect of any substantive improvement in its domestic situation and also in its relations with the rest of the world.

On the advice of the Germans, Litvinov and Chicherin called on Lloyd George on 8 May, where they received definitive information: there would be no Allied loan to Russia.[27] Early the next morning, instructions arrived from Moscow that unless the delegation could secure "exceptional advantages," there must be a break.[28] The telegram angered Chicherin and provoked an animated discussion with Litvinov.

The long-delayed Russian response, written with the help of the Germans and with revisions suggested by Schanzer and possibly also by Lloyd George,[29] was completed on 11 May. It was a tour de force whose purpose was

24. Ibid., 45:530; Italian intercept, IGPS Boll. no. 21, 9 May, IMAE 52/31; Litvinov tel., 6 May, in S.I.S. report, Russia, Apr.–Aug., GB FO 371 N10682/246/38, summarized in Lenin, *Collected Works*, 45:738; Lenin to Litvinov, 8 May, in Lenin, *Collected Works*, 45:740.

25. S.I.S. report, Russia Apr.–Aug., GB FO 371 N10682/246/38; Georgii Chicherin, "Soviet Diplomacy since the War," *The Living Age* (22 March 1924): 547–51; E. M. Chossudovsky, *Chicherin and the Evolution of Soviet Foreign Policy and Diplomacy* (Geneva: Graduate Institute of International Studies, 1973), pp. 15–16.

26. IGPS Boll. nos. 11, 13–16, and 19, for 26, 28, 29 Apr., 1, 3, 7 May, IMAE 52/31; N. N. Lyubimov and A. N. Erlikh, "The 1922 Genoa Conference," *International Affairs* (Moscow) (June, Aug., Sept., Oct. 1963): 72; Barthou to MAE, Genoa, 9 May, #444–45, FMAE B 111; Anthony Rhodes, *The Vatican in the Age of Dictators* (London: Hodder and Stoughton, 1973), p. 133. The cordial though fruitless Chicherin-Ninčić talks in Fischer Papers.

27. Litvinov to People's Commissariat for Foreign Affairs, Genoa, 8 May, *DVP SSSR*, 5:360.

28. IGPS Boll. no. 22, 10 May, IMAE 52/31; original text in Lenin, *Collected Works*, 45:541–42.

29. IGPS Boll. nos. 16, 21, 21A, and 22, for 3, 8–10 May, IMAE 52/31; Rathenau diary, 10 May, Germ. AA T-120 3398/1735/D739181; text in Germ. Pol. Arch. AA, DDG, bd. 19.

to thwart a general agreement based on the Allied memorandum but keep channels open for exceptional offers.[30] It consisted of two parts. The first and longest, a brilliant piece of propaganda probably written by Chicherin, attacked the Allies' memorandum of 2 May for violating the Villa d'Albertis discussions, the London Report, and the Cannes Resolutions. The Russians criticized the entire procedure of the Genoa Conference, especially the Allied experts' refusal to discuss the "whole series of plans and proposals" the Russians had brought to Genoa; they had concentrated instead almost exclusively on Russia's obligations.

The Russian statement recalled that "more than one of the S: es represented at Genoa have repudiated debts and confiscated the property of foreigners," and it accused "certain powers" of attempting to deny Russia political and economic equality, thus resulting in injury both for Russia and Europe. In a point aimed at stirring Western public opinion, the Russians insisted that "the problems of the future which interest everyone have been subordinated to the interests of the past, which affect only certain groups of foreigners." Evenhandedly, their response also mentioned the recent oil scandals and the efforts of those who wished, contrary to the Cannes Resolutions, to impose a political and social system on Russia. It maintained that Russia was neither isolated nor desperate and would not accept the principle of one-sided sacrifice.

The Russian reply cut the heart out of the Allies' preamble, which had provided no concrete plan or credits for Russia's restoration. It noted that while there was only vagueness in the passages dealing with help, there was nothing but precision in the text on obligations. The statement also took issue with the political material that had been introduced, rejecting the clauses about propaganda, Rumania, and Asia Minor. It argued against the principle of forcing the Soviet government to assume czarist debts, citing the precedents of revolutionary America and France, and the Allies who had seized enemy property without compensation during and after World War I. Insisting that Russia was not legally responsible for debts, restitution of nationalized property, or damage caused to the Allies' property during the civil war, the Russians again raised their own counterclaims. By withdrawing from the agreement of 15 April, the Allies had given Russia freedom to renege on Chicherin's note of 21 April.

There was a brilliant attack, no doubt aided by the Germans, against the property clause, which made the sovereignty of the Russian state "the plaything of chance." The Russians warned that the capitalists returning to Russia without a "friendly agreement . . . would soon feel a general hostility toward themselves." The note chided France for "subordinating the interests of small

30. Litvinov to People's Commissariat for Foreign Affairs, Genoa, 10 May, *DVP SSSR*, 5:360; IGPS Boll. no. 23, 12 May, IMAE 52/31. Text in Jane Degras, ed., *Soviet Documents on Foreign Policy* (London and New York: Oxford University Press, 1951), pp. 308–18, and *FRUS, 1922*, 2:792–803.

holders of Russian bonds to those of certain groups who demand the restitution of property." The Russians offered former owners only "a preferential right" to future concessions.

Suddenly, the last two paragraphs contained the germ of conciliation. The Russians endorsed Lloyd George's proposal (which had originated with various individuals, including Child, Skirmunt, Karnebeek, and Beneš) to appoint "mixed commissions of experts" to conduct a "deeper study" of two matters: the claims presented to Russia and the credits Russia needed. The British noticed that in these final paragraphs Moscow had dropped its counterclaims against the Allies as well as the question of war debts.

Closing with a propagandistic flourish, the Russians once more insisted on reciprocity. At Genoa there had been an opening for rapprochement between Moscow and the West, and it could lead to reconstruction and peace. It was an amazing document—"wooly and argumentative," fumed Hankey[31]—that was open to a myriad of interpretations. The Russians had dared not accept the Allies' terms because of orders from Moscow, but they dared not break off completely. They had therefore penned a document that was "useful in their country and dangerous in others."[32] Whatever happened, the Russian delegation had succeeded in satisfying doctrinaire hard-liners but also, by leaving the door open to further negotiations, in pacifying the proponents of detente with the West. However, in so doing, they had demolished the spirit of the Genoa Conference. The meeting of world statesmen would be superseded by a convocation of experts, who were to deliberate over the two problems that separated the two worlds—the past and the future.

On to The Hague

The fiery propaganda in the Russian memorandum of 11 May cheered Poincaré, depressed Schanzer, and stirred the British to action.[33] The *Wall Street Journal* announced that the memorandum "would form the basis of discussion" and Schanzer so assured the Genoa press. However conciliatory its conclusion, and whoever its authors, it required a firm, collective response. Most important, Lloyd George and Schanzer had to patch up a plausible end to the Genoa Conference: to avoid a rupture, prevent the conclusion of more separate agreements, and avoid the blame for the failure.[34]

31. Hankey to Chamberlain, Genoa, 11 May, GB FO 371 N4775/646/38.
32. Lloyd-Greame to Baldwin, Genoa, 14 May, LGrP.
33. Hankey to Chamberlain, Genoa, 13 May, HP.
34. Barthou to MAE, Genoa, 7 May, FMAE PM G/VI; Litvinov tel., Genoa, 10 May, *DVP*

Even Lloyd-Greame, one of Lloyd George's severest critics, supported the salvaging mission: "I feel strongly in favor of going on. . . . . If we keep contact we keep the peace, and this means a great deal because there is no doubt that a complete break will not now leave the position the same as before, but would leave it definitely worse. . . . A break now would leave all the border states nervous, anxious, and unable to settle down. They will go on inflating. They will fail to produce exportable surpluses."[35]

The British needed to demonstrate to their own fellow citizens some result of five weeks' labor. Though anxious to hurry home, Lloyd George required "something substantial," for his position in the cabinet and in the country depended on visible success.[36] Schanzer was in a similar position. Should the Genoa Conference fail to produce a collective agreement, he would have to face Chicherin by himself, to resume the negotiations to renew the Russo-Italian trade treaty that was about to expire in June.[37] The shadow of Rapallo would affect any future dealings with Moscow unless the West could devise some holding action. It was not enough to blame France.

Poincaré held Barthou on a tight leash. He badgered him to protest the long delay in the Russian reply, sent detailed instructions, and stressed the need to avoid making any further dangerous commitments. Barthou nevertheless worked conscientiously in a vain attempt to work out a property formula that would be acceptable to Belgium. He also reestablished ties with the Little Entente, Japan, and the neutrals.[38] Poincaré received reassuring news from London: although Labour continued to attack France, the British public was alarmed that its government might wreck the Entente for the benefit of Russia or Germany. The king, who was then visiting Belgium, was reportedly critical of Lloyd George's policies at Genoa. With the pro-French Arthur James Balfour replacing the ailing Curzon at the Foreign Office, Poincaré chose this time to reintroduce the issue of the Anglo-French pact.[39]

Yet despite Poincaré's desire to capitalize on Lloyd George's apparent set-

SSSR, 5:360; Rathenau diary, 11 May, Germ. AA T-120 3398 / 1735 / D739182; IGPS Boll. no. 23, 12 May, IMAE 52/31; Kessler, *Tagebücher*, pp. 314–18.

35. Lloyd-Greame to Baldwin, Genoa, 14 May, LGrP.

36. US MID Weekly Summary, 13 May; Lloyd George, *My Darling Pussy*, pp. 51, 52.

37. Charles-Roux to Poincaré, Rome, 9 May, FMAE Z GB 49; Barthou to MAE, Genoa, 12 May, #479, FMAE B 111, 12 May, FMAE Z It. 121; Charles-Roux to MAE, Rome, 13 May, FMAE Z It. 121, and 16 May, FMAE PM G/VIII; van den Steen to MAE, Rome, 17, 18 May, BMAE 10991.

38. Poincaré to Delegation, Paris, 6 May, #327–28, FMAE Y 32, 7 May (2 tels.), FMAE PM G/VI, 9 May, #380–82, FMAE B 111, 10 May, FMAE PM G/VIII, 11 May, #407, #414, FMAE B 97; Barthou to Poincaré, 9 May, #431–32, FMAE B 111.

39. Margerie to MAE, Brussels, 10 May, FMAE Z GB 49; Poincaré to Saint-Aulaire, Paris, 11 May, and to Barthou, 11 May, FMAE PM G/VIII.

backs, there was a deeper reality across the Channel: Britain largely favored Lloyd George's Genoa policy. In a *Times* article on 14 May, even Leslie Urquart, head of the Association of British Creditors in Russia, defended the principle of long-term leases over the Franco-Belgian demand for full restitution of nationalized properties. Britain, a nation of salaried workers, leaseholders, and freeholders, had recognized Rumania's and Czechoslovakia's expropriations and had written paragraph 1 of the Cannes Resolutions; it thus did not share France's scruples on the "sanctity of property."[40] This was illustrated by the oil conflict, where Britain was investigating ways of capitalizing on the new situation in Soviet Russia, even at the expense of former owners. Lloyd-Greame, though a solid Conservative, was very evasive on this point in his talks with Eynac; he avoided any commitment to joint Franco-British action in Russia on the model of the San Remo agreement for the Near and Middle East.[41]

As Poincaré later admitted to parliament, France could have used the Russian reply as a pretext for leaving Genoa and "slamming the door," but no doubt it would have walked out alone. Among the delegates there was a generalized sympathy for and lingering fear of Lloyd George, whose crusade for European peace and disarmament had won many supporters throughout Europe.[42] On the eve of a potential reparations crisis with Germany, France could not afford the luxury of isolation. Its allies, Czechoslovakia, Rumania, Yugoslavia, and Poland, were reluctant to antagonize Soviet Russia; and the neutrals, concerned about their public opinion, wanted to continue to the end.

The solution came from an unexpected quarter. On 6 May, accompanied by his wife and daughter, Lloyd George had lunched with Child at the Cafe Righi overlooking the city of Genoa. Their hopes for a private tête-à-tête were spoiled when Barthou arrived to host a luncheon for British and American journalists. Child tried to cheer the despondent Briton with a suggestion: should Genoa break up, he suggested that the Allies consult and appoint a commission of their experts to investigate Russia's economic and financial needs and also to determine whether foreign interests could safely reenter Russia. While this investigation took place, they must pledge no separate agreements with Moscow. Child hinted strongly that American participation would be conditional on the last stipulation.[43]

40. Saint-Aulaire to Poincaré, London, 16 May (2 letters), FMAE B 98 and Z GB 49.

41. Note of interview, Genoa, 13 May, GB FO 371 N4969/50/38; Barthou [Eynac] to MAE, Genoa, 14 May, #502–5, FMAE B 111.

42. Édouard Bonnefous, *Histoire politique de la Troisième République*, 2d ed. (Paris: Presses Universitaires de France, 1968), 3:307; also Poincaré to Delegation, Paris, 11 May, #414, FMAE B 97; Kessler, *Tagebücher*, 14 May, p. 316; and Lloyd George, *My Darling Pussy*, p. 51.

43. Child, *Diplomat*, pp. 45–46; Child to State Dept., Genoa, 7 May, USDS 550 E1/250; *DBFP*, 19:776–77.

Hughes approved Child's initiative as a "safe, practical course of action" but warned against committing the United States in advance, adding that there was "no change" in American policy toward Russia.[44] Hughes had never taken the oil rumors seriously. There was nonetheless the danger that should the protracted Genoa Conference end suddenly, there would be a scramble for concessions by the Western governments. A Czechoslovak or an Italian agreement with Moscow would be innocuous; but if the credit-hungry Russians offered Britain something substantial, America's interests might be injured. Child, who had delayed meeting with Krassin until the Russians answered the Allies, wrote the night the negative Soviet answer was published, "I am now reasonably certain Lloyd George will try a way out along the lines I suggest."[45]

A day before the Russian reply was actually received, Lloyd George unveiled to the British delegation a confidential memorandum drafted by Hurst. Though cloaked in the form of an "international" action, his plan to send investigatory commissions to Russia was designed to ease the way of British capitalists.[46] On 11 May he showed Schanzer a more detailed proposal: the Genoa Conference would appoint three separate commissions to investigate the questions of credits, debts, and private property, and would report back to the powers. Meanwhile, there would be a provisional peace pact on Russia's borders and pledges from both sides to refrain from hostile propaganda. Schanzer suggested two important modifications. Lloyd George accepted Italy's right to conclude a separate agreement with Moscow, even while the international investigations were proceeding. Also, given Chicherin's likely refusal to admit commissions into Russia, they decided to convene these in a neutral capital and to have Russian representation.[47]

When Barthou joined them that evening, Lloyd George bombarded him with threats. He raised the Soviet menace to Poland, Rumania, and "perhaps Czechoslovakia." He reminded Barthou of the domestic repercussions of a deadlock; they would be reproached with the fact that "for five weeks the Powers have been engaged not in discussing the business before them, but in protecting the owners of property and the bondholders." Lacking instructions from Paris, Barthou could not dispute or present counterproposals. He was maneuvered into suggesting that Lloyd George draft the reply to the Russian note of 11 May.[48] Britain quickly assembled representatives from the key neu-

44. Hughes to Child, Washington, 11 May, USDS 550 E1/263, 350; also unsigned memorandum, 10 May, Millspaugh to Poole, Harrison, and Phillips, 10 May, and Phillips memorandum, Washington, 11 May, USDS 550 E1/247, 250, 328.
45. Child, *Diplomat*, p. 48.
46. *DBFP*, 19:792–96.
47. Ibid., pp. 846–50.
48. Ibid., pp. 851–53; Barthou to Poincaré, Genoa, 12 May, #471–73, FMAE B 111.

tral and East European countries and won their consent to the commission plan. Child seemed agreeable, and Chicherin gave his guarded assent.[49]

There were significant details still to be worked out before Genoa could reach a dignified closing. Where would the commissions meet? How would they be composed? Could the French and Belgians be induced to meet once more with the Russians and would the Germans agree to be excluded? What about the knotty problem of separate agreements, raised by Italy, Sweden and others, which was at the heart of Soviet aims and the basis of American resistance? How would a mutual renunciation of hostile propaganda be enforced? Finally, and most controversial, how would the again-revived nonaggression pact apply during this interim period, and where?

Lloyd George proceeded to settle everything hurriedly with an improvisatory plan. On 13 May he put three tidy proposals to the political subcommission, which was called officially to respond to the Russian reply. He recommended a clear and vigorous rebuttal to the Soviets' propagandistic attacks on the West; but he also pleaded for the three commissions, a prompt meeting in a neutral capital, a universal pledge against propaganda, and a nonaggression pact based on the de facto boundaries of Eastern Europe.[50]

Barthou, ordered by Paris not to sign any more memoranda, continue any talks with the Russians, or do anything to prolong the Genoa Conference, rejected the British proposals as an attempt to "recommence under much worse conditions." At Genoa they had a solid base, the Cannes Resolutions; tomorrow this would be gone, and the Russians, having "rejected everything," would create another sorry spectacle in which France could not participate. However, faced with the overwhelming sentiment of the subcommission to approve Lloyd George's improvisation, Barthou agreed to meet privately with the British premier and work out a compromise.[51]

With a series of crafty offers, Lloyd George overrode Barthou's reservations. He endorsed Brătianu's suggestion that the Russian experts participate in the commissions only upon invitation. He conceded that France did not have to sign anything further but merely indicate its approval of the projected talks. Finally, he posed as spokesman for the United States, reviewing its conditions for participation but inventing one: that the Soviets be part of the negotiations. Barthou allowed himself to be persuaded.[52]

49. *DBFP*, 19:868–70; Hankey to Chamberlain, Genoa, 11 May, HP.

50. *DBFP*, 19:871–82; Hankey to Chamberlain, Genoa, 13 May, HP.

51. *DBFP*, 19:876–78, 882–85; Barthou to MAE, Genoa, 13 May, #493, and Colrat to MAE, Genoa, 13 May, FMAE B 98.

52. Seydoux note, "Négociations avec les russes depuis 2 Mai," Genoa, 16 May, FMAE B 98; Colrat to MAE, Genoa, 13 May, ibid.; *DBFP*, 19:883; Hankey to Chamberlain, Genoa, 13 May, HP; Lloyd George, *My Darling Pussy*, p. 52: "Very hard day—but a very good day. Beat French hip & thigh."

That afternoon the political subcommission worked more harmoniously. There still was considerable interest in resuming commercial ties with Russia or at least in not slamming the door at Genoa.[53] Despite America's cautions, Belgium's suspicion of despoilment, and France's hesitations, there was a general conviction among the small countries of the necessity to exploit Chicherin's presence and Lloyd George's energies to keep the negotiations going. Whether the spirit of conciliation would survive Genoa was, of course, unknown.

On the last Sunday of the Genoa Conference, 14 May, four weeks after the Rapallo treaty, the inviting powers assembled at the Villa d'Albertis to formulate a conclusion.[54] Barthou had a surprise: ordered by Paris to retain his "freedom of action," he withdrew from the agreement of the day before. He recommended that Genoa end with the simple proposal to the various governments represented there that the commissions would be convened at some future date, setting neither a time nor a place. No one would be obligated to attend, especially the United States, which France was now actively wooing.[55]

Startled and angry, Lloyd George termed the proposed procedure a "farce" and disputed whether it would appeal to America. Claiming that Child had promised him an official reply to his commissions proposal within twenty-four hours, he disingenuously insisted that the Americans expected a specific plan.[56] Trapped and again isolated Barthou gave way, accepting Lloyd George's assurances that France could at any time withdraw from the commissions before or even during the talks with the Russians.[57] That roadblock removed, the inviting powers worked all day. They decided that the expert commissions would be convened on 15 June at The Hague, and the Russians would be invited to participate eleven days later. They drew up the official communication to the Russian delegation. However, Belgium, which had not signed, and France, which had withdrawn from the memorandum of 2 May, would not officially endorse this new document.[58]

On the same day, 14 May, Chicherin made a formal protest against the Allies' procedures. His letter to Facta, leaked in the press, censured the rumored pledges against making separate agreements with Moscow. In private the Russians were still trying to be conciliatory. Nevertheless, this piece of

---

53. *DBFP*, 19:885–95; Barthou to Poincaré, Genoa, 13 May, #487–92, FMAE B 98.
54. *DBFP*, 19:895–902.
55. Poincaré to Barthou, Paris, 12 May, #420–21, #422, #423, FMAE B 97, 13 May, FMAE PM G/VIII, 13 May, #433, #443, FMAE B 98; Barthou's statement in *DBFP*, 19:896–97; contacts with Child: Barrère to MAE, Genoa, 14 May, #500, FMAE B 98, and Child, *Diplomat*, p. 49.
56. *DBFP*, 19:898; cf. Child to Hughes, Genoa, 14 May, *FRUS, 1922*, 2:804.
57. Barthou to MAE, Genoa, 15 May, #503–11, FMAE B 98.
58. *DBFP*, 19:902–16; Gregory to FO, Genoa, 14 May, GB FO 371 N4675/646/38.

bombast made Barthou's retreat (which Poincaré eventually approved) all the more painful.[59]

France won a few victories. Paris had chosen the Hague location over the other possibilities, Copenhagen or Stockholm. It had prevented mixed commissions that included the Russians from the outset. It had determined that each government and not the Genoa Conference would appoint the experts that would go to The Hague. Because of the Rapallo treaty, Germany would be excluded. There would be no restrictions in the nonaggression pact on possible punitive actions against the Reich. As to Russia, Barthou felt certain that he had made no commitments on the recognition question by agreeing to Lloyd George's scenario for the closing of the Genoa Conference. France's sole concession was its agreement that the nonaggression pact would not be limited to Russia's immediate borders but would apply to the general tenor of relations between Russia and the rest of the world.[60]

The political subcommission, without France, Belgium, or Germany, finally met with the Russians on 17 May. Chicherin was in top form, asking for a full reading of the Allies' proposals, challenging German and not Polish exclusion from the Hague Conference, rebuking the Allies for their high-handed decision making, and questioning details about the projected Hague meeting and the nonaggression pact. At his request there was a twenty-four-hour adjournment, after which he attacked the pact, provoked Poland, Rumania, and Japan, and accused the West of plotting aggression against the Soviet state.[61]

Lloyd George had indulged the Russians enough; now he raised his own accusations. Admitting they had failed to reconcile their divergent points of view, he blamed the deadlock on the "events of 1 May," the demonstrations in Russia that had reinforced the Bolsheviks' intransigency. The Hague meeting would give them a fresh opportunity to discuss matters and come to "practical" conclusions. In the meantime, he pleaded for his pact with force and wit:

> There was Chicherin describing Russia: innocent, harmless, patient, tolerant, attacking nobody, giving no offense or trouble to any country in the world, only seeking to lead a quiet life, in fact a model of all the Christian virtues. On the other hand, there [were] M. Brătianu and M. Skirmunt describing their countries. They [too] only wanted to lead a quiet life. . . . After sixteen years in office—and he had been minister longer, he thought, than anyone else present—he had come to the con-

59. Chicherin to Schanzer, Genoa, 14 May, *DBFP*, 19:923–24; IGPS Boll. no. 23, 12 May, IMAE 52/31; and Lenin to Chicherin, in Lenin, *Collected Works*, 45:547; Poincaré to Barthou, Paris, 15 May, #451, #452, #453, FMAE B 98.

60. Barthou to MAE, Genoa, 15, 16 May, #503–11, #521–23, FMAE B 98.

61. *DBFP*, 19:925–35, 954–57; Hankey to Chamberlain, Genoa, 16 May, GB FO 371 N5332/646/38; Barthou to Poincaré, Genoa, 16 May, #525–28, FMAE B 98.

clusion that it was more than one could do to mind one's business. . . .
To attack or to attempt to reform other countries, or to organize missionary expeditions whether under the command of Wrangel or anyone else
to convert the heathens in Russia, or for M. Chicherin or M. Litvinov to
organize a band of missionaries to convert the cannibals of Western Europe would result in a great deal of trouble. They each had as much trouble in their countries as they could manage, and if they looked after their
own countries and left other countries to look after their affairs, they
would get on much better. If they would help one another in the direction where it was possible, it would be to their mutual advantage. That is
what he meant by a pact of non-aggression, and he hoped that after they
had signed it they would abide by it faithfully.[62]

Chicherin, who intended to exploit the pact proposal both to strengthen the
Soviet regime and challenge the status quo, was not intimidated by Lloyd
George's rhetoric. With Britain's complicity and over Japan's objections, he
succeeded in extending the pact to Asia and limiting its duration to four months
after the closing of the Hague meeting, at which time everyone would regain
his freedom of action. Finally, by disputing interminably the Hague location,
Chicherin obtained a pledge from the subcommission that the Dutch, who had
resolutely refused all official contact with the Soviet government, would extend all the customary guarantees and privileges to the Russians. With so few
cards to play, Chicherin had nevertheless won some points.[63]

Lloyd George prematurely claimed a victory in his "fight for peace," and
Genoa seemed assured a decent burial.[64] However, America spoiled his
strategy by refusing to attend the Hague meeting. Deeming it "a continuance
under different nomenclature of the Genoa Conference and destined to encounter the same difficulties," Hughes again said no. He objected, above all, to the
Russians' presence. This would emphasize political rather than "scientific"
questions. Assured that France and Belgium would automatically stymie any
major separate agreements, Washington could now withdraw, even at the cost
of undercutting Child's initiative, frustrating the British, and casting off
France's overtures for joint action.[65] Lloyd George continued to hope that in a
month Washington would change its mind.

62. *DBFP*, 19:963; Gregory to FO, Genoa, 17 May, GB FO 371 N4797/646/38.
63. Lenin to Chicherin, Moscow, 14 May, in Lenin, *Collected Works*, 45:547; Gregory to FO,
Genoa, 17 May, GB FO 371 N4792, N4817/646/38; Barthou to MAE, Genoa, 17 May,
#539–44, FMAE B 99.
64. Lloyd George, *My Darling Pussy*, p. 52.
65. Hughes to Child, Washington, 15, 17 May, *FRUS, 1922*, 2:807–8, 811–12; Child to
Schanzer, Genoa, 15 May, IMAE 52/4 (USA); Child, *Diplomat*, pp. 49–52; Hankey to

There was unfinished business relating to Eastern and Central Europe. Lloyd George had once hoped, on the basis of paragraphs 5 and 6 of the Cannes Resolutions, to allow Genoa's Political Commission to discuss specific problems such as the borders of Lithuania, the status of Vilna, Eastern Galicia, and Bessarabia, and the minority problems raised by Hungary and Bulgaria. Barthou had strongly resisted any widening of Genoa's agenda, thereby giving an audience to revisionist propaganda and reducing the prerogatives of the Supreme Council or the League.[66] When Russia replied on 11 May and an improvised truce was established, there was no longer any urgency to discuss complicated political and territorial questions. Genoa handed some complaints over to the League and the rest to the Allies, leaving still-gaping holes in the East. Though certain grievances had been aired, the governments that were the targets of these complaints were only made uneasy, and nothing was settled. Russia was temporarily too weak to remake its borders, and the Allies were too divided to formulate positions on Eastern Europe.[67]

In return for their considerable services, the Italians had hoped that Lloyd George would lend his support to them against Yugoslavia, but they were to be disappointed. The harried British leader turned the Fiume problem over to a junior representative of the Foreign Office, who knew little about the Adriatic. Lloyd George himself met briefly with Italian and Yugoslav leaders but could not break the stalemate. Schanzer failed to convince Ninčić to agree to a special economic regime for the Italian enclave in Zara or for special rights of the Italian minority in Yugoslavia. Italy, which itself had failed to carry out the provisions of its Rapallo treaty, was left frustrated and disappointed.[68]

Chamberlain, Genoa, 16 May, GB FO 371 N5332/646/38; memorandum of conversation (Lloyd George, Schanzer, Child), 18 May, GB CAB 29/92; Jusserand to Poincaré, n.d. [14–15 May], #568–72, n.d., no # [received 16 May], n.d. [received 16 May], #577–78, #579–81, FMAE B 98.

66. *DBFP*, 19:678–80, 744–47, 798–812, 937–42.

67. Ibid., pp. 938–39, 941–42, 806–8, 838–40, 938, 939–40. East European reactions in: Mariner to State Dept., Bucharest, 3, 23 June, USDS 550 E1/342, 350; Dering to Balfour, Bucharest, 12, 21 June, GB FO 371 C8738, C9019/458/62; Dodge to State Dept., Belgrade, 18 May, USDS 550 E1/335; Strang to Curzon, Belgrade, 18 May, Gregory to FO, Genoa, 21 May, GB FO 371 C7477, C7443/458/62; Hoffinger to BMA, Belgrade, 24 May, A HHSt 687; Clerk and Gregory memoranda, Prague, 19 July and London, 27 Oct., GB FO 371 N9694/646/38; Hoare to Curzon, Warsaw, 18 May, GB FO 371 N4926/1876/55; Hoare to Balfour, Warsaw, 1 June, GB FO 371 N5454/5233/55; Panafieu to MAE, Warsaw, 25 May, FMAE B 99; Picot to MAE, Sofia, 6 May, #64, FMAE Y 32; Erskine to Balfour, Sofia, 28 May, GB FO 371 C8136/769/7.

68. J. D. Gregory, *On the Edge of Diplomacy* (London: Hutchinson, 1928), pp. 209–11; *DBFP*, 19:728–29, 787–89; Dodge to State Dept., Belgrade, 1 May, Dominion to Hughes, Genoa, 19 May, USDS 550 E1/288, 320; Child to Schanzer, 11 May, IMAE 52/26 (Rapallo); Pagliano to Schanzer, Rome, 11 May, ibid.

On the eve of Genoa's close, Lloyd George met one final time with Wirth and Rathenau at the Villa d'Albertis to acknowledge Germany's mediation efforts. In an awkward conversation, Lloyd George conveyed a mixed message to the Reich leaders: while he assured them that their fulfillment policy had saved the Reich from being broken up and encouraged more of the same, the British prime minister held out little hope for the future. He now doubted that Berlin would obtain a substantial American loan or that France could be restrained from a coup de main in the Ruhr; he nevertheless recommended "patience" and not "defiance," for presumably a ruined and passive Reich would ultimately obtain support from the West. He was still impatient with Rathenau's complaints about the various Allied commissions and the Conference of Ambassadors and disappointed with Wirth's evasive attitude toward Germany's joining the League.[69] Awaiting the end of his labors at Genoa—which German actions had made more difficult—Lloyd George squelched Wirth's threat to make trouble at the final plenary and rushed the Germans out after a seventy-five-minute interview in order to make a final abortive effort to settle Fiume.[70]

Finis Genua

> Behold all the delegates in the same places they occupied on the first day. Everyone whispers that this session will be short. Perfunctory speeches, thanking Italy as host and manager of the Conference. Eternal chatter from the Italian spectators, so that no one can hear what is being said. Interpreters putting more zest into the repetition than appeared in the original discourse. Chatter, chatter, chatter. A conference which failed![71]

At 9 A.M. on Friday, 19 May, the Genoa Conference reassembled for its third and last plenary session in the Palazzo San Giorgio. Bags were packed. The delegates were anxious to return home to their legislative and political duties, to their families and loved ones. With little respite, Lloyd George had worked diligently, sometimes ruthlessly, for forty-two days. He had failed at Genoa. In the cynical commentary of the *Nieuwe Rotterdamsche Courant* on 4 June, he was compared to a ruined gambler whom the saloon had lent money for his return home. He had obtained a first-class fare: the Hague Conference.

69. *DBFP*, 19:990–98; Wirth to Ebert, Genoa, 19 May, Germ. AA T-120 3398/1735/ D739406–8 (remarking on Lloyd George's "obvious fatigue"); Wigram to Grigg, Genoa, 16 May, Grigg Papers, roll 10.
70. *DBFP*, 19:1001–4.
71. Diary, 19 May, in Child, *Diplomat*, p. 52.

What had caused Genoa's failure? Soviet intransigence, French nervousness, German perfidy, the machinations of certain East European leaders, and America's aloofness were all contributing elements, but Lloyd George's methods were the critical factor. Although few doubted the honesty of his struggle for peace, there was considerable criticism of the faulty design of the Genoa Conference. Its agenda was unrealistically large and its organization haphazard; time was squandered on posturing for political motives while insufficient preparation and attention were given to complex issues. Conference diplomacy, which he had championed over the more narrow Allied councils, showed its weakness at Genoa.[72]

Lloyd George himself bore some of the responsibility for Genoa's failure. Although he was a statesman with energy, insight, flexibility, verve, and persuasiveness over his colleagues and the public, he had nevertheless fallen prey to the overconfidence that had defeated Woodrow Wilson. In addition, like Wilson, Lloyd George was inordinately influenced by certain members of his palace guard, by their advice but also by their prejudices. Moreover, as brutally described in the once-sympathetic *Nieuwe Rotterdamsche Courant* on 4, 7, and 9 June, Lloyd George's ignorance of East European affairs was abysmal. He raised frantic alarms of war scares between the Black and Baltic seas, but he cast out Beneš for his more practical pact proposal, alternately wooed and frightened the Poles, made Rumania anxious, left Italy and Yugoslavia in a stalemate, and allowed the League to handle the unsettled border, minority, economic, and health problems of Eastern Europe. Finally, the Welsh wizard, who knew Britain could do little to restore peace in Europe without France's full cooperation, decided to exaggerate France's dependency and ignore Britain's.

Failure also loomed at home. On 16 May a government-sponsored bill imposing obligatory pension contributions on British school teachers had been narrowly defeated by three votes. Chamberlain gently needled his chief, hoping that the setback, though not too serious, would not add to his "difficulties at Genoa."[73] There was grumbling in London from the anti-Bolsheviks Curzon and Churchill and the francophiles Derby and Chamberlain.[74] On 16 May the cabinet expressed its "profound admiration of the courage and resource"

---

72. Jürgen Heideking, "Oberster Rat-Botschaftskonferenz-Völkerbund: Drei Formen multilateraler Diplomatie nach dem Ersten Weltkrieg," *Historische Zeitschrift* 231 (December 1980): 593–603.

73. Chamberlain to Lloyd George, London, 16 May, Grigg Papers, roll 10, 17 May, GB CAB 23/30; Lloyd George, *My Darling Pussy*, p. 53.

74. Curzon to Chamberlain, 13, 15 May, ACP 23/6/33; Derby to Churchill, 9, 13 May, WSCP; Churchill to Birkenhead, 6 May, ibid., and to Chamberlain, 13 May, ACP 23/6/38; Chamberlain to Curzon, 15 May, ACP 23/6/40.

Lloyd George had displayed at Genoa but also its "appreciation of the way in which, *working within the limits of the policy laid down by the Cabinet*, he has dominated the proceedings by his great personal gifts, raised the influence and authority of all our representatives and officials and enhanced the prestige of the British Empire among all the nations represented at the Conference."[75]

Lloyd George, who had attempted a great diplomatic effort to save the tottering coalition, had now given its enemies a weapon for attack. On 18 May the *Times* printed a letter by former Foreign Secretary Sir Edward Grey depicting Genoa as "an example of what should be avoided": alienating France and America for a foolhardy gamble on the Bolsheviks. Die-Hard Conservatives joined Wee Free Liberal critics in deploring the Genoa "fiasco."[76] Britain had grave economic problems, aging, uncompetitive industries, and high unemployment, and faced the resumption of violence in Ireland and a restive empire. It was a matter of time before Lloyd George's six years of coalition leadership would end. His supporters, the *Daily Chronicle* and the *Observer*, labeled his work heroic and indispensable; nevertheless, except for a stormy reparations conference that summer, this would be Lloyd George's last appearance at a major international gathering.

The final session of the Genoa Conference lasted four hours. First came the report of the Economic Commission, which gave Rathenau his only opportunity to speak, Chicherin the chance to taunt France and Switzerland, and Facta, in a repeat of the opening day, the role of disciplinarian. Schanzer then presented the recommendations of the Political Commission. Placing Genoa's meager achievement in a more favorable light than the French desired, Schanzer emphasized the importance of the Hague meeting and characterized the truncated peace pact as a first step to a general peace. "We are not . . . abandoning our task. . . . Our confidence in a final solution of the great problem remains unshaken. The torch of that confidence is not extinguished. Genoa will pass it on to The Hague."[77]

Even the modest pact temporarily preserving the status quo was challenged. The Lithuanian delegate once more complained about Vilna and Chicherin about Bessarabia, Baron Hayashi brought up the problem of Siberia, and Estonia, Finland, Latvia, and Poland reminded the gathering of their formal though delicate relations with Soviet Russia. Norway, Belgium, and France accepted

---

75. GB CAB 23/30, emphasis added.

76. Younger to Lloyd George, London, 19 May, LGP F 48/5/5; *New Statesman*, 20 May; Sthamer to AA, London, 18 May, Germ. AA T-120 3398/1735/D739403–5; Staatskommissar für öffentliche Ordnung, Berlin, 24 May, Germ. BA R 38/329; Saint-Aulaire to Poincaré, London, 20 May, FMAE Z GB 49.

77. *DBFP*, 19:1019–20; Barthou to MAE, 19 May, #551–53, FMAE B 99.

the commission's resolutions ad referendum. Finally, Chicherin made another nasty remark about the League, which no one refuted.[78]

Then came the speeches. A voluble Lloyd George intended to slap the Russians' hands. Despite their obvious need, they had trampled on the precious "prejudices" of the Western mind: to be paid for what one has sold, to be repaid for what one has lent, and to refuse to sell or lend to a party who had refused the first two conditions. He also held out hope, shrewdly and eloquently:

> I implore the Russian delegation, when they go to The Hague, not to trample upon those sentiments and principles that are deeply rooted in the very life of Europe. At Cannes, we threw out a lifeline. We have not drawn it in, as I thought we might; neither has it been snapped; neither has it been let go. It is still there, and we would like to draw all the distressed, all the hungry, all the suffering in the East of Europe back to life with all the help that the accumulated energy and skill of other lands can give.[79]

Ignoring the earlier rumblings, he emphasized his quest for peace and lauded his peace pact:

> We have decided to have peace amongst warring nations. Once you establish it, nations are not going back upon it. We have decided to give peace a trial on our hearthstones, and when she has been there for seven months, we will not turn her out again. The psychological effects upon the peoples of the world will be electrical. The thrill of peace has gone through the veins of Europe, and you are not going to get nation lifting up hand against nation again.[80]

Barthou's address, less grandiloquent, praised the "satisfactory" conclusions of the four commissions. He pledged the "absolute and loyal intention" of his government to carry out the Genoa Resolutions, assured the Russian *people* of France's immense gratitude for their wartime sacrifices and continued goodwill, and, in response to Rathenau's lofty rhetoric, assured Germany and Europe of France's desire for peace.[81]

Chicherin, joining in the chorus of thanks to Italy for its hospitality, announced bluntly that the "results of the conference do not fulfill the expectations which it aroused amongst the peoples of all nations." Genoa had failed to

78. *DBFP*, 19:1027–28.
79. Ibid., p. 1031.
80. Ibid., pp. 1031–32.
81. Ibid., pp. 1032–33.

make a "bold step towards new political and economic methods" outlined in his opening speech, particularly on the question of disarmament. The conference had failed to "add anything to existing facts, or to the resolutions adopted by previous conferences" and failed especially to adhere to the principle of equality among nations that had been stated in the Cannes Resolutions. Russia, which had obtained the Genoa Conference's sole victory, emphasized and evaded responsibility for its failure.[82]

Chicherin bludgeoned Lloyd George: "The British premier tells me that if my neighbor has lent me money I must pay him back. Well, I agree, in that particular sense, in a desire for conciliation; but I must add that if this neighbor has broken into my house, killed my children, destroyed my furniture, and burnt my house, he must at least begin restoring to me what he has destroyed."[83] Having attacked his hosts, Chicherin repeated Russia's massive need for credits and pledged further "efforts at conciliation." Facta then closed the Genoa Conference on a somber note: they had *not* finished their work or resolved their disagreements. Genoa had simply opened the way to a "new European policy," but a "long road is still to be travelled."[84]

Lloyd George hurried back to Britain, stopping briefly in Paris to confer with Hardinge and Bradbury on the state of the reparations talks. He did not see Poincaré.[85] On 20 May he was given a "hero's welcome" at Victoria Station that sympathetic observers compared with Balfour's triumphant return from Washington.[86] Three days later, he faced the cabinet after a long seven weeks' absence. Claiming to have adhered to the government's directives in his dealings with Russia, he also admitted that his Genoa policy had more or less failed. His presentation to his colleagues was dominated by other matters: the 31 May reparations deadline, the impending debt negotiations with America, and the revived question of the Anglo-French pact.[87]

Two days later, on 25 May, Lloyd George faced the House of Commons, where his weak speech was judged "courageous" by the *Manchester Guardian*.[88] His left-wing Liberal supporters were split by the Soviet reply: some insisted that the Genoa Conference should have continued, some insisted that

82. Ibid., p. 1035; also Lenin, *Collected Works*, 45:739, n. 670.

83. *DBFP*, 19:1038.

84. Ibid., p. 1038. Gregory to FO, Genoa, 19 May, GB FO 371 C7353, C7354, C7356, C7357, C7359/458/62, reviews the final session.

85. Barthou to MAE, Genoa, 18 May, #548, FMAE B 99; Poincaré to Saint-Aulaire, Paris, 22 May, FMAE Z GB 49; De Gaiffier to MAE, Paris, 29 May, BMAE 366 VII.

86. Frank Owen, *Tempestuous Journey: Lloyd George, His Life and Times* (New York: McGraw-Hill, 1955), p. 620; George Allardice Riddell, *Lord Riddell's Intimate Diary of the Paris Peace Conference and After, 1918–1923* (London: Gollancz, 1933), p. 369.

87. GB CAB 23/30.

88. Saint-Aulaire to MAE, London, 26 May, #504, FMAE B 99.

The Genoa Conference

Moscow's insolence and the high risk of further negotiations had made a rupture inevitable. British public opinion again rallied around the embattled prime minister who still commanded a majority in the House. Nevertheless, the support of British industry was waning. Trade journals recommended that Britain save itself through rigorous government economies, heightened productivity, and investment in the non-European world instead of falling into the murky traps of "sterile resolutions" and diplomatic maneuvers.[89] The Genoa Conference had become a negative model for British policy, and Lloyd Georgian diplomacy, which had conceived it, suffered a stunning if not fatal setback.[90]

89. Christoph Stamm, *Lloyd George zwischen Innen- und Aussenpolitik: Die britische Deutschlandpolitik 1921/1922* (Cologne: Verlag Wissenschaft und Politik, 1977), p. 320.

90. Still, hopes had not died; see Grigg memorandum, "The Political Aspect of the Genoa Conference," 23 May, Grigg Papers, roll 10.

10

The Aftermath

The end of the Genoa Conference stirred reactions of relief and disappointment in Europe. Allied unity had held before the Bolsheviks, but all the unsettled problems had yet to be faced.[1] Where Genoa had represented Lloyd George's attempt to create a collective solution, its improvised ending at once suggested the alternative: *sauve qui peut*. The Bolsheviks' memorandum of 11 May indicated the limits of Moscow's concessions for an international agreement: there would be no debt repayment or restoration of property without the promise of substantial loans and recognition. Russia nevertheless gave no indication that it intended to withdraw into isolation; indeed, the disappointing results of the Genoa Conference signified that Moscow would seek separate agreements with renewed energy.[2]

Separate Arrangements with Moscow?

The first Western government to break Allied unity after Genoa was Czechoslovakia. It had neither major claims nor significant resources but was simply seeking to pacify certain domestic interests, maintain its security, and assert its independence. At Genoa Beneš negotiated a commercial treaty with Chicherin, which was signed at Prague on 5 June.[3] While refusing to grant de jure recognition to the Soviet regime, Beneš agreed to sever ties with all anti-Soviet organizations, establish commercial and diplomatic relations with Russia on a basis equal to other states, support and cooperate with private Czechoslovak enterprises working to restore trade with Russia, and recognize the Soviets' state trading monopoly. The Russians conceded little. Both sides agreed to refrain from hostile propaganda. Moscow promised to grant those it would permit on its territory complete personal freedom and protection of their prop-

---

1. See, e.g., Stork to BMA, Bucharest, 15 May, Di Pauli to BMA, Berne, 24 May, and Wurzian to BMA, Lvov, 29 May, A HHSt 687.
2. Wiedenfeld to AA, Moscow, 22 May, Germ. AA T-120 6700H/3045/H111501-4.
3. Provisional Commercial Treaty between Czechoslovakia and Soviet Russia, signed at Prague, 5 June, GB FO 371 N7880/242/38; Clerk to Balfour, Prague, 9 June, *DBFP*, 20:886.

erty, and it accepted Czechoslovakia's right to participate in any future international settlement. Although Beneš termed this a "purely commercial agreement" with no effect whatsoever on the impending deliberations at The Hague, his critics in London, Paris, and Rome resented his supple and successful small-power diplomacy.[4] The June 1922 agreement governed Czechoslovak-Soviet relations for thirteen years.

Italy's effort to secure a permanent commercial treaty with Moscow had a less happy outcome. The preliminary pact of December 1921 signed in Rome by Della Torretta and Vorovsky was about to expire in June. On 20 May Senator Ettore Conti, a leading industrialist, arrived in Genoa to head an Italian negotiating team of businessmen and government officials that included the Genoa veterans Jung, Giannini, and Scialoja. Though their Soviet partners were the moderates Chicherin, Krassin, and Vorovsky, the talks were difficult, even acrimonious. Having signed with the Germans and concluded commercial agreements with the Swedes and Czechs, the Russians no longer had to be accommodating to Rome.[5]

The Italians considered themselves bound by the terms of the Allies' note of 2 May, by the impending Hague talks, and especially by their loyalty to Britain. Schanzer insisted that they therefore eliminate political questions from their negotiations. Krassin demanded that Rome honor its pledge of the past December, drop all relations with anti-Soviet and separatist representatives, and grant Moscow at least de facto recognition. Italy, though hoping to secure an important commercial role in southern Russia, stuck to the line established at the Villa d'Albertis, demanding full debt repayment and property restitution, and the rights of individual capitalists reentering Russia.[6]

On 24 May Chicherin and Giannini signed a treaty in the Palazzo San Giorgio. There were significant elements of reciprocity, such as a free port for Russia at Trieste and for Italy on the Black Sea. It also included considerable opportunity for Italian bankers and exporters, a guarantee of personal rights and most-favored-nation treatment to all Italian nationals, the option for concessions of Russian oil wells not already assigned, and—Conti's special

---

4. Clerk to FO, Prague, 30 May, Clerk to Balfour, 14 June, unsigned memorandum, 19 July, Gregory minute, 27 Oct., GB FO 371 N5297, N5896/242/38, N9694/646/38; Couget to MAE, Prague, 7 June, FMAE B 100; Aufzeichnung, Prague, 3 May, Germ. BA R 43 I/132, Dieckhoff to AA, Prague, 6 May, Germ. AA T-120 L1468/5118/L415946–49, Koch to AA, Prague, 20 May, Dieckhoff to AA, Prague, 31 May, Germ. AA T-120 L488/4540/L142287, L142588, Aufzeichnung, Berlin, 1 Aug., Germ. BA R 43 I/132; Piotr S. Wandycz, "Foreign Policy of Eduard Beneš, 1918–1938," in *A History of the Czechoslovak Republic, 1918–1948*, ed. Victor S. Mamatey and Radomír Luža (Princeton: Princeton University Press, 1973), p. 223.

5. Schanzer to all Italian representatives abroad, Rome, 24 May, IMAE 52/4; negotiations, 21–23 May, #2, #3, #4, Verbale, IMAE 52/37. The provisional Russo-Swedish trade agreement signed on 1 Mar. was turned down on 30 May by both houses of the Swedish parliament: Barclay to Balfour, Stockholm, 1 June, *DBFP*, 20:880–82.

6. Verbale, 21–23 May, #2, #3, #4, IMAE 52/37.

achievement over Russian resistance—grants of about one thousand hectares each in the Ukraine and the Kuban, with twenty-four-year renewable leases, for exclusive development by Italians.[7] The Palazzo San Giorgio agreement never came into force. On Schanzer's insistence, the Italian cabinet voiced its reservation to Article 14, which provided a government guarantee for the industrialists' investments. This undercut Conti's work, for few individuals were prepared to accept the risks of entering the Soviet market without official backing. Moscow would have an excellent pretext to back off.[8]

More important, two days after the treaty was signed, Lenin had a stroke. Severely incapacitated, he was unable to complete the enterprise he had earlier supported.[9] On 8 June the Council of People's Commissars rejected the new Italo-Soviet agreement, and the old treaty was simply renewed. The acting Soviet leadership, the triumvirate of Kamenev, Rykov, and Stalin, trod warily in international affairs. The opportunity to crack Western unity by wooing Rome was apparently outweighed in this instance by the Kremlin's fear of submitting to blatantly prejudicial terms. Schanzer's refusal to grant de facto recognition would have given the ascendant leftist opposition in Russia a powerful weapon against the trio; thus the Kremlin concluded it was better to wait than to accept an inferior status vis-à-vis Rome.[10]

After calling on Italian nationalist leader Gabriele D'Annunzio, Chicherin departed for Berlin. There, to compensate for Moscow's repudiation of his treaty with Italy, he celebrated his reward for Rapallo: the new Soviet embassy was about to be unveiled. Recuperating from his strenuous labors and temporarily eclipsed by his subordinate Litvinov, Chicherin spent five months in Berlin conducting negotiations with various powers while the situation at home was clarified.[11]

7. Barrère to MAE, Rome, 25 May, FMAE Z It. 121; Graham to Balfour, Rome, 2 June, GB FO 371 N5422/57/38.

8. On Schanzer's reservations: Schanzer to Visconti Venosta, Genoa, n.d., IMAE 52/4 (Russia); Drago note, Genoa, 26 May, ibid.; and Danilo Veneruso, *La vigilia del fascismo: Il primo ministero Facta nella crisi dello stato liberale in Italia* (Bologna: Il Mulino, 1968), p. 412. On nonratification by Moscow: note, Berlin, 1 June, FMAE Y 37; Hodgson to Balfour, Moscow, 13 June, GB FO 371 N5924/57/38; and US MID Report, no. 6444, 29 May (Italy), and no. 6486, 19 June (Italy).

9. V. I. Lenin, *Collected Works* (Moscow: Progress Publishers, 1967–71), 45:546, 551.

10. Young to State Dept., Riga, 6, 7 June, report by ARA representative Goodrich, Moscow, 14 June, USDS 861.00/9454, 9547, 9460; Hodgson to Balfour, Moscow, 13 June, *DBFP*, 20:889; report on the triumvirate, GB FO 371 5755/3416/38.

11. Romano Avezzana to Schanzer, Rome, 27 May, and Genoa prefect's report, 29 May, IMAE 52/4 (Russia); Harry Graf Kessler, *Tagebücher, 1918–1937* (Frankfurt-am-Main: Insel-Verlag, 1961), 11 June, p. 32; Houghton diary, 12 July, Houghton Papers; Lago to De Martino, Rome, 24 Sept., IMAE Amb. Lond. F 532/21 (Russia); Richard K. Debo, "George Chicherin: Soviet Russia's Second Foreign Commissar" (Ph.D. diss., University of Nebraska, 1964), pp. 258–66.

Schanzer, who had risked and now regretted the failure of the Russo-Italian treaty, proceeded with the Hague preparations. He appointed Giannini Italy's chief delegate, and Rome continued its loyal cooperation with London. Schanzer feared the resurrection of Franco-British detente, which would leave Italy "in the cold." When there was an announcement of Poincaré's visit to London to discuss reparations, Schanzer requested an early interview with Lloyd George and other British officials. He still hoped to redeem the prime minister's promises at Genoa.[12] It was an urgent mission. Italy's troubled and violent political scene, the poor rewards of its exertions at Genoa, the setbacks to its Russian policy, and the gloating sounds of France and its allies forced Schanzer to Britain's side, to The Hague, and to one more effort at appeasement.[13]

Again Reparations

Wirth and Rathenau did not hasten their departure from Genoa. They passed the afternoon and evening after the final plenary session with journalists and various statesmen, and they sought Italian support in the impending reparations talks.[14] Bypassing Munich (whose government had requested an official visit) because of threats of rightist violence, the delegation reached Berlin on 21 May and reported immediately to Ebert. Except for *Vorwärts*, which on 20 May had welcomed Wirth and Rathenau with praise for an extraordinary performance of their duties at Genoa, the Reich press meted out harsh judgments to the returning ministers: the Genoa Conference had done little to clarify Germany's situation as the deadline of 31 May approached. There was no cabinet discussion of the conference for two days. Instead, the government plunged immediately into discussions about the negotiations in Paris between Hermes and the Reparations Commission. German politics underwent a temporary truce awaiting the outcome.[15]

The Hermes mission caused division within the German government. The outspoken finance minister had departed Genoa a strong critic of Rapallo; back

12. Graham to Balfour, Rome, 5 June, GB FO 371 C8348/8348/22; Barrère to Poincaré, Rome, 8 June, FMAE Z It. 121; Schanzer to De Martino, Rome, 11 June, IMAE Amb. Lond. (2-Aja); Schanzer's remarks to the Senate on 16 June quoted in Graham to Balfour, Rome, 19 June, GB FO 371 C9100/366/22.

13. Graham to Balfour, Rome, 8 June, GB FO 371 C8410/366/22; cf. Veneruso, *La vigilia*, pp. 319–91.

14. Rathenau diary, 19 May, Germ. AA T-120 3398/1735/D739189; Rathenau to Haniel, Genoa, 19 May, Germ. AA T-120 9233H/3493/H253161; Schanzer to MAE and Sforza, Genoa, 20 May, IMAE 52/20.

15. *Deutsche Allgemeine Zeitung*, 22 May; Addison to Balfour, Berlin, 23 May, GB FO 371 N5198/646/38; Ernst Laubach, *Die Politik der Kabinette Wirth, 1921/1922* (Lübeck and Hamburg: Matthiesen, 1968), pp. 222–23; *Akten-Wirth*, 2:816–18, 818–22, 826–27; Saint Quentin to Poincaré, Berlin, 23 May, Tirard to MAE, Koblenz, 28 May, FMAE B 99.

in Berlin in the beginning of May, he had fueled public opposition to Wirth and Rathenau's policies at the Genoa Conference. With the remainder of the cabinet's approval, Hermes had decided to leave for Paris on 12 May without consulting the chancellor still at Genoa or including a representative of the Foreign Ministry in his difficult and important mission.[16] Hermes believed that Germany *had* to negotiate with the Allies in order to avert a crisis on 31 May and that nothing would be accomplished at Genoa. The Belgian representative on the Reparations Commission, Léon Delacroix, had assured him that any agreement would be purely "formal," designed to provide the backdrop for the coming meeting of international bankers in Paris, which had been called to discuss a loan for Germany.[17]

The negotiations with the Reparations Commission proceeded less smoothly than expected. Germany had to make amends for its refractory note on the eve of Genoa and satisfy the Allies by agreeing to higher taxes and some form of control over its finances and its budget. On learning of these demands, Hermes' compliance, and Lloyd George's approbation, Wirth became bitter and hinted at defiance. He had labored tirelessly at Genoa to prevent any new burdens, still hoping to broaden his government with the support of the DVP.[18] The majority of the cabinet defended Hermes. Socialist Vice-Chancellor Gustav Bauer derided Wirth's complaints and ridiculed the delegation's achievements at Genoa. Rathenau, joining the conciliators, recalled Lloyd George's last remarks: that only a fulfillment policy would save the Reich from invasion.[19] Though Germany had good cause to believe that the French would not act alone on 31 May,[20] there was no reason to tempt Poincaré or further antagonize the British or Italians with an empty gesture of defiance.

Hermes returned to Berlin to defend his compromise. In the end, the German cabinet accepted the commission's rather mild proposals, though this acceptance was conditional on a foreign loan.[21] The partial moratorium for the remainder of 1922 was formally established by an exchange of notes between

16. Haniel to Rathenau, Berlin, 1 May, Germ. Pol. Arch. AA, Bur. R.M., bd. 11; Wever to Wirth, Berlin, 3 May, Germ. AA T-120 K1946/5372/K505634–35. Though Wirth claimed on 22 May that he had no advance warning of Hermes' departure for Paris (*Akten-Wirth*, 2:809), see the following: Germ. AA T-120 K1946/5372/K505633, K505636; K9233/3493/H253127, H253129, H253130–31, H253135–36; 3398/1735/D739133–39.

17. Hermes to AA, Paris, 17 May, Germ. AA T-120 9233H/3493/H253200–9.

18. Statement to cabinet, 22 May, *Akten-Wirth*, 2:807–8, 809–11; Max Reiner to Stresemann, 8 June, Germ. Pol. Arch. AA, Stresemann Nachlass, bd. 246, H143749–55.

19. *Akten-Wirth*, 2:808–11, 816–18, 818–22; also Rathenau to Raumer, Genoa, 5 May, Germ. Pol. Arch. AA, Bur. R.M., bd. 11.

20. Müller to AA, Genoa, 20 May, Germ. AA T-120 9233H/3493/H253225–26.

21. Reich Chancellery to Hermes, Berlin, 23 May, Germ. AA T-120 9233H/3493/H253312; Hermes to Government, Paris, 24 May, Hermes' statement to party leaders, Berlin, 26 May, and cabinet meeting, 27 May, *Akten-Wirth*, 2:828–41; Laubach, *Kabinette Wirth*, pp. 233–34.

Wirth and the Reparations Commission on the eve of the 31 May deadline. News of the Hermes-Wirth dispute leaked in the press and was treated with special sensationalism by the Right. Appearing before the Reichstag on 29 May with his belated report on the Genoa Conference, Wirth wisely refused to discuss the Paris talks. Instead he boasted of Germany's "equal treatment" at Genoa, the success of Rapallo, and the alleged "abandonment" of Britain's nonaggression pact as a result of Germany's objections to the threat of French sanctions. He nevertheless appealed to parliament to support his "policy of conciliation."[22]

The Loan Committee, consisting of Belgian, British, French, German, Italian, and Dutch representatives, and with J. P. Morgan from America, finally opened its deliberations on 1 June. There was a general reluctance to bail out Germany because of the flight of its capital and its ruinous financial policies. Moreover, with America's refusal to link interallied debts to the discussion of Germany's reparations bill and France's resultant refusal to reduce Germany's obligation, the committee could agree neither on a small nor a large international loan. While the committee reached its negative verdict, both the extreme Left and Right in Germany loudly questioned the desirability of any loan. Only when it proved impossible did the Germans appreciate the "theoretical importance" of the failure of the Loan Committee; Wirth in his Stuttgart speech on 9 June and Rathenau in his statement to the cabinet on 13 June emphasized this new "evidence" of the untenability of the London Schedule.[23]

There was a search for villains. In its report on 10 June, the Loan Committee blamed France for its obduracy though also indicating that the question of "international indebtedness" lay at the root of the reparations problem.[24] After this expected announcement, the mark began to tumble again. The Wirth government took steps to protect the currency, which provoked resistance from the newly independent Reichsbank and from the industrialist Hugo Stinnes. On 18 June a committee of guarantees dispatched by the Reparations Commission to establish a system of control was scheduled to arrive in Berlin. *Erfüllungspolitik* was in shambles, Germany's *Ostpolitik* had not yet produced palpable benefits, and the Hague Conference was about to open with Germany blatantly excluded.[25]

22. Saint Quentin to Poincaré, Berlin, 29 May, #893–98, FMAE B 99.

23. Étienne Weill-Raynal, *Les réparations allemandes et la France* (Paris: Nouvelles Éditions Latines, 1947), 2:166–71; John M. Carroll, "The Paris Bankers' Conference of 1922 and America's Design for a Peaceful Europe," *International Review of History and Political Science* 10 (August 1973): 43; Melvyn P. Leffler, *The Elusive Quest: America's Pursuit of European Stability and French Security, 1919–1933* (Chapel Hill: University of North Carolina Press, 1979), pp. 73–75; Laubach, *Kabinette Wirth*, pp. 236–42.

24. Weill-Raynal, *Réparations*, 2:176–79.

25. Lucius to AA, The Hague, 22, 26 May, Germ. Pol. Arch. AA, Abt. IVA (Russ) Akten, bd. 6.

Violence now erupted in the Reich, first with an attack on former Chancellor Philip Scheidemann on 4 June in Cassel, then, on 24 June in Berlin, with the assassination of Rathenau by two young right-wing extremists. The night before his death, Rathenau had debated with Stinnes over the necessity of curbing the inflation, the desirability of continuing to seek a foreign loan, and the importance of demonstrating conciliation to prevent a showdown with France. His biographer Kessler wrote on the day of Rathenau's death, "A new chapter of German history begins, or at least should begin."[26]

However, Germany continued to drift between confrontation and collapse. Wirth, who again took over the Foreign Ministry, introduced emergency legislation after the shooting, but his government was neither broadened nor strengthened that summer. On 4 July, after a fervent defense by Maltzan, the Rapallo agreement—Germany's sole gain at the Genoa Conference and Rathenau's most controversial achievement—was ratified by the Reichstag. Eight days later, following another plunge in the mark, Wirth asked the Reparations Commission for a moratorium through 1924.[27] The Weimar Republic and the Allies were headed for a collision, and only American intervention would bring relief two long years after Genoa.

The Entente and the Opening of the Hague Conference

Following two years of self-imposed exile during which he had either traveled abroad or remained in the countryside, Georges Clemenceau returned to Paris in mid-May 1922. The still-robust eighty-two-year-old *tigre* seemed delighted to vent criticism on the failed Genoa Conference, on Poincaré's "timidity," and on his former diplomatic partner Lloyd George's "domineering" attitude toward France. Yet the great war leader could offer no alternative program for his country in peacetime. Doubting the efficacy of a punitive expedition into the

26. Kessler, *Tagebücher*, 24 June, pp. 332–34; Rathenau-Stinnes talks in Houghton diary, 24 June, Houghton Papers; Houghton to Hughes, Berlin, 25 June, USDS 862.00/1129; David Felix, *Walther Rathenau and the Weimar Republic: The Politics of Reparations* (Baltimore: Johns Hopkins University Press, 1971), pp. 168–72. On 22 July Stresemann confided to DVP leaders his fear that as a result of Rathenau's murder, "international Jewry" would dissuade British and American bankers from aiding Germany: Germ. Pol. Arch. AA, Stresemann Nachlass, bd. 248. Earlier, however, he correctly predicted that the United States would eventually press its allies for a viable reparations solution: letter to Crown Prince, 14 May, Germ. AA T-120 7012H/3110/H143690-701.

27. Weill-Raynal, *Réparations*, 2:191–92; Laubach, *Kabinette Wirth*, pp. 246–49; D'Abernon to Balfour, Berlin, 5 July, GB FO 371 N6621/646/38, on Rapallo. D'Abernon to Hankey, 11 July, to Balfour, 12 July, and to Hankey, 13 July, LGP F 54/2/26, 27, 29, described Germany's desperate and distracted state but also its ingratitude for "the assistance we have given."

Ruhr, which inevitably would galvanize all Europe against France, he called for "another method" but failed to specify what. Time, he admitted, was on Germany's side. The Rapallo treaty served as a warning of the eventual dangers to peace.[28]

Poincaré was more concerned with Britain than with Germany. He wanted to renew the earlier lapsed discussions on an Anglo-French pact. He believed that France, which had neither caused a rupture at Genoa nor absolutely refused to attend the Hague meeting, could expect Britain's gratitude or at least a more positive response to its security demands. Poincaré failed to realize the depth of Britain's resentment of French policy and the degree to which this had become a major part of its public posture during the Genoa Conference.[29]

French politics heated up as the Chamber reopened on 23 May after a long Easter break. The Communists renewed the attacks on *Poincaré-la-guerre*, and Socialist deputy Léon Blum blamed Poincaré for the Rapallo treaty as well. Spurred by its electoral victories in the 14 and 21 May cantonal elections, the Left criticized the Quai d'Orsay's "artificial distinction" between Europe's victors and vanquished, rejected a policy of coercion against Germany, and called for reconciliation between France and Russia. Joined by leading Radicals Édouard Herriot and Édouard Daladier and by the left-wing Republicans, this *bloc des gauches* urged the government to endorse Lloyd George's diplomacy of appeasement and to seek security not through more military alliances but in an enlarged, invigorated League of Nations.[30]

The French Right, shocked by Rapallo and stung by the leftist offensive as well as the ineffectiveness of the prefects in the May elections, criticized Poincaré à la Clemenceau for his timidity. Maintaining the correctness of France's hard line toward Germany and Russia and led by André Tardieu and Léon Daudet, it attacked Anglo-Saxon diplomacy, which, behind its seemingly "economic" goals, ruthlessly pursued a dangerous, essentially revisionist purpose.[31]

Poincaré steered a deft course between the two extremes. Although neither was strong enough to provide him with a permanent base of support, the criti-

28. De Gaiffier to MAE, Paris, 15 May, BMAE 10991; conversation between Clemenceau and an American journalist, n.d., LGP F 8/8/16; letter to Pieri, 22 Apr., quoted in Georges Wormser, *La république de Clemenceau* (Paris: Presses Universitaires de France, 1961), p. 445.

29. Interview with Poincaré by an American correspondent, 18 May, LGP F 5/8/14; Vansittart to Curzon, London, 13 June, GB FO 371 W4880/50/17.

30. Blum, in *Le Populaire*, 25 Apr., Cachin, in *Humanité*, 26 Apr., "La fin de Gênes," *Le Populaire*, 21 May; Édouard Bonnefous, *Histoire politique de la Troisième République*, 2nd ed. (Paris: Presses Universitaires de France, 1968), 3:303–4; De Gaiffier to MAE, Paris, 16 May, 3 June, BMAE Fr.

31. De Gaiffier to MAE, Paris, 24 May, BMAE 10991; Hardinge to Curzon, 23 May, GB FO 371 W4609/4/17; US MID Report, no. 5584W, 29 May (France).

cism of both produced a menace that could not be ignored.[32] On 1 June, in his three-hour-long speech to the Chamber on foreign policy, he performed a masterful acrobatic. By citing all the directives he had sent Barthou during the Genoa Conference, he assumed responsibility for all that had happened, including France's remaining until the bitter end. He evaluated Genoa's technical accomplishments as positive, even repeating Worthington-Evans's characterization of its financial "Justinian code"; but he viewed its political results as largely negative, and urged the United States to join in the reconstruction of Europe. Though he took a tough line on reparations, insisting that France could use force (preferably in concert with its allies) if Germany continued to default, this was mere rhetoric since the current crisis had already passed. Poincaré easily won a vote of confidence, 436 to 92.[33]

On 27 May Facta sent invitations to all the governments represented at the Genoa Conference except Germany and Russia (scheduled to arrive later) to attend a preliminary meeting at The Hague on 15 June. The Dutch were reluctant hosts, fearing another drawn-out squabble between the Allies and the Russians. Karnebeek asked for the League's assistance in setting up the Hague Conference, which Drummond declined.[34]

As in the period before Genoa, Poincaré dispatched a long memorandum to London listing the conditions for France's participation in the preliminary meetings at The Hague. These included: (1) limiting the conference to a gathering solely of experts; (2) eliminating the Russian memorandum of 11 May as a basis of discussion; (3) drawing up a "definite scheme" for the reconstruction of Russia, with clear indications of the role each country would play that would be universally agreed upon before the Russians arrived; and (4) extending the time of the non-Russian talks to do the necessary work.[35] The French memorandum was published in the *Times* on 5 June.

Poincaré's note, with its hint of an ultimatum, worried the Italians and angered the British, who took a week to prepare their response.[36] Grigg's original

32. Hardinge to Curzon, Paris, 1 Nov., GB FO 371 W9078/4/17; Charles S. Maier, *Recasting Bourgeois Europe: Stabilization in France, Germany, and Italy in the Decade after World War I* (Princeton: Princeton University Press, 1975), p. 290.

33. *JO Ch. Déb. Par.*, 1 June, pp. 1641–51; Hardinge to Balfour, 2 June, GB FO 371 C8190/99/18.

34. De Martino to Balfour, London, 27 May, GB FO 371 C8190/99/18; Marling to FO, The Hague, 30, 31 May, Wise to Chapman, The Hague, 5 June, GB FO 371 N5310, N5311, N5661/646/38; Karnebeek to Drummond, The Hague, 3 June, Drummond to Karnebeek, Geneva, 6 June, LNA 30A 20161/20836; Karnebeek diary, 14, 17 June, *DBPN*, nos. 338, 340.

35. Hardinge to Balfour, Paris, 3 June, GB FO 371 N5377/646/38.

36. Graham to Balfour, Rome, 4 June, GB FO 371 N5382/646/38; Crowe and Balfour minutes, 7 June, Maxse memorandum, 10 June, and Balfour to Hardinge, London, 10 June, GB FO 371 N5381/646/38.

tendentious reply was toned down by the Foreign Office and by Britain's two designated delegates to The Hague, Lloyd-Greame and Sir E. Hilton Young, a former Wee-Free Liberal serving as financial secretary to the Treasury. In its reply, London reassured Paris on the purely technical nature of the Hague discussions and also on the supersession of the 11 May document; but it opposed "presuming the right to dictate to Russia," insisting that "consultation and cooperation with the representatives of Russia [were] absolutely necessary if the Hague is to give any practical results." The British disapproved of "the method proposed by the French government not only because . . . it is impractical, but also because it [is] inconsistent with another principle to which the French Government itself attaches the greatest importance—namely the avoidance of politics."[37]

"Business at The Hague" would be conducted according to the "conclusions reached after full discussions at Genoa." There would be practical arrangements for the repayment of Russia's debts, which incorporated the prior decision that prewar debt repayment be arranged with the bondholders. As far as Britain was concerned, the agreement of 15 April that reduced a considerable portion of Russia's war debts still held. As to property, London was noncommittal. On credits, the British declared that "the need of Russia to borrow is out of all proportion to the desire of Europe and America to lend"; nevertheless, without any specifics, London indicated that the Hague Conference should consider terms not only for private investors but also what their governments might do to assist.[38]

Britain's statement, which was published in the *Times* on 12 June and distributed to the representatives in London of all the governments invited to The Hague, ended on a dual note: it raised the threat that "concession hunters" could endanger relations between otherwise friendly Western governments, and it also reiterated the great principles of Cannes—the cause of humanity, the "practical necessity of European reconstruction, the urgency of good relations between the Allies, and the need for a genuine peace in Europe." It was an eloquent document, in contrast to the actual confusion among Britain's leaders about what might yet be accomplished at The Hague.[39]

Poincaré answered promptly and again published his response. His tone was more moderate. He had decided to send a study commission (*mission d'étude*) to The Hague, but it arrived after the other main powers.[40] In the meantime, a

37. Memorandum in reply to the French memorandum of 2 June, *DBFP*, 19:1044–49; quotation is on p. 1047.
38. Ibid., p. 1048.
39. Ibid., p. 1049; cf. minutes of British Empire delegation, 12 June, *DBFP*, 19:1050–57.
40. Hardinge to Balfour, Paris, 13 June (2 tels.), GB FO 371 N5712, N5714/646/38; Poincaré to French Missions in London, The Hague, Brussels, Washington, and Rome, Paris, 13 June, FMAE PM La Haye II; De Gaiffier to MAE, Paris, 13 June, BMAE 10992.

new Anglo-Belgian combination was forming. Belgium, seeking to revive the earlier talks with Britain on a pact, signaled that it wished to separate itself from France and work cooperatively with the British at The Hague. Cattier, the chief Belgian delegate, who had distinguished himself at Genoa with his inquisitorial talents against the Russians, now seconded Britain's plans for the Hague Conference. He sought to play mediator between London and Paris and also tried to ensure his government an important role at the Hague Conference.[41]

The preliminary conference opened on 15 June at the Peace Palace. Karnebeek welcomed the delegates with a warm speech that emphasized the practical nature of their deliberations. The formalities over, the British, French, Belgian, Italian, and Japanese representatives met with Karnebeek to organize the Hague Conference. There would be one main "Non-Russian" Commission and three subcommissions dealing with debts, credits, and property. Their six governments would participate on all three subcommissions, and five additional members would be appointed from all the other invited governments.[42]

The next morning Cattier presented these proposals to the full conference. Because of the objections of the small powers, membership on the three subcommissions was slightly enlarged. The French representative stressed that his government had not yet decided to participate; thus there was no general debate over the goals of the Hague Conference. The preliminary meeting then adjourned for three days, ostensibly to enable the delegates to consult with their governments but in fact to allow France to decide.[43]

Poincaré now sought assurances from London that France's participation at the Hague Conference would involve no binding obligations. Still fearing the shadow of Lloyd George's virtually defunct nonaggression pact, he asked for Britain's pledge that it apply only to Russia. Furthermore, he insisted on France's right to withdraw from the conference should the Russians again prove obstreperous.[44] The pressure on France to join mounted. Italy, the East

41. Grahame to Balfour, Brussels, 29 May, 2, 13 June, Balfour to Grahame, London, 15 June, GB FO 371 W4578/431/4, C8224/458/62, N5711/646/38, W4959/432/4; Gregory to Balfour, The Hague, 14 June, *DBFP*, 19:1058–59; Lloyd-Greame to Lloyd George, Scheveningen, 17 June, LGP F 46/3/10; Gallopin, Witmeur, et al. to Jaspar, The Hague, 14 June, Ligne to Jaspar, The Hague, 18 June, and telephone message from Cattier, The Hague, 19 June, BMAE 10992.

42. Gregory to Balfour, The Hague, 15 June (2 tels.), *DBFP*, 19:1059–61; Netherlands, Ministerie van Buitenlandsche Zaken, *Conference at the Hague: Minutes and Documents* (The Hague: M.B.Z., 1922), pp. 12–14.

43. Gregory to Balfour, The Hague, 16 June (3 tels.), *DBFP*, 19:1062–64; Benoist to MAE, The Hague, 17 June, unsigned note for Peretti, Laroche, Fromageot, Paris, 17 June, and Peretti [Millerand] to Saint-Aulaire [Poincaré], Paris, 17 June, FMAE B 131.

44. Balfour to Saint-Aulaire, London, 10 June, GB FO 371 N5323/646/38; Poincaré to Benoist, Paris, 16 June, FMAE PM La Haye II; Poincaré to all French Missions, Paris, 17 June, FMAE B 131.

European states, and the neutrals all supported the Hague meeting, and Belgium was taking part actively. Moreover, Poincaré was about to ply the route to London in the hope of reviving Britain's interest in an Anglo-French alliance and to discuss the Near East and reparations.

The Anglo-French talks went smoothly, and both sides concluded that they had prevailed over the other.[45] Lloyd George, disenchanted with the talkative and inflexible Russians, predicted a meager outcome for the Hague Conference; but he warned that the Allies had to demonstrate that Moscow and not Paris had caused the failure. Poincaré insisted that by sending the *mission d'étude* to The Hague without parliament's consent, he had already demonstrated "a mark of friendship toward the British government." In fact, the day before he had telephoned Paris and agreed to France's full participation in the Hague meeting. This was hedged with conditions, including the prohibition against "political" subjects and France's right to pull out.[46] Despite Poincaré's hope, there was no opportunity to discuss the Anglo-French pact; they agreed tacitly to wait on events in Germany and the Near East.

Lloyd George's government was besieged with domestic problems. There was a new eruption of violence in Ireland, underscored by the assassination on 21 June of one of the government's most outspoken right-wing critics, Sir Henry Wilson. Also there were press attacks, emanating from the Honors scandals, the Arab-Jewish tensions in Palestine, and the debate over funding Britain's debt to America. Lloyd George therefore was not concentrating on the Hague Conference to any great extent. Wise was in the Dutch capital to watch over the proceedings, and the seasoned Lloyd-Greame represented Britain's interests with tact, firmness, and skill.[47]

France was therefore again in the position of a watchful principal participant, reluctant either to contribute to or sabotage the Hague Conference. The delegation was officially headed by Charles Alphand, with the assistance of Ambassador Charles Benoist. Poincaré assigned René Massigli, a junior official of the Quai d'Orsay and a veteran of the Genoa Conference, the tasks of defending France's main interests and of "preventing any surprises."[48]

45. "Notes . . . d'une conversation entre Poincaré et Lloyd George," London, 19 June, FMAE Y 686; the British résumé is in *DBFP*, 19:1070–71 (The Hague), 20:68–69 (Reparations), 17:859 (Near East). Also Frances Lloyd George, *Lloyd George: A Diary* (New York: Harper and Row, 1971), p. 242; and De Gaiffier to MAE, Paris, 21, 27 June, BMAE Fr.

46. Instructions du Président du Conseil telephonées de Londres à M. Peretti de la Rocca, and Peretti to all French Missions, Paris, 18 June, FMAE B 131.

47. Lloyd-Greame to wife, Scheveningen, 24 June, LGrP; Viscount Swinton (Lloyd-Greame), *I Remember* (London and New York: Hutchinson, 1949), pp. 24–25.

48. Alphand, compte rendu #1, The Hague, 15 June, FMAE Alphand Papers, IV; Poincaré to Alphand, Paris, 20 June, #180, FMAE B 131; Charles Benoist, *Souvenirs de Charles Benoist*, (Paris: Plon, 1934), 3:431–36; and Lloyd-Greame to Lloyd George, Scheveningen, 17 June, LGP F 46/3/10.

The formal arrangements for the conference followed the earlier Anglo-Belgian discussions. There would be one Non-Russian Commission, consisting of all twenty-six nations and presided over by a Dutch chairman (Patijn) and a Belgian vice-chairman (Cattier). The subcommissions on debts, property, and credits were chaired by a Frenchman (Alphand), a Briton (Lloyd-Greame), and an Italian (Romano Avezzana). These five individuals, who constituted the conference's bureau, would act also as liaison with the "Russian Commission," which would consist solely of the Soviet delegates who were due to arrive on 26 June.[49]

The three subcommissions set to work in an informal and harmonious atmosphere. The debts subcommission attempted to clarify various classifications of debts and agreed on a procedure for negotiating with the Russians. The property subcommission established guidelines for ascertaining what industries the Russians were willing to restore, the conditions of restitution, and the means of dealing with difficult and contested cases. The credits subcommission produced an Anglo-French plan involving no specific types of credit but aimed simply at eliciting from the Russians the amount and purposes of their needs.[50]

The Anglo-Belgian strategy, which was approved by the other delegates, was as follows: when the Russians arrived, the debt issue would be discussed first in order to ascertain any changes in Moscow's position. There would be no plenary meetings that might give the Russians or the French a chance to haggle or debate. Throughout the subcommission meetings, *amitié* prevailed between the French and British delegations.[51] However, once more the representatives at The Hague suffered from misunderstandings with the home front. The British complained of receiving insufficient information from London about the state of Lenin's health and on general conditions in Russia. The French delegation again objected to the insinuations of the Paris press.[52]

Litvinov arrived in The Hague on 26 June ahead of the more moderate

49. Gregory to Balfour, The Hague, 20 June, *DBFP*, 19:1071–72. The property subcommission included Finland, Norway, Rumania, Sweden, Switzerland, and Yugoslavia; the debts subcommission, Denmark, Lithuania, and Spain, and the credits subcommission, Bulgaria, Estonia, Czechoslovakia, Greece, Poland, and Latvia, GB FO 371 N5981/646/38; British Empire Delegation, notes on work to be done by the committees, *DBFP*, 19:1065–69, A. S[ylvester] to Lloyd George, The Hague, 21 June, LGP F 93/4/4.

50. Gregory to Balfour, The Hague, 22, 23, 24, 26 June, *DBFP*, 19:1072–73, 1074–75; Benoist to MAE, The Hague, 22, 24, 26 June, FMAE PM La Haye II.

51. Cattier to Jaspar, The Hague, 21 June, BMAE 10992; A. S. to Lloyd George, The Hague, 21 June, LGP F 93/4/4; Hilton Young to Lloyd George, Scheveningen, 23 June, LGP F 28/8/13; Massigli to Poincaré, The Hague, 24 June, FMAE B 131.

52. Gregory to Balfour, The Hague, 23 June, *DBFP*, 19:1073–74; Marling to FO, The Hague, 26 June, GB FO 371 N6166/646/38; Lloyd-Greame to Harmsworth, The Hague, 26 June, GB FO 371 N6261/646/38; Benoist [Massigli] to MAE, The Hague, 24 June, #33, FMAE B 131.

Krassin, and he immediately tossed some fireworks. The chief Soviet delegate confirmed Lenin's illness and his "temporary" replacement but also announced that Russia wanted cash before discussing principles. Once credit arrangements were made, he assured the press that Moscow would be conciliatory on the questions of debts and private property. Again Russia raised the subject of disarmament.[53]

Litvinov's bombast succeeded. At Britain's urging, the Allies reluctantly agreed to reverse the order of the procedure, and the first meeting between a non-Russian subcommission and the Russian Commission dealt with the question of credits.[54] There was little indication that either the Soviet or the Western attitude had changed. Indeed, when the Bolsheviks arrived, the Dutch government ordered the hotels to remove the national banners of all the delegations in order not to display the red flag,[55] a small though significant prophesy of the fate of the Hague Conference.

Non-Russians Meet the Russians

The Russians faced a unified and determined Allied camp. Under British direction, the West's aim was to force the Soviet delegates to provide information and answer questions, while making no commitments at all. When Litvinov and his colleagues first faced the credits subcommission, the atmosphere was electric. Ignoring the Bolsheviks' truculence, the subcommission asked for a definite plan for the restoration of Russia. British delegate Hilton Young was firm but amiable, describing his role of "build[ing] bridges and carry[ing] oil cans [sic] across to them . . . so they could trot across very tractably and tell us all we need to know about Russian reconstruction."[56]

The other two subcommissions worked according to plan. The debts subcommission asked for a copy of the Russian state budget to enable it to make recommendations on a "possible" moratorium, although the French delegate announced that his government was not bound by the debt-reduction offer made at Genoa. On the property subcommission, Lloyd-Greame confronted Litvinov with Krassin's statement at Genoa that 90 percent of the expropriated

53. British Delegation to Balfour, The Hague, 26 June (2 tels.), GB FO 371 N6200, N6201/646/38; Benoist to MAE, The Hague, 26 June (2 tels.), 27 June, FMAE B 131; Cattier to MAE, The Hague, 26 June, BMAE 10992.

54. Marling to Balfour, The Hague, 27 June, GB FO 371 N6254/646/38; Hilton Young to Lloyd George, Scheveningen, 28 June, LGP F 28/4/14; Lloyd-Greame to Balfour, The Hague, 30 June, GB FO 371 N6340/646/38; Benoist to MAE, The Hague, 26 June, FMAE B 131.

55. Lucius to AA, The Hague, 27 June, Germ. AA T-120 6700H/3045/H118530–31.

56. British Delegation to Balfour, The Hague, 27 June, GB FO 371 N6236/646/38; Benoist to MAE, The Hague, 28 June, FMAE PM La Haye II; Hilton Young to Lloyd George, Scheveningen, 28 June, LGP F 28/8/14.

properties could be restored to their former owners. When Litvinov equivocated and asked the Allies for precise figures of their property claims, they refused the request.[57] Finally, Litvinov returned to the credits subcommission with a demand for 3 billion, 224 million gold rubles, representing Russia's immediate needs for transport, agriculture, commerce, and banking. This provoked sarcastic comments by the Belgian delegate on the utter destruction of Russia's economy, gave Litvinov the opportunity to accuse the Allies of contributing to Russia's ruin, and offered British and Italian members the chance to play mediator.[58]

The British felt that the Russians could be persuaded to do business. Though Moscow had sent the pugnacious Litvinov to The Hague, it had also sent the conciliatory Krassin, Sokol'nikov, and Krestinsky. Despite their noisy xenophobia and their continued efforts to sow dissension among the Allies, the Russians' very presence indicated their need.[59] Germany's observer, its minister in The Hague, was concerned about the amicable atmosphere of the early Allied-Russian negotiations. He was disturbed by rumors that an agreement at the conference sacrificing Germany's interests would be sealed before the Rapallo treaty could be ratified. In Paris Poincaré was also alarmed at the Bolsheviks' insolence and Britain's continued obsession with a settlement.[60]

Lloyd-Greame attempted to move things along. On 30 June he met privately with Litvinov, who affected ignorance of Krassin's pledge, surprise at Britain's reluctance to open its government's coffers to the Russians, and astonishment at Allied solidarity over debts and property. Two days later, Lloyd-Greame, Hilton Young, and Cattier met with a more conciliatory Krassin. The Allied representatives hammered the theme that if Russia refused to restore property, the negotiations would be over.[61]

57. Debts subcommission: Benoist [Alphand] to Poincaré, The Hague, 29 June, FMAE PM La Haye II; British Delegation to Balfour, The Hague, 28 June, GB FO 371 N6250/646/38; Hilton Young to Lloyd George, Scheveningen, 28 June, LGP F 28/8/4; Lloyd-Greame to wife, Scheveningen, 28 June, and to Leeper, 28 June, LGrP; property subcommission: Gregory to Balfour, The Hague, 29 June, British Delegation to Balfour, The Hague, 30 June, GB FO 371 N6283, N6339/646/38.

58. British Delegation to Balfour, The Hague, 30 June (2 tels.), GB FO 371 N6341, N6342/646/38.

59. Hodgson to Balfour, Moscow, 29 June, *DBFP*, 19:1082–83.

60. Germany: Lucius to AA, The Hague, 29, 30 June, Mueller to AA, Berne, 30 June, Scheffer to Maltzan, The Hague, 30 June, Germ. AA T-120 6700H/3045/H118558, H118542, H118577, H118538–39. France: Poincaré to Delegation, Paris, 28 June (2 tels.), #209, #210, FMAE B 131, and to French Representatives in London, Brussels, and Rome, 28 June, FMAE PM La Haye II; telephone message from The Hague, 30 June, Alphand note on Massigli-Urquart conversation, 30 June, FMAE B 131.

61. Lloyd-Greame memorandum, The Hague, 1 July, GB FO 371 N6382/646/38; the interviews were related on 3 July to the Belgian, French, Italian, and Japanese delegates: Chasles note, FMF F 30/1376; Cattier to Jaspar, The Hague, 3 July, BMAE 10992.

Britain's strategy was to drive the Russians into a corner where they would either do business or separate. Given Russia's difficult situation, Britain would be neither conciliatory nor patient.[62] However, as at Genoa, the Russians had once more gained the weapon of pacing the negotiations. The longer they delayed their answers, the greater the opportunity for stimulating disunity among their adversaries. Though crediting the fears of Russia's East European neighbors of an attack that summer by the Red Army (and therefore willing to prolong the negotiations for a reasonable period), the Allies, with other more pressing problems, were unwilling and unable to remain at The Hague for interminable haggling.[63]

The Hague Conference posed opposite priorities and strategies. The Russians wanted credits and promised to be accommodating if they could obtain cash. The French wanted Russia to acknowledge its full debt to the bondholders, with details of repayment to be decided later; and the Belgians demanded the restoration of former properties under conditions that ensured security of tenure. The British, in the most difficult and exposed role, had a goal different from the other three: it was to reach a collective settlement whereby their nationals might penetrate Russia and play a leading role in the revival of its economy and industry, in collaboration with the others that wished to follow. Any of the first three might cause a rupture because of the powerful domestic mainsprings of their policies. The Russians needed to proclaim firmly that only a portion of the czarist debt would be funded and that nationalization was permanent. France and Belgium had to resist offering any succor to a government that had violated capitalist principles. However, Britain and Italy needed to apply the maximum of flexibility to the negotiations to prove to their home audience that all means had been exhausted and that the other side was at fault for the failure of a collective agreement.[64]

Hilton Young to Lloyd George, Scheveningen, 2 July, LGP F 28/8/16: "We shall continue . . . long enough . . . to make sure no possible avenue of reconciliation is unexplored [and] carefully stage the decease of the conference so the guilt of the Russians will not be in doubt. Who killed Cock-Conference? I said Mr. Krassin."

62. Maxse to Ovey, The Hague, 6 July, GB FO 371 N6559/646/38. Pelt [League observer] to Attolico, The Hague, 1, 8 July, and Attolico to Pelt, Geneva, 11 July, LNA 40A 21887/X.

63. There were repeated questions in the House of Commons on the progress and duration of the Hague Conference; for example, on 4 July, Unionist M. P. William Ormsby-Gore inquired and Lloyd George replied evasively, citing the "recentness" of the Soviets' arrival. Poincaré, nervous over the revival of talk about forming an international corporation, warned his delegation to be vigilant and called for a speedy end to the Hague: cf. Benoist [Alphand] to MAE, The Hague, 7 July, #111–13, FMAE B 132; Poincaré to Delegation, Paris, 7 July, FMAE PM La Haye III; Benoist [Alphand] to MAE, The Hague, 8 July, ibid.; Poincaré to Delegation, Paris, 8 July, #230, FMAE B 132.

64. Hilton Young to Lloyd George, Scheveningen, 9 July, LGP F 28/8/15; Maxse to O'Malley, The Hague, 10 July, Dashwood, Gregory minutes, London, 12 July, and Tyrrell minute, 14 July, GB FO 371 N6696/646/38; Hilton Young to Grigg, The Hague, 14 July, Grigg Papers, roll 2.

The French delegation was again in an isolated position. From the start, Paris insisted that the Allies pledge that if no agreement were reached, their governments would condemn separate arrangements or private negotiations with Moscow. Alphand was confronted with many problems: the eagerness of the Belgian delegate to support Britain, mediate between Britain and France, and prevent a rupture; the continuous private negotiations between British and Italian representatives and the Russians; and, once more, Paris's suspicions and impatience with any signs of delay or surrender. With a new crisis brewing in Germany after Rathenau's assassination, this was an unpropitious time for Allied disunity. Poincaré insisted on the pledges that Lloyd George had made in London.[65]

The Hague Conference reached its critical stage between 10 and 14 July.[66] The Russians received a negative reply from the credits subcommission: there would be no direct loans and no government guarantees of private investments unless the Soviet government "inspired confidence" by signaling its willingness to make concessions in other areas.[67] The property subcommission examined what the Russians had to offer. France, now with Belgium at its side, insisted on "precision." On 7 July Litvinov presented a list to the subcommission of the concessions that his government was prepared to grant to foreigners; it included only a small percentage of former holdings and excluded whole industries. Krassin and Litvinov outlined the conditions under which concessions would be conveyed and the terms of compensation for dispossessed owners. These were deemed unacceptable by the Allies. Again, as at Genoa, the Soviets attempted a diversionary tactic by hinting that a large oil concession was being offered to Shell. A Franco-Belgian group combined with the Shell company and others to check the Russians' effort to provoke a concessions scramble.[68]

The negotiations on the debts subcommission also broke down. Litvinov refused to recognize Russia's obligations until he knew what credits would be

65. Cattier to Jaspar, The Hague, 26 June, BMAE 10992; Benoist [Alphand] to MAE, The Hague, 11 July, Peretti note, n.d., and Poincaré to Delegation, Paris, 11 July, FMAE PM La Haye III; Cattier to MAE, The Hague, 11, 12 July, Jaspar to Cattier, Brussels, 12 July, Hervy minute, 12 July, BMAE 10992; Lucius to AA, The Hague, 10 July, Germ. AA T-120 6700H/3045/H118613.

66. Lloyd-Greame to wife, The Hague [10 July], LGrP; Lucius to AA, The Hague, 10, 11 July, Germ. AA T-120 6700H/3045/H118616, H118661–62; Pelt to Attolico, The Hague, 11 July, LNA 40A 21887/X.

67. British Delegation to Balfour, The Hague, 10 July, *DBFP*, 19:1094–96.

68. Sussdorff to State Dept., The Hague, 6 July, USDS 550 E1/Russ./3 (minutes); British Delegation to Balfour, The Hague, 7, 10, 12 July, *DBFP*, 19:1090–92, 1093–94, 1097–1102; Lucius to AA, The Hague, 8 July (2 tels.), 10, 11, 12 July, Germ. AA T-120 6700H/3045/H118596, H118614–15, H118616, H118617, H118633, H118635; Benoist [Alphand] to MAE, The Hague, 11 July, #137, FMAE B 132; Hahn Aufzeichnung, Berlin, 13 July, Germ. BA R 43 I/132; Louis Fischer, *Oil Imperialism: The International Struggle for Petroleum* (New York: International, 1926), pp. 73–91.

forthcoming. He rejected a debt commission on the lines formerly imposed upon Turkey. The Allies on their part refused a new Russian proposal to establish a "global figure" of Russian indebtedness, allow Moscow to accept an agreed portion, and empower a tribunal set up by the West to deal with private claims.[69] On 14 July, in its final encounter with the Russians, the credits subcommission announced that according to the information received from the other two subcommissions, there could be no further negotiations with the Soviet delegates. In response to Litvinov's protests and criticisms, Hilton Young and Romano Avezzana defended the proceedings, leaving the door open, however, for "new facts or proposals."[70]

The Hague Conference was dying. Despite the hopes of Wise and Giannini for a continuation, the Russians admitted they had nothing new to offer.[71] The subcommissions began drafting their negative reports. Suddenly, "at the eleventh hour and fifty-ninth minute," Litvinov asked to speak at a full plenary session. The British and the Belgians persuaded the French to continue.[72]

The Non-Russian Commission met for the last time with the Russian Commission on the morning of 19 July. Litvinov's improvised announcement consisted of this garbled statement:

> If the other delegations represented at The Hague agree to refer the proposal at the same time to their governments, the Russian delegation will at once refer to the Russian government the question whether the Russian government cannot be given (1) to acknowledge the debts due by the Russian government or its predecessors to foreign nationals, and (2) to agree to give effective compensation to foreigners for property previously owned by them which has been nationalized by the Russian government provided that terms of payment of the debts and terms of compensation . . . be left to be agreed upon between the Russian government and the persons concerned in the course of two years.[73]

69. Benoist [Alphand] to MAE, The Hague, 13 July, FMAE PM La Haye III ("We have not progressed from Chicherin's statement of 28 Oct. [1921]."); British Delegation to Balfour, The Hague, 12 July, *DBFP*, 19:1102–4.

70. British Delegation to Balfour, The Hague, 14 July, *DBFP*, 19:1107–10; Benoist to MAE, The Hague, 14 July, FMAE PM La Haye III.

71. Pelt to Attolico, The Hague, 15 July, LNA 40A 21887/X2; Lloyd-Greame to wife, The Hague, 16 July, LGrP; Marling [Lloyd-Greame] to FO, The Hague, 14 July, GB FO 371 N6767/646/38.

72. Litvinov to Patijn, The Hague, 16 July, British Delegation to Balfour, The Hague, 17 July, Knatchbull-Hugessen [Lloyd-Greame] to FO, The Hague, 17 July, GB FO 371 N6923, N6827, N6855/646/38; Hilton Young to Lloyd George, Scheveningen, 17 July, LGP F 28/8/11; Lucius to AA, The Hague, 12, 18 July, Wiedenfeld to AA, Moscow, 17 July, Germ. AA T-120 6700H/3045/H118669, H118675, H118687–89; unsigned note, Brussels, 18 July, De Gaiffier to MAE, Paris, 18 July, Davignon to De Gaiffier, Brussels, 19 July, Cattier to MAE, The Hague, 20 July, BMAE 10992.

73. Marling [Lloyd-Greame] to Balfour, The Hague, 19 July, *DBFP*, 19:1120.

It was a tour de force convincing even his severest critics of Litvinov's talent as a virtuoso Soviet negotiator, and was well designed to sow dissension among the Allies, prolong the Hague Conference, and write in the historical record that Russia was conciliatory to the very end. The Allies refused the bait, which on closer analysis would have left their nationals at the mercy of Russian decisions.[74] Litvinov, on further questioning after the meeting, admitted that his unauthorized statement might not be accepted by Moscow and that his government would probably attach the condition of de jure recognition to any concessions it agreed to. Having been given fairly wide latitude by London as to how and when to break off, Lloyd-Greame, like Lloyd George, lost patience with his cunning Russian partners.[75]

The Non-Russian Commission met on the evening of 19 July and adopted the resolutions of the subcommissions. It took note of Litvinov's declaration and unanimously rejected it as a basis for an agreement, but announced that the "lines of conduct indicated in [the] declaration can, if it is accepted by [the] Russian government and loyally carried out, contribute to the restoration of confidence which is necessary for [the] collaboration of Europe in [the] restoration of Russia."[76] They tossed the ball back to the Russians' court.

There was also a final clause, inserted on the insistence of the British, noting that "this declaration can help to create a favorable atmosphere for any further negotiations which may be considered expedient by the various governments."[77] To clarify how they intended to proceed with these "further negotiations" and any separate agreements, the French and Belgians pressed for another plenary session of the Non-Russian Commission. On the next day, 20 July, the closing of the Hague Conference, the Non-Russian Commission adopted the "Cattier resolution," which recommended that the governments represented at The Hague "not assist their nationals in attempting to acquire property in Russia which belonged to other foreign nationals and [was] confiscated since November 1917 without [the] consent of such foreign owners or concessionaires provided that the same recommendation is made by the governments not so represented and that no decision shall be come to jointly except with these governments."[78]

The Cattier resolution, a nonbinding and innocuous gesture, was the closing

74. Pelt to Attolico, The Hague, 21 July, LNA 40A 21887/X; British Delegation to Balfour, The Hague, 19 July, GB FO 371 N6977/646/38; Romano Avezanna to Schanzer, Scheveningen, 23 July, IMAE 54 (Aja).

75. Benoist résumé of the Hague Conference, Paris, 12 Aug., FMAE Y 37.

76. Marling [Lloyd-Greame] to Balfour, The Hague, 19 July, *DBFP*, 19:1121–22; "Report to the Council of People's Commissars of the Soviet Delegation to the Hague Conference," 22 July, in Jane Degras, ed., *Soviet Documents on Foreign Policy* (London and New York: Oxford University Press, 1951), pp. 322–27.

77. *DBFP*, 19:1122. Lloyd-Greame to Lloyd George, Scheveningen, 20 July, LGP F 46/3/10.

78. *DBFP*, 19:1123.

act of the Hague Conference. It signified the gulf that separated the Allies from each other. Britain, still anticipating an arrangement with Russia, had both acquiesced in the resolution and insisted on the last clause, that American and German compliance were essential. France, Britain, and Belgium squabbled over the wording. The French insisted strongly though futilely that there be no acknowledgment of the Russians' right to nationalize property. The capitalist world was still far from united: by specifying the date November 1917 as establishing eligibility for restitution, the Allies excluded both German property confiscated before the Russian Revolution and properties acquired by American and other speculators thereafter.[79]

In time the Cattier resolution quietly disappeared. London, though reluctant to disown it, was unwilling to promote its universal ratification. Western capitalists and oil companies bid separately to enter Russia. They produced and marketed goods and resources from confiscated properties and concessions, and only occasionally displayed concern for their expropriated fellows.[80]

The Hague Conference had failed. France again could claim a victory: there had been no progress in the West's relations with Soviet Russia, and Britain was back at its side in time for the impending new crisis over Germany.[81] The Anglo-Soviet connection was withering. Litvinov announced that he was "tired of conferences" and would now deal strictly with individuals and single governments. However, when Krassin called on Lloyd George on 28 July, the British prime minister, though still keen to settle, gave him little encouragement; two days earlier, Churchill had slammed the door on the question of de jure recognition of Soviet Russia. Soon afterwards, Moscow renounced Litvinov's bizarre declaration of 19 July.[82] The "spirit of Genoa" had expired.

79. Hilton Young to Lloyd George, The Hague, 9 July, LGP F 28/8/15; Marling [Lloyd-Greame] to Balfour, The Hague, 13 July, Gregory, Tyrrell, and Crowe memoranda, London, 14 July, GB FO 371 N6733/646/38; Balfour to Marling [Lloyd-Greame], London, 15 July, GB FO 371 N6733/646/38; Balfour memorandum to Lloyd George, 15 July, GB FO 371 N6883/646/38; British Delegation to Balfour, The Hague, 15 July, GB FO 371 N6824/646/38; Balfour to Belgian Ambassador Moncheur, London, 17 July, GB FO 371 N6889/646/38; Poincaré to Saint-Aulaire, Paris, 14 July, FMAE PM La Haye III; Peretti to Alphand, Paris, 14 July, ibid.; British Delegation to Balfour, 20 July, *DBFP*, 19:1123.

80. Ovey minute, London, 11 Aug., Ovey to Lloyd-Greame, 24 Aug., GB FO 371 N7644/646/38; Curzon to Knatchbull-Hugessen, London, 16 Nov., Knatchbull-Hugessen to Curzon, The Hague, 22 Nov., *DBFP*, 20:944–45, 950; Poincaré to Governments represented at the Hague Conference, Paris, 30 Dec., FMAE B 132; cabinet memorandum by pres. of Board of Trade, on purchase of Russian oil, 22 Nov. 1929, GB BT POW 33/340, but also a notice offering compensation to former owners of expropriated oil properties in Baku and Grosny in *Daily Telegraph*, 7 Mar. 1932.

81. Benoist, Conférence de la Haye, 29 July, FMAE Y 37; US MID Intell. Summary, 1922, p. 9451. Cf. Posonby to Morel, [1923], Morel Papers.

82. Ligne to Jaspar, The Hague, 24 July, BMAE 10992; Litvinov statement, Moscow, 10 Aug. (intercept), GB FO 371 N7647/646/38; Churchill to Lloyd George, London, 26 July, WSCP;

Epilogue

During the last third of 1922, while the reparations question, the related problem of interallied debts, and the new crisis in the Near East all dominated the major capitals, the issues framed at the Genoa Conference began to unravel. There was no further discussion of an Anglo-French or an Anglo-Belgian pact. The League of Nations dealt very generally with the problems of disarmament and minorities in the September assembly. On 20 November 1922, four months after the Hague Conference, the Genoa nonaggression pact expired. Lloyd George had resigned a month earlier, his successor made no effort to prolong it,[83] and his quest for European peace and stability was suspended. After Chanak, Mussolini's advent to power, the invasion of the Ruhr, and Lenin's death, revisionism took on an entirely new face.

Russia and the powers drew apart. After the Hague Conference, the United States offered to send a technical commission to Russia to investigate the possibility of purely commercial bilateral relations. On 16 September Chicherin not unexpectedly refused.[84] At the same time, Leslie Urquart, who had attended the Genoa and Hague Conferences and who was chairman of the Russo-Asiatic Consolidated Corporation and head of the Association of British Creditors in Russia, negotiated an agreement with Krassin that provided a ninety-nine-year lease and restored to his company all its former properties and rights. Rising from his sickbed, Lenin, who had first encouraged this arrangement, tried to extract political concessions from Britain. Failing this, he swung his weight against what would have been the crown of Lloyd George's efforts for detente with the Bolshevik state.[85] Urquart never got his agreement, and Britain failed to achieve a head start in Russia.

French Radical leader Herriot journeyed to Russia in October 1922 and wrote glowingly of the "stability" of the Bolshevik regime. Nonetheless, as long as Poincaré headed the Quai d'Orsay, there was no improvement in

---

Churchill memorandum for cabinet, 4 Aug., LGP F 204/1/17; Churchill to Curzon, London, 2 Sept., CzP; Curzon to Hodgson, London, 10 Aug., *DBFP*, 20:908–9, and note of 28 July conversation, GB FO 371 H7372/646/38; Hodgson to FO, Moscow, 17 Aug. (2 tels.), GB FO 371 N8060/646/38.

83. Gregory memorandum, London, 1 Dec., *DBFP*, 20:954–55.

84. Harvey to Harding, London, 26 May, Harding Papers, roll 228; Hughes to Harding, 15, 25 July, Houghton to Hughes, Berlin, 28 July, Hughes to Harding, 31 July, Harding to Hughes, 31 July, 1 Aug., ibid., roll 231; Hughes to Harding, 21 Aug., Phillips to Harding, 30 Aug., Harding to Phillips, 30 Aug., J. G. Harbard to Christian, 31 Aug., Phillips to Harding, 15 Sept., and Houghton to State Dept., Berlin, 16 Sept., ibid., roll 181; also *Washington Post*, 16 Sept.

85. Wise to Grigg, 14 Sept., Grigg Papers, roll 2; Peters to Curzon, Moscow, 10 Oct., *DBFP*, 20:928–31; Lenin, *Collected Works*, 4 :562–63, 565–66; Giannini to MAE, London, 23 Oct., IMAE Amb. Lond. F532/21 (Russia); Thomas S. Martin, "The Urquart Concession and Anglo-Soviet Relations, 1921–1922," *Jahrbücher für Geschichte Osteuropas* 20 (1972):551–70.

Franco-Soviet relations.[86] The German government, which dutifully extended the Rapallo treaty to all the Soviet republics, was too embroiled with the reparations problem to expand its relations in the East.[87] Mussolini's Italy, though reviving Giannini's contacts with the Russians, held back from granting de jure recognition out of concern for angering Britain.[88] The Union of Soviet Socialist Republics was formed at the end of 1922. It considered itself still blockaded by the West, which had judged its conduct at Genoa and The Hague sufficient proof to suspend the process of detente. Russia consolidated its position in Europe as the foremost revisionist power next to Germany.[89]

After Lloyd George's fall, coalition government ended in Britain. Subsequent conference diplomacy, as practiced at Lausanne, London, and Locarno, reflected an entirely different conception of European appeasement: Russia was excluded, the United States remained outside, and the former enemies—first Turkey, then Germany—joined the Allies to formulate practical regional settlements. No statesman ever attempted an enterprise like the Genoa Conference again. Against the opposition of his Tory coalition partners and Churchill, an aloof and suspicious America, a fearful France, Belgium, Germany, and Russia, with the lukewarm support of Italy, the neutrals, and the East European states, the British prime minister had attempted a grand but flawed improvisation. The ruin of Lloyd George's Genoa policy became manifest three months after his resignation with the invasion of the Ruhr—the climax of a prolonged and bitter struggle among the victors of World War I as well as with the vanquished. The resulting settlement, however, laid the seeds for another, more deadly conflict.

86. Herriot to Millerand, Moscow, 2 Oct., BN PM/70; Peters to Curzon, Moscow, 9 Oct., *DBFP*, 20:927–28; Édouard Herriot, *La Russie nouvelle* (Paris: J. Ferenczi et fils, 1922); unsigned note, Berlin, 30 Oct., Germ. AA T-120 6700H/3045/H118818; Curzon to Hardinge, London, 13 Oct., Hardinge to Curzon, 24, 26 Oct., *DBFP*, 20:933–34, 938–41.

87. Maltzan Aufzeichnung, Berlin, 25 July, Germ. AA T-120 L690/4783/L204072–76; D'Abernon to Curzon, Berlin, 27 Oct., *DBFP*, 20:941–43.

88. Curzon to Graham, London, 4 Dec., Graham to Curzon, Rome, 7 Dec., *DBFP*, 20:955–57, 958–60. Italy finally granted de jure recognition on 31 Jan. 1924, one day before Britain.

89. Peters to Curzon, Moscow, 5 Dec., McNeill to Morel, London, 16 Dec., and especially Curzon to Crowe, Lausanne, 17 Dec., ibid., pp. 957–58, 965–67, 967–68; E. H. Carr, *The Bolshevik Revolution* (Baltimore: Penguin, 1966), 3:422–61.

Conclusion

The Genoa Conference in Retrospect

What were the fruits of the Genoa Conference? The Rapallo treaty, long antici-pated, was surprising only in its timing. Definition of the future relationship between Soviet Russia and the West was based on an uneasy, competitive coex-istence. The sharp accentuation of Anglo-French differences was long estab-lished and would remain a fixture of interwar history. Italy once more had failed to obtain special privileges from Britain.[1] The apparent crystallization of new territorial boundaries in Eastern Europe was achieved without any actual stability in the area or any specific commitment by the Great Powers. Finally, several resolutions were passed on financial, transport, and economic prob-lems; these formed the basis of attempts at international cooperation and were continued by the League of Nations. Though styled an international economic conference, Genoa was primarily a political gathering designed to reshape the postwar order, mitigate national antagonisms, reduce economic barriers, and create a durable peace. In the end, it unquestionably contributed not only to reestablishing contacts between nations but also toward sharpening differ-ences.

The Genoa Conference was based on a vision of Europe that had its roots in the period before World War I, of an affluent, stable continent led by six great powers in virtual balance that dominated the world with their arms, wealth, and culture. The Great War had changed everything, including the face of Europe itself: America's intervention, the Russian Revolution, the collapse of the Habsburg monarchy, and Germany's surrender created the new Europe re-flected in the Paris peace treaties. However, once the ink was dry, more funda-mental realities resurfaced: that the United States was more aloof from Europe than its contributions to the war and peace had indicated; that Russia would not permanently retreat from Europe; that the new order of Eastern Europe was

1. Schanzer went to London at the end of June, presented a list of requests for concessions in Africa and the eastern Mediterranean, received a cold reception from the British government, and returned to Rome a bitter and defeated man: Graham to Balfour, Rome, 13 July, GB FO 371 C10160/8635/22, and the accompanying minutes.

weak and unstable; and that Germany, potentially stronger than the sorely divided victors, would eventually seek its place in Europe.

At Genoa, Britain attempted to reshape Europe for its own benefit. Timing, political realities, and his own ambition and shortcomings worked against Lloyd George. Because of its long imperial tradition, Great Britain had no well-defined "European" policy, and its role at the Genoa Conference reflected London's indecision over whether to defend the treaties or join the revisionists. Lloyd George and his entourage conceived an activist British commercial and political leadership in Europe at a time when London was experiencing strong competition from America as well as anticolonial pressures in its empire. Lloyd George used conference diplomacy—hurried, ill prepared, and often fusing important but unrelated issues—to galvanize and direct British and European public opinion. His purpose, to promote accommodation, appeasement, and coexistence with former enemies, was aimed at restoring the ostensibly unified continent of prewar days and especially at reviving Britain's prosperity. This visionary goal developed too late to alter the realities of the recent past and too early to set bold directions for Britain and Europe's future.[2]

Under his successors, Britain's Conservative leadership returned to the ways of more traditional diplomacy, looking primarily to the empire for Britain's world role and attempting to maintain the more neutral position of balancer of forces in Europe. Genoa, the apotheosis of Lloyd Georgian diplomacy, lived on only in its details: the tendency to accept the inevitability of Germany's rejoining the powers, without Lloyd George's insistence that this be integrated into a broader European settlement that included Russia, and an enduring British uneasiness with both the peace treaties and the League, without any further efforts either to revitalize or replace them. Moreover, Lloyd George had always insisted, however vaguely, that European peace was indivisible. After Genoa, Britain endorsed the policy enunciated at Locarno, that peace was conditional on special arrangements devised by the powers.

When Briand fell in January 1922, a victim to some extent of his adherence to Lloyd George's Genoa policy, France, under the cautious and politically threatened Poincaré, became an unwilling partner in Britain's enterprise. Paris feared the consequences of success but also of failure. Genoa, stressing the

2. Kenneth O. Morgan, *Consensus and Disunity: The Lloyd George Coalition Government, 1918-1922* (Oxford: Clarendon Press, 1979), pp. 147–48 and 328, compares the "active" appeasement of Cannes and Genoa with the piecemeal and passive traditionalism of the Tories and the Foreign Office that led to Munich. A perhaps more fruitful approach would be to compare the *objects* of appeasement: Lloyd George sought primarily to bring Russia back into Europe, using Germany as an accessory and accomplice, accommodating France where possible, and hoping that the United States would cooperate. His successors, facing an isolationist Soviet state that was deemed hostile to the British Empire, staked all their appeasement efforts on Germany. America remained aloof, and Britain towed a bitter and reluctant France in the wake.

themes of "neither victors nor vanquished" as well as coexistence with the Soviet state, threatened France's security, its allies, its investors, and its conservative leadership. The underlying basis of the Genoa Conference called for the renunciation of France's hard-won victory on behalf of a needed liaison with more powerful Britain, which refused repeatedly to make a prior commitment to an alliance.

Poincaré, who disliked the unpredictability of conference diplomacy, worked consistently during the Genoa and Hague meetings to protect France's interests while carefully avoiding precipitate acts that would cause a rupture. More realistic and flexible than his detractors admit, Poincaré believed that France's security and economic problems could not be solved by improvised conferences but through patient use of traditional channels of diplomacy. Existing treaties and obligations might conceivably be altered to take in new conditions if the essential French interests were maintained. The Ruhr invasion of 1923 and its aftermath changed things drastically. Afterwards, a weakened and chastened France submitted more meekly to British direction than it had at Genoa. It admitted Germany to the Great Powers of Europe, but without relinquishing its rigid public posture of the treaties' defender, and lost the perhaps improbable opportunity Genoa had offered to rebuild Europe on the basis of universal acceptance of the status quo.

For Germany and Russia, the two outcast nations, Genoa embodied both progress and danger. Since neither could concede anything that could be represented as gains for the Allied side, the most prudent course was a negative one. The Rapallo treaty undercut Lloyd George's design for a collective agreement and, even more, for an agreement conditional on German and Russian submission to the West's commercial and political designs. Rapallo thwarted Lloyd George's strategy of controlling the Russian negotiations, forcing the West to continue the talks with Chicherin and Litvinov beyond any chance of success. Though Rapallo distorted the Genoa Conference and contributed to its failure, it left its signers still searching for economic aid and firm direction of their foreign policy.

Germany, to which Rapallo gave only temporary advantage, headed toward default, invasion, hyperinflation, and a new reparations settlement formulated by the bankers. Under Stresemann's leadership, which began one year after Genoa, Germany soon regained a major role in Europe. In 1926 it joined the League as a permanent council member, although it was still uncommitted to the new order, which most Germans were determined to revise eventually. Similarly, Russia, after undergoing the struggle for power following Lenin's death, under Stalin's leadership pursued a Great Russian *Machtpolitik*, first cautious, then overt. In 1922 neither Germany nor Russia could have been coerced into reentering the Concert of Europe; but Genoa's failure was the failure of *both* sides to take the first steps.

Italy, Belgium, Japan, the East European states, and the neutral countries were largely bystanders at the Genoa Conference, with occasional moments on the stage. They could exert little influence over the proceedings except to slow things down. Genoa solved none of their immediate problems and indeed exacerbated some. The fall of governments in Austria, Czechoslovakia, Poland, Bulgaria, Japan, and Italy was at least indirectly related to the protracted, inconclusive proceedings at Genoa. Italy, which had gambled recklessly on trading tremendous exertion and expense for quick rewards—a treaty with Russia, a settlement with Yugoslavia, the expansion of its influence in the Eastern Mediterranean—bore the greatest brunt of Genoa's failure; in the ensuing months, Mussolini, who had attended both Cannes and Genoa as a journalist, made capital of the liberal government's blunders. Czechoslovakia, which also played a prominent role in 1922 under Beneš's direction, was another significant loser. Confident that Britain and France would defend Eastern Europe against the resurgence of Germany and Russia, Beneš placed his trust too credulously in his own personal diplomacy and in the League of Nations. After Genoa, Eastern Europe, with its contested boundaries, discontented minorities, and internal and external rivalries, remained virtually unprotected against the revival of the two great revisionist powers.

The United States neither expected Genoa to succeed nor contributed measurably to its failure, but the American relationship with Europe was much strengthened by the results. Washington proceeded to demand debt repayment from its former allies and to propose and contribute to a new reparations settlement but also arranged its own immigration, tariff, and financial policies independently of Europe. The United States wanted a peaceful Europe, but its vision of Europe, more limited than Britain's, excluded Soviet Russia and largely ignored the intractable political and security problems of France and its allies. Washington's foreign interests lay primarily in Asia. Europe was of minor strategic and economic importance, and the League was considered of little consequence.[3] Genoa's end brought relief and some satisfaction. Its failure eventually caused Lloyd George's demise; and the Ruhr crisis gave the opportunity for an American solution without binding Washington politically to the Old World.

The Genoa Conference has been dismissed by Lloyd George's critics as a pipe dream and exaggerated by his supporters as one of history's important lost opportunities. The reality was somewhere in between. This study has attempted to discuss and analyze what actually happened at one of the most conspicuous diplomatic gatherings of the twentieth century. On 15 and 21 April, the West and Russia indicated a willingness to concede to the other; on 2 and

3. Child to Harding, Genoa, 22 May, Harding to Child, 24 July, 9 Oct., Harding Papers, roll 231.

11 May, they formally stated their positions, that although they were loath to break off, they could not satisfy the other side. Was there a chance Genoa could have succeeded? Probably not. Like the agreement at Helsinki in 1975, it might have established certain ground rules of coexistence and territorial stability and certain follow-up procedures, but it was unlikely that statesmen in the confused era after World War I had the ability to reshape Europe, to transcend Wilsonian and Leninist ideology with a cohesive concept of a new European order. The statesmen and experts who went to Genoa and The Hague did make some modest statements: they asserted the interconnection between economic and political stability; they accepted, at least for the sake of a growing segment of their public opinion, the opportunity to discuss rather than fight over territory, resources, and conflicting ideologies; and they acknowledged that peace meant not simply the absence of war but a quest for structure, leadership, and principles to guarantee the security of nations.

The personae at the Genoa Conference were, except for Beneš, men in their fifties whose values had been molded in the prewar era; even Chicherin, despite his fierce Bolshevik loyalties, represented a figure from the past age. The diplomats, cautious and self-conscious actors before a highly expectant public, promised "results" at Genoa that could not be produced. War and revolution, destruction of people, property, capital, and hopes, made European restoration a difficult if not impossible goal. The Genoa Conference demonstrated the limits of a daring diplomatic enterprise: a collective effort to revise the peace and strengthen the European order. Rapallo was the first step in another direction: the overturning of the decisions of 1918 by force.

Bibliography

This bibliography is organized as follows:

A. Manuscript Sources
  1. Government Archives (Austria, Belgium, Canada, France, Germany, Great Britain, Italy, United States)
  2. International (League of Nations)
  3. Private Collections and Personal Papers (listed by repositories)
B. Published Documents
  1. Government Collections and Papers (Belgium, Canada, France, Germany, Great Britain, Italy, the Netherlands, Russia, United States)
  2. International (League of Nations)
  3. Speeches
  4. Diaries, Journals, Letters, Memoirs, and Miscellaneous Writings by Contemporaries
C. Books, Articles, Dissertations
  1. International Affairs
  2. Austria
  3. Belgium
  4. Eastern Europe
  5. France
  6. Germany
  7. Great Britain
  8. Italy
  9. Near East
  10. Russia
  11. United States
D. Contemporary Press Publications
  1. Periodicals (Austria, France, Germany, Great Britain, Italy, Poland, Switzerland, United States)
  2. Newspapers (Belgium, France, Germany, Great Britain, Italy, Switzerland, United States)

A. Manuscript Sources

1. Government Archives

Austria
Österreichisches Staatsarchiv, Vienna
    Abteilung Haus-, Hof-, und Staatsarchiv
        Neues Politisches Archiv, Präsidal- und Politische Akten des Bundeskanzler
        Amtes, Auswärtiges Angelegenheiten, 1919–38: Deutschland, Italien (includes the Genoa Conference), Österreich, Rapallo, Tschechoslowakei, Vatikan
    Finanz- und Hofkammerarchiv
        Akten des Dept. 17 aus dem Finanzarchiv

Belgium
Ministère des Affaires Étrangères et du Commerce Extérieur, archive, Brussels
    Classement B
        Sér. 10991: La Conférence de Gênes
        Sér. 10992: La Conférence de la Haye
        Correspondance Politique, 1922: Allemagne, États-Unis, France, Grande-Brétagne, Italie

Canada
Public Archives of Canada, Ottawa
    Department of Finance
        Genoa Economic Conference, 1922
    Department of External Affairs
        Genoa Economic Conference, 1922

France
Ministère des Affaires Étrangères (since 1981, Ministère des Relations Extérieures), archive, Paris
    Sér. B: Relations Commerciales, Déliberations Internationales, 1920–29
        Conférence de Cannes
        Conférence de Gênes
        Réunion de la Haye
    Sér. Y: Internationale, 1918–40
        Conversations de Londres, 19 juin 1922
        Direction des affaires politiques et commerciales: Conférences politiques,
            Conférence de Gênes
        Entretiens de Londres, 19–22 déc. 1921
        Paix: États-Unis
        Ravitaillement et matières premières: pétroles
        Société des Nations
        Société pour la restauration économique de l'Europe
    Sér. Z: Europe, 1918–29
        Allemagne, Belgique, États-Unis, Grande-Brétagne, Italie, Russie, Tchécoslovaquie

Ministère de l'Économie et des Finances, archive, Paris
Sér. F [30]
   Banque russe pour le commerce étranger; société pour la reconstruction de
     l'Europe
   Cannes: Réparations
   Conférence de Gênes
   Conférence de la Haye
   Négociations anglo-russes
   Projet de reconstruction de la Russie, 1919–22; renseignements fournis par
     M. Poncet
   Russie: Correspondance, 1918–43
   Russie: Pétrole
Service Historique de l'Armée, Château de Vincennes, Vincennes
   Conseil supérieur de la défense nationale: Pétrole, Nov. 1922

Germany
Bundesarchiv, Koblenz
   R 2: Reich Finanzministerium
     Ausführung des Friedenvertrags von Versailles . . . Konferenz in Genua in
       April 1922
   R 38: Reichsministerium für Wiederaufbau
     Deutsch-Italienische Wirtschaftsverhandlungen, 1920–22
     Französische Finanzpolitik: Nachrichten über finanzielle Lage und Finanz-
       politik Frankreichs
     England: Nachrichten über wirtschaftliche Lage und Wirtschaftspolitik
       Grossbritanniens und Irelands, 1920–24
     Vorbereitung und Verhandlungen der Konferenz von Genua, Jan.–Nov. 1922
     Verhandlungen über die Regelung der Beziehungen mit Sowjet-Russland,
       1922–23
     Nachrichten über wirtschaftliche und rechtliche Verhältnisse in Sowjet-
       Russland
     Frankreich: Nachrichten über Wiederaufbau, wirtschaftliche Lage und Wirt-
       schaftspolitik Frankreichs, 1920–22
   R 43: Reichskanzlei
     Antisemitismus
     England, 1921–26
     Frankreich, 1919–23
     Handelspolitik, 1919–32
     Innere Politik im allgemeinen und politische Lage, 1920–23
     Internationale Wirtschafts- und Finanzkonferenzen, 1922
     Kabinettsprotokolle, 1922
     Konferenz von Genua: Handakten, Bde. 1–4
     Sowjet Union, 1922–23
     Vatikan
     Wirtschaftspolitik und Wiederaufbau, Apr. 1921–Oct. 1922
Politisches Archiv des Auswärtigen Amtes, Bonn
   Akten des R. M. Dr. Rathenau, Bde. 7–11

Deutsche Delegation in Genua, Bd. 16: Frankreich/Russland
Deutsche Delegation in Genua, Bd. 17: England/Russland
Deutsche Delegation in Genua, Bd. 18: Rapallo: Deutschland/Russland
Deutsche Delegation in Genua, Bd. 19: Russland: Genua
Abteilung IV Russland, Bde. 6–9
U.S. National Archives, Washington, D.C., Captured Records of the German
Foreign Ministry, 1920–45, on microfilm, Series T-120
    3398: Büro des Reichsministers, Akten betreffend Cannes, Genua, und der
      Haag
    4597H: Büro des Staatssekretärs Karl von Schubert: England (Ganz geheim)
    6192H: Geheimakten, Abteilung IV Polen Akten (Kleine Entente)
    6700H: Geheimakten, Abteilung IV A Russland: Wirtschaftliche Wiederaufbau
      Russlands (Konferenz im Haag)
    7605H: Nachrichten-Abteilung, R. M. Rathenau
    9233H: Abteilung W (Wirtschaft) Reparationen: Die Pariser Reparations-
      verhandlungen (1922)
    9234H: Abteilung W Reparationen: London, Aug. 1922
    9235H: Abteilung W Reparationen: Cannes
    9263H: Abteilung W Reparationen: Genua
    K128: Geheimakten: England, Personalien (Hutchinson)
    K130: Geheimakten: England, Botschafterkonferenz
    K131: Geheimsache: England
    K362: Abteilung II Politische Akten: Wirtschaftskonferenz . . . in Portorose
    K367: Abteilung II Politische Akten: Kleine Entente
    K1946: Alte Reichskanzlei: Konferenz in Genua
    L309: Deutsche Delegation Genua: Rapallo-Vertrag
    L311: Deutsche Delegation Genua: Rapallo (Römer/Radek)
    L312: Deutsche Delegation Genua: Rapallo
    L488: Abteilung IV Russland: Beziehungen zwischen Russland und
      Tschechoslowakei
    L640: Abteilung IV Russland: Rapallo Vertrag
    L690: Abteilung IV Russland: Rapallo Vertrag
    L751: Deutsche Delegation Genua: Deutsches Eigentum in Italien
    L752: Deutsche Delegation Genua: Italienische Sachverlieferungen
    L753: Deutsche Delegation Genua: Italienischer Wanderungsvertrag
    L754: Deutsche Delegation Genua: Abkommen mit Italien
    L755: Presse Abteilung Akten: Genua Konferenz
    L989: Sonderreferat A (Arbeit) Akten: Genua
    L989–99: Sonderreferat W (Wirtschaft) Akten: Genua
    L1464: Sonderreferat W (Wirtschaft) Akten: Genua
    L1465–67: Deutsche Delegation: Genua
    L1468: Presse Abteilung: Genua

Great Britain
Public Record Office, London
Board of Trade

BT 60:
Department of Overseas Trade
BT 90:
Advisory Committee to DOT
Confidential Minutes, DOT
BT POW 33:
Anglo-French Agreement
Anglo-Persian and Shell
Fuel Research Board
Imperial Economic Conference
Inter-Departmental Petroleum Committee
Petroleum situation, British Empire
Purchase of Russian Oil
Russia
San Remo
Shell
Washington Conference

Cabinet Papers
CAB 23:
Cabinet Conclusions, 1921–22
CAB 24:
Cabinet Memoranda
CAB 29:
Allied and International Conferences (Dec. 1921–Feb. 1923)
CAB 31:
Genoa International Conference, 1922
CAB 35:
Miscellaneous Memoranda, A.J. Ser.

Foreign Office Papers
FO 371:
General Correspondence, Political
Genoa Conference, 1922; Belgium, France, Germany, Italy, League of
Nations, Oil and Oilfields, Royal Dutch, Russia, United States
FO 800:
League of Nations, Feb. 1918–Oct. 1924
Private Office Papers from various sources: Conferences, 1922

Italy
Ministero degli Affari Esteri, archive, Rome
Conferenza di Cannes
Colloquio a Londra tra Lloyd George e Schanzer (Mar. 1922)
Conferenza di Genova
Colloquio a Londra (June–July 1922)
Conferenza Aja
Ambasciatra di Londra, 1921–22

United States of America
National Archives, Washington, D.C.
Department of State Decimal File, 1910–29
France, Genoa Conference, Germany, Great Britain, Italy, Russia
Military Archives Division, Records of the War Department, General Staff,
Military Intelligence Division, 1917–41
Political Conditions, General: Czechoslovakia, France, Italy, League of
Nations, Russia
Weekly Intelligence Summaries, vol. 18, 1922: Czechoslovakia, England,
France, Germany, Italy, Poland, Russia

2. International: League of Nations

Archives of the League of Nations, United Nations Library, Geneva
League of Nations and the Genoa and Hague Conferences
League of Nations: Special Circulars
Minutes of the Directors' Meetings, 1922

3. Private Collections and Personal Papers

Birmingham, England
Birmingham University Library
Sir Joseph Austen Chamberlain Papers

Bonn, Germany
Politisches Archiv des Auswärtigen Amtes
Ulrich von Brockdorff-Rantzau Papers
Edgar von Haniel Papers
Ernst von Simson Papers
Gustav Stresemann Papers

Brussels, Belgium
Archives Générales du Royaume
Henri Jaspar Papers

Cambridge, England
Churchill College Archive, Cambridge University
Maurice Hankey [1st Baron Hankey] Papers
Philip Lloyd-Greame [1st Viscount Swinton] Papers

Columbus, Ohio
Ohio Historical Society
Warren G. Harding Papers (microfilm edition)

Corning, New York
The Knoll
Alanson B. Houghton Papers

Geneva, Switzerland
United Nations Library, League of Nations Archives
Eric B. Drummond Papers
Alexander Loveday Papers
Paul Mantoux Papers

Kingston, Ontario, Canada
Queens University Library
Sir Edward Grigg [1st Lord Altrincham] Papers (microfilm edition)

London, England
Beaverbrook Library
William Maxwell Aitken [1st Baron Beaverbrook] Papers
British Library
Arthur James Balfour [1st Earl of Balfour] Papers
Edgar A. R. G. Cecil [1st Viscount Cecil of Chelwood] Papers
Edgar Vincent [1st Viscount D'Abernon] Papers
House of Lords, Record Office
Andrew Bonar Law Papers (consulted at Beaverbrook Library)
David Lloyd George [1st Earl Lloyd George of Dwyfor] Papers (consulted at
Beaverbrook Library)
India Office Library
George Nathaniel Curzon [1st Marquess Curzon of Kedleston] Papers
London School of Economics, Library
E. D. Morel Papers
Public Record Office
Sir Eyre Alexander Crowe Papers

New Haven, Connecticut
Sterling Memorial Library
Louis Fischer Papers

Ottawa, Ontario, Canada
Public Archives of Canada
Loring Christie Papers
William Lyon MacKenzie King Papers

Oxford, England
The Map House, Residence of Martin Gilbert
Sir Winston S. Churchill Papers

Paris, France
Bibliothèque Nationale
Alexandre Millerand Papers
Raymond Poincaré Papers
Ministère des Affaires Étrangères, Papiers d'Agents
Charles Alphand Papers
Joseph Avenol Papers

Camille Barrère Papers
François Charles-Roux Papers
Jean Goût Papers
Joseph-Fernand Grenard Papers
Édouard Herriot Papers
Henri de Jouvenel Papers
Jules Jusserand Papers
Charles Laurent Papers
Pierre de Margerie Papers
Alexandre Millerand Papers

Rome, Italy
  Archivio Centrale dello Stato
    Amedeo Giannini Papers
    Carlo Schanzer Papers
    Carlo Sforza Papers

Stanford, California
  Hoover Institution on War, Revolution, and Peace
    Louis Loucheur Papers

Washington, D.C.
  Library of Congress
    Charles Evans Hughes Papers

West Branch, Iowa
  Herbert Hoover Presidential Library
    Herbert Hoover Papers, Department of Commerce

B. Published Documents

1. Government Collections and Papers

Belgium
Ministère des Affaires Étrangères. *Documents Diplomatiques Belges, 1920–1940.*
  Vol. 1, *1920–1924.* Brussels: Palais des Académies, 1964.

Canada
Delegation to the Economic and Financial Conference at Genoa, 1922. *The Genoa
  Conference . . . April 10–May 19: Joint Report of the Canadian Delegates, Sir
  Charles Bordon and Prof. Édouard Montpetit.* Ottawa: F. A. Acland, 1922.

France
*Journal Officiel de la République Française. Chambre des Députés, Débats Par-
  lementaires.* Paris: Imprimerie des Journaux Officiels, 1919–24.
Ministère des Affaires Étrangères. *Documents Diplomatiques. Conférence de
  Washington, juillet 1921–février 1922.* Paris: Imprimerie National, 1923.
———. *Documents Diplomatiques. Conférence économique internationale de
  Gênes, 9 avril–19 mai 1922.* Paris: Imprimerie Nationale, 1922.

_____. *Documents Diplomatiques. Documents relatifs aux négociations concernant les garanties de securité contre une agression de l'Allemagne, 10 janvier 1919– 7 décembre 1923*. Paris: Imprimerie Nationale, 1924.

Germany
Akten der Reichskanzlei, Weimarer Republik. Die Kabinette Wirth I und II. Vols. 1–2. Boppard am Rhein: Boldt, 1973.
Auswärtiges Amt. *Material über die Konferenz von Genua*. Berlin: Reichsdruckerei, 1922.
Ministerium für Auswärtige Angelegenheiten der DDR/Ministerium für Auswärtige Angelegenheiten der UdSSSR. *Deutsch-sowjetische Beziehungen von den Verhandlungen in Brest-Litowsk bis zum Abschluss des Rapallo-Vertrages*. Vol. 2, *1919–1922*. (East) Berlin: Staatsverlag der DDR, 1971.
Reichstag. *Verhandlungen des Reichstags. Stenographische Berichte*, vols. 344–74. Berlin: Reichsdruckerei, 1921–24.

Great Britain
Foreign Office. *Documents on British Foreign Policy, 1919–1939*, 1st ser.
Vol. 14 (1920–22): *Far Eastern Affairs*. London: HMSO, 1966.
Vol. 15 (1921): *International Conferences and Conversations*. London: HMSO, 1967.
Vol. 16 (1921–22): *Upper Silesia, 1921–22; Germany 1921*. London: HMSO, 1968.
Vol. 17 (1921–22): *Greece and Turkey*. London: HMSO, 1970.
Vol. 18 (1922–23): *Greece and Turkey*. London: HMSO, 1972.
Vol. 19 (1922): *Conferences of Cannes, Genoa, the Hague*. London: HMSO, 1974.
Vol. 20 (1921–22): *German Reparation and Allied Military Control, Russia*. London: HMSO, 1976.
Parliament. House of Commons. *Parliamentary Debates*. 5th ser., vols. 138–59, 1921–22. London: HMSO, 1921–22.
Parliament. Papers by Command.
Cmd. 1207: *Trade Agreement between His Majesty's Government and the Government of the Russian Socialist Federal Soviet Republic*. London: HMSO, 1921.
Cmd. 1546: *Correspondence with M. Krassin respecting Russia's Foreign Indebtedness*. London: HMSO, 1921.
Cmd. 1570: *Correspondence between His Majesty's Government and the French Government Respecting the Angora Agreement of 20 October 1921*. London: HMSO, 1921.
Cmd. 1621: *Resolutions Adopted by the Supreme Council at Cannes, January 1922*. London: HMSO, 1922.
Cmd. 1637: *Telegram from M. Chicherin, Moscow, to the Governments of Great Britain, France, and Italy Respecting the Genoa Conference*. London: HMSO, 1922.
Cmd. 1641: Miscellaneous No. 3. *The Pronouncement by Three Allied Ministers for Foreign Affairs Respecting the Near Eastern Situation, Paris, 27 Mar. 1922*. London: HMSO, 1922.
Cmd. 1650: *Resolutions of the Financial Commission*. London: HMSO, 1922.
Cmd. 1657: *Memorandum sent to the Russian Delegation, Wednesday, 3 May 1922*. London: HMSO, 1922.

Cmd. 1667: *Papers Relating to the International Economic Conference of Genoa, April–May 1922*. London: HMSO, 1922.

Cmd. 1724: *Papers Relating to the Hague Conference, June–July 1922*. London: HMSO, 1922.

Cmd. 1742: *Correspondence between His Majesty's Government and the French Government Respecting the Genoa Conference*. London: HMSO, 1922.

Cmd. 2169: *Papers Respecting Negotiations for an Anglo-French Pact*. London: HMSO, 1924.

Italy

Commissione per la Pubblicazione dei Documenti Diplomatici. *I Documenti Diplomatici*. Ser. 7, vol. 1. Rome: Libreria dello Stato, 1953.

Ministero deglo Affari Esteri. *Les Documents de la Conférence de Gênes*. Rome: MAE, 1922.

The Netherlands

Departement van Buitenlandsche Zaken. *Conference at the Hague. Minutes and Documents*. The Hague: M.B.Z., 1922.

Departement van Buitenlandse Zaken. *Documenten betreffende de Buitenlandse Politiek van Nederland, 1919–1945*. Ser. A, *1919–1930*. Vol. 2, *July 1920–Aug. 1921*. The Hague: Martinus Nijhoff, 1977. Vol. 3, *Sept 1921–July 1922*. The Hague: Martinus Nijhoff, 1980.

Russia

Degras, Jane, ed. *Soviet Documents on Foreign Policy*. London and New York: Oxford University Press, 1951.

Communist Internationale. *The Communist Internationale, 1919–1943*, ed. Jane Degras. Vol. 1. London: Oxford University Press, 1956.

————. *Compte rendu de la conférence de l'executif élargi de l'internationale communiste, Moscou 24 fév.–4 mars 1922*. Paris: Librairie de l'Humanité, 1922.

————. *Protokoll des internationalen Executivkomitees in Berlin vom 2. bis 5. April 1922*. Vienna: Kommunistische Internationale, 1922.

Ministerstvo Inostrannykh Del (Ministry of Foreign Affairs). *Dokumenty vneshnei politiki SSSR*, Vol. 4, *Mar.–Dec. 1921*. Moscow: Gosizdat, 1961. Vol. 5, *Jan.–Nov. 1922*. Moscow: Gosizdat, 1962.

————. *Dokumenty e materialy po istorii sovetsko-chekhoslovakskikh otnoshenii*. Vol. 1. Moscow: MID, 1973.

Narodnyi Komissariat po Inostrannym Delam (People's Commissariat of Foreign Affairs). *Gaagskaia Konferentsiia, Iun' Iul' 1922*. Moscow: NKID, 1922.

————. *Genuezkaia Konferenciia*. Moscow: NKID, 1922.

————. *Materialy Genuezkoi Konferentsii*. Moscow: NKID, 1922.

Soviet Delegation, Genoa Conference. *Les réclamations de la Russie aux états responsables de l'intervention et du blocus*. Genoa: NKID, 1922.

United States

Department of State. *Conference on the Limitation of Armament, Washington, Nov. 12, 1921–Feb. 6, 1922*. Washington: GPO, 1922.

————. *Papers Relating to the Foreign Relations of the United States. 1921*, Vol. 2.

Washington: GPO, 1936. *1922*, Vols. 1–2. Washington: GPO, 1938.
Federal Reserve Board. *Federal Reserve Bulletin: The Genoa Conference*. Washington: GPO, 1922.
Senate Subcommittee on Disarmament. *Disarmament and Security: A Collection of Documents, 1919–1955*. Washington: GPO, 1956.

2. International: League of Nations

League of Nations, Assembly. *Plenary Meetings of the Third Assembly*. Geneva: League of Nations, 1922.
League of Nations, Economic, Financial, and Transit Department. *Commercial Policy in the Interwar Period: International Proposals and National Policies*. Geneva: League of Nations, 1942.
League of Nations, Secretariat. *La Conférence de Gênes et la Société des Nations: Mémorandum du Secrétaire-Général*. Geneva: Secretariat, League of Nations, 1922.

3. Speeches

Beneš, Edvard. *Exposé de M. Beneš au sujet de la Conférence de Gênes, fait devant la Chambre des Députés et la Sénat, le 23 mai 1922*. Prague: Orbis, 1922.
Brătianu, Ionel. "Discours au 29 juillet au parlement roumain." *L'Europe Nouvelle* (26 August 1922).
Briand, Aristide. *Paroles de paix*. Paris and Brussels: E. Figuière, 1922.
Hughes, Charles Evans. *The Pathway to Peace: Representative Addresses Delivered during his Term as Secretary of State, 1921–1925*. New York and London: Harper, 1925.
La politique française en 1922. Paris: Dunod, 1923.
Radek, Karl. *Die Einheitsfront des Proletariats und die kommunistische Internationale*. Hamburg: Kommunistische Internationale, 1922.
————. *Die Liquidation des Versailles Friedens: Bericht an den IV Kongress der kommunistischen Internationale*. Hamburg: Kommunistische Internationale, 1922.
Rathenau, Walther. *Cannes und Genua*. Berlin: S. Fischer, 1922.
————. *Gesammelte Reden*. Berlin: S. Fischer, 1924.
Schanzer, Carlo. *Sulla conferenza di Genova e sulla politica estera dell' Italia: Discorsi raccolti a cura di Amedeo Giannini*. Rome: Libreria di Scienze e Lettre, 1922.
Wirth, Joseph. *Reden während der Kanzlerschaft*. Berlin: Germania, 1925.
Zinoviev, Georgi. *Die Taktik der kommunistischen Internationale gegen die Offensive des Kapitals*. Hamburg: Kommunistische Internationale, 1922.

4. Other Documentary Sources

Lenin, V. I. *Collected Works*. Vols. 32, 33, 42, 45. Moscow: Progress Publishers, 1965–71.
————. *Selected Works: 1922*. Moscow: Progress Publishers, 1967.
Stalin, J. V. *Works*. Vol. 10. Moscow: Foreign Languages Publishing House, 1954.

The Trotsky Papers, 1917–1922. Edited by J. M. Meijer. Vol. 2, *1920–1922.* The Hague and Paris: Mouton, 1971.

5. Diaries, Journals, Letters, Memoirs, and Miscellaneous Writings by Contemporaries

Albertini, Luigi. *Epistolario, 1911–1926.* Vol. 3, *Il dopoguerra, 6 Nov. 1918–28 Ott. 1922.* Milan: Mondadori, 1968.

Benoist, Charles. *Souvenirs de Charles Benoist.* Vol. 3, *1902–1933.* Paris: Plon, 1934.

Bergmann, Carl. *The History of Reparations.* London: E. Benn, 1927.

Beyens, Auguste Baron. *Quatre ans à Rome, 1921–1925.* Paris: Plon, 1934.

Bonn, Moritz. *Wandering Scholar.* New York: John Day, 1948.

Bonnet, Georges. *Le Quai d'Orsay sous trois républiques, 1870–1961.* Paris: A. Fayard, 1961.

Charles-Roux, François. *Souvenirs diplomatiques: Une grande ambassade à Rome, 1919–1925.* Paris: A. Fayard, 1961.

Child, Richard W. *A Diplomat Looks at Europe.* New York: Duffield, 1925.

Churchill, Winston. *The World Crisis.* Vol. 4, *The Aftermath.* London: Butterworth, 1929.

Conti, Ettore. *Dal taccuino di un borghese.* Milan: Garzanti, 1946.

D'Abernon, Viscount Edgar. *Versailles to Rapallo, 1920–1922: The Diary of an Ambassador.* Garden City, N.Y.: Doubleday, Doran and Co., 1929.

Davidson, J. C. C. *Memoirs of a Conservative.* Edited by Robert R. James. London: Weidenfeld and Nicolson, 1969.

Eastman, Max. *Love and Revolution: My Journey through an Epoch.* New York: Random House, 1964.

Ebert, Friedrich. *Schriften, Aufzeichnungen, Reden.* 2 vols. Dresden: C. Reissner, 1926.

Einaudi, Luigi. *Cronache economiche e politiche di un trentennio, 1893–1926.* Vol. 6, *1921–22.* Turin: G. Einaudi, 1966.

Fischer, Louis. *Men and Politics: An Autobiography.* London: Cape, 1941.

Fraser, W. Lionel. *All to the Good.* Garden City, N.Y.: Doubleday, 1963.

Giolitti, Giovanni. *Quaranti' anni di politica italiana.* Vol. 3, *1910–1928.* Milan: Feltrinelli, 1962.

Gregory, J. D. *On the Edge of Diplomacy.* London: Hutchinson, 1928.

Guariglia, Raffaele. *Ricordi, 1922–1946.* Naples: Edizioni Scientifiche Italiane, 1949.

Hardinge, Charles. *Old Diplomacy.* London: J. Murray, 1947.

Hemingway, Ernest. *Hemingway By-Line: 75 Articles and Dispatches of Four Decades.* London: Penguin, 1968.

Herriot, Édouard. *Jadis: D'une guerre à l'autre.* Paris: Flammarion, 1952.

Jones, Thomas. *Whitehall Diary.* Vol. 1, *1916–1925.* London and New York: Oxford University Press, 1969.

Kennedy, A. L. *Old Diplomacy and New.* London: J. Murray, 1922.

Kessler, Harry Graf. *Tagebücher, 1918–1937.* Frankfurt-am-Main: Insel-Verlag, 1961.

Keynes, John Maynard. *The Collected Writings of John Maynard Keynes.* Vol. 17, *Activities, 1920–1922, Treaty Revision and Reconstruction.* Edited by Elizabeth Johnson. London and New York: Macmillan, 1977.

Laroche, Jules. *Au Quai d'Orsay avec Briand et Poincaré, 1913–1926.* Paris: Hachette, 1957.

———. "La grande déception de Cannes (Souvenirs de 1922)." *La Revue de Paris* (June 1957): 39–51.

Lloyd George, David. *Memoirs of the Paris Peace Conference.* 2 vols. New Haven: Yale University Press, 1939.

———. *The Truth about Reparations and War Debts.* London: Heinemann, 1932.

Lloyd George, David and Frances. *My Darling Pussy: The Letters of Lloyd George and Frances Stevenson, 1913–1941.* Edited by A. J. P. Taylor. London: Weidenfeld and Nicolson, 1975.

Lloyd George, Frances. *Lloyd George: A Diary.* Edited by A. J. P. Taylor. New York: Harper and Row, 1971.

———. *The Years That Are Past.* London: Hutchinson, 1967.

Lloyd George Family Letters, 1885–1936. Edited by Kenneth O. Morgan. Cardiff and London: University of Wales Press, 1973.

Lochner, Louis P. *Stets das Unerwartete: Erinnerungen aus Deutschland, 1921–1953.* Darmstadt: F. Schneekluth, 1955.

Loucheur, Louis. *Carnets secrets, 1908–1932.* Brussels: Brepols, 1962.

Lyubimov, N. N., and Erlikh, A. N. *Genuezkaia Konferenciia.* Moscow: Instituta Mezhdunarodnikh Otnoshenii, 1963.

———. "The 1922 Genoa Conference." *International Affairs* (Moscow) (June, Aug., Sept., Oct. 1963): 65–70, 97–103, 78–83, 71–78.

Monnet, Jean. *Memoirs.* Translated by Richard Mayne. Garden City, N.Y.: Doubleday, 1978.

Oeri, Albert. *Sorge um Europa: von Versailles bis Potsdam.* Basel: Schwabe, 1977.

Peretti de la Rocca, Emmanuel. "Briand et Poincaré (Souvenirs)." *La Revue de Paris* (16 Dec. 1936): 767–88.

Pierrefeu, Jean de. *La saison diplomatique: Gênes (Avril–Mai 1922).* Paris: Éditions Montaigne, 1928.

Rathenau, Walther. *Briefe.* Vols. 1–2. Dresden: C. Reissner, 1926.

———. *Tagebuch, 1907–1922.* Edited by Hartmut Pogge von Strandmann. Düsseldorf: Droste Verlag, 1967.

Ribot, Alexandre. *Journal et correspondances inédites, 1914–1922.* Paris: Plon, 1936.

Riddell, George Allardice. *Lord Riddell's Intimate Diary of the Paris Peace Conference and After, 1918–1923.* London: Gollancz, 1933.

Saint-Aulaire, August Félix Charles de Beaupoil. *Confession d'un vieux diplomate.* Paris: Flammarion, 1953.

Salandra, Antonio. *Memorie politiche, 1916–1925.* Milan: Garzanti, 1951.

Schanzer, Carlo. "La vicende e il risultati della Conferenza di Genova." *Vita Internazionale* 25 (10 July 1922): 237–45.

Scheffer, Paul. *Augenzeuge im Staate Lenins: Ein Korrespondent berichtet aus Moskau, 1921–1930.* Munich: R. Piper, 1972.

Schlesinger, Moritz. *Erinnerungen eines Aussenseiters im diplomatischen Dienst.* Cologne: Verlag Wissenschaft und Politik, 1977.

Scott, Charles Prestwick. *The Political Diaries of C. P. Scott, 1911–1928.* Edited by Trevor Wilson. London: Collins, 1970.

Seydoux, Jacques. *De Versailles au Plan Young.* Paris: Plon, 1932.

Sforza, Carlo. *L'Italie telle que je l'ai vue.* Paris: Grasset, 1946.

Steed, Henry Wickham. *Through Thirty Years, 1892–1922.* Vol. 2. London: Heinemann, 1924.

Stein, B. E. *Genuezkaia Konferenciia.* Moscow: Gosizdat, 1922.

Stockhausen, Max von. *Sechs Jahre Reichskanzlei: von Rapallo bis Locarno.* Bonn: Athenäum-Verlag, 1954.

Stresemann, Gustav. *Vermächtnis.* 3 vols. Berlin: Ullstein, 1932–33.

Swinton, Viscount [Philip Lloyd-Greame]. *I Remember.* London and New York: Hutchinson, 1949.

––––––. *Sixty Years of Power.* London: Hutchinson, 1966.

Sylvester, A. J. *The Real Lloyd George.* London: Cassell, 1948.

Troeltsch, Ernst. *Spektator-Briefe: Aufsätze über die deutsche Revolution und die Weltpolitik 1918/22.* Tübingen: Mohr, 1924.

Trotsky, Leon. *Mein Leben.* Berlin: S. Fischer, 1930.

Weiss, Louise. *Mémoires d'une européene.* Vol. 2, *1919–1934.* Paris: Payot, 1969.

Wiedenfeld, Kurt. *Zwischen Wirtschaft und Staat: Aus den Lebenserinnerungen von Kurt Wiedenfeld.* Berlin: W. de Gruyter, 1960.

C. Books, Articles, Dissertations

1. International Affairs

Aldcroft, Derek. *From Versailles to Wall Street, 1919–1929.* Berkeley and Los Angeles: University of California Press, 1977.

Artaud, Denise. "Die Hindergründe der Ruhrbesetzung, 1923: Das Problem der interallierten Schulden." *Vierteljahrshefte für Zeitgeschichte* 27, no. 2 (1979): 241–59.

––––––. *La question des dettes interalliées et la reconstruction de L'Europe (1917–1929).* 2 vols. Lille: Atelier Reproduction des Thèses, Université de Lille III, 1978.

––––––. "La question des dettes interalliées et la reconstruction de l'Europe." *Revue Historique* 262, no. 2 (April–June 1979): 363–82.

Bariéty, Jacques. *Les relations franco-allemandes après la première guerre mondiale.* Paris: Éditions Pedone, 1977.

Baumont, Maurice. *La faillite de la paix.* 2 vols. Paris: Presses Universitaires de France, 1951.

Bertrand, Charles L., ed. *Revolutionary Situations in Europe, 1917–1922.* (Proceedings, 2d International Colloquium, 25–27 March 1976, at the Inter-University Centre for European Studies.) Montréal: ICES, 1977.

Campbell, F. Gregory. *Confrontation in Central Europe: Weimar Germany and Czechoslovakia.* Chicago: University of Chicago Press, 1975.

Carr, E. H. *International Relations between the Two World Wars, 1919–1939.* New York: Harper and Row, 1966.

Cassel, Gustav. *Money and Foreign Exchange after 1914.* London: Constable, 1922.

Cassels, Alan. "Repairing the Entente Cordiale and the New Diplomacy." *Historical Journal* 23, no. 1 (1980): 133–53.

Clarke, Stephen V. O. *Central Bank Cooperation, 1924–1931.* New York: Federal Reserve Bank of N.Y., 1967.

La Conferenza di Genova e il Trattato di Rapallo (1922), Atti del covegno italo-sovietico, Genova-Rapallo, 8–11 guigno 1972. Rome: Edizioni Italia-URSS, 1974.

Craig, Gordon A., and Gilbert, Felix, eds. *The Diplomats, 1919–1939.* Vol. 1. Princeton: Princeton University Press, 1953.

Dingman, Roger. *Power in the Pacific: The Origins of Naval Arms Limitation.* Chicago and London: University of Chicago Press, 1976.

Dulles, Eleanor Lansing. *The Bank for International Settlements at Work.* New York: Macmillan, 1932.

Duroselle, Jean-Baptiste. *Histoire diplomatique de 1919 à nos jours.* Paris: Dalloz, 1962.

Fabre-Luce, Alfred. *La crise des alliances: Essai sur les relations franco-britanniques depuis la signature de la paix (1919–1922).* Paris: B. Grasset, 1922.

Fischer, Louis. *Oil Imperialism: The International Struggle for Petroleum.* New York: International, 1926.

Gathorne-Hardy, G. M. *A Short History of International Affairs, 1920–1939.* 4th ed. London and New York: Oxford University Press, 1950.

Gatzke, Hans W., ed. *European Diplomacy Between Two Wars, 1919–1939.* Chicago: Quadrangle Books, 1972.

Gilbert, Martin. *The Roots of Appeasement.* New York: New American Library, 1966.

Heideking, Jürgen. "Oberster Rat-Botschaftskonferenz-Völkerbund: Drei Formen multilateraler Diplomatie nach dem Ersten Weltkrieg." *Historische Zeitschrift* 231 (December 1980): 589–630.

―――――. "Vom Versailler Vertrag zur Genfer Abrüstungskonferenz: Das Scheitern der allierten Militärkontrollpolitik gegenüber Deutschland nach dem Ersten Weltkrieg." *Militärgeschichtliche Mitteilungen* 28 (1980): 45–68.

"The International Financial Conference at Brussels and Its Lessons." *Round Table* 11 (December 1920): 50–86.

Jacobson, Jon. *Locarno Diplomacy: Germany and the West, 1925–1929.* Princeton: Princeton University Press, 1972.

Joll, James. *Three Intellectuals in Politics.* New York: Pantheon, 1960.

Jordan, W. M. *Great Britain, France, and the German Problem.* London and New York: Oxford University Press, 1943.

Keynes, John Maynard. *The Economic Consequences of the Peace.* London: Macmillan, 1919.

―――――. *A Revision of the Treaty.* London: Macmillan, 1922.

Krüger, Peter. "Das Reparationsproblem der Weimarer Republik in fragwürdiger Sicht." *Vierteljahrshefte für Zeitgeschichte* 29 (January 1981): 21–47.

Launay, Jacques de. *Histoire contemporaine de la diplomatie secrète, 1914 à 1945.* Lausanne: Éditions Rencontre, 1965.

Maier, Charles S. *Recasting Bourgeois Europe: Stabilization in France, Germany, and Italy in the Decade after World War I*. Princeton: Princeton University Press, 1975.

Marks, Sally. *The Illusion of Peace: International Relations in Europe, 1918–1933*. New York: St. Martin's, 1976.

————. "The Myths of Reparations." *Central European History* 17, no. 3 (1978): 231–55.

Mayer, Arno J. *Politics and Diplomacy of Peacemaking: Containment and Counterrevolution at Versailles, 1918–1919*. New York: Knopf, 1967.

Meyer, Richard. *Bankers' Diplomacy: Monetary Stabilization in the 1920s*. New York: Columbia University Press, 1970.

Mills, John Saxon. *The Genoa Conference*. New York: Dutton, 1922.

Mourin, Maxime. *Les relations franco-soviétiques, 1917–1967*. Paris: Payot, 1967.

Nelson, Keith L. *Victors Divided: America and the Allies in Germany, 1918–1923*. Berkeley and Los Angeles: University of California Press, 1975.

Newman, William J. *The Balance of Power in the Interwar Years, 1919–1939*. New York: Random House, 1968.

Nitti, Francesco S. *Peaceless Europe*. London and New York: Cassell, 1922.

Palyi, Melchior. *The Twilight of Gold, 1914–1936: Myths and Realities*. Chicago: Regnery, 1972.

Rhodes, Anthony. *The Vatican in the Age of Dictators*. London: Hodder and Stoughton, 1973.

Roskill, Stephen. *Naval Policy between the Wars*. Vol. 1, *1919–1929*. London: Collins, 1968.

Rossler, Helmuth, ed. *Die Folgen von Versailles, 1919–1924*. Göttingen: Musterschmidt-Verlag, 1969.

Rowland, Benjamin M., ed. *Balance of Power or Hegemony: The Interwar Monetary System*. New York: New York University Press, 1976.

Rüge, Wolfgang. "Zum Platz der revolutionären Nachkriegskrise, 1917–1923 im revolutionären Weltprozess." *Zeitschrift für Geschichtswissenschaft* 26 (1978): 771–84.

Schmidt, Royal J. *Versailles and the Ruhr: Seedbed of World War II*. The Hague: Martinus Nijhoff, 1968.

Schuker, Stephen A. *The End of French Predominance in Europe: The Financial Crisis of 1924 and the Adoption of the Dawes Plan*. Chapel Hill: University of North Carolina Press, 1976.

Schultz, Gerhard. *Revolutions and Peace Treaties, 1917–1920*. London: Methuen, 1972.

Selsam, John Paul. *The Attempts to Form an Anglo-French Alliance, 1919–1924*. Philadelphia: University of Pennsylvania Press, 1936.

Silverman, Dan P. *Reconstructing Europe after the Great War*. Cambridge: Harvard University Press, 1982.

Simonds, Frank. *How Europe Made Peace without America*. London and Garden City, N.Y.: Heinemann and Doubleday, 1927.

Sontag, Raymond. *A Broken World, 1919–1939*. New York: Harper and Row, 1971.

Stambrook, Fred G. " 'Resourceful in Expedients'—Some Examples of Ambassadorial Policy Making in the Inter-War Period." *Historical Papers* (1973): 301–20.

Strakosch, Sir Henry. "The Money Tangle of the Postwar Period." In *The Lessons of*

Monetary Experience, edited by Arthur D. Gayer, pp. 153–78. New York: Farrar and Rinehart, 1937.

Taylor, A. J. P. *The Origins of the Second World War*. London: Hamilton, 1961.

Temperley, H. W. V. *A History of the Peace Conference of Paris*. 6 vols. London: H. Frowde, Hodder & Stoughton, 1920–24.

Toscano, Mario. *Lezioni di storia dei trattati e politica internazionale*. Vol. 1. Turin: G. Giappichelle, 1958.

Toynbee, Arnold J. *Survey of International Affairs, 1920–1923*. London and New York: Oxford University Press, 1925.

Trachtenberg, Marc. *Reparation in World Politics*. New York: Columbia University Press, 1980.

Traynor, Dean Elizabeth. *International Monetary and Financial Conferences in the Interwar Period*. Washington: Catholic University of America Press, 1949.

Truchanowski, W. G., ed. *Geschichte der internationalen Beziehungen, 1917–1939*. Berlin: Deutscher Verlag der Wissenschaften, 1963.

Ullman, Richard H. *The Anglo-Soviet Accord*. Princeton: Princeton University Press, 1973.

Waites, Neville, ed. *Troubled Neighbors: Franco-British Relations in the Twentieth Century*. London: Weidenfeld and Nicolson, 1971.

Walters, F. P. *A History of the League of Nations*. London: Oxford University Press, 1952.

Wandycz, Piotr S. *France and Her Eastern Allies, 1919–1925*. Minneapolis: University of Minnesota Press, 1962.

Weill-Raynal, Étienne. *Les réparations allemandes et la France*. Vol. 2, *mai 1921– avril 1924*. Paris: Nouvelles Éditions Latines, 1947.

Wolfers, Arnold. *Britain and France between Two Wars: Conflicting Strategies of Peace since Versailles*. New York: Harcourt, Brace and Co., 1940.

Wüest, Erich. *Der Vertrag von Versailles in Licht und Schatten der Kritik: Die Kontroverse um seine wirtschaftliche Auswirkungen*. Zurich: Europa Verlag, 1962.

Zimmern, Alfred S. *Europe in Convalescence*. London: Mills and Boon, 1922.

2. Austria

Benedict, Henrich, ed. *Geschichte der Republik Österreich*. Vienna: Verlag für Geschichte und Politik, 1954.

Hochenbichler, Eduard. *Republik im Schatten der Monarchie*. Vienna, Frankfurt, Zurich: Europa Verlag, 1971.

Ladner, Gottlieb. *Seipel als Überwinder der Staatskrise vom Sommer 1922*. Vienna: Stiasny Verlag, 1964.

Malfer, Stefan. "Die Beziehungen zwischen Italien und Österreich, 1919–1922." *Annali del' Istituto Storico Italo-Germanico in Trento* 4 (1978): 161–73.

Rothschild, K. W. *Austria's Economic Development between the Two Wars*. London: F. Muller, 1947.

Schmidt, Peter E. "The Relief of Austria, 1919–1922." Ph.D. diss., Case Western Reserve University, 1977.

Zöllner, Erich. *Geschichte Österreichs*. Vienna: Verlag für Geschichte und Politik, 1970.

3. Belgium

Helmreich, Jonathan. *Belgium and Europe: A Study in Small Power Diplomacy.* The Hague: Mouton, 1976.

_____. "From Paris to Cannes: Belgium's Fight for Priority Reparation Payments, August 1921–January 1922." *Studia Diplomatica* 33, no. 4 (1980): 383–410.

Höjer, Carl-Henrik. *Le régime parlementaire belge de 1918 à 1940.* Uppsala and Stockholm: Almquist and Wiksells, 1946.

Jaspar, Henri. "La Conférence de Cannes de 1922." *La Revue Générale* 138 (1937): 129–47.

_____. "The Keystones of Belgium's Foreign Policy." *New York Times Magazine* 19 (March 1924): 1032–37.

Marès, Roland de. "M. Theunis et M. Jaspar." *Annales Politiques et Littéraires* 81 (9 December 1923): 683–84.

Marks, Sally. *Innocent Abroad: Belgium at the Paris Peace Conference of 1919.* Chapel Hill: University of North Carolina Press, 1981.

Miller, Jane K. *Belgian Foreign Policy between Two Wars, 1919–1940.* New York: Bookman Associates, 1951.

Shepherd, Henry L. *The Monetary Experience of Belgium, 1914–1936.* Princeton: Princeton University Press, 1936.

4. Eastern Europe

Alexander, Manfred. "Die Tschechoslowakei und die Problem der Ruhrbesetzung, 1923." *Bohemia* 12 (1971): 308–17.

Beneš, Eduard. "The Little Entente." *Foreign Affairs* 1 (September 1922): 66–72.

Berend Iván T., and Ránki, György. *Economic Development in East Central Europe in the 19th and 20th Centuries.* New York: Columbia University Press, 1974.

Codresco, Florin. *La petite entente.* Paris: P. Bossnet, 1930.

Gajanová, Alena. *ČSR a středoevropska politika velmocí (1918–1938).* Prague: Academia, 1967.

_____. "La politique extérieure tchécoslovaque et la 'question russe' à la Conférence de Gênes." *Historica* (Prague) 8 (1964): 135–76.

Gasiorowski, Zygmunt. "Czechoslovakia and the Austrian Question, 1918–1928." *Sud-Ost Forschungen* 16 (1957): 87–122.

_____. "Poland's Policy towards Soviet Russia, 1921–1922." *Slavonic and East European Review* 53, no. 131 (April 1975): 230–47.

_____. "Polish-Czechoslovak Relations, 1918–1922." *Slavonic and East European Review* 35 (1956): 172–93.

Gruber, Josef. *Czechoslovakia: A Survey of Economic and Social Conditions.* New York: Macmillan, 1924.

Hiden, John W. "The Significance of Latvia: A Forgotten Aspect of Weimar *Ostpolitik.*" *Slavonic and East European Review* 53, no. 130 (January 1975): 389–413.

Korbel, Josef. *Poland between East and West: Soviet and German Diplomacy towards Poland, 1919–1933.* Princeton: Princeton University Press, 1963.

Korczyk, Henryk. "Dyplomacja czechosłowacka w czasie konferencji economicznej w Genui." *Studia Historyczne* 21 (1978): 561–86.

Lederer, Ivo. *Yugoslavia at the Paris Peace Conference.* New Haven: Yale University Press, 1963.

Longu, Dov B. "Soviet Rumanian Relations and the Bessarabian Question in the Early 1920s." *South Eastern Europe* 6, no. 1 (1979): 29–45.

Macartney, C. A., and Palmer, A. W. *Independent Eastern Europe.* London: St. Martin's, 1966.

Machray, Robert. *The Little Entente.* London: Allen and Unwin, 1929.

Mamatey, Victor S., and Luža, Radomír, eds. *A History of the Czechoslovak Republic, 1918–1948.* Princeton: Princeton University Press, 1973.

Mikulicz, Sergiusz. *Od Genui do Rapallo.* Warsaw: Książkà i Wiedza, 1966.

Pasvolsky, Leon. *Economic Nationalism of the Danubian States.* New York: Macmillan, 1928.

Pearton, Maurice. *Oil and the Romanian State.* Oxford: Clarendon Press, 1971.

Plaschka, Richard Georg, and Mack, Karlheinz. *Die Auflösung des Habsburgerreiches: Zusammenbruch und Neuorientierung im Donauraum.* Vienna: Verlag für Geschichte und Politik, 1970.

"Polens Aussenpolitik zwischen Versailles und Locarno: Runderlass des polnischen Aussenministers Skirmunt an alle Missionen (Warschau, 2 Aug. 1921)." *Berliner Monatshefte* 18 (January 1940): 17–23.

Roberts, Henry L. "International Relations between the Wars." In *Challenge in Eastern Europe,* edited by C. E. Black. New Brunswick, N.J.: Rutgers University Press, 1954.

Rodgers, Hugh. *Search for Security: A Study in Baltic Diplomacy.* Hamden, Conn.: Archon Books, 1975.

Rose, Adam. *La politique polonaise entre les deux guerres.* Neuchâtel: Éditions de la Baconnière, 1945.

Rothschild, Joseph. *East Central Europe between the Two Wars.* Seattle: University of Washington Press, 1974.

Sakmyster, Thomas. "István Bethlen and Hungarian Foreign Policy, 1921–1931." *Canadian-American Review of Hungarian Studies* 5, no. 2 (1978): 3–16.

Seton-Watson, Hugh. *Eastern Europe, 1918–1941.* Hamden, Conn.: Archon Books, 1962.

Szurig, Georges. "Quelques observations à la veille de la Conférence de Gênes." *L'Est Européen* (5 April 1922): 92–97.

Teichova, Alice. *An Economic Background to Munich: International Business and Czechoslovakia, 1918–1939.* London and New York: Cambridge University Press, 1974.

Vondracek, Felix J. *The Foreign Policy of Czechoslovakia, 1918–1935.* New York: Columbia University Press, 1937.

Wandycz, Piotr S. *Soviet-Polish Relations, 1917–1921.* Cambridge: Harvard University Press, 1969.

5. France

Andrew, Christopher M., and Kanya-Forstner, A. S. *The Climax of French Imperial Expansion, 1914–1924.* Stanford: Stanford University Press, 1981.

Artaud, Denise. "À propos de l'occupation de la Ruhr." *Revue d'Histoire Moderne et Contemporaine* 17 (1970): 2–21.

Binion, Rudolf. *Defeated Leaders.* New York: Columbia University Press, 1960.

Blatt, Joel. "French Reaction to Italy, Italian Fascism, and Mussolini, 1919–1925." Ph.D. diss., University of Rochester, 1977.

Bonnefous, Édouard. *Histoire politique de la Troisième République.* 2d ed. Vol. 3, *L'Après-guerre, 1919–1924.* Paris: Presses Universitaires de France, 1968.

Bournazel, Renata. *Rapallo: Naissance d'un mythe. La politique de la peur dans la France du bloc national.* Paris: Fondation Nationale des Sciences Politiques, 1974.

Carley, Michael Jabara. "Anti-Bolshevism in French Foreign Policy: The Crisis in Poland in 1920." *International History Review* 2, no. 3 (1980): 410–31.

Celtus [André François-Poncet, Guillaume de Tarde, and Jean Benoist]. *La France à Gênes: Un programme français de reconstruction économique de l'Europe.* Paris: Plon, 1922.

Chaumeix, André. "Le nouveau ministère." *La Revue de Paris* 29, no. 1 (February 1922): 663–72.

Jacobson, Jon. "Strategies of French Foreign Policy after World War I." *Journal of Modern History* 55 (March 1983): 78–95.

Kaplan, Jay L. "France's Road to Genoa: Strategic, Economic, and Ideological Factors in French Foreign Policy, 1921–1922." Ph.D. diss., Columbia University, 1974.

Keeton, Edward D. "Briand's Locarno Policy: French Economics, Politics, and Diplomacy, 1925–29." Ph.D. diss., Yale University, 1975.

Kemp, Tom. *The French Economy, 1913–1939: The Story of a Decline.* London: Longman, 1972.

Leonhardt, Fritz Hermann. "Aristide Briand und seine Deutschlandpolitik." Inaugural diss., Heidelberg University, 1951.

McDougall, Walter A. *France's Rhineland Diplomacy, 1914–1924.* Princeton: Princeton University Press, 1978.

Miquel, Pierre. *La paix de Versailles et l'opinion publique française.* Paris: Flammarion, 1971.

———. *Poincaré.* Paris: A. Fayard, 1961.

Osgood, Samuel M. "Le mythe de 'la perfide Albion' en France, 1919–1940." *Cahiers Historiques* 20 (1975): 5–20.

Paul-Boncour, Joseph. *Entre deux guerres: Souvenirs sur la III. République.* Paris: Plon, 1945.

Pinon, René. *Le redressement de la politique française, 1922: Chroniques du ministère Poincaré.* Paris: Perrin, 1923.

Sauvy, Alfred. *Histoire économique de la France entre les deux guerres.* 4 Vols. Paris: A. Fayard, 1965–75.

———. "L'inflation en France jusqu'à la dévaluation de 1928." In *Mélanges d'Histoire Économique et Sociale en Hommage au Professeur Antony Bebel.* Vol. 2. Geneva: n.p., 1963.

Shorrock, William I. "France and the Rise of Fascism in Italy, 1919–23." *Journal of Contemporary History* 10 (1975): 591–610.

Siebert, Ferdinand. *Aristide Briand: Staatsmann zwischen Frankreich und Europa.* Zurich and Stuttgart: E. Rentsch, 1973.

Soulié, Michel. *La vie politique d'Édouard Herriot.* Paris: A. Colin, 1962.

Soutou, Georges. "Un autre politique? Les tentatives françaises d'entente économique avec l'Allemagne, 1919–1921." *Revue d'Allemagne* 8 (1976): 21–34.

————. "Die deutschen Reparationen und das Seydoux-Projekt, 1920–21." *Vierteljahrshefte für Zeitgeschichte* 23, no. 5 (1975): 237–70.

————. "L'imperialisme du pauvre: La politique économique du gouvernement français en Europe centrale et orientale de 1918 à 1929." *Relations Internationales* 7 (1976): 219–39.

————. "La politique économique de la France en Pologne (1920–1924)." *Revue Historique* 251 (1974): 85–116.

Suarez, Georges. *Briand: sa vie, son oeuvre.* Vol. 5, *L'artisan de la paix, 1918–1923.* Paris: Plon, 1941.

Wandycz, Piotr S. "French Diplomats and Poland, 1919–1926." *Journal of Central European Affairs* 23 (1964): 440–50.

Wormser, Georges. *La république de Clemenceau.* Paris: Presses Universitaires de France, 1961.

Zimmermann, Ludwig. *Frankreichs Ruhrpolitik von Versailles bis zum Dawesplan.* Göttingen: Musterschmidt-Verlag, 1971.

6. Germany (including Rapallo)

Anderle, Alfred. *Die deutsche Rapallo-Politik: Deutsch-sowjetische Beziehungen 1922–1929.* (East) Berlin: Rütten and Loening, 1962.

————. *Rapallo und die friedliche Koexistenz.* (East) Berlin: Akademie-Verlag, 1963.

Benz, Wolfgang, and Graml, Hermann, eds. *Aspekte deutscher Aussenpolitik im 20. Jahrhundert.* Stuttgart: Deutsche Verlags-Anstalt, 1976.

Blücher, Wipert von. *Deutschlands Weg nach Rapallo.* Wiesbaden: Limes Verlag, 1951.

Bresciani-Turroni, Constantino. *The Economics of Inflation: A Study of Currency Depreciation in Post-War Germany.* London: Allen and Unwin, 1937.

Brink, Marianne. "Deutschlands Stellung zum Völkerbund in den Jahren 1918/19 bis 1922." Diss., Free University of Berlin, 1962.

Craig, Gordon A. *From Bismarck to Adenauer: Aspects of German Statecraft.* Rev. ed. New York: Harper and Row, 1965.

Erdmann, Karl Dietrich. "Deutschland, Rapallo und der Westen." *Vierteljahrshefte für Zeitgeschichte* 11, no. 2 (April 1963): 105–65.

Euler, Heinrich. *Die Aussenpolitik der Weimarer Republik, 1918–1923.* Anschaffenburg: Pattloch-Verlag, 1957.

Eyck, Erich. *A History of the Weimar Republic.* Translated by H. P. Hanson and R. G. L. Waite. 2 vols. Cambridge: Harvard University Press, 1962.

Favez, Jean-Claude. *La Reich devant l'occupation franco-belge de la Ruhr en 1923.* Geneva: Droz, 1969.

Feldman, Gerald D. *Iron and Steel in the German Inflation, 1916–1923*. Princeton: Princeton University Press, 1977.

_____. "The Social and Economic Policies of German Big Business, 1918–1929." *American Historical Review* 75 (1969): 47–55.

Felix, David. *Walther Rathenau and the Weimar Republic: The Politics of Reparations*. Baltimore: Johns Hopkins University Press, 1971.

Freund, Gerald. *Unholy Alliance*. London: Chatto and Windus, 1957.

Gatzke, Hans W. "Russo-German Military Collaboration during the Weimar Republic." *American Historical Review* 63, no. 3 (1957): 565–97.

_____. *Stresemann and the Rearmament of Germany*. Baltimore: Johns Hopkins University Press, 1954.

"The German Inflation of 1923." *Midland Bank Review* (November 1975): 20–29.

Grottian, Walter. "Genua und Rapallo, 1922: Entstehung und Wirkung eines Vertrages." *Aus Politik und Zeitgeschichte* B25/26 (June 1962): 305–28.

Helbig, Herbert. *Die Träger der Rapallo-Politik*. Göttingen: Vandenhoeck and Ruprecht, 1958.

Helfferich, Karl. *Die Politik der Erfüllung*. Munich-Berlin-Leipzig: Schweitzer, 1922.

Hilferding, Rudolf. "Die Weltpolitik, das Reparationsproblem und die Konferenz von Genua." *Schmollers Jahrbuch* 46, nos. 3–4 (1922): 1–28.

Hilger, Gustav, and Meyer, Alfred G. *The Incompatible Allies*. New York: Macmillan, 1953.

Holtfrerich, Carl-Ludwig. *Die deutsche Inflation, 1914–1923*. Berlin and New York: W. de Gruyter, 1980.

Jacobsen, Hans-Adolf. *Misstrauische Nachbarn: Deutsche Ostpolitik, 1919–1970*. Düsseldorf: Droste Verlag, 1970.

Jones, Larry Eugene. "Gustav Stresemann and the Crisis of German Liberalism." *European Studies Review* 4, no. 2 (1974): 141–63.

Kessler, Count Harry. *Walther Rathenau: His Life and Work*. New York: Harcourt, Brace and Co., 1930.

Krüger, Peter. *Deutschland und die Reparationen, 1918–19*. Stuttgart: Deutsche Verlags-Anstalt, 1973.

Laubach, Ernst. "Maltzans Aufzeichnungen über die letzten Vorgänge vor dem Abschluss des Rapallo-Vertrags." *Jahrbücher für Geschichte Osteuropas* 22, no. 4 (1975): 556–79.

_____. *Die Politik der Kabinette Wirth, 1921/1922*. Lübeck and Hamburg: Matthiesen, 1968.

Linke, Horst-Günther. "Deutschland und die Sowjetunion von Brest-Litovsk bis Rapallo." *Aus Politik und Zeitgeschichte* 16 (1972): 23–37.

_____. *Deutsch-sowjetische Beziehungen bis Rapallo*. Cologne: Verlag Wissenschaft und Politik, 1970.

Maxelon, Michael-Olaf. *Stresemann und Frankreich*. Düsseldorf: Droste Verlag, 1972.

Mommsen, Hans; Petzina, Dietmar; and Weisbrod, Bernd, eds. *Industrielles System und politische Entwicklung in der Weimarer Republik*. 2 vols. Düsseldorf: Droste Verlag, 1974, 1977.

Morsey, Rudolf. *Die Deutsche Zentrumspartei, 1917–1923*. Düsseldorf: Droste Verlag, 1966.

Mueller, Gordon H. "Rapallo Re-Examined: A New Look at Germany's Secret Military Collaboration with Russia in 1922." *Military Affairs* 40 (1976): 109–17.

Pederson, Jörgen. "Einige Bemerkungen zur deutschen Inflation von 1919–1923." *Zeitschrift für die gesamte Staatswissenschaft* 122 (July 1966): 418–30.

Riekhoff, Harald von. *German-Polish Relations, 1918–1933*. Baltimore: Johns Hopkins University Press, 1971.

Rosenfeld, Gunter. *Sowjet Russland und Deutschland, 1917–1922*. (East) Berlin: Akademie-Verlag, 1960.

Salewski, Michael. "Das Weimarer Revisionssyndrom." *Parlament* 30, no. 2 (1980): 14–25.

Schieder, Theodor. "Die Entstehungsgeschichte des Rapallo-Vertrags." *Historische Zeitschrift* 204 (June 1967): 545–609.

———. *Die Probleme des Rapallo-Vertrags*. Cologne: Westdeutscher Verlag, 1956.

Schulin, Ernst. "Noch etwas zur Entstehung des Rapallo-Vertrages." In *Was die Wirklichkeit lehrt: Golo Mann zum 70. Geburtstag*, edited by Hartmut von Hentig and August Nitschke, pp. 179–202. Frankfurt: S. Fischer, 1979.

Stampfer, Friedrich. *Die vierzehn Jahre der ersten deutschen Republik*. Offenbach: Bollwerk-Verlag, 1947.

Stolper, Gustav. *German Economy, 1870–1940*. New York: Reynal and Hitchcock, 1940.

Strandmann, Hartmut Pogge von. "Grossindustrie und Rapallopolitik: Deutschsowjetische Handelsbeziehungen in der Weimarer Republik." *Historische Zeitschrift* 222 (April 1976): 265–341.

———. "Rapallo—Strategy in Preventive Diplomacy: New Sources and New Interpretations." In *Germany in the Age of Total War*, edited by Volker R. Berghahn and Martin Kitchen. London: Croom Helm, 1981.

Turner, Henry A. *Stresemann and the Politics of the Weimar Republic*. Princeton: Princeton University Press, 1963.

Uschakow, W. F. *Deutschlands Aussenpolitik, 1917–1945*. Berlin: Deutscher Verlag der Wissenschaften, 1964.

Weinberg, Gerhard L. "The Defeat of Germany in 1918 and the European Balance of Power." *Central European History* 2 (1969): 248–60.

Weisbrod, Bernd. "Economic Power and Political Stability Reconsidered: Heavy Industry in Weimar Germany." *Social History* 4 (May 1979): 241–63.

———. *Schwerindustrie in der Weimarer Republik*. Wuppertal: Hammer, 1978.

Williamson, John. *Karl Helfferich*. Princeton: Princeton University Press, 1971.

Zimmermann, Ludwig. *Deutsche Aussenpolitik in der Ära der Weimarer Republik*. Göttingen: Musterschmidt-Verlag, 1958.

Zsigmond, László. *Zur deutschen Frage, 1918–1923*. Translated by P. Félix. Budapest: Akadémiai Kiadó, 1964.

Zwoch, Gerhard. "Die Erfüllungs- und Verständigungspolitik der Weimarer Republik und die deutsche öffentliche Meinung." Inaugural diss., Christian-Albrechts University, 1950.

7. Great Britain

Aldcroft, Derek H. "The Impact of British Monetary Policy, 1919–1939." *Revue Internationale d'Histoire de la Banque* 3 (1970): 39–65.

―――. *The Interwar Economy: Britain, 1919–1939.* London: Batsford, 1970.

Andrew, Christopher. "British Secret Service and Anglo-Soviet Relations in the 1920s: From the Trade Negotiations to the Zinoviev Letter." *Historical Journal* 20, no. 3 (1977): 673–706.

Bardoux, Jacques. *Lloyd George et la France.* Paris: F. Alcan, 1923.

Beaverbrook, Lord. *The Decline and Fall of Lloyd George.* London: Collins, 1963.

Bertram-Libal, Gisela. *Aspekte der britischen Deutschlandpolitik, 1919–1922.* Göttingen: Kummerle, 1972.

―――. "Die britische Politik in der Oberschlesienfrage, 1919–1922." *Vierteljahrshefte für Zeitgeschichte* 20, no. 2 (1972): 105–32.

Butler, James R. M. *Lord Lothian, Philip Kerr, 1882–1940.* London: Macmillan, 1960.

Cairns, John C. "A Nation of Shopkeepers in Search of a Suitable France, 1919–1940." *American Historical Review* 79 (June 1974): 710–43.

Catterall, Ross E. "Attitudes to and Impact of British Monetary Policy in the 1920s." *Revue Internationale d'Histoire de la Banque* 12 (1976): 29–53.

Chirol, Valentine. "Four Years of Lloyd Georgian Foreign Policy." *Edinburgh Review* (Jan. 1923): 1–20.

Conte, Francis. "Lloyd George et la Traité de Rapallo." *Revue d'Histoire Moderne et Contemporaine* 23 (January–March 1976): 44–67.

Cowling, Maurice. *The Impact of Labour, 1920–1924.* Cambridge: Cambridge University Press, 1971.

Dohrmann, Bernd. *Die englische Europapolitik in der Wirtschaftskrise, 1921–1923.* Munich and Vienna: Oldenbourg, 1980.

Elcock, H. J. "Britain and the Russo-Polish Frontier, 1919–1921." *Historical Journal* 12, no. 1 (1969): 137–54.

Fisher, Herbert A. L. "Mr. Lloyd George's Foreign Policy, 1918–1922." *Foreign Affairs* 1, no. 3 (15 March 1923): 69–84.

Fritz, Stephen E. "Lloyd George and Britain's Search for Peace, 1918–1922." *International Review of History and Political Science* 13, no. 1 (February 1976): 31–70.

―――. "Lloyd George and Peacemaking, 1918–1922." Ph.D. diss., University of Kentucky, 1972.

―――. "*La politique de la Ruhr* and Lloyd Georgian Conference Diplomacy: The Tragedy of Anglo-French Relations, 1919–1923." *Western Society for French History, Proceedings* 3 (1975): 566–82.

Fry, Michael G. *Illusions of Security: North Atlantic Diplomacy, 1918–1922.* Toronto: University of Toronto Press, 1972.

Gallagher, John. "Nationalisms and the Crisis of Empire, 1919–1922." *Modern Asian Studies* 15, no. 3 (1981): 355–68.

Gilbert, Martin. *Winston S. Churchill.* Vol. 4, *The Stricken World, 1916–1922.* Boston: Houghton Mifflin, 1975.

Goold, J. Douglas. "Lord Hardinge as Ambassador to France and the Anglo-French

Dilemma over Germany and the Near East, 1920–1922." *Historical Journal* 21, no. 4 (1978): 913–37.

Hall, Hines, III. "Lloyd George, Briand, and the Failure of the Anglo-French Entente." *Journal of Modern History* 50, no. 2 (December [June] 1978): Supplement D1121–38.

Jones, G. Gareth. "British Government and Oil Companies, 1912–1924: The Search for an Oil Policy." *Historical Journal* 20, no. 3 (1977): 647–72.

Jones, Thomas. *Lloyd George*. Cambridge: Harvard University Press, 1951.

Kinnear, Michael. *The Fall of Lloyd George: The Political Crisis of 1922*. London: Macmillan, 1973.

Larew, Karl. "Great Britain and the Greco-Turkish War, 1912–1922." *The Historian* 35, no. 2 (1973): 256–70.

Lowe, C. J., and Dockrill, M. L. *The Mirage of Power: British Foreign Policy, 1914–1922*. Vol. 2. London: Routledge, 1972.

Lundgreen, Peter. *Die englische Appeasement-Politik bis zum Münchener Abkommen*. Berlin: Colloquium Verlag, 1969.

Martin, Thomas S. "The Urquart Concession and Anglo-Soviet Relations, 1921–1922." *Jahrbücher für Geschichte Osteuropas* 20 (1972): 551–70.

Medlicott, W. N. *British Foreign Policy Since Versailles, 1919–1963*. London: Methuen, 1968.

Moggridge, D. E. *British Monetary Policy, 1924–1931: The Norman Conquest of $4.86*. Cambridge: Cambridge University Press, 1972.

Montgomery, A. E. "Lloyd George and the Greek Question, 1918–22." In *Lloyd George: Twelve Essays*, edited by A. J. P. Taylor, pp. 257–84. London: Hamilton, 1972.

Morgan, E. Victor. *Studies in British Financial Policy, 1914–1925*. London: Macmillan, 1952.

Morgan, Kenneth O. *Consensus and Disunity: The Lloyd George Coalition Government, 1918–1922*. Oxford: Clarendon Press, 1979.

————. "Lloyd George's Premiership: A Study in 'Prime Ministerial Government.' " *Historical Journal* 13, no. 1 (1970): 130–57.

Mowat, Charles L. *Britain between the Wars, 1918–1940*. Chicago: University of Chicago Press, 1955.

Nicolson, Harold. *Curzon: The Last Phase, 1919–1925*. Boston and New York: Houghton Mifflin, 1934.

Nish, Ian H. *Alliance in Decline: A Study in Anglo-Japanese Relations, 1908–1923*. London: Athlone, 1972.

Northedge, F. S. *The Troubled Giant: Britain Among the Great Powers, 1916–1939*. London and New York: Praeger, 1966.

Orde, Anne. *Great Britain and International Security*. London: Royal Historical Society, 1978.

Owen, Frank. *Tempestuous Journey: Lloyd George, His Life and Times*. New York: McGraw-Hill, 1955.

Recker, Marie-Luise. *England und der Donauraum, 1919–1929*. Stuttgart: Klett, 1976.

Roskill, Stephen. *Hankey: Man of Secrets*. Vol. 2, *1919–1931*. London: Collins, 1972.

Rowland, Peter. *David Lloyd George: A Biography.* New York: Macmillan, 1975.

Schmidt, Gustav. "Britische Strategie und Aussenpolitik: Wahlchancen und Determinenten britischen Sicherheitspolitik im Zeitalter der neuen Weltmächte, 1897–1929." *Militärgeschichtliche Mitteilungen* 9 (1971): 197–218.

————. "Strategie und Aussenpolitik des 'Troubled Giant.'" *Militärgeschichtliche Mitteilungen* 14 (1973): 200–220.

Sharp, Alan J. "The Foreign Office in Eclipse." *History* 61, no. 202 (June 1976): 198–218.

Stamm, Christoph. *Lloyd George zwischen Innen- und Aussenpolitik: Die britische Deutschlandpolitik 1921/1922.* Cologne: Verlag Wissenschaft und Politik, 1977.

Steinbach, Lothar. "Britische Aussenpolitik in der Ära Lloyd George." *Neue Politische Literatur* 15 (1969): 534–46.

Taylor, A. J. P. *Beaverbrook.* London: Hamilton, 1972.

————. *English History, 1914–1945.* London and New York: Oxford University Press, 1965.

Williams, David. "Montagu Norman and Banking Policy in the 1920s." *Yorkshire Bulletin of Economic and Social Research* 2 (1959): 38–55.

Wilson, Trevor. *The Downfall of the Liberal Party, 1914–1935.* London: Collins, 1966.

Wise, E. F. "Anglo-Russian Trade and the Trade Agreement." *Empire Review* 38 (September 1923): 995–1104.

Zwehl, Konrad von. *Die Deutschlandpolitik Englands von 1922–1924.* Augsburg: Blasatitsch, 1974.

8. Italy

Calboli, Paulucci de. "La Conferenza di Genova e l'Italia." *Nuova Antologia* 210 (1 July 1922): 63–70.

Cassels, Alan. *Mussolini's Early Diplomacy.* Princeton: Princeton University Press, 1970.

Castronovo, Valerio. *Giovanni Agnelli.* Turin: Unione tipografico-editrice torinese, 1971.

Coppa, Frank J. "Francesco Saverio Nitti: Early Critic of the Treaty of Versailles." *Risorgimento* (Belgium) 2 (1980): 211–19.

De Felice, Renzo. *Mussolini.* Vol. 2, *Il Fascista,* Part 1: *La conquista del potere, 1921–1925.* Turin: G. Einaudi, 1965.

Giannini, Amedeo. *Saggi di storia diplomatica, 1920–1940.* Milan: Istituto per gli studi di politica internazionale, 1942.

Giusti, Ugo. *Le grandi città italiane nel primo quarto del XX^{mo} secolo.* Florence: Alfani e Venturi, 1925.

Hermon, Elly. "L'Italia di fronte all'occupazione franco-belga della Ruhr (1923)." *Storia Contemporanea* 10 (April–May 1979): 697–766.

Italy, Ente Nazionale per le Industrie Turistiche. *Ten Towns of Italy.* Rome: ENIT, 1933.

Johnson, Virginia W. *Genoa the Superb.* Boston: Estes and Lauriat, 1892.

Lopez, Robert. *Storia della colonie genovesi nei Mediterraneo*. Bologna: Zanichelli, 1938.

———. *Studi sull'economia genovese nel medio evo*. Turin: S. Lattes, 1936.

Lowe, Cedric J., and Marzari, F. *Italian Foreign Policy, 1870–1940*. London and Boston: Routledge, 1975.

Macartney, Maxwell H. H., and Cremona, Paul. *Italy's Foreign and Colonial Policy, 1914–1937*. London: Oxford University Press, 1938.

Marsico, Giorgio. "L'Italia e la preparazione della Conferenza di Portorose (24 ottobre–23 novembre 1921)." *Risorgimento* 30 (June 1978): 54–75.

Petrarchi, Giorgio. "Ideology and Realpolitik: Italo-Soviet Relations, 1917–1933." *Journal of Italian History* 2, no. 3 (1979): 473–519.

Pizzigallo, Matteo. "L'Italia alla Conferenza di Washington, 1921–1922." *Storia e Politica* 14, nos. 3–4 (1975): 408–48, 550–89.

Rodgers, Allan L. *The Industrial Geography of the Port of Genova*. Chicago: University of Chicago Press, 1960.

Rosen, Edgar R. "Mussolini und Deutschland, 1922–1923." *Vierteljahrshefte für Zeitgeschichte* 5 (1957): 17–40.

Rumi, Giorgio. *Alle origini della politica estera fascista, 1918–1923*. Bari: Laterza, 1968.

Salvemini, Gaetano. *Mussolini diplomatico*. Rome: De Luigi, 1945.

Veneruso, Danilo. *La vigilia del fascismo: Il primo ministero Facta nella crisi dello stato liberale in Italia*. Bologna: Il Mulino, 1968.

Vivarelli, Roberto. "Revolution and Reaction in Italy, 1918–1922." *Journal of Italian History* 1 (Autumn 1978): 235–63.

9. Near East

Anderson, M. S. *The Eastern Question, 1774–1923*. London: Macmillan, 1966.

Busch, Briton Cooper. *Mudros to Lausanne: Britain's Frontier in Asia, 1918–1923*. Albany: State University of New York Press, 1976.

Cumming, Henry H. *Franco-British Rivalry in the Postwar Near East*. London: Oxford University Press, 1938.

Evans, Laurence. *United States Policy and the Partition of Turkey, 1914–1924*. Baltimore: Johns Hopkins University Press, 1965.

Finefrock, Michael M. "Atatürk, Lloyd George and the *Megali* Idea: Cause and Consequence of the Greek Plan to Seize Constantinople from the Allies, June-August 1922." *Journal of Modern History* 52, no. 1 (March 1980) Supplement D1047–66.

Frangulis, A. J. *La Grèce et la crise mondiale*. 2 vols. Paris: F. Alcan, 1926.

Howard, Harry N. *The Partition of Turkey*. Norman, Okla.: University of Oklahoma Press, 1931; New York: Fertig, 1966.

Jäshke, Gotthard, and Pritsch, Erich. *Die Türkei seit dem Weltkrieg. Geschichtskalender: 1918–1928*. Berlin: Deutsche Gesellschaft für Islamkunde, 1929.

Krüger, Wilhelm. *Die englisch-französischen Spannungen bei der Lösung der orientalischen Frage*. Berlin: Ebering, 1940.

Paillarès, Michel. *Le kémalisme devant les alliés*. Paris: Édition du "Bosphore," 1922.

Pech, Edgar. *Les alliés et la Turquie*. Paris: Presses Universitaires de France, 1925.

Sforza, Carlo. "How We Lost the War with Turkey." *Contemporary Review* 32 (November 1927): 583–89.

Sonyel, Salahi Ramsdan. *Turkish Diplomacy, 1918–1923*. London and Beverly Hills, Calif.: Sage, 1975.

10. Russia

Achtamzan, A. A. "Genuezkaia Konferenciia i Rapall' skii dogover." *Voprosy Istorii* 5 (1972): 42–63.

_____. Lenin's Foreign Policy Activity (April–October 1921)." *International Affairs* 2 (1969): 50–53.

Bihl, Wolfdieter. "Die Sowjetunion aus der Sicht eines österreichischen Diplomaten (Apr. 1922)." *Österreichische Osthefte* 17, no. 3 (1975): 217–24.

Burakov, V. "Lenin's Diplomacy in Action." *International Affairs* 5 (1972): 92–97.

Buzinkai, Donald. "Soviet-League Relations, 1920–1923: Political Disputes." *East European Quarterly* 13, no. 1 (1979): 25–45.

Carr, E. H. *The Bolshevik Revolution*. 3 vols. Baltimore: Penguin, 1966.

Chicherin, Georgii. "Soviet Diplomacy since the War." *The Living Age* 320 (22 March 1924): 548–51.

Chossudovsky, E. M. *Chicherin and the Evolution of Soviet Foreign Policy and Diplomacy*. Geneva: Graduate Institute of International Studies, 1973.

_____. "Genoa Revisited: Russia and Coexistence." *Foreign Affairs* 50, no. 3 (April 1972): 554–77.

_____. "Lenin and Chicherin: The Beginnings of Soviet Foreign Policy and Diplomacy." *Millennium* 3, no. 1 (Spring 1974): 1–16.

Chubaryan, A. O. *Peaceful Coexistence: The Origin of the Notion*. New York: Arno, 1976.

_____. *V. I. Lenin i formirovaniye sovietskoy vneshney politiki*. Moscow: Nauka, 1972.

_____. "V. I. Lenin i Genua." *Istoriia SSSR* 2 (1970): 36–50.

Clemens, Walter C., Jr. "Ideology in Soviet Disarmament Policy." *Journal of Conflict Resolution* 8, no. 1 (1964): 7–22.

_____. "Lenin on Disarmament." *Slavic Review* 23 (September 1964): 504–25.

_____. "Origins of the Soviet Campaign for Disarmament: The Soviet Position on Peace, Security, and Revolution at the Genoa, Moscow, and Lausanne Conferences." Ph.D. diss., Columbia University, 1961.

Cohen, Stephen F. *Bukharin and the Bolshevik Revolution: A Political Biography, 1888–1939*. New York: Knopf, 1973.

Conte, Francis. "Autour de la polémique Rakovskij-Staline sur la question nationale, 1921–1923." *Cahiers du Monde Russe et Soviétique* 16, no. 1 (1975): 111–17.

_____. "Christian Rakovskij: Commissaire aux affaires étrangères de l'Ukraine, janvier 1919–aôut 1923." *Cahiers du Monde Russe et Soviétique* 12, no. 4 (1971): 439–66.

_____. *Christian Rakovski (1873–1941), Essai de biographie politique*. 2 vols. Lille: Atelier reproduction des thèses, Université de Lille III, 1975.

Davis, Kathryn W. *The Soviets at Geneva*. Geneva: Geneva Research Center, 1934.

Day, Richard B. "Leon Trotsky and the Politics of Economic Isolation." Ph.D. diss., University of London, 1970.

———. *Leon Trotsky and the Politics of Economic Isolation*. Cambridge: Cambridge University Press, 1973.

———. "Trotsky and Preobrazhensky: The Troubled Unity of the Left Opposition." *Studies in Comparative Communism* 10, nos. 1–2 (Spring–Summer 1977): 69–86.

Debo, Richard K. "Dutch-Soviet Relations, 1917–1924: The Role of Finance and Commerce in the Foreign Policy of Soviet Russia and the Netherlands." *Canadian Slavic Studies* 4, no. 2 (Summer 1970): 199–217.

———. "George Chicherin: Soviet Russia's Second Foreign Commissar." Ph.D. diss., University of Nebraska, 1964.

Deutscher, Isaac. *The Prophet Unarmed: Trotsky, 1921–1929*. London and New York: Oxford University Press, 1970.

Edmondson, Charles M. "The Politics of Hunger: The Soviet Response to Famine, 1921." *Soviet Studies* 29, no. 4 (October 1977): 506–18.

Eudin, Xenia J., and North, Robert C. *Soviet Russia and the East: A Documentary Survey, 1920–1927*. Stanford: Stanford University Press, 1957.

"La famine en Russie: Une manoeuvre déjouée." *Revue Politique et Littéraire* 60, no. 7 (1 April 1922): 193–96.

Fischer, Louis. *The Life of Lenin*. New York: Harper and Row, 1964.

———. *The Soviets in World Affairs*. Vol. 1. Princeton: Princeton University Press, 1951.

Fisher, H. H. *The Famine in Soviet Russia, 1919–1923*. New York: Macmillan, 1927.

Goldbach, Marie-Luise. *Karl Radek und die deutsch-sowjetischen Beziehungen, 1918–1923*. Bonn–Bad Godesberg: Verlag Neue Gesellschaft, 1973.

Grieser, Helmut. *Die Sowjetpresse über Deutschland in Europa, 1922–1932*. Stuttgart: Klett, 1970.

Griffiths, Franklyn. *Genoa Plus 51: Changing Soviet Objectives in Europe*. Toronto: Canadian Institute of International Affairs, 1973.

Herriot, Édouard. *La Russie nouvelle*. Paris: J. Ferenczi et fils, 1922.

Heymann, Hans. "Oil in Soviet-Western Relations in the Interwar Years." *American Slavic and East European Review* 7, no. 4 (1948): 303–16.

Jackson, George D. "Lenin and the Problem of Psychohistory." *Canadian Slavonic Papers* 2 (1977): 207–22.

K [Archibald C. Coolidge]. "Russia after Genoa and the Hague." *Foreign Affairs* 1, no. 1 (1922): 133–55.

Katzenellenbaum, S. *Russian Currency and Banking, 1914–1924*. London: P. S. King and Son, 1925.

Kennan, George F. "Peaceful Coexistence: A Western View." *Foreign Affairs* 38, no. 2 (1960): 171–90.

———. *Russia and the West under Lenin and Stalin*. New York: New American Library, 1961.

Krasina, Lîubov'. *Leonid Krassin: His Life and Work*. London: Skeffington, 1929.

Lang, David Marshall. *A Modern History of Soviet Georgia*. New York: Grove, 1962.

Lenin, V. I., and Trotsky, Leon. *Kronstadt*. New York: Monad Press, 1979.

Lerner, Warren. *Karl Radek: The Last Internationalist*. Stanford: Stanford University Press, 1970.

Linder, I. "Lenin's Foreign Policy Activity (October 1921–March 1922)." *International Affairs* 12 (1969): 46–51.

Möller, Dietrich. *Karl Radek in Deutschland*. Cologne: Verlag Wissenschaft und Politik, 1976.

Morse, William P., Jr. "Leonid Borisovich Krassin: Soviet Diplomat, 1918–1926." Ph.D. diss., University of Wisconsin, 1971.

Niedhart, Gottfried. "Die westlichen Allierten und das bolshewistische Russland." *Neue Politische Literatur* 15 (1970): 460–70.

Norton, H. K. *The Far Eastern Republic of Siberia*. London: Allen and Unwin, 1923.

Pasvolsky, Leo, and Moulton, Harold G. *Russian Debts and Russian Reconstruction*. New York: McGraw-Hill, 1924.

Payne, Robert. *The Life and Death of Lenin*. New York: Simon and Schuster, 1964.

Pipes, Richard. *The Formation of the Soviet Union*. Rev. ed. New York: Atheneum, 1968.

Rakovsky, Christian. "The Foreign Policy of Soviet Russia." *Foreign Affairs* 4, no. 4 (1926): 574–84.

_____. *Roumanie et Bessarabie*. Paris: Librairie du Travail, 1925.

Remington, Thomas. "Trotsky, War Communism, and the Origins of NEP." *Studies in Comparative Communism* 10, nos. 1–2 (Spring/Summer 1977): 44–68.

Rigby, T. H. *Lenin's Government: Sovnarkom, 1917–1922*. Cambridge and New York: Cambridge University Press, 1979.

Schapiro, Leonard. *The Origin of the Communist Autocracy: Political Opposition in the Soviet State. First Phase: 1917–1922*. Cambridge: Harvard University Press, 1955.

Schub, David. *Lenin*. Baltimore: Penguin, 1966.

Stein, B. E. "V. I. Lenin i Genuezkaia Konferentsiia 1922." *Vestnik Moskovskogo Universiteta* 2 (1960): 15–39.

Tarulis, Albert N. *Soviet Policy toward the Baltic States, 1918–1940*. Notre Dame: University of Notre Dame Press, 1959.

Trishka, Jan F. "A Model for the Study of Soviet Foreign Policy." *American Political Science Review* 52 (March 1958): 64–83.

Trush, M. "Lenin's Foreign Policy Activity (Apr.–July 1922)." *International Affairs* 1 (1970): 63–66.

_____. "Lenin's Foreign Policy Activity (Aug. 1922–Mar. 1923)." *International Affairs* 2–3 (1970): 34–47.

Ulam, Adam. *Lenin and the Bolsheviks: The Intellectual and Political History of the Triumph of Communism in Russia*. London: Collins, 1969.

Uldricks, Teddy J. *Diplomacy and Ideology: The Origins of Soviet Foreign Relations, 1917–1930*. London and Beverly Hills, Calif.: Sage, 1979.

_____. "Russia and Europe: Diplomacy, Revolution, and Economic Development in the 1920s." *International History Review* 1, no. 1 (January 1979): 55–83.

Varga, Eugen. "Die Wendung in der Wirtschaftspolitik Sowjet Russlands." *Die kommunistische Internationale* 18 (1921): 90.

Walling, William. "The League of Nations and Soviet Responsibility for the Russian Famine." *American Federationist* 30 (April 1923): 297–302.

White, John Albert. *The Siberian Intervention*. Princeton: Princeton University Press, 1950.

White, Stephen. "Colonial Revolution and the Communist International, 1919–1924." *Science and Society* 40, no. 2 (1976): 173–93.

11. United States

Artaud, Denise. "Aux origines de l'Atlantisme: La recherche d'un équilibre européen au lendemain de la première guerre mondiale." *Relations Internationales* 10 (1977): 115–26.

Brandes, Joseph. *Herbert Hoover and Economic Diplomacy: Department of Commerce Policy, 1921–1928*. Pittsburgh: University of Pittsburgh Press, 1962.

Burke, Bernard V. "American Economic Diplomacy and the Weimar Republic." *Mid-America* 54, no. 4 (1972): 211–33.

Carroll, John M. "The Paris Bankers' Conference of 1922 and America's Design for a Peaceful Europe." *International Review of History and Political Science* 10 (August 1973): 39–47.

Costigliola, Frank. "The United States and the Reconstruction of Germany in the 1920s." *Business History Review* 50 (1976): 477–502.

Davenport, E. H., and Cooke, Sidney R. *The Oil Trusts and Anglo-American Relations*. New York: Macmillan, 1924.

Dayer, Roberta Allbert. "The British War Debts to the United States and the Anglo-Japanese Alliance, 1920–1923." *Pacific Historical Review* 45 (1976): 569–95.

Feis, Herbert. *The Diplomacy of the Dollar*. Baltimore: Johns Hopkins University Press, 1950.

Filene, Peter G. *Americans and the Soviet Experiment, 1917–1933*. Cambridge: Harvard University Press, 1967.

Gelfand, Lawrence, ed. *Herbert Hoover: The Great War and its Aftermath, 1914–1923*. Iowa City: University of Iowa Press, 1979.

Gescher, Dieter B. *Die Vereinigten Staaten von Nordamerika und die Reparationen*. Bonn: L. Röhrscheid, 1956.

Gillette, Philip S. "American Capital in the Contest for Soviet Oil, 1920–23." *Soviet Studies* 24, no. 4 (April 1973): 477–90.

Hoffman, Karl. *Ölpolitik und angelsächsischer Imperialismus*. Berlin: Ring, 1927.

Hogan, Michael J. "Informal Entente: Public Policy and Private Management in Anglo-American Petroleum Affairs, 1918–1924." *Business History Review* 48, no. 2 (1974): 187–205.

―――――. "The United States and the Problem of International Economic Control: American Attitudes towards European Reconstruction, 1918–1920." *Pacific Historical Review* 44 (1975): 84–103.

Holtfreich, Carl-Ludwig. "Amerikanischer Kapitalexport und Wiederaufbau der deutschen Wirtschaft 1919–1933 im Vergleich zu 1924–1929." *Vierteljahrsschrift für Sozial- und Wirtschaftsgeschichte* 64 (1977): 497–529.

Kane, N. Stephen. "American Businessmen and Foreign Policy: The Recognition of Mexico, 1920–1923." *Political Science Quarterly* 90 (1975): 293–313.

―――――. "Bankers and Diplomats: The Diplomacy of the Dollar in Mexico, 1921–1924." *Business History Review* 47 (1973): 335–52.

Leffler, Melvyn P. "American Policy Making and European Stability, 1921–1933."
    Pacific Historical Review 46 (May 1977): 207–28.
————. *The Elusive Quest: America's Pursuit of European Stability and French Sec-
    urity, 1919–1933.* Chapel Hill: University of North Carolina Press, 1979.
————. "Origins of Republican War Debt Policy, 1921–1923." *Journal of American
    History* 59, no. 3 (1972): 585–601.
————. "Political Isolationism, Economic Expansionism, or Diplomatic Realism:
    American Policy toward Western Europe, 1921–1933." *Perspectives in American
    History* 8 (1974): 413–61.
Link, Werner. *Die amerikanische Stabilisierungspolitik in Deutschland, 1921–1932.*
    Düsseldorf: Droste Verlag, 1970.
Marks, Sally, and Dulude, Denis. "German-American Relations, 1918–1921." *Mid-
    America* 53, no. 4 (October 1971): 211–26.
Parrini, Carl P. *Heir to Empire: United States Economic Diplomacy, 1916–1923.*
    Pittsburgh: University of Pittsburgh Press, 1969.
Toinet, Marie-France. "La politique pétrolière des États-Unis à l'égard de l'U.R.S.S.,
    1917–1927." *Revue Française de Science Politique* 17 (1967): 689–712.
Van Meter, Robert H., Jr. "The United States and European Recovery, 1918–1923."
    Ph.D. diss., University of Wisconsin, 1971.
————. "The Washington Conference of 1921–22: A New Look." *Pacific Historical
    Review* 46 (1977): 603–24.
Vinson, John C. *The Parchment Peace: The United States Senate and the Washington
    Conference, 1921–1922.* Athens: University of Georgia Press, 1955.
Watt, D. C. "American 'Isolationism' in the 1920s: Is It a Useful Concept?" *Bulletin
    of the British Association of American Studies*, no. 6 (1958): 3–19.
Weissman, Benjamin. *Herbert Hoover and Famine Relief to Soviet Russia, 1921–
    1923.* Stanford: Hoover Institution Press, 1974.
Williams, William A. *American-Russian Relations, 1781–1947.* New York: Rinehart,
    1952.
————. "The Legend of Isolationism in the 1920s." *Science and Society* 18, no. 1
    (1954): 1–20.
————. "A Note on American Foreign Policy in Europe in the Nineteen Twenties."
    Science and Society 22 (1958): 1–20.

D. Contemporary Press Publications

1. Periodicals (* indicates extensive coverage of the Genoa Conference)

Austria
  Der österreichische Volkswirt

France
  Le Correspondant
  L'Économie Nouvelle
  L'Économiste Européen
  L'Économiste Français

L'Europe Nouvelle
La Grande Revue
Journal des Économistes
L'Opinion
La Paix par le Droit
Parlement et Opinion
Revue Contemporaine
*Revue des Deux Mondes
Revue d'Économie Politique
Revue Économique Internationale
Revue Économique des Soviets
*Revue des Études Coopératives
La Revue de France
La Revue Hebdomadaire
La Revue de Paris
Revue Politique et Parlementaire
Revue Universelle

Germany
Archiv für Politik und Geschichte
Der deutsche Ökonomist

Great Britain
Communist International (London)
Contemporary Review
Economist
Fortnightly Review
Headway
Journal of the British Institute of International Affairs
Journal of the Parliaments of the Empire
*Manchester Guardian Commercial
*Nation
*New Statesman
*Petroleum Times
Round Table
Saturday Review
Spectator
Statist
Times Trade Supplement

Italy
*Il Comune di Genova: Bollettino Municipale Mensile
Critica Fascista
Politica
Rivista Bancaria
*La Vita Internazionale
*La Vita Italiana

Poland
L'Est Européen
L'Est Polonais

Switzerland
Bibliothèque Universelle (Geneva)
Schweizer Blätter für Handel und Industrie
Schweizerische Monatshefte
Société de Banque Suisse

United States
American Economic Review
American Review of Reviews
Annalist
Atlantic Monthly
Current History
Federal Reserve Bulletin
Foreign Affairs
The Nation
New Republic
North American Review
World Affairs

2. Newspapers

Belgium
Le Peuple
Le Soir

France
Le Matin
L'Oeuvre
Le Temps

Germany
Frankfurter Zeitung
Deutsche Allgemeine Zeitung
Vorwärts

Great Britain
Daily Telegraph
Manchester Guardian
The Observer
The Times

Italy
Corriere della Sera

Switzerland
Neue Zürcher Zeitung

United States
New York Times
Washington Post

Index

Adler, Viktor, 127
Afghanistan, 13
Africa, 32, 254; northern, 143
Ahmedabad, 67
Albania: at Genoa, 144
Alexander, king of Yugoslavia, 110
Allgemeine Elektrizitäts-Gesellschaft, 20
Allied experts' meeting, 20–28 March, London, 76, 121–26, 213; postponement, 89. *See also* London Report
Allied foreign ministers' conference on Near East, 119–20
Allied Military Control Commission, 62
Allied-Russian talks, 161–62, 167–70, 177, 185–90; catalyst for Russo–German talks, 166; Russian response to 15 April offer, 187–88; experts' committee, 189–90; 2 May memorandum, 209–10, 213, 226, 229, 262; Seydoux amendment, 226, 229; Russian response, 11 May, 264–66, 281
Allies: heavy debt to United States, 16; and Polish borders, 109; attitude toward Russia, 210–11; Russia policy alternatives, 211–13; reluctance to revise treaties, 242
All-Russian Central Executive Committee of Soviets, 204, 263
All-Russian Congress of Metalworkers, 95
All-Russian Extraordinary Commission. *See* Cheka
All-Russian Famine Relief Committee, 8, 10; dissolved, 11
Alphand, Charles, 292, 293, 297
American Relief Administration, 13, 26; aid to Russia, 8–9, 10, 11, 56, 77, 94, 124
Anatolia, 64, 119, 120
Anglo-Belgian pact, 61, 291, 301
Anglo-French disunity: and Eastern European security, 107
Anglo-French pact, 22, 33, 41, 45, 46, 57, 69,

70–71, 82, 87, 134, 136, 267, 279, 292, 301; French public opinion, 37–38; British public opinion, 38. *See also* Great Britain: relations with France; France: relations with Britain
Anglo-German collaboration in Russia, 19–20
Anglo-German conversations, 80–81
Anglo-Japanese alliance, 98
Anglo-Persian oil company, 225
Anglo-Soviet trade agreement, 30
Ansaldo complex, 143
Anschluss, 77, 107, 240
Appeasement, 302, 304n
ARA. *See* American Relief Administration
Armenia, 39, 64
Arms, French, 71
Army of Occupation on the Rhine, 48
Asia, 11, 27, 32, 254
Asia Minor, 67, 217, 265
Asquith, H. H., 136
Asquithites, 31, 46
Association of British Creditors in Russia, 268, 301
Association of Former French Investors in Russia, 73
Attolico, Bernardo, 252, 253, 254, 257
Austria, 76, 77, 78; at Genoa Conference, 41, 144; on transport subcommission, 159; need for exchange controls, 238; liens on assets, 239–40; need for credits, 239–42; pan-Germanism, 240; socialism, 240; receives credits, 241; and Porto Rosa Conference, 247; and minority rights, 255; fall of government, 306

Baku, 226
Baldwin, Stanley, 137
Balfour, Arthur James, 29, 267, 279
Baltic, 109